THE EARLY YEARS HANDBOOK FOR STUDENTS AND PRACTITIONERS

The Early Years Handbook for Students and Practitioners is a comprehensive and accessible course text for all students studying at levels 4 and 5, including those on Foundation degrees and Early Childhood Studies degrees. Designed and written by the Chair of the SEFDEY (Sector-Endorsed Foundation Degree in Early Years) network and a team of expert contributors, this book covers the essential skills, knowledge and understanding you need to become an inspiring and effective early years practitioner.

Divided into four parts 'The Student-Practitioner-Professional', 'The Learning and Development of Children 0–5', 'The Child, Family and Society', and 'The Senior Practitioner-Professional', the book covers all aspects of working with young children and engages you with theory that is explicitly linked to your practice. Throughout there is a strong emphasis on supporting your transition to undergraduate study, developing your academic skills and encouraging you to be an active learner.

In every chapter, the book seeks to help you develop your professional identity. It features:

- Activities to help you to reflect on your own practice
- 'Provocations' to promote discussion and debate
- Case study examples and photographs to illustrate key points
- 'From Research to Practice' boxes outlining key research in the field and implications for practice.

The book is supported by a companion student website featuring links to useful websites and video material, and an interactive flashcard glossary. Online support for lecturers includes ideas for tasks and activities to use in class and the diagrams and images in the book are available to download.

Lyn Trodd (editor) is Associate Dean, UK and International Collaboration in the School of Education at the University of Hertfordshire, UK. She is also Chair of the SEFDEY network.

Routledge
Companion Websites

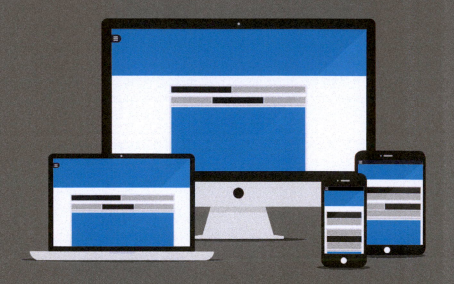

Enhancing online learning
and teaching.

 www.routledge.com/cw/trodd

THE EARLY YEARS HANDBOOK FOR STUDENTS AND PRACTITIONERS

An essential guide for the foundation degree and levels 4 and 5

Edited by
Lyn Trodd

Routledge
Taylor & Francis Group

LONDON AND NEW YORK

First published 2016
by Routledge
2 Park Square, Milton Park, Abingdon, Oxon OX14 4RN

and by Routledge
711 Third Avenue, New York, NY 10017

Routledge is an imprint of the Taylor & Francis Group, an informa business

British Library Cataloguing-in-Publication Data
A catalogue record for this book is available from the British Library

Library of Congress Cataloging-in-Publication Data
Names: Trodd, Lyn, author.
Title: The early years handbook for students and practitioners : an essential
guide for the foundation degree and levels 4 and 5 / Lyn Trodd.
Description: Milton Park, Abingdon, Oxon ; New York, NY : Routledge, 2016.
Identifiers: LCCN 2015027513| ISBN 9781138776395 | ISBN 9781138776401
Subjects: LCSH: Early childhood educators–Training of–Great Britain.
| Early childhood teachers–In-service training–Great Britain. | University
extension–Great Britain. | Education, Cooperative–Great Britain. |
Continuing education–Great Britain.
Classification: LCC LB1775.6 .T76 2016 | DDC 372.21–dc23LC record
available at http://lccn.loc.gov/2015027513

ISBN: 978-1-138-77639-5 (hbk)
ISBN: 978-1-138-77640-1 (pbk)
ISBN: 978-1-315-77320-9 (ebk)

Typeset in Interstate
by Florence Production Ltd, Stoodleigh, Devon, UK

Printed and bound by CPI Group (UK) Ltd, Croydon, CR0 4YY

CONTENTS

PREFACE

Lyn Trodd

If you have just opened this book it is likely that you identify in some way with people who work with very young children. You might be a student or someone who is already working within an Early Years setting, or both. You might be a tutor, a mentor or a manager in an Early Years setting, or all three. You might also be an Early Years tutor and a practitioner as well as an author of one of these chapters. The writers of this book are all people who are immersed in the field of Early Years and feel passionately that Early Years practice must be of the highest quality. Their aim has been to contribute to the kind of book they would like to have for their students and Early Years colleagues.

Choosing what to include in this book has been fraught with difficulties. We know that professional identities are shaped by expectations of what a particular professional should know. Once upon a time it was an expectation that people working with very young children were kind, responsible and clean, and that was probably enough. Nowadays we still want kind, responsible, clean people but we expect a great deal more of them. Part I, The Student-Practitioner-Professional, explores the potential professional identity of someone working in the Early Years sector and embarking on higher level study. Part II, The Learning and Development of Children 0–5, offers starting points for the professional knowledge and values that are the key expectations of people working with young children.

As it has become more widely understood that experiences in the first years of life are fundamental to people's happiness, wellbeing, life chances and contributions to their community, expectations of those of us working with the youngest children have grown. We are expected to know why we do things in our work with children and what the likely impact of actions will be. It is considered important that we reflect on how we work in order to spot ways to improve and do things in a better way. Part III, The Child, Family and Society, explores these 'bigger picture' perspectives in order to promote the kind of 'extended' professionality described by Eric Hoyle (1974).

Children and their families trust us to have their best interests at heart and to provide a wealth of interesting, creative ideas of ways to engage children in activities that they enjoy and from which they may learn. Society expects our work to prevent crime, integrate people into the community, develop parenting skills, promote good health, increase educational attainment, be on the front line of safeguarding and play a part in ensuring that children grow up to contribute to the economic success of the country. Part IV, The Senior Practitioner-Professional, introduces some of these significant responsibilities.

Hoyle, E. (1974) 'Professionality, professionalism and control in teaching', *London Educational Review*, 3(2), 13–19.

A VISUAL TOUR OF *THE EARLY YEARS HANDBOOK FOR STUDENTS AND PRACTITIONERS*

Pedagogical features

The Early Years Handbook for Students and Practitioners offers an array of features specifically designed to enhance your teaching and learning experience.

Learning Outcomes

Each chapter begins by outlining the key Learning Outcomes that the reader will achieve after reading the chapter. These also serve to map out the reader's journey through the chapter.

Provocations

Each chapter contains 'Provocation' boxes, promoting discussion and debate and challenging the reader to think about the key issues raised.

'Reflective Practice' activities

'Reflective Practice' activities promote self-awareness and encourage the reader to think about the implications of their actions, assumptions and practice.

Case Studies

Case Studies put the topics under discussion into context and help to illustrate key points.

'From Research to Practice' boxes

'From Research to Practice' boxes outline key research in the field and explain the implications for practice.

Suggestions for Further Reading

Each chapter concludes with a carefully selected and annotated list of recommended further reading, including relevant books, articles and reports. This feature serves as a guide to independent study and provides a useful point of departure for students and practitioners wishing to deepen their knowledge of a particular area.

Useful websites

An annotated list of recommended websites follows the suggestions for Further Reading, highlighting the most useful websites related to the topic. These can also be found on the book's companion website www.routledge.com/cw/trodd.

Illustrations

The book contains a number of supporting figures, tables and diagrams to help the reader to visualise the material described in the text. Lecturers can download these from the book's companion website, www.routledge.com/cw/trodd, to use in class.

Figure 13.1 The Communication Tree

Glossary of key terms and acronyms

A helpful glossary of key terms and acronyms allows the reader to quickly look up definitions. An interactive version of the glossary can be found on the book's companion website, www.routledge.com/cw/trodd, allowing the reader to test their knowledge.

Companion website

Visit the companion website for a whole host of student and lecturer resources that support and enhance the textbook, including:

Routledge Companion Websites

Enhancing online learning and teaching.
www.routledge.com/cw/trodd

For students

- Links to useful websites, organised by chapter
- Links to useful video material
- An interactive flashcard glossary, allowing you to test your knowledge of key terms
- Interviews with students discussing challenges they have faced and how these were overcome.

For lecturers

- Ideas for tasks and activities to use in class
- All the figures, tables and diagrams from the book available to download for your own use.

www.routledge.com/cw/trodd

ACKNOWLEDGEMENTS

Thank you to all of the contributors to this book – both to those who are named and also those who are not. I am particularly grateful to the Early Years students and practitioners who shared their case studies with the authors of the chapters. Thank you as well to members of the SEFDEY Committee for their support, especially to Dr Gill Goodliff, Head of Qualifications in Early Years at the Open University, for her friendship and encouragement.

It is important to acknowledge the painstaking work of the publishing team at Routledge who were brave (foolhardy?) enough to go forward with the rather daunting task of developing this complex, multi-authored book and its companion website.

This book is dedicated to all those who work with and for children in order to improve their life chances.

ABBREVIATIONS

BERA	British Educational Research Association
CAMHS	Child and Adolescent Mental Health Services
CPD	Continuing Professional Development
DCSF	Department for Children Schools and Families
DfE	Department for Education
DfES	Department for Education and Skills
EAL	English as an Additional Language
EYE	Early Years Educator
EYTS	Early Years Teacher Status
ECM	Every Child Matters
EPPE	The Effective Provision of Pre-School Education
EPPSE	Effective Pre-School, Primary and Secondary Education
EY	Early Years
EYE	Early Years Educator
EYFS	Early Years Foundation Stage
EYP	Early Years Practitioner
EYFS	Early Years Foundation Stage
EYT	Early Years Teacher
FDEY	Foundation Degree in Early Years
FEC	Further Education Colleges
FEU	Further Education Unit
FSM	Free school meals
GLF	Graduate Leader Fund
HCP	Healthy Child Programme 2009
HEI	Higher Education Institutions
HFAC	Health For All Children Policies
HLTA	Higher Level Teaching Assistant
IMR	Infant Mortality Rate or death rates between 0-1 years
LIS-YC	Leuven Involvement Scale for Young Children
NHS	National Health Service
NICE	The National Institute for Health and Care Excellence
NSF	National Service Frameworks
NVQ	National Vocational Qualification
ONS	Office of National Statistics

PSED	Personal, Social and Emotional Development
PSHE	Personal, social and health education
QCA	Qualifications and Curriculum Authority
QTS	Qualified Teacher Status
REPEY	Researching Effective Pedagogy in Early Years
SCR	Serious Case Review
SEN	Special Educational Needs
SENCO	Special Educational Needs Coordinator
SES	Socio-economic status
SSCC	Sure Start Children's Centre
SSLP	Sure Start Local Program
UNCRC	United Nations Convention on the Rights of the Child
WBL	Work-based learning
WHO	World Health Organization
WP	Widening Participation
ZPD	The Zone of Proximal Development

CONTRIBUTORS

Karen Appleby is a Principal Lecturer in the Institute of Education (Centre for Early Childhood) at the University of Worcester. She teaches across a variety of Early Childhood programmes and modules. Her current responsibilities include leadership for learning, teaching and student experience. Previously she has held the position of Partnership Co-ordinator for the SEFDEY foundation degree in Early Years and Course Leader for the BA (Hons) Integrated Early Childhood Studies and HND in Early Childhood programmes. She has authored publications on reflective practice and takes a particular interest in the way reflective learning is positioned within undergraduate study.

Pere Ayling is a lecturer and a researcher in the University Campus Suffolk (UCS), Ipswich. She is a trained sociologist with seven years of teaching experience in Higher Education. Her areas of specialisation include inequality and class (re)production strategies. She is particularly interested in how social class, gender and race intersect to (re)produce 'inequality' in education.

Catherine Barker studied Early Childhood Studies and obtained a BA (Hons) from Bradford University. On graduation she was employed within the Early Years sector before becoming a lecturer within a Further Education college and now having worked in the area for 14 years is programme manager of the Foundation Degree Early Years Practice.

Viki Bennett is Programme Leader for the Early Years Foundation degree at Bath Spa University and also works for Bristol City Council supporting the development of self-improving Early Years local networks. Her areas of interest are play, the pre-schools of Reggio Emilia and practitioner narratives.

Claire Beresford trained and worked as a primary school teacher, then as an advisory teacher for primary, nursery and special schools in Lancashire. She is the course tutor for Foundation Degree and BA (Hons) Top-up Young Children's Learning and Development at Craven College, Skipton.

Allison Boggis's specialist teaching areas broadly relate to Childhood Studies. As an Early Years practitioner herself and a senior lecturer in various aspects of Early Childhood, she has played an active role in developing and leading the current FdA in Early Years Practice at the University Campus Suffolk. Allison is an ambassador for the Child Exploitation and Online Protection Centre (CEOP) and she is also a panel member on their educational advisory board.

Jill Brown worked in the Primary sector for ten years before teaching in Further Education on NNEB and BTEC courses and being involved in setting up and running the SEFDEY Early Years Foundation Degree. For nine years she was an Open University Associate Lecturer on the Child Development psychology unit. Before retiring Jill worked at Bath Spa University on the Early Years Professional programme.

Joe Brown has worked in a variety of roles with children aged between birth and twelve and taught on the Sector Endorsed Foundation Degree in Early Years at City of Bristol College for ten years. Joe now leads the Foundation Degree and Early Years Teacher programmes at Bath Spa University.

Danielle Carey worked in the Children's Workforce for 20 years before becoming a lecturer in Early Years. Her current position is Dean of the School of Education and Community at University College, Birmingham where she has overall responsibility for Early Year's qualifications ranging from Level 2 to Level 7.

Alix Coughlin teaches on the Foundation Degree in Young Children's Learning and Development at Craven College and enjoys seeing the development of the students into thoughtful and knowledgeable practitioners as they progress through the course. She has worked with children all her life, and is passionate about encouraging reading for pleasure.

Jo Dallal began her career as a social worker before moving into teaching at Kingston College. Her interest in facilitating widening participation for all has led her to being at the forefront of developing new higher level courses in child care. Her present post is that of Head of Higher Education and Counselling at Kingston College.

Jonathan Doherty has worked as a teacher, lecturer and EYFS adviser with the National Strategies. He is currently Head of Primary Education at Leeds Trinity University. His research interests are around inequality. He is passionate about improving the life chances of children and breaking the link between disadvantage and educational underachievement.

Mary Dyer is a Senior Lecturer in Early Years and has been teaching and training early years practitioners for over 25 years. She has also worked in the early years sector as a Development Officer, then Project Co-ordinator, supporting early years settings in developing and improving provision. Her research focuses on how practitioners develop and describe their professional identity, particularly at this time of significant change for the sector.

Dawn Evans trained as a Primary Teacher with QTS and Early Years specialism at the University of Wales Institute Cardiff. She also holds an assessor award and a Masters Post-Graduate Certificate in Early Childhood gained at Bath Spa University. Additionally, she has spent time working in a day nursery with under-fives. For the past 12 years she has worked at New College, Swindon where she is Programme Leader for the Early Years Foundation degree in partnership with Bath Spa University.

Sharon Friend qualified as a teacher before moving into research, investigating inclusion and young children's use of technology in play. Following lecturing positions at Swansea University and on Foundation degrees, she is now a senior lecturer in Early Childhood at University of West of England, Bristol, specialising in play and childhood in different cultures.

Katherine Goodsir worked in both nurseries and primary schools before joining the Early Years Professional team at Bath Spa University. She currently teaches on the Education Studies degree at Bath Spa and is programme leader on the Sector Endorsed Foundation degree at City of Bristol College. Katherine's research interests are around health and physical development and she is currently completing her MA dissertation on the importance of Fundamental Movement Skills.

Karen Hanson is the Head of the Centre for Early Childhood at the University of Worcester. She has extensive professional experience, which has included her roles as a teacher and registered child-minder, and also her work for the Preschool Play Association. Karen's published research interests have encompassed the way reflective practice can be made visible to students as part of their academic and professional engagement with early education.

Janet Harvell is a Senior Lecturer at the Centre for Early Childhood, University of Worcester. She is also a practising HMI. A qualified teacher, Janet has worked in the Early Years sector for the last 26 years with experience as a childminder, pre-school supervisor and nursery manager. Janet worked with the Bridgwater Sure Start programme and set up the first accredited Childminding Network in Somerset before moving into further and higher education where she has managed the Foundation Degree and BA in Early Years. Janet's research interests are focused on international education, particularly in China, and she has presented at national and international conferences.

Carol Hayes has been the Academic Group Leader for Early Childhood Studies at the University of Staffordshire until her recent semi-retirement. Carol is the Chair of the Sector-Endorsed Foundation Degree in Early Years Professional Association (SEFDEY). She has worked in Early Years education for the last 40 years starting out as a nursery teacher. Carol's specialist area of interest is cognitive development, language, literacy and communication and her main research interests are dyslexia and communication difficulties and the role of graduate teaching assistants in the workforce.

Nicki Henderson has recently been appointed Head of School at River Mead School and is committed to moving the school ever forward, creating a school culture that supports inspired teaching, effective learning, respectful relationships and high expectations of learning behaviours. Formerly Programme Leader for the PGCE at Bath Spa University, Nicki is a passionate advocate for the rights of children and understands the importance of providing children with opportunities to play, explore and be active.

Wendy Holland has 30 years of experience of Early Years teaching, and is currently lecturing in Bradford on Early Years HE programmes, including initial teacher training. She is editor and author of the *Early Years Professional's Complete Companion*, soon to be republished as *The Early Years Graduate Leader's Complete Companion*.

Kate Hulm is a lecturer in Early Years Education at City of Bristol College and a private Early Years and play consultant. Kate's experience includes working for Barnardo's to promote parental involvement with vulnerable children and she has researched the voice of the child for Bristol City Council to understand children's views on their Early Years experiences outside their homes.

Pam Jarvis writes and teaches in the field of psychological, sociological and historical issues relating to children and families. She is currently working as a Senior Lecturer at Leeds Trinity University and has a range of publications including *Perspectives on Play*, recently internationally published in a second edition.

Tricia Johnson qualified as a nurse and diversified into childcare and education. She worked at the Norland College for 14 years managing various childcare areas. She gained a Master's Degree in Early Years and moved into Further Education as Head of school for Early Years and then into Higher education as a senior lecturer and subject specialist for the FdA Early Years and BA Practice Development (Early Years) at Buckinghamshire New University. Her main area of interest and research is the emotional needs of very young children.

Caroline Jones is a former teacher and currently lectures part-time at the University of Warwick. She owns a small group of private nurseries on school sites in Warwickshire and Solihull (established 1989). Caroline operates as an independent Early Years consultant. Her international expertise is in Leadership and Inclusive Education.

Kawal Kaur is a lecturer in Kingston University and is also an experienced manager in the childcare sector. She holds a double Masters in both nutrition and education as well as Early Years Professional Status. Using action research Kawal aims to bring together the best practices of both the nutrition and education sectors in order to inform practice with young children.

Alaina Lally has worked as a midwife and an FE and HE lecturer in both Early Years and Health and Social Care. She is currently a Senior Lecturer for Teaching and Learning in the School of Education and Community at University College Birmingham. Her current doctoral research is using the Capability Approach to enhance understanding of student experiences of studying on university-based foundation degrees.

Shan Lockwood first got involved in childcare after having her own children. Since then she has worked as a playgroup assistant and PLA field worker, a self-employed childminder, a parent support worker and a tutor in an FE college teaching students from Level 3 to Level 6.

Isobel MacDougall worked as a primary school teacher before having children. She became involved in toddler groups and pre-school which inspired her to work in early years education. Isobel led the Sector Endorsed Foundation Degree in Early Years in Bristol for many years and has taught at various universities. She is completing a PhD in culture, language and identity.

Samantha McMahon is course leader for the BA (Hons) Early Years at Huddersfield University and has been teaching children and young people for 20 years in a variety of contexts, HE, FE, Primary and pre-school. She has worked at the university for ten years and been instrumental in the growth and development of early year's provision from Foundation degrees to EYPS. She works closely with practitioners and providers to enhance provision and improve practice. Her research interests are the professionalisation of the Early Years workforce and leadership in Early Years.

Eva Mikuska is a senior lecturer at the University of Chichester. She worked with children for many years and now leads the Sector Endorsed Foundation Degree in Early Childhood. Her doctoral research interest is exploring the role of emotion in education and the construction of 'good' within the Early Years context.

Yasmin Mukadam trained in Early Years before moving into Further and Higher Education. Currently, she is Liaison Officer and Senior Lecturer at Kingston University. Her research interests are yoga and mindfulness for children's holistic health and wellbeing. She specialises in collaborative working with employers and key stakeholders with a focus on the impact on personal and professional practice for work-based learners.

Jonathan Ratcliffe was a primary school teacher before moving into Further and Higher Education. Currently, he is a curriculum leader at Blackpool and the Fylde College; leading degree programmes. He has a particular interest in the transition from Level 3 to Level 4 and believes that creative approaches to study can support students in being successful.

Anne Rawlings is an Associate Professor at Kingston University. Anne's professional background is in nursing and she has taught on various Early Years programmes for many years. Anne's passions are multi-disciplinary working and to ensure the prevention of child protection issues. Recently Anne has been involved looking at serious child protection case reviews in order to identify ways that services for children can be improved.

Debbie Reel trained as a primary school teacher before moving into Initial Teacher Education 13 years ago. She specialises in early years and primary mathematics teaching on both undergraduate and postgraduate courses. Debbie is particularly interested in the impact of university and school-based training on the newly qualified teacher.

Janine Ryan trained in Early Years before qualifying as a teacher. She holds the post of Academic Lead and Programme Leader for Early Years provision at University Centre Doncaster. She has an MA in Early Years and is undertaking doctoral studies at Leeds Beckett University. Her research interest is Men in Early Years.

Nicola Smith worked as a Y1, Reception and Nursery teacher before studying for a PhD, researching relationships between nursery teachers and parents from minority ethnic backgrounds. She works as an Early Years lecturer at University College Birmingham, supporting students on undergraduate Childhood Studies degrees and PGCE programmes.

Dianne Solly began her career as a teacher specialising in Primary and Early Years education. Following this she became a senior lecturer at the University of Hertfordshire working with trainee teachers and students from a range of Early Years settings who wanted to develop their practice. She is now a visiting lecturer and supports trainee teachers during their school-based training.

Caroline Tobbell has been a teacher for 30 years and worked in a diverse range of schools. She was a Head teacher in two schools, one a primary school and one an Infant and Nursery school. She moved into teacher education in 2006 and currently works as a senior lecturer in Primary Education at Leeds Trinity University where she lectures primarily on the Early Years degree course with QTS.

Ute Ward worked in a pre-school, Sure Start local programme and children's centre before becoming Senior Lecturer in Early Years at the University of Hertfordshire. She now leads the BA (Hons) Early Childhood Education and undertakes research into supporting practitioners and practitioner-parent relationships in a range of early childhood settings.

Part I

The Student-Practitioner-Professional

1 Your emotional, personal life and your achievements as an undergraduate

Eva Mikuska

LEARNING OUTCOMES

After reading this chapter, you will be able to:

✔ Understand the complexity of studying at a degree level, especially when you need to combine working responsibilities and family commitments.
✔ Become more aware of how undergraduates, particularly mature students, experience the transition from Level 3 to Level 4.
✔ Reflect on parallels between your experiences as you start out as an undergraduate with those of young children entering day care, pre-school, nursery or reception.

Introduction

This chapter discusses the way students who are also practitioners-professionals see themselves as undergraduates. It explores possible issues Foundation Degree in Early Years (FDEY) students face while studying but these apply equally to any students engaged in undergraduate study. Where the term 'mature student' is used it refers to those who are 21 years old and above and eligible to apply for a government maintenance grant and student loan as an 'independent' student (DfES, 2012). The chapter draws on **case studies** of 42 mature students across three Higher Education Institutions (HEIs) in the South East of England, in which their experiences were examined.

The prime focus was on analysing students' emotional experiences while studying at degree level. You may find it surprising to focus on this. You probably expect the primary focus of this chapter should be on children. However, this chapter aims to give you an insight into the multi-layered nature of the emotions of students in order to prepare you for the potential challenges ahead. It highlights the complex issues you may face in balancing the multiple demands of your professional work, personal life and the academic requirements of your course. This chapter links to your personal achievements as an undergraduate to the enhancement of the quality of **Early**

Years (EY) education. In the study of 42 students it was clear that doing their Foundation Degrees in Early Years provided them with real depth of relevant knowledge, competence and professional confidence.

The context

In the last two decades a large number of students like you have entered HEIs to study on the FDEY. National political initiatives such as the 'Widening Participation' (DfES, 2006) agenda and programmes mounted by individual HEIs, have enabled access into higher education for '**non-traditional entrants**' of all kinds drawn from a wide range of backgrounds (Basit and Tomlinson, 2012) including those who missed their opportunity to study when they were younger. What was once seen as the preserve of students straight from school has now become open to a wider range of applicants.

Motives *v* obstacles faced by students when studying

There may be several motives for students returning to education after a break, such as wishing to become a role model for their children, improving their financial situation or sustaining their employment (Hoult, 2006; Johnson and Robson, 1999; Giancola *et al.*, 2008). Whatever the reason, participation in education appears to be **transformative**, especially for mature students. Studying at HE level appears to improve their performance in their employment, their self-esteem and their social functioning (Carney, 2001; Christie *et al.*, 2007). Mature students returning to learning after a long break from formal education may experience significant life changes and, as a result, a range of sometimes extreme emotions. Carney and McNeish (2000, cited in Carney, 2001) identified mature students as a group prone to having more problems with emotions and social functioning in the University environment than younger students. An interesting link can be made between the experiences of children starting pre-school or reception class and mature students starting HE. Riccardi (2013, cited in Trodd, 2013) argues that the **transition** process in the EY setting is a constant feature having an impact on the family, child and staff. In many ways mature students joining HEIs experience similar challenges.

Carney (2001) carried out a small scale research project based on information gathered from 756 mature students, and discovered that mature students often deal with family childcare responsibilities alongside their work responsibilities. Carney's study showed that although students might have positive aspirations, female students are more likely to feel insecure about expressing their anxieties and their concerns about adapting to classroom life. Furthermore Carney's study (2001) revealed that students rated feelings related to financial pressures as their most significant emotional challenge.

New understanding and policies are required if HEIs are to support effectively the increasing numbers of mature students (particularly those studying Early Years). Educational researchers have made progress in identifying the impact that emotional turbulence has on the process of learning.

As a student entering higher education, particularly if you are from a non-traditional background, you may have to adopt new ways of learning such as **e-learning**, **blended learning** and the '**e-brary**'. Supporting students who are struggling with writing an academic piece of work, or who are hostile to the idea of using modern technologies, is a concern for educators (DfES, 2006). Left to their own devices without support, students may obstruct their own learning. Universities are more responsive to the diverse needs of students, and they recognise that age may be an aspect of diversity within their student population. Barnett and Coate (2005, p. 126) advise that Universities and lecturers should adopt the '**empathy in advance**' approach towards mature students taking into account their socio-cultural, material and emotional needs.

There is substantial evidence of a strong link between the learner's emotion and the learning process (Dirkx, 2006; Leibowitz, 2009). Yet limited literature is available on the impact of emotion on students' learning and everyday lives, particularly mature students. Shultz and DeCuir (2002) explain that traditionally UK HEIs have been designed as an 'emotion-free sector' focusing on students' academic achievements. Leathwood and Hey (2009) and Beard *et al.* (2007) point out that this is probably because in general HEIs reject emotion as being irrational and subjective and so it is under-theorised. If starting a University degree in an unknown context and environment involves a transition, it must also be seen as an emotional process (Trodd, 2013).

The role of emotion in education

There are numerous attempts to explain the role of emotion within higher education (Mikuska, 2013) with different approaches to how emotion is conceptualised. The term 'emotion' is used differently according to which discipline is using it. In psychology Plutchik (2001) suggests that emotion is considered from an individual and private viewpoint reducing emotion to a very internal and personal part of human life. In contrast, from a sociological perspective the concept of emotion has been theorised in a cultural and social context (Williams, 2001). Turner and Stets (2005) emphasise that cultural factors are dominant when theorising emotions. Burkitt argues that emotions are 'multidimensional' and cannot be separated from social, cultural, and individual factors. 'They ... cannot be reduced to language alone ... and cannot be reduced to biology, relations or **discourse** alone, but belong to all these dimensions' (1999, p. 115)

How emotion is viewed

A number of studies have investigated how emotions are perceived by HE students (Zembylas, 2008; Carney, 2001; Shuck *et al.*, 2006; McMillan, 2013; Christie *et al.*, 2007). What emerges is that struggling with transitions to HE without support may obstruct learning and teaching. Indeed an ongoing **post-structuralist feminist** debate increasingly questions the way the contemporary

REFLECTIVE PRACTICE

In your work with children do you think there is a case for the dualities listed above? For example, are there links between a child's physical development and his or her cognitive development or can they be separated? Are there links between a child's emotional well-being and their learning?

PROVOCATION

Furedi (2004) argues that the embrace of a 'therapeutic ethos' in education is in danger of turning students into vulnerable and anxious individuals rather than aspiring and resilient adults. Ecclestone and Hayes (2009) identified a potential risk of over emphasising emotion in education saying that such a view is based on an assumption that we are emotionally fragile and vulnerable and, as a consequence, we need emotional support, even counselling to cope with aspects of university life. Not everyone accepts this. Whilst accepting the idea of a general shift from purely academic to the emotional Bigger (2000) argues that evidence for a therapeutic turn in higher education is very weak. Amsler (2011) identifies concerns about student satisfaction in universities as evidence of the rise of therapeutic education while Leathwood and Hey (2009) argue that it reaffirms the importance of emotion to learning.

What do you think? As an undergraduate do you think that your tutors need to be concerned about your emotional well-being? Should tutors spend time advising students about their personal problems or should one-to-one meetings be for the benefit of students' academic progress – in your view?

discourses contrast emotion and education and argue that they reflect an unnatural **dualism** of 'rational/emotional, mind/body, public/private, masculine/feminine split' (Leathwood and Hey, 2009, p. 429).

Dirkx (2006), Perkun *et al.* (2009) and Perkun and Stephens (2010) argue that only a few scholars in adult and higher education regard emotion as an integral part of learning. While Beard *et al.* (2007, p. 235) call for a 'clear theorisation of the role of emotion in education', Kristjánsson (2000) found that very few leading education journals or books that consider seriously emotion within education exist and Lynch and Lodge (2002) found that little or no attention was paid to addressing emotion in educational theory and in social research. They found that differences were examined in terms of gender, religion or race 'but not in terms of affective relations' (p. 11).

REFLECTIVE PRACTICE
REFLECTIVE PRACTICE

It seems that educators themselves are not confident about how to support students with their emotional needs and they find studying emotion difficult due to its fluid character.

Reflect on your experiences since you decided to become an HE student (enrolment process, induction day, academic requirements) and discuss how you could have been supported better.

This chapter draws on a small-scale qualitative research project with 42 mature female students, who finished their study in 2011 after joining an HEI after a number of years of being without any formal education. The research project illustrated how being a University student is an emotional process and how a broader understanding of the emotional impact of becoming a student is necessary. It showed that learning and achievement depended not just upon an individual's commitment to developing new learning strategies, but on emotions arising from interaction between the student, their changed learning environment, their workplace and their personal 'circle' of friends and family.

PROVOCATION

Do you identify with the findings below?

The study showed that all participants expressed concern about being out of formal education for a number of years where that was the case. Most of the participants suggested that the main reason for studying was to prove to themselves and to others (such as family members, colleagues and former teachers) that they were capable of finishing the degree. According to this research, the financial support from their local authority and government requirements provided only a secondary motive. Only two participants stated that they had joined higher education due to government requirements to upgrade their qualification. Both participants were also owners of an EY setting so it could be argued that consequently investing in their own education might result in financial gain. Participants had concerns about academic writing.

CASE STUDY 1

Before joining the HEI

Student 1: I can clearly remember the first day of attending university and coming out thinking, what on earth have I done but also being quite excited by the journey. I had left school at 16 and I kept thinking – people like me don't go to university. It was scary. I left school after I had failed my exams with the feeling that I am not intelligent at all. I desperately wanted to do the Foundation Degree for many reasons, but most of all, to prove to myself I could do it. I was particularly concerned about going back to essay writing after so long (32 years gap). As a mature student it had been many years since I have written an essay and I had much doubt about my ability to do so and how this would compare with the other students. I knew I had to learn fast but felt I was on my own.

In the research study all 42 participants wrote or spoke about their positive emotions associated with their sense of pride related to being able to pass assignments and being able to fulfil the academic requirements of their degree. Participants expressed their pleasure at being more knowledgeable within the EY's field resulting in increased confidence and self-satisfaction at work. This was especially evident when they were talking to parents about child development or dealing with children with challenging behaviour. Alongside these positive feelings participants expressed feelings of negative emotions. Among their main concerns were stress and doubt about their ability and also feelings associated with finding the time for studying, and combining their study with other family and work commitments whilst struggling to cope with the numerous demands of the programme, such as meeting assignment deadlines. Table 1.1 below summarises the positive and negative emotions they experienced.

Table 1.1 Students' positive and negative emotions

Positive emotions	Negative emotions
Enthusiastic, comfortable at work, gained professional confidence, feeling skilled, relaxed because I know now, excited, enjoyment of studying, happy to have a degree, feeling strong bond, settled quickly, sense of relief, challenging positively, reassured, valued by peers, feeling knowledgeable, good feeling at work, pride for passing a module, more confident at work, being able to understand children more, pleased to achieve, love studying, been supported, feeling of security	Stressed because of the deadline, anxious of not knowing if I passed, panicky to use the computer, scared of not knowing what is expected, feeling tired, helpless, increasingly restless, shocked by the result, upset not getting a better grade, concerned, disappointed, unsettled, sense of failing, exhausted, frustrated, nervous, pressured, worried, terrified , angry, unsure, unconfident of writing academic 'stuff', feeling unsupported, doubt about the ability, at the beginning I felt incompetent, confused, guilty leaving my own children at home, lonely

CASE STUDY 2

Positive outcome of studying the degree

Student 2: Although I had a broad range of experience in Early Years practice, completing the degree has provided real breadth and depth to my knowledge and built my professional confidence. I have seen myself progress in a way that I can only attribute to participation in the course. I have made progress in understanding and managing my emotions during difficult situations and I have developed greater empathy and ability to recognise and meet the emotional needs of others (children, other professionals, families). In my book these are key requirements of an Early Years professional.

Recently I had the opportunity to reflect on what I have learnt through participating on this course as I applied (and was offered) a position as the Deputy Manager. During an interview I was asked many questions that required reflection and evaluation of my professional development. The depth of my knowledge in current Early Years practice and child development was assessed, together with my responses to challenges requiring emotional intelligence. I was offered the post within an 'outstanding' Nursery and Children's Centre due, I believe, to the high level of confidence, skill and knowledge instilled in me through participating in a Foundation Degree in Early Years.

CASE STUDY 3

Negative emotions

In the early days the greatest challenge was getting the referencing right, particularly in the early hours of the morning when you knew you had run out of time and all you wanted to do was sleep but you had to think 'how did you reference a quote from an edited chapter again'! Time management was the major issue all the way through the course.

One of the themes identified in the study was concern about how to balance the university workload with family commitments and employment. Entering university was a challenge due to low self-esteem as was learning how to become a university student by learning the rules of the university and how to manage time effectively. Stress was an issue for some students (Giancola *et al.*, 2008 and Pryor *et al.*, 2011).

'I did spend many nights in a complete fluster and there were tears too, especially when the deadline date was approaching.'

Another source of stress was competing commitments to family, employment and university workload as suggested in the quotes below.

'I felt I was balancing my time effectively as I was on maternity leave; however when I went back to work I felt my family and my daughter were missing out. Not only was I putting my daughter in childcare when I was at work but I also had to sort childcare so I could do my university work. This made me feel extremely guilty.'

'I become increasingly restless within my current setting, perhaps a result of having been there for the last eight years. I acknowledged there were areas within the setting's professional practice that I disagreed with ... As this was a full-time course the time management required for study placed immense pressure on my work life balance.'

'I recall that every time I entered another piece of work for marking, there was a pressure in the few weeks before it was due in, and a bit of adrenaline as deadlines loomed and a sense of relief when the work went in. This feeling was the same all the way through each year.'

REFLECTIVE PRACTICE
REFLECTIVE PRACTICE

- What are your current strategies for dealing with these competing pressures?
- What could you do differently to make life easier for yourself?

Self-esteem

The study used in this chapter shows that participants' confidence was threatened by a lack of ICT knowledge and by lack of confidence in writing an academic piece of work. This accords with research by Leibowitz (2009) about mature students' self-esteem and motivation in higher education. As you can see from the quotes below students experienced some distress from not knowing, or being uncertain about, how to write an essay or how to use the ICT.

> 'Being unconfident on computers put a big barrier in the way for me when I started . . . I felt stupid and incompetent and walked away . . . My first essay I had sleepless nights over it, I had never written an essay academically.'

> 'I was initially nervous and concerned that I would not be able to engage my brain in the academic work I was undertaking.'

However the study showed that once the requirements of what was needed to complete the course were made clear, students became much more confident.

Feeling proud and confident at work

While reports from participants focused mainly on stress-related experiences, they also commented on the feeling of being immensely proud of becoming a university student and achieving a university degree. They reported that they felt more confident at work. For example, a student said:

> 'I feel very proud of what I have achieved and what I have done and this will stay with me for life. I was very close to giving up during the first module as it was so difficult balancing everything; however the pride I felt handing over a completed essay and then receiving my first grade was powerful. Especially when the penny was dropped – I understood *why* we do the learning journey, *why* we observe. Suddenly talking to families and other professionals became an easy task. Reflecting on the course now I can certainly see how important it is to continue with the professional development. My next step is to complete the whole degree.'

REFLECTIVE PRACTICE
REFLECTIVE PRACTICE

This chapter has tried to reveal some of the connections between emotions, entering higher education and practitioners' personal lives.

- Reflect on your journey as a student and give examples of how your HE course has changed or shaped your personal life and professional practice.
- What did you change in your setting as a result of the course?

When they see the difference engaging in degree level study makes to their own confidence and competence, many undergraduate students realise that continuous professional development of all staff is crucial in raising the quality of the EY setting (Nutkins *et al.*, 2013).

FROM RESEARCH TO PRACTICE

As has already been mentioned, there is increased interest in researching the role of emotion in education especially in HEIs. Although this research theme is under-researched and under-theorised, Quinlan (2014) notes that existing theories are 'scattered in pockets in various disciplines that are focusing on different levels of education' (p. 1). Quinlan (2014) categorised them from five different positions:

1   A therapeutic stance, i.e. exploring how emotions and education can interact to improve an individual's well-being.
2   Using an **emotional intelligence** perspective which examines how students learn to regulate and manage their own emotions and those of others.
3   Researching from a socio-cultural view point, i.e. how society and sub-groups of society view emotions in education.
4   Exploring how emotional experiences in education can be a **catalyst** for changes in individuals and groups in society.
5   Enquiring how achieving or failing to achieve our goals influences our feelings and confidence.

Quinlan argues that education is a **holistic** experience which involves feelings and that each of the five stances above suggests different implications for learning. She argues that emotions are an integral part of our everyday life and learning and that once we acknowledge this it has important implications for our professional practice and for teaching and learning. You will find evidence of the influence of this view in Part II of this book when authors consider children's development from a holistic perspective.

Read Quinlan's five research stances again.

*   *In relation to becoming an undergraduate student, is there one that you think needs to be researched more urgently than the others? Which is it?*
*   *Why? What does your selection of this stance tell you about your priorities and your experience of education so far?*

Conclusion

The research study upon which this chapter is based showed that students experienced an emotional journey, 'a real emotional rollercoaster', during their undergraduate courses in Early Years. The courses had an invaluable impact on their professional practice. Although they found studying at a degree level challenging, especially combining working responsibilities and family commitments, their degree level study provided all participants with a depth of relevant knowledge and professional confidence and competence. Participants in the study reported a strong dynamic between their emotions, achievements and personal and professional lives. This formed a particular emotional climate that influenced their learning by making them more self-aware and resilient.

Further reading

Baxter, A. and Britton, C. (2011). Risk, identity and change: Becoming a mature student. *International Studies in Sociology of Education*, 11(1), pp. 87–104.
  This article investigates the stories mature students tell about the risks of higher education, in terms of its effects on identity and the implications for relationships with their families and former friends.

Carney, C. (2001). *The Challenge of Being a Mature Student.* Glasgow: University of Glasgow.
  This research report offers a detailed analysis of the impact on the quality of life and academic work of part-time and full-time undergraduate mature students. From this original report mature students were identified as a group who seem, in general, to have more problems with emotions, social functioning, mental health and energy/vitality than students in the younger age group.

Nutkins, S., McDonald, C. and Stephen, M. (2013). *Early childhood education and care. An introduction.* London: Sage.
  This book offers an excellent insight into early years topics and includes chapters on issues of professional autonomy and on personal qualities and interpersonal skills.

Useful websites

www.hefce.ac.uk/whatwedo/wp/
  This website of HEFCE offers an explanation and promotes the opportunity of successful participation in higher education to everyone who can benefit from it.

www.gov.uk/mature-student-university-funding
  This government website offers guidance for mature students where the government promotes the right to study even if you don't have traditional qualifications.

References

Amsler, S.S. (2011). From 'therapeutic' to political education: the centrality of affective sensibility in critical pedagogy. *Critical Studies in Educations*, 52 (1), pp. 47–63.

Basit, T.N. and Tomlinson, S. (2012). *Social Inclusion and Higher Education*. Bristol: The Policy Press.

Barnett, R. and Coate, K. (2005). *Engaging the Curriculum in Higher Education*. Buckingham: SRHE.

Baxter, A. and Britton, C. (2011). Risk, identity and change: Becoming a mature student. *International Studies in Sociology of Education*, 11 (1), pp. 87–104.

Beard, C., Clegg, S. and Smith, K. (2007). Acknowledging the affective in higher education. *British Educational Research Journal*, 33, pp. 235–252.

Bigger, S. (2000). 'Motivating students to succeed', in *Values in Education and Cultural Diversity*, ed. by Leicester M., Mogdil S. and Mogdil C., RoutledgeFalmer: London. Available online: www.heacademy.ac.uk/resources/detail/subjects/escalate/4866_Book_review_-_The_dangerous_ri [accessed 23 January 2013].

Burkitt, I. (1999). *Bodies of Thought, Embodiment, Identity & Modernity*. London: Sage.

Burman, E. (2009). Beyond 'emotional literacy' in feminist and educational research. *British Educational Research Journal*, 35 (1), pp. 137-155.

Carlson, N.R. (2010). *Foundations of Behavioural Neuroscience*. 8th edn. New York: Pearson Education.

Carney, C. (2001). *The Challenge of Being a Mature Student*. Glasgow: University of Glasgow.

Christie, H., Tett, L., Cree, E.V., Hounsell, J. and McCune, V. (2007). *A real rollercoaster of confidence and emotions: learning to be a university student*. Online papers archived by the Institute of Geography, Schools of Geoscience, University of Edinburgh.

Department for Education and Skills (DfES) (2006). *Widening participation in higher education: creating opportunity, releasing potential, achieving excellence*. London: HMSO.

Dirkx, J. M. (2006). Engaging emotions in adult learning: a Jungian perspective on emotion and transformative learning. *New Directions for Adult and Continuing Education*, 109, pp. 15-26.

Ecclestone, K. and Hayes, D. (2009). *The Dangerous Rise of Therapeutic Education*. London: Routledge.

Furedi, F. (2004). *Therapy Culture, Cultivating Vulnerability in an Uncertain Age*. London: Routledge.

Giancola, K., Munz, J. and Trares, D.S. (2008). First- versus continuing-generation adult students on college perceptions: are differences actually because of demographic variance? *Adult Education Quarterly*, 58 (3), pp. 214-228.

Hoult, E. (2006). *Learning Support for Mature Students*. London: Sage.

Johnson, S. and Robson, C. (1999). Threatened identities: the experiences of women in transition to programmes of professional higher education. *Journal of Community & Applied Social Psychology*, 9, pp. 273-288.

Kristjánsson, K. (2000). Teaching Emotional Virtue: a post-Kohlbergian approach. *Scandinavian Journal of Educational Research*, 44 (4), pp. 405-422.

Leathwood, C. and Hey, V. (2009). Gender/ed discourses and emotional sub-texts: theorising emotion in UK higher education. *Teaching in Higher Education*, 14 (4), pp. 429-440.

Leibowitz, B. (2009). What's inside the suitcase? An investigation into the powerful resources students and lecturers bring to teaching and learning. *Higher Education Research & Development*, 28 (3), pp. 261-274.

Lynch, K. and Lodge, A. (2002). *Equality and Power in Schools: Redistribution, Recognition and Representation*. London: Routledge.

McMillan, W. (2013). Transition to university: the role played by emotion. *European Journal of Dental Education*. 19 (1), pp. 1-35.

Mikuska, E. (2013). The relationship between higher education, emotion and gender: a qualitative study using text and interviews. Available online http://srmo.sagepub.com/view/methods-case-studies-2014/n137.xml [accessed 2 August 2015].

Nutkins, S., McDonald, C. and Stephen, M. (2013). *Early Childhood Education and Care. An introduction*. London: Sage.

Perkun, R., Elliot, A.J. and Maier, M.A. (2009). Achievement goals and achievement emotions: testing a model of their joint relations with academic performance. *Journal of Educational Performance*, 101, pp. 115-135.

Perkun, R. and Stephens, E. J. (2010). *Achievement Emotions in Higher Education, Higher Education: Handbook of Theory and Research*, Vol. 25, pp. 257-306.

Plutchik, R. (2001). The nature of emotions. *American Scientist*, 89, pp. 344-350.

Pryor, J. H., DeAngula, L., Blake, L.P., Hurtado, S. and Tran, S. (2011). The American Freshman: National Forums Fall 2011. *Cooperative Institutional Research Programme at the Higher Education Research Institute at UCLA*. Los Angeles: University of California.

Quinlan, K.M. (2014). Conceptualising emotion in research on teaching and learning in higher education. SRHE Conference, 10-12 December, Newport, Wales.

Shuck, B. Albornoz, C. and Winberg, M. (2006). *Emotions and their Effect on Adult Learning: A Constructivist Perspective*. Florida: Florida International University.

Schultz, A.P. and DeCuir, T.J. (2002). Inquiry on emotion in education. *Educational Psychologist*, 37, pp. 125–134.

Turner, J.H. and Stets, E.J. (2005). *Sociology of Emotions*. Cambridge: Cambridge University Press.

Trodd, L. [Ed.] (2013). *Transitions in the Early Years, working with children and families*. London: Sage.

Williams, S. (2001). *Emotion and Social Theory*. London: Sage.

Zembylas, M. (2008). Adult learners' emotions in online learning. *Distance Education* 29 (1), pp. 71–78.

2 Becoming an undergraduate: the transition from Level 3 to Levels 4 and 5

Jonathan Ratcliffe

LEARNING OUTCOMES

After reading this chapter, you should have:

✔ Developed and increased your awareness of the differences in academic rigour and expectations of the foundation degree: and the contrast between a Level 3 and Level 5 qualification.
✔ Been challenged to consider your expectations and goals and to approach your study from different perspectives in order to discover how you can maximise your potential.
✔ Considered realistic strategies in terms of your personal target setting and become aware of the importance of careful and honest management of your work, study and life.
✔ Considered adopting alternative approaches to your time management with a focus on maintaining honesty, clarity and creativity in terms of your approach to study.

Introduction

'Study' – noun: The pursuit of knowledge, as by reading, observation or research

This chapter is not only about learning how to study, but how to manage what you study and how you study. Your degree will cover a host of **assessment** methods, some of which will suit your learning preferences more than others. It is important to understand that the academic journey on which you are now embarking will have its ups and downs. This chapter has been written to help you combat the times when you are struggling and also to help you get through them.

One of the main reasons for writing this chapter was to try to prepare you for the 'jump' from Level 3 to Level 4. Some students struggle at first to adapt to the requirements of Level 4 and they are often surprised by the expectations and academic rigour that Level 4 requires of them. This chapter aims to support and guide you through your experience of this transition and enable you to succeed.

This chapter challenges you to be open to taking risks, and to try different approaches to your study to encourage you out of your 'comfort zone'. As Early Years practitioners you are most probably juggling many aspects of work and life and therefore you need to find the right strategies so that you achieve your potential.

Level 3 to Levels 4 and 5 - What is the difference?

There are two main differences between Level 3 and Level 4 academic study; the first is that within Level 3 your writing style is largely descriptive, whereas at Levels 4 and 5 you are expected to develop a critical and analytical writing style that is supported by evidence.

Second, at Levels 4 and 5 you are expected to become a more proactive and independent learner. You will find that you are much more responsible for finding things out for yourself and managing your study. You will not find all you need to know within one textbook, for example! At Levels 4 and 5 there is an expectation that you should be researching the content gained from each lecture in order to deepen your knowledge and understanding. What you learn in each taught session is not exhaustive. You need to take responsibility for widening your knowledge and challenging yourself using reading and research.

One of the first things you will discover at Level 4 is that there is a difference in the academic language you will be expected to understand and use. Words such as 'describe' and 'outline' can be replaced by 'compare', 'analyse' and 'evaluate' and so on. You can no longer rely on description to form your discussion or response to essay questions; instead you need to show your understanding using various viewpoints and perspectives on the subject matter. The only way you can achieve this is to read, read and read!

Here is a breakdown of some key academic words that you will come across throughout your Level 4 and Level 5 studies. Please use it as a guide to help you to understand the requirements of your assessment.

Analyse   Break an issue into its constituent parts. Look in depth at each part using supporting arguments and evidence for and against as well as how these interrelate to one another.

Compare   Identify the similarities and differences between two or more phenomena. Say if any of the shared similarities or differences are more important than others. 'Compare' and 'contrast' will often feature together in an essay question.

Critically evaluate   Give your verdict as to what extent a statement or findings within a piece of research are true, or to what extent you agree with them. Provide evidence taken from a wide range of sources which both agree with *and* contradict an argument. Come to a final conclusion, basing your decision on what you judge to be the most important factors and justify how you have made your choice.

Define   To give in precise terms the meaning of something. Bring to attention any problems posed with the definition and different interpretations that may exist.

Describe   Provide a detailed explanation as to how and why something happens.

Discuss   Essentially this is a written debate where you are using your skill at reasoning, backed up by carefully selected evidence to make a case for and against an argument. Or you could point out the advantages and disadvantages of a given context. Remember to arrive at a conclusion.

Identify   Determine the key points to be addressed and their implications.

Justify   Make a case by providing a body of evidence to support your ideas and points of view. In order to present a balanced argument, consider opinions which may run contrary to your own before stating your conclusion.

Outline   Convey the main points placing emphasis on global structures and interrelationships rather than minute detail.

Review   Look thoroughly into a subject. This should be a critical assessment and not merely descriptive.

Summarise   Give a condensed version drawing out the main facts and omit superfluous information. Brief or general examples will normally suffice for this kind of answer.

The list above is not exhaustive. You may come across other Level 4 and 5 words. The key thing is to make sure that you are completely clear about what you are being asked to do so take some time to check the definition of any such words.

Another important feature to grasp when writing your Level 4 assignments is that your personal opinion matters but you must support and back-up your opinions and arguments with evidence from a wide range of relevant reading and literature. It is essential that you realise from the outset that you must develop your academic thinking and writing techniques to embrace and tackle the requirements of Level 4.

Expectations and making things happen

CASE STUDY 1

Recently I have been studying a concept that the GB Cycling Team and Team Sky successfully adopted and that contributed to them winning the Tour de France and, shortly after, the Great Britain Cycling Team were the most successful cycling team at the Olympics in London 2012, securing eight gold, two silver and two bronze medals and also securing 22 medals including 8 golds in the Paralympic games (British Cycling, 2014).

This concept has been named 'Marginal Gains' (Hoye *et al.*, 2015) and is a theory that has been developed by Sir David Brailsford who was the Performance Director for the Team GB Cycling Team. Brailsford explained it as 'the 1% margin for improvement in everything you do' (Clear, 2013). His plan was meticulous and his belief was that if you improved every area related to cycling by just 1 per cent those small gains add up to remarkable improvement. Brailsford was determined that if they could successfully execute this strategy, then Team Sky would be in a position to win the Tour de France in five years' time. He was wrong. They won it in three years.

Some of the aspects that Team GB focused on were making sure cyclists washed their hands properly – this would limit their chances of becoming ill; each cyclist took their own pillow to each hotel they stayed in whilst on tour – this improved the likelihood of a more restful sleep; and even searching for the best types of massage gels to use after training (Clear, 2013). These improvements were some of many they considered and with each consideration may have improved their performance by 1 per cent at a time. If you improve ten minor aspects of your performance you have then increased your overall performance by 10 per cent.

You may be wondering at this point what the relevance of cycling performance theory is to a chapter about study skills for Early Years Practitioners. The answer to that is simple; you can apply this same approach to your studies and performance whilst on your degree.

Consider an essay where you were graded 57 per cent. If you were to improve your essay by 5 per cent it would then take your grade to the next assessment boundary. By applying the marginal gains concept you would need to consider what five things you could do to improve your essay – when you consider it this way it seems achievable and realistic. Supposing you identified that you need to add more critical analysis to your discussion or maybe you just need to edit and proof-read your work more thoroughly or could you improve your conclusion slightly. All these things are achievable and within your reach. With limited improvement, this could be the difference between a Commendation and a Distinction!

Marginal gains does not have to be something that you focus on just in terms of improving your grade by making changes to the essays you write, it could be that you make marginal gains by getting more sleep the night before your attendance at lectures, making sure that you get to University or College 10 minutes before a lesson in order to relax and focus, making sure you eat breakfast and take in lots of fluids throughout the day. These small improvements could increase your performance and concentration slightly and after a while your performance may have improved by 1 per cent with very little effort.

Likewise don't waste time and energy on worrying about your studying, about what or how well your peers are doing or panicking about how you are going to fit in all of your studying. This is time and energy wasted and it is not a positive mind-set. Instead, concentrate on what you can do to combat these issues. Spend time figuring out how you can solve these problems. The fact that this method of producing success in various sports and skills in life shows it's a transferable and adaptable methodology which can be moulded into most walks of life (CSC, 2014).

Identifying how you learn best

Every year at graduation ceremonies students collect their degree certificates knowing that one of the major influences in helping them to gain their degree qualification was the help and support they received from their family and friends. It is important that you recognise this in the early stages of your studies and that you accept support from the people who are close to you. For some students it is small things that help; asking someone to look at your spelling and grammar in an essay or asking someone to look after your children for a few hours while you get some valuable studying done. When you consider how to improve your chances of success and add to your enjoyment of your course, it is important to communicate with friends and family in terms of the rigour and requirements of your programme. Don't keep family and friends in the dark. Then they will be aware that from time to time you may feel some strain and they will be able to empathise and support you.

ACTIVITY

✔ Look back at the feedback that you received for your last essay and determine what aspects your tutor is suggesting you could improve on or what areas of the essay were lacking. This will give you the basis to begin improving your performance 1 per cent at a time.

✔ Take a few minutes now to compile a list of things that you believe you could make small changes to – remember that marginal gains can add up to significant improvements.

✔ Don't compare yourself to other students . . . focus on yourself.

✔ Have an open mind in terms of **marginal gains.** Don't rule it out until you have tried it!

One of the most important aspects of how we learn best is based on knowing and understanding our own learning styles and preferences. Identifying and understanding these learning styles and preferences will help you to personalise your learning and tailor your studies to suit your individual and personal needs. There are many different theories related to learning styles such as the work of Kolb and Honey and Mumford. As a Level 4 or 5 student who takes responsibility for his or her own learning you should be proactive in discovering your preferences, identifying your needs and using this information to help you study effectively.

REFLECTIVE PRACTICE
REFLECTIVE PRACTICE

Consider the following:

What do I tend to prefer?

1 Someone talking to me and telling me how something is done? (Auditory learner)
2 Someone letting me try something myself, using my hands and getting stuck in! (Kinaesthetic learner)
3 Watching someone, seeing and visualising how something is done. (Visual Learner)

While studying and attending your lectures, seminars and workshops you will encounter all of the above strategies for teaching and learning. You will find yourself preferring different styles of learning in different situations. It is really important that you do not label yourself as just one of these and as a result resist other teaching and learning styles. You need to consider which style or styles you lean towards and then use this knowledge to your advantage. It is very common for students to identify their learning style but to fail to consider what they need to do next. It is pointless to apply a label yourself but not to ask the questions:

– What do I need to do about this?
– How can I make this work for me?
– What do I need in order to succeed?

Learning styles are not fixed and may change over time. As your undergraduate experience progresses, take responsibility for challenging yourself about how your learning preference may be changing and developing.

PROVOCATION

You find yourself in a lesson and you are struggling to concentrate and understand while listening to a lecturer explain a theory related to practice. The lecturer does not use visual aids or practical activities. What should you do?

- Do you just listen harder and then tell yourself you will ask your friend at break time to explain what has been 'taught' to you?
- Do you write a note to yourself to have a look at your notes later in your own time?
- Do you ask the lecturer to explain the theory again?

None of these things are wrong, but in this situation when you are struggling to learn from auditory teaching you could take responsibility for your own learning. You could ask the lecturer if they would give a practical example of the theory in terms of your Early Years practice. You could ask for a diagram or visual representation of the theory or if you are daring, role play the theory in small groups!

By taking charge of your learning and using your knowledge of how you learn to overcome obstacles and barriers that you may face, you are being a proactive learner. You are identifying that you have a study challenge but you are going one step further and trying to overcome it.

The environment in which you study is usually an important factor of success. You need to identify what features of your environment help you to feel comfortable and able to concentrate. Factors like the amount of noise, how light the room is, how comfortable your chair is and time of day or evening can all be influential on our capacity to study. When is the right time for you? Are you an early bird or a night owl? Such issues may seem trivial but, in terms of marginal gains, they could be the 1 per cent of difference that is crucial to your success. Usually people have a preference for a particular type of environment but it may change from day to day.

REFLECTIVE PRACTICE
REFLECTIVE PRACTICE

Use the following exercise to identify what particular type of environment is conducive to your studies.

As you pack up your books after a study session jot down what helped and hindered your ability to think, read and write. What helped you to start? What meant you were not distracted? What took you off task? Read the rest of the chapter jotting down your reflections on how the content applies to you and then review your notes. Are there common themes?

Studying: the work-life balance

Balancing work, study and life as a practitioner student is a huge challenge. You will need to be honest and realistic with yourself about what you are going to achieve. Some students set themselves unrealistic goals and targets. While this makes them feel better in the short term, when they do not achieve these goals and targets the disappointment and failure they experience affects their motivation. Such students are more likely to doubt themselves and start to question their ability to succeed. When time is a rare commodity you have to make the most of the time you do have. Ask yourself: *What do I really believe I will be able to achieve today*? *Do I feel like writing today and can I concentrate enough*?

Perhaps if you have only a little time or are finding it particularly hard to concentrate you should spend some time gathering resources, photocopying, organising, reading – something that does not require you to think and concentrate at a high level. If you are self-aware in this way at least you will do something productive with your time and you may feel better than if you had wasted time struggling to concentrate and making little progress.

– *What are my immediate priorities?* Do you need to get to grips with the requirements of the assignment before you start reading? Do you fully understand the learning outcomes? Do you know what you are trying to find out when you are reading or are you reading without a purpose?
– *Are my motivation levels low?* Are there some 'quick wins' to be achieved? Success may give you a lift and help to motivate you.

These questions are starting points. You know yourself better than anyone else. Consider other questions you could ask of yourself in order to study successfully. Perhaps you need to find a way to remind yourself that sacrifices made now will pay off in the long term.

Time management

There has been a lot of literature published over the years and many websites created that give advice on managing your time more effectively. Little has been written about being honest and realistic about the time available. Students who are most successful with their time management and enjoy their studies are those who are most honest and realistic about how much study time they can really fit into their busy schedule.

REFLECTIVE PRACTICE
REFLECTIVE PRACTICE

The following table will help you identify exactly how much time you apply to the different areas of your life. Complete the table below making sure you are honest in order to help effective time management.

Estimate your average for the following:	Write down how many hours per day:	Weekly total	Conclusions
How many hours are you at work?			
How many hours are you spending with family and friends?			
How many hours of free time do you have?			
For how many hours do you have other pressing commitments?			
How many hours a day do you sleep?			
Totals			

Are you surprised by the results from your table? Have you identified how much time left to study you actually have? You need to note areas of concern when looking at the hours you have estimated for the different aspects of your life.

You need to have a balance of time for you, your family, rest time, fun time and study time. Are there some small changes you can make to your day that would enable you to increase the time you can dedicate to studying? Are you a last minute.com person? Some students are organised and submit their work before the deadline. However, some students are the 'last minuters'. Ask yourself the two questions below.

- *Are you spending little time preparing for study and assignments and having to work as the deadline looms, perhaps producing work that is not as good it could be?*
- *Is this just the way you are and you enjoy 'taking things up to the wire'? Or do you have to admit that you know you need to do things differently but you don't know how to change?*

Set yourself short timed tasks. This will get you started and prevent you spending too much or too little time on particular elements of your studying. For example, give yourself 10 minutes to read a chapter that is linked to the learning outcomes of your assignment and then only 10 minutes to write up your thoughts in your notes.

Being creative with how you learn and study

Craft et al. (2001) define being creative as 'seeing the world differently . . . happy to experiment, to take risks and to make mistakes. They make connections often unseen by others' (2001, p. 38). A successful student adopts a creative approach to his or her studies. Experiment and take risks with how you approach your reading or structure your notes and assignments in order to find the most effective way for you.

REFLECTIVE PRACTICE
REFLECTIVE PRACTICE

Question: *Do you take risks in terms of where you look for information? Or do you stay with the recommended titles within your reading lists? Have you ever considered using a different method to plan the structure of your essay; a mind-map or brainstorm, a list and so on?*

Being creative in this way is aligned to being independent in the way you learn and having the independent mind expected when you are studying at Levels 4 and 5. A creative approach reaps benefits in all aspects of your studies including in your class discussions, your assignments and your own **reflective practice**. Asking creative questions helps you develop a broader understanding of something you are studying, it helps you to see and appreciate things from a different perspective and it can also help you to develop your thinking. You might ask, for example:

- What does that really mean?
- Do I agree with it or not and why?
- What if I did it another way? What can I do differently? How can I improve that? Is there another way to approach it?
- Is there another side to that story (theory)?
- Why did I do that? What made me make that decision?

Some experts call this 'thinking outside the box'. Perhaps it would be better to call it 'thinking outside *your* box'. Such questions are fundamental to developing the **criticality** expected at undergraduate level, that is, demonstrating the ability to look at the world from different perspectives from the obvious ones or the ones with which you are presented. Some fairly simple questions can support the development of criticality in your studies, such as:

- Who says?
- What is the evidence for their claims?

- Can we trust the evidence?
- Can we trust the logic of what is presented?
- What will they get out of saying this and convincing others of it?
- So what?
- Who disagrees with this and why?
- What are the assumptions behind this statement?

Adopting these questions and applying them to all aspects of your study and practice will enable you to stretch yourself and develop different perspectives.

FROM RESEARCH TO PRACTICE

Think about what you know about how the brain develops especially with regard to the formation of neural pathways. Does this support a view that we are creatures of habit?

Fisher and Williams challenge us to avoid doing things in the same way. They suggest that doing things differently avoids unquestioning habits of mind. They argue that when we do things that we have not done before, and they are effective, we begin to develop an 'individual mind' (2006, p. 9).

Think of something you have done differently. How did it make you feel? What was the impact on others? Was doing something differently associated with more or less learning?

Writing good assignments

Whole books are dedicated to how to write better assignments. This chapter will only touch on a few of the most important points. To write a good assignment, you first need to have a clear understanding of what the essay question or task is asking you to do and especially understanding the learning outcomes it is asking you to address. In HE assignments and examinations you have to assess the learning outcomes for the module. Looking at the essay question in close detail will help you to identify the topic and the significant 'directive words' which instruct you how to answer the question. As stated earlier in this chapter, understanding the full meaning of these directive words is a vital first step to producing a relevant essay.

Thinking in a critical and creative way enables you to consider the future audience for your assignment. For example, when writing an essay make sure that you always consider the person who will mark and moderate the assignment. How well are you communicating with the reader? Have you written the assignment in an appropriate style? Have you taken the time and trouble to number pages, set out paragraphs properly and write in complete sentences? Rather than putting a pretty picture on the front of your assignment, put your time into creating a helpful contents page. Are all your pages in plastic wallets? That usually annoys the marker. Have you included lots of unnecessary appendices to make your assignment look bigger? That also usually annoys the marker.

Did you read the feedback your tutor gave you on your previous assignment? Do not miss this opportunity to learn from feedback and improve your performance in your next assignment. Try to discern what each tutor is looking for. Take on board comments and make sure you take actions to reflect what has been said in your next assignment. What does the feedback tell you? Does your tutor want more evidence of more reading? Do you understand what is meant if your tutor suggests that your critical analysis could be improved? If not, you need to seek guidance. Is your tutor saying that a lack of proof-reading made it difficult to read and understand?

CASE STUDY 2

Tutor: 'It is surprising how often I repeat the same feedback to a student. I include in my feedback in year 1 that they need to improve their conclusions in order to achieve a higher grade and I find that I am still making the same suggestion on their final assignment feedback of their degree. I spend a great deal of time writing comments on assignments and students don't bother to read them. Yet we know that responding to feedback is the most important way for students to improve their success on their degrees. I feel like giving up!'

What technique could you use to make sure you are not one of these students? Have you ever had any of the following comments on your assignment?

- Make sure your assignment is always supported with reading, using different viewpoints to create a balanced argument.
- Keep a consistent approach throughout your assignments; are you giving each learning outcome an appropriate amount of attention?
- Always leave time to proof-read your work before submission, preferably a day or two before the deadline. This will help you to read your assignment with 'fresh eyes' and it will help you to see your mistakes and anomalies.
- Make sure you are within your word count. If your essay is under length it is likely that you have not done enough reading or critical analysis!
- Don't rush your conclusions – always ensure you have enough words left to write a thorough conclusion for each assignment.
- You need to describe, show evidence of analysis, compare and contrast and showcase your understanding via the wide range of literature you have used to compile your assignment.
- Try different strategies in terms of how you manage your reading – find a way that suits you.
- Get to know the assessment criteria well before you even start reading for your assignment, know the learning outcomes . . . keep referring to them. This will prevent you from straying off the path and digressing from the assignment title.
- Make sure that your paragraphs are well structured and that you conclude one paragraph before moving on to the next.

How did you address the points made?

Conclusion

In this chapter it has been argued that in order to maximise your potential and achieve success, you may need to trial and adopt new strategies and think differently about how you manage your study. As you reflect on the elements of the chapter you might apply to your learning consider starting with the most 'appealing' strategies or the one that you believe would be easiest to adopt, a 'quick win'. Perhaps you can manage to make a 1 per cent increase to an aspect of your study without a great deal of effort. It could make a great deal of difference to your success and enjoyment of your undergraduate studies.

Further reading

Cottrell, S. (2011) *Critical Thinking Skills: Developing Effective Analysis and Argument*, Basingstoke: Palgrave Macmillan.

This book helps students to develop reflective thinking skills, improve their critical analysis and construct arguments more effectively. It breaks down a complex subject into easily understood blocks, providing easy-to-follow, step-by-step explanations and practice activities to develop your understanding and practise your skills at each stage. It is essential for students who are mystified by tutor comments such as 'more critical analysis needed'.

Weyers, J. and MacMillan, K. (2011) *How to Write Dissertations and Project Reports*, Essex: Pearson.

This book helps the student to assess and address their particular weaknesses in researching and writing dissertations and longer pieces of coursework. It offers detailed tips, techniques and strategies to enable you to improve your abilities and performance in skills such as how to structure and plan your writing proposal, how to undertake field research, how to read and analyse information and take notes effectively, how to improve your academic writing style, how to cite references and avoid plagiarism, how to review, proof-read and present your dissertation or project for maximum impact and results.

Useful websites

www.educationscotland.gov.uk/studyskills/

This website works through study skills in a series of levels in order to help the reader become an effective learner at undergraduate level.

www2.open.ac.uk/students/skillsforstudy/

A very useful open access website specially designed to help undergraduates to develop their study skills.

www.gre.ac.uk/studyskills

A very worthwhile website that will assist you with your study skills as an undergraduate.

References

British Cycling (2014) *Great Britain Cycling Team – The Performance Pathway* [Online] Available at www.britishcycling.org.uk/performancepathway [Accessed (2/4/15)]

Clear, J. (2013) 'This Coach Improved Every Tiny Thing by 1 Percent and Here's What Happened' [Online] Available at http://jamesclear.com/marginal-gains [Accessed (4/2/15)]

Craft, A., Jeffrey, B. and Leibling, M. (eds), (2001) *Creativity in Education*. London: Continuum.

Craft, A., Jeffrey, B. and Liebling, M. (2009) *Creativity in Education*, London, Continuum.

CSC (2014) With Small Changes Comes the Aggregation of Marginal Gains in Business Process Outsourcing [Online] Available at www.csc.com/life_sciences/blog/101149/107529-with_small_changes_comes_the_aggregation_of_marginal_gains_in_business_process_outsourcing [Accessed (4/2/15)]

Fisher, R. and Williams, M. (2010) *Unlocking Creativity: Teaching across the Curriculum*. Oxford, David Fulton Publishers.

Hoye, R., Smith, A. and Nicholson, M. (2015) *Sport Management: Principles and Applications,* London: Routledge.

Robinson, K. (1999) National Advisory Committee on Creative and Cultural Education, *All Our Futures: Creativity, Culture and Education*, Report to the Secretary of State for Education and Employment and the Secretary of State for Culture, Media and Sport, NACCE.

3 Work-based learning

Caroline Jones and Jo Dallal

LEARNING OUTCOMES

After reading this chapter you should be able to:

✔ Understand theoretical perspectives on the notion of work-based learning.
✔ Explain the connection between work-based learning and the Foundation Degree in Early Years.
✔ Discuss the role of the mentor in the early years.
✔ Justify the role of work-based learning in relation to professional development.
✔ Recognise the importance of researching practice as an element of work-based learning.

Introduction

This chapter examines the notion of work-based learning as an integral feature of Foundation Degrees, with particular reference to the Foundation Degree in Early Years. It encourages undergraduate students to embrace work-based learning, in their own contexts, as integral to the spirit of the Foundation Degree in Early Years and not view it as a 'bolt on' to academic study. The chapter begins by acknowledging that there is a lack of consensus about the meaning of work-based learning in theory and in practice. It examines the notion of work-based learning, highlighting the shift in thinking from traditional ideas of work experience as being primarily about 'practice', to more recent and radical views of work-based learning as an increasingly significant and critical element of learning at higher education (HE) level.

Farrelly (2010) argues that a fundamental principle underpinning work-based learning is to acknowledge and reward higher learning wherever it has taken place, within a university qualification. Drawing on case studies and student voices we exemplify this in this chapter and identify the potential value of work-based learning, specifically in relation to the Foundation Degree in Early Years programme. While it is beyond the scope of this chapter to provide detailed consideration of the role of the mentor, the chapter recognises the relationship between Foundation Degree in Early Years student and mentor in supporting work-based learning.

The latter part of the chapter illustrates the potential of work-based learning as a tool for professional development, enabling you to think critically about your own practice and recording your own work-based learning journey. The final section examines work-based learning in the context of researching an aspect of practice, with particular reference to undergraduate research projects. Such projects reinforce the view that the workplace as a learning environment not only provides a vehicle for the application of knowledge but for the generation of new knowledge.

The chapter concludes that, in spite of the constraints, effective work-based learning can be an empowering experience for students and can result in the emergence of a different practitioner. We suggest that the potential of work-based learning in developing new higher level professional knowledge and skills remains undervalued. We argue that the Foundation Degree in Early Years, characterised by the interaction between academic and work-based learning, is crucial in the development of new knowledge and can make a significant contribution to the government's aspirations to create a 'world class' children's workforce.

What is work-based learning?

It is important to acknowledge from the outset that work-based learning is a mode of study that takes place in a variety of contexts, ranging from block work placements, sandwich courses, day release and voluntary work, to paid employment while studying at the same time. Work-based learning cannot be simply defined, as it is a complex, messy process taking place in a context which Schön (1987, p. 71) and Moore and Workman (2011) refer to as the 'swampy low land of practice', representative of the reality of the real world of work. The term 'workplace' is used to cover the diverse range of voluntary, independent, private and state maintained settings where practitioners on Foundation Degree in Early Years will be applying their knowledge and skills in their paid or voluntary work with children.

Work-based learning has become an umbrella term encompassing a range of meanings and contexts. However, even at senior management level in universities the concept of work-based learning is not wholly understood and students on these courses are often considered to be on placements rather than in employment. A number of commonly used terms are located under the auspices of work-based learning, for example, professional practice, vocational learning, work-experience, workplace, experiential or work-related learning. The common denominator is that work-based learning is related to learning that takes place in a real 'work' context, rather than learning in a classroom. Moore and Workman (2011) define experiential learning as embracing the 'knowledge skills and behaviours acquired in a planned or unplanned way throughout life (p. 70). Work-based learning is distinct from experiential learning as the location is specifically a workplace environment.

For the purposes of this chapter, we use the term **'institutional-based learning'** to refer to student learning experiences, including work-related learning and academic learning, within the Higher Education (HE) classroom context, for example at a Further Education (FE) college or at a university. Work-based learning is used to indicate learning taking place in your work context, where the workplace as opposed to the classroom is the learning environment but where there is a strong link between the two.

Reflective practice and work-based learning

Traditionally, universities have been viewed as seats of knowledge where specialist lecturers transmit information. Graduates have found themselves with in-depth knowledge but no experience of applying their knowledge in a work context. Work-based learning provides the link between work and learning. It increases the practitioner's ability to reflect. One student on a **Leadership** and Management course reflected on her handling of a situation that occurred with one of her members of staff. She reflects on how she dealt with the situation without extensive consideration and immediately reprimanded the member of staff for her behaviour. This was not the best way of handling the matter. Reflection enabled her to see the error of her action and improved her handling of future incidents.

PROVOCATION

Is time to reflect important? Does it make a difference to the outcome for practitioners? Think of some examples where you have reflected and as a result your practice has been refined or developed.

On the other hand work-based learning has been viewed as the poor relation to academic learning. In the last two decades there has been a growing acceptance that traditional, didactic methods of teaching with a focus on the transmission of knowledge have not always met the needs of employers (Helyer, 2010, p. 17). The legacy of a content-heavy, didactic approach appears to be shifting in favour of a more interactive, flexible and dynamic process, which acknowledges and meets the diverse needs of learners. Hence, there has been a significant cultural shift in thinking about the workplace merely as a location for practising what has been learnt in a classroom, through to the notion of experiential learning, and more recent acknowledgement of the workplace as a site for the application of knowledge and skills. It is useful to locate work-based learning as referring to 'what is learned by working' not by reading, not by observing but actually doing *real* work (Heller, 2010, p. 2).

REFLECTIVE PRACTICE
REFLECTIVE PRACTICE

Consider the meaning of work-based learning:

- Do you believe in the concept of 'learning by doing' as stated by Rawlings (2008)? Why might it be better for the practitioner than other modes of learning?
- By engaging in this form of practice are you becoming an agent for change?

This chapter takes this a step further, and starts from the premise that the workplace is not only a site for practical experience or experiential learning. Instead, we argue that it is vital in ensuring not only the application of knowledge and skills, but crucially a place where new knowledge can be generated. Seagraves *et al.* (1996) (see Rawlings, 2008, p. 23), differentiate between three strands that can be used to examine personal and professional learning in your own context:

- **Strand 1** Learning for work – theory, knowledge, skills and understanding.
- **Strand 2** Learning at work – roles, responsibilities and relationships.
- **Strand 3** Learning through work – looks at the application of knowledge and skills in the workplace.

Learning for, through and in work contexts offers flexible, student-centred and relevant opportunities for learning.

PROVOCATION

With reference to your own learning, identify some examples for each of the above three strands.

The Sector-Endorsed Foundation Degree in Early Years and work-based learning

Moore and Workman (2011, p. 67) claim that notwithstanding the complexity of work-based learning it encourages meaningful 'individual led investigation' and 'a creative, imaginative, and collaborative, approach to lifelong learning that enables the development of a workforce that is 'fit for purpose'. Rawlings (2008, p. 2) suggests that work-based learning can be viewed as an element of 'a structured learning course, taking place in a voluntary or paid position that connects career opportunities and interests with academic aspirations and qualifications'.

This was exemplified by the introduction of the HE **Sector-Endorsed Foundation Degree in Early Years** (SEFDEY) in 2001, a new employment-related higher education qualification, which acknowledged that a combination of broad-based rigorous academic learning and relevant work specific skills was the essential ingredient to developing high calibre Early Years practitioners. A core feature of the foundation degree model is the timely application of knowledge and skills in the world of work, as opposed to studying an academic degree and developing knowledge of theory without an opportunity to apply the new knowledge until three or more years later. Furthermore there was a clear official acknowledgement of the value of the workplace as an environment for learning as well as experience, and that work-based learning should be creditworthy in the Higher Education context,

There should be procedures for valuing work-based learning not purely for its experiential dimension, but for its worth in terms of achieving credit towards the learning requirements of the degree.

(DfES, 2001, p. 11)

The Statement of Requirement (DfES 2001) heralded a set of core learning outcomes for Foundation Degrees in Early Years and clearly stated that 'By the end of the Foundation Degree a learner should be able to demonstrate appropriate knowledge and understanding and have demonstrated in the workplace' that these outcomes had been achieved. The Statement of Requirement determined that within an effectively planned framework work-based learning was of equivalent value to institution based learning stating that,

The term work-based learning derives from the fact that fulfilling a role in the workplace is itself an educative experience. Just as what is learned in lectures or seminars, or arises from independent study, can be credited in relation to the requirements of the Foundation Degree, so can what is learned in the workplace. For this reason it needs to be reflected upon and related to theory in a systematic way – it will be important that learners are provided with an appropriate framework. Similarly important is that work-based learning is carefully integrated with 'traditional' learning, so that learners can be clear that both are of *equal value*.
(my italics) (DfES, 2001, p. 4)

CASE STUDY 1

Student feedback confirms that the concept of work-based learning does not detract from the academic rigour of the Sector-Endorsed Foundation Degree in Early Years but rather enhances the learning and the practice. Many students have commented on their increased knowledge as a result of their studies which then creates a different atmosphere in the workplace. Fellow practitioners begin to regard them differently, with more respect, as having more accurate knowledge. One of the strengths of work-based learning is the potential immediate effect of being able to put learning into practice and to be able to implement new initiatives and legislation. The interface between institution-based learning and work-based learning creates a synergy which enhances the skills of the practitioner and ultimately benefits the child and the workplace.

For me this module has been all consuming in the best possible way. I have been fascinated by the way stories can awaken children's thinking and learning. The school has enabled me to use stories and storytelling all term in literacy session.

'How Children Learn and Develop' was useful and made me look at my work in a different light. I have gained knowledge and understanding and am now able to use critical thinking and questioning in my setting as to why children behave in certain ways. I have been more reflective on my practice.

I always thought I had enough knowledge about children but I have deepened my knowledge and understanding of the needs and characteristics of young children. I have gained knowledge of why 'play' is an important part of a child's life.

I am so impressed with the session on 'sustained shared thinking'. Of course, it's what I do naturally or should do, but do I? Now having brought the concept to the front of my mind I can actively steer the conversation and learning task to the child's way of thinking and level of understanding.

As a result of this new knowledge (on computers) I am more confident when supporting children.

I have gained so much not only academically and professionally but personally.

I have been able to improve my teaching skills and I am now so much more aware of the child as an individual.

A positive experience that has helped to improve confidence, strengthen my knowledge and given me a greater understanding of legislation.

Learning and experience went hand in hand and helped to inform practice.

I no longer feel disempowered and feel that I have an important place in the care and education hierarchy.

REFLECTIVE PRACTICE

Below is a list of the benefits of work-based learning (adapted from Helyer, 2010, p. 8). Which (if any) of these features matters to you?

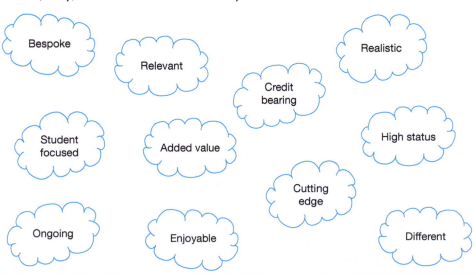

In pedagogical terms the Foundation Degree in Early Years is based on a developmental, process-based curriculum model that focuses on reflective enquiry-based study, couched in the term work-based learning. In practice, programmes have incorporated work-based learning in a variety of ways. For example, on some programmes specific modules focus on workplace learning, while others embed work-based learning across the programme. The common denominator for students is that work and study are combined and there is a continued attempt to acknowledge

CASE STUDY 2

The feedback from employers and mentors signals the benefits in the workplace environment.

This module has consolidated and reinforced Cheryl's knowledge, substantiating the reasons why children behave as they do. She is more proficient now at observing and assessing children and relating these observations to theory.

Christine is finding the module challenging but very interesting and it is causing her to reflect on her professional practice.

She is more confident and reflective in her practice.

The Foundation Degree in Early Years model, of systematically integrating institution-based learning and work-based learning, enabling the application of new knowledge gained in the academic context can be a process which not only benefits employers, but empowers students.

My students feel empowered by their new-found knowledge and that they can apply it in the workplace.

The subjects I am learning about are relevant to my work, I look at things differently because I question myself.

I feel energised. I am far more reflective within my daily practice and am able to monitor, extend and expand children's learning further.

An awesome and inspiring night – practical strategies, reflection, theory and pure delight!

PROVOCATION

- Can you think of any examples of how the integration of institutional-based learning and work-based learning has had an impact in your professional context?
- What constraints might inhibit the potential benefits of work-based learning?

not only the link between theory and practice but the link between practice and theory. Helyer (2010, p. 3) highlights the unusual benefits to students on work-based learning programmes, combining the traditional benefits of HE study, intellectual, personal, critical and analytical skills, which can then be used to inform and support practical skills and knowledge.

Garnett (2004, cited in Moore and Workman 2011, p. 64) states that work-based learning,

> is a learning process which focuses University level critical thinking upon work (paid or unpaid) in order to facilitate the recognition, acquisition and application of individual and collective knowledge, skills and abilities to achieve specific outcomes of significance to the learning, their work and the University.

The notion of work-based learning is pushing the boundaries of traditional understandings of learning at HE level. It has been described as a 'marrying' process which brings theory outside the classroom – to the shop floor or wherever individuals seek to '*build* and *use' knowledge* (italics in original) (Nicolou-Walker, cited in Helyer, 2010, p. 21). This implies that work-based learning is far more than just the application of knowledge to practice but is instrumental in creating new

CASE STUDY 3

The Warwick model – a tripartite relationship

The Warwick tripartite model originated from the pilot Foundation Degree for teaching assistants. The Warwick Partnership system was well-established in relation to initial teacher training and the placement of students on teaching practice in primary and secondary schools. It was adapted to the Foundation Degree in Early Years students and has evolved over the last 12 years, to provide a clear framework for the integration of work-based and institution-based learning. Students are required to be paid for directed voluntary work with children under eight for a minimum of 150 hours a year. At the point of application students, wherever possible, select a mentor to support them in the workplace. The workplace signs to confirm they are aware of and support the application and are prepared to support the student in the work-based elements of the course. Each student is assigned a university link tutor who visits the setting three or four times a year and forms the bridge between the student, the workplace and university. If possible, students keep the same link tutor throughout the three years and build up a strong partnership with our settings, some lasting for several years. Students keep a record of their professional development, and the university link tutor and mentor jointly support this. Workplace elements are embedded in all modules with varying levels of emphasis. Work-based tasks are formatively and summatively assessed. The mentor and university link tutor reflect with the student on their progress each term. The programme culminates in a workplace project in which students investigate an aspect of practice involving a small-scale study jointly supervised by the link tutor and the mentor.

knowledge through the application of theory to practice, notably through 'live interrogation' of practice. From this perspective work-based learning arises from action and problem-solving within a work environment, live projects and the generation of new knowledge through a tripartite interaction between the HE institution, the setting as a community of practice and the student.

The role of mentor

One of the cornerstones of work-based learning is the role of the workplace mentor. Since the inception of the Foundation Degree in Early Years, there have been various models of mentoring used in work-based learning. Mentoring occurs in a variety of forms, ranging from informal to formal adviser and from a 'critical friend' offering support to a line manager and lasting varying amounts of time. Mentors may be assigned to a particular student or may be chosen by the students themselves. In most cases, mentors are considered to have more experience than the student, but it is possible for peers to mentor each other (Murray, 2006). Rodd (2006, p. 173) points out that the early **childhood** profession has 'endorsed informal and formal mentoring as a key leadership strategy because it focuses on helping practitioners to realize their professional potential'. Callan endorses this view and describes the mentor as a 'bridge between the academic forum and the day-to-day experience encountered by practitioners in early years settings'. suggesting that the mentor 'assists in the transmission of knowledge and skills and encourages practitioners to develop **reflective practice**' (Callan, 2006, p. 8).

Doan (2013, p. 22) argues that successful mentoring can result in a culture of learning, where knowledge gain occurs for both the mentor and the mentee. Clutterbuck (2005, p. 19) states that 'the essence of effective mentoring is that mentors have the facility to move along the dimensions in response to their observations of the learner's needs at the time'. However, the role of a mentor is not unproblematic and can be difficult to sustain. Finding a mentor can be difficult, if as a student you are the most senior person in the setting. Inconsistency of mentor training, knowledge, experience and levels of support may disadvantage those students who receive lower-quality support.

CASE STUDY 4

The Kingston University model of mentoring

The Kingston model was developed in 2003 when the first Foundation Degree in Early Years was developed. One of the strengths of this model is its collaborative nature. Nine colleges are involved, each delivering the same programme. Again it was a tripartite model. Employers were part of the development process lending their expertise to the content. However there is no obligation for them to offer more than nominal support for the student. During the interview process, students are asked to acknowledge support from their workplace and are given information about the role of work-based mentors. Students have the opportunity, with guidance from the setting and their tutor, to select an appropriate mentor. When the student first applies for one of the Foundation Degrees they are required to nominate a person who will fulfil this role. However, this person might change over the years that the student is studying. Experience demonstrates that it has become apparent how much students value this support. As a staff team we also find this support invaluable. It is a good idea to arrange regular time slots to see the mentee. We are aware of busy lifestyles and understand that this might not happen on a weekly or even a fortnightly basis. Once a month would be sufficient and might prove particularly useful around the time for submission of an assignment. The student might be asking for advice about observation and/or assessments and certainly for time to undertake them. If the mentor has completed a similar qualification it would be useful to share resources or give advice as to where relevant documents might be available. An opportunity to attend meetings or to go on relevant courses might be offered, which might possibly help them with the writing of their assignments. It might also prove useful for the student to share some of their learning at staff development sessions if this was felt to be appropriate.

Kingston University 'roadshows' provide a forum for both students and mentors to discuss issues with support from programme tutors and university staff. For students at Kingston, the mentor acts as someone (usually with a higher qualification) who can calm the practitioner's nerves, who can listen to and guide their ideas and make suggestions which might add depth to their learning. Nurturing relationship confidence and self-esteem develops confidence. Professional dialogue and critical conversations support the development of pedagogical practice. The mentor aids the practitioner in an essential skill, that of reflection. Where a mentor is a senior colleague they may be able to act as an advocate, using their power, influence and authority on behalf of the mentee.

A list of ways that a mentor might support work-based learning:

- Helping find answers to challenges
- Promoting, guiding and nurturing as well as cognitive, affective support
- Sustaining motivation
- Supporting in keeping up-to-date
- Observing practice and giving feedback
- Authenticating practice
- Offering guidance with written oral work-based assessment
- Enabling access talk to parents or other professionals
- Enabling access to other age groups or settings
- Supporting with work-related tasks
- Being a link between the setting and the Higher Education Institutions or university
- Passing on information about your course to others in the setting
- Keeping you up-to-date with external and internal changes in policy
- Supporting the maintenance of a record of professional development
- Reviewing targets set
- Offering positive, constructive criticism if necessary
- Enabling visits to other age groups

- Encouraging reflection
- Helping mentees to identify and solve problems for themselves
- Liaising with the programme leader and personal tutor regarding any problems that may affect the mentee's progress on the course
- Being partners in the reflection process, not only in the formally logged meetings but on a day-to-day basis.

It is important to remember that the mentor role is also a form of work-based learning. Mentors will often be part of the process for work-based formative assessment in co-operation with the colleges. This does not involve marking assignments or discussing the intricacies of referencing. It involves offering support for work-based learning, i.e. the professional elements of the course.

As a student it is important that you take the initiative and make the most of your mentor's time and talents. Mentors may be busy people and students may be reluctant to ask for time. The student must initiate a professional dialogue in order to benefit from the relationship, remembering that it may be a voluntary one which is often entered into for purely altruistic reasons. The onus is on the student to take responsibility for their own learning and not wait for the mentor to make things happen. It is advisable that students establish the reasons for a meeting by providing an agenda, summarising what they have discussed, and agreeing actions for the next meeting, also that they are proactive in fixing the date for the next meeting.

CASE STUDY 5

Students from two different universities comment on the role of mentor

My mentor is able to look at the module guidelines and make sure I understand the requirements of the brief; she can make suggestions, in order to draw out further details. (Foundation Degree in Early Years Student, Kingston University 2014)

Through termly meetings with my mentor, I have been able to look at what I would like to achieve during the following term and modules, and have set targets to help me achieve these goals accordingly. Towards the end of the term, I have met with my mentor again, to review the targets and to consider their effectiveness and establish whether further strategies or action need to be taken, for me to be able to achieve them. (University of Warwick Foundation Degree in Early Years 2013)

PROVOCATION

Consider your relationship with your mentor – how could you both make the process more effective?

Work-based learning and professional development

Rawlings (2008) suggests that interpersonal, inter-professional, intellectual and practical skills are developed though each learner's recognition and reflection on their professional development. On your work-based practice it is likely that you will be required to keep some sort of record of your learning journey. A common model for recording this process is the maintaining of a record of professional development or professional development plan (PDP). These are primarily practitioner led and the documentation can be used as evidence to demonstrate the personal and professional outcomes that have been achieved. This could be an e-portfolio, a collection of work-related tasks, and a series of reflections, profiles or a structured diary. Common elements are that it documents a learning journey, contains a range of evidence and demonstrates continuous reflection and self-evaluation at a deeper level. Whether it is formally assessed or used as a tool for reference, it takes the practitioner though a process of self-expression.

Foundation Degree in Early Years students at the University of Warwick, for example, are required to keep a record of professional development from the first day on the course. This provides a systematic approach for documenting professional development. It also provides a personal tool in which students can record their thoughts, feelings, comments and reflections during a period of learning. They can also include an account of professional growth and development. The record of professional development includes, for example, termly target-setting and self-evaluation records, logs of review meetings with mentors, termly reflective learning diaries, and link tutor reviews. Students can develop this record according to their own needs, ultimately creating a comprehensive and progressive as well as a reflective, critical and analytical overview of the work-based learning elements of the course. A key purpose of developing this type of record is to provide a tool for you to manage and evaluate your own learning and critically reflect on your own practice. Through this process students' experiential knowledge and skills are valued, and reflection on the underpinning values and attitudes of their professional practice is promoted. The Open University (E105) states that the professional development plan 'should relate to your own practice taking into account your values and beliefs, strengths and weaknesses – in terms both of aspects of your knowledge and practice. It should acknowledge constraints, build on opportunities and contain short- and long-term goals'.

Farrelly (2010) suggests that work-based learning is not necessarily about being taught by someone else, but demands higher level independent learners, who need to take responsibility for understanding and developing their own learning priorities in relation to their practice. As students, it is important to subscribe to these processes, even if you are not sure at the start about their benefits.

CASE STUDY 6

Some students are motivated from the outset and look forward to everything that is on offer, albeit somewhat scary. One student, after an induction evening, recorded how she felt about her record of professional development.

I can't believe I am at university, I just can't wait to begin the reflective journal. I think it will be my friend for the next 4 years. A lamb to the slaughter springs to mind.

Others do not see the value or purpose of documenting reflections, and may be perplexed by the requirement to keep a record of professional development, seeing it as a time-consuming paper exercise.

When I learned that it was a requirement of my degree course to keep a reflective practice diary as part of a more general Record of Professional Development, I was irritated by the idea. I saw this as an annoying task which would serve no personal purpose and would take up valuable time.

Others find the target-setting process somewhat daunting.

This was the first time I have ever been faced with initiating my own learning. It was a new experience for me and took a lot of consideration.

However, later in the programme most students recognise the benefits.

During the last three years whilst working towards a Foundation Degree in 'Early Years' at the University of Warwick, I have been required to compile a record of professional development during my period of studies. As part of the process, I have compiled an ongoing learning diary in which I have recorded my progression both academically and personally since starting my degree. When reading through the diary and reflecting upon my journey through the last three years, the progress and development I have made academically, professionally and personally is self-evident. Another valuable method to support my professional development has been target setting. (Year 3 Student, Warwick 2013)

REFLECTIVE PRACTICE
REFLECTIVE PRACTICE

- Think about your own records and written reflections.
- How did they develop your knowledge of theory and practice?
- What key or transferable skills did you gain from recording and reflecting on your experience?

FROM RESEARCH TO PRACTICE

The knowledge and skills gained on the Foundation Degree in Early Years are *transferable* across contexts. A particularly striking, creative and innovative part of many programmes is the workplace-based project and other opportunities to research your own practice.

Whether this is through carrying out small-scale observations, case studies, or conducting an extensive project, you are in a privileged position to interrogate practice in detail. In common with a number of programmes, Sector-Endorsed Foundation Degree in Early Years students at Warwick and Kingston conduct an **action research** project, using research techniques and use their findings to develop their practice. Without exception students say this has a profound influence leading to innovation and change, not only in their settings but in their communities. The Open University provides a similar opportunity, 'The purpose of this activity is to think critically about the purpose of your research to identify its contribution to practice and impact on work-based learning and **continuing professional development**' (Activity 6.3 E210 139). The benefits of practitioner research are well established. It has the potential to make a valuable contribution to professional development and practices. Investigating a topic in depth not only encourages you to critically interrogate and challenge day-to-day practice but to develop 'fresh insights and understandings' (Cooper and Ellis, 2011, 141 E210 paraphrased). These can then be shared with colleagues formally and informally, further illustrating the power of work-based learning in generating knowledge, influencing not only the learner, but a wider group of professionals. Many Higher Education Institutions organise conference and presentation events where students each present a synopsis of their project to tutors, mentors, and other students.

Conclusion

Postmodern theory has weakened the traditional claims of what is classed as 'knowledge' and of value. This chapter has argued that the workplace is equally valid as a learning environment as the classroom in the Higher Education Institution. It has traced a cultural shift from learning being confined to institutions, to a more fluid and flexible concept. The past two decades have seen an unprecedented growth in the professionalisation of the children's workforce and a wider acknowledgement that working with children is a complex, demanding role requiring not only high levels of knowledge but also the ability to apply that knowledge in a professional context.

There has been a growing realisation of the need for a combination of rigour and an increase in reflective practice. The term 'work-based' learning is no longer regarded as a simple matter of experience but a notion with the potential to make an important contribution to the generation of knowledge, not only from an academic postgraduate research point of view but at undergraduate level. This chapter has argued that work-based learning builds self-confidence, empowering the learner and that it encourages non-traditional student entry and success. Work-based learning offers students an opportunity to think in the abstract about the complexities of the role and the multi-faceted nature of interactions between theory, policy and practices set within a particular socio-cultural historical context.

This chapter has suggested that work-based learning is a relational process which 'mediates power relationships' and is not a context-neutral activity – 'a terrain of interacting phenomena' (Darmon *et al.* cited in Wang, 2008, p. 192). The challenge remains that in some contexts knowledge emerging from practice is undervalued when, conversely, it should be recognised that content-driven programmes may actually limit new knowledge generation. Knowledge increases confidence and self-esteem. Link this to experience and there results a potent cocktail of creative energy and benefits for the child. Practitioners and academics work together to push the boundaries of learning and practice so that the two create the best possible environment for the child.

Further reading

Clutterbuck, D. (2005) *Everyone Needs a Mentor,* London, CIPD.
> *An innovative source, although now slightly dated, this book highlights the important role of the mentor in the development of work-based learning.*

Helyer, R. (2010) *The Work-Based Learning Student Handbook*, Basingstoke, Palgrave Macmillan.
> *An accessible and comprehensive guide for students on courses that include work-based elements.*

Rawlings, A. (2008) *Studying Early Years: A Guide to Work-Based Learning*, Maidenhead, Open University Press.
> *This was one of the first sources to explore work-based learning. Edited by Anne Rawlings with contributions made by three other Early Years lecturers, it provides a framework for understanding this concept and links work experiences with work-based assignments.*

References

Callan, S. (2006) 'What is mentoring?', in Robins, A. (ed.) *Mentoring in the Early Years*, London, Sage.

Clutterbuck, D. (2005) *Everyone Needs a Mentor,* London, CIPD.

Cooper V. and Ellis, C. (2011) 'Ethnographic practitioner research', in Callan, S. and Reed, M. (eds) *Work-based Research in the Early Years*, London, Sage.

Department for Education and Skills DfES (2001) *Statement of Requirement,* Nottingham DfES Publications.

Doan, L.K. (2013) 'Mentoring: a strategy to support novice early childhood educators', *Canadian Children*, 38 (2) pp. 21–23.

Farrelly, P. (ed.) (2010) *Early Years Work-Based Learning*, Exeter, Learning Matters.

Helyer, R. (ed.) (2010) *The Work-Based Learning Student Handbook*, Basingstoke, Palgrave Macmillan.

Moore T. and Workman, B. (2011) 'Work-based learning: Creative, imaginative and flexible approaches', *The International Journal of Learning* 17(12) pp. 67–79.

Murray J. (2006) 'Designing and implementing a mentoring scheme', in Robins, A. (ed.) *Mentoring in the Early Years*, London, Sage.

Open University (E105) *Professional Practice in the Early Years Book 2 Developing Reflective Practice: Key Themes*, The Open University.

Open University (E210) *Extending Professional Practice in the Early Years, Book 2, Extending Practice: Promoting Participation and Evaluating Professional Roles,* The Open University.

Rawlings, A. (2008) *Studying Early Years: A Guide to Work-Based Learning*, Maidenhead, Open University Press.

Robins, A. (ed.) (2006) *Mentoring in the Early Years*, London, Sage.

Rodd (2006) *Leadership in Early Childhood*, 3rd edition, Maidenhead, Open University Press.

Schön, D. (1987) *Educating the Professional Practitioner*, San Francisco, CA: Jossey-Bass.

Seagraves, L., Osborne, M., Neal, P., Dockrell, R., Hartsham, C. and Boyd, A. (1996) *Learning in Smaller Companies. Final Report.* Available at: files.eric.ed.gov/fulltext/ED415350.pdf [accessed 5/9/2015].

Wang L. (2008) 'Work-based learning: A critique', *The International Journal of Learning*, 15(4) pp. 189–196.

Workman, B. (2010) 'Work-based projects', (p. 127) in Helyer (ed.) *The Work-Based Learning Student Handbook*, Basingstoke, Palgrave Macmillan.

4 Developing the practice of staff in partnership with employers

Yasmin Mukadam and Eva Mikuska

LEARNING OUTCOMES

After reading this chapter, you will be able to:

✔ Understand the impact of foundation degrees within the Early Years sector.
✔ Recognise the role of higher education institutions in developing partnerships with employers.
✔ Reflect on an employer's perspectives of the Foundation Degree Early Years **(FDEY)** to determine whether it is fit for purpose.
✔ Make informed choices as an Early Years employer or student in developing the Early Years sector and enhancing both practice and career prospects.

Introduction

Foundation Degrees were introduced by the Department for Education and Skills (DfES) in 2000 to provide graduates with relevant skills to address shortages in particular sectors such as the Early Years (EY) (Quality Assurance Agency for Higher Education, 2010).

The Foundation Degree in Early Years (FDEY) is a qualification that integrates academic and work-based learning through collaborations between employers and training providers. They build upon a long history of vocational qualifications in higher education and intend to equip learners with the skills and knowledge relevant to their employment, satisfying the needs of employees and employers.

This chapter invites you to reflect on and recognise the role of higher education institutions (HEIs) in developing partnerships between further education colleges (FECs) and employers to support higher education opportunities for the Early Years (EY) sector. It also provides you with the opportunity to understand the emergence of the FDEY and reflect upon employers' and students' perspectives of the programme. There is a focus on findings from empirical research conducted at a London University summarising whether the FDEY meets employers' needs. There is a summary of reactions and examples of impacts on practice from different categories of employers. The chapter continues with a focus on emerging views of FDEY students with the relevance of a growing graduate workforce being explored within the complexities of the current political framework.

The chapter will introduce the notion of continual professional development (CPD) and what this means for the EY profession. Case studies and examples to show the skills in planning and facilitating self-managed learning are explored. The chapter concludes with suggested strategies for employers to support staff and colleagues with their CPD requirements.

The role of higher education institutions in developing partnerships with employers

In the last decade higher education institutions and further education colleges have played a pivotal partnership role in designing a programme with employers to meet the professional development needs of Early Years practitioners.

A fundamental component in building partnerships and developing the Early Years workforce was the introduction of the FDEY with the National Childcare Strategy Green Paper (DfES, 1998) asserting a clear objective:

> We want to ensure that all childcare is of good quality, so that it meets the needs of children, and parents can have confidence in it. We aim to increase very substantially the number of skilled, qualified people working with children.
>
> (cited in Taylor *et al.*, 2006, p. 20)

At a national level, the collaboration between universities, further education colleges and key stakeholders including local authorities and employers led to the creation of a 'fit for purpose' work-based learning programme, the FDEY. The Department for Business, Innovation and Skills (BIS) (2012) reported that the location of higher education in FECs has become increasingly visible. According to the research 'Understanding Higher Education in Further Education Colleges', carried out by the University of Sheffield and Institute of Education in 2012, FECs offered a cost-effective, flexible and more accessible way of expanding places in higher education. BIS (2012) also revealed that many FECs have delivered degree-level higher education successfully for a number of years, and that a high proportion of those enrolled are mature students (HEA, 2012; BIS, 2012). Collaborative provision between HEIs and FECs is a key element in delivering higher education opportunities to those wishing to study locally via a work-based route, and who may have returned to learning through the familiar setting of local college.

Enrolments on Foundation Degree programmes grew at a greater rate (Harvey, 2009) which was reflected through UCAS applications for the FDEY programme at a London University, showing a considerable increase in numbers. Maisey (2014) suggests this is because the intention of the FDEY programme was to enable access to a recognised qualification and to support the CPD for those working within the EY sector. In addition, the introduction of the Levels 4 and 5 qualification enabled a government target for Widening Participation and Lifelong Learning by encouraging participation by learners who may not previously have considered studying for a higher level qualification.

PROVOCATION

What is your view on Widening Participation? How far should the Government go to encourage and enable people from groups who do not usually enter Higher Education to study for a degree?

- Require Universities to lower entry requirements?
- Provide funds for fees for people from groups who do not usually enter Higher Education?
- Monitor Universities and name and shame those who do not widen participation?
- Do nothing?

What is your view on this issue? What should be done? Why?

If you think something should be done, which groups should be prioritised for encouragement and support so they enter Higher Education? Why?

A brief history of the development of the Early Years labour market

Since the end of the 1980s there has been a rapid expansion of Nurseries (QAAHE, 2010). Alongside this expansion has come an awareness of the need for the employment of a larger, but more skilled EY workforce as both the quality and quantity of childcare services depend in large measure on the workforce. Since 1997, public policy has for the first time during the post-war period been actively committed to support working parents (DfES, 2007). The Labour Government strategy was 'paid employment for all' including women with children; this was underlined in policies such as the New Deal and the National Childcare Strategy (DfES, 2007).

Consequently there was an urgent need for a skilled EY workforce to be employed in an increasing number of EY settings (Miller and Cable, 2008) which show the introduction of the National Childcare Strategy (DfES, 2007) document. This aimed for high-quality, affordable childcare for children aged 0–14 in every neighbourhood. The introduction of the FDEY was a direct consequence of the WP (DfES, 2006) agenda following the Dearing Report (1997), which aimed at addressing the shortage of higher technical skills in the UK.

However, at this time, work-based learning was a relatively new concept to Early Years employers and only gained recognition through being promoted by HEIs and FECs through collaboration with local authority Early Years childcare teams and employer feedback for CPD following a Level 3 qualification. Political influence from The Rumbold Report (1990) and the Effective Provision of Pre-School Education (EPPE) (Sylva *et al.*, 2004) project urged for quality in all Early Years **childhood** provision. This is in line with the Early Years Foundation Stage (EYFS) guidance, where it has been clearly articulated that 'the daily experience of children in Early Years settings and the overall quality of provision depends on all practitioners having appropriate qualifications, training, skills and knowledge and a clear understanding of their roles and responsibilities (DfE, 2014, p. 16).

This is also in line with the statement from the Department for Education, where the former minister for education and childcare, Elizabeth Trust, highlighted within the Government's policy report (More Great Childcare) that 'Providing children with good quality education and care in their earliest years can help them succeed at school and later in life, contributing to a society where opportunities are equal regardless of background' (DfE, 2013).

In contradiction to this statement, considering the level of responsibility and skills required by EY practitioners for children's care, education and well-being, training has never been a statutory requirement for employment in, or the provision of childcare services. Changes that occurred with The Children Act 2004, empowering local authorities to provide training for those engaged in childcare, still did not make it statutory. Curtis (1998) sums up succinctly the pre-conceptions of many other professionals in the early 1990s and still today that the care of young children is often not regarded as 'real work' but as an extension of the mothering role which is assumed to come naturally to women without the need for training. With the government's focus on a graduate led workforce still at the forefront of EY policy, funding enabled the growth towards a higher degree qualified and skilled workforce. Despite the coalition government's agenda to raise tuition fees in 2010 it was important to explore employers' perspectives of the value of considering entering higher education for staff despite financial constraints and being part of an inherent low paid sector. For example, Cameron *et al.* (2002) addressed an important issue saying that continuous change in the EY sector raises a number of issues about childcare work, such as low payment, a highly gendered industry and low social value (Osgood, 2005). Not only is the childcare workforce gender segregated, but compared with other occupations (social work for example), the workforce has a low level of educational qualification (Rolfe *et al.*, 2003).

This however contradicted the DfES (2003) White Paper which recognised that employers' **perceptions** of Foundation Degrees (FDs) were of importance with suggestions stressing the need to embed the FD within the job role, and to ensure that they are widely accepted and valued by employers. The contradictory messages from the government may have impacted upon employers' interpretations of the purpose of FDEY resulting in differing levels of **engagement** and understanding. For example university liaison visits to employers identified concerns where the value and purpose of a FDEY was not clearly understood or perceived to have particular impact on practice. A Day Care Nursery Manager (2008) spoke frankly saying: 'It seems like a lot of work to do for someone working full-time and raising a family.'

Work-based learning: a cultural shift for the Early Years sector

Under the former Labour government the FD was introduced in order to tighten the link between universities and business, and to up-skill the workforce. Tony Blair (2003, in Beckman and Cooper, 2004, p. 1), said that 'the university sector is no longer simply a focus of educational opportunity; it is also a very, very important part of the future of the British economy' (p. 1).

This was supported by the Quality Assurance Agency (DfES, 2004) who identified the need for qualification pathways for employees that would enable them to remain in work whilst studying for a higher education award. National demand and growth of a work-based learning route to a degree qualification was applauded by EY employers with an EY work-based model designed by universities in partnership with key stakeholders (Burke and Hayton, 2011). The

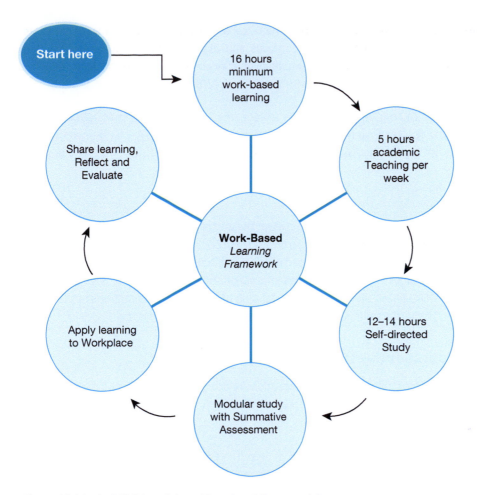

Figure 4.1 A typical FDEY work-based learning delivery model

uniqueness of this model was the professional engagement between the EY employers and key education stakeholders in understanding and supporting both the political aims (Widening Participation and Technical Skills) as well as supporting career pathways for the sector beyond Level 3 awards.

HEIs and FECs introduced a model of **work-based learning** (**WBL**) to support learning for work, learning at work and learning through work (Gray, 2001). For example, Figure 4.1 shows a typical FDEY work-based learning delivery model.

The work-based nature of this qualification not only provided opportunities for career development but a model of learning that supported engagement with higher level knowledge, reflection upon practice and understanding of the wider political framework.

Employer involvement at design and development stage was fundamental to enhance their understanding of how to support employees in the workplace. Taylor *et al.* (2006) assert that employer confidence about supporting WBL varied with some having a lack of prior understanding of work-based qualifications.

Active engagement between the university, local authorities and further education colleges ensured that the philosophy of FDs was recognised and described by Thurgate and MacGreg (2008) as one which, crucially, involves the employer playing a central role in developing and delivering this new initiative. This aligned with the QAAHE (2010) benchmark:

> that employers are fully involved in the design and regular review Foundation Degree programmes. It is beneficial if employers are involved, where possible, in the delivery and **assessment** of the programme and the monitoring of students, particularly within the workplace.
>
> (p. 5.)

Without the commitment and participation between these stakeholders the success of the FDEY may not have been possible. A national research study (DfES, 2006) to evaluate employers' and mentors' experiences of the FDEY set the partnership role between universities and employers as fundamental to the success of evidence based practice. However, concerns have been raised by Morgan *et al.* (2004) about the limited understanding of employers' perceptions of the FD and Ooms *et al.* (2009) regarding uncertainty of the demand for FDs by industry.

Employers' perspectives: findings from the study

This research explored in depth employers' perceptions relating to six key areas of enquiry relating to FDs. The list below shows the six key areas of enquiry forming the basis of the employer interviews:

1   Relevant content – fit for purpose and of value to the Early Years labour market.
2   The development of higher level skills and technical knowledge.
3   Flexible work-based delivery model to support business needs of employers.
4   Appropriate employer engagement to facilitate work-based learning.
5   High quality teaching, learning and assessment.
6   Evidence of professional and personal impact on practice.

The response was overwhelmingly positive and suggested that the FDEY has an important role to play in raising aspirations and continuing to develop a graduate-qualified profession. The findings showed that over the years the FDEY has grown in recognition as a vocational qualification, offering work-based practitioners a flexible means of achieving an academic qualification and work towards a full degree. Many employers perceived that it has become an important part of the aspiration for a graduate-led workforce, supported by local authorities under the former Graduate Leader Fund (GLF). Responses from individual interviews provided evidence from practice that learning on the course is relevant to the work setting. Perceptions of WBL showed that it was regarded as 'the best feature of the FDEY; however interpretation of the meaning of both WBL and employer engagement varied across employer groups interviewed. The reason for this disparity was that some employers who were interviewed had completed the FDEY themselves and responded to questions first from their own experiences as students then their engagement as employers supporting existing staff; whereas those who had not studied on the FDEY provided a less detailed understanding of WBL as a delivery model and their role as employers was perceived as one offering support when staff asked. All employers however regarded WBL as the best feature of the FD, with day nursery and pre-school employers in agreement that the EYFD provides the only educational opportunity for many non-traditional work-based learners to gain a degree. Although employers took an active and interested role in supporting staff, to some employers the FDEY was deemed very different from their experiences of accommodating NVQ students.

The research identified strong recognition among employers that the FDEY gave a good return on investment, with qualified individuals ensuring that their settings were up to date with legislation, policy and practice. Significantly, employers provided examples of individuals who were able to motivate other team members, creating a positive, aspirational culture. Table 4.1 below summarises the responses from sixteen Early Years employers relating to their perceptions of the FDEY within six key areas of enquiry.

Most employers emphasised that the content of the FDEY is relevant and fit for purpose, and they all pointed out the immediate impact on practice evident through shared knowledge and the dissemination of evidence-based practice. Employers' interpretations of work-based learning and its impact on practice and personal development were regarded as the best features of the FDEY.

Table 4.1 Sixteen Early Years employers' perceptions of the FDEY within six key areas of enquiry

Six aspects of the Foundation Degree in Early Years	Day Care	Pre-school	Children's centre	Schools	Total responses
The content of the FDEY is relevant, fit for purpose and of value to the Early Years labour market	✔✔✔	✔✔✔✔	✔✔✔✔	✔✔✔✔	15
The FDEY develops higher level skills and technical knowledge	✔✔✔✔	✔✔✔	✔✔	✔✔✔	12
The FDEY provides a flexible work-based learning model	✔✔✔✔	✔✔✔✔	✔✔✔✔	✔✔✔	15
There is appropriate employer-engagement with HEIs and FECs to facilitate work-based learning	✔✔✔	✔	✔✔✔	✔✔✔	10
There is high quality teaching, learning and assessment	✔✔✔✔	✔✔✔	✔✔✔✔	✔✔✔	14
There is an impact on personal and professional practice	✔✔✔✔	✔✔✔✔	✔✔✔✔	✔✔✔✔	16

FROM RESEARCH TO PRACTICE

The research findings suggested that the two-year FDEY has earned its place within the qualifications framework for higher education and was considered 'the best' qualification for anyone aspiring to gain a degree to broaden their knowledge as well as their career prospects. Significantly, employers identified that the FDEY is a relevant and purposeful progression route into higher academic work, aligning with the Wilson Report (2012) that highlighted how business and university collaboration during the past decade has seen important cultural changes whereby gradual workforce reform has been delivered through belief, commitment and **leadership** in universities, in business and in government. The research recommended that FDs should be reaffirmed as a qualification in their own right rather than as a stepping stone to an honours degree. Most importantly, employers considered that opportunities for the sector have increased since the FDEY was introduced and has continually helped raise recognition of the profession among teachers, the health sector and other professionals working with children.

Immediate impact on practice identified by all employers

- A high level of theory is applied to the work and the level of **professionalism** has developed.
- An up-skilled workforce is the main benefit as the FDEY inspires the other staff and makes a difference to everyone.
- Learning is shared at team meetings, during inset and planning days for example:
- A better understanding of the key person role, understanding of theory shared with other staff and also the benefits to building relationships with parents.
- Improved confidence in what they are doing with more leadership in managing the planning of activities.
- Communication with the children is more in-depth with a universal approach being taken to interact with parents and other professionals.
- Staff now have an up-to-date understanding of legislation and the law.
- It raises confidence and gives a new perspective on working with children, really understanding their individual needs.
- They fully understand **reflective practice** and demonstrate these skills to other staff, so that we all benefit.

Three important messages emerged from this research

1   For policy makers to acknowledge that employers regarded this vocational qualification as the key driver to recognising the Early Years workforce as a profession in its own right.
2   Employers' appreciation of the funding received within the last decade through active participation and engagement with universities, local authorities and colleges.
3   The lasting impact of training on work-based learners has inspired them to develop their practice further, leading to a continuum of support for fellow staff within their settings.

Gittus and Hemsworth (2006) stated that partnershp and collaboration are central to the concept of FDs, not least because of the requirement to engage employers in the development of the qualification. More recently, the Nutbrown (2012) Review of Early Education and Childcare Qualifications stated that, 'The roles of learning centres (Further Education Colleges, Higher Education Institutions, and other training providers) ... are all critical to ensuring that a qualification that looks good on paper is experienced in the best way by learners' (p. 31). This research has highlighted the importance of the work-based learning approach as it has allowed people working in the Early Years sector to build on existing expertise and continue working as they study for a higher level qualification (Knight, 2002).

Collaborative advantage of the employer and university/college partnership

Key findings showed that better partnership working between employers and the university and colleges was a key development to improve Early Years educational practice. Employers recommended communication at the start of the academic years as significant in developing the

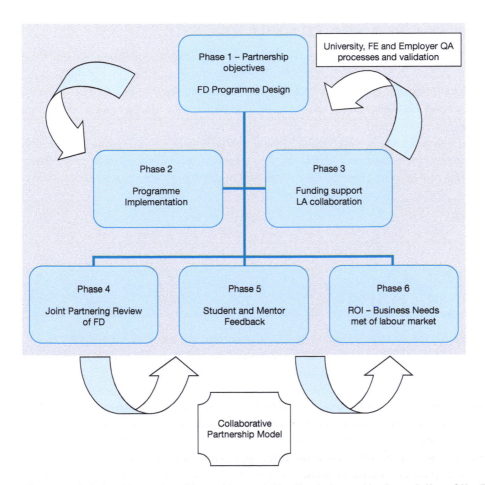

Figure 4.2 Collaborative partnership working model for the design and implementation of the FDEY

partnership role. Figure 4.2 depicts a model for collaborative advantage from partnership working with the role of the university as a centrally co-ordinated system to inform and monitor the programme quality and learning.

To support enhanced partnership engagement with employers, the positive impact of effective partnership working between the training provider, the employers and other key stakeholders is demonstrated in the Partnership Advantage Model above which provides a systematic process to achieving higher educational opportunities towards building a graduate-led workforce.

REFLECTIVE PRACTICE

- How much evidence of employers engaging with Higher Education institutions have you noticed?
- What might be the barriers that prevent HE and employer engagement?
- If you were in charge how would you overcome these barriers?

Your Continuing Professional Development (CPD)

This section of the chapter will help you to understand how to take responsibility for your own professional development, or that of others within your setting, with an awareness of the growing importance of self-managed learning for Early Years practitioners. You will look at ways to continuously develop knowledge, skills and methods to enhance your practice as an Early Years practitioner.

Undertaking training, including accredited training, such as the FDEY, is one way of accessing CPD opportunities. There are many other valuable ways of developing yourself and others. Farrelly (2010) identifies three common CPD areas for today's Early Years practitioners:

- **Action Research**
- Reflection
- Leadership skills

CASE STUDY 1

A children's centre manager identified that it is important before planning any CPD to recognise the outcomes of what you want to achieve, both for the practitioners involved and for relating it to the children and families you are working with.

The manager defines CPD as a collaborative continual process for providing the highest standards of care and education through reflection on an individual's personal development needs and career planning. It is an important way to keep your skills, knowledge and working practices up to date.

A planned package of CPD is identified at this children's centre between the manager and individual staff on a six-weekly basis.

Other forms of CPD are buddying, coaching, mentoring, short course training and visiting other settings.

REFLECTIVE PRACTICE

REFLECTIVE PRACTICE

Consider practice in your own setting, identifying the various possible approaches to support the development of staff/colleagues. You may have considered some of the following:

- Attending in-house training and workshops
- Attending local authority conferences and courses
- Undertaking an accredited award such as a Level 3 or FDEY
- INSET training and team away days
- Visiting other settings
- Shadowing and working with other staff
- Networking with other professionals
- Sharing knowledge through presentations and staff meetings
- Reading articles and accessing relevant information websites
- Reflecting on practice
- Peer observation
- Mentoring and coaching new staff and students
- Staff supervision meetings (held every 6 weeks)
- Enabling staff to lead a change within the setting

It is important to remember that CPD is important and your role as a work-based learner will enable you to become a thinking, reflective practitioner. Students who are currently studying on the FDEY or accessed CPD training have shared their experiences below of immediate impact on practice and personal gains.

The students' perspective on Foundation Degrees: enabling continual professional development?

While quality is closely linked with qualifications and with the need to up-skill the profession, there are suggestions that the FDEY has been seen as a CPD in general. Day (1999, cited in Goodall *et al.*, 2005) has defined CPD as, 'all natural learning experiences and those conscious and planned activities which are intended to be of direct or indirect benefit to the individual, group or school, which constitute, through these, to the quality of education in the classroom' (p. 6). Professional development should be a purposeful endeavour. Through evaluation, professionals can determine whether these activities are achieving their purposes. Guskey (2000) suggests that evaluation of impact takes place at five different levels: participant reaction, participant learning, organisational support and change, participant use of new knowledge and skills and pupil learning outcomes. Sometimes the difficulty is to find a relevant course that fits the purpose, but in this case, the FDEY works for them as it provides the necessary skills which professionals are able to apply correctly in their work. For example the narratives from a student who finished the degree clearly highlight this in the following quotes:

> I am more confident in my writing abilities and I am able to support my colleagues far better with theories and can refer them to reading for themselves. The conversations in the nursery are more professional and I am able to enhance the provision that we offer the children and families. . . . The past three years have been exciting, exhausting, interesting, challenging, thought provoking and supportive. I have had a great 3 years at my University and I am confident that it has set a secure foundation on which I will continue to grow as a practitioner.
>
> (Yvonne)

> After the final assessment I actually felt different – more professional and validated which enable me to take a much more positive and productive outlook for me future.
>
> (Nikki)

Students reflected on their study and they felt that they were more confident at work due to the knowledge they had gained from the programme. They have also said:

> I feel more confident now. It changed my practice. I always thought I am a reasonably good practitioner, but now I just 'get' the children more. I just 'get' the way how to work with children who have challenging behaviour, where a few years ago I would have found it more difficult.
>
> (Jo)

Therefore, as an Early Years employer it is imperative that the support is available for active planning and support of all staff's learning experiences in order to accelerate development and career opportunities.

The research highlighted that well over three-quarters (84 per cent) of Early Years professionals reported that they felt that their CPD activities related directly to their work in settings. Therefore CPD can be seen as a career-long obligation for practising professionals and it is widely acknowledged to be of great importance in the life of the Early Years professionals. It is a personal responsibility of professionals to keep their knowledge and skills current so that they can deliver the high quality of Early Years setting that safeguards the children and meets the expectations of parents/carers. Has the Foundation Degree in Early Years therefore been seen as part of the **continuing professional development** programme?

Whatever the answer is, the programme helps the professional/practitioner to manage not only their own learning and growth but also that of other members of staff and with it the children's. For example, one practitioner has said:

> I suppose each time I got my grade through I got a strong sense of achievement. And not only passing the modules but maintaining my grades and constantly improving my practice. But the real joy is on the daily basis when I put in practice what I have learnt.
>
> (Elizabeth)

This quote indicates that as an Early Years practitioner the gained skill and up-to-date knowledge with a focus on meeting the needs of children and families is paramount.

Therefore, professional development brings benefits at a personal as well as an organisational level. The most important message is that one size does not fit all. To support the CPD of all staff within a setting, wherever they are in their career right now and whatever they want to achieve, their CPD should be their responsibility, supported by the employer.

Taking responsibility for self-development

In recent years, particularly within the last decade, managers, leaders and practitioners in the sector have taken responsibility for their own self-development. Universities, local authorities and government intervention have all helped to raise qualification levels and the quality of provision in Early Years through workforce development initiatives identified through the Children's Workforce Strategy. The results have been evident with the increase in numbers of graduates and skilled professionals within the sector. Local authority input has enabled practitioners to approach and manage their own portfolio of CPD short courses. As Farrelly (2010) suggests, 'we are living in a culture of lifelong learning and constant change. It is not possible to sit back and consider yourself fully qualified and think no more need of further knowledge' (p. 32). This shift since 2003 has led to practitioner comments such as 'learning to take responsibility for my own learning has been empowering and enabled me to manage myself better'. A group of practitioners at an in-house positive behaviour management training recently said, 'it is good to know strategies that we can use. It has given us more confidence when we are managing children's behaviour'.

Self-development is an area of increasing importance and is becoming embedded within the EY culture as the government encourages lifelong learning and supporting the workforce towards achieving the Early Years Teachers (EYT) and more recently the Early Years Educator (EYE)

CASE STUDY 2

A nursery manager from a London day nursery setting identified that the CPD within her setting is made up of a combination of planned techniques including a training matrix of staff needs followed by a range of approaches to address areas for development for staff such as in-house or local authority training, mentoring, role modelling practice and shadowing.

Reflect: *Do all these bring benefits at a personal as well as organisational level?*

The most important message from this setting is that one size does not fit all settings and their developmental needs whereby a mixed approach is beneficial to support the CPD of all staff within a setting. Wherever they are in their career right now and whatever they want to achieve, their CPD should be their responsibility supported by the employer.

Do you agree with this statement?

qualification. As an Early Years employer it is imperative that you are actively planning and supporting the learning experiences of all staff in order to accelerate development and career opportunities.

Here are the benefits of CPD to Early Years practitioners within this London-based setting consisting of 18 staff:

- It builds practitioners' confidence and credibility.
- Learning and progression can be tracked.
- It enables job promotion and additional responsibilities leading to potential salary increase.
- It offers a tool for supervision and **appraisal**.
- Being more reflective and focusing on training and development helps individuals achieve their career goals.
- Constantly updating your skill set improves your ability to cope positively with change.
- Reflecting on your learning and highlighting gaps in your knowledge and experience makes you more productive and efficient.

Here are the benefits of CPD to *employers* within a London-based setting consisting of 18 staff:

- Employers are willing to support staff financially as CPD is adding value to the organisation.
- Opportunities for staff to reflect and be responsible for their own personal growth and development.
- Confident staff maximising their potential by linking their learning to actions and applying theory to practice.
- At appraisals staff are able to set SMART targets and it is a good tool to help focus on achievements during the year.
- Training activity can be more closely linked to business needs.
- A positive staff development culture develops, with better staff morale and a motivated workforce.
- Staff are learning to apply learning to their role – this adds value to the setting, achieving high quality provision.

Conclusion

The FDEY was established to equip students with both academic knowledge and the technical transferable skills required by employers. Research on the impact of this work-based programme demonstrates increasing evidence that the degree is proving effective in its contribution to the development of staff and as a successful mode of learning. Universities' engagement with employers and students is continuing to grow and develop the workforce, providing a work environment in which learning and effective change take place creating an immediate and valuable impact on practice.

The value of the FDEY to work-based learners has been outlined by employers and students as significant for the personal growth of individuals and at practice level. This catalyst for change qualification is a result of effective partnership working between employers and key stakeholders and remains a distinct qualification within universities today.

CPD was traditionally viewed as 'going on training' or undertaking a qualification, but the case studies highlight that CPD can include a range of approaches including mentoring, peer observation, supervision and workshops. For continued development of practitioners, setting managers responsible for workforce development need to be able to recognise existing strengths within the team and work collaboratively with staff to identify areas of practice and knowledge that require improvement or development. When an area of development has been identified, an appropriate package of support and learning should be planned, implemented and its effectiveness reviewed. In May 2010, the coalition government pledged to lay the foundations for better lives for our children. The EY sector remained unsettled by the changes introduced by the government, and continues to create a culture of learning and CPD which is growing as an integral part of a settings ethos to give children the best start in life.

Further reading

Goodall, J., Day, C., Lindsay, G., Muijs, D. and Harris, A. (2005). *Evaluating the Impact of Continuing Professional Development (CPD)*. Nottingham: DfES.

This two-year project offers a detailed evaluation of the impact of continuing professional development in schools where the findings shows that CPD is most likely to be effective when it includes choice, ownership and active participation, when demonstrations of new techniques are practically based, when theory is aligned to real-life situations or arises from their examination, when there is a chance for ongoing feedback, and when staff are not isolated in their training and development.

Cameron, C., Mooney, A. and Moss, P. (2002). The child care workforce: current conditions and future directions, *Critical Social Policy*. 22 (4) pp. 572–595.

The article provides an analysis of the situation of the current workforce, including the highly gendered nature of the work, low pay and high job satisfaction, and how the work is understood.

Illeris, K. (2011). *The Fundamentals of Workplace Learning. Understanding How People Learn in Working Life*, Oxon: Routledge.

This book is a comprehensive guide on how people learn in the workplace, and the issues and challenges involved. Especially in Part 1 there is an analysis of the workplace as a learning space and workplace learning as competence development.

Useful websites

www.gov.uk/government/uploads/system/uploads/attachment_data/file/32425/12-905-understanding-higher-education-in-further-education-colleges.pdf

This summary presents the main findings from research undertaken for the Department for Business, Innovation and Skills (BIS) to understand the current nature of higher education (HE) in further education colleges (FECs) in England.

www.gov.uk/professional-development-for-work-based-learning-practitioners-apprenticeships

Work-based learning is training or development which is delivered in the workplace, usually through a university, college or training provider. This government web site gives you a clear guidance what it really means and what the options are for a practitioner who is employed to help others with their training in the workplace.

References

Beckman, A. and Cooper, C. (2004). 'Globalisation', the new managerialism and education: rethinking the purpose of education in Britain, *Journal for Critical Education Policy Studies.* 2 (2).

BIS (2012). *Understanding Higher Education in Further Education Colleges.* London: Department for Business, Innovation and Skills.

Burke, L., Marks-Marana, D. J., Ooms, A., Webb, M. and Cooper, D. (2009). Towards a pedagogy of work-based learning: perceptions of work-based learning in foundation degrees. *Journal of Vocational Education & Training.* 61 (1) pp. 15-33.

Burke, P. J. and Hayton, A. (2011). Is widening participation still ethical? *Widening Participation and Lifelong Learning.* 13 (1) pp. 8-26.

Cameron, C., Mooney, A. and Moss, P. (2002). The child care workforce: current conditions and future directions, *Critical Social Policy.* [online] Available at: http://csp.sagepub.com/content/22/4/572 [Accessed: 10 May 2014].

Curtis, A. (1998). *A Curriculum for the Pre-school Child.* London: Routledge.

Dearing, R. (1997). *The Dearing Report.* London: HMSO.

Department for Education and Skills (DfES) (1998). Meeting the childcare challenge: A framework and consultation document. London: HMSO.

Department for Education and Skills (DfES) (2003). The Future of Higher Education. White Paper on Higher Education. London: HMSO

Department for Education and Skills (DfES) (2004). Curriculum and Qualification Report: The Final Report. London: HMSO.

Department for Education and Skills (DfES) (2005). The children's workforce in England: A review of the evidence. Version 1.0. London: HMSO.

Department for Education and Skills (DfES) (2006). Widening participation in higher education: creating opportunity, releasing potential, achieving excellence. London: HMSO.

Department for Education and Skills (DfES) (2007). Aiming high for young people: a ten year strategy for positive activities. London: HMSO.

Department for Education (DfE) (2013). More great childcare: raising quality and giving parents more choice. London: HMSO.

Department for Education (DfE) (2014). The Early Years Foundation Stage. London: DfE.

Farrelly, P. (2010). *Early Years Work-based Learning.* Exeter: Learning Matters.

Gittus, B. and Hemsworth, D. (2006). *Engaging Employers in Foundation Degrees Skills.* Active: London.

Goodall, J., Day, C., Lindsay, G., Muijs, D. and Harris, A. (2005). *Evaluating the Impact of Continuing Professional Development (CPD).* Nottingham: DfES.

Gray, D. (2001). *A Briefing on Work-Based Learning.* LTSN Generic Centre Assessment Series 11.

Guskey, T. R. (2000). *Evaluating Professional Development.* Thousand Oaks, CA: Corwin.

Guskey, T. R. (2001). The backward approach. *Journal of Staff Development.* 22 (3) pp. 60-68.

Harvey, L. (2009). *Review of Research Literature focussed on Foundation Degrees.* Staffordshire: Foundation Degree Forward.

Higher Education Academy (2012) *Pedagogy for Employability.* [online] Available at: https://www.heacademy. ac.uk/sites/default/files/pedagogy_for_employability_update_2012.pdf [Accessed 15 February 2014]

Knight, P. (2002). A systemic approach to professional development: learning as practice. *Teaching and Teacher Education.* 18 (3) pp. 229-241.

Maisey, D. (2014). Professionalism in early years, in Johnson, Jessica, *Becoming an Early Years Teacher.* Maidenhead UK: Open University Press.

Miller, L. and Cable, C. (2008). *Professionalism in the Early Years.* Oxon: Hodder Education.

Nutbrown, C. (2102). *Foundation for Quality*. The independent review of early education and childcare qualifications. Final Report. London: DfE.

Morgan, A., Jones, N. and Fitzgibbon, K. (2004). Critical reflections on the development of a foundation degree. *Research in Post-Compulsory Education*. 9 (3) pp. 353-70.

Ooms, A., Webb, M., Burke, L., Marks-Maran, D.J., and Cooper, D. (2009). Students' perceptions of Foundation Degrees. *Journal of Further and Higher Education*. 13 (2) pp. 89-95.

Osgood, J. (2005). Who cares? The classed nature of childcare. *Gender and Education*. 17 (3) pp. 289-303.

The Quality Assurance Agency for Higher Education (QAAHE) (2010). *Foundation Degree Qualification Benchmark*. London: Southgate House.

Rolfe, H., Metcalfe, H., Anderson, T. and Meadows, P. (2003). *Recruitment and Retention of Childcare,Early Years and Play Workers: Research Study*. London: National Institute of Economics and Social Research.

Rumbold, A. (1990). *The Rumbold Report*. London: HMSO.

Sylva, K., Melhuish, E., Sammons, P., Siraj-Blatchford, I. and Taggart, B. (2004). *The Effective Provision of Pre-School Education* (EPPE) *Project: Final Report*. London: Institute of Education.

Taylor, J., Brown, R. and Dickens, S. (2006). *Evaluating the Early Years Sector Endorsed Foundation Degree: A Qualitative Study of Employers'*. London: Department for Education and Skills.

Thurgate, C. and MacGregor, J. (2008). Collaboration in Foundation Degree provision: a case study in Kent. *Journal of Further and Higher Education*. 32 (1).

Wilson, T. (2012). *A Review of Business-University Collaboration*. London: HMSO.

5 Research and ethics

Joe Brown

LEARNING OUTCOMES

After reading the chapter you should be able to:

✔ Identify the distinct role of the practitioner as researcher.
✔ Reflect on the main issues to address when choosing a research topic and question.
✔ Consider the benefits and challenges of participatory early years research.
✔ Consider ethical frameworks and some of the challenges and debates when designing ethical research.
✔ Reflect on the main considerations in the research design process.
✔ Assess the main methods used in educational research.
✔ Consider the main issues when analysing research findings and drawing conclusions.

Introduction

Educational research has been influencing policy and practice, both nationally and internationally, for many years. Multi-disciplinary in nature, researchers have sought to provide answers and solutions to many aspects of children's lives. *The Plowden Report* for example (DES, 1967) gathered data from professionals about the importance of a child-centred approach in primary education, whereas the Department of Health report *Messages from Research* (DoH, 1995) focused on how to improve child protection services in the UK. However, as the early years sector has become increasingly professionalised there has been a greater focus on research pertaining to very young children, meaning that many of the elements of early years practice which settings now take for granted have their roots in research. The Early Years Foundation Stage (DfE, 2014) was developed after evidence was gathered from professionals in the sector, while the Effective Provision of Pre-School Education (EPPE) Project (Sylva et al., 2004) used a variety of data collection methods such as child **assessments** and parental interviews to identify the main indicators of quality in early years settings. While these examples were large national studies undertaken by paid and experienced researchers, studies on a smaller scale can hold just as much value, allowing practitioners to address specific issues about practice and place this within the context of the families and communities they work with.

While recognising the numerous forms **educational research** can take, this chapter is specifically designed as a guide for practitioners and students who are undertaking small-scale research projects, many for the first time. The main stages of planning and organising your own research project are outlined and the distinct role of the **practitioner-researcher** is explored. In particular this chapter will seek to assist practitioners and students in developing their own ethical and value-based framework for early years research, and explore some of the challenges and dilemmas which need to be addressed to ensure your own research project benefits all those involved.

The practitioner as researcher

Costley *et al.* (2010) define research as a systematic process which is designed to create and judge knowledge, whereas Cohen *et al.* (2011) state it is a systematic and controlled search for the truth. These definitions point to a planned, purposeful process but the way this process is conducted can vary enormously, depending on the discipline, scale of the research and, crucially, the role of the researcher. The growth of undergraduate programmes such as the Sector Endorsed Foundation Degree in Early Years (SEFDEY) has led to an increasing number of early years professionals becoming practitioner-researchers. Practitioner-led research can support **reflective practice** and inform change and improvement in early years settings, as practitioners are in a **unique** position to be able to study work-based issues in-depth and frame theoretical positions in the 'real world' of their practice.

Practitioner-led research and the dual role

While this model of practitioner-led research has numerous benefits, would-be researchers also need to reflect on the challenges of this approach. Practitioners need to take on a dual role, one where the researcher is first and foremost an insider or practitioner, with established relationships with children, parents and staff and an understanding of the practices, cultures and **pedagogical values** of the setting. In undertaking research practitioners also become outsiders with a responsibility to investigate and challenge long-established practices and assumptions, including their own if necessary. This dual role can lead to **conflicts** and contradictions as staff can feel their practice is being criticised, parents can feel bombarded with forms and questions and children can wonder why adults are busy gathering data rather than spending time engaging in play.

This dual role should be at the forefront of practitioner-researchers' minds as they plan and carry out their project. The following standpoints are crucial to reflect upon when planning an early years research project as a practitioner-researcher:

*   Researchers need to think critically and in a reasoned way (Carr and Kemmis, 1986).
*   Be sceptical (MacNaughton and Rolfe, 2010: 8).
*   Be prepared to challenge yourself and others.
*   Be prepared for the unexpected.

- Maintain a clear understanding as to the purpose of your research.
- Reflect on how your research will impact on others in the setting such as children and parents.
- Be prepared for research to change professional practice.
- Understand how your professional values can affect your research.

Research as a process

Of course, beyond these **conceptual** standpoints research is a carefully planned process, and one which researchers need to reflect on and review throughout. The diagram below highlights the main stages of a typical early years project.

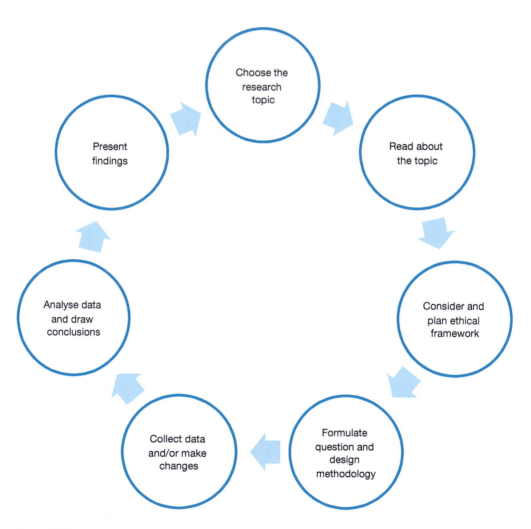

Figure 5.1 The research process

Choosing a research topic and question

Many practitioner-researchers say that choosing a topic and formulating the research question is the hardest part of the whole research process. It is true that failure to get this right might mean that you are spending significant time trying to answer the unanswerable or, worse, studying something which really doesn't interest you. The size and scope of the research question is also an important factor to get right at the start to ensure your project is achievable.

CASE STUDY 1

Choosing a topic and question – Amy

Amy's research concerned how her Children's Centre could work more effectively in partnership with the local Teenage Parent Midwives service. Amy describes some of the issues she faced in choosing her topic and question.

Supporting teenage parents is a real interest of mine but also part of my professional role at the Centre. At the time of the research we were not reaching any so choosing a research topic was very easy for me. The question was a little more difficult as there was a danger of making the research too broad so it needed to be focused in order to get the results I intended. In particular I needed to ensure my question could be answered in a way that would not impact on people's workload.

Amy discusses how her personal and professional worlds converged when reflecting on a topic – meaning her interest would be maintained throughout the project. She also highlights how careful thought needs to be given to the question to ensure the research project is possible within practical and time constraints. When choosing a topic reflect on the following issues:

- Choose something which is interesting and meaningful for you.
- Choose something which is relevant professionally – remember practitioner-led research is about improving practice and ultimately the experiences of children.
- Discuss it with other staff – it is crucial that the setting and staff support the research, especially if it will challenge current practices.
- Discuss any ideas with your tutor, a mentor or fellow students – if you can provide strong reasons to them why this is the right project then it probably is.
- Read widely about the topic – this supports your understanding of the different perspectives and enables you to decide if this is the right topic for you.
- Where is the child in this research topic – what benefits does it have for them?
- Is the idea ethical – can it be undertaken and do no harm at the same time?
- What principles and values will you bring to the research?

The research question

Once the broad topic area has been decided, practitioner-researchers need to reflect on how to focus this down into an answerable question. In practice issues such as research **ethics**, intended benefits of the project and research **methodology** all need to be considered when reflecting on a question so it is not uncommon for research questions to change as the planning process proceeds. Many first-time researchers start with an idea which is too ambitious (MacNaughton and Rolfe, 2010), but there is also a danger that some questions can be so specific as to lack depth and clarity of purpose. Finding this balance can take time and one strategy is to break the topic down into component parts. For example, practitioner-researchers sometimes say they want to research children's learning and make changes to improve how it is supported in the setting. To turn this idea into an achievable question, the researcher needs to reflect on making their terms more specific, for example:

- What do I mean by children? Am I working with a specific age range, gender or group?
- What do I mean by learning? Which aspect needs addressing in the setting? Is it about one area of provision?
- What do I mean by improvement? For example, is the issue one of resourcing, or adult interactions, or planning?

Other issues to consider when devising research questions include:

- Avoid questions which can be answered yes or no – they will not give you the depth needed for a research project.
- Ensure the research question can meet practical considerations – such as timescale, access to participants and **data collection methods**.
- Avoid terms which are difficult to quantify such as 'impact' or 'best practice'.
- Avoid making generalisations or assumptions in the research question.

PROVOCATION

Think about the broad topic you have in mind for your research project.

- Can you break this down so you can highlight exactly what you are trying to find out?
- Are all your terms specific and measurable?
- What data could you collect to find the answers you need?
- Can you work out who who are the main participants of this research?

Participatory early years research

As previously stated, research in the early years is increasingly seen as a critical tool in understanding the lives and experiences of young children and, more importantly, to improve our practice both in settings and societally through policy development. Early **childhood** research approaches have advanced in line with our developing understanding about the way young children develop and learn, and about their ability to participate and be powerful agents in their own lives (Mayall, 2002). In particular, the **social constructivist** approach espoused by Vygotsky and others (MacNaughton, 2009) which proposes that children's learning is contextualised through their experiences, relationships and interactions, gives weight to the idea that the child's voice is a critical element in many early years research studies.

> **REFLECTIVE PRACTICE**
>
> Think about how you use children's voices in your setting.
>
> - What do you consult children on in your setting?
> - How do you seek their views?
> - What are some of the challenges with seeking the opinions of young children?
> - How do you ensure that the children's views are valued and acted upon?

The participatory methodology

The social constructivist approach links to a model of research sometimes known as 'social research' (James and Prout, 1997). Within **social research** the voices and attitudes of the participants define the answers to the questions posed by the researcher and the context of these voices is crucial. From an early years perspective this changes the focus of research from something which is traditionally *about* children to something which is undertaken *with* children (Kellett, 2010), and this places an increased importance on the specific context of the research.

This approach leads to a number of assumptions pertaining to **participatory early years research**:

1   The voices of young children are a reliable and genuine research tool (Alderson, 2008).
2   Young children are able to voice how they think and feel.
3   Researchers must find a way of capturing children's views, even from very young children.
4   Research in early years settings takes account of children's contexts and specific experiences.

Using children's voices in research

Research based in settings and involving children means practitioner-researchers need to think about the implications of this throughout the whole research process, as this approach can be

FROM RESEARCH TO PRACTICE

Clark, A. and Moss, P. (2011) *Listening to Young Children. The Mosaic Approach.* (2nd edn). London: National Children's Bureau

First published in 2001, the Mosaic Approach is a multi-method system of capturing the voices and views of young children which has become widely embedded in participatory early years practice. Originally derived from research undertaken in an early years setting in London, the Mosaic Approach uses a range of methods to gather the perspectives of children including observation, cameras and child conferencing. Like other participatory approaches it treats young children as experts in their own lives who are able to make informed decisions about the issues which affect them.

The Mosaic Approach is now widely used nationally and internationally to capture the views of young children. In particular many practitioner-researchers have used the Mosaic Approach to gather data from children, parents and practitioners about aspects of professional practice in search of improvement. As seen below, gathering the views of children has a number of practical and ethical issues which the Mosaic Approach can help address.

fraught with challenges. Research involving children must adhere to a strict ethical code which is discussed in more detail in the next section. However there are a number of other issues which need to be considered. First, researchers need to ensure children's voices are given as much weight as adult voices; while there is sometimes a tendency for researchers to 'talk down' to children and restrict their responses because of perceived immaturity, researchers must also take care to avoid over-complicated terms or research methods which will stop children from fully participating. This may also include consideration of how research methods are culturally appropriate for the children in the setting. In addition, researchers and other staff may find what children have to say challenging and must resist the temptation to ignore or downplay it. Second, is the question of power; practitioner-researchers have a dual role within the setting and children will be aware of the authority wielded by adults professionally. Practitioner-researchers need to reflect on how this may affect children's participation and how they can address it (Palaiologou, 2012). Finally, researchers should reflect on the level of child involvement in any project; will children be collecting their own data or even devising the data collection methods themselves for example? If so, practitioner-researchers need to reflect on the support children may need to do this.

Research ethics

Ethics are of course a key concern in all types of research across all disciplines, with many areas having their own specific ethical codes. In particular, the medical professions have ethical frameworks which have developed over time, and often as a direct result of unethical research undertaken by professionals (Gray, 2012). Arguably however it is research involving children and other vulnerable groups which poses the most ethical challenges to the researcher. Changing attitudes towards the ability of even very young children to make accurate, informed judgements about their own lives (Langsted, 1994) have to be balanced against the continuing power of adults to decide what is best for children (McDowall-Clark, 2010). These subtle shifts in understanding about the abilities of young children have led to the growth of participatory early years research, however this must go hand in hand with the development of the participatory rights of children.

CASE STUDY 2

Karen noticed that not many boys were using the role play area in her setting. She decided to change the role play area to include resources which interested boys to discover if more of them would use it. First Karen decided to seek the views of the boys in the setting, to ask them what they would like to see in the role play area. She decided to hold a group discussion with the boys and borrowed a video camera so the boys could film each other talking about the changes they would like to see.

- What might be some of the ethical challenges with this research?
- What do you think of Karen's methods for seeking the views of the boys?
- What other voices might Karen have to consider when planning her research?

The legal and ethical framework

The basis of modern research ethics can be traced back to the Nuremburg Code (1949) which was established in response to the experiments carried out by the Nazis. The key aspects of the code include:

- The need for voluntary consent from all research subjects.
- The need to ensure all research is for the good of society.
- Avoid any unnecessary suffering.
- Research subjects must be allowed to withdraw from the research at any time (Roberts-Holmes, 2011).

However, it is the United Nations Convention on the Rights of the Child (UNCRC), (UN, 1989), which is widely regarded as the watershed in *children's* **rights** to involvement and participation (Gray, 2012). Across 54 articles the UNCRC covers most aspects of children's lives including the right to care, protection and education. However, it is three specific articles which arguably have the biggest impact on the practitioner-researcher:

- Article 12 – '[T]he right [for the child] to express those views freely in all matters affecting the child, the views of the child being given full weight in accordance with the age and maturity of the child' (UN, 1989: 5).

- Article 13 – 'Children's right to express their views in any way they wish' (UN, 1989: 5).
- Article 36 – 'Children's right to protection from all forms of exploitation. This includes protection from exploitation through research processes' (UN, 1989: 10).

Shortly after the UNCRC the UK government passed the 1989 Children Act. A wide-ranging piece of legislation, this also contains sections which specifically highlight children's rights to a voice, as Section One states that 'the ascertainable wishes and feelings of the child concerned (considered in the light of his age and understanding)' should be considered (HM Government, 1989). However, it could be argued that this falls a long way short of the active participation highlighted in the UNCRC. The Children Act 2004 (HM Government, 2004) took these ideas further, with the development of the role of Children's Commissioner, specifically designed to 'proactively consult children' about their lives and the decisions which affect them (HM Government, 2004).

PROVOCATION

While the UNCRC states that children should be actively involved in decisions which affect them, this is not always easy in practice.

- How might the role of the parent challenge a child's right to participation?
- How might the setting make active participation more difficult?
- How could you ensure that all children have an equal opportunity to take part?
- Is there a limit to the issues children should be consulted about?

Ethical codes

In addition to the legislative framework described above, a number of research bodies linked to different professional disciplines have created their own codes for researchers. For example the British Psychological Society's ethical code contains a clear set of principles including; respect, responsibility and integrity (British Psychological Society, 2009). For research involving children the British Education Research Association (BERA, 2011) has an ethical framework which includes guidelines for voluntary **informed consent**, privacy and openness which goes some way to address the specific ethical challenges research in the early years can bring. The development of many of these codes is derived from the medical ethical principles of 'do no harm'. According to Naidoo and Wills (2009) these are:

- Autonomy – the right of research participants to self-determination, and the right for participants to make informed decisions about issues which affect them.
- Beneficence – to ensure that everything is done in the best interests of the research participants.
- Non-maleficence – the concept of 'first, do no harm' that it is more important to do no harm than it is to do good.
- Justice – act fairly to all involved.

PROVOCATION

Think about the 'do no harm' principles and what some of the challenges may be in ensuring these are upheld. In particular:

- How does the right of autonomy sit with young children? Does this conflict with the rights of parents or professionals who are expected to care for them?
- Are there conflicts between autonomy and beneficence? Do children always have their own best interests at heart?
- Early years research often entails making changes to practice. How can researchers be sure that these changes will do no harm?
- How do researchers ensure that justice is done? Can all children hold equal power within a research process?

Clearly these principles interact and in reality research is often a juggling act where choices between the principles may have to be made and where sometimes they can contradict each other. Add in the complex ethical considerations of involving children and these principles can often pose as many questions as they answer.

In addition to national ethical codes, Universities and Colleges have developed their own guidelines to support students in undertaking research. The following issues are typically highlighted in these documents.

Informed consent

Despite the legislative background such as the UNCRC and Nuremburg Code and the increasing importance of children's participation, the issue of consent in research involving children is still one which is largely controlled by the child's significant adults (Coady, 2010). The reason why children cannot legally give informed consent seems to centre around the issue of whether children are 'competent' and at what age competence occurs (Gray, 2012). Clearly competence depends not only on the age of the child but the context of what, and how, they are being asked. Indeed studies have claimed that the very process of gaining consent gave researchers strong evidence of children's own competence in understanding the research process (Alderson, 2000). However, this question of competence is why children's consent is called 'assent'. Although **assent** doesn't seem to have the same status as full informed consent it is still a vital component of all early years research.

While seeking children's 'assent' is vital, there are also two groups who need to be consulted about access to children for the purposes of research. The first are what are called '**gatekeepers**' - these are groups of professionals such as head teachers, social workers or setting managers who have a **duty of care** towards the children (Cohen, Manion and Morrison, 2011). The second is the child's parent or carer. Clearly this relationship is a key one when involving young children in research and the following issues are crucial for the parent to feel fully informed:

- The nature of the research – what is it about?
- The voluntary nature of the research and the right to withdraw at any time.
- Confidentiality and the limits to this.
- Who will see the data and research.
- The nature of the commitment from all participants.
- The benefits and consequences of the research (Roberts-Holmes, 2011: 48; Denscombe 2010: 333).

Clearly there is a requirement here for the practitioner-researcher to build positive relationships with gatekeepers and parents and continue these throughout the project and beyond. However, even with the best ethical planning unexpected things can happen. A Foundation Degree student had gatekeeper and parental consent for a child study but near the hand-in date the parents withdrew consent due to the child leaving the setting – as participation in the research was of course voluntary, the project had to be abandoned and a new child found.

Confidentiality and anonymity

The privacy of children, parents and practitioners is something that early years practitioners are concerned with on a daily basis but during research this can be particularly challenging. For students undertaking research there is an expectation the project will be shared with marking tutors, university moderators and perhaps even other students. This all needs to be carefully communicated to all stakeholders including children (Coady, 2010). Furthermore, how the project will attempt to protect anonymity and the challenges of this will also need to be shared. Confidentiality can be particularly difficult to achieve in small-scale setting-based studies, where the context of the setting is crucial to the project but also where the small number of participants can make it easier for them to be identified. In particular the researcher needs to consider:

- Who will the research be shared with?
- How will privacy be maintained (use of initials for example)?
- How might the data be coded?
- What are the limits to confidentiality?
- How might the setting's identity be protected?

Storage of data

Alongside confidentiality, researchers need to ensure that any data gathered is stored in an ethical and legal manner. The primary legislation to adhere to is the Data Protection Act (1988) which sets out principles for the collection and storage of data. In particular it highlights that data must be up to date and relevant for the purpose it was collected and that data must be stored securely.

Perspectives of stakeholders

Within these ethical frameworks the researcher must also reflect on the differing perspectives of all the people involved with, and affected by, the research. This can be complex as views can often contradict and a balance needs to be found. In particular, undertaking research involving children can often feel like navigating between competing agendas where parental and practitioner views and values, the rights of parents and children and the aims of the researcher all need to be accommodated.

Designing Early Years Research

Designing research which is ethical, fair and **valid** can be seen as a process of refining and defining. Once a topic has been selected the overarching ideas about the researcher's understanding of knowledge and how it is constructed need to be considered before focusing in on the research approach and eventually the practical data collection strategy. The following diagram illustrates how this refining and defining process works.

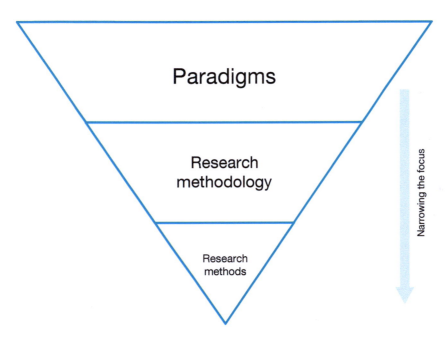

Figure 5.2 The research design process

Paradigms

When reflecting about the word research it is often easy to picture a scientist in a white coat putting liquids into test tubes. However, the social research approach centres on people and their thoughts, feelings and actions and has long been an important part of research in education. These two different approaches influence the way researchers choose to design their study, the methods they choose and how data is analysed in search of an answer.

Positivism

The positivist approach views the world as rational, measurable and scientific. Researchers believe that humans will behave in a predictable and consistent way. According to Opie positivists believe that 'no knowledge exists beyond that which is objectively, immediately observable' (2004: 13). This approach is also often called **quantitative research** as the data the researcher seeks is often numerical or objectively and scientifically measured.

Interpretivism

Conversely, the interpretivist view of research maintains that the world is much more random than that and knowledge is constructed when humans interact. These interactions can vary depending on the context, and help construct shared meanings. According to Lowe interpretivists believe '[w]e create and construct our world by negotiating with others the meaning of our interactions' (2007: 11). This approach can also be known as **qualitative research** as the methods employed are often about the voices and attitudes of the participants and as such are not easy to generalise.

PROVOCATION

Think about your attitudes to knowledge and how it is constructed. Do you think you are a positivist or an interpretivist?

- How might your approach influence what you want to research?
- Which might be the best approach when undertaking research which involves children?
- What might it mean for the types of methods you want to use?
- Will it limit what you can find out in an early years setting?

Arguably, much of the research in education takes an interpretivist view of knowledge and places participants' attitudes or feelings at the centre of the research design. This view is synonymous with the social constructivist view of the world which is particularly pertinent in early years. However, researchers need to be cautious about completely discounting one approach in favour of another and this particularly applies to qualitative and quantitative research. While these two approaches seem poles apart it is important to note that they also relate to data gathering. Many researchers will choose to collect a mix of qualitative (words) and quantitative (numbers) data.

Research methodology

While it is important to think about how your attitudes to knowledge will influence the research project, the next step is to focus in on the research design. This brings together ideas about paradigms with considerations such as the intended audience, purpose of the research and data collection methods. Roberts-Holmes calls this 'the principle and values, philosophies and **ideologies** that underpin your research' (2011: 22). However, this next step has also been called 'research strategy' (Denscombe, 2010: 4), or the 'design frame' (Thomas 2009: 99).

Action research

Increasingly popular in the field of education, action research is sometimes known as the 'practitioner as researcher model' (Campbell *et al.,* 2004). It is work-based enquiry and has two main features. First, it enables professionals to focus on an issue or dilemma in their work and address this in search of improvement (McNiff and Whitehead, 2011). Second, it is seen as an emancipatory process, that is, anyone can undertake it, making it 'participatory and **democratic**' (Macnaughton *et al.*, 2010: 69). Broadly speaking this methodology is concerned with making changes to practice and assessing whether these changes have enriched the experiences of children, parents and practitioners.

Case study

This can be defined as an in-depth study surrounding a specific group, instance or phenomenon. It could be argued that many practitioner-researchers select a case study approach by virtue of their professional identity – they don't have the access to a wide variety of settings for example, or don't have the time to collect data across large cohorts. It can help the practitioner-researcher look in depth at a single issue to provide answers; 'it lends itself to the study of processes and relationships within a setting' (Denscombe, 2010: 55)

Ethnography

This is the study of specific cultures or groups of people and has its roots in the studies of distinct groups such as isolated tribes (Demscombe, 2010: 79). Transferred to an educational perspective it could be the study of a specific class or age group within a setting. For example many SEFDEY students have focused on boys and their play or learning and it could be argued that the specific group being studied makes these projects ethnographic.

Evaluation research

This methodology is concerned with judging how well something is working and making recommendations for improvement. This could also be seen as surveying – finding out how well a policy or a routine works for example. Data for **evaluation research** is often based on the experiences and feelings of the participants, and so is largely qualitative. Early years researchers need to consider how evaluation research may work with young children – evaluating an aspect of practice will usually mean the voice of the child is a crucial part of any evaluation and so ethical issues are often paramount.

REFLECTIVE PRACTICE
REFLECTIVE PRACTICE

Reflect on your own research project. When thinking about which research design to use, consider the following:

- Will the design fit with your ethical considerations?
- Does it reflect your personal views of the way knowledge is created?
- Will it help you answer your questions?
- Does it fit with the purpose of your research?

Research methods

Beyond the research design or methodology considerations lie the research methods. Described by Cohen *et al.* as; 'instruments for collecting data . . . to enable researchers to gather useful and usable data' (2011: 375). Choosing the right methods for the task is not easy as each one has particular strengths and weaknesses and all have specific ethical issues to consider. Different methods also provide different forms of data, and particular attention needs to be paid to whether they are qualitative or quantitative, or a mix of both. It is important to consider how many research projects use a mix of methods to obtain the information required. This section will briefly outline three of the main methods used in early years research namely, questionnaires, interviews and observations.

Questionnaires

There is a huge number of different questionnaires, and not all are suitable for research purposes. However they can offer the researcher a way of reaching larger numbers of people and offer the opportunity for asking different types of questions such as open or closed questions, scales and multiple choice options. They need to be carefully planned to ensure responses are honest and clear.

Advantages

- A good way of reaching larger numbers of people fairly easily.
- Can be anonymous, meaning that respondents may be more honest.
- Can provide a mix of both qualitative and quantitative data.
- Can be organised and coded for analysis.
- Questions are standardised and the same for everyone.

Disadvantages

- Questions can be unclear to the participant – leading to inaccurate answers.
- Participants need to be able to read and write to complete them.
- Return rate can be low.

- Long questionnaires or difficult questions can lead to respondents 'giving up'.
- There is no way of checking that the answers given are truthful.

Ethical issues

- Informed consent and the right to withdraw need to be made clear.
- The possibility of questions appearing sensitive or offensive to the respondent (Cohen *et al.*, 2011: 378).
- The need for confidentiality – how will they be stored for example?

Interviews

Again there are a number of different types of interviews – structured, semi-structured and unstructured in particular. Interviews provide detailed in-depth responses, and the feelings and experiences of respondents can be fully explored (Denscombe, 2010: 174). However, they can be time-consuming and are usually suitable for a smaller number of participants.

Advantages

- Can provide in-depth information.
- Subjects can be 'probed' and clarification and further detail sought.
- There is a high response rate to due to the fact they are organised in advance.
- They can be flexible.

Disadvantages

- Can be time-consuming and as result can only reach limited numbers of people.
- Takes skill and practice to become a good interviewer.
- Respondents can feel nervous or challenged during interviews.
- As the data is likely to be deeply personal analysis can be difficult.

Ethical issues

- Confidentiality and who will see the results.
- The interviewer interpreting the answers differently from the interviewee.
- Will the interview be conducted in a sensitive and stress-free way?

Observations

This is a widely used method of data collection in early years and has become embedded in practice on a daily basis. However, the type of observation you wish to use and how this dovetails with research design needs careful consideration. Again, observations can be a good way of gathering both qualitative and quantitative data, depending on the format used.

Advantages

- Early years settings are used to this method and staff are usually skilled in it.
- Can provide a 'real-time' view of what is happening and how participants are responding in a naturalistic way.
- A useful tool in gathering data from children in a setting context.

Disadvantages

- Can be open to interpretation by the observer – making the data unreliable.
- Can be open to interpretation from the observer.
- Can take a lot of skill to observe, especially in an early years context.

Ethical issues

- Access and informed consent are needed.
- Observers need to try to take an objective approach.
- Subjects may not behave naturally when being observed.

Analysing findings

Once the researcher has done all the hard work in choosing a topic and research question, designing the study and gathering data, the process of organising and analysing what the data tells you can be challenging but should enable you to answer the question you have set. Good research often has different forms of data from a variety of sources, for example, questionnaires from parents, observations on children and staff interviews, and it is important to use all the data available to make the research findings honest and valid (Roberts-Holmes, 2011; 189).

Using themes

One of the clearest ways to analyse data is to use themes to organise and present what has been collected. Researchers should already have a good idea of the themes linked to the topic area from background reading and this is a good place to start. Many researchers find the process of drawing diagrams helpful in deciding what pieces of data link to which topic themes.

Tips for data analysis

- Try to use data from a variety of methods (a process known as **triangulation**).
- Don't split your data up into 'types' but bring it together around themes.
- Use your reading on your topic to help you decide your key themes.
- Don't use all your data – use the data which is 'rich' in terms of answering the question.
- Keep an open mind and be prepared to be challenged by the findings – it is better to be honest than to try to make your data 'fit' your own position.
- Ensure the data you analyse is ethical – for example, that you have consent to use it all.

Drawing conclusions and making recommendations

Concluding your research project is a process of drawing the main findings together and providing some answers to the research questions. Small-scale projects in early years settings will naturally need to be cautious about the scope of any findings and be careful not to generalise, however it is also important to celebrate the success of any project which leads to new knowledge or an improvement to practice. In particular, conclusions should include:

- Reflect on the process you went through and what you would improve next time.
- Suggest some areas for further research around this topic.
- Focus on your personal experience of research – what do you think you have learnt about your own values, assumptions and decision-making?
- Provide recommendations arising from the findings – for example should practice be changed or adapted?

CASE STUDY 3

Jo

Jo's research concerned the routines within a privately run day nursery and in particular the number of transitions from room to room the children were expected to make during a typical day. Jo was concerned that these transitions made it difficult for children to have autonomy to choose the content of their own play and that this might have an adverse effect on the development of independence and their self-esteem. Jo decided to set up an action research project and make significant changes to the way the nursery day operated to assess whether children's independence and self-esteem could be improved. In particular Jo had to consider:

- How these major changes might affect children, staff and parents.
- How she could address the principle of non-maleficence (do no harm), particularly if the research was unsuccessful.
- How staff and managers might be feeling when having their practice questioned in this way.
- What methods she could use to gather all the voices in the setting, particularly those of children.
- What consent and assent she needed and how to obtain it.
- How to keep all participants fully informed of the research throughout the process.
- How to ensure the confidentiality of the participants and assess the possible limits of this.
- How to analyse her data to find out if the project was successful.

Conclusion

This chapter has looked at some of the key issues to reflect on when undertaking research in the early years as a practitioner-researcher. In particular we have examined some of the key ethical issues which are crucial in research involving children, and addressed some of the key dilemmas and challenges which early years researchers face. Above all practitioner-researchers need to recognise that research is a state of mind, one which can be fraught with difficulties but when properly planned can also provide key answers to issues surrounding all aspects of young children's lives. However, it is important to note that research is such a broad area that it cannot be fully covered in just one chapter – students need to read more widely to address many of these issues in more depth.

Further reading

Palaiologou, I. (2010) (ed.) *Ethical Practice in Early Childhood*. London: SAGE.
 This text addresses the key ethical issues in research with children, as well as ethical practice more generally.

Denscombe, M. (2010) *The Good Research Guide. For Small-Scale Social research Projects*. (4th edn). Berkshire: OUP.
 Looks at the whole research process in detail, with a particular focus on research strategies.

Thomas, G. (2013) *How to do Your Research Project*. (2nd edn). London: Sage.
 An accessible text which covers the research process step by step.

Useful websites

www.bera.ac.uk/
 The British Educational Research Association. This website has some useful resources for researchers, including an ethical guide.

www.nfer.ac.uk/research/early-years
 The National Foundation for Educational Research. Has good examples of early years research projects.

References

Alderson, P. (2000) *Young Children's Rights.* London: Jessica Kingsley.

Alderson, P. (2008) 'Children as Researchers' in: Christensen, P. and James, A., *Research with Children: Perspectives and Practices* (2nd edn). London: Routledge.

BERA (2011) *Revised Ethical Guidelines for Educational Research*. London: BERA, Available from: www.bera.ac.uk/publications/Ethical%20Guidelines.

British Psychological Society (2009) *Code of Ethics and Conduct.* Leicester: BPS.

Campbell, A. McNamara, O. and Gilroy, P. (2004) *Practitioner and Professional Development in Education.* London: Paul Chapman.

Carr, W. and Kemmis, S. (1986) *Becoming Critical: Education, Knowledge and Action Research.* London: Falmer Press.

Clark, A. and Moss, P. (2011) *Listening to Young Children. The Mosaic Approach* (2nd edn). London: National Children's Bureau.

Coady, M. (2010) 'Ethics in Early Childhood Research' in MacNaughton, G., Rolfe, S.A. and Siraj-Blatchford, I. *Doing Early Childhood Research. International Perspectives on Theory and Practice* (2nd edn). Berkshire: OUP.

Cohen, L., Manion, L. and Morrison, K. (2011) *Research Methods in Education* (7th edn). London: Routledge.

Costley, C., Elliott, G. and Gibbs, P. (2010) *Doing Work-Based Research. Approaches to Inquiry for Insider-Researchers.* London: Sage.

Denscombe, M. (2010) *The Good Research Guide. For Small-Scale Social Research Projects* (4th edn). Berkshire: OUP.

Department for Education (DfE) (2014) *Statutory Framework for the Early Years Foundation Stage. Setting the Standards for Learning, Development and Care for Children from Birth to Five.* London: Crown Copyright.

Department of Education and Science (DfE) (1967) *Children and their Primary Schools (The Plowden Report).* London: Crown Copyright.

Department of Health (DfE) (1995) *Child Protection: Messages from Research.* London: Crown Copyright.

Farrell, A. (2013) 'Early Years Research', in Veale, F. (ed.) *Early Years for Levels 4 and 5* Oxon: Hodder Education.

Gray, C. (2012) 'Ethical Research with Children and Vulnerable Groups', in: Palaiologou, I. (ed.) *Ethical Practice in Early Childhood.* London: Sage.

HM Government (1989) *Children Act 1989.* London: Crown Copyright. Available from: www.legislation. gov.uk/ukpga/1989/41/contents.

HM Government (2004) *Children Act 2004.* London: Crown Copyright. Available from: www.legislation.gov.uk/ ukpga/2004/31/contents.

James, A. and Prout, A. (1997) *Constructing and Reconstructing Childhood: Contemporary Issues in the Sociological Study of Childhood.* (2nd edn) London: Falmer Press.

Kellett, M. (2010) *Rethinking Children and Research: Attitudes in Contemporary Society (New Childhoods).* London: Continuum.

Langsted, O. (1994) 'Looking at Quality from the Child's Perspective', in Moss, P. and Pence, A. (eds) *Valuing Quality in Early Childhood Services: New Approaches to Defining Quality.* London: Paul Chapman.

Lowe, M. (2007) *Beginning Research, A Guide for Foundation Degree Students.* Oxon: Routledge.

MacNaughton, G. (2009) 'Exploring Critical Constructivist Perspectives in Children's Learning', in Anning, A., Cullen, J. and Fleer, M. (2009) *Early Childhood Education Society and Culture* (2nd edn). London: Sage.

MacNaughton, G. and Rolfe, S. A. (2010) 'The Research Process' in MacNaughton, G., Rolfe, S. A. and Siraj-Blatchford, I. *Doing Early Childhood Research. International Perspectives on Theory and Practice* (2nd edn). Berkshire: OUP.

MacNaughton, G., Rolfe, S. A. and Siraj-Blatchford, I. (2010) *Doing Early Childhood Research. International Perspectives on Theory and Practice* (2nd edn). Berkshire: OUP.

Mayall, B. (2002) *Towards a Sociology for Childhood. Thinking from children's lives.* Buckingham: OUP.

McDowall-Clark, R. (2010) *Childhood in Society for Early Childhood Studies.* Exeter: Learning Matters.

McNiff, J. and Whitehead, J. (2011) *All You Need to Know About Action Research* (2nd edn). London: Sage.

Naidoo J. and Wills, J. (2009) *Foundation for Health Promotion* (3rd edn). Edinburgh: Balliere Tindall.

Nutbrown, A. (2012) *Foundations for Quality: The Independent Review of Early Education and Childcare Qualifications.* London: Crown Copyright.

Opie, C. (2004) (Ed.) *Doing Educational Research.* London: Sage.

Palaiologou, I. (2012) (Ed.) *Ethical Practice in Early Childhood.* London: Sage.

Roberts-Holmes, G. (2011) *Doing your Early Years Research Project* (2nd edn). London: Sage.

Sylva, K., Melhuish, E., Sammons, P., Siraj-Blatchford, I., Taggart, B. and Elliot, K. (2004) *Effective Provision of Pre-School Education (EPPE).* London: Institute of Education.

Thomas, G. (2013) *How to do Your Research Project* (2nd edn). London: Sage.

United Nations (1989) *UN Convention on the Rights of the Child.* London: Unicef. Available from: www. unicef.org.uk/crc?gclid=CNnqmMypgLOCFUsUwwodmTQAVA&sissr=1.

6 Reflective practice

Karen Hanson and Karen Appleby

LEARNING OUTCOMES

After reading this chapter you should be able to:

✔ Question your current understanding of **reflective practice**.
✔ Understand the relevance of reflective practice for practitioners working with children and families.
✔ Examine your current value base and professional responsibility as a reflective practitioner working with others.
✔ Apply different perspectives on how to develop a reflective disposition; reflective practice as a 'way of being'.
✔ Examine your identity and role as a **reflective thinker, learner** and **'activist'**.
✔ Examine the significance of socio-cultural factors impacting on your role as a reflective practitioner.
✔ Examine the significance of being a creative reflective practitioner.

Introduction

As a student, tutor, employer or employee working with or for children and families, you will be aware of the expectation for you to be a reflective practitioner. The intention of this chapter is to help you to develop and deepen your understanding of your role as a reflective practitioner within the context of working and learning with and for others. You will be asked to engage with different ways of thinking about the nature of **reflective practice** and what this means for you both personally and professionally. There is a particular focus on you taking responsibility for the development of your own **reflective identity** and practice within the context of working with and for others.

beyond a 'technical' application of theory to practice to the active process of developing a 'theory for action' (Argyris, 1995) which is specific to your context. McIntosh (2010) examines the limitations of 'evidence-based practice' and argues instead for practitioners engaging in professional inquiry to inform 'practice-based evidence'. This means you are creating knowledge in collaboration with others which is specific to the needs of your setting. It requires 'a real sense of being in the moment' (McIntosh, 2010: 25) as an active participant within your professional community and a commitment to working with others to make a difference. This places the role of the reflective practitioner within the practice community and recognises the complex social relationships, needs and perspectives of others impacting on choices, decisions and actions. The reflective practitioner will embrace these complexities, work hard to understand them and use insights gained from the process to inform practice.

The qualities demonstrated by **'reflexive' practitioners** support a deeper understanding of the impact you have on and within your practice community. Developing a critical awareness of the impact of self; 'focusing close attention upon one's own actions' and the way I am 'experienced and perceived by others' (Bolton, 2005: 10) can be emotionally challenging but potentially very rewarding. Significantly for reflective practitioners, this 'way of being' can nurture a strong sense of identity and empowerment. It enables insight into your role within complex social situations which in turn can be used to inform creative and purposeful solutions.

Reflective practitioners who demonstrate these qualities can play a significant role in responding positively to challenges from outside of the setting such as the implementation of externally imposed guidelines. A practitioner who applies a 'technical' approach to practice may implement policy without much thought to the consequences. A reflective practitioner will work collaboratively with the practice community to critically examine guidelines, consider the needs of their children, identify different possibilities and develop practice which is informed by a range of different perspectives.

PROVOCATION

- How much of your practice is based upon externally imposed targets and expectations?
- Do these compromise your professional principles and values?
- If so, how do you manage these challenges?

Reflective practice as a 'way of being'

The reflective practitioner who understands their own identity and the needs of their community will respond to challenges from a 'deep' rather than 'surface' approach. They can be described as a 'reflective professional practitioner in marked contrast to the worker-as-technician' (Moss, 2008: xiii). As Leitch and Day (2000: 181) argue,

> what defines the effective [critically] reflective practitioner is more a set of attitudes towards practice based upon broader understandings of self, society and moral purposes than those

which seek simply to increase efficiency in relation to 'delivery' and narrowly conceived achievement targets.

This identifies the significance of a 'way of being' as a **reflective thinker** and learner; someone who is constantly striving to develop a deeper understanding of practice within and beyond the setting. As an **agent of change**, reflective practitioners require this 'set of attitudes' or **reflective dispositions** to identify and evaluate meaningful and appropriate creative solutions to complex issues within their settings. This focus on action emerging from thinking and learning can be described as **'reflective activism'** (Hanson and Appleby, 2015) involving:

> an active engagement in continual review and repositioning of assumptions, values and practice in light of evaluation of multiple perspectives, including the wider socio-cultural perspectives influencing the context; transforming and transcending self and practice in order to effect change and improvement.

(Hanson, 2012: 144)

Reflective activity: exploring your value base

PROVOCATION

What informs your identity and role as a reflective practitioner?

Represent the story of your role as a practitioner. This can be in any form you choose.

- What motivates you as a practitioner? What is your purpose; your reason for being a reflective practitioner?
- What do you value? What do you believe is important and why?
- What has informed your position?
- How does this inform your practice?
- What, if anything, has challenged your position; your values and beliefs and why?
- How does your position relate to the values and beliefs of those you work with?

A reflective disposition

A reflective disposition builds on a strong value base that assumes personal and professional responsibility for improving the quality of provision for children and families. Reflective practitioners actively engage with interests, concerns and issues. Their engagement is stimulated and informed by their values, an inherent need to act and make a difference in the most appropriate way for all involved. This requires energy and drive.

Dewey (1910: 13) identifies that 'reflective thinking is always more or less troublesome because it involves overcoming the inertia that inclines one to accept suggestions at their face value; it involves willingness to endure a condition of mental unrest and disturbance'.

PROVOCATION

- How often do you question what, how and why things are as they are?

CASE STUDY 1

Karen

Central to Karen's reflective disposition and related research was the moral commitment to enabling others to improve their practice. This value base informed the development of her research project into how she could support her students in developing as reflective practitioners (Hanson, 2012). McNiff (2011: 280) describes this as moral justification: *'trying to live one's values of moral commitment in practice'.*

Karen's dilemma
A group of students discussed one of her fellow tutors in a very uncaring, disrespectful and damaging way, on a social media site. This caused her considerable concern as their espoused identity was as caring, collegiate, empathic and suitable to work with young children.

Karen's reflection
In her role as a tutor and practitioner researcher she recognised the need to be honest with herself and with others; to know and constantly evaluate her 'espoused self'. Through reflection Karen identified that students sometimes struggle to bring together their personal and professional identities.

What did Karen learn?
This event highlighted the significance of 'social media' within the students' personal lives. It also reinforced the need for espoused professional values to be at the core of who you are as a person. From reflection on this experience Karen realised that sometimes there are challenges involved in transferring values and guiding principles from one context to another. Karen realised that she was making assumptions about the students and had not considered the world from their perspective. This prompted her to develop her existing theory for practice which recognised what students bring to their journey as developing reflective practitioners.

Karen's contribution to our understanding of reflective practice
Karen developed a framework to support the development of reflective dispositions which included recognition that the socio-cultural context in which we live is a significant factor (See Figure 6.1).

This disposition to question also recognises the importance of a reflexive approach to your reflective practice. This involves an examination and 'theorisation' of what you do and why and the impact this has on self and others. It is useful here to consider Hanson's (2012) exploration of her own identity as a reflective practitioner and rationale for researching reflective practice.

Developing your reflective disposition: accessing our natural resources

Understanding reflective practice as a 'way of being' rather than a mechanistic or 'technical' approach encourages a deeper examination of reflective activity as a human capacity. Dewey (1910, 1933) refers to us having 'natural resources' that can be used to develop our ability to be reflective. He states that *curiosity*, *depth* and *suggestion* are the three natural resources which enable us to develop the ability to be **reflective thinkers**.

- **Curiosity** is the predominant resource; the need to investigate, question, understand and make sense of our experiences is presented as an essential characteristic of someone who wants to learn. *Are you naturally curious*?
- **Depth** is another of these three resources. Dewey states that to establish substantial ideas time is required to digest and translate impressions. *Do you give yourself time to think*?
- **Suggestion** is the other natural resource identified by Dewey and is probably the most difficult to explain. As curious human beings we cannot stop ourselves from responding to stimulus (suggestion) within our environment. '*Thinking is rather something that happens in us*' (Dewey, 1910: 34). Our responses to suggestion are dependent upon the nature of the stimulus and whether we perceive it as meaningful and relevant. *What stimulates your thinking?*

At this point it is important to note that while these resources can be found within us, we are social beings whose 'natural resources' are stimulated and developed through interaction with others; therefore the nature of learning and professional working communities is significant. As human beings we have the potential to consider possibilities, for our curiosity to motivate us to explore and develop new connections and insights. As we are working with young children we need our curiosity and interest to be provoked within our working environment. Sometimes this will be motivated by our disposition as thinkers and learners and at other times driven by our value base and the need to act on this for the benefit of others.

FROM RESEARCH TO PRACTICE

The aim of this research is to understand how reflective dispositions can be developed in Early Childhood Studies students in order to create a reflective learning community and culture. The objective is to understand Early Childhood students' **perceptions** of reflective practice. These perspectives may support your own insight into your role as a reflective practitioner.

Hanson, K. (2011) 'Reflect' – is this too much to ask? *Reflective Practice*, vol. 12, no. 3: 293–304, London: Routledge.

Reflective thinking, learning and action

Understanding reflective practice as a process involving reflective thinking, learning and action helps us to describe what we do. Rather than a recipe for how to be a reflective practitioner, it creates a framework for questioning, explaining and validating our role and identity as Early Years practitioners. This understanding also helps us know how we can continue to develop both personally and professionally.

- Identify a meaningful purpose for reflective activity.
- Engage in reflective thinking (reflection) as a meaning-making process which in turn informs learning and actions.
- Stimulate and inform purposeful reflective activity through professional conversation and dialogue with others within your practice community.
- Critically evaluate personal and collective 'theories for action' (Argyris, 1995) (the values, principles and knowledge underpinning choices, decisions and actions in practice).

Being a reflective thinker and learner

Mezirow (1998) believes that critical reflection is integral to **transformative learning** and this happens through a change occurring in the learners' existing habit of mind. For some, whose past learning experiences have been dominated by a transmission approach based on receiving, rehearsing and recapitulating information, reflective thinking and learning may require a transition period. Reflective practice requires ownership and active engagement as thinkers and learners who are open and responsive to learning opportunities.

> ## REFLECTIVE PRACTICE
>
> - **How do you learn?**
> - **Do you take time to think about issues within practice?**
> - **What resources do you use to help you make sense of these issues?**
> - **Now, take time to consider how you use them.**

At this point it is helpful to consider how reflective thinking and learning can be developed. Models of reflective practice discussed previously can support evaluation of current practice to inform change and improvement. However, thinking about what is working and what can be improved can happen at a surface level. Experiences, problems and solutions are described rather than investigated more deeply through engagement with a range of resources. This deeper level of thinking requires a disposition to research a range of relevant evidence and to be open to new ways of understanding. What is learned from this process can then inform decisions and actions in practice.

Reflective practice as a 'way of being' recognises its potential for enhancing practice. Ghaye (2005: 177) states that many of us have a *predisposition to more readily reflect on past problems and failures'*. However, success can also serve as a catalyst for change and improvement. Knowing what is working well can be used to inform decisions about the nature or need for change. This does not mean that we should be complacent and assume what has worked well in the past will continue to do so in the future. It is important that reflective practitioners recognise the need for on-going review of all aspects of practice which is provoked by their own and others' learning.

Reflective practitioners therefore need to be self-critical and self-motivated, resilient and creative problem solvers who are actively engaged in thinking and learning in collaboration with others. They need to research and engage critically with a range of knowledge from different sources to 'transform' their thinking and learning and to use what they have learned for the benefit of their professional community. As developing reflective practitioners it is helpful to use a framework for understanding and developing a more critical level of reflective thinking and learning. The aim is to support your use of natural resources, as Dewey (1910) describes them. However, it is your choice and responsibility to actively use them to stimulate your own 'way of being' as a reflective practitioner.

Seeing things from different perspectives

Brookfield's (1995) four lens theory provide a significant tool for reflective thinking and learning. These are explained below.

Autobiographical lens

Brookfield (1995) identifies the need to recognise and value what we bring to our role as reflective practitioners. We should celebrate and utilise our diverse experiences and potential for the benefit of children and their families rather than assessing and comparing ourselves with others. This perspective recognises and values practitioners as individuals and the significance of different personal and professional journeys. It recognises that difference in what we believe is important and how this is reflected in our practice.

Use a timeline to record your personal and professional journey. Identify the impact of your journey on your practice. How have your experiences informed what you believe is important? How do they affect your decisions and actions in practice?

Colleagues lens

Brookfield (1995) discusses how learning from others who have similar experiences to you will enrich your understanding of your own interpretation of a situation. Experience provides a rich resource of practice narratives; stories of practice which can be shared. These have the potential to stimulate and inform dialogue, critical thinking and reflective learning. This highlights the significance of practice based learning and the need for the less experienced to reflect, discuss, learn and 'theorise' through engagement with different perspectives.

Do you listen to and engage with your colleagues' stories/perspectives?

Students/children/families lens

Brookfield (1995) considers what he calls the 'student' lens. For the reflective practitioner this will include those we are aiming to support. Often central to our 'dilemmas' and catalysts of the need to reflect, the perspectives of these people are crucial in understanding the situation from their point of view. It is not always easy to find ways to gain the views of very small children or some of our most vulnerable families; however, it is possible and essential.

Think about ways in which you can or have included the perspectives of this group within your reflective process.

Theoretical/literature

Brookfield (1995) also identifies the significance of engaging with theoretical perspectives. You will be regarded as experts in your field but this does not mean you will know everything about every aspect of your work. Many people research specific aspects of working practices relevant to your own. The outcome of these inquiries can be used to inform our own knowledge and support the decisions we make. Other literature such as policies and legislation also impact upon how we practice, and therefore should be considered alongside the other perspectives.

How deeply do you think about what you have read? Does your reading provoke thinking about your practice? Does it make you question or challenge practice or help you to develop new approaches?

Seeing things from an additional perspective

The socio-cultural lens

As discussed previously, experiences with students' use of social media led Hanson (2012) to review her own ability to effectively reflect and use these reflections to make decisions. The explanation of her approach to reflective thinking and learning revealed the limitations of her practice and led her to identify an additional dimension. She had examined the issue from her own autobiographical perspective, her colleagues' perspectives, her students' perspectives and the perspectives from existing theory and literature upon the concepts affecting the particular concern (Hanson, 2012). The nature of this issue, which is clearly located in the specific nature of the students' life experience, highlighted the significance of the wider **socio-cultural context** and resulted in Karen developing the Peripheral Socio-Cultural Lens within the concept of Evolutionary Critical Reflection (see Figure 6.1).

The four perspectives identified by Brookfield (1995) can stimulate a critical level of reflective practice, however, the missing fifth lens, that Hanson (2012) refers to as the Peripheral Socio-Cultural Lens (see Figure 6.1), takes that criticality to a different level. To use this lens you have

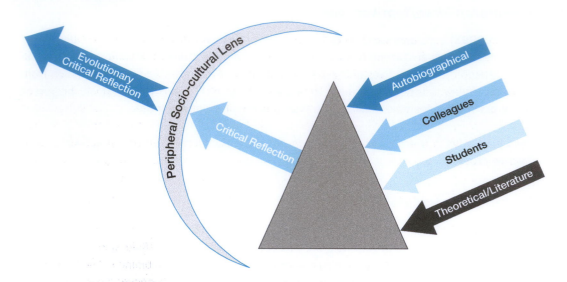

Figure 6.1 The peripheral socio-cultural lens (Hanson (2012: 144)

to be prepared to step outside your own 'world' and view the world as the people who are the subjects of your enquiry would view it. In Hanson's case, as her world (era) did not involve engaging with the social media concept she was unable to understand her students' behaviour and their difficulty with the concept of reflective practice. The world and people's lives have continually evolved and sometimes we become entrenched in the traditions of the decades of our most formative years. Therefore, we have to be committed to what Hanson terms 'Evolutionary Critical Reflection' to ensure we are viewing things from a current perspective (as demonstrated in Figure 6.1). A new line of enquiry was established which posed the question – does continuous engagement with social media sites develop attitudes that have a negative impact upon the development of reflective dispositions? For instance, the immediacy and instant reactive nature of sharing to a worldwide community on a social media site does not encourage the depth (Dewey, 1910) and thinking needed to really understand the consequences of actions. You might think about this question from a personal viewpoint.

REFLECTIVE PRACTICE

Try using all of the lenses, including the peripheral socio-cultural lens (Hanson, 2012), when you are next faced with a dilemma.

Creative reflective practice: 'professional artistry'

Developing critical self-awareness as a learner is important as highlighted in the example above. Schön (1983) describes this as developing **'professional artistry'**. Schön (1983: 49) compares the concepts of 'Technical Rationality' and 'Professional Artistry'. He suggests that technical rationality does not support the practical competence required in 'divergent' situations and states that there is a need for 'an **epistemology** for practice implicit in the artistic, intuitive processes which some practitioners do bring to situations of uncertainty, instability, uniqueness, and value **conflict**' (Schön, 1983: 49). This requires you to be creative and theorise your practice, building a capacity for creating new meanings and consequently exploring different possibilities and solutions. This might be described as creative reflective practice. Thompson and Pascal (2012: 312) also critically examine the concept of 'technical rationality' which in their view 'demeans professional practitioners, by relegating them to the status of unthinking followers of instructions and procedures'. Their argument for 'artistry in practice' clearly reflects Schön's (1983) 'Professional Artistry'. Thompson and Pascal (2012: 313-14) describe a 'fluid approach in which there is a greater emphasis on integrating theory and practice' and becoming a 'knowledgeable doer'. This position is also evident within Hanson and Appleby's (2014) concept of the 'Reflective Activist' explained earlier in the chapter. Development of your own self-awareness and professional artistry requires an objective and inclusive overview of everything and everyone involved within the context you are working. Your professional artistry will develop from understanding the wider issues impacting upon your everyday actions.

In summary

- Those who choose to work with and for children and families have a responsibility to understand how to meet their needs. These needs and the situations in which they are realised are diverse and complex which means we need as reflective practitioners to make well-informed decisions before acting.
- Being a reflective practitioner is an essential part of being a professional who endeavours to improve practice and to make a positive difference to the lives of others.
- Reflective practitioners need to understand and evaluate their role and identity within the context of their practice community.
- Reflective practice is synonymous with professional inquiry which is driven by a need to practise our values. If these values are compromised it acts as a catalyst to explore how we can make improvements to fulfil our beliefs and professional principles.
- A reflective disposition is ever evolving. As social, institutional, political, economic and individual landscapes continually change so should our thinking and practice in light of reviewing and repositioning our assumptions and values. What might have worked well last year might be completely the wrong action this year.
- To be a critically reflective practitioner, who acts as an agent of change, requires a set of attitudes and skills to think critically, learn and act for themselves and others.

Conclusion

The development of your own identity as a reflective practitioner is central to your role as an agent of change with the ability to make a positive contribution in collaboration with your professional community. It is important that there is a continual link between practical experiences relating to theoretical knowledge and the development of theory from and for your own practice. The environment within practice and within the educational institution in which you are studying should enable you to develop the confidence to question and challenge both practice and theory and to be critical in the contradictions between the theory and the practice. As a consequence your reflective way of being will be forever evolving. You cannot expect to reach a point where you can claim you are a completed 'finished' critically reflective practitioner. The nature of this way of being is that you will be examining your existing 'frames of reference' and existing assumptions continually. You will keep adjusting your thinking as a result of new experiences, research, and new knowledge and create a broader, deeper and richer understanding. This will require you to embrace critically reflective practice as a way of being.

Further reading

Appleby, K. (2010) 'Reflective Thinking; Reflective Practice', in Canning, N. and Reed, M. (eds), *Reflection in the Early Years*, London: Sage Publications, 7-23.
   This chapter provides an introduction to reflective practice informed by students studying Early Childhood.

Appleby, K. and Andrews, M. (2012) 'Reflective Practice is the Key to Quality Improvement', in Reed, M. and Canning, N. (eds), *Implementing Quality Improvement and Change in the Early Years*, London: Sage Publications, 57-72.
   This chapter examines the significance of reflective practice for improving quality in Early Years settings.

Hanson K. and Appleby, K. (2014) 'Reflective Practice', in Reed, M. and Walker, R. (eds), *Early Childhood Studies: A Critical Reader*, London: Sage Publications, 7-13.
   This chapter examines the concept of 'reflective activism' in more depth.

Useful websites

The following websites provide ways of developing your understanding of your role as a reflective practitioner in collaboration with others.

http://wenger-trayner.com/introduction-to-communities-of-practice/
   This website provides further information on the concept of 'Communities of Practice' mentioned briefly in this chapter.

https://www.youtube.com/watch?v=qn3joQSQm4o
   Wenger has more recently developed the concept of 'Landscapes of Practice' which he discusses in this YouTube video.

References

Argyris, C. (1995) *Journal of Managerial Psychology*, 10(6): 20-26, MCB University Press.
Bolton, G. (2005) *Reflective Practice: Writing & Professional Development*, (2nd edn). London: Sage Publications.
Brookfield, S. (1995) *Becoming a Critically Reflective Teacher*, San Francisco: Jossey-Bass.

Dewey, J. (1910) *How We Think,* Boston/New York/Chicago: D.C. Heath & Co.

Dewey, J. (1933) *How We Think: A Restatement of the Relation of Reflective Thinking to the Educative Process,* Chicago: Henry Regnery.

Edwards, G. and Thomas, G., (2010). Can Reflective Practice Be Taught?. *Educational Studies*, 36(4): 403–414.

Ghaye, T. (2005) 'Reflection as a Catalyst for Change', *Reflective Practice*, 6(2): 177–187.

Gibbs, G. (1988) *Learning by Doing: A Guide to Teaching and Learning Methods*, Oxford: Oxford Polytechnic.

Hanson, K. J. (2012) *How Can I Support Early Childhood Studies Undergraduate Students To Develop Reflective Dispositions?,* University of Exeter: Exeter Availale from: https://eric.exeter.ac.uk/repository/handle/10036/3866 (accessed 4 August 2015).

Hanson, K. and Appleby, K. (2015) 'Reflective Practice', in Reed, M. and Walker, R. (eds), *Early Childhood Studies: a Critical Companion*, London: Sage Publications, 7–13.

Lahav, R. (2008) 'Philosophical Practice: Have we gone far enough?' *Practical Philosophy*, 9(2): 13–20. Online. Available from: www.society-for-philosophy-in-practice.org/journal/pdf/9-2%20013%20Lahav%20-%20Far%20enough.pdf (accessed 20 March 2015).

Leitch, R. & Day, C., 2000. Action Research and Reflective Practice: Towards a Holistic View. *Educational Action Research*, 8(1): 179–193.

McIntosh, P. (2010) *Action Research and Reflective Practice: Creative and visual methods to facilitate reflection and learning*, Abingdon: Routledge.

McNiff, J. (2011) 'New Cultures of Critical Reflection in Qatar', *Educational Action Research*, 19(3): 279–296.

Mezirow, J. (1998) 'On Critical Reflection', *Adult Education Quarterly*, 48: 185–198.

Moon, J. (2008) *Critical Thinking: An exploration of Theory and Practice*, London: Routledge.

Moss, P. (2008) 'Foreword', in Paige-Smith, A. and Craft, A. (eds.) *Developing Reflective Practice in the Early Years,* Maidenhead: Open University Press.

Schön, D. A. (1983) *The Reflective Practitioner,* London: Ashgate Publishing Ltd.

Schön, D. A. (1987) *Educating the Reflective Practitioner,* San Francisco: Jossey Bass.

Thompson, N. and Pascal, J. (2011) 'Reflective Practice: An existentialist perspective', *Reflective Practice,* 12(1): 15–26.

Thompson, N. & Pascal, J. (2012) Developing critically reflective practice. *Reflective Practice: International and Multidisciplinary Perspectives.* 13(2): 311–325

Wenger, E. (1998) *Communities of Practice: Learning, meaning, and identity,* Cambridge: Cambridge University Press.

Part II

The Learning and Development of Children 0-5

7 The Foundation Years: babies

Isobel MacDougall and Jill Brown

LEARNING OUTCOMES

After reading this chapter you should be able to:

✔ Explain some important theories and influences on the development of babies during the first year of life.
✔ Understand the enormous changes that take place during that time and the adult role in supporting the baby through them.
✔ Recognise the vital importance of building a relationship with the family and other carers of the baby.
✔ Understand how to engage with babies in order to meet their needs and interests and enable them to develop their learning through play.
✔ Try different methods of recording this development.
✔ Know and understand brain development, attachment theory, the formation of a child's identity, relationships and strategies for learning and the role of the Key Worker or Key Person.

Introduction

From the moment a baby is born, she tries to make sense of the world around her. Her senses are bombarded with new stimuli, but her priority is to form a relationship with the important people around her that will sustain her through the first year of her life. Knowledge of development in the first year of life is fundamental for everyone working in any capacity with children. This chapter will start by investigating the importance of the development of the brain and its impact on a child's social and **emotional development** and the theory of **attachment**. It will consider the significance of **culture** in the formation of individual identities and highlight some of the strategies for learning in the first year of life.

Development and learning are **holistic** and interconnected. For the young child, experience is not separated into different compartments, every aspect of life being dependent on the others, so that no single area should be considered in isolation. However for the purposes of this book, you will notice that areas of development are compartmentalised in order to interrogate issues in more depth. It is important to be aware of this when reflecting on children to view them as a whole child. This chapter highlights the significant features affecting babies in the first year of life but, due to the limitations of the chapter, cannot study them to the depth they deserve. You are expected to do further reading and research as indicated within the chapter.

Brain development

Are the theories of Piaget and Vygotsky still relevant? Theories of child development are constantly developing as more detailed research is carried out. Many long-held theories are being disproved and new ones evolving. The Swiss biologist Piaget realised that **neonates** had powerful learning mechanisms that allowed them to construct ideas about the world, **assimilate** that knowledge and develop new theories as they met different experiences. It was thought for a long time, as Piaget suggested, that this development was innate and followed a strict sequential pattern and that one stage must be reached before the next one developed (known as developmental stages theory or constructivism). In his theory of Cognitive Development, Piaget called the first two years of life the 'sensory motor stage'. Babies use all their senses to explore their environment and they especially use their mouths to explore objects, because there are many nerve endings in the lips which tell the child if objects are hard, soft, hot or cold and provide much more information.

A contemporary of Piaget's, but living in Russia, was Lev Vygotsky. He was more interested in how much society shaped babies' development and realised that the role of the adult was a vital component in a child's learning (known as social constructivism). The culture into which the baby is born, as well as the quality of social interactions she experiences, shape the brain's development. Vgotsky coined the term **Zone of Proximal Development** to emphasise the difference between a child learning alone or with a 'co-learner' who could be an adult or more experienced child (Nutbrown and Clough: 2014). He considered that learning is a social and cultural activity, often being 'scaffolded' or supported by a more knowledgeable 'other' (Jordan: 2009).

REFLECTIVE PRACTICE
REFLECTIVE PRACTICE

So what do you think? How relevant today are Piaget's ideas of child development and is Vygotsky's social constructivism nearer the truth as we understand it now?

Of course, it's not a simple matter of right or wrong as these theories are complex and both have much to offer our understanding of child development. Read more about these theories. As you read more about neuroscience, consider the importance of both Piaget's and Vygotsky's ideas today. What examples have you observed of these theories in practice?

In the last decade or more, a new element to this research, **neuroscience**, has enabled techniques such as brain scans to help us reach a more accurate theory of development. Scientists can use this technology to observe electro-chemical activity in the brain. They can now see that there is no fixed timescale for brain development or a genetic blueprint for it, but that everything a baby experiences changes the physiology of the brain. So during what Piaget called the sensory-motor stage, when babies use all their senses to explore and learn about the world, this influences the wiring of the brain.

What has neuroscience discovered about the way babies develop?

Our brains are composed of one hundred billion nerve cells called neurons and glial cells. Neurons have fibrous branches called dendrites for transmitting information to other neurons and axons which receive incoming signals. As thoughts are initiated and repeated, neurons continually process this and build stronger and stronger network pathways between dendrites and axons called a synapse. Synapses are covered in a myelin sheath to protect them. It is the number and type of these synaptic connections that make healthy brains. With more stimulation, the connections become stronger and can undertake further learning. Neurons that do not form synapses die off. Babies' brains are much busier than ours and more than double in weight in the first year while these connections are being formed. The number of neurons remains the same from birth but what changes is the wiring of those new synaptic connections that continue to be made throughout our lives. One of the things that influences that wiring is interaction with you!

Have you ever wondered what is going on in a baby's brain when they smile at you? If you think it is just wind you may not smile back. This has a massive consequence for that baby as your response has a major impact on their physical brain development. What neuroscience tells us is that the brain of a baby forms these synapses in response to what the adults around them do. In other words we all function best when linked to another brain. Consider Vygotsky's theory about peer learning and social construction (Nutbrown: 2010).

'The kind of brain each baby develops is the brain that comes out of his or her particular experiences with people' (Gerhardt: 2006: 38).

REFLECTIVE PRACTICE
REFLECTIVE PRACTICE

Next time you change a nappy, or go to pick a small baby up, notice every small change of facial expression: was there a frown? Did the baby make eye contact and hold it even if you moved to one side? Are the arms and legs moving? Are they coordinated? What is the baby trying to tell you?

- Now think about your response. Was it loud or soft, excited or soothing, encouraging, calm or busy?
- Consider the effect on the baby when you speak to them. The baby is trying to understand the way your mind is working (Zeedyk and Robertson: 2011).

Attachment and the developing brain

John Bowlby was the originator of attachment theory that contributed to our understanding of early relationships and the necessity of feeling secure before venturing forth to explore the world. Bowlby postulated the 'Maternal Deprivation' hypothesis which suggested that between the ages of 6 months and 3 years, babies need continuous love from a primary care-giver. Bowlby thought this should be the mother, and that serious **separation** from her would have considerable impact on the baby's emotional development. He proposed that there is a pre-disposition in babies to maintain proximity to their care-givers and in order to do this, babies engage in behaviour which attracts the attention of their care-giver. They therefore perceive separation from this caregiver as a threat and activate attachment behaviours.

Bowlby worked with a psychologist, Mary Ainsworth, to develop the 'Strange Situation Technique, 'a system of assessing the extent and quality of an infant's attachment to the parent. Subsequently, a great deal of research has suggested that babies are capable of forming a secure attachment with a primary care-giver who need not be the mother (Rutter: 1985).

Babies are programmed to be socially cooperative, but will only be so if treated warmly and sensitively by a primary carer. The child must feel the attachment figure will be available, responsive and supportive when difficulties or frightening situations occur. This secure attachment gives a child confidence to become increasingly adventurous and able to tolerate brief separations. This gives her freedom to learn.

Conversely, when the baby is unwillingly responded to, ignored or even rejected, insecure attachment can result in anxiety about separation, clinginess and inability to take risks involved in undertaking new experiences.

REFLECTIVE PRACTICE

Read more about the theory of attachment and think about these questions yourself.

- What makes some attachments secure and others insecure?
- Can babies form attachments with more people than their primary care-giver?
- To what extent do early attachments affect behaviour in adulthood?

Thinking about infants with whom you have worked, consider how day care experiences may affect a baby's attachments and future social and emotional development.

It is clear that from birth babies need to attract adult attention and form attachments, either by aversive behaviours such as crying or screaming or attractive behaviour such as smiling, eye gaze and cooing. Their behaviour is triggered by some sort of stress, hunger, discomfort or absence of the primary care-giver. It is also clear that the response of the adult to that behaviour is key: a baby is unable to regulate her own stress so when an adult can respond by soothing, cuddling, relaxing and playing with the baby this actively develops the brain. Cairns (2004) suggests that trauma is caused not by what happens at the time but what happens around and after the event and that traumatised children who recover develop extra resilience. Adults who know how to respond sensitively play a large part in this recovery.

As we have seen, secure attachment relationships build healthy brains because the brain is a social organ stimulated by interactions with others but environmental, socio-economic conditions and political policy factors such as dietary deficiency, housing, poverty and inequality all affect brain development pre-birth as well as throughout life. If the mother is under stress because of her financial situation, a poor environment, marital difficulties or worse, **abuse**, the stress hormone cortisol passes through the placenta to the developing brain. Babies exposed to these sorts of difficulties in the womb are more likely to be demanding and termed as 'difficult', making it harder for an already stressed parent to handle (Cairns: 2004).

If a pregnant or breast-feeding woman has a poor diet, drinks alcohol heavily, takes drugs or smokes, this all affects the developing brain, sometimes with disastrous outcomes (failure of myelination). There is a robust link between pre-natal smoking or alcohol abuse and later antisocial behaviour of the child (Gerhardt: 2006). The food we eat affects brain wiring; low levels of fatty acids passed on through the placenta or breastmilk can cause depression and lack of concentration. When working with babies and young children, it is vital to keep informed about healthy feeding and nutrition. See the NHS website to check the latest guidance for parents.

PROVOCATION

- So what can be done in practice to ensure healthy brain development and synapse connections?
- How could you improve practice in the workplace to ensure secure attachments, and emphasise the importance of strong relationships of the children with the adults?
- Review the settling in policy in a nursery and consider what strategies you could employ to strengthen the relationships between home and nursery.

Identities and culture

Who am I? Where do I belong? These are philosophical questions that have persisted in Western thought over the years. When we consider the young baby, how do they form their sense of self in the first year of life? At a first glance, we may think that babies are born as helpless beings, dependent on others for their survival: yet babies are born with senses and **reflexes** that enable them to respond to the world around them. They react to light, sound, touch and have the skills for rooting, sucking and swallowing. These involuntary reflexes are part of the building blocks of voluntary actions that support the young baby in their quest for survival and their physical development.

However, the emotional and **social development** of the baby, and their developing sense of self is more dependent on the baby's relationship with their primary carers. Although babies are born with reflexes and senses that help them to learn quickly, they are totally dependent on their primary carers for food, warmth and love, all of which they need for survival. Babies need unconditional acceptance in order to become confident and resilient as they grow. Roberts, (cited in Dowling: 2009: 13) comments that the young baby experiences a range of conflicting emotions that they cannot control, needing their primary carer to help them to understand and accept them. She states that:

> *The mother's face and body are like a mirror to the baby. This very early mirroring process, which can reflect the mother's acceptance, forms the basis of the baby's* **self-concept**; *the mother's responses are the first 'brush strokes' for the developing picture.*

FROM RESEARCH TO PRACTICE

www.centreforum.org/assets/pubs/parenting-matters.pdf (publ.2014)

This research by Chris Paterson relates to government policy for tackling the widening gap in opportunity and how children's life chances are most determined in their first year of life. The plasticity of the brain in the first year means that interventions and prevention are most effective during that time. It is important that the setting provides consistent interaction with a baby and that the key person understands and provides for individual needs.

www.nspcc.org.uk/globalassets/documents/research-reports/all-babies-count-spotlight-perinatal-mental-health.pdf (publ. 2015)

This research conducted by the NSPCC discusses the impact of mental illness suffered by 10 per cent of the population after birth and how it can affect the mother's capacity for building a positive relationship with her child. If not treated it can lead to emotional, social and behavioural difficulties for the child and ultimately prevent him/her from reaching their full potential. Practitioners need to be aware of any possible problems and sensitively support families. They need to know where to suggest mothers can go for help if needed.

As we have seen, the way the baby is nurtured influences brain development, and the environment in which they are nurtured also has an impact on their development. Babies are not born into neutral environments, but into the cultural, geographical and socio-economic environment of their parents or carers; and parents and carers have the privilege and the responsibility of helping to shape the lives of very young children.

In his work in 1979, Urie Bronfenbrenner developed a theory that took account of children growing up in a given time and place. His research described the impact of the child's environment on their development, while maintaining the individuality of the child. In 'The Ecological Systems Theory' Bronfenbrenner (1979) endeavoured to consider the impact of issues such as religion and culture on the developing child as well as considering the impact of local, national and global policies. This theory suggests that individual babies and families cannot be understood in isolation, but within the complex network in which they exist. Bronfenbrenner's theory is described as a set of concentric circles: the microsystem includes the people and contexts that are closest to the child; the mesosystem includes the interrelationship of two or more groups that the child participates in; the exosystem includes the social system and social networks of the child in which the child is not a direct participant; and the macrosystem includes the broader national social structures such as education, health, and economic and cultural values. As his thinking and research developed, Bronfenbrenner's Ecological Systems Theory evolved, focusing more on the development of individuals in ever-changing, multi-level contexts, and accounting for the influence of time and culture. He added the chronosystem to his theory and renamed his theory the Bioecological Model (Bronfenbrenner: 2005), highlighting the importance of **biological** processes in development although he only acknowledged biology as producing a person's potential. His evolving studies over the years demonstrate the complexity of the environmental influences on the young child as they develop and establish their own identities.

CASE STUDY 1

Anne was born in Nigeria to white British parents. They were both teachers and lived and worked in a small educational community where her father trained teachers and her mother taught women basic literacy skills. When her parents were working, Anne was looked after by a couple of local women who spoke with her, played with her and sang to her in their own home languages. Anne has no memories of early years of life, but despite spending most of her **childhood** from the age of 6 years in England, she has chosen to work with very young children who are becoming bilingual in an area where most of the families have immigrated from Africa.

As we can see through this case study, the formation of identity is a complex process that continually evolves as the baby has more experiences and relationships. Culture, gender and class all affect the formation of identity. However, it is important that each child is seen as ____ and that 'babies' are not seen as a **homogenous** group, but that each baby has its own shifting identities and is born with different personalities and temperaments (Brooker and Woodhead: 2010).

Culture is important in developing our sense of who we are and our developing identities. Positive self esteem and identity in young children under two in day-care depends on the attitudes of the people who care for them in their setting – the way that staff respect and genuinely value the cultural background of each child.

So what is culture? Culture is made up of the beliefs, behaviours, artefacts, traditions and other characteristics that are shared by members of a particular group or society. Through culture, people groups define themselves and conform to their society's shared values; these include language, customs, values, rules, accepted norms, technologies and organisations.

So what about attitudes towards gender? It is interesting to note that despite critical research around **equality** of opportunities for all children in recent decades and the importance of nonstereotypical treatment of girls and boys, buying clothes, equipment and toys for babies in the UK is frequently discriminated as blue for boys and pink for girls. Although this may be seen purely as colour coding, the underlying beliefs and values have a powerful influence on the way that babies are nurtured, highlighting the softer gentle handling of female babies and the tougher physical handling of male babies. Attitudes towards babies have profound effects on the developing child and their view of themselves as males or females. What happens in the first year of life has a lasting impact on later life. Different cultures have their own stereotypical views of gender, boys frequently being valued more highly than girls.

PROVOCATION

So what about you? Think about the influences on your own early life, then using Bronfenbrenner's Ecological Systems Theory (1979) try to plot the influences in your early life into his concentric circles: the micro system, the mesosystem and the exosystem; and continue to consider the geographical, political and historical context of your early years. Consider how these different influences have shaped who *you* are becoming.

Child development

It is important for any Early Years student to have sound knowledge about child development in the first year of life. In this first year the baby becomes mobile; sitting, standing alone and possibly walking; can manipulate objects; expresses their feelings, communicates effectively with others; is a participant member of the family and is an explorer, experimenter and hypothesiser. A foundational knowledge of child development will support you in evaluating, analysing and critically reflecting on your reading, research and practice with children. For example, you will know that during the first year of life the baby is constantly developing receptive language, so it is important to talk to them about what is going on around them, even if you think they will not understand. They are hearing the rhythm and cadence of sentences. Whatever age of child you are working with, it is helpful to know what developmental processes they have been through. Developmental psychology has developed biological maturation theories, environmental learning theories and social learning theories. These theories will not be discussed in this chapter, but you are advised to revisit or read about child development using core texts from the further reading list.

Traditionally, child development has been studied through the lens of developmental psychology, however, it is important to note that these theories do not usually take account of cultural diversity and are often proposed by psychologists from the West, based on research carried out in the West. Consider how this knowledge may be biased and, at times, discriminatory against people from other cultural and geographical backgrounds. Bruner (2000) proposes that childcare practices and beliefs are more marked than most cultural matters. Why do you think this is? In this book you will read about other **paradigms** or **discourses** of childhood such as the Emergent Paradigm (Dahlberg, Moss and Pence: 1997) and reconceptualisation of childhood

(Cannella: 2005). These will enable you to consider a postmodern approach to childhood in which the child is viewed within a cultural context and considered from a position of social justice and equity.

So, the formation of identities is a complex process that is never completed. Factors such as gender, race, position in the family, culture, language and ability interconnect to shape our shifting identities. Perhaps you are forming a new identity as a student or an early years educator to add to your identity as a friend, a sibling or a parent. We are unique and always evolving. Even the youngest baby is starting to form their identities within their family group (Robinson: 2011).

CASE STUDY 2

A student's experience

A student who was studying on a work-based Foundation Degree in Early Years while working in a city-centre nursery had been learning about the importance of language, culture and identity. She worked in the 'baby room' and had observed that a new baby was very unsettled. She knew that the baby's family had recently arrived from Eastern Europe but knew very little about them. She asked the parents if they had any favourite music that they played frequently at home, and asked them to bring it into the nursery. She then observed that as she played the music in the nursery, the baby began to settle. The student then realised the importance of getting to know about the family's cultural background and incorporating aspects of this into the daily life for the child in the nursery.

Relationships and strategies for learning

The family and community that make up the baby's world are at the heart of their culture and learning. It is important to recognise that there are cultural differences in care-giving for the very young, variations on the family structure globally and locally, diverse discourses of childhood and various approaches to interacting with the young baby. Therefore it is critical that adults working with children in their first year of life know the family well, have carried out home visits and engage in a collaborative relationship with the main carers so that the baby receives consistent care. The ways that children under one year feel about themselves is neither innate nor inherited, it is learned.

So how do babies learn? We have considered the importance of neuroscience to help us understand the way that the brain develops, dependent as it is on interaction and relationships with key people. The baby develops from interdependence to a capacity for independence in their first 5 years of life, moving from a focus on themselves to a focus on others. The young baby initially learns about being acceptable through their relationships with others in their first language – body language, before developing their spoken language. Babies converse with their caregivers through turn-taking interactions, termed 'co-regulation' by Trevarthan (1998). In his study on the interaction between young babies and their mothers, Trevarthan noted the finely tuned, **reciprocal** interactions in which babies were participants and active. This is known as intersubjectivity, defined as the 'meeting of minds' that takes place between the infant and the caregiver enabling the infant to be inducted in the culture of the caregiver. Intersubjectivity is dependent on an acute awareness of the emotional state of the infant, the caregiver sensitively tuning into the young child and articulating their needs and feelings. Trevarthan (1998) describes this reciprocal and sensitive interaction as 'the dance' between the mother and the infant, developing throughout the first year of life.

Babies also learn through their senses, using sight, sound, touch, taste, smell and physical movement to discover the world around them. Piaget's constructivist theory of cognitive development suggests that children go through stages of constructing understandings. He proposed that mental structures, known as *schema*, help us to organise our knowledge about the world. As we take in new information we *assimilate* it into our existing knowledge. However, if we take in information that challenges our existing knowledge we have to *accommodate* our schema to accept the changes. Piaget used the term *equilibration* to explain the continuous adjustments to our existing schema when we learn new concepts and acquire new information. Vygotsky, as we have already seen, regarded learning as a social activity, depending on being supported by a more knowledgeable 'other'. It has been argued that this approach is more adult-directed whereas co-construction, in which the child and adult are learning together is reciprocal with shared control of the learning process.

Chris Athey developed the concept of schemas in more depth in her research into children's thinking. She stated that schemas are both biological and socio-cultural, and defined schemas as 'a pattern of repeatable behaviour in which experiences are assimilated and that are gradually co-ordinated. Co-ordinations lead to higher-level and more powerful schemas' (Athey: 2011: 50). An example of a schema is a containment schema in which a child may put objects into boxes or baskets take them out and then put them back in again. There are many different schemas or more commonly, clusters of schemas.

CASE STUDY 3

A student's experience

A student was working with several young babies in a Baby Room in a Children's Centre. She had recently learned about Treasure Baskets on her Foundation Degree and decided to 'try them out'. She prepared a Treasure Basket using *People Under Three* by Elinor Goldschmied and Sonia Jackson (2004) as her guide and sat back to observe a baby of 11 months, as directed by Elinor Goldschmied. She was amazed to see how long the young baby spent taking objects out of the basket, examining them with her mouth then replacing them before taking out another. The baby then took each object out of the basket, one by one, and then replaced them all. He then tipped the basket out.

The student recorded that she had identified schematic behaviour and later noted that she observed this pattern of behaviour repeated at the child's lunchtime, with his food!

REFLECTIVE PRACTICE
REFLECTIVE PRACTICE

Read about schemas using sources listed at the end of this chapter. Reflect on your observations of children you are currently working with. Can you identify any schemas or schematic behaviour?

- What does this tell you about how the child is learning?
- What does this tell you about how the child may be thinking?
- How does this help you to plan more effectively for that child's learning opportunities?

So babies learn through their senses and schematic behaviours. However, babies are highly relational, needing to form strong relationships to support their learning and development. From their earliest moments, babies seek out relationships, wanting to connect with their primary carers. The notion of an active learner was originally coined by Piaget (1962), who emphasised the use of curiosity to investigate and solve problems as a way of accommodating and assimilating new knowledge, with little focus on the social nature of learning. Vygotsky highlighted the social aspect of learning and it has been argued that this approach is more adult-directed whereas co-construction, in which the adult and child are learning together, is reciprocal, with shared control of the learning process.

Barbara Rogoff, an American educator who has studied children in different cultural contexts, focuses on how culture influences the classic areas of human development such as cognitive development and social relations among children and their families and peers. Rogoff (1990) defines culture as '*the organised and common practices of particular communities in which children live*'. She uses the image of the child as an apprentice, and presents the child as an active learner, who will use the support of knowledgeable others and their socio-cultural context to make sense of the world. Dewey (cited in Rogoff: 2003: 207) suggests that guiding children does not imply that adults must control them; but rather work in collaboration with different roles and responsibilities. This is empowering for all participants. This notion of co-constructing learning, valued by the Reggio Emilia approach, views the child as competent, powerful, rich in potential and connected to adults and other children. Young infants learn competently as apprentices alongside confident, respectful and sensitive adults.

REFLECTIVE PRACTICE
REFLECTIVE PRACTICE

Read about the work of Rogoff in *Apprenticeship in Thinking* (1990).

- Reflect on the ways that a young baby learns alongside a more knowledgeable other.
- How does the young child learn to stack cups, feed themselves, learn to talk?
- What is the role of the adult in this process?
- In what way is the young child an apprentice?

A key person or a key worker?

Although fewer babies are in child-care settings in their first year of life due to the changes in maternity and paternity entitlements in the last decade, the role of a key worker or key person is critical for the young infant. Are the terms key worker and key person interchangeable? For the purposes of this chapter the roles are significantly different. The key worker ensures that records are maintained, the environment is appropriate for the infant, health and safety **assessments** are monitored and all the 'work' around caring for a young baby is completed. It is predominantly an organisational role. The role of the key person is a relational role. This is the person who forms an attachment with the infant and is able to 'tune into' them and be 'present' for them. The key person is able to be their advocate and support their learning and development.

For the young baby in a childcare setting, attachments to a key person are critical for their sense of well-being and a positive learning experience. This notion of 'the key person approach' was proposed by Elinor Goldschmied and Peter Elfer, based on Attachment Theory and Neuro-science, in which they describe the key person approach as 'a way of working in nurseries in which the whole focus and organisation is aimed at enabling and supporting close attachments between individual children and individual nursery staff' (Elfer, Goldschmied and Selleck: 2003: 18).

This means that the key person will work with their key child, carrying out all the personal tasks such as feeding, changing, comforting and stimulating. They will communicate with the parents so that both parents and staff know about the 24/7 experiences and needs of the infant. They will be the advocate for the infant within the child-care setting and take on the emotional responsibility of their care during this time.

This is a demanding role, and can be challenging for child-care settings and key people. What if the infant or their parents and delegated key person do not get on with each other? Elfer and Dearnley (2007) propose that where possible, the child-care setting is flexible and responds to the needs of the family. They also suggested that where members of staff do shift or part-time work, key people could work in pairs, so that each infant has two key people, ensuring that one of them is always available. The role of key person is intense and can be emotionally demanding and Elfer and Dearnley (ibid) discuss the importance of supervision for staff within a nursery context.

The role of the adult caring for infants in their first year of life is critical. The adult needs to be well qualified with a sound knowledge of child development, the needs of the developing child, how children learn and how to assess children's learning and development (Sylva *et al*.: 2004) to ensure the best outcomes for the infant. The adult needs to be emotionally intelligent, able to establish respectful and reciprocal relationships with parents and know how to seek support for any issues they find hard to deal with, for example, feeling that the child is not loved by their parent, or has a weak attachment.

Goldschmied and Jackson (2004) discuss the importance of the key person carrying out the home visits, being present to settle the infant into the care-setting and supporting the parents through this process. This will support the infant's social, emotional and cognitive development and ensure that their care is consistent between home and the setting, and that the infant feels secure and confident.

You may have noticed that very young babies appear to be happy being passed from one person to another, but as they get older they become more anxious when their main carer leaves.

PROVOCATION

Carry out research both in your reading and in discussions with colleagues on your degree course and in the work place on the difference between a 'key worker' and a 'key person'. How can both of these roles be maintained in a Baby Room caring for children under the age of 18 months?

- What are the advantages and disadvantages of each role?
- How can a busy nursery manage staff work and shifts alongside continuity of care for the young baby?

CASE STUDY 4

A student's experience

A mature student working in the baby room of a private nursery was disappointed to see that a nine-month-old baby for whom she had been a key person for 2 months suddenly started to be very upset when his mother left him. One afternoon when playing 'peepo' with him and his favourite soft toy, she noticed that when she hid the toy under a blanket, the child would now lift up the blanket to look for it, whereas previously he had not. He was realising that the toy was still there even if he couldn't see it. The student remembered something she had learnt in college about object permanence and began to understand why the behaviour had changed. How is this linked to separation anxiety? Carry out more research on this.

Their lack of anxiety in the early months does not mean that separation is a good thing for them; as we have seen, forming strong attachments is critical for their well-being and builds the pathways in the brain. However, the baby is developing their understanding of how their minds work in relation to the presence of others. There comes a stage when babies become distressed when an attachment figure is no longer present.

Conclusion

In this chapter we have considered the importance of the developing brain and its dependence on nurturing relationships for healthy growth and development. We have discussed the importance of attachments; those powerful relationships that provide security and support the development of a positive sense of self and self esteem. We have identified the importance of a healthy lifestyle with appropriate levels of exercise, sleep and rest and a healthy diet. All these factors are influenced by culture and environment and this in turn affects the infants' developing identities and their cognitive development, as they become skilful communicators, critical thinkers and intrepid explorers and discoverers of their worlds.

Further reading

Elfer, P., Goldschmied, E. and Selleck, D. (2003) *Keypersons in the Nursery. Building Relationships for Quality Provision.* London: Fulton Publishers.
  Detailed rationale, information and analysis of the role of the keyperson.

Gerhardt, S. (2006) *Why Love Matters.* London: Routledge.
  Informative early chapters on brain development and the importance of attachment and early relationships.

Nutbrown, C., Page, J. and Clare, A. (2013) *Working with Babies and Children. From Birth to Three* (2nd edition). London: Sage.
  A comprehensive book on policy and practice in work with very young children.

Roberts, R. (2010) *Wellbeing from Birth.* London: Sage.
  This book is a valuable source of information about the needs of the young baby and the role of the practitioner in meeting these needs and supporting the family.

Robinson, M. (2011) *Understanding Behaviour and Development in Early Childhood. A Guide to Theory and Practice.* Abingdon: Routledge.
  This book has a very clear chapter on brain development as well as information on early development.

Useful websites

www.rosemaryroberts.co.uk/links.html
  This website gives you details of the publications by Rosemary Roberts and also a very helpful list of relevant websites.

www.katecairns.com/?carousel=main
  This website will provide you with information about supporting babies and vulnerable young children. You will also find useful additional resources.

www.literacytrust.org.uk/talk_to_your_baby/news/1856_let_s_talk_about_working_with_babies
  The Literacy Trust provide helpful information and guidelines about communicating with babies and supporting their language development.

www.nhs.uk/conditions/pregnancy-and-baby/pages/solid-foods-weaning.aspx#close
  Guidelines for feeding babies.

References

Athey, C. (2011) *Threads of Thinking: Schemas and Young Children's Learning* (4th edn). London: Sage.

Bronfenbrenner, U. (1979) *The Ecology of Human Development. Experiments by Nature and Design.* Cambridge, Massachusetts: Harvard University Press.

Bronfenbrenner, U. (2005) *Making Human Beings Human. Bioecological Perspectives on Human Development.* London: Sage.

Brooker, L. and Woodhead, M. (2010) *Culture and Learning.* Early Childhood in Focus 6 Series. Milton Keynes: The Open University.

Bruner, J. (2000) 'Foreword' in DeLoache, J.S. and Gottlieb, A. (eds) *A World of Babies,* Cambridge, Cambridge University Press.

Cairns, K. (2004) *Attachment, Trauma and Resilience – Therapeutic Caring for Children*. London: BAAF.

Cannella, G. (2005) 'Reconceptualising the field of early care and education: if "western" child development is a problem, then what do we do?' in Yelland, N. (ed) *Critical Issues in Early Childhood Education*. Maidenhead: Open University Press pp. 17–39.

Dahlberg, G., Moss, P. and Pence, A. (2006) *Beyond Quality in Early Childhood Education and Care: Languages of Evaluation* (2nd edition). Abingdon: Routledge.

Dowling, M. (2009) *Young Children's Personal, Social and Emotional Development*. London: Sage.

Elfer, P. and Dearnley, K. (2007) 'Nurseries and emotional well being: Evaluating an emotionally containing model of continuing professional development', *Early Years: An International Journal of Research and Development*, 27 (3).

Elfer, P., Goldschmied, E. and Selleck, D. (2003) *Keypersons in the Nursery. Building Relationships for Quality Provision*. London: Fulton Publishers.

Gerhardt, S. (2006) *Why Love Matters*. London: Routledge.

Goldschmied, E. and Jackson, S. (2004) *People Under Three. Young Children in Daycare*. London: Psychology Press.

Gopnik, A., Meltzoff, A., Kuhl, K. (2001) *How Babies Think*. London: Phoenix.

Jordan, B. (2009) 'Scaffolding learning and co-constructing understandings', in Anning, A., Cullen, J. and Fleer, M. (eds) *Early Childhood Education. Society & Culture*. London: Sage.

Nutbrown, C. and Clough, P. (2014) *Early Childhood Education History, Philosophy and Experience*. London: Sage.

Nutbrown, C. (2010) *Key Concepts in Early Childhood Education and Care*. London: Sage.

Piaget, J. (1962) *Play, dreams and imitation in childhood*, New York: Norton Library.

Robinson, M. (2011) *Understanding Behaviour and Development in Early Childhood. A guide to theory and practice*. Abingdon: Routledge.

Rogoff, B. (1990) *Apprenticeship in Thinking. Cognitive Development in Social Context*. Oxford: Oxford University Press.

Rogoff, B. (2003) *The Cultural Nature of Human Development*. Oxford: Oxford University Press.

Rutter, M. (1985) 'Resilience in the face of adversity: protective factors and resistance to psychiatric disorder', *British Journal of Psychiatry*, 147: pp. 598–611.

Sylva, K., Mellhuish, E., Salmons, P., Siraj-Blatchford, I. and Taggart, B. (2004) *The Effective Provision of Pre-school Education (EPPE) Project. Findings from the Early Primary Years. Available from:* www.ioe.ac.uk/RB_Findings_from_early_primary(1).pdf

Trevarthan (1998) 'The Child's Need to Learn a Culture' in Woodhead, M., Faulkner, D. & Littleton, K. (eds) *Cultural Worlds of Early Childhood*. London: Routledge.

Zeedyk, S. and Robertson, J. (2011) *The Connected Baby*. www.theconnected baby.org

8 The Foundation Years: 2-3-year-olds

Janine Ryan

LEARNING OUTCOMES

After reading this chapter you should be able to:

✔ Identify the prime areas of development.
✔ Explain attachment theory and the impact this has on emotional well-being.
✔ Identify language skills that 2-3 year-olds develop.
✔ Describe physical development.
✔ Identify the role of the practitioner in supporting the learning and development of children aged 2-3 years.
✔ Explain how the enabling environment can be planned to support children's holistic development.

Introduction

The *Birth to Three Matters* framework (2001) demonstrated the government's commitment to the care and education of the youngest children. A review of research literature demonstrated that all areas of a child's learning and development are intricately intertwined, but that emotional and **social development** are the bedrock of other areas. This framework was used to develop the subsequent **Early Years Foundation Stage** (EYFS) framework (DCSF, 2008) for children aged 0-5 years.

In order for children to develop and learn they must have solid foundations on which to build. The EYFS (DfE, 2014a) outlines the developmental stages that children 0-5 should be working towards, setting out Early Learning goals that children should be achieving by the time they progress to Key Stage 1. The primary areas of learning (**Emotional Development**, Communication and Language, and Physical Development) are fundamental building blocks for higher-level cognitive development, and these will be a focus in this chapter. The coalition government's extension of the **Early Education Entitlement** (15 hours' free nursery education a week) to the poorest 2-year-olds has enabled 100,000 children to access early education. Research has identified that too many toddlers from disadvantaged backgrounds lack stimulation and exposure to the vocabulary which is readily available to children from advantaged backgrounds. Field (2010) identified that by the age of 3 there are large and systematic differences in children's outcomes and gaps persist through school with a negative impact on children's attainment. Field identified the significance of the early years in supporting achievement; it is difficult to undo the disadvantages experienced in the earliest years. Analysis of outcomes in the UK education system shows that 55 per cent of children who were in the bottom 20 per cent at age 7 remain there at age 16 and less than 40 per cent of them moved into the top 60 per cent (*Department for Education Internal Analysis of National Pupil Database*, cited in Field, 2010). Children who perform poorly at the start of school tend to continue to perform badly throughout. Therefore a good start in life is of great importance to later educational attainment. The focus on early years was also endorsed by Graham Allen in *Early Intervention* (2011). Sylva *et al.* (2004) reported that high quality pre-school education could have a significant impact on outcomes for children, positively impacting on children's social, intellectual and emotional development.

Theory

Attachment and emotional well-being

The first three years of a child's life constitute a period of phenomenal growth. They learn to walk and talk and are able to make their feelings known in addition to starting to manage many of their own personal care needs. These foundation years hold significant potential for learning and development. Warm and responsive relationships are crucial in supporting young children's development. Recent research in the field of neuroscience reveals the impact on brain development that love and a sense of safety and security have on a young child's cognitive development (Gerhardt, 2004). By age 3, 80 per cent of a child's brain is already developed, as connections between different parts of the brain are formed; neurological pathways are rich sources of activity and support brain structure and future cognitive development. Through a loving and safe base a young child is able to explore and experience the world around them with the security of a significant other being close by. These experiences enable a young child to engage socially with their environment and develop their own sense of self-awareness, self-esteem and sense of agency, i.e. they can act on their own behalf. This positive experience supports a child's ability to regulate their responses to stress and their capacity for self-regulation, which is a catalyst for learning. Bowlby's work on **attachment** identified the impact this relationship has on a child's ability to learn. His pioneering work identified different attachment models: *secure*, *avoidant*, and *resistant*, and later this was extended by further research to include *disorganised*.

- **Secure:** These children often cry when the parent leaves but actively greet them on their return. Sensitive parents respond to their child's needs in a consistent manner.
- **Avoidant:** These children leave their parent readily and act in a similar way with other adults. On the parent's return they avoid contact, tending to show minimal affective expression. Parents of these children find it difficult to respond to their child with physical contact. They

do not respect their child's autonomy and are not able to see things from the child's perspective. The child learns to suppress their feelings and switches them off.

- **Resistant or ambivalent**: These children are clingy to parents, tending not to explore their surroundings. They demonstrate resistant behaviour on their return, often hitting and crying even after they are picked up. Resistant attachment is the result of parent unresponsiveness and withdrawal of affection as a means of control. These children learn that help with regulating their feelings is unavailable. They often have feelings bubbling away on the surface waiting for their bid for parental attention. Rather than learning to suppress their feelings they exaggerate them, being overly aware of their fears and needs which can undermine their sense of self and independence.
- **Disorganised**: These children show a lack of **engagement** with adults and their environment. They are of most concern as their behaviour towards their parent is confused. These parents are unable to provide for the basic needs of their child, protecting them and providing safety and security.

A child's emotional well-being is crucial to their future learning. Laevers (1997) has discussed emotional stability as fundamental in underpinning a child's responsiveness to learning. A confident child with high levels of self-esteem will be content and effective in their lives. Supporting a child's emotional development enables them to develop confidence to explore, interact and play. The **key person approach** identified within the EYFS (DfE, 2014a) and championed by Peter Elfer (2007) ensures that children are able to rely on a particular practitioner for comfort, support and love; attuned and **reciprocal** interactions with children should be consistent, responsive and sensitive in order to nurture a positive and secure attachment (Bradford, 2012). This special relationship supports the child's emotional well-being and enables them to flourish, leading to the development of empathy, trust and well-being. In contrast inconsistent and unresponsive care by constantly changing practitioners may cause stress and impact on how children can monitor and control their own behaviour, emotions and thoughts.

The practitioner's role is to: act as a key person, develop positive relationships with parents, communicate sensitively with children and maintain a flexible and balanced routine in accordance with children's needs.

PROVOCATION

1. What are the benefits of the key person approach for the:
   a) children?
   b) practitioner?
   c) setting?
2. How does the key person approach operate in your setting?
3. Does your setting operate a key person buddy system to ensure a child has two points of contact in case of holiday, sickness etc?
4. Ask a key person in your setting what they think about the effectiveness of this approach.

CASE STUDY 1

Sally, aged 2 years 2 months, has joined our setting today. Her parent came to register her the day before and attended a settling-in visit for an hour. When she is dropped off today Sally is distressed when her parent leaves. She is inconsolable and unable to settle. Sally shows signs of distress and refuses to be picked up or comforted. She sits in the book corner and rocks herself, sucking on her thumb. She is unable to connect with anyone around her, feeling insecure and vulnerable she withdraws and shows signs of disconnection. Unable to comfort the child, the manager telephones the parent. However the parent states she is unable to collect the child as she is at work.

Communication and language

Language and thought are developmentally interlinked and toddlers use a variety of ways in which they communicate their feelings, thoughts and experiences. Between and ages of 24 and 36 months memory and language develop at a phenomenal rate as toddlers express themselves through verbal communication. They tell narratives about their experiences and learn the social rules of conversation, such as turn taking. At 16–26 months toddlers are able to listen, understand and begin to put two words together but at 22–36 months they rapidly expand their vocabulary, using questions such as *What?*, *Where?* and *Who?* and they form their own simple sentences. They are beginning to be able to express their feelings and share experiences and thoughts. Their repertoire of vocabulary develops from 50 to 300 words during this time, but their understanding of words is far greater at around 5,000 (Every Child a Talker, DCSF, 2009). The communication chain is complex, made up from processes involved in understanding spoken language (receptive language) and talking (expressive language). Children need to develop skills in listening and attention, comprehension, expressive language and speech.

Key features

Phonological awareness is a general ability to attend to the sounds of language. It is developed through the initial awareness of speech sounds and rhyme, recognition of sound similarities, and phonemic awareness. A 2-year-old will demonstrate this through developing listening.

Comprehension is the process of understanding that what is being learned is largely linked to what is already known. This is supported by social interaction and children's engagement with their immediate environment. A 2-year-old will demonstrate this through developing friendships and speech through play opportunities.

An effective way of supporting language development is the use of narratives. Early Years practitioners should encourage children to recall and retell experiences in their own lives. This supports development of memory and thinking skills as well as a sense of self, **self-efficacy** and independence. A 2-year-old will do this through immediate talking about what they are doing and as children get older they will be able to recount and retell their experiences.

The **High Scope** approach is implemented by many settings and rests on the fundamental premise that children are active learners who learn best when able to pursue their own interests whilst being supported and challenged by adults. Central to the High Scope approach is the *plan-do-review* sequence, in which children have a choice of experiences in order to plan and carry out ideas and reflect on their learning. When children make plans they carry out a range of mental processes. They establish a goal, such as 'I am going to play with the boat'. This intention impels them to engage in a series of actions that lead to this goal. When a child plans there is a pause between impulse and action which shapes the intention into purposeful action. During play the child will deliberate and often make modifications based on past experiences (Hohmann and Weikart, 2002). Children as young as 2 can make decisions about what they want to play with; using a planning basket containing concrete things can facilitate this. Each item in the basket is a concrete representation of an area of continuous core provision, e.g. a teapot/kettle for the home corner, a building block for construction, a pair of gloves for outside, a piece of fabric for the cosy corner, a car for the small world and a paint brush for the art area. These items should remain constant. The opportunity to make decisions encourages children's thinking and promotes initiative and independence, which supports their emotional development. Sensitive practitioners ask children about their play experiences and provide opportunities for children to recount and retell. For older children this may take the form of small group discussion. Children need to have the means, reasons and opportunities to develop speech and communication skills.

Figure 8.1 Planning basket

Story-telling and role play support children's ability to retell narratives. By using imaginary stories or recreating roles during pretend play, children can develop listening and attention skills as well as social skills through cooperating with others. Other activities that support communication include dance, arts and games. Reading stories, sharing a book and using familiar songs and rhymes foster children's early literacy skills.

Skilled practitioners balance their interactions to support and encourage children's language and communication and help children develop their ideas and thinking skills. Sensitive interactions using open-ended questioning provide opportunities for children to talk about what they are doing. Questions should encourage their thought processes, allowing enough time for children to respond. **Sustained shared thinking** has been identified as a process that occurs between practitioners and children and is frequently observed in high quality practice (Sylva *et al.*, 2004). Your participation in play should be child-led, assuming roles suggested by children, following their cues and extending their play through suggestion but remaining within the child's play theme.

The practitioner's role is to: support children with language through commentary and provide opportunities for language through story, song and small-group interactions.

Physical development

Physical activity is important to children's developing skills. *EYFS* outlines two aspects to this (DfE, 2014a): Moving and Handling, and Health and Self-care. Toddlers require opportunities to develop gross motor skills as well as **fine motor skills**. Before children are able to develop the control required to hold a pencil they need to be able to control their large muscle movement. It is recommended that toddlers should access three hours physical activity a day (Mathers *et al.*, 2014). Toddlers require access to outdoors for physical experiences to support their learning and development and engagement with natural resources. This also provides opportunities to develop their immune system. From 2 to 3 children become more confident and steady in their movements and can skilfully negotiate space. This is a foundation skill for later literacy skills. They can turn the page of a book and show control by using jugs to pour and mark-making tools.

Bilton (2004) gives three reasons for having outdoor play:

- Outside is a natural environment for children; there is freedom associated with the space that cannot be replicated inside.
- The environment in which children and adults play and work affects emotions, behaviour, personality and the ability to learn, and affects different children in different ways.
- Outdoors is a perfect place to learn through movement, one of the four vehicles through which children can learn, the others being play, talk and sensory experience.

The EYFS (DfE, 2014a) continues the vision of learning outdoors, insisting that children have daily opportunities to be outdoors. If your outdoor space is limited you should supplement with activities inside that will enable children to experience a range of natural resources. A 'tuff spot' or builder's tray with free and found seasonal resources such as pine cones, conkers, leaves and twigs can make for an enjoyable sensory experience (see Figure 8.2).

The practitioner's role is to: plan and evaluate activities, join in with children's play, carry out observations of children, teach new skills and support children's development. It is imperative to assess risk and ensure a safe environment.

Figure 8.2 Builder's tray

 FROM RESEARCH TO PRACTICE

Two-year-olds are bundles of energy, inquisitive and exploratory. As an Early Years practitioner you should be offering a range of experiences that support active learning, play and exploration, and creative and critical thinking – the *characteristics of effective learning* (DfE, 2014b). Recent research supports the idea that children should have access to developmentally appropriate practice and play-based pedagogy in their early years (Walsh *et al.*, 2010). Recent training provided by Mary Barlow at The Totem Pole™ ('I'm Two Having Fun on the Floor'™) supports practitioners in developing provision for 2-year-olds that supports active, participatory learning. There are five key elements to planning your day:

Materials: a variety of interesting materials including everyday items.
Manipulation: children learn through their senses. Support this by offering opportunities to explore and work with different materials, both indoors and outside.
Choice: children should be able to make choices and decisions about what and who they play with, and what they want to achieve.

> *Language from the children*: children should be given opportunities to communicate verbally and non-verbally throughout the day, in 1:1 interactions and small group activities.
>
> *Adult support*: supportive practitioners tune into children's thinking and support them through interacting sensitively, joining in with their play and supporting them in solving problems by developing different thinking skills (Hohmann and Weikart, 2002).
>
> You will find commonality with some of these features within the EYFS.

Creating the right pace

The space you create for 2-3-year-olds should have a homely feel which will support a smooth transition. The area provided should be labelled and stocked with diverse materials to help children develop **conceptual** and linguistic representations of their environment. Materials should be accessible and stored in labelled clear boxes or baskets to promote children's initiative and independence. The environment should be maintained, enhanced and restocked as required. It should be an appealing place for a toddler to be. The room should be divided into core areas of continuous provision that support children's holistic development. Core areas can be enhanced throughout the year following children's interests and should provide opportunities to offer different types of play, providing for the five senses: touch, smell, sight, taste and sound, and also reflect diversity.

The routine

Babies, toddlers and young children thrive on routine. Regularity, predictability and consistency provide feelings of security and safety as they recognise what comes next. A routine should be flexible to a toddler's needs but a few core aspects can be built in:

Hello, greeting: A welcome song gets the day off to a good start. This should be brief, five-minutes maximum small-group time with your three or four key children. You may want to inform the children of a particular activity or special event happening and you should include this at this time. Each key group should have a range of ways to communicate. A greetings board with images is effective to use with very young children. This small-group time provides opportunities for interaction, language and literacy development. The adult will be modelling writing, supporting language through interaction and questioning.

The core provision

The home corner/kitchen: This area provides opportunities for practitioners to recreate a home environment. The use of a small table and chairs, real fruit and vegetables, real small pans and utensils makes a lot more sense than a world of plastic fantastic! The home corner supports children's re-enactment of their own experiences and enables them to retell their own narratives through social learning. You should use parents as a resource to provide clean empty fabric conditioner bottles, empty packets and small containers. A small china cup, saucer and plate enable children to learn to handle things with care. Providing real everyday items has much more

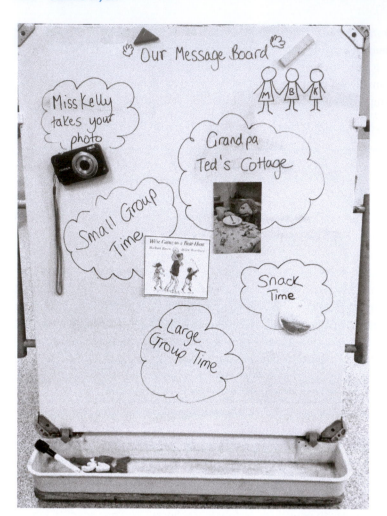

Figure 8.3
Greetings board

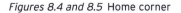

Figures 8.4 and 8.5 Home corner

Figures 8.6 and 8.7 Home corner with child

meaning to children and will enable them to be safe in their own home environment as they will be able to explore the feeling of lifting a small saucepan. Real vegetables like cabbage leaves are great for tearing and cutting with scissors, an aubergine provides opportunities for peeling and a pineapple is a wonderful sensory experience. A few teabags with the teapot will support the real life context. A basil plant provides further sensory experiences. This area of core provision can be inexpensive to resource; if you speak to the local supermarket you should be able to pick up discounted quick sale items.

The art area: A well-planned and resourced area located on the floor allows small children to have access to explore. The provision of natural materials as well as paints and mark-making resources offers open-ended opportunities. Including messy play with gloop or shaving foam provides a tactile opportunity for children's sensory exploration, supporting mark-making. You might decide to vary the materials available. Practitioners need to consider where to position this area with some natural boundaries as there is every chance your toddlers will transport these items around the room as they explore and you will need to support this schematic learning.

Figures 8.8 and 8.9 Art areas inspired by Andrew Goldsworthy.

The cosy corner: A small basket of books provides easy access for children. Often this area can be over-filled and inaccessible to children. A cosy seating arrangement is most suitable to share a book with other children or a practitioner. Provision of blankets, fabrics and cushions can provide an intimate place. This can be extended with puppets, a story board or a range of resources that support children's retelling of stories.

You might develop an area that is devoted to a familiar story. Props and resources allow children independently to retell their own version. Providing Communication Friendly Spaces™ focuses on the role of the environment in supporting speaking and listening skills, emotional well-being, physical development and general engagement (Jarman, 2015).

Figure 8.10 'Stripy Horse' book corner

Figure 8.11 Construction

Construction: Open-ended resources are the key to this investigation area. Providing blocks, tubes and piping along with suitable methods to construct and join can ignite all sorts of possibilities. This area supports children's large muscle development, balance and fine motor skills. It also provides opportunities for problem-solving and early mathematical concepts of size and shape.

Small world: Providing children with natural resources as well as conventional small-world resources gives children open-ended opportunities to explore and develop imaginative play. Small baskets containing a small amount of carefully selected resources enable children to access a range of small-world objects, and tell their own narratives through open-ended opportunities. A basket of fir cones, small twigs, soft toys and small pieces of fabric will support children's imagination.

Outdoors: Children should have opportunities to play outdoors with a range of resources. The selection of resources will depend on the space available. However, even if you have just a tarmaced back yard, free and found items can enhance your provision. Outdoors encourages children to relive their experiences through movement, and provides a context for role play. It provides **unique** opportunities for learning and supports children's emotional well-being.

Figure 8.12 Small-world dinosaur inside

Figure 8.13 Small-world dinosaur outside

Tidy-up time: It is important that children help to put things back ready for the next session. It is an important part of the Plan, Do, Review schedule and takes place before reviewing what children have been doing.

Snack time and quiet times should be built into the day, meeting the individual needs of each child. A rolling snack time is best practice and fits well with individual children's needs. A flexible approach to when children choose their snack is important as it values children's sense of choice, and does not cut across or interrupt deep levels of involvement in play. Children aged 2 to 3 years develop likes and dislikes to food and drink. They should be exposed to a wide variety of foods to prevent faddy eating habits. You play a significant role in this as you can provide a range of different foods through snack times. Raisins, cheese and breadsticks, carrot sticks and hummus, and chopped fresh fruit are suitable choices. When children can be involved in food preparation they develop self-help skills, so providing a knife to spread butter onto toast is very appropriate. As children learn within a social context, seeing others try different foods encourages them to do the same. Between the ages of 2 and 3 children start to gain control over their personal care and, when supported by adults, this provides opportunities for increasing their independence and self-confidence.

Goodbye: This is an important time to develop partnerships with parents through sharing information on their child's day.

REFLECTIVE PRACTICE

- Audit your setting's areas of core provision. Are these areas distinct and well resourced?
- Consider your setting's daily routine. Does this provide for children's individual needs?
- How do you provide for children's interests and different developmental stages in relation to the prime areas of development?
- What sensory experiences are available for children?
- What natural resources are incorporated into your setting's core provision?

Child's name: Amanda (example)	Date of Birth: 19.12.12	Date: 28.01.2014
	PERSONAL, SOCIAL AND EMOTIONAL DEVELOPMENT	
Self-confidence and self-awareness	**Managing feelings and behaviour**	**Making relationships**
Amanda is a confident child who enters nursery happily. She separates well from Mum although will often bring in a favourite toy as a comfort. Amanda accesses all the available play space freely and enjoys exploring new resources making choices. She is beginning to engage in imaginative play, e.g. using a brick as a telephone. Amanda is gaining confidence and will happily express her wants and needs through using 'yes' and 'no'.	Amanda is very expressive. She uses her facial expressions, body language and also her arms and legs in order to express how she is feeling. Amanda knows the nursery routine and follows it accordingly. She has an understanding of some boundaries but needs support at times. Amanda has an understanding that things need to be shared and will sometimes initiate.	Amanda has begun to form relationships with other children and will actively seek them out to play. She will initiate games and try to involve her peers but sometimes she can become upset when the other children don't cooperate. Amanda has a particular group of friends she likes to play with and will seek these out. Amanda has formed strong trusting relationships with the staff and her key person. She will actively seek her key person out of she is upset or has a particular want or need.
Developmental stage: 22–36 months	**Developmental stage: 22–36 months**	**Developmental stage: 22–36 months**
	COMMUNICATION AND LANGUAGE	
Listening and attention	**Understanding**	**Speaking**
Amanda is very aware of what is going on around her and will react to different noises and voices that she hears with interest. She enjoys stories and her favourite is 'The Hungry Caterpillar'. She will join in with repeated refrains with enthusiasm. Amanda enjoys circle time and loves to choose what we are doing. She confidently joins in and will listen and follow the directions given.	Amanda shows a good understanding of the language used towards her and can follow simple directions e.g. 'let's sit down'. She is beginning to gain an understanding of simple concepts e.g. 'big' and 'little'.	Amanda has a lot to say but it is not always clear leaving her sometimes very frustrated. She tends to use 2–3 word sentences such as 'want drink' or 'Manda's ball' but the words used are not always understandable. Amanda is copying more of what is said to her and tends to repeat phrases that are familiar e.g. 'Oh dear'. Her vocabulary is growing on a weekly basis and she is able to make her wants and needs known to that staff through the use of words, facial expressions and Makaton signs.

Developmental stage: 22–36 months	Developmental stage: 22–36 months	Developmental stage: 16–26 months

PHYSICAL DEVELOPMENT

Moving and handling

Amanda has a good control of her gross motor skills and is able to negotiate space safely. She runs on her whole foot and can change direction with ease. She enjoys being outside and will use the climbing equipment confidently either through climbing up the climbing wall or using the steps alternating feet with each step.

Amanda uses the small equipment also such as throwing and kicking large footballs, rolling balls at skittles or balancing stepping on the stepping stones.

Amanda enjoys the craft activities and is able to manipulate the equipment to her satisfaction. She can hold a pencil comfortably between her first two fingers and thumb when drawing and has shown preference for her right hand. She is gaining increasing control as she draws. She enjoys using one handed tools such as scissors.

Developmental stage: 22–36 months / 30–50 months

Health and self-care

Amanda is very clear about her wants and needs and will ensure she makes these clear to adults. She will say when she is tired, hungry, or thirsty either through basic language or using Makaton signs or pointing.

Amanda has very strong feelings about what she likes to eat and drink and needs persuading to try new foods. She is able to use cutlery and drinks confidently from an open cup. Amanda is able pour her drink from a small jug in to her cup.

Amanda has been toilet trained for two months now and has very few accidents. She will access the toilet area independently needing little support knowing that she needs to flush the toilet and wash hands once finished. This was initiated by Amanda herself and parents were very encouraging allowing the process to go at Amanda's pace.

Amanda is able to put on her own coat and can fasten some buttons. If the zip is started for her she is able to pull it up to fasten.

Developmental stage: 22–36 / 30–50 months

Characteristics of effective learning:

Amanda is a very curious child and is always interested in what is going on around her. She likes to explore her environment and new activities and is always willing to 'have a go'.

She is very strong willed and likes to be in control of what she is doing and how she is going to do it.

Is the child meeting developmental milestones?

All areas except for speaking. Both areas of physical development are strengths.

What next?

Follow up concern regarding speech with a possible referral to speech and language therapist.

Continue to build on level of development at same rate to ensure Amanda's progression.

Parent's comments including child's interest:

Completed by (Key person)

Signature of key person:

Signature of Parent/Carer

Figure 8.14 An example of a completed two-year report

The adult role

An Early Years practitioner's role is vital in supporting children's development. Through observations of children you will be able to map their progress against the EYFS and with a sound understanding of child development you will be able to plan for the next stage of their learning. This may be through consolidation of new and developing skills, through practising or moving onto the next steps of their learning journey. Your observations will inform the child's two-year check as well as forming part of the child's on-going development file. You may use narrative observations that provide details of the child's development or a range of other methods, which might include video recordings.

Two-year progress check

The two-year progress check is a written summary of a child's progress in the three prime areas: Personal, Social and Emotional Development; Physical Development; and Communication and Language. The EYFS requires practitioners to complete this when a child is aged 24–36 months and share it with parents. It should reflect a child's individuality, personality and characteristics and identify a clear picture of the child's development and any areas where progress is less than expected. The report should be a truthful but sensitive representation of a child's development based on on-going observations in a range of contexts in the setting, and if possible it should include observations from parents. The importance of parental involvement is a key principle in the EYFS and positive partnerships will support children's future learning. The review should be easy to read and understand, avoiding unfamiliar jargon. It is important to be sensitive to the needs of your parents and ensure that the material is in a form that is accessible.

The progress check has been introduced to enable early identification of developmental needs so that additional support can be provided to address any developmental concerns. However it should avoid labelling a child. This report should set out the setting's plans which might include working with other professionals, should this be beneficial to the child's future progress.

REFLECTIVE PRACTICE
REFLECTIVE PRACTICE

Review the two-year report that your setting completes. Compare your setting's review with that above in Figure 8.14.

1. How does your setting:
    a) Gain parents' input into the two-year review?
    b) Engage hard to reach parents?
    c) Communicate with parents with poor literacy skills?
2. How does your setting meet the needs of parents with EAL?

Conclusion

This chapter has identified the development that occurs between the ages of 2 and 3 and focused on the primary areas of development. It has outlined the significance of emotional development and the role of the key person in supporting children's emotional well-being through sensitive and supportive interactions that foster children's language and cognitive development. It has outlined physical development, both gross motor and fine motor as part of the foundation skills to learning. The enabling environment and core areas of provision have been described. The provision for children needs to be carefully planned so that it is both developmentally appropriate and stimulating. The Foundation Years 2 to 3 is a significant stage in its own right and can determine the life chances for the most deprived children.

Further reading

Allen, G. (2011) *Early Intervention: The Next Steps*. Available from www.gov.uk
   This report provides you with greater understanding of the impact Early Intervention can have.

David, T., Goouch, K. Powell, S. and Abbott, L. (2003) *Birth to Three Matters: A Review of Literature*. Available from: http://webarchive.nationalarchives.gov.uk/20130401151715/ and www.education.gov.uk/publications/eOrderingDownload/RR444.pdf
   This review of literature underpinned the development of a framework to support children 0–3.

Dowling, M. (2013) *Young Children's Thinking*. London: Sage.
   This book will provide you with a firm understanding of child development that will underpin your work as an Early Years practitioner.

Gerhardt, S. (2004) *Why Love Matters: How affection shapes a baby's brain*. East Sussex: Routledge.
   This book provides you with a detailed insight into the power of love in shaping a child's future.

Mathers, S., Eisenstadt, N. Sylva, K., Soukakou, E. and Ereky-Stevens, K. (2014) *Sound Foundations*. Available from: http://ox.ac.uk.
   This report provides evidence from international research into the dimensions of quality in Early Years education and care that facilitate the learning and development of children from birth to three, and what the implications are for policy and practice.

Walsh, G., Sproule, L., McGuinness, C. Trew, K. and Ingram, G. (2010) *A Literature Review of Research and Practice*. Available from www.nicurriulum.org.uk.
   This review of research and practice provides a useful critique of the emerging consensus on early years curriculum, pedagogy and the theoretical framework that underpins developmentally appropriate practice.

Useful websites

www.foundationyears.org.uk/files/2012/03/Development-Matters-final-print-amended.pdf
   Development Matters in the Early Years Foundation Stage (EYFS)

www.elizabethjarmantraining.co.uk/
   The Communication, Friendly Spaces approach focuses on the role of the environment in supporting speaking and listening skills, emotional well-being, physical development and general engagement.

http://www.thetotempole.co.uk/
   This website provides information and resource ideas that can stimulate the youngest of children.

www.ican.org.uk/ and www.elklan.co.uk/
These two websites provide useful research and information on speech, language and communication programmes.

References

Allen, G. (2011) *Early Intervention: The Next Steps*. Available from www.gov.uk.

Bilton, H. (2004) *Playing Outside*. David Fulton Publishers.

Bowlby, J. (1969) *Attachment and Loss, Volume 1*. London: Pimlico, p. 177.

Bradford, H. (2012) *The Well-being of Children Under Three*. Oxon: Routledge.

DCSF (2008) *The Early Years Foundation Stage*. Nottingham: DCSF.

Department for Education (DCSF) (2009) *Every Child a Talker*. Available from http://webarchive.nationalarchives.gov.uk/20110202093118/ and http:/nationalstrategies.standards.dcsf.gov.uk/node/153355. [Accessed 25/8/2015].

Department for Education (2012) *Know How Guide: the EYFS progress check at age two*. Available from www.gov.uk. [Accessed 25/8/2015].

Department for Education (2013) *More Great Childcare Raising Quality and Giving Parents More Choice*. Available from www.gov.uk/government/publications/more-great-childcare-raising-quality-and-giving-parents-more-choice. [Accessed 25/8/2015].

Department for Education (2014b) *Development Matters*. Available from www.foundationyears.org.uk/ [Accessed 25/8/2015].

Department for Education (2014a) *The Statutory Framework for the Early Years Foundation Stage*. Available from https://www.gov.uk/.../ [Accessed 25/8/2015].

Field, F. (2010) *The Foundation Years: Preventing poor children becoming poor adults*. Available from webarchive.nationalarchives.gov.uk.

Gerhardt, S. (2004) *Why Love Matters: How affection shapes a baby's brain*. East Sussex: Routledge p. 43.

Hohmann, M. and Weikart, D.P. (2002). *Educating Young Children: Active learning practices for preschool and child care programs*. 2nd ed. Ypsilanti, MI: High/Scope Press.

Jarman, E. (2015). Elizabeth Jarman: The Communication Friendly Spaces Approach Website http://www.elizabethjarmantraining.co.uk/.

Laevers, F. (1997) The project experiential education: wellbeing and involvement make a difference. *European Early Childhood Research Journal*, 1, pp. 53–68.

Mathers, S., Eisenstadt, N. Sylva, K., Soukakou, E. and Ereky-Stevens, K. (2014) *Sound Foundations*. Available from http://ox.ac.uk.

Siraj-Blatchford, I., Sylva, K., Taggart, B., Sammons, P. and Nelhuish, E. (2002) The EPPE case studies Technical Paper 10 University of London, Institute of Education/DfEE.

Sylva, K., Siraj-Blatchford, I., Taggart, B., Melhuish, E., Sammons, P. and Elliot, K. (2004) *The Effective Provision of Preschool Education (EPPE)* Available from: /www.education.gov.uk/publications.

Walsh, G., Sproule, L., McGuinness, C. Trew, K. and Ingram, G. (2010) *A Literature Review of Research and Practice*. Available from www.nicurriulum.org.uk.

Acknowledgements

Photographs and images from: Mary Barlow, The Totem Pole, Grantham; Lincolnshire; Little Learners Day Nursery, Doncaster; Little Oaks Day Nursery, Doncaster; and The Toybox Nursery, Doncaster.

9 The Foundation Years: 4-5-year-olds

Nicola Smith and Debbie Reel

LEARNING OUTCOMES ✔

After reading this chapter, you should be able to:

✔ Reflect on the most effective ways to support the learning of 4- and 5-year-olds, with particular reference to personal, social and emotional development.

✔ Understand some of the issues involved in transition experiences, for example from home to school or from a Reception class to Key Stage One.

✔ Think about how to build relationships with children as individuals, including effective behaviour management.

Introduction

This chapter will examine what it means to be a 4- or 5-year-old in the Early Years Foundation Stage (EYFS) (DfE, 2012). It will address key issues and consider what we as practitioners do to develop appropriate pedagogical practice based upon three themes:

*   Learning and developmental expectations with a particular focus on personal, social and emotional development (PSED).
*   The impact of **transition** on development.
*   The role of the adult.

Each theme will be considered in light of the principles of the EYFS (DfE, 2012) and its **characteristics of effective learning**. We will also consider the importance of '**the unique child**' with his or her individual needs, including those of the child with Special Education Needs or Disability (SEND) or English as an Additional Language (EAL).

What does it mean to be 4 and 5? Learning and developmental expectations

As practitioners we need to develop a clear understanding of the type of learners 4- and 5-year-olds are capable of being and to embrace this through strong pedagogical beliefs and approaches. The EYFS outlines how children learn effectively as well as acknowledging that children learn at different rates and at different stages. Within this document, there is a strong focus on three key aspects: Active learning, critical thinking and play, each of which has a crucial role in shaping 4- and 5-year-old children's learning experiences. In considering these characteristics of effective learning, we can make links to the importance of learning dispositions in young children (Katz, 1993).

A learning disposition is a pattern of behaviour which indicates how children feel about learning; curiosity, humour and creativity are all examples. Katz (1993) points out that developing positive learning dispositions is important because they make the difference between having knowledge and skills and applying knowledge and skills. So at the ages of 4 and 5, children are developing what they know and can do, but they are also developing the motivation to use this knowledge. This is sometimes referred to as 'learning to learn'.

One of the challenges in supporting children as they 'learn to learn' is that each child is **unique** and will need support tailored to their individual needs, circumstances and personalities. Early years settings must ensure that adults plan for learning opportunities which allow all 4- and 5-year-olds to experience the characteristics of effective learning. This will mean careful planning for children with specific needs, or children who speak English as an Additional Language, for example. We will explore practical examples in the section entitled 'The role of the adult'.

Bandura's (1977) **social learning theory** is useful to help us understand how 4- and 5-year-olds are 'learning to learn' and making sense of the world around them. By the age of 4, most children will have developed a strong sense of who they are. They will be engaged in the process of learning about the people and environment around them, as supported by Erickson (Batra, 2013). Some 4-year-olds will be having new experiences outside of their immediate family and home for the first time as they begin school. Bandura demonstrated that children learn from 'models' around them. So they will look at their parents, siblings, teachers and peers and imitate their behaviour and attitudes. They need positive reinforcement, such as verbal praise, when they imitate these behaviours and attitudes. The role of the adult in acting as the model who is imitated and observed indicates the proactive role that we have to play in understanding and supporting the foundations needed for all 4- and 5-year-olds to learn effectively. We should also remember that children also look to their peers as models. As Reception practitioners, we need to support children to build positive relationships with one another and to develop the ability to regulate their behaviour as part of a group; this is discussed later in the chapter, in the section on Personal, Social and Emotional Development (PSED).

PSED

Children are social in nature and from birth their **engagement** with others supports their emotional and **social development** and well-being. The EYFS recognises PSED as a prime area of learning and identifies three key elements:

PROVOCATION

Analyse this conversation between a practitioner and a 5-year-old. How does the practitioner use effective questioning to support and challenge this child?

C: Can you make the batman car with me now?

P: OK, have you got the box? . . . Let's get a tray so we don't lose anything . . . Right, shall we sort the colours out first so we don't get in a muddle?

C: You do that and I'll look at the book.

P: Well, I'll do some of the colours and you do the others. Which one do you want to do?

C: I'll do yellow.

P: Have you got the book then? What do we need first? That's it .

C: Now we need a 'special' . . . this one.

P: Are you sure it's that one? How many buttons are on it?

C: One, two, three, four, oh, we need six.

P: Whoops, oh that's it. Will it fit on? Now what do we need?

C: We just need . . . two of these . . . There you go.

P: Does that one go on this side? Is it the same as the picture?

C: Can you see a black one like that?

P: Yes, look in that corner.

C: This is going to be awesome.

P: Well, it is for Batman, isn't it? Try that one on here, look, is that right?

This example highlights the importance of demonstrating our own positive dispositions for learning by joining in with learning experiences alongside children. At the same time, we can use talk and questioning to support children's progression in their thinking and to support their involvement in the learning opportunity.

- self confidence and self awareness
- managing feelings and behaviour
- making relationships

(DfE, 2012)

It is important that a secure foundation within each of these areas is laid. Without this there is potential for a negative impact on the holistic development of the child as they grow as individuals, as part of a family, a school and a community. At the ages of 4 and 5, young children need support to build relationships with their peers and with adults in the setting. They also need to be nurtured as individuals in order to maintain a positive sense of their own worth.

As you identify with **social constructivists** such as Vygotsky (Gray and MacBlain, 2012) or Bruner (Smidt, 2011), you will begin to develop in your understanding that children's development is dependent upon significant others who support, build confidence and create challenge in a safe environment where failure is reassuringly used to build confidence and resilience. Roberts (2010) writes about the importance of developing a sense of 'resilient wellbeing' in young children. In other words, children need to feel confident in themselves, their relationships and their environments. If they have these strong foundations in their earliest years, then children will be able to cope with challenges and difficulties in their lives as they grow and develop. When working with 4- and 5-year-olds, this means encouraging a 'trial and error' approach to learning rather than providing all the answers for children. It also means working alongside children to support them in solving problems as they arise. This might mean asking open ended questions such as 'How do you think we could do this?' However, we also need to spend some time 'teaching' 4- and 5-year-olds in a more direct manner. A recent review of research into early years education tells us that, 'the most effective pedagogy combines both "teaching" and providing freely chosen yet potentially instructive play activities' (Pascal *et al.*, 2013, p. 31). For Reception practitioners, planning a careful balance between child-initiated or child-led tasks and adult-led tasks is an important part of their role. You will need to develop your understanding of when and how to involve yourself in a child's play and when to take a step back and observe.

The work of Bowlby and Ainsworth (1965) demonstrated that children need secure **attachments** in order to manage how they are feeling and that these attachments will influence their behaviour. Children who are emotionally supported by a significant other outside of the home will form increasingly secure relationships as they become more independent. They will become more adept at adjusting to changing relationships and will eventually engage positively in solving issues. It therefore makes sense to consider the importance of children having a significant adult or key person with whom they can form a secure attachment when at school. Elfer *et al.* (2012) refer to the vital role a **key person** can play in children's development as this significant adult is charged with rich opportunities to respond to children's needs be they cognitive, **emotional**, **developmental** or physical. The role of the key person can be difficult to manage as a Reception practitioner, as most classes will have higher adult:child ratios than a Nursery or home-based setting. This means that we need to work hard to build relationships with individual children, as well as supporting them to make **trusting relationships** with their peers.

REFLECTIVE PRACTICE

Think about these questions in relation to your own experiences of working with 4- and 5-year-olds:

- How do you build relationships with young children you work with?
- What can you do to show children that you value them as individuals? This could be to do with the way you talk to them, or to do with the way you organise the learning environment, for example.
- What do you find challenging about getting to know children as individuals and how can you address this in your practice?

Children have been making relationships well before they have turned 4 and then 5. Your role, when working with 4- to 5-year-olds is to support children in making relationships in a new context, to **scaffold** the decisions children make in the relationships they form and to be mindful of the differences in the ways in which adults and children might perceive relationships. For example, because a 4- or 5-year-old plays regularly with another over a week but then chooses to play with someone else does not necessarily mean that they have 'fallen out' nor does it mean that they are not considering the needs of the other. At 4 and 5, they are too young to form 'mutual friendships', these are still abstract in nature and coincide with levels of maturity (Bennett and Palaiologou, 2013).

At the same time, children at the ages of 4 and 5 need consistent boundaries for acceptable behaviour. Clear understanding of acceptable and unacceptable behaviour helps young children to feel secure. This is why many settings and schools will create and share rules with new children. If rules are negotiated, clear, reasonable and manageable in number, they can contribute to the building of positive relationships between children and adults. Rewarding children when they behave in an acceptable way can also help to reinforce positive behaviour; this process is known as **operant conditioning** (Skinner, 1948). This is why practitioners may use stickers or certificates to encourage positive attitudes to learning. However, we need to make sure that we reward effort as well as final achievements if we are going to nurture the sense of 'resilient wellbeing' which we know is important. We also need to consider the importance of **intrinsic** as well as **extrinsic motivation**. Four- and five-year-olds need to be supported to manage their own feelings and behaviour, rather than always relying on reinforcement from an adult. Another important finding from the EPPE study (Sylva *et al.*, 2010) is that behaviour management is most effective in settings where practitioners talk to children about their behaviour and help them to understand their own feelings and those of others. Developing understanding in this way can support children to begin to manage their own behaviour; in other words, self-regulation.

Transition

'Big school', 'growing up', 'harder work' : these phrases may be associated with children aged 4 and 5 as they move from one phase of the education system to the next. However, these **perceptions** of change can cause **conflict** with the realities of being a young child, at this age and at this stage of their development. Brooker (2008) refers to these children having to learn how to adapt in a very different learning environment rather than the learning environment adapting to meet their needs. This research highlighted the importance of making sure that we are prepared to support children during key transitions.

When working with 4- and 5-year-olds, the first major transition you will need to consider is the move from home, pre-school, nursery or a childminder to the Reception class. If well supported in this transition, the vast majority of children will cope effectively and settle happily into their new Reception class. In order to support children through this transition, you will need to plan how you will manage the change, both before and after the official date for starting school. This might mean visiting children and parents at home or in their pre-school setting to get to know them and talk to them about the Reception class. Most schools also arrange for children to visit the school and experience their new classroom before their official start date. However, you should consider that not all children and families will need or want the same transition programme. For example, Greenfield's (2006) research demonstrates that not all families or communities find home-visits supportive. As with all areas of practice with 4- and 5-year-olds, we need to tailor support to individual children and their families.

Although the child is at the centre of concerns around transition, as a practitioner you also need to consider the needs of parents. As Bateson (2013, p. 52) points out, 'If schools can support parents effectively by decreasing the stress and worry of childcare and ensuring a smooth transition to "big school" children would be happier, healthier, more successful learners.' This may mean talking to parents about their childcare arrangements and demonstrating flexibility with regard to starting dates and whether children come to school on a part-time or full-time basis in the first few weeks.

As well as preparing children for the change to a new physical environment, you will also need to consider their emotional wellbeing during the transition to school. Remember that transition is a process and not an event (Hard *et al.*, 2010). In other words, young children need time to prepare for and to adjust to new experiences. By supporting children in the process of transition to school you are building their sense of resilience which they will need to cope with the many transitions they will experience in life. You should bear in mind that children do not always worry about the things we might expect them to in preparation for 'big school'. For example, in her research into transition, Fisher (2012) found that one of children's biggest worries was that there might be spiders in the school toilets! As a practitioner, you need to find out about children's individual concerns and acknowledge them as important to the child. You also need to work with them to overcome any worries.

More recently, the emphasis on children being 'school ready' at the age of 5 has caused some debate around what 4- and 5-year-olds should be learning and doing in the Early Years Foundation Stage. PACEY's (2013) school ready research project identified three key areas of development for improving the transition into a Reception class; a stronger emphasis on play-based learning, more effective communication, and better information provided for parents. However, this might be difficult for Reception teachers to take action on at the same time as managing changes to **assessment** from September 2015, when it is proposed that children will be assessed on entrance to Reception, with an emphasis on communication and language, literacy and mathematics.

As Fisher (2012) points out, there is no evidence to suggest that developmentally, children need a change in pedagogic approach at the age of 5. However, in the current school system, many Year 1 classes are taught in a more structured, formal manner than Reception classes in order to meet the expectations of the National Curriculum. Young children, particularly those who are 'summer-born', can struggle with the move from Reception to Year 1 in school. This is another key transition which needs careful management by practitioners and parents. The National Foundation for Educational Research (NFER) study on transition from the EYFS to KS1 publicised the impact of this transitional process on the lives of children (Sanders *et al.*, 2005). Their revealing portrayal of children's feelings suggested that a child's ability to move from one learning environment into another should not be taken for granted.

CASE STUDY 1

The following case study demonstrates how a school managed a change in its transition process from the EYFS to KS1.

The EYFS unit is part of an inner city two-form entry school. It hosts its own outdoor learning area and runs as a successful example of early years practice. The KS1 coordinator has recently been asked to consider the differences in learning environments between the EYFS and KS1 which have been highlighted as a possible cause for a fall in children's progress in Year 1. After careful analysis, the following changes were implemented:

- Teaching Assistants worked with each class on a three-year rolling process through the two years in the EYFS and the first year in KS1.
- Year 1 and Reception teachers have carried out a half a day teaching swap for half a day per week for the final half of the summer term.
- The outdoor learning area in the EYFS was also timetabled for use by Year 1.
- The reception class have made an ongoing book throughout their Reception year – this will be given to their new teacher welcoming him/her to 'their' way learning over the last two years. This book details children's work and includes photographs of their learning experiences, likes and dislikes.
- All Year 1 teachers have attended CPD on the importance of play.
- Parents are invited to a 1:1 meeting with the new Year 1 teacher at the end of the Reception year.

Consider the impact of each of these changes on children's personal, social, emotional and cognitive development as they move from the EYFS to KS1. How has the coordinator taken key theories into consideration when deciding how to continue an effective learning journey?

The role of the adult

The role of any adult working with 4- and 5-year-olds is to ensure that effective learning opportunities are provided. The opportunity for effective individual learning to take place arises from adults' active responses that encourage children to shape and lead their experiences. In order for any child to do this successfully they need to be secure both in themselves and their learning environment. This security is formed through strong attachments which allow children to feel safe to take risks, face challenges and lead learning.

As we have already discussed, learning begins from positive relationships between children and the adults in the classroom. Observation is a key tool in enabling us to get to know the children we work with and to plan real, valuable and appropriate interventions that will support learning. Adult interactions with children need to support, encourage and challenge whilst promoting a sense of competence and independence amongst the children. This has been demonstrated in the findings of the Effective Pre-school and Primary Education (Sylva *et al.*, 2010) project which has championed **sustained shared thinking** as an effective tool for supporting children's learning. Adults working with children, modelling and promoting sustained shared thinking through questioning and discussion has had a huge impact on the importance of the role of the adult when working with young children. The findings of this longitudinal study suggest that adults play a significant role in the way in which children learn and this is far more powerful when secure relationships are embedded.

FROM RESEARCH TO PRACTICE

The Effective Pre-school and Primary Education project (Sylva *et al.*, 2010) identified the features of high quality teaching and learning in early years settings which lead to good outcomes for children. One of the ideas from this study which has influenced practice in the EYFS is the notion of 'Sustained shared thinking' (Siraj-Blatchford *et al.*, 2002). This refers to interactions between an adult and a child or children, in which the adult reinforces, discusses and extends the child's thinking about an area of shared interest. This might be in the context of solving a problem together, evaluating an idea or project together, or telling a story together, for example. An important point to remember about sustained, shared thinking is that it is a process of collaboration. This means it is not about asking children a series of questions and expecting them to provide answers.

Consider the following case studies: How can the attachment already formed between teacher and child support the learning experience? How could the adult build on Eleanor and Adeel's strengths as well as addressing their learning needs?

CASE STUDY 2

Eleanor

Eleanor is 4 years old and is in her second term in a Reception class. She has an older brother who is in Year 2 in the same school and is making good progress in all curriculum subjects. Eleanor enjoys coming to school and separates happily from her mother or father in the mornings. She plays willingly with other children in the class and is also content to spend some time playing on her own. Eleanor likes painting and playing in the sand and water trays.

The children in Eleanor's class are encouraged to find their own name card and self-register each morning. Eleanor could find her name card last term, when a picture was attached. Now that the picture has been removed, Eleanor needs support from an adult to find her name card. Eleanor enjoys looking at books on her own and with an adult but struggles to concentrate during whole class or group story sessions. She can hear the initial sound in a word, e.g. the 'C' sound at the beginning of the word 'Cat'. However, Eleanor cannot recognise individual letters of the alphabet.

- *If you were working with Eleanor how would you build on her strengths and address her learning needs?*
- *How would you encourage the characteristic of active learning within your practice?*

 CASE STUDY 3

Adeel

Adeel was 5 years old when he joined his Reception class at the beginning of September. Adeel is of Pakistani origin and lives with his parents, grandmother and two younger sisters. Adeel's father and mother are both fluent English speakers. At home the family speak Mirpuri, as this is their home language, spoken by Adeel's grandmother.

Adeel has only spoken a few words in English since he started at school four weeks ago. He is reluctant to leave his mother when she brings him to school, but will say goodbye if his bilingual teaching assistant takes him to play on the computer. Adeel plays alongside other children in the class but does not attempt to engage them in conversation.

Adeel enjoys mathematical activities and in assessments carried out by the teaching assistant in his home language, he demonstrates a high level of understanding of calculations and can add numbers together up to ten.

- *If you were Adeel's teaching assistant, how would you build on his attachment to you to support his learning?*
- *How would you use the characteristic of 'Playing and Exploring' to develop his mathematical abilities?*

Conclusion

In summary, the learning and development of children who are 4 and 5 is complex and is immersed in theoretical and practical expectations. This chapter has drawn upon just three key aspects that impact upon their lives:

- Learning and developmental expectations
- Transition
- The role of the adult.

This chapter has challenged you to consider the importance of learning theory and how this has shaped key characteristics of learning associated with children at this age. The focus on an active, play based approach to learning challenges you to consider your role in supporting children's progress in learning. This is inextricably linked with the need to consider well-being and resilience in 4- and 5-year-olds so that their personal, social and emotional needs are supported alongside their learning.

This chapter has also drawn upon the theoretical work of Bowlby and Elfer, again encouraging you to evaluate how a strong attachment can create a sense of belonging and safety so that children's resilience can develop within a safe environment. There will be challenges, and managing appropriate behaviour was highlighted as key. The management of a learning environment that encourages appropriate behaviour is further challenged by the transitional phase that children of this age experience from Reception to Year 1. It is here that you as practitioners are encouraged to analyse theory, PSED and the role of the adult to ensure that this process maintains and promotes a positive learning culture for children. Building on learning experiences which we know and understand to be effective can only have a positive impact on children's development as they progress though their primary years.

Further reading

Canning, N. (2011) *Play and Practice in the Early Years Foundation Stage*, Sage, London.
   This book will help you to understand the values and beliefs that underpin a play-based curriculum. It includes detailed consideration of the themes and principles of the EYFS, linking theory to practice in an accessible manner.

Fisher, J. (2013) *Starting from the Child*, Open University Press, Maidenhead.
   This book looks at how we can use the notion of 'The Unique Child' to support children's learning. It is particularly useful in suggesting ways in which early years practitioners can plan for a balance of child-initiated, child-led and adult-led learning in the classroom.

Lindon, J. (2012) *What Does it Mean to be Four?* Practical Pre-School Books, London.
   This book will support you in your knowledge and understanding of developmental expectations of four-year-olds.

Useful websites

www.foundationyears.org.uk/
   Information and documents relating to the EYFS and some useful advice for working with parents.

www.pre-school.org.uk/
   Up-to-date news and publications relating to the EYFS and working with pre-school children.

www.early-education.org.uk/
   The website of the British Association for Early Childhood Education, with some useful downloadable resources, for example, 'Helping children with their behaviour'.

References

Bandura, A. (1977) *Social Learning Theory*, Pearson, New Jersey.

Bateson, J. (2013) 'From nursery to reception', in Trodd, L. (ed.) *Transitions in the Early Years*, Sage, London.

Batra, S. (2013) 'The psychosocial development of children: implications for education and society', Erik Erikson in *Context Contemporary Education Dialogue*, vol. 10, no. 2, pp. 249–278.

Bennett, J. and Palaiologou, I. (2013) 'Personal, social and emotional development', in Palaiologou, I. (ed.) in *The Early Years Foundation Stage*, Sage, London.

Bowlby, J. (1991) *Attachment and Loss*, volume 1: Penguin, London.

Bowlby, J. and Ainsworth, M.D.S. (1965) *Child Care and the Growth of Love* (2nd edn), Penguin Books, Harmondsworth.

Brooker, L. (2008) *Supporting Transitions in the Early Years*, McGraw-Hill, Maidenhead.

Child, D. (2011) *Psychology and the Teacher Continuum*, International Publishing Group, London.

Department for Education (DfE) (2012) *Statutory Framework for the Early Years Foundation Stage*, Department for Education, London.

Elfer, P., Goldschmied, E. and Selleck, D. (2012) *Key Persons in the Early Years: Building Relationships for Quality Provision in Early Years Settings and Primary Schools* (2nd edition). Routledge, Oxon.

Fisher, J. (2012) *Moving On To Key Stage One. Improving Transition from the Early Years Foundations Stage*, McGraw-Hill, Maidenhead.

Gray, C. and MacBlain, S. (2012) *Learning Theories in Childhood*, Sage, London.

Greenfield, S. (2006) 'Home visiting: The beginning of a home–school partnership', *Early Childhood Practice Journal*, vol. 8, pp. 5–12.

Hard, L. *et al.* (2010) 'Exploring transition through collective biographical memory work: considerations for parents and teachers in early childhood education', *Australasian Journal of Early Childhood*, vol. 35, no. 3, pp. 24–30.

Katz, Lilian G. (1993) *Dispositions: Definitions and Implications for Early Childhood Practices*. ERIC Clearinghouse on Elementary and Early Childhood Education, Illinois.

PACEY (2013) *What Does 'School Ready' Really Mean? A Research Report from Professional Association for Childcare and Early Years*. Available from: www.pacey.org.uk/Pacey/media/Website-files/school%20ready/School-Ready-Report.pdf (accessed 20 November 2015).

Pascal, C., Bertram, T., Delaney, S. and Nelson, C. (2013) *A Comparison of International Childcare Systems*, Department of Education, London/CREC, Birmingham.

Roberts, R. (2010) *Wellbeing from Birth*, Sage, London.

Sanders, D., White, G., Burge, B., Sharp, C., Eames, A., McEune, R. and Grayson, H. (2005). *A Study of the Transition from the Foundation Stage to Key Stage 1*, DfES, London.

Skinner, B.F. (1948) 'Superstition in the pigeon', *Journal of Experimental Psychology*, vol. 38, pp. 168–172.

Smidt, S. (2011) *Introducing Bruner: a Guide for Students and Practitioners in Early Years Education*, Routledge, London.

Sylva, K., Melhuish, E., Sammons, P., Siraj-Blatchford, I., and Taggart, B. (eds) (2010) *Early Childhood Matters: Evidence from the Effective Pre-school and Primary Education Project*, Routledge, Oxon.

10 Holistic development: children playing

Viki Bennett, Sharon Friend and Nicki Henderson

LEARNING OUTCOMES

After reading this chapter you will have:

✔ Made progress in developing and articulating a personal framework for the place of play in your professional practice.
✔ Considered your own feelings about play.
✔ Explored some case studies of play in order to extend your understanding of its place in children's lives, development and learning.

Introduction

Much has been written about the value of play in children's learning and play is widely acknowledged as an essential and innate aspect of young children's development. Bruce, for example, concludes that 'Play is the highest form of learning in early **childhood**' (2005: 128). Moreover every child's opportunity 'to relax, play and join in with a wide range of cultural and artistic activities' is internationally recognised in the United Nations Convention as the right of every child (UNICEF).

In this chapter we will offer strategies to support you in navigating the myriad of information, research and theory about children's play in order to help you develop and articulate a personal framework for the place of play in your professional practice. We acknowledge what Moyles succinctly describes as the 'possible confusions about play' (2010: 4) and using two quotations concerning play will support you to critically analyse the underpinning messages and then, through the exploration of two illustrative case studies, reflect upon the implications for you as an early years professional. This process will enable you to rationalise, justify and promote the role of play in your own practice and provision.

The place of reflection as a powerful medium for making sense of experiences, deepening understanding and considering different perspectives is seen as integral to developing and sustaining effective practice (Paige-Smith and Craft, 2011).

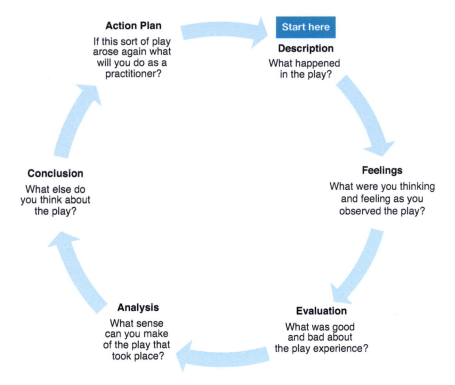

Figure 10.1 Using Gibbs' 'Reflective Cycle' to reflect upon play (adapted from Gibbs, 1988)

In this chapter we use Gibbs' (1988) Reflective Cycle, a highly effective and proven model to structure your reflective process with the aim of supporting you to develop the critical skills needed to help formulate a personally relevant insight of children's play. Throughout, as you explore play through scenarios, quotations, theory and research, you will be supported by a recurring use of Gibbs' Reflective Cycle. In so doing, you will develop a secure reflective approach for your practice.

In order for you to begin to engage with reflections on play, the six stages of Gibbs' Reflective Cycle, as seen in Figure 10.1, have been adapted and are explained below.

Description

At this stage of the reflective process you are asked to gather all the information you can about the quotation or experience and explore the underpinning messages.

- What is the quotation saying?
- What happens in the play experience in the case study?
- What is the context within the case study?

Feelings

The emotional response that we have when reflecting upon play is a key aspect for us to consider since interpretations of play are bound up with both cultural and personal contexts, beliefs and experiences. Views of children and childhood are culturally and personally framed. Else helps us understand possible current cultural views of children and their play by acknowledging that, 'the trouble is, when we grow up we become serious, rational and logical, and we start to think that children and young people's play is not important because it looks frivolous, irrational, "just playing"' (2009: 8). In this chapter we take a child-centred stance, with a view to contesting this notion of childhood play being unimportant, of children 'just playing' (Moyles, 2008), believing children to be competent creative, active learners (Rinaldi, 2006). Questions that will support you in this chapter for exploring your feelings about play will be:

- What did the quotation/case study make you think about?
- What resonated with your previous experiences?
- What 'emotional wake' did reading this leave you with?

Evaluation

For the evaluation stage, consider your understanding of the quotation and case study play experience.

- What aspects are relevant? Irrelevant? Effective? Ineffective?
- Are there alternative opinions or viewpoints to consider such as colleagues', tutors', authoritative opinion and theorists'?
- What evidence do you need to consider?
- How might you reason your thinking and understanding?

Analysis

In your analysis, examine what might have helped or hindered your understanding of the quotation or situation.

- Do you agree with what is being said? Why?
- Has it challenged your previous beliefs or assumptions or affirmed them?
- Again, why?

Crucially, you should ask how your own values and attitudes impacted on what you think about the quotation.

Conclusion

Here you will be able to summarise what you have learned from the quotation or case study.

- How has it contributed to your own professional and personal development?
- What are the implications for your own practice?

Action plan

Action planning will enable you to continuously capture everything that you need to know to improve your play practice and revise your views. For both of the quotations and case studies used in this chapter, you should capture your responses in a play action plan designed to include the following:

- Areas to focus on next
- Benefits for your practice and for the children
- Tasks to be done for areas of focus

(Bristol City Council, 2013)

Conceptual confusion

There is no unified theoretical or pedagogical base to guide practice in relation to play ... which has resulted in 'conceptual confusion' regarding the role of play within an educational setting.

(Haughton and Ellis, 2013: 74)

Description

First let us explore what this quotation is saying. There has never been one single model of play that has been universally agreed and this wide range of play research and theory has resulted in children's play being 'conceptualized in terms of creativity, adaptation, exploration, experimentation, learning, communication, socialization, acculturation, and mastery' (Ashiabi, 2007: 200). Here, Haughton and Ellis suggest that this range of thinking has created confusion and anxiety about the purpose and significance of children's play amongst current Early Years practitioners which warrants reflection in your professional journey.

Feelings

Do you agree with the quotation? Are you also unsure about the understanding of play in your setting in particular and its place in education in general? Do you see this same confusion in colleagues? It might well be a relief to feel that your confusion is acknowledged. Do you worry that it is difficult to have one argument to promote play or do you feel that having many reasons to promote play helps to indicate just how important it is? Do you think play is important for learning and development? Is it a purely recreational activity, or 'the child's work' (Isaacs, 1929: 9)? By recording your emotional response, you are acknowledging that being alongside young children when they play is indeed an emotional experience and that reflecting upon what sort of play provision we offer helps us understand our personal views of play in the midst of possible 'conceptual confusion'.

Evaluation

Let us now evaluate how accurately the quotation captures practitioners' understanding of play. Play is a complex aspect of childhood, and perhaps of humanity in general too, and yet, how much opportunity have you had in your career so far to focus in depth through your practice on children playing? It could be said that the very fact that play is recognised to be complex, provides a barrier to some students to engaging in analysis of play and can bring about a simplification of play in the early years resulting in broad but vague statements such as 'We do everything through play as children learn all they need from play'.

Analysis

In order to analyse Haughton and Ellis' statement further, we can focus on what it is that we see and hear when children play that makes us realise that, even though there is a range of theories

PROVOCATION

The Early Years Foundation Stage (EYFS) notes that, 'play is essential for children's development, building their confidence as they learn to explore, to think about problems, and relate to others' (DfE, 2014: 9). Can you find evidence of the above aspects from observations from your own practice of young children playing? For instance:

- A baby putting a wooden spoon in and out of a bucket.
- A toddler hiding from and then peeking out from behind a chair.
- A group of 5-year-olds playing heroes outside.
- An older child helping their younger sibling catch a ball.
- Two 3-year-olds 'cooking' at a pretend kitchen.
- A toddler exploring 'gloop' with his hands.
- A 4-year-old engrossed in small-world play with a toy farm.

about play, most of us are still able to agree that play is one of the most important aspects of children's learning.

You are most probably confident that what you have seen and heard demonstrates an important process. You know that play (in all the variety of forms) sustains children's interest and enjoyment over long periods of time.

On your Foundation Degree, you will explore topics such as schematic interests, children's representation, and emotional and **social development**, all of which can be apparent in play. As well as labelling the play type, it is essential for you as a reflective practitioner to analyse why you think you have witnessed something important in play. For this analysis, an holistic viewpoint is required in order that you are fully mindful that children's learning and play encompasses all domains of their experience: social, cultural, emotional, physical, spiritual, intellectual and moral.

REFLECTIVE PRACTICE

When you have observed a play experience, consider these questions to support your reflective thinking:

- Is the play stemming from a cognitive basis? Does it seem to be a schematic interest?
- Is the play driven by the child's personal topic-based interests (e.g. transport, animals, story)?
- Is the child exploring an emotional concern such as fear, anger, excitement, friendship, family, care?
- Is the play allowing children to explore real or imagined fantasy worlds?

When observing children playing, you will also know that you are witnessing something that is fast moving and requires the management of swift changes of focus. These changes might be connected to new and unexpected circumstances such as another child joining the play, the finding of an inviting object with possibilities to be explored or a change of location for the play. Children are often so motivated to sustain the play that they will creatively incorporate these unplanned events into the experience. So, when witnessing play we can usually see that children are deeply involved, highly imaginative and appear to enjoy the experience, whether it seems fun or serious, or, as can often the case, both of these.

We also see children exploring emotional domains through role play, taking on roles and life experiences which enable them to pursue a wide range of opportunities, contexts and emotions. Children are responsive to each other and to their environment in play and communicate effectively. They are able to maintain the momentum of play by negotiating, reframing and reforming the play to make it work.

In order to affirm just how important play is, we can turn to the **Leuven Involvement Scale for Young Children** (**LIS-YC**) developed by Laevers (1998). He has identified Signals of Involvement that young children display when engaged in their everyday activities, including play (Table 10.1). Scales from 1-5 (low to high) are used by the observers to identify the intensity of the child's involvement in an activity. If you take a moment to consider these Signals of Involvement, it is most probable that you have seen children showing these signals in play. Since

Table 10.1 The Leuven Involvement Scale for Young Children (adapted from Laevers, 1998)

1) Low Activity	Activity at this level can be simple, stereotypic, repetitive and passive. The child is absent and displays no energy. There is an absence of cognitive demand. The child characteristically may stare into space. N.B. This may be a sign of inner concentration.
2) A Frequently Interrupted Activity	The child is engaged in an activity but half of the observed period includes moments of non-activity, in which the child is not concentrating and is staring into space. There may be frequent interruptions in the child's concentration, but his/her Involvement is not enough to return to the activity.
3) Mainly Continuous Activity	The child is busy at an activity but it is at a routine level and the real signals for Involvement are missing. There is some progress but energy is lacking and concentration is at a routine level. The child can be easily distracted.
4) Continuous Activity with Intense Moments	The child's activity has intense moments during which activities at Level 3 can come to have special meaning. Level 4 is reserved for the kind of activity seen in those intense moments, and can be deduced from the 'Involvement signals'. This level of activity is resumed after interruptions. Stimuli, from the surrounding environment, however attractive cannot seduce the child away from the activity.
5) Sustained Intense Activity	The child shows continuous and intense activity revealing the greatest Involvement. In the observed period not all the signals for Involvement need be there, but the essential ones must be present: concentration, creativity, energy and persistence. This intensity must be present for almost all the observation period.

Source: Laevers (1998)

Laevers' ongoing research connects high levels of involvement (at the upper end of the scales, 4-5) to deep level learning, the Leuven Involvement Scale for Young Children can be used to support you in identifying just how important a play situation is for a child or group of children.

Conclusion

As Moyles suggests then, we do not need to strive for an elusive definition of play, but should actually 'see play as a process that, in itself, will subsume a range of behaviours, dispositions, motivation, opportunities, practices, skills and understandings' (2010: 5). She invites us to explore play as an all-encompassing process through a cycle of reflection on our day to day practice.

Action plan for play

Now you understand that it is crucial for Early Years practitioners to acknowledge play as multifaceted. Rather than attempt to simplify it, you should plan to read regularly about play, analyse your observations of children playing and discuss play with colleagues, parents and children themselves (Howard, 2010). You should aim to develop co-constructed understandings, which means that you will encourage and value play for children, in all its diverse forms rather than discourage or constrain it (Bruce, 2013) and embrace the complexity of play rather than shy away from it.

CASE STUDY 1

Flour play and 'conceptual confusion'

We can now study this 'conceptual confusion' further through Helen's experience.

Description

Helen, the room leader of the 3/4 year-old room in a nursery, wanted to offer an open-ended sensory play opportunity to the children. She had noticed that some of them had been particularly interested in the feel of flour during a cooking activity the day before. She poured a small amount of flour on a table and briefly introduced the children to the offer of flour play. Helen sat at the table with a few children and she watched as they used their fingers and palms to push, pull, pour and sprinkle the flour across the table. The children also made patterns with the flour and Helen poured more flour onto the table. Inevitably the flour went onto the floor and also into the air! There were up to five children at the table at a time, two of whom remained engrossed for 30 minutes. Child A, who was new to the setting, selected a small world dinosaur which he 'walked' through the flour. Helen laughed and pointed out the dinosaur footprints in the flour and he smiled and carried on. He then covered the dinosaur with flour, and another child joined in with this covering. A further two children were engrossed using building bricks to make a 'construction' with bricks which they then enjoyed covering with flour. Helen sat with the children, showing her interest with her expressions and her body language and used relevant descriptive vocabulary (such as more, push, pour, float and sprinkle), swept the floor and looked calm throughout, even though there was a growing layer of flour on the floor!

Feelings

Helen felt uncertain during this time, not sure about whether to allow children time to explore or whether to be 'safe' and take more control over the situation. She did acknowledge that she was *excited* about what she was seeing, since the children were clearly engrossed, enjoying the sensory and physical experience, and also engaged in small world play. However, at the same time, she was also *worried* about what was happening; there was flour on the floor and she did wonder if the children might slip over. Primarily, then, she was concerned that she did not fully understand her role as children played – was it to tidy up, to talk to them, to use appropriate vocabulary, to observe them or to play with the flour too?

Does this remind you of feelings you have experienced when supporting children's play? To help you manage these conflicting feelings, and conceptual confusion, we must evaluate Helen's experience further.

Evaluation

When Helen reflected upon this play event afterwards, she focused on an evaluation of her role and then on the learning and development for Child A.

When reflecting upon her role, Helen felt that she had needed to manage her worries (about what her role was) in order to successfully facilitate the continuation of the play. Such worries may well be familiar to many Early Years practitioners, since it is recognised that it is difficult to participate effectively in children's play without taking over or becoming too regulatory (Whitebread, 2010). However, Helen was certain that her role as an adult was to facilitate the play (Rose and Rogers, 2012) as the children took it from adult-initiated play (the flour as a provocation) to child-led play (children choosing to select more resources and ways of playing with the flour). The children were able to choose this activity (or not) and determined what to do with the flour, whether other resources should be brought to the table, who they would play with and how long they would stay there. Helen supported this child-managed transition to child-led play through offering a calm, observing and attentive presence and some commentary. In this way, as she commented upon what the children were doing, Helen used relevant vocabulary, affirmed their play explorations with the flour and stayed in close contact with them, and was able to foster 'sustained shared thinking', a critical concept which should be explored and used by all Early Years practitioners. Identified in the Effective Provision of Pre-School Education (EPPE) Project, '"Sustained shared thinking" occurs when two or more individuals "work together" in an intellectual way to solve a problem, clarify a concept, evaluate an activity (or) extend a narrative' (Sylva *et al.*, 2004) and occurs when children are with an adult or another child in a 1:1 situation or in small groups. Through this **reciprocal** discussion, questioning and active ongoing **engagement**, children's understanding of concepts within the experience is enhanced.

When reflecting upon the flour play for Child A, Helen felt that the play had offered an emotionally sustaining context for him. He was able to follow his own play interest (the dinosaur) whilst being alongside other children and a supportive adult. In this way, the play offered him a medium to experience a sense of belonging and to feel connected to Helen and the children nearby.

To support her understanding further, Helen interpreted his play against the characteristics of effective learning outlined in Development Matters (Early Education 2012) and in particular within the area of Playing and Exploring. She identified that the aspects below had been evident in his play:

1   Playing and exploring – children investigate and experience things, and 'have a go'.
2   Active learning – children concentrate and keep on trying if they encounter difficulties, and enjoy achievements; and
3   Creating and thinking critically – children have and develop their own ideas, make links between ideas, and develop strategies for doing things.

Analysis

Helen drew upon her certainty that this play was important for the child, which supported her to continue to offer the experience. In so doing, she was able to explore her understanding that 'children learn by leading their own play, and by taking part in play which is guided by adults' (DfE, 2012 p. 6).

Helen was also driven to explore the interesting question of who directs or influences the play. Was this play child-led or adult-led?

When thinking about whether play is adult-led or child-led, it can often be helpful to think about it as both. To help us in this thinking, we can turn to Vygotksy's (1978) assertion that in play children will achieve success at challenges that they themselves have set when they are supported by an adult (or knowledgeable peer). This theoretical concept, known as the Zone of Proximal Development (ZPD), is frequently affirmed by Early Years practitioners who have seen children they have been playing alongside solve significant problems with their guidance. Pascal (2014) further recognises that often there is an interplay between adults and children in play, and that the lead is handed back and forth between adults and children, calling this exchange a 'dialogic dance'. This idea of a sharing of the lead is a helpful way for us to plan to offer a balance of child- and adult-led play.

Conclusion

Helen felt that this flour play experience has given her a greater personal confidence for offering open-ended play opportunities to children. Her reflection upon the experience enabled her to understand that the flour activity was a 'valuable learning and developmental' experience for children and she now has more professional assurance that 'letting go' (Moyles, 2010: 3) in such a situation can bring about high quality learning.

Action plan

By reflecting in depth upon this experience, and by acknowledging that she felt uncertain as to her role, Helen now feels that she will not be surprised or worried 'if the play takes off on a life of its own that leaves us behind' (Else, 2009: 12) and she intends to work to establish an environment in her practice that offers children opportunities for play that is rich and well developed in order to foster their creative drive, their learning and imagination (Bruce, 2013). Helen will also work to develop her role as a practitioner, who will support children to achieve and succeed in challenging situations which they have embarked upon themselves.

Tuning into child's play

> Through observing and becoming part of a child's play, we discover an individual child's personal play style and 'tune in' to what we, as practitioners, can do to help that child develop the dispositions that support active learning through play.
>
> (Bruce, 2005: 255)

Description

Here, Bruce is describing the process of immersing ourselves in children's play. She suggests that as practitioners we should familiarise ourselves with the ways that children play, not only through observation, an essential part of Early Years practice, but also by actively 'becoming part of a child's play'. She is urging us to be with the children as they play and to be open to, and receptive of, the children's play interests. In so doing, we will find out about children as individuals, see them in their own individual holistic context and then be best able to support them in their ongoing learning and development.

Feelings

We hope that this quotation inspires you to continue to do just as Bruce says – to observe and also become part of children's play. This can be exciting, but practitioners can also feel worried about both these aspects. In terms of observing play, many practitioners can worry about how to manage time when playing and also about how to observe unobtrusively. Furthermore, as discussed earlier, practitioners also have to consider how to join in with children sensitively and support their play rather than hindering or indeed curtailing it. With these feelings in mind, let us evaluate further what Bruce is suggesting.

Evaluation

Bruce is advocating that practitioners seek to understand children as individuals through observation of them in their play in order to meet their needs – a critical aspect of the role of the practitioner (Fawcett, 2009). To help us gain a deep insight into children's interests in play, we can turn to a robust framework for recognising, promoting and analysing high quality play contexts devised by Bruce: The Twelve Features of Play.

By interpreting observations of children playing using the Twelve Features of Play, practitioners can identify children's interests and achievements. Equipped with information about what children are exploring though play, practitioners can then organise an environment that offers high quality play opportunities, affirms children's interests and needs, and supports ongoing learning and development.

Analysis

Not only does Bruce advocate us observing play, she also asks us to 'tune in' to children's play. This suggests an active involvement of play which again reminds us of Vygotsky's proposition that adults (or knowledgeable others) are essential to support children's learning within the Zone of Proximal Development. Building upon this, and recognising that learning for children involves a sequence of actions and thought, Bruner (1966) encourages adults to structure learning experiences for children into carefully organised sequences, offering guidance throughout.

Table 10.2 The 'Twelve Features of Play' (Bruce, 2013)

1	The crucial combination of first-hand and direct experience of life and the natural world	- This is at the heart of play
2	Play depends on rules – but who makes the rules?	- Children do not like to feel boundary-less - Children make decisions about the importance of rules - Children are motivated to solve problems
3	Play props – representing – making one thing stand for another	- The best play props are those which can be transformed - Play props support imagination and creativity
4	The moment and conditions must be right in order for play to develop	- Children cannot be forced to play
5	Play allows children to escape from the here and now, and to move in time and space	- Children move from literal play to advanced and sophisticated forms of play
6	Literal play changes into symbolic, pretend play	- Children's play becomes more engaged with imaginative possibilities, alternative ways of living and being
7	Playing alone helps children to reflect and know themselves	- Children need personal space, time and possibilities to develop their ideas
8	Play with one other child, or one other adult, has an important contribution to make	- Children seem to benefit from playing with one another - Children are emotionally engaged
9	Collaborative, social play demands each player can develop and sustain their play agenda, and make it resonate and chime with that of others so that the play flows	- Children are motivated to engage with and sustain free-flow creative group play
10	Deep play means deep involvement in the play by the players	- Involvement means great concentration in the play - Children wallow in their play, being difficult to distract - Babies and toddlers can be involved in free-flow play too
11	Play helps children to apply their learning	- Children apply what they know inside the play situations they create (outer to inner) - Children view themselves in the play role and narrative of the play scenario (inner to outer)
12	Play is an integrating mechanism	- Children experiment safely with life, ways of living and being, possible alternatives and impossibilities - Children are able to do things in different ways, freeing their mind to be creative and thoughtful

Rose and Rogers (2012) similarly advocate that, as facilitators, Early Years practitioners should be active, as opposed to passive, and that they should offer sensitive and respectful guidance to children in their learning, based upon careful observation and attentive **listening to children**.

Conclusion

It is apparent, then, that active engagement with children's play, coupled with a commitment to interpreting what has been observed, are vital aspects of Early Years practice. Using the Twelve Features of Play, practitioners will have a basis for 'tuning into' children as they play and for reflecting upon how the environment and the role that adults take can be designed to promote ongoing effective play-based learning experiences.

Action plan

Following on from Bruce's idea of 'tuning into play', ensure you consider opportunities whereby you/practitioners can become (more fully?) involved in the play that you have planned and facilitated. This may require under, rather than over planning, allowing a greater degree of responsiveness and flexibility.

FROM RESEARCH TO PRACTICE

In her recent paper for the Cambridge Primary Review Trust, Goswami (2015) reviews research illustrating how young children learn, and the impact of early experiences on cognitive development, particularly social interaction, play and scaffolding, and she explores the implications for education. A key factor is dialogue with and feedback from the practitioner, helping the child to reflect upon their own learning and develop their self-esteem. In what ways are the implications relevant to your understanding of the value of play, and how can you best model reflection to the children about their own learning through play?

Goswami, U. (2015) *Children's Cognitive Development and Learning*, York: Cambridge Primary Review Trust

CASE STUDY 2

Tuning into child's play – Boats and Floods

We can now study this aspect of *tuning into child's play* through Maria's experience.

Description
Below, Maria, an Early Years Foundation degree student in her first year, describes how she set up, observed and then analysed a loose parts play experience for children. This

opportunity enabled her to significantly develop her understanding of the children in her group:

'I chose to research the value of loose parts play following my observation of a small group of children who used any loose parts they could find to support their role play. To gain a better understanding I decided to provide a variety of loose parts in the most spacious area of the classroom, including:

- Wooden blocks
- Different sized netting
- A large piece of blue material
- Different sized ropes
- Cardboard boxes and cubes
- Wooden circle shapes

I set up the loose parts so they looked inviting and so it was easier for the children to explore and make a choice. The children arrived and instantly two boys approached the loose parts. 'Wow let's do that,' one boy said. They both began to explore the parts and spontaneously one child said 'we can build a real Octo-pod with all this' and both children began to move the parts and construct an enclosure. Two girls and another boy joined in and engaged with the same play theme. Together they came up with a plan and built another enclosure. The wooden circle block was now 'a steering wheel that makes it go super-fast'. The wooden block became 'a chair for everyone to sit on' and also 'the door where the Gups go'. Together the children worked cooperatively to build the Octo-pod. Throughout this they all demonstrated high levels of energy and involvement. Together they negotiated with each other about the roles that they would take on and once organised they became further engaged in their role play.

The loose parts were still a significant feature of their play; the rope was used to attach to the toy then to a child so they could jump into the sea and it was used as a seat belt. Two of the children were able to independently tie a knot! Amazing! One boy who usually asks an adult to support him in trying new things then set himself the challenge of being able to tie a knot by himself. This was wonderful for me as his key worker to see. The other children offered him help and he refused it saying, 'no I can do it'. He was evidently so proud when he achieved the knot.

After twenty minutes, the theme then began to change. Two children spread out the large blue material, 'it's the sea' one girl said. One boy then used the gaps in the wooden blocks as a place to store some of the loose parts that he liked, naming it 'his treasure' and this then developed the role play theme into pirates and ships. From here the loose parts took on a whole new meaning. The children recognised that their theme had changed so using language they began to re-label the loose parts. One piece of fabric became the pirate flag that 'scares the other pirates away'. The rope was now used to tie up the 'baddies' and to be an anchor for the boat. The children constructed a plank with the wooden blocks shouting 'walk the plank, walk the plank!'. This developed into the children setting up their own treasure hunt. The children took it in turns to hide the treasure and then find it. I saw them settle **conflict** and negotiate turn-taking without an adult.

Forty minutes into play the theme developed again and for the final time. This section was the longest. The theme then developed into the children rescuing each other from a flood (there was much coverage of severe flooding nationally and locally in the media at the time). One girl lay on the blue material and began to swim, 'help help I'm in a flood' she said, repeating this several times. Once again as the play evolved so did the value of the loose parts. The children used the boxes as 'speedboats' and with the 'rescue rope' they rescued the girl from the water. This was repeated several times. The children were using language such as 'deeper', 'shallow end' – specific language I have never heard from them before. The children made the most of their space and any available space they could find in the room. The play was ended by the routine, however the children asked to keep their construction so that they could continue with it later and they did.

Feelings

Maria had an overwhelming sense of excitement throughout this experience. She knew that the play experience was facilitating deep-level learning and that this was connected to the resources that she had selected carefully and also to the time and space for exploration that she had offered the children. She could see that the children were highly involved (consider the LIS-YC) and motivated since they showed persistence and sustained the play. She was impressed with how creatively the children used the resources, and with their language and ongoing sophisticated shared communication.

Evaluation

Maria evaluated the experience in the following way:

This particular observation gave me such an holistic view of the children's knowledge, previous experiences they have had, their dispositions and attitude towards new activities and learning. All children displayed dispositions towards self-motivation by becoming deeply involved. Some children set their own challenges and met them. They were all confident in their ability to communicate, interact, make suggestions and to turn-take in conversation. All the children were imaginative, spontaneous and innovative. They expanded on their own ideas and the ideas of others. Once they made plans they were confident to follow them through. During a moment when peers accidently knocked down part of their construction the children demonstrated resilience by remaining with a positive sprit and dealing with their frustration by thinking of new ways to build the boat.

Later, when this play ended, the girl spoke to me about her Nan and Granddad who lived in an area of a flood. I was then able to see she used this play experience to make sense of this situation. During the play she said 'but it's ok because floods won't hurt you, people can rescue you and then you're safe'. I felt this play was emotionally satisfying for her and she was clarifying her thoughts through play. This prompted another boy to discuss what he had seen on the TV relating to the flood. This play provided a great opportunity for the children to have this conversation with each other and adults during reflection time soon after the activity.

I feel that loose parts are valuable to the child and therefore valuable to the practitioners in gaining a better understanding of the child. Loose parts provide a 'blank canvas' upon which children can place their own meaning and ideas. It provides a good opportunity to truly see a child's interest. Loose parts allow children to become independent and self-sufficient as they can organise and manipulate the objects. The value and meaning of the loose parts can evolve as the children's play does.

When playing with loose parts children are able to be imaginative and give objects a new meaning that is separate from their true meaning in the real world. Through the use of loose parts children can create something unique or original. However, I also believe that the time and space the children were given allowed this play to evolve.

By carrying out this evaluation, Maria identified that the range of good quality resources, the physical space and her desire not to interrupt the play were key to the learning she witnessed (Whitebread, 2010).

Analysis

The loose parts resources offered a flexibility of use and interpretation which supported children's imagination and their 'individual play trajectories' (Robinson, 2011: 74) and enabled them to make connections to their lived lives (television and family): in this way they were able actively to investigate real experiences in all their complexity (water, fear, excitement, rescue, help, together, being alone) in a truly meaningful context which resulted in them making sense together of floods and adventure through a process co-constructing meaning. Furthermore, with the resources and space becoming a flooded world, this symbolic play corresponds to Piaget's proposal that children aged 2–7 years play symbolically and explore the world through concrete experiences – the 'pre-operational stage' (Piaget, 1965).

It is also most apparent that this play offered the children a communication-rich experience. Their vocabulary was contextually relevant, and their communication strategies were effective and wide-ranging, encompassing elements of organisation, problem-solving, imagination, creativity and description as well as supporting them to feel a sense of participation, achievement and to explore emotions such as excitement and fear.

As the facilitator of this play, Maria was able to develop her understanding of her role – she thoroughly enjoyed observing the children's interests and social actions. Crucially, she knew that her offer of these resources and of the time for the children to play with them enabled the play to develop in depth. Taking an 'in action' reflective stance (Schön, 1991), that of actively considering an event in the moment, she decided that she did not need to intervene in the play and did not want to stop it abruptly.

In order to develop Maria's evaluation further, now use the Twelve Features of Play (see Table 10.2) to analyse what took place in the play.

- What features are present?
- What do you think the children were learning?
- How could you share your observations and analysis with children, their parents and carers, and your colleagues?

Action plan

Maria was obviously keen to share her learning with colleagues. The group of children were so engrossed that they were able to coordinate and sustain their own play independently and successfully. She says that this experience confirmed her belief in the value of open ended, flexible, inviting resources, and the use of space in order to 'create and sustain an environment in which choice is facilitated' (Broadhead *et al.*, 2010: 178).

Conclusion

Maria took a risk with this entirely open-ended offer, by exploring how children engaged with the loose parts offered to them in this way. Taking a reflective approach, she managed this risk by acknowledging her principles that children's play is essential for their learning and that children are highly adept at play.

This boats and floods case study provides an inspiring example of actively valuing play in practice (Sayeed and Guerin, 2000). By researching one's own play practice practitioners will be able to continually reflect upon their understandings of play in order to support children's holistic learning.

Play	*Children*	*Practitioners*	
	Reflection ⟷		**Actions** Implications for pedagogy: environment and interactions.
Play is inspiring and motivating	Children are highly motivated to play. Children are deeply involved when they play.	Practitioners are fascinated by what they see when children play. Supporting play is an emotional aspect of Early Years practice.	
Play is complex	Play operates across the holistic spectrum – social, cultural, emotional, physical, spiritual, intellectual and moral aspects of children's lives and learning. Children adeptly manage the varied experiences and swift pace of play.	Analysis of observations is rewarding as so much can be revealed in play. Play operates on many domains and in many contexts.	
Play is for learning	Play is the work of children. It is about exploring the world and learning to learn.	Practitioners aim to promote play for young children as a rich learning medium.	

(Vertical arrow label between Children and Practitioners columns: Observe and research)

Figure 10.2 A framework for a reflective and holistic approach to play

Conclusion: Developing your own 'Framework for a reflective and holistic approach to play'

Using two quotations and two illustrative case studies, this chapter has supported you to engage in a reflective cycle for analysing play. In so doing you will have been able to begin to relate theory to play experiences observed in your own practice. Taking a child-centred stance, that of recognising the child as a competent learner, we have highlighted key aspects of play principles for Early Years practitioners that are outlined in our framework for a reflective and holistic approach to play (see Figure 10.2).

By adopting this reflective framework, our aim is that you will be better equipped to observe and then analyse children at play, take account of your own **perceptions** and developing understanding of play, and actively plan for children in your setting to learn through play. In this way, as you continually reflect upon your understandings of play you enhance your 'play related skills' (Springate and Foley, 2008: 116).

Further reading

Roberts-Holmes, G. (2012) ' "It's the bread and butter of our practice": Experiencing the Early Years Foundation Stage', *International Journal of Early Years Education,* vol. 20, issue 1, pp. 30–42.
This article captures the realities of working in the Early Years in England today by exploring both the highly positive aspects of the Early Years Foundation Stage along with the more difficult areas of practice. Discontinuities in practice across a range of sectors and between the Foundation Stage and KS1 are identified. The article will enable you to begin to join in with ongoing debates about Early Years policy.

Rogers, S. (ed.) (2011) *Rethinking Play and Pedagogy in Early Childhood Education: Concepts, Contexts and Cultures,* London: Routledge.
The authors encourage you to critically reflect upon the value and role of play in children's development and learning. They question the distinction between play and work and explore play from a range of cultural and conceptual stances. The book will enable you to further reflect on the tensions between play and pedagogy and will immerse you in fascinating international debates on play.

Wood, E. (2013) *Play, Learning and the Early Childhood Curriculum* (3rd edn) Sage: London.
Recent research and theory concerning play is shared in this book, with focus areas ranging from pedagogical constructs of play, the role of play in learning, international play perspectives and Early Years policy and play. The problematic notion of 'educational play' is explored in depth. Practitioner generated research and theory forms the basis of this exploration, which will be particularly inviting to Foundation Degree students.

Useful websites

www.bristolearlyyearsresearch.org.uk/index.asp
The Bristol Early Years Research and Development website aims to promote opportunities for rich professional learning and innovation through reflective practice and setting-based research and enquiry. There are a range of specialist 'hubs' exploring areas of interest, and an excellent range of links to further reading.

www.earlychildhoodaction.com
The members of Early Childhood Action offer an alternative curriculum which proposes that imaginative play is at the heart of children's learning. The group express concern over strict age related outcomes

for children in the Early Years and stress the importance of the key person approach and opportunities for children to explore their physical development, outdoor learning and the arts.

References

Ashiabi, G.S. (2007) *Play in the Preschool Classroom: Its Socio-Emotional Significance and the Teacher's Role in Play*. Early Childhood Education.

Bristol City Council (2013) *The Bristol Standard: A Self Evaluation Framework for Early Years settings* (5th edn). Bristol: Apple Litho Bristol Ltd.

Broadhead, P., Howard, J. and Wood, E. (2010) 'Conclusion: Understanding Playful Learning and Playful Pedagogies – Towards a New Research Agenda', in Broadhead, P., Howard, J. and Wood, E. (eds) *Play and Learning in the Early Years: From research to practice*. London: Sage.

Bruce, T. (2005) 'Play, the universe and everything!', in Moyles, J. (ed.) *The Excellence of Play* (2nd edn). Maidenhead; McGraw-Hill/Open University Press: pp. 255–267.

Bruce, T. (2013) 'Play and creativity in the early years', in Veale, F. (ed) *Early Years: for Level 4 & 5 and The Foundation Degree*. London: Hodder Education: pp 377–398.

Bruner, J.S. (1966) *Towards a Theory of Instruction*. MA: Harvard University Press.

DfE (2014) *The Early Years Foundation Stage Framework*.

Else, P. (2009) *The Value of Play*. London: Continuum.

Fawcett, M. (2009) *Learning through Child Observation* (2nd edn). London: Jessica Kingsley Publishers.

Gibbs, G. (1988) *Learning by Doing: A Guide to Teaching and Learning Methods*. London: Further Education Unit.

Goswami, U. (2015) *Children's Cognitive Development and Learning*. York: Cambridge Primary Review Trust.

Haughton, C. and Ellis, C. (2013) 'Play in the Early Years', in Palaiologou, I. (ed) *The Early Years Foundation Stage; Theory and Practice* (2nd edn). London: Sage, pp. 73–87.

Howard, J. (2010) 'Making the Most of Play in the Early Years; The importance of Children's Perceptions', in: Broadhead, P., Howard, J. and Wood, E. (eds) *Play and Learning in the Early Years: From Research to Practice*. London: Sage, pp. 145–160.

Isaacs, S. (1929) *The Nursery Years: The Mind of the Child from Birth to Six Years*. London: Routledge and Kegan Paul.

Laevers, F. (1998) *The Leuven Involvement Scale for Young Children: LIS-YC:* Manual Issue 1, of the Experiential Education Series: Centre for Experimental Education.

Moyles, J. (2010) *The Excellence of Play* (3rd edn). Maidenhead: McGraw-Hill/Open University Press.

Pascal, C. (2014) *Two Year Olds are Serious Business*, Bristol Early Years May Conference in partnership with ECHO, The Voice of Early Childhood and Bristol Early Years Teaching Consortium (BEYTC) 'Being Two: The Age of Enchantment', St George's Church Bristol 10 May.

Paige-Smith, A. and Craft, A. (eds) (2011) *Developing Reflective Practice in the Early Years* (2nd edn). Maidenhead: Open University Press.

Piaget, J. (1965) *The Child's Conception of the World*. Totowa, NJ: Littlefield, Adams & Co.

Rinaldi, C. (2006) *In Dialogue with Reggio Emilia: Contextualising, Interpreting and Evaluating Early Childhood Education (Contesting Early Childhood)*. Abingdon: Routledge.

Robinson, M. (2011) *Understanding Behaviour and Development in Early Childhood: A Guide to Theory and Practice*. Abingdon: Routledge.

Rose, J. and Rogers, S. (2012) *The Role of the Adult in Early Years Settings*. Maidenhead: Open University Press.

Sayeed, Z. and Guerin, E. (2000) *Early Years Play*. London: David Fulton Publishers.

Schön, D. (1991) *The Reflective Practitioner: How Professionals Think in Action*. Aldershot: Ashgate Publishing Ltd.

Springate, D. and Foley, P. (2008) 'Play Matters', in Collins, J. and Foley, P. (eds) *Promoting Children's Wellbeing: Policy and Practice*. Milton Keynes: Open University Press, pp. 111–141.

Sylva, K., Melhuish, E., Sammons, P., Siraj-Blatchford, I. and Taggart, B. (2004) *The Effective Provision of Pre-school Education (EPPE) Project: Findings from Pre-school to end of Key Stage 1*. Research Brief.

UNICEF A summary of the United Nations Convention on the Rights of the Child. Article 31. Available online at www.unicef.org/crc/files/Rights_overview.pdf (Accessed 15 April 2015).

Vygotsky, L. (1978) *Mind in Society*. Cambridge MA: Harvard University Press.

Whitebread, D. (2010) 'Metacognition and Self Regulation', in Broadhead, P., Howard, J. and Wood, E. (eds) *Play and Learning in the Early Years: From Research to Practice*. London: Sage.

11 Holistic development: enabling learning and cognitive development

Kate Hulm

LEARNING OUTCOMES

After reading this chapter you should be able to:

✔ Consider the value of the characteristics of effective learning.
✔ Identify the characteristics as the foundations of children's learning.
✔ Recognise the characteristics of effective learning as observable behaviours.
✔ Analyse the characteristics of effective learning against learning theories.
✔ Evaluate interactions in promoting sustained shared thinking.

Introduction

A key message from Tickell's (2011) review of the Early Years Foundation Stage was that practitioners should focus more on how children approach play opportunities in order to better understand their learning. In this chapter we will examine how the characteristics of effective learning are attitudes, or **cognitive qualities**, required not only for learning but for life. Comparisons will be made with learning dispositions, an integral aspect of Te Whariki, the early **childhood** curriculum in New Zealand. Connections with wider **psychological perspectives** and educational models, such as Experiential Education will help you consider the value of understanding how children approach their learning. Links with Piaget's and Vygotsky's thinking about the importance of cognitive development and social interactions will allow you to consider how the characteristics of effective learning are rooted in developmental theories that have stood the test of time. Siraj-Blatchford *et al.* (2002) recognise how interactions which enable children to examine their own and others' ideas in depth contributed significantly to their cognitive development, and called these exchanges 'sustained shared thinking'. Valuing children's communication and responding appropriately are **pedagogical qualities** identified as crucial for supporting effective learning. Overall, this chapter will enable you to consider all the ways you can encourage children's positive attitudes to learning as well how you engage in meaningful communication with them. It should help you see connections between underpinning ideas about cognitive development and the processes of children's learning; and recognise implications for your practice.

The value of the characteristics of effective learning

Dame Clare Tickell (2011) offered the early years' sector a gift with her review of the Early Years Foundation Stage (EYFS) by highlighting that practitioners should pay more attention to the ways children approach learning. Arguably perhaps, it is an opportunity that appears not to have been seized wholeheartedly by either the workforce or those responsible for making judgements about the quality of practice and provision. The characteristics of effective learning are no new concept; they have been part of the EYFS learning and development requirements since 2008 and were embedded within the Birth to Three Matters framework before then. However, it was Tickell's review that raised the profile of these characteristics as essential when thinking about how children learn.

The characteristics as the foundations of children's learning

Much has been written about the value of understanding children's learning from their perspective and Tickell is by no means the first to highlight the role of **intrinsic motivation** as crucial for learning to occur. Lillian Katz, an American developmental psychologist, identifies how dispositions can underpin all potential for effective learning:

> A disposition is a tendency to exhibit frequently, consciously, and voluntarily a pattern of behaviour that is directed towards a broad goal. They are ... relatively enduring habits of mind or characteristic ways of responding to experiences across types of situations.
>
> (Katz, 1985, cited in Katz, 1993: 16)

Katz acknowledges that dispositions towards learning can develop in both positive and negative ways. While positive dispositions can enhance learning opportunities, negative ones can result in poor academic outcomes and problematic behaviour. McDermott *et al.* (2012: 66) refer to 'observable mannerisms that facilitate or inhibit a child's **engagement**' in learning situations. In other words, the ways in which children engage with learning and begin to self-regulate. In her review, Tickell (2011: 87) identifies self-regulation as one of the 'principal determinants of later academic success'. It is, along with managing feelings and behaviour 'a concept that involves attitudes and dispositions for learning (the motivation or "will"'), and an ability to be aware of one's own thinking (cognitive strategies, or skill)'.

Clearly, what we want for children is to be motivated towards their learning or as Claxton and Carr (2004: 87) say 'ready, willing and able to learn'. While character traits such as shyness or exuberance are more about **temperament** and personal qualities, Katz (1993) argues that dispositions for learning, such as giving up quickly or trying harder when things get difficult, are affected by emotional states learnt as a result of interactions and experiences.

Adult responses are pivotal in how children learn to approach life. Social psychologist, Carol Dweck's research in the 1980s identifies how acknowledging and encouraging a child's effort

REFLECTIVE PRACTICE

REFLECTIVE PRACTICE

1: Learning mind sets

- How do you respond to children who frequently ask you to do things for them, give up easily or say 'I can't' when faced with tasks that they find difficult?
- What are your reasons for responding in this way?

instilled in them a sense of self-belief that praising outcomes or ability (cleverness) simply did not (cited in Katz, 1993). Dweck (2006) suggests that children develop a fixed and **negative mind set** about their own learning potential if the way they strive to make sense of their world, in other words their effort, remains unacknowledged. This can put limits on their motivation or willingness to learn. Lafferty (cited in Dowling, 2013: 122) endorses this point suggesting that praise is an external judgement of approval, while 'encouragement is about motivating the child within', which creates an 'ongoing desire to learn'. Recent collated research acknowledges 'a growing body of evidence emerging, which suggests that educational interventions, particularly in early childhood, can change children's dispositions and self-beliefs in lasting ways' (OECD, 2013: 33).

Encouraging positive attitudes to learning in young children is imperative. Curiosity can be stifled for babies who are not given opportunities to independently investigate and explore; resilience hampered for toddlers who are not encouraged to problem solve and feel they can do things. Thinking can be hindered for pre-schoolers who are continually instructed by adults, rather than having time and space to test their own ideas. In order for children to develop effective characteristics you should encourage excitement, puzzlement, honest attempts and surprise, as well as valuing wrong outcomes. Duckworth (1996: 69), an educationalist who worked with Piaget, argues that being wrong is a 'legitimate and important element of learning' that leads to further development.

REFLECTIVE PRACTICE

REFLECTIVE PRACTICE

2: Supporting positive learning mind sets

Drawing on the previous paragraph write down some implications for how you interact with young children.

The characteristics of effective learning as observable behaviours

While recognising that your response to children is crucial in supporting the development of characteristics of effective learning, it is also necessary to consider the lenses through which you view how children do what they do. When the Early Years' curriculum in New Zealand was

Te Whariki Positive learning dispositions		Early Years Foundation Stage Characteristics of Effective Learning		
Disposition	Behaviours to look for	Playing and exploring	Active learning	Creating and thinking critically
Taking an interest	Courage, inquisitiveness, purposefulness, curiosity	A child who shows curiosity	A child with physical and mental energy	A child who has ideas and tries something new
Being involved	Trust, playfulness, concentration, resourcefulness	A child who engages with their senses	A child who concentrates and stays involved	A child who can connect ideas
Persisting with difficulty	Perseverance, resilience, self-motivation	A child who is willing to have a go	A resilient and persistent child who keeps on trying	A child who can choose different ways to do things
Expressing a feeling	Communication, confidence, optimism	A child who has a positive, 'can do' attitude	A child who enjoys and believes in him/herself	A child who shows or tells you what they know
Being responsible	Co-operation, testing a theory, self-control	A child who uses their experiences	A child who achieves what they set out to do	A child who can problem solve

Figure 11.1 Te Whariki compared with Characteristics of Effective Learning

rewritten in 1998, a then new observational method of interpreting children's development through Learning Stories was developed by Margaret Carr. Learning Stories provide a theoretical framework that enables practitioners to look at the process of learning and respond appropriately by paying attention to learning dispositions. Carr (2001: 5) specifies 'outcomes of interest' for children, which begin with what they know and can do. She argues that when there is also 'intent' learning strategies develop. If children's learning strategies are well supported through 'social partners, practices and tools', they become 'situated'. She goes on to say that when children have 'situated learning strategies plus motivation', positive learning dispositions follow and this is how children build on existing knowledge and skills. Positive learning dispositions and the characteristics of effective learning are interchangeable terms really. Behaviours to look for, such as curiosity and persistence, are common to both (see Figure 11.1).

Today, Learning Stories have been adapted by many settings in England for best fit with the EYFS. This can mean that the scope for looking at how children learn is reduced because they focus predominantly on what children are learning (prime and specific areas). It is interesting see how the positive dispositions for the original Learning Stories are expressed as ways of behaving or positive 'habits of mind'; the ways, in fact, that we want children to characteristically respond to all the different learning opportunities in their lives. It is, of course, essential to recognise children's developmental progress in prime and specific areas of learning but a great shame if we miss valuing the processes of how they make decisions or their capacity for thinking things through, as a result of focusing too much on learning outcomes. Duckworth (1996: 64) explains it thus:

Of all the virtues related to intellectual functioning, the most passive is the virtue of knowing the right answer. Knowing the right answer requires no decisions, carries no risks, and makes no demands. It is automatic. It is thoughtless.

Being thoughtless is clearly not an effective characteristic of learning while being prepared to problem solve, take risks and make choices are attitudes we want to encourage. Identifying children's developmental or academic 'success' through measuring or testing their knowledge and skills against a set of predetermined outcomes or goals may limit our ability to value 'imagination and intellectual daring' (Duckworth, 1996: 65). Creating a holistic picture that pays as much attention to their approach to learning as it does to what they can do, enables us to see children as motivated and competent individuals. More recently, Rosemary Roberts, a founder of PEEP (Peers Early Education Partnership) has identified five Thinking Dispositions as key in the development of agency in children. These are Caring, Empowerment, Decision-making, Learning dispositions, and **Self-concept** and confidence. Roberts (2014: 31) emphasises the importance of well-being for children and believes that 'repeated rich experiences of well-being play nurture positive thinking dispositions'.

FROM RESEARCH TO PRACTICE

Companionable learning

Rosemary Roberts (2010) has researched the value of resilient well-being for children's learning from an early age and the implications of this into adolescence. She has identified 'companionable learning' opportunities, or *'diagogy'* as fundamental for the development of individual well-being.

- What do you understand by well-being?
- Reflect on the links you feel there are between the characteristics of effective learning and resilient well-being.
- Consider your own diagogy, explained as 'learning by child and companion together', and identify strategies that you use or can implement to grow companionable learning with children.
- Read *Wellbeing from Birth* by Rosemary Roberts.

Learning theories and the characteristics of effective learning

To help us focus on children's learning processes more clearly, the guidance document *Development Matters* (Early Education, 2011) interpreted the messages from Tickell's review. This provides a clear framework to support our understanding of the characteristics of effective learning. It is perhaps unfortunate that the change of government at that time led to confusing communication about the use of *Development Matters* (DM), which has subsequently led to the

PROVOCATION 1

Characteristics of effective learning (CoEL)

A year 1 Foundation Degree student commented on completing an assignment that asked her to focus on the characteristics of effective learning in relation to play:

The assignment made me feel more equipped to explain how children learn through play to parents and colleagues and how important effective learning is: It also helped me to understand how interconnected all learning is and that the outcome is not the important part of learning, instead it is how the children get to the outcome.'

What do you do to help parents and colleagues understand what the characteristics of effective learning look like and what they mean for children's development? What could you do or what else could you do?

dilution of Tickell's original message. DM (Early Education, 2011) helps us to unpick what might at first appear to be arbitrary identifiers of children's actions.

By themselves, the titles of the characteristics are perhaps a little perfunctory: *Playing and Exploring; Active Learning* and *Creating and Thinking Critically.* Surely, all children play and are active, except when asleep, eating or watching the television or computer games. They create play situations, models or pictures, which they need to think about. However, it is the descriptors of what the characteristics really mean to which we should pay more attention. Perhaps a more helpful way to depict the characteristics is as an interconnected model with the child at the centre (see Figure 11.2). Stewart (2011) suggests that focusing on children as agents of their own development enables us to see them as active participators in learning, which is rooted in well-established theory. In the mid-twentieth century, Swiss psychologist, Jean Piaget's research on children's cognitive development opened up a whole new way of thinking about learning from birth, which remains influential today (Gray and MacBlain, 2012). Much of Piaget's work was based on observation and listening to his own young children in natural environments. Constructivism, the way his theory is described, proposes 'that humans generate knowledge and meaning from an interaction between their experiences and their ideas' (Gray and MacBlain, 2012, p. 44). A fundamental premise is that children are powerful, exploratory thinkers actively engaged in the process of learning. To help you think more deeply about how you might use the CoEL in your **assessments** of children's learning, carry out Reflective practice Task 3.

Another constructivist, and influential thinker during the twentieth century was Russian psychologist, Lev Vygotsky. Like Piaget, he recognised children as active agents in their own learning but also proposed that learning had significant cultural context and believed that children develop within a 'social matrix' framework (Gray and MacBlain, 2012). Children's interactions with other children form the basis of their **social matrix** 'complemented by the adult's willingness to help and instruct'. Vygotsky believed that play allowed children to understand objects, imagine, form relationships and adopt cultural norms; so strong was his belief about the value of play he defined it as 'self-education' (ibid, pp. 71–76).

Characteristics of Effective Learning

These characteristics overlap and are interconnected with one another

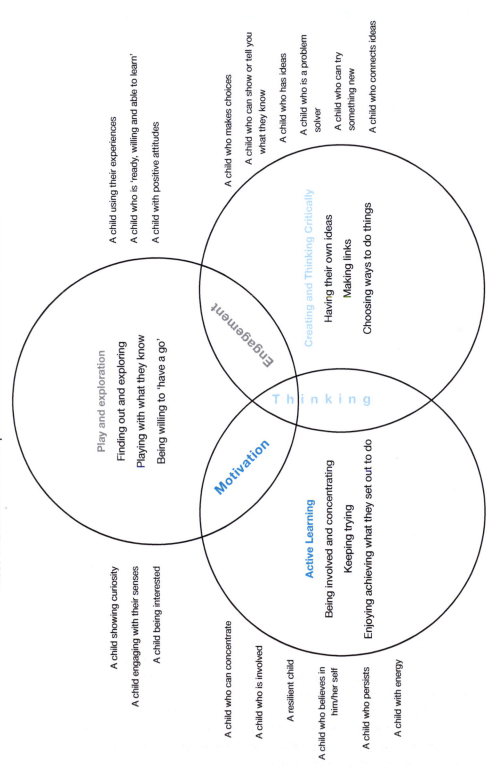

Figure 11.2 Characteristics of Effective Learning: An interconnected model

REFLECTIVE PRACTICE
REFLECTIVE PRACTICE

3 Characteristics of effective learning

Think of three children for whom you are key person; make a blank copy of the diagram for each child and write their name in the centre. Next write in examples of their behaviour or approaches to learning that fit the descriptors of the characteristics of effective learning (CoEL). Try and recall at least three examples for each CoEL or circle for each child.

Playing and exploring

When we look at some of the descriptors of playing and exploring, the connections with Piaget's ideas are clear; for instance, a child who finds things out by using his experiences and engaging with his senses. Stewart (2011) challenges us to think hard about the play dilemma when focusing on this particular characteristic. Play is defined as being an intrinsically motivated activity, with children biologically programmed to engage with it for its own sake (Hughes, 2011, Skills Active, 2005). The EYFS is a play based framework but there is perhaps a tension between the kind of play identified as intrinsic and self-motivated and the 'planned, purposeful play' depicted by the EYFS (DfE, 2013: 6). Howard and McInnes (2010) consider research relating to emotional and environmental cues about what play means to children, which clearly shows the distinctions children make between play and work. Play is voluntary, fun and under their control while work is compulsory, under an adult's control and can be fun too but not always! Whenever Foundation Degree students are canvassed for their ideas about what play means, the idea that it should be 'fun' is a consistent response.

On the other hand, play theorist, Bob Hughes (2011) tells us this is not always so; play poses dilemmas and challenges for children as they test out physical and mental capabilities. This idea is perhaps more connected with cultural context or social construction identified by Vygotsky, as children inevitably play within the scope of their social matrix and cultural norms. There are times when play may be scary; for some children this could mean jumping off a high wall or pretend games about monsters or witches that become too real. For other children whose experiences have been influenced by trauma such as war or death scary or 'deep' play takes on a whole different meaning. It is how children manage their responses, or 'self-regulate', in the context of their play situations that enables them to learn from and make sense of their experiences.

Stewart (2011: 22) recognises that children learn through all of their experiences and play is just one way this can happen. Through looking at the work of Bruner she considers that 'play may be less a particular behaviour or activity and more a state of mind'. We can see the connection with Katz's ideas about responses or 'habits of mind' children learn to take with them as they engage in different experiences whether planned or freely chosen. There will be times when you provide particular resources or set up an environment in a specific way using learning provocations, or fascination traps, for children. This has elements of the planned and purposeful, as you will base your ideas on observations and assessments of children playing and exploring

Figure 11.3 Socially constructed play between friends
Source: iStock

to extend their learning interests according to what you have found out. At other times children have opportunities to choose more freely whether they play inside or outside, with mud or trucks, in the home corner or cycling a bike. Paying attention to the different ways children choose to engage in the opportunities that come their way; looking for their interests, how curious they are to find things out, how willing they are to have a go, are the essential ingredients for us to understand the significance of this characteristic for effective learning.

Active learning

Again the concept of active learning is not new, both Piaget and Vygotsky understood the value of this characteristic for development. Piaget proposed that children should be able to discover and find things out for themselves in a hands-on, practical way; **assimilating** and **accommodating** new experiences in order to learn (Siraj Blatchford *et al.*, 2002). Vygotsky also understood the value of active involvement in learning in the context of children's social interactions, linked to the development of thought (Gray and MacBlain, 2012). He understood the process of learning as requiring interactive instruction and shared thinking; he claimed that children assimilated knowledge by basing their thinking and actions on 'the understandings of others' (Siraj Blatchford *et al.*, 2002: 34). Social construction recognises that as children gain in knowledge, they gain more control over it. In other words, they come to believe in themselves as cognitive processors (ibid). Self-belief along with concentration and involvement are key identifiers of active learning (Early Education, 2011). Piaget is typically not credited with paying sufficient attention to active learning within social contexts. However, he did in fact argue 'that the child's **intellectual adaptation** was as much an adaptation to the social environment as it was an adaptation to their physical and material environment' (cited in Siraj Blatchford *et al.,* 2002: 32–3).

During the 1970s and 1980s Belgian professor, Ferre Laevers, founded the Experiential Education (EXE) programme, which has involvement and well-being at its heart. Aspects of this model were later incorporated into the Effective Early Learning Project used widely in the UK, elements of which have been subsumed into the Accounting Early for Lifelong Learning or AcE framework (Pascal and Bertram, 1995; CREC, 2014). EXE focuses on how learning feels from the point of view of the learner and specifies that the degree to which children 'feel at ease' because their 'basic needs are satisfied' influences the extent to which they can be properly involved in their learning (Laevers, 2011: 1). Laevers' (1994) view is that deep, lasting learning takes place when children are fully involved with what they are doing. He developed a way of looking for involvement called the Leuven Involvement Scale (LIS). The main premise of his scale is that involvement is a quality available to all (OECD, 2004); from a four-month-old baby playing with her toes to creating a computer motherboard in adulthood. Similarly, involvement does not discriminate in terms of ability, home language or behaviour in the way that pre-determined developmental outcomes can and, all too often, do.

Pascal and Bertram (1995) developed the Child Involvement Scale based on the LIS enabling those who work with children to look for nine signals of involvement. These signals are:

- Concentration
- Energy
- Complexity and creativity
- Facial expression and posture
- Persistence

- Precision
- Reaction time
- Language
- Satisfaction

Figure 11.4 Involvement signals

The observable behaviours of concentration, persistence, energy and involvement are all identifiers of active learning (see above). They are in fact the self-regulated motivations that children use to facilitate their own learning. Stewart (2011: 52) defines these motivations as 'the driving force that propels and maintains interest and engagement towards achieving a goal'. Here it is easy to see the connection with Katz's ideas about 'patterns of behaviour directed toward a broad goal' mentioned earlier in this chapter. Stewart (2011) also identifies the essential nature of protecting and fostering these motivations to learn, recognising that intrinsic motivation, which comes from within, aids self-regulation and purposefulness in children far better than external rewards or consequences, otherwise known as extrinsic motivation. Consider Provocation 2 in order to reflect on practice implications in your setting.

Supporting active learning means giving children opportunities to be **autonomous** and independent, players and explorers; it is about providing experiences for children to investigate, experiment and find things out for themselves. As adults we must take a back seat and relish their 'virtue of not knowing' (Duckworth, 1996: 68). From our perspective it is easy to answer the

PROVOCATION 2

Intrinsic motivation

Think about a typical day in your setting from when children arrive to when they leave.

- Make a list of all the different ways you value children's intrinsic motivations to learn. For instance, acknowledging effort or telling a child's parent about an act of kindness by the child in front of them.
- Now list all the ways you may provide extrinsic motivations in the form of rewards or consequences. For instance, not choosing children who don't put their hand up or giving out stickers for tidying up.
- Which list is longer? If the second list is longer what do you think the reasons are for this?
- Discuss intrinsic and extrinsic motivations with colleagues. Agree a way of auditing this in your setting or with co-workers for a period of two weeks to find out whether your responses are similar or different.

From this small scale practitioner research develop an action plan that challenges everyone to increase by two strategies how they support children's intrinsic motivation and reduce extrinsic motivation, also in two ways.

Agree to discuss what has happened and what you will do next after another two weeks.

question, do up the coat or understand that two plus two makes four. It can be harder by far to be puzzled, patient and excited when we know the action or answer required. In order for them to actively learn, we must empower children to arrive at their own understandings, in their own time or perhaps 'to come honestly to terms with their own ideas' (ibid: 69).

Creating and thinking critically

Ideas, of course, are at the heart of the third characteristic of effective learning. It has been suggested that pre-school children's brains are at least three times more active than those of adults (Gopnik *et al.,* 1999). Creativity, as defined by Craft (2002: 56), is a way of coping with everyday challenges, innate in all humans, because of our ability to use '**possibility thinking**', which helps us to wonder 'what if?' Malaguzzi (1998: 76), the first director of the world-renowned pre-schools of Reggio Emilia, valued creativity as 'a characteristic of thinking, knowing and making choices'. The Development Matters descriptors of creating and thinking critically are both implicit and explicit within the definitions above, and it has long been recognised that for any society to successfully flourish we need people who are possibility thinkers (Whittaker, 2006). Adaptability and flexibility of thought are in fact associated with a country's national and international stability, along with the potential for economic growth (OECD, 2013). Stewart (2011: 78) explains the importance of creative and critical thinking thus: 'Effective learners move beyond unconscious mental processes to become aware of themselves as thinkers and learners, and they learn how to think about things in the most constructive ways.' Stewart (2011) also identifies a difference between creativity, which applies across the breadth and depth of play and learning experiences, and critical thinking. The latter she specifies 'involves rational approaches' to decision-making or evaluating ideas. However, she is clear that for the majority of activities that require problem-solving or choice both qualities are needed. Duckworth (1996: 19) argues that infants are able to make intelligent choices through refining actions and seeking consistencies long before they talk, in other words 'thinking in their actions'. Piaget identified this cognitive way of understanding the world as schemas. He recognised that as very young children explore their world they make connections, initially perhaps by accident (ibid). For instance, a baby reaching out on a blanket accidentally pulls an object resting on it close enough to touch and hold. The satisfaction of grasping the toy helps her to understand that her action had a positive consequence and gives her a purpose to repeat the action. As she refines and develops these skills, perhaps by using a different hand when next near an object beyond her reach, Piaget would argue that a schema has developed for this child (ibid). Athey (1990: 37) furthered this idea by describing schemas as: 'Patterns of repeatable behaviour into which experiences are assimilated and gradually co-ordinated. Co-ordinations lead to higher-level and more powerful schemas'.

This way of children making sense of their world through actions has been described as an organised grouping of knowledge, or constructive memory, about what is known and perhaps it is how creativity and critical thinking begins. Duckworth (1996) distinguishes between what is in children's minds; for instance, ideas, logic, awareness, feelings and what they make explicit through language. She suggests that there are times when the logic or 'rational approach' in children's actions and minds may not necessarily be revealed by the language they use. This is perhaps an especially pertinent point for us in understanding the value of this characteristic for children when English is not their mother tongue or those who have difficulties with speech. Vygotsky proposed that children are born with the foundations of cognitive development in place (Gray & MacBlain, 2012). He saw language as a cultural tool used in social, collaborative activity moving children from lower order thinking; for instance memory and attention, to higher order thinking; such as problem solving and logical reasoning. Age and the influence of societal and cultural norms are critical factors leading to 'cognitive independence, flexibility and freedom' (ibid: 75). Perhaps Vygotsky's idea of independent thought, coupled with flexibility and freedom, are useful ways to help us reflect on what creative and critical thinking really means for children.

Meaningful interactions as the basis for promoting sustained shared thinking

The previous discussions in this chapter have focused on the different characteristics children may use in their approach to learning. These happen everywhere; at home, at pre-school and nursery or in the park; with siblings, parents, friends and, of course, key people in a child's early years setting. Researchers into early years pedagogy first coined the phrase 'sustained shared thinking', while the Effective Provision of Pre-school Education research (EPPE) identified this as an aspect of practice that impacted positively on children's learning opportunities (Siraj-Blatchford *et al.,* 2002; Sylva *et al.,* 2004a). Put more simply, it is 'the sharing of thinking', which recognises the *'particularly sustained nature of some of these interactions'* (Siraj-Blatchford, 2009: 1).

Figure 11.5 Pretend play as the basis for a joint involvement episode.
Source: iStock

Interactions are at the root of Vygotsky's ideas about how children learn and he identified language as the most significant cultural tool at their disposal. He especially believed that through 'talking and listening to others, children develop and extend their own understanding' (cited in MacBlain, 2014: 46). In other words, it is through their conversations with other people that children learn the most. Sustained shared thinking is also inextricably linked to Vygotsky's concept of the **zone of proximal development** (ZPD). His idea here was that all children had an actual level of development and the potential for more. The ZPD is how children can, with enabling and knowledgeable support, consolidate and develop their ideas or skills in order to progress to a new level of understanding, and language is central to how this happens (ibid).

Jerome Bruner, a key theorist in the fields of education and psychology, also sees language as an essential tool for learning. He recognises that by using language children can engage in 'problem solving and critical reflection, both of which are fundamental to higher order thinking' (cited in Gray and MacBlain, 2012: 110). It is possible to see connections with characteristics of effective learning here and recognise the flexibility and freedom of thought that Vygotsky viewed as pivotal for learning. Bruner also understands the value of enabling support or 'scaffolding' that helps children arrive at a new understanding or achieve something that they could not do alone; he specifies the relevance of '**joint involvement** episodes' for children's learning (Gray and MacBlain, 2012; Siraj Blatchford *et al.*, 2002). Entering into a joint involvement episode with children, one that helps them to think, to problem-solve or try a new way of doing something, is a key part of your role as an early years practitioner. This can also be recognised within sustained shared thinking, which Sylva *et al.* (2004b: iv) explain in this way:

> An episode in which two or more individuals 'work together' in an intellectual way to solve a problem, clarify a concept, evaluate activities, extend a narrative, etc. Both parties must contribute to the thinking and it must develop and extend the understanding.

Some examples of verbal pedagogical strategies to share and sustain thinking with children:

- Tuning-in
- Genuine interest
- Inviting children to elaborate
- Recapping
- Offering own experience
- Clarifying children's ideas
- Offering suggestions

- Reminding
- Using encouragement to further thinking
- Offering alternate view
- Speculating
- Reciprocating
- Open questions
- Modelling thinking

(Sylva *et al.*, 2004a)

Figure 11.6 Sustained shared thinking

In order for positive learning dispositions and emergent thinking, or perhaps as we should call them now, characteristics of effective learning, to develop, various supportive verbal pedagogical practices have been clearly identified. These include modelling language, values and practices with children through sensitive questioning, discussion, interaction, encouragement and reinforcement identified in Figure 11.6 above. As the previous quotation suggests, sustained shared thinking is about how a practitioner and a child can become immersed in a process of deliberation or reflection, aided by dialogue. Undertake the Reflective Practice task below to enable you to see connections between different pedagogical strategies and consider the implications for your practice.

REFLECTIVE PRACTICE

4: Connecting different perspectives

Compare and contrast sustained shared thinking with companionable learning (from the Research into Practice box earlier in this chapter). Think especially about the differences between verbal and pre-verbal children.

CASE STUDY 1

Sustained shared thinking

Read through the case study and respond to the questions at the end.

Two-and-a-half-year-old Joe was being cared for by his mother's friend, Jane, an early year's practitioner. He had arrived at Jane's house via the drive and back door, one he did not normally use when visiting her home with his parents. Jane and Joe were involved in digging in the front garden where the front door that Joe usually used was clearly observable. Joe stopped digging and began paying close attention to the front of the house, a semi-detached cottage. Joe lived in a detached house. Noticing his thinking Jane starts a conversation:

Jane: What are you thinking about Joe? (*A pause while he continues studying the houses.*)

Joe: So – you got three doors on your house Jane?

Jane: Why do you think we have three doors Joe? (*Joe points to the two doors he can see and turns his head to the pathway leading to the back garden.*)

Jane: (*realising that Joe was adding on their neighbour's door to the front door he could see as well as the remembered back door*) The green door there (*pointing*) doesn't go into our house, it goes into our neighbour's house. (*A pause . . . Joe continues looking at the front of the cottages.*)

Joe: So that's not your door (*pointing at the neighbour's green door*)

Jane: That's right Joe, the green door goes into our neighbour's house. Which one do you think is our door?

Joe: (*pointing*) So that's your door, the blue one?

Jane: Yes, that's our front door. The blue one. (*A pause while Joe thinks a little more.*)

Joe: So, their house is 'stucked' on your house then.

- Which of the strategies from the box above has Jane used?
- What does this discussion tell you about Joe's thinking as well as his mathematical aptitude?
- Identify three ways you could extend his thinking.

Through conversations children can be supported to ponder, speculate and plan as well as consider what worked and what they might do differently in the future. It is perhaps sensible to recognise '**metacognition**' here, or how children are encouraged to think about their own thinking, and the importance of supportive interactions that raise children's own consciousness about how they think. Dowling (2013) recognises this point and links it with how children control and direct their thinking, and learn to self-regulate. With this in mind, we come full circle back to Tickell's idea at the start of this chapter that self-regulation is essential if children are to engage successfully, and learn from their play opportunities. If we follow the thread of ideas through this chapter it would appear that how children approach their learning cannot be separated from how we approach them. Watching and **listening to children** will provide you with insights into their thinking, and help you recognise when and how children understand the world differently or in a similar way to you. You will be surprised at how much you can learn from children; having proper conversations and paying close attention allows you to hear their ideas, this can let you know when verbal or physical scaffolding is needed or when just to stand back and be amazed.

> The more we help children to have their wonderful ideas and to feel good about themselves for having them, the more likely it is that they will some day happen upon wonderful ideas that no one else has happened upon before.
>
> (Duckworth, 1996: 14)

Conclusion

There is so much more that could be written about how children learn and the many ways that theorists and educationalists have chosen to look at learning and how these are influenced by, and interconnected, with one another. This chapter has very deliberately considered established, proven, perhaps 'old' theories and ideas about young children's approach to their learning and linked these with how the characteristics of effective learning should be reflected upon and valued within practice today. The pedagogical quality of sustained shared thinking has been linked to socio-constructivist learning, recognising that high quality verbal exchanges with children will empower them as expert thinkers. How children approach their learning; their typical characteristics and ways of thinking are not new concepts. They provide the foundations for everything else that happens in children's lives including their academic success and life chances; they are too fundamental, too important to ignore. If we pay less attention to the 'how' of learning because we are focusing too much on the 'what', as the emphasis on outcomes or testing knowledge leads us to believe, we are doing a huge disservice to children now, and to all our futures.

Relish children's ideas, questions, attempts, deliberations and dilemmas. Recognise that by valuing and encouraging them to be people who can help themselves and others, in terms of their attitudes, actions and thinking you are enabling them to see themselves as people who *can* do things. It is essential to appreciate the uniqueness of how this may happen for individual children you work with and critical to understand that early dispositions become lifelong habits of mind. For their own success as well as the common good, children should be empowered to develop a positive and effective approach that becomes characteristic, both for learning and to life.

Further reading

Duckworth, E. (1996) *'The Having of Wonderful Ideas' and Other Essays on Teaching and Learning*, New York: Teachers College Press.
This book provides insightful views into Piaget's ideas and helps you to consider why your responses are pivotal to how children learn. This book is written as a series of essays so you dip in and out at will.

Gray, C. and MacBlain, S. (2012) *Learning Theories in Childhood*, London: Sage.
This text will easily help you get to grips with key theorists and learning theories.

Stewart, N. (2011) *How Children Learn: The Characteristics of Effective Learning*, London: The British Association for Early Childhood Education.
Written to support Development Matters, the author of this book advised the review of the Early Years Foundation Stage. Characteristics of effective learning are interrogated in depth and detail.

Useful websites

www.early-education.org.uk/development-matters

Early Education: The British Association for Early Childhood Education, *Development Matters* [online]
This links you to Development Matters (DM) guidance where the characteristics of effective learning are described in context of the Early Years Foundation Stage as well as other useful links to Nancy Stewart's book and a page explaining the currency of DM.

http://eprints.ioe.ac.uk/6091/1/Siraj-Blatchford2009Conceptualising77.pdf

Siraj-Blatchford, I. (2009) 'Conceptualising progression in the pedagogy of play and sustained shared thinking in early childhood education: A Vygotskian perspective', in *Educational and Child Psychology*, Volume 26, No. 2 [online]
This will help you better understand the value and practices of sustained shared thinking from a primary source.

www.educate.ece.govt.nz/learning/exploringPractice/EducationalLeadership/LeadingProgrammes/
Environment/LearningDispositions.aspx

NZ Ministry of Education: ECE Educate, *Learning Dispositions* [online]
Here you can read more about the value of learning dispositions, which this chapter identifies as closely aligned to characteristics of effective learning. There is also a link to characteristics of effective practice, which is interesting.

www.thinkingschoolsinternational.com/thinking-resources/thinking-tools/dispositions/

Thinking Schools International, *Learning Dispositions* [online]
Here you can watch short film clips in which American educational consultants discuss habits of mind, critical thinking and metacognition. There are links to some free resources that will help you think about thinking.

References

Athey, C. (1990) *Extending Thought in Young Children*, London: Paul Chapman Publishing.

Carr, M. (2001) *Assessment in Early Childhood Settings: Learning Stories*, London: Paul Chapman Publishing.

Claxton, G. and Carr, M. (2004) 'A framework for teaching learning: the dynamics of disposition', in *Early Years: An International Journal of Research and Development*, Volume 24, Number 1, pp. 87–96.

Craft, A. (2002) *Creativity and Early Years Education: A Lifewide Foundation*, London & New York: Continuum.

CREC (Centre for Research in Early Childhood) (2014) Accounting Early for Lifelong Learning (AcE) [online]. Available from www.crec.co.uk/AcE-accounting-early-for-lifelong-learning [Accessed 1/3/2014].

DfE (Department for Education) (2013) *Statutory Framework for the Early Years Foundation Stage: Setting the standards for learning, development and care for children from birth to five*, Runcorn: Department for Education.

Dowling, M. (2013) *Young Children's Thinking*, London: Sage.

Duckworth, E. (1996) *'The Having of Wonderful Ideas' and Other Essays on Teaching and Learning*, New York: Teachers College Press.

Dweck, C. (2006) *Mindset: The New Psychology of Success*, London: Random House.

Early Education (2011) *Development Matters*, London: The British Association for Early Childhood Education.

Gopnik, A., Meltzoff, A. and Kuhl, P. (1999) *How Babies Think*, London: Phoenix.

Gray, C. and MacBlain, S. (2012) *Learning Theories in Childhood,* London: Sage.

Howard, J. and McInnes, K. (2010) 'Thinking through the challenge of a play-based curriculum: Increasing playfulness via co-construction', in Moyles, J. (ed.) *Thinking about Play: Developing a Reflective Approach,* Maidenhead: Open University Press.

Hughes, B. (2011) *Evolutionary Playwork* (2nd edn), Abingdon: Routledge.

Katz, L. (1993) *Dispositions: Definitions and Implications for Early Childhood Practices*, Washington DC: ERIC Clearinghouse on Elementary and Early Childhood Education.

Laevers, F. (2011) *Experiential Education: Making Care and Education: More Effective Through Well-Being and Involvement* [online] Available from www.oecd.org/dataoecd/23/36/31672150.pdf [Accessed 1/3/2014].

Laevers, F. (1994) 'The innovative project Experiential Education and the definition of quality in education', in Laevers, F. (ed.) *Defining and Assessing Quality in Early Childhood Education*, Belgium: Laevers University Press.

MacBlain, S. (2014) *How Children Learn,* London: Sage.

Malaguzzi, L. (1998) 'History, Ideas and Basic Philosophy: An Interview with Lella Gandini', in Edwards, C., Gandini, L. and Forman, G. (eds) *The Hundred Languages of Children; The Reggio Emilia Approach: Advanced Reflections,* Connecticut & London: Ablex Publishing.

McDermott, P., Rikoon, S., Waterman, C. and Fantuzzo, J. (2012) 'The Preschool Learning Behaviours Scale: Dimensionality and External Validity in Head Start', in *School Psychology Review*, Volume 41, No. 1, pp. 66–81.

OECD (Organisation for Economic Cooperation and Development (2013) *PISA 2012 Results: Ready to Learn: Students' Engagement, Drive and Self-Beliefs (Volume III),* [online] Pisa, OECD Publishing Available from http://dx.doi.org/10.1787/9789264201170-en [Accessed on 2/4/14].

OECD (Organisation for Economic Cooperation and Development) (2004) *Starting Strong: Curricula and Pedagogies in Early Childhood Education and Care: Five Curriculum Outcomes;* Paris: OECD Publishing.

Pascal, C. and Bertram, T. (1995) '"Involvement" and the Effective Early Learning Project: a Collaborative Venture', in Laevers, F. (ed.) *An Exploration of the Concept of 'Involvement' as an Indicator of the Quality of Early Childhood Care and Education.* Dundee: CIDREE Report, Volume 10, pp. 25–38.

Roberts, R. (2010) *Wellbeing from Birth*, London: Sage.

Roberts, R. (2014) *The Role of the Adult as a Companion in Learning.* [Power Point Slides]. Presented for ECHO: The Voice of Early Childhood Seminar at Bristol University Graduate School, 4 October 2014.

Siraj-Blatchford, I. (2009) 'Conceptualising progression in the pedagogy of play and sustained shared thinking in early childhood education: A Vygotskian perspective', in *Educational and Child Psychology*, Volume 26, No. 2 [online] Available from http://eprints.ioe.ac.uk/6091/1/Siraq-Blatchford2009Conceptualising77.pdf [Accessed on 9/3/2014].

Siraj-Blatchford, I., Sylva, K., Muttock, S., Gilden, R. and Bell, D. (2002) *Researching Effective Pedagogy in the Early Years (REPEY)*, Nottingham: DfES.

Skills Active (2005) *The Pocket Guide to Playwork,* [online] Available from www.playboard.org/Uploads/document/290620110857-1455693788.pdf [Accessed on 21/2/2014].

Stewart, N. (2011) *How Children Learn: The Characteristics of Effective Learning*, London: The British Association for Early Childhood Education.

Sylva, K., Melhuish, E., Sammons, P., Siraj-Blatchford, I., Taggart, B. and Elliot, K. (2004a) *The Effective Provision of Pre-School (EPPE) Project; Findings from the Early Primary Years,* Nottingham: DfES Publications.

Sylva, K., Melhuish, E., Sammons, P., Siraj-Blatchford, I. and Taggart, B. (2004b) *The Effective Provision of Pre-School (EPPE): Final Report,* London; DfES and Institute of Education, University of London.

Tickell, C. (2011) *The Early Years: Foundations for life, health and learning: An Independent Report on the Early Years Foundation Stage to her Majesty's Government,* Department for Education.

Whittaker, S. (2006) (Director, Imperial Oil) A New Statesman Round Table – The role of private-sector business, *Educating for Creativity;* [online] Available from http://asp.readspeaker.net/cgibin/new statesmanrsone?customerid=1003373&lang=en&url [Accessed on 29/10/06].

12 Holistic development: children's creativity

Dianne Solly

LEARNING OUTCOMES

After reading this chapter you will have increased your understanding of the factors which contribute to the development of children's creativity. You will:

✔ have considered the meaning of creativity and why it is important
✔ understand the need to provide a physical and emotional environment which encourages children to explore and investigate
✔ be familiar with the role of practitioners in supporting children's creativity
✔ appreciate the need to involve parents in their children's creative development
✔ be able to reflect on your own practice and consider ways in which you can implement changes based on your learning.

Introduction

Supporting young children's creativity has become increasingly significant in early years practice during recent years. This chapter outlines some of the ways in which practitioners can provide an environment where children can investigate and begin to understand aspects of their world through first-hand experiences. In order to develop children's creativity, practitioners themselves need to think creatively. The chapter will consider the roles of adults in fostering children's enquiries, encouraging risk taking and co-constructing possible ways forward. Throughout, there are references to the Reggio Emilia approach and its influence on the Early Years Foundation Stage (EYFS) (2014).

Many people believe creativity is only associated with the arts; that is, art, music, dance and drama. This is not so. Creativity has a much wider scope. We are all creative in some form or another on a daily basis. This may be evident, for example, when choosing colours to decorate a room, arranging furniture in a particular way, decorating a cake or combining items of clothing to make a complete outfit. What is important to remember is that we will all make different choices and this individuality should be recognised and encouraged. Pre-schools in Northern Italy which follow the Reggio Emilia approach are renowned for encouraging children's creativity and believe that children have '100 languages and more' with which to express themselves. The founder of the approach, Loris Malaguzzi, believed that giving children the freedom to represent their ideas in whatever form they choose (for example, dance, paint, clay, written or spoken word to name but a few) would result in them becoming powerful and competent learners, willing to share ideas and learn from each other. Practitioners' recording of observations of children also take a number of forms such as videos, photographs or written transcripts, as the child's thinking may be represented through a dance or mime. The influence of Reggio can be seen in current Early Years practice in the UK as the EYFS states that adults should 'provide children with opportunities to use their skills and explore concepts and ideas through their representations' (EYFS, 2014: 46). This culminates in their achievement of the Early Learning Goal (ELG) 'children use what they have learnt . . . in original ways . . . representing their own ideas, thoughts and feelings' (EYFS, 2014: 46). When working with young children, adults must be aware of the range of expressions available.

Creativity is relevant in all areas of learning. This is particularly true in early years as young children do not have subject boundaries and are continually faced with situations which require them to think of possible ways to solve a problem. The National Advisory Committee for Creative and Cultural Education (NACCCE) which produced the report 'All Our Futures' (1999), believed that everyone has the capacity to be creative and that all learning involves aspects of creativity. Creativity involves a number of processes, some of which happen unconsciously and some of which are the result of determined efforts. Imagination is an essential element as implied by Robinson (NACCCE, 1999: 30) whose definition of creativity is 'imaginative activity fashioned so as to produce outcomes that are both original and of value'. The work of Csikszentmihalyi centres around children being in flow, fully engrossed in their play and thus also demonstrating creative thinking. It is important to remember when considering this thought process in young children, that although someone else may have created something similar previously, the thinking is 'new' for each individual at that time.

REFLECTIVE PRACTICE

When did you last draw on your own creativity? Jot down your current thoughts on what constitutes creativity and attempt to write a definition of what the term means to you. Share your ideas/reflections with colleagues. Do they see creativity in the same way that you do?

Why is creativity important?

Since 1999, the government has introduced a number of policies promoting a creative approach to education. The QCA/DfEE (2000: 118) stated that creativity 'begins with curiosity and involves children in exploration and experimentation . . . they draw upon their imagination and originality'. This was further developed with the introduction of the Early Years Foundation Stage (EYFS) (DfE, 2007) which emphasised that play-based learning provided endless opportunities for children to demonstrate creativity and critical thinking. However, the revised Early Years Foundation Stage (EYFS) (DfE, 2012, 2014) further emphasised the importance of encouraging children's creativity by naming 'creating and thinking critically' as one of the three characteristics of effective learning. The area of learning previously named 'Creative Development' was replaced by 'Expressive Arts and Design', which, although it includes guidance about exploration of media and materials, also highlights the need for children to be imaginative. The intention is now extremely clear – opportunities for children to think creatively should always be available and permeate all aspects of their learning. Research into brain development has shown that more connections and synapses are made in the first years of life than at any other time. If these connections are not made the synapses will fade, this being one of the reasons why enabling children to think creatively is particularly important in early years.

As adults we find some activities we undertake more challenging than others, but we have a number of skills and attributes which support us through the tasks. Not having the appropriate skills or attributes may cause us to give up when not being successful. Hence the need for adults to interact with children, supporting them in whatever way is necessary to take them to the next stage in their learning. In a creative environment with creative adults, young children can develop self-confidence, increased self-esteem and positive learning dispositions alongside skills. Successful learning is more than memorising information; a key factor to achievement depends on the presence of motivation, particularly intrinsic motivation. It is often said that young children have a very short concentration span, but when children are self-motivated they can remain focused for much longer.

Children need to be 'active learners' from birth if they are to grow into confident, motivated, imaginative adults. Children are innately curious and it is essential that adults build on this and encourage children to be inquisitive. It is thought that young children who display an eagerness to learn and positive approaches to challenges are more likely to retain this in adulthood (Lai, 2011). Through allowing children to take an active part in their learning, adults are giving them opportunities to do this.

All creative thinking involves **engagement** with the thinking of others, whether this is an adult or a child. Dialogue between children and adults not only encourages communication skills, but also enables children to see things from a different perspective and perhaps try something which they may not have thought of themselves. There are times when a child will benefit from learning alone but there are many advantages to collaborative learning. I have often observed children working as a pair on a project and the opportunity to ask for someone's help or suggestions when unsure, has ensured that the task has been continued rather than being abandoned when a solution was not immediately apparent.

In a changing world it is essential that we develop individuals who are capable of thinking differently and a creative approach will promote this. When faced with a problem the confident child will face the task eagerly, seeing it as a challenge to be overcome rather than something to ignore; these children are said to have a growth mindset. However, less confident children avoid such challenges because they feel they do not have the ability to solve them and are said to have a fixed mindset. Dweck (2008) attributes some of the reasoning for fixed mindsets to children's interpretation of an adult's praise. If children have been praised for completing relatively simple tasks then they want to repeat this and will only attempt tasks which they know they can complete successfully. However, the child with a growth mindset will want to attempt more difficult challenges seeing these as an opportunity to try out different strategies, confident that if they approach the task positively they will find a solution. They also realise that there is quite often not just a single right answer but a number of solutions and that the process they have undergone is more important than the end product. These children are also demonstrating the attributes of Claxton's 4Rs, namely resilience, resourcefulness, reflectiveness and reciprocity. Claxton (2010) believes in building children's learning power (BLP), concentrating on developing the skills, attitudes and dispositions which will prepare the child for the future.

The Researching Effective Pedagogy in the Early Years project (REPEY) (Siraj-Blatchford *et al.*, 2002) identified child-initiated play as the most effective form of learning in young children. Chapter 13 looks in detail at the different types of play which children engage in. When following their interests children will not only spend a longer time focused on an activity, but will concentrate more fully. Laevers (2005) has researched the effect of children's well-being on their development and learning and believes that children who feel comfortable in their surroundings will be more open to learning. If children feel 'like a fish in water', then learning will be at a deeper level. Laevers' scale of involvement (2005) is used in many settings. It is a way of identifying in a very short observation whether the child is really involved in an activity, or simply carrying it out with little or no interest and thus, limited concentration and probably no learning.

Csikszentmihalyi (2002) refers to individuals being 'in flow', that is, so immersed in an activity that nothing will distract them. Children can often be seen doing the seemingly boring, laborious task of filling and emptying a container with sand or water but this is what Csikszentmihalyi believes to be a rewarding experience in itself. An important aspect of creative practice is the provision of times such as these when the mind can be free to wander and imagine without the need for a goal. Through these and similar repeated experiences children begin to explore and extend their understanding of different objects and materials. They are also demonstrating aspects of 'flow', engagement, absorption, concentration and, again, their learning will be at a deeper level. Remember enjoyment is important too. Children are more likely to maintain the enthusiasm and motivation for learning if they are enjoying the experience.

REFLECTIVE PRACTICE

Research Claxton's thoughts on Building Learning Power (BLP) in more depth and consider his ideas on what makes a good learner. Now consider what *you* believe are the essential qualities, skills and dispositions which will help children to become successful learners.

How can practitioners support children's creativity?

Children are active constructors of their world and have a drive to be creative, which should be nurtured and developed. However, it is possible that inexperienced adults could inadvertently diminish rather than extend this quality in young children. Adults can support children's developing creativity in two ways, first by creating a *physical* environment which allows, promotes and extends creativity as well as a secure *emotional* environment in which children can take risks. The second, equally important role of the adult, is as a trusted friend with whom to share discoveries or difficulties.

Creating the environment for creativity

Children learn through play and being actively involved in their learning. Therefore creating an environment conducive to exploration and investigation is an essential part of the adult role in early years' settings. Babies are ready to begin their journey of discovery from the moment of birth, hence the introduction of **'heuristic' play** (from the Greek word to discover). Babies and very young children enjoy handling objects and will be curious to find out what they can do with each, especially as some objects will produce interesting sounds on touching each other. Whatever the age of the child, they will repeat their actions hoping for similar results, while also developing cognitive and physical skills. As mentioned earlier, it is during the first years of life that the brain develops at an incredible rate and requires stimulation from the environment and people to ensure this. Loughton and Teather (2010: 47) believe that **childhood** play 'creates a brain that has greater behavioural flexibility and improved potential for later learning', so it is extremely important that practitioners ensure an appropriate environment for play is provided.

The environment is extremely important in Reggio Emilia and is often referred to as 'the third teacher'. Adults believe that the surroundings should be aesthetically pleasing and resources attractively arranged as well as accessible. Every space is considered carefully with places planned for communication as well as privacy, and outdoor learning is encouraged so that the children begin to make connections with nature.

Creativity is central to learning experiences in Reggio Emilia. Rather than providing a large range of toys for children to play with, adults prefer the children to have access to more open-ended resources, many of them natural objects such as wood, leaves and shells, thus inviting them to explore, imagine and create. This idea has been adopted by settings in the UK so that children have similar opportunities to be creative, with few or no restrictions. Anna Craft suggests that children should not be asking the questions 'What is this?' and 'What does it do?' but, rather, 'What can I do with this?' (Craft, 2007). Craft's notion of 'possibility thinking' changes the emphasis from children simply gathering information to one which enables the child to take full control of his/her learning as begun during heuristic play sessions. There will be successes and failures but if children are aware that failure is part of the learning process, they are more likely to persevere and look for other 'possibilities'. Providing children with a range of interesting resources will stimulate new ideas and be the starting point for new creations and different ways of working or looking at things. Bruce (2011) supports this, believing that creativity develops from our previous experiences and that children will develop their own form of creative expression given the time and opportunity.

An important factor in developing children's creativity is the balance between structure and freedom. In the past it was common to see tables set out with specific resources as the activities for the session had been decided upon by the adults with no child involvement. Different coloured papers, pencils and templates were placed for the children to use, the templates ensuring (or almost), that the elephant looked like an elephant and the triangle had three sides. We have all witnessed the mass production of the Christmas card or calendar where children simply reproduce the example created by the adult, often by sticking pre-cut shapes on pre-folded card. This situation has almost disappeared as adults have begun to appreciate that this kind of activity does not encourage children to be creative. Compare this with a situation where an activity has evolved naturally from a child's interest and the adult has listened closely to the child's ideas before working together on the task. The child has the perfect opportunity to be creative in whatever way he chooses.

However, there are children for whom too much choice can be overwhelming and it may be appropriate for them to be initially supported by an adult with a limited number of materials. Once the child feels confident in his/her ability to make decisions and choices independently, the support or scaffolding can be removed. Enabling children to feel confident when working in this way is dependent upon the emotional environment of the setting. The physical environment has been prepared carefully but the relationships between adults and children take a much longer period of time to develop. Close observations of individual children will provide adults with information about children's approaches to learning and this in turn will contribute to the amount and type of interaction that would be appropriate at a particular time. Chapter 26 will further examine the subject of observing children. Bayley (2008: 45) believes that 'if we want children to become creative thinkers we must support them to take risks, tolerate uncertainty and persevere'. Part of the reason for developing a safe environment and a secure relationship with children is to promote the risk-taking necessary when involved in experimentation. If uncertainty is introduced as an expected part of exploration children will be more likely to persevere, trying alternative ways to solve the problem. Praising children's efforts (rather than the end result) and showing their attempts are valued throughout the process, will enable children to feel comfortable in taking risks in the future. If a child has experienced negative responses then he/she will naturally shy away from attempting anything new.

REFLECTIVE PRACTICE

REFLECTIVE PRACTICE

Think back to the early part of the chapter when the importance of creativity was discussed and consider how you are going to provide the opportunities for children to develop the numerous skills and attributes necessary in today's world.

- What do you believe to be essential constituents of the environment, both indoors and outdoors?
- Together with colleagues at your setting, step back and look through the child's eyes at what is on offer? What do you see?

The adult role in developing children's creativity

According to NACCCE (1999), the adult role is to recognise children's creative possibilities and to provide the conditions for them to be realised. To be successful in promoting creativity in children, I believe it is essential for adults to have the same attitudes and dispositions as those required by the children with whom they are working, for example, curiosity, imagination, flexibility, enthusiasm and willingness to try new things. These will enable the adult to 'put themselves in the children's shoes' and feel the uncertainty, the risks involved and the unease that these bring.

Robson (2006) believes the creative process can be broken down into four stages: familiarisation, incubation, insight and verification, and an adult may choose to become involved at any one of these stages depending on the confidence and security of the child in question. Children spend much of their time at nursery or pre-school choosing their own activities and using the environment within which they find themselves, whether indoors or outdoors. They choose their own equipment, they decide whether they want to work alone or with a friend, and eventually they decide when to end the chosen activity. All of these decisions allow the child to remain in control of their learning and to place it into contexts which are meaningful to them. Duffy's (2006) definition of creativity, 'connecting the unconnected in ways that are meaningful to the individual', being relevant here. Children do not see the world in the same way as adults and it is extremely important that the starting point for supporting and extending learning is based around the child's current achievements and interests. A child may not have a definite goal in mind when beginning an activity but be content to experiment and see what evolves. The child is not placing any limits on the learning but simply following an original idea to satisfy his/her curiosity. Encouraging children's efforts will be the incentive needed for them to continue.

When thinking about developing children as creative learners, we have to consider and value the different ways that children approach their learning. Lucas (2000: 44) states that 'an understanding of how we learn to learn . . . will be the means of unlocking the creative potential within us all'. It is essential that adults are fully aware of the child's capabilities in order to gauge the moment for interaction or intervention. I distinguish between interaction and intervention as there are times when an intervention is necessary, for example, when demonstrating a particular skill such as holding scissors correctly for cutting, or how to move the handlebars to steer a tricycle. The interactions must show the adult's interest in and appreciation of the child's activity. **Listening to children** enables the adult to become involved in a learning conversation where each person's contributions are important and valued.

As important as the exchanges are the 'spaces for thought'. An experienced practitioner understands this and will allow time for children to consider the questions posed rather than expecting an instant response. The co-construction of ideas continues, the adult carefully showing their appreciation of the child's opinions and ideas and working with the child to find a range of possible solutions to any problems which have arisen. The experienced adult will be well aware of how to support children through open-ended questioning, more often than not responding to one question with another one, promoting and extending critical thinking. Chapter 14 will consider many aspects of the adult role in extending children's thinking skills. This emphasis on adult and child constructing ideas and moving forward by experimenting together is a key part of the Reggio Emilia approach and has had a strong influence on EYFS practice. Jeffery and Craft's (2004) research also suggests that children and adults working closely together in **co-participation** is an effective strategy in fostering children's creativity.

Adults should not take over the child's explorations and experimentations or guide them in a specific direction, but observe the child closely, identifying the most appropriate time and way in which to interact with the child. The interest the adult shows will often affect whether a child continues with the task or not.

CASE STUDY 1

Read the following observation of a 4-year-old child and consider the following questions.

1   Is the child being an 'active' learner?
2   What other characteristics of effective learning are evident?
3   Is the child demonstrating aspects of creativity?

JP is working independently in the creative area. He is collecting an assortment of materials which includes two sticks, a large square sheet of paper, a pair of scissors and some string. He makes the sticks into a cross and puts them on the paper. He cuts a piece of Sellotape using the dispenser and uses it to secure the sticks to the paper. He appears to be making a kite. The sticks move but he rearranges them and adds another piece of Sellotape. He does this once more. JP goes to collect some felt-tipped pens and draws a face on the paper. He tries to cut a piece of string but is unsuccessful. He pulls at the string which falls to the floor and unwinds. He picks it up and tries again but cannot manage to cut the string. He looks around and watches other children for a while. He goes to the scrap box and finds a piece of tissue paper. He begins to tear a sliver from the edge but it tears quite quickly and he has to try again. He attaches the short length of tissue paper to the bottom of the kite with Sellotape and takes it outside.

JP used his knowledge of the parts of a kite to support him when making his own. The activity arose out of a personal interest which enabled him to maintain concentration during the activity except for a slight pause when he observed other children. He obviously faced a challenge when he could not cut the string he intended to use but showed persistence as he made another attempt to do this. In order to complete the kite JP needed to adapt his original idea and find an alternative to the string for the tail. He demonstrated the ability to make choices regarding materials and appeared organised at the beginning of the activity. JP did not seek help from an adult or peer but this may not have been the situation had he not been satisfied that the tissue paper tail would suffice.

What next?
The child in the observation demonstrated a number of positive dispositions (flexibility, originality, inventiveness, self-determination and independence). Alongside these there is also a strong sense of personal achievement. What would you do now to support and extend JP's learning?

During the last century adults working with young children had a caring role, their main concern being to ensure that the children's physical needs were met. However, the role has changed considerably as theorists have realised the importance of early brain stimulation and other factors which have an effect on later learning. Government reports and research have shown that well–qualified staff and their commitment to **continuing professional development** have a huge effect on the quality of children's learning. It is essential therefore that we reflect on and adapt our practice regularly to ensure we offer children the opportunities needed to think creatively.

PROVOCATION

'There is no creativity in the child if there is no creativity in the adult: the competent and creative child exists if there is a competent and creative adult' (Rinaldi, 2006: 120).

Do you agree?

Involving parents in children's creative development

Parental involvement in their children's education is a requirement of the revised EYFS (2014). This chapter has considered the environment and adult support that is provided for young children in their settings but it must be remembered that parents too have a powerful effect on children's learning. Research (DfE/ DoH, 2011) has shown that the home environment has more influence on future achievement than innate ability or the quality of pre-school provision. The Reggio Emilia approach recognises the important role that parents play in their children's education and values their contributions highly.

Many parents in the UK feel their role in a child's education is to prepare them for the 'real' learning which they believe begins at school. They do this by encouraging them to write their name, read word for word from story books or keep within the lines provided in colouring books. This is of course, exactly the opposite of what we are aiming for when encouraging children to be creative. Where are the opportunities for really expressing yourself through making patterns in sand or other substances, becoming an author by using pictures or puppets to create an exciting story of your own, or using play dough or clay to invent your own shapes and forms? Gardening and cooking are perfect opportunities to let children explore and discover but may be in danger of too much adult intervention. Parents (and I do not include all in this) need help in seeing the potential learning from these and many other child-initiated activities and to become familiar with how they can support, not lead, in a similar way to practitioners. You may wish to have a conversation with colleagues to consider ways in which you currently work with parents and to identify new ideas you could implement.

What are the challenges to working creatively?

Time is often considered to be a barrier to working creatively, but as adults responsible for organising the structure of the day we should not let this be the case. A sustained engagement with an activity is more effective than a succession of short bursts, but adult constraints inevitably impose limits upon children's play. Imagine how frustrated we would feel if we had just collected a large number of components required for an idea we had, only to hear that it is now time to tidy everything away. Children need time to assimilate ideas, to think things through and to have several attempts if things do not immediately work as planned. Consideration of time is therefore an important aspect of the adult role when organising the day.

Space is also often listed as a barrier to learning and I am sure even the practitioner with access to a large indoor and outdoor area would always ask for more. Following the earlier discussion on preparing the environment I would urge you to consider whether full use is being made of the space available to you and your colleagues, or if there are changes which could be made which would offer a more enabling environment where opportunities for creativity could be enhanced.

The range of resources varies enormously from one setting to another and sometimes practitioners feel they cannot be creative as they do not have enough resources. I have even heard practitioners comment that they do not have the 'right' resources although I am unsure what these are. Resources do not have to be costly items selected from a glossy catalogue and many settings are appreciating their visits to local recycling centres. Here practitioners can gather huge amounts of reclaimed materials (at a minimal cost per year) which are perfect for children's investigative play and inventions.

It may be that you are working with practitioners who are reluctant to change their way of working as they feel more confident in leading children's activities as they have done previously. Allowing children to take more control of their learning does not feel comfortable to some as it is outside their experience and they are not aware of the benefits of this approach.

REFLECTIVE PRACTICE

- Do you feel confident that you are able to distinguish between creative practice and practice which fosters creativity?
- Are there practitioners in your team who have a negative attitude to change and are unwilling to become a little more creative themselves?
- How will you encourage these practitioners to embrace the notion of supporting children's creativity in the ways discussed throughout the chapter?
- Is continuing professional development recognised as important in your setting?

Completing the table below may help you to identify the challenges in your setting. Discussions with colleagues will then enable you to think of ways to resolve these.

Challenge	Possible solution

As with anything new which may challenge some individuals, it is important to approach the issue carefully and to discuss concerns as a team. In this way, everyone has the opportunity to share their thoughts and work together to find a solution. Introducing change gradually is always more effective than a complete overhaul. The outcomes and benefits to the children should be discussed within the team regularly and should also lead to further successful changes.

Although some of these barriers may be difficult to overcome at times, they are not insurmountable and the determined practitioner will find solutions.

FROM RESEARCH TO PRACTICE

Research into brain development has shown that babies' brains appear to grow in response to creative environments, particularly between birth and 3 years. Babies use their experiences to see patterns and make links as they make sense of their world, thus it is extremely important that parents and practitioners provide the opportunities to do this. You may like to read the following article by Ruth Churchill Dower (July 2013)

Early Arts – Nurturing Children's Creativity. Where is the social, emotional and brain science behind our early education? Available at: www.earlyarts.co.uk

Conclusion

Learning is a journey of personal discovery and thus every child will follow a different pathway. However, it is hoped that every child will have had a rich and stimulating environment during his or her early years, and also the support and encouragement of interested, well-qualified and enthusiastic adults. This chapter has suggested many ways in which children's creativity can be nurtured but it must be remembered that for maximum learning the child must take the lead, creating their own pathway. Adults should provide the time, space and opportunities for children to explore things which interest them, answer questions which have arisen, think about problems and how to solve them, whilst always showing appreciation of the ideas that evolve.

You may find that your views on what constitutes creativity or creative practice have now changed slightly. Discussions with colleagues following your personal reflections and engagement with the tasks in the chapter may stimulate you to be more imaginative in your own setting.

Further reading

Fumoto, H., Robson, S., Greenfield, S. and Hargreaves, D. (2012) *Young Children's Creative Thinking*, London: Sage.
  This book examines the meaning of creative thinking from the perspectives of children, parents and practitioners. It identifies the importance of children's play in encouraging creative thinking and within this, stresses the importance of practitioners providing appropriate time, space and choices.

Rose, J. and Rogers, S. (2012) *The Role of the Adult in Early Years Settings*, Maidenhead: Open University Press.

This book discusses seven specific aspects of the practitioner role and considers how to enhance the interactions and relationships between adults and children. It begins with the 'Critical Reflector' in the hope that this will emphasise the importance of reflecting on personal practice but also examines the need for individuals to be part of a successful learning community.

Thornton, L. and Brunton, P. (2005) *Understanding the Reggio Approach*, London: David Fulton Publishers. *This is a good source of information if you are not familiar with the Reggio Emilia approach to Early Years education.*

Useful websites

www.demos.co.uk/files/Born_Creative_-_web_-_final.pdf?1289392179

Tims, C. (ed) *Creative Learning in the Early Years is not just Child's Play . . .* , Born Creative Collection. This consists of 11 articles by a range of authors on the subject of creativity in early years. There are many links from theory to practice and it should encourage you to reflect further on your own practice.

www.early-arts.co.uk

This site has information on how children learn and the place of arts and creativity in this. There are ideas for practitioners wanting to be creative in their practice as well as access to a range of articles which include developing creativity in early years and brain development.

References

Bayley, R. (2008) *Creative Thinking in EYE*, Volume 9, No. 11, March.

Bruce,T. (2011) *Cultivating Creativity: For Babies, Toddlers & Young Children* (2nd edn) London: Hodder Education.

Claxton, G. (2010) Building Learning Power. Available at: www.buildinglearningpower.co.uk/what_it_is.html [Accessed 27 May 2014].

Craft, A. (2007*) Creativity and Possibility in the Early Years*, TACTYC. Available at: www.tactyc.org.uk/pdfs/Reflection-craft.pdf [Accessed 27 May 2014].

Csikszentmihalyi, M. (1997) Creativity: Flow and the psychology of discovery and invention. Available at www.bioenterprise.ca/docs/creativity-by-mihaly-csikszentmihalyi.pdf [Accessed 17 April 2014].

Department for Education (DfE) and Department of Health (DoH) (2011) *Supporting Families in the Foundation Years*. Available at: media.education.gov.uk/assets/files/pdf/s/supporting %20families%20in%20the %20foundation%20years.pdf [Accessed 13 August 2014].

Department for Education and Skills (2007) *The Early Years Foundation Stage: Setting the Standards for Learning, Development and Care for Children from Birth to Five.* Nottingham: DfES Publications.

Department for Education (DfE) (2012) *Statutory Framework for the Early Years Foundation Stage: Setting the Standards for Learning, Development and Care for Children from Birth to Five.* Available at http://www.foundationyears.org.uk/early-years-foundation-stage-2012 [Accessed 17 May 2014].

Department for Education (DfE) (2014) *Statutory Framework for the Early Years Foundation Stage: Setting the Standards for Learning, Development and Care for Children from Birth to Five* Available at: www.gov.uk/government/uploads/system/uploads/attachment_data/file/335504/EYFS_framework_from_ 1_September_2014 [Accessed 17 May 2014].

Duffy, B. (2006) *Supporting Creativity and Imagination in the Early Years,* (2nd edn) Maidenhead: Open University Press.

Dweck, C. (2008) *Mindset: The New Psychology of Success*, New York: Random House Publishing.

Early Education (2012) *Development Matters in the Early Years Foundation Stage* (EYFS) London: Early Education. Available at www.early-education.org.uk [Accessed 20 May 2014].

Jeffery, B. and Craft, A. (2004) 'Teaching Creatively and Teaching for Creativity: distinctions and relationships', *Educational Studies*, 30(1): 77–87.

Laevers, F. (2005) *Deep-level Learning and the Experiential Approach in Early Childhood*, Leuven: Katholieke Universiteit.

Lai, E. (2011) *Motivation: A Literature Review*, Research Report, Harlow: Pearson.

Loughton, T. and Teather, S. (2010) 'Creating the conditions: trusted professional and targeted resources for creativity in the early years', in Tims, C. (ed.) *Creative Learning in the Early Years is not just Child's Play* . . . , Born Creative Collection 29 DEMOS. Available at www.demos.co.uk/files/Born_Creative_-_web_-_final.pdf?1289392179 [Accessed 28 May 2014].

Lucas, B. (2001) 'Creative Teaching, Teaching Creatively and Creative Learning', in Craft, A., Jeffrey, B. and Leibling, M. *Creativity in Education*, London: Continuum.

National Advisory Committee on Creative and Cultural Education (NACCCE) (1999) *All Our Futures: Creativity, Culture and Education*, London: DfEE.

Paige-Smith, A. and Craft, A. (2007) *Developing Reflective Practice in the Early Years*, (2nd edn) Maidenhead: Open University Press.

Qualifications and Curriculum Authority (QCA)/Department for Education and Employment (DfEE) (2000) *Curriculum Guidance for the Foundation Stage*, London: QCA/DfEE.

Rinaldi, C. (2006) *In Dialogue with Reggio Emilia: Listening, Researching and Learning*, Abingdon: Routledge.

Robinson. K. (1999) *All Our Futures: Creativity, Culture and Education.* The report of the National Advisory Committee on Creative and Cultural Education London: DfEE/DCMS.

Robson, S. (2006) *Developing Thinking and Understanding in Young Children*, London: Routledge.

Siraj-Blatchford, I., Sylva, K., Muttock, S., Gilden, R. and Bell, D. (2002) Researching Effective Pedagogy in the Early Years (REPEY). Available at: www.ioe.ac.uk/REPEY_research_report.pdf [Accessed 10 May 2014].

13 Holistic development: communication, language and literacy

Claire Beresford and Alix Coughlin

LEARNING OUTCOMES

After reading this chapter you should be able to do the following:

✔ Identify the building blocks for communication, language and literacy development.
✔ Recognise the adult role in supporting communication, language and literacy development.
✔ Provide an appropriate environment and resources to support the development of communication, language and literacy skills.
✔ Discuss major theories and debates regarding communication, language and literacy.
✔ Identify barriers to children developing communication, language and literacy skills and the ways to support all children's learning.

Introduction

This chapter shows how communicating, speaking, listening, engaging in stories and singing rhymes alongside beginning to write must be supported because these skills underpin much of children's holistic learning and development. It offers examples of how practitioners can provide children with opportunities and encouragement to use their skills with increasing confidence in a variety of situations and for a range of purposes. The chapter outlines the major theories and debates regarding communication, language and literacy, drawing out the implications for early years practice. In addition, barriers to children's learning are identified and strategies are suggested. Throughout the chapter, case studies, provocations and exercises are included to encourage reflection on your own practice.

Communication, language and literacy development have significant influences upon children's learning in all areas. This is emphasised within the Statutory Framework for the Early Years Foundation Stage (EYFS) (DfE, 2014) which recognises communication and language as a prime area. Literacy is a specific area which is supported by the three prime areas. Communication, language and literacy should be viewed as part of a child's holistic development and supporting this is one of the most important roles for the early years practitioner.

Building blocks for communication and language development

Early years practitioners recognise that 'Language can be spoken, heard, read, written or signed' (Neaum, 2012, p. 7) and that The Statutory Framework for the EYFS divides communication and language development into listening and attention, understanding and speaking (DfE, 2014). The skilled practitioner supports children to make progress in all these areas. They know that learning to communicate effectively is cumulative: each new skill must build on previously learnt skills to develop the complex system of **non-verbal** and **verbal** communication that children need to interact with others. Therefore, in their workplace, early years practitioners strive to provide the building blocks for communication and language development.

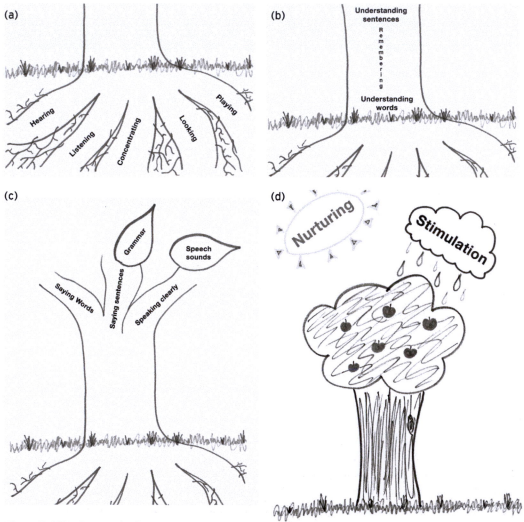

Figure 13.1 The Communication Tree

Source: *Supporting the growth of the communication tree* (Bolton, 2013, after Whitworth and Carter, 2004)

Speech and language therapist, Ben Bolton, explains the development of children's language to early years practitioners through *The Language Tree* developed by Whitworth and Carter (2004). Figure 13.1 (Bolton, 2013, after Whitworth and Carter, 2004) shows the importance of the roots of the tree: developing children's looking, hearing, listening, concentrating and of course playing in the early communicator stage of development. The child is dependent on the adults around for interactions to develop specific skills through games, for example peek-a-boo, to encourage shared interaction. Just as a tree cannot grow without its roots a child cannot develop clear speech without developing essential skills (Figure 13.1a).

By the age of twelve months the roots of language are well established if they have been nourished by adults around the child. Next, the child who shows understanding of familiar words is able to remember a couple of items at a time, and then, up to around eighteen months, the child starts to understand short sentences. Remembering is shown on the trunk because this skill needs to be strong in order to support the rest of a child's language development; remembered words used in context will develop understanding (Figure 13.1b).

The branches show the more visible signs of the ground work done so far. The spreading branches are the single words, leading on to two words together, then short phrases and longer sentences. Leaves grow and represent the plural markers and tenses, alongside the further development of speech sounds leading to ever increasing clarity (Figure 13.1c).

By the time the child is five, the fruits appear as children are ready to use their language to learn, to participate in everything school has to offer them, from friendships to literacy lessons. However, none of this growth will occur without language stimulation, or without shared experiences represented by the rain on the diagram. The sun, as every child learns, is also crucial to the growth of a plant. The sun represents nurturing, praise, successful social contacts and a loving circle of people. If children's attempts to communicate are rejected or seen as irritating, then they may communicate less. Language only develops through experience; if the child is not encouraged they may attempt less and reduce their experience. There is a window of opportunity for these skills to develop and if it is missed children may struggle to catch up (Figure 13.1d).

The importance of developing communication, language and literacy skills

The Bercow Report (2008), *Every Child a Talker* (DCSF, 2009), The Tickell Report (2011), Jean Gross' work as communication champion and Roulstone *et al.* (2011) all emphasise the importance of communication and language development for every child. They recognise the long term and various consequences associated with poor communication and language skills including lower qualifications, behavioural and **mental health** issues plus reduced opportunities for securing employment. Research shows that differences in vocabulary and language use at age two continues and increases as shown by **assessment** when children enter school (Roulstone *et al.*, 2011). Indeed Gascoigne reports a 16-month difference between the vocabulary of children from high and low income backgrounds when they start school (2012). Children's home experience varies; at best it provides exposure to a wide vocabulary and a variety of language uses in contexts which have meaning for the child, combined with positive interactions with significant others.

Providing up to fifteen hours of fully funded childcare for disadvantaged two-year-olds represents one response to raising standards in language and communication (DfE, 2013). The overarching aim of the two-year-old funding programme has been 'improving disadvantaged children's social and cognitive outcomes' (Gibb *et al.*, 2011, p. 11) including within that social confidence and verbal skills. The pilot study focused on children who were identified as having more difficulties with speech and language than the general population; and after the intervention, their language ability scores had risen from the 34th percentile to the 46th percentile (Smith *et al.*, 2009). However, Mathers *et al.* (2014) warn that improvements for such children only occur when they are provided with quality childcare.

Table 13.1 Strategies for developing good communication and language skills

Strategies for the adult to use	Pitfalls for the adult to avoid
Select a **quiet** area without background noises.	Avoid playing music because the child is so quiet. It is more difficult for young children to listen and respond when there are many sounds.
Wait and **observe** what the child is focused on in their play. Use this as the basis of the communication as children are more likely to talk about what interests them.	Avoid interrupting the child who is engrossed in their play and don't try to make the play into something different.
Ensure that you are at the child's height, near to them and that the child will see your face and **non-verbal** cues when they look up from their play.	Avoid standing or sitting looking down on the child.
Ensure that your body language is friendly. Be prepared to have fun, smile and laugh! Show **playfulness.**	Avoid carrying a clip board and pen ready to write an observation.
Wait for the child to show they are ready to engage when they look at you.	Avoid becoming frustrated and talking to the back of the child's head.
When the child seeks a word provide it, say it clearly and **repeat** it.	Avoid forcing the child to use a word you have provided.
Show that you are **genuinely interested** to play with the child and to follow their lead.	Avoid trying to take over the play.
Describe or provide a **commentary** on what you observe the child doing. 'You've parked the car at the petrol pump. I wonder if the car needs some petrol?'	Avoid asking assessment questions such as what colour is that? How many . . .? The child will simply move away.
Pause for the child to speak. Smile and wait up to 10 seconds (count elephants).	Avoid speaking all the time.
Recast what the child says correctly in order to emphasise new vocabulary.	Avoid repeating the child's pronunciation mistakes even if they make you smile.
Adapt your speech so that it is appropriate and make your voice interesting (use **intonation**).	Avoid saying too much in a complicated way.
Positive responses encourage more engagement by the child (feedback loop).	Avoid negatively correcting all the language mistakes the child makes.
Extend and **expand** the child's vocabulary through joining in the activity and playing.	Avoid using too many closed questions and directives.

The adult role in supporting communication and language development

Practitioners are required to work with families to support children's communication and language development. Recent research in America (Hart Research Associates, 2009) highlighted the fact that parents need more guidance about the importance of talking and singing to a baby, and suggests that it is the quality and not the quantity of language that a child hears that aids language development. For example, parents benefit from support in how to talk to their baby in one to one conversations rather than using standard adult-directed speech. Part of the practitioner's role is to support parents to develop knowledge about how to increase their child's full and varied vocabulary, and to give advice on methods of encouraging communication between parent and child. This chapter provides strategies in order to achieve this, and later discusses working with other professionals in order to overcome challenges in supporting the development of communication techniques. Websites including Talking Point, I CAN, Talk for Meaning and the Communication Trust all offer useful guidance.

REFLECTIVE PRACTICE

Select a positive interaction you have had with a child recently and identify successful strategies used to support the child's communication and language development.

To extend your reflection use the four activities from *Every Child a Talker: Guidance for Early Language Lead Practitioners* (DCSF, 2008) in order to audit practice within your setting and to identify areas to develop.

Expanding children's vocabulary using S.T.A.R.T

One strategy for increasing children's vocabulary is suggested by Bryce-Clegg (2014). It could be used to introduce a particular word related to a topic, or to clarify understanding of a word which has been misused by a child. It emphasises the importance of the adult role in modelling language, although should be used in moderation together with child-led conversations.

Choose a word to extend the child's already basic understanding, for example, 'beautiful'.

Stress the word	'This is a pretty flower; it has beautiful colours in its petals.'
Tell them what it means	'The petals are so colourful and attractive, and really make me want to look at it!'
Act it out using gestures or tone of voice	'It's so pretty and beautiful, I just want to touch it!'
Relate it to something personal	'It's as beautiful as that rainbow we saw when it rained and we were outside, do you remember?'
Talk it again and again	'What else can you see that is beautiful? Let's have a look inside and outside for things we think are beautiful and make us want to look closer.'

REFLECTIVE PRACTICE
REFLECTIVE PRACTICE

Select a routine from daily practice and identify the key phrases used. Develop a list of phrases to be used by all practitioners during the routine. After a week discuss with your colleagues whether this has supported the children's listening, understanding and usage of the key words and phrases.

Theories of children's communication and language development

There is no definitive answer about how children become competent communicators in a remarkably short time but a number of theories have furthered understanding of how this happens. The theories and research are important as they should inform daily practice with children.

Behaviourists including Skinner (1957) considered that children learn language through a process involving **stimulus and response** combined with imitation and reinforcement. The rewards that children receive for saying a word will encourage them to continue using the word; for example, saying 'snack' when hungry and being given something to eat combined with the adult's positive verbal and non-verbal reaction. This argument does not, however, explain why young children use phrases they have never heard spoken or had reinforced.

The influence of the behaviourist approach and particularly positive reinforcement is evident when practitioners working with babies encourage the early stages of communication development. A practitioner, for example, may have a 'conversation' with a baby by listening to the sounds that the baby makes, repeating the vocalisation and adding new ones, together with facial expressions, smiling, nodding and laughing which encourage the baby to repeat the vocalisation and join in the proto-conversation.

The sequential nature of language acquisition is emphasised by theorists including Piaget (1959) who viewed language development as part of the stages children progressed through at different ages and as part of their intellectual development. As a **cognitive** theorist Piaget suggested that when a child's thinking develops in the pre-operational stage this allows the child to use language in an increasing variety of ways.

Young children's ability to learn language was emphasised by **nativists** including Chomsky (1965) who proposed that children are born with an in-built Language Acquisition Device (LAD). Chomsky suggested that the LAD enables all children to learn the language spoken around them and to quickly apply the grammatical rules for their language. This theory has been used to explain the speed with which children learn language and also the grammatical mistakes children make. For example, a child may say 'mouses' and 'goed' which they are most unlikely to have heard said but the errors are evidence that children apply the grammatical rules for their language. The impact of this theory is evident in the way practitioners expose children to language from the very first day they enter a setting, recognising that all children are ready to communicate and the adult role is to provide a language rich environment. This positive approach leads practitioners to recognise each child's potential for communication.

The importance of the adult role in supporting children's communication was highlighted by Bruner (1983). He suggested that language development was not just dependent upon an innate mechanism in the brain but was shaped through parent-child interactions which he termed the language acquisition support system (LASS). He argued that both the LAD and LASS were required for communication to develop and that language was learnt as part of the culture where the child lived. The interactionist theory recognises that 'it is the interaction between LAD and LASS that makes it possible for the infant to enter the linguistic community – and, at the same time, the culture to which the language gives access' (Bruner, 1983, p. 19). This theory encourages practitioners to engage in meaningful interactions to expand children's vocabulary and means of expression through conversations which interest and are relevant to each child.

The importance of providing young children with opportunities to use language was emphasised by Tomasello (2003) who argued that it is through usage that children learn the structure of language and grammar. Hearing language is not enough as children need to be encouraged to participate and be supported in their efforts by the adult. Practitioners encourage this aspect of development by using songs, rhymes and sound games to **scaffold** the child's development of language skills and to allow the child to use and rehearse language. Similarly, it is through play that practitioners support children's development of language skills because this is when children are actively involved. For example, young children use an object to represent another: a box becomes a telephone and the child and adult use words as part of the role play scenario which expose the child to the structure and grammar of language.

The role of language in supporting thinking and cognitive development was considered by Vygotsky (1962). He emphasised the importance of when the child and the practitioner have a shared focus and seek to communicate about it, and also how a child can achieve more through the support of a more knowledgeable adult or peer in the **zone of proximal development**. Through **contingent strategies** the adult can support the child's language development and thinking. For example, during child-led activities the practitioner may use a commentary, open ended questions and prompts to draw out the children's ideas or decide jointly on what resources are needed to carry out the activity. The language and vocabulary used will be shared between the children and

FROM RESEARCH TO PRACTICE

Neuroscientists and researchers including Malloch and Trevarthen (2010), Gopnik (2010) and Kuhl (2007) have confirmed what many mothers and carers of babies always felt, that young babies are ready to communicate if the adult tunes in to them. Kuhl suggests that even before they are born, babies are tuning in to the phonetical sound of their mother's natural language. Recordings of such exchanges have demonstrated the musicality of interactions between mothers and their babies (Malloch and Trevarthen, 2010). The sound a baby makes becomes a joint focus involving **intersubjectivity**. This is seen in **Motherese** or infant directed speech with gazing, turn-taking, body language, raising and lowering the pitch and listening to each other. The importance of these proto-conversations is emphasised by the work of The National Scientific Council on the Developing Child, available from http://developingchild.harvard.edu/

the adult, with the practitioner modelling new words, thinking strategies and reflecting the children's own words back to them.

An overview of theories of communication and language development has been provided but theories of learning are complex. Use the recommended books and websites available at the end of the chapter to further your own knowledge and to assess the contribution of each writer to current understanding of children's development of communication and language.

Figure 13.2
Amandine's first language is French. She reads with Chlöe in both French and English and they enjoy sharing books together

Bilingual and multilingual children

Whitehead (2010) emphasises the benefits of **bilingualism** and **multilingualism** for the child's communication and thinking skills. Practitioners' attitudes are significant in demonstrating that home languages and cultures are both valued and welcome in the setting.

To support a child learning to speak English

- Support the child to develop understanding by using props, actions and photos.
- Use clear short words or phrases in context.
- Emphasise and repeat key words which are of interest to the child.
- Respond positively to all attempts to communicate, whether they are through sounds, pointing or looking at the chosen item rather than insisting on words. Respond to any sound the child makes as part of the play, possibly by repeating it.
- Model examples for children to use in their speech.
- Offer limited and simple choices which interest the child (holding both ask 'Would you like an apple or an onion for snack?')
- Allow the child plenty of time to process a choice, to decide on their answer and time to rehearse their response in their head before indicating their decision to you.

PROVOCATION

Read the account of Kelly's practice and then consider the questions. Use *Development Matters in the EYFS* (Moylett and Stewart, 2012) to identify how Kelly met the communication needs of the families.

'I want to talk to my children' was Kelly's title for her research into how to support the development of communication skills for children from families where Mandarin was spoken in the home. As the key person for children starting the setting unable to speak any English she was keenly aware of the challenges. Through reflection Kelly identified that she wanted to be able to talk to the children but also to value the children's first language. She enrolled at night school to learn some basic Mandarin.

In the setting nursery rhymes with actions were included on a daily basis. Kelly observed that many children requested rhymes by performing the actions associated with a particular rhyme. The setting already had some story sacks for families to borrow so that songs, rhymes and stories could be shared by children with their families at home. Kelly decided to extend this provision by offering song sacks to include a CD sung in both English and Mandarin. She worked with a child's mother who spoke some English to translate the words into Mandarin and recorded the mother's singing onto a CD. Families were eager to borrow the sacks, plus the child's mother now assists the setting in translating key words to display in the setting and letters for families.

Figure 13.3
The song bag, CD and props made by Kelly to promote communication with the children

- Why do you think that Kelly chose to learn some Mandarin?
- How do you think that the family felt when they heard Kelly attempting to speak Mandarin?
- Identify the benefits of providing nursery rhymes in Mandarin and English for children, families and the setting.

CASE STUDY 1

The importance of communication to enable children to settle and to participate in the routines of the setting became clear to a room leader, Lois. Recently, several children who spoke Polish in their homes had joined the setting. Recognising the importance of security for children to enable them to play and learn she reflected on the children's progress through the four stages of additional language learning described by Tabors (1997). Using a Talking Photo Album Lois photographed key areas and routines in the setting. The father's voice was recorded naming the photographs in Polish and she recorded the English words. All children could press the button beside each photo to hear its name in both languages.

REFLECTIVE PRACTICE

Imagine that you enter your workplace as a child unable to speak English. Identify the communication techniques currently used by practitioners. Are there any signs that home languages are valued?

The adult role and good practice in approaching the challenges faced by children developing communication, language and literacy skills

- Gain the child's attention first by using their name to ensure that they turn towards the speaker.
- Talk about daily routines as repetition is useful for learning key words and phrases.
- Use the actual object to explain the routine; for example, show a real nappy before a nappy is changed.
- If the child understands when the object is shown with the word consider whether they are ready to progress to photographs of objects or actions in order to explain routines. These may be combined to form a visual timetable for the child to re-visit at relevant points during the session.
- Support communication and understanding by using many strategies including signing and Makaton. More information is available from www.makaton.org/
- Use one instruction at time.
- Prepare children for talk by stating 'Now we are going to talk about . . .'
- When children are relaxed in routine or physical tasks they are more likely to initiate talk. Be ready to listen while they are putting on their coat or hand washing and while they engage in pouring water, cutting and sticking.

Part of the role of the practitioner is to observe a key child and to recognise if there is any cause for concern regarding the child's development of communication, language and literacy skills. It is important to be aware of the difference between a concern and common **childhood** ailments which can temporarily restrict a child's hearing and impact on their communication. Involving the child's family ensures that an accurate picture of the child is created. Such observations are vital to plan next steps for learning but also to provide evidence for discussion with other professionals to determine whether early intervention is required. Speech and language therapists may provide strategies for practitioners and families to use in order to support a child's language development. Similarly, working with other professionals helps practitioners to understand specific learning needs, syndromes and conditions. Throughout these processes the aim is not to label the child but to provide the best learning opportunities to meet individual needs appropriately. For further information consult **Early Support** for children, young people and families. Information about speech, language and communication needs (DfE, 2012).

Figure 13.4 Example of a visual timetable

Using language and communication to support sustained shared thinking

The EPPE project confirmed the importance of adults supporting sustained shared thinking with children (Sylva *et al.*, 2004). Through observing and listening carefully to children practitioners identify next steps for each child. Practitioners scaffold and extend children's language through elaborated talk as they add new vocabulary, model language, think out loud and discuss. Collaborative activities such as construction and role play are particularly suitable because they provide opportunities for meaningful social interaction, support the child's confidence and self-esteem and offer opportunities to both consolidate and extend the child's vocabulary. The practitioner replaces closed questions with speculative, open-ended pondering.

- I wonder … ?
- What would happen if … ?
- What do you suppose … ?
- How did that happen … ?
- What do you think about … ?
- How did you … ?
- What should we do next … ?

Figure 13.5
Thomas and a practitioner talking
about their shared activity

Practitioners agree that supporting interactions is important and most believe that is what they do on a daily basis. Fisher and Wood's practitioner-led **action research**, however, showed that the reality was not quite as expected (2012). Through the use of video recordings, logs and both individual and collaborative reflection practitioners were surprised by their interactions and were able to identify areas for improvement in their own practice as they became 'more sensitive to the extent of their own contributions in interactions ... and more aware of when to instigate conversation and when to be responsive to children's conversational overtures' (2012, p. 125).

Using technology

One way to increase children's communication is through the use of new technologies – tablets, laptops, touch screens and recording devices. There are many apps and programs that are directed at young children's communication skills, which encourage letter and word recognition, listening skills, repeated fine motor skill action, and ways of expressing themselves on screen through art activities.

Research by the Literacy Trust (Formby, 2014a) shows that practitioners both recognise the increasing use of technology in children's lives and are gaining confidence in their own use of it. It is an aspect of practice that practitioners in the twenty-first century need to utilise in order to develop children's communication in a way that is familiar to them at home. The Literacy Trust's research with parents (Formby, 2014b) shows that three quarters of those surveyed had access to touch screens at home, that over a quarter used them to access stories, and that 41 per cent played games on screen at least once a week. So how does this affect children's experiences of technology in a setting? Although eight out of ten practitioners believe that technology is supplemental to play rather than instrumental in assisting children's communication, studies of children's interactions with digital text highlight the playfulness, agency and creativity used when engaging with them (Burnett, 2010). The Characteristics of Effective Learning encourage finding out and exploring, and being willing to have a go (Moylett and Stewart, 2012). Should practitioners make more use of technology in promoting communication and literacy? The Literacy Trust research states that to be literate in today's society children must be able to use a range of media effectively and that 'touch screen technology is more age appropriate for young children to use' (Formby, 2014a, p. 2) than print-based media. Worries about the impact of technology in hindering children's language should be 'mediated by teachers' use of the same developmentally appropriate principles and practices that guide the use of print materials and all other learning tools and content for young children' (National Association for the Education of Young Children, 2012, p. 4).

Highly qualified and knowledgeable practitioners use their skills to help children engage with any new toy, game, experience or activity in an interactive and developmentally appropriate way, and ensure that is relevant to each individual child. Why should this change because the new activity is using technology? (Coughlin, 2014). Use the same techniques in encouraging children's interest in technology as would be used if their interest was in pirates and dinosaurs – talk about it!

Literacy

The Statutory Framework for the EYFS (DfE, 2014) divides the specific area of literacy into reading and writing.

PROVOCATION

Letters and Sounds vs Michael Rosen

What methods of teaching reading have you experienced? What do you consider is the most successful way of encouraging children to read?

The phonics resource *Letters and Sounds* (DfES, 2007) aims to help children become fluent readers. Synthetic phonics, based on the simple view of reading, is the approach advocated currently as the best way to teach children the basics of working out sounds (phonemes) and combining (synthesising) them into words. Phase One is used within the EYFS and focuses on seven aspects; environmental sounds, instrumental sounds, body percussion, rhythm and rhyme, alliteration, voice sounds and finally oral blending and segmenting (DfES, 2007, p. 4). It involves 'supporting linking sounds and letters in the order in which they occur in words, and naming and sounding the letters of the alphabet' (DfES, 2007, p. 1).The systematic programme has been criticised as a 'prescriptive, rigid and limited view of what it means to teach early reading' (Wyse and Styles, 2007, p. 41). Some settings have excluded other materials and approaches for encouraging reading and used *Letters and Sounds* exclusively, rather than a holistic approach of stories, songs, rhymes and sustained shared talking to help children make sense of texts (Rosen, 2013). The author Michael Rosen has been critical of the synthetic phonics approach, arguing that it just teaches children to read aloud and to decode, without deriving any meaning from the words.

Consider the two sides of the argument. How do you foster in children a love of reading books and also ensure that all children become fluent readers? What must a practitioner do to achieve both?

Reading

'Literature is a powerful medium for communicating ideas, transmitting emotions and finding out about other people's culture, language, religion and life experiences' (Brock and Coughlin, 2012, p. 90). Some settings have a list of core texts to ensure all children become particularly familiar with a few books and rhymes as well as providing a range of others. Selecting stories, rhymes and songs to use with young children should involve informed and deliberate choices.

One of the most popular activities in early years provision is sharing books with children but is it being used as an opportunity to develop children's communication, language and literacy skills or as an excuse for some quiet time? Story time, book sharing, the book corner, rhyme time, singing and action songs all contribute to developing children's literacy through the introduction of simple and repetitive vocabulary and identifiable words in a familiar and safe context. Children love to have the same book read to them over and over again, because they start to recognise the words on the page, to learn that text has meaning and to use literacy skills such as **prediction, inference, deduction and interpretation**. These are all skills which they will need to become fluent readers. Other benefits include the extra-contextual development of language as practitioners and children discuss the story after sharing the book, giving children a chance to use the words in their own context, with exploration of the vocabulary in their own world (Gonzalez *et al.*, 2013). Practitioners can also enhance children's comprehension by using questioning that goes beyond the literal to the inferred meaning behind the story; don't just ask, 'What?'and 'Who?' type questions that test children's recall of facts, use questions that enable the children to answer 'Why?' and 'What do you think?' These types of questions allow children to give explanations and develop their thinking and reasoning skills (Zucker *et al.*, 2010).

It is important to remember to give children an opportunity to develop and retell the stories that they experience in their own context, *storying* (Brock and Rankin, 2008, p. 122) in order to encourage the skills they will need for communicating their personal experiences. Children are excellent story tellers if given time and someone who will listen to them. Storytelling, reading role models and sharing familiar books are some ways to develop a lifelong love of reading for pleasure and for knowledge. Practitioners should choose stories that can be discussed, added to, amended and adapted by a child to fit their own purpose and to tell their own story, and the practitioner should be prepared to listen to the child's version.

Sharing stories and storytelling in a setting

- Create a book area that changes regularly with bright, attractive books on display.
- Make time to share stories with children in small groups and individually and wherever they feel comfortable listening – don't confine stories to a story corner, they can happen anywhere.
- Show enthusiasm for reading through the choice of books, how you read them, how you treat books and your responses to children's choices.
- Allow children to revisit stories by re-reading, no matter how many times, and by talking about the stories and characters afterwards.
- Listen to the children's own stories.
- Provide children with props and space to develop the story with their own ideas, in the role play area, small world play and outdoors.
- Don't assume that children know traditional tales and nursery rhymes. Introduce and re-visit them; include those which reflect children's home culture.

PROVOCATION

Core texts

Everybody has their own favourite books to read with children. Do you know these? Which other books would you include?

The Very Hungry Caterpillar – Eric Carle
The Gruffalo – Julia Donaldson
Kipper's Toy Box – Mick Inkpen
Owl Babies – Martin Waddell
We're Going on a Bear Hunt – Michael Rosen
Where's My Teddy? – Jez Alborough
Rosie's Walk – Pat Hutchins
Dear Zoo – Rod Campbell
Hairy Maclary – Lynley Dodd
An Oliver Jeffers book
An Anthony Browne book
A collection of nursery rhymes
A collection of traditional tales – *Goldilocks and the Three Bears, The Gingerbread Man, The Three Little Pigs, Billy Goats Gruff*

Writing

Language and print rich environments both indoors and outside are essential for supporting children's literacy development. Children should be surrounded by texts that give meaning to their world in the setting and that draw attention to the words used every day, while reflecting the status of the written word. A print rich environment will reflect 'the interdependent nature of the four aspects of language development: speaking, listening, reading and writing' (National Strategies, 2009, p. 1). A skilled practitioner will enable children to become increasingly familiar with words that they see every day and encourage them to begin to mark make for meaning using the prompts around them, valuing the process that the children go through to make marks as well as the result.

Children need stimuli in order to find a reason to write which will quite often come out of the talking that has taken place in the setting. 'Writing is only the talk that comes out of the end of your pencil instead of your mouth' (Bryce-Clegg, 2014). Place interesting objects, pictures or labels around the setting, giving children a chance to ask questions, explore the objects, discuss them with friends and practitioners, laugh at them, feel them or smell them. Then give them the prompts to start writing about what they have found out, what they would like to find out, what they thought about the smell, taste, touch and sound of the object.

Developing skills for mark making in a setting

- Provide opportunities for children to develop gross motor skills and large body movements, for example, large wall paper brushes to 'paint' with water or using water sprays to mark out shapes on the ground.
- Encourage children to feel shapes with their body and encourage spatial awareness, balancing, climbing and stretching, curling and rolling.
- Develop physical movements of the fingers through a dough disco, dancing with fingers, rolling, squidging and squeezing to strengthen the muscles.
- Provide hand-eye coordination activities, for example, using tweezers to sort small items, transferring liquids with a pipette and weaving.
- Encourage children to make marks, patterns and letter shapes through pressing onto paint within sealed plastic on table tops, in trays of wet sand, with paint using a variety of mark making tools and with pens on whiteboards.
- Provide meaningful opportunities through play for children to mark make and write throughout the provision including large sheets of paper on the ground or at child height, chalks on the ground, cards to write, envelopes to address and menus for the role play café.
- Recognise the importance of children using symbols in their drawings and paintings.
- Value all children's mark making and emergent writing.
- Let children see you writing and explain your purpose in writing.
- Write down the words children say about their picture or photo and read the words back to them.
- Mark making should be fun, developed from play and have meaning for the child.

CASE STUDY 2

Case studies focused on encouraging boys to mark make and write

Using writing and drawings to communicate for a purpose

In the construction area three children with a particular interest in model making were provided with clipboards, paper, graph paper and large pens to record how to make their models. The practitioner discussed the sketches with individuals as they worked and provided a commentary about what the child was drawing, to remind them of the order in which they built and as positive encouragement to sustain their concentration. Elaborate sequences of drawings were produced with annotations. Other children were then invited to make the models using the drawings and notes with enthusiastic prompting from the original designers.

Starting with the children's interests and providing opportunities to mark make

Cassie observed that a group of boys spent most of their time outside dressed as builders, transporting building materials, using tools and that they rarely chose to mark make unless guided by an adult. She offered the children some clipboards and tool belts which held large pens, rulers and chunky pencils. Cassie showed the boys a book about builders and pictures of a construction site where people were writing. Later she observed the boys incorporate mark making into their play as they measured materials, drew plans and wrote bills for their construction work.

Listening to children

Andrea had been asked to focus on writing with a group of children. She decided to listen to the children and use their ideas to develop a role play area. Andrea showed the children photographs of possible scenarios and the group decided to create a police station. She scribed for the group on a large sheet as they selected the resources including those for writing. Soon the children were busy creating identity cards and badges, choosing note pads and recording crimes; one child made road signs and another wrote a list of rules.

Working with parents and carers to support literacy development

Parents and carers may require encouragement to promote literacy with their child at home. The importance of regular reading, storytelling and singing with children at all ages should be promoted by practitioners. Similarly, appropriate mark making activities should be shared with parents and carers. It is important that practitioners provide information about realistic expectations based on the child's stage of development to ensure that children have positive literacy experiences both in the setting and at home. Support can be found from programmes including Early Words Together (National Literacy Trust, 2014) which empowers families to encourage their children's literacy skills.

Conclusion

The **reflective practice** activities, case studies and provocations should have led you to consider your practice to improve children's communication, language and literacy holistically. Have you considered the following?

- The adult role in supporting communication, language and literacy?
- Where, when and how you talk with children?
- The vocabulary you use in the setting?
- How you overcome barriers to communication for all children and their families including those with English as an additional language?
- The resources you use to develop communication and literacy?
- Strategies and opportunities to encourage communication, reading and writing with children at all stages of development?
- How you ensure that your setting is a communication rich environment where all children are comfortable to communicate?

It is important to remember that children do not compartmentalise their learning and that communication, language and literacy development will also be part of their social, emotional and physical development. Practitioners must be alert to all the ways children communicate 'thinking, playing, speaking, listening, marvelling, loving, singing, understanding' (Loris Malaguzzi, *The Hundred Languages of Childhood*, cited in Edwards *et al.*, 2012, p. 3)

Further reading

The following books contain information about theories, practical application, research and more detailed knowledge of children's communication, language and literacy development.

Brock, A. and Rankin, C. (2008) *Communication, Language and Literacy from Birth to Five*. London: Sage.
　This book is accessible and provides a detailed view of children's development of communication, language and literacy.

Neaum, S. (2012) *Language and Literacy for the Early Years*. London: Sage.
　This book is a valuable resource for practitioners as it presents theory linked to practice in the early years.

Whitehead, M. (2010) *Language and Literacy in the Early Years 0-7*. 4th edn. London: Sage.
　This book has been revised and it provides comprehensive coverage of the development of language and literacy.

Useful websites

www.ican.org.uk
　I CAN is the children's communication charity. It provides useful information and guidance for practitioners and families in order to support speaking and understanding.

www.talkformeaning.co.uk/
　Talk 4 Meaning. Supporting children's language, communication and learning.
　Through the website Michael Jones offers guidance and inspiration for all who seek to provide support for children's language and communication.

www.talkingpoint.org.uk/
　Talking Point is run by I CAN. It provides valuable information about supporting children's speech, language and communication.

www.thecommunicationtrust.org.uk/
　The Communication Trust. Every Child Understood. The website brings together fifty organisations working to support children's speech, language and communication.

www.literacytrust.org.uk/
　National Literacy Trust. Words for Life. The charity is dedicated to improving literacy levels in the UK.

References

Bercow, J. (2008) *The Bercow Report. A review of services for children and young people 0-19 with speech, language and communication difficulties*. Nottingham: DCSF.
Bolton, B. (2013) *Early Language Development*. Unpublished conference paper. Skipton: Craven College.

Brock, A. and Coughlin, A. (2012) 'Libraries, literacy and popular culture – what's cool to read?', in Brock, A. and Rankin, C. (2012) *Library services for children and young people. Challenges and opportunities in the digital age*. London: Facet Publishing, pp. 89–107.

Brock, A. and Rankin, C. (2008) *Communication, Language and Literacy from Birth to Five*. London: Sage Publishing.

Bruner, J. (1983) *Child's Talk: Learning to Use Language*. Oxford: Oxford University Press.

Bryce-Clegg, A. (2014) Talk for Mark Making and Writing – Granny's teeth. ABCDoes [online] Typepad. Available from: http://abcdoes.typepad.com/ [Accessed 5 February 2014].

Burnett, C. (2010) 'Technology and literacy in early childhood educational settings: a review of research', *Journal of Early Childhood Literacy*. 10(3) pp. 247–270.

Chomsky, N. (1965) *Aspects of Theory of Syntax*. Cambridge, MA: MIT Press.

Coughlin, A. (2014) 'Communication using new technologies: the tip of the iceberg', in Brock, A. (ed.) (2014) *The Early Years Reflective Practice Handbook*. Abingdon: Routledge. pp. 270–275.

Department for Children, Schools and Families (2008) *Every Child a Talker: Guidance for Early Language Lead Practitioners*. Nottingham: DCSF Publications.

Department for Children, Schools and Families (2009) *Every Child a Talker*. Nottingham: DCSF Publications.

Department for Education (2012) *Early Support for children, young people and families. Information about speech, language and communication needs*. (2nd edn). Available from: www.ncb.org.uk/media/875224/earlysupportslcnfinal.pdf [Accessed 20 December 2014].

Department for Education (2013) *92,000 2-year-olds already receiving free childcare* [online]. Available from: www.gov.uk/government/news/92000-2-year-olds-already-receiving-free-childcare [Accessed 15 March 2014].

Department for Education (2014) Statutory Framework for the Early Years Foundation Stage (EYFS). Setting the standards for learning, development and care for children from birth to five. [online]. Available from: www.gov.uk/government/publications/early-years-foundation-stage-framework–2 [Accessed 12 March 2014].

Department for Education and Skills (2007) *Letters and Sounds: Principles and Practice of High Quality Phonics*. National Strategies: Crown Copyright.

Edwards, C., Gandini, L. and Forman, G. (eds) (2012) *The Hundred Languages of Children: The Reggio Emilia Experience in Transformation* (3rd edn). Oxford: Praeger.

Fisher, J. and Wood, E. (2012) 'Changing educational practice in the early years through practitioner-led action research: an Adult-Child Interaction'. *International Journal of Early Years Education*. 20(2) pp. 114–129.

Formby, S. (2014a) *Practitioner Perspectives: Children's Use of Technology in the Early Years*. London: National Literacy Trust.

Formby, S. (2014b) *Parent Perspectives: Children's use of technology in the early years*. London: National Literacy Trust.

Gascoigne, M.T. (ed.) (2012) *Better Communication – Shaping Speech, Language and Communication Services for Children and Young People*. London: RCSLT.

Gibb, J., Jelicic, H., La Valle, I., Gowland, S., Kinsella, R., Jessiman, P. and Ormston, R. (2011) *Rolling out free early education for disadvantaged two year olds: an implementation study for local authorities and providers* [online]. London: National Children's Bureau with National Centre for Social Research. Available from: www.education.gov.uk/publications/RSG/publicationDetail/Page1/DFE-RR131 [Accessed 20 November 2014].

Gonzalez, J, E., Pollard-Durodola, S., Simmons, D., Taylor, A., Davis, M., Fogarty, M. and Simmons, L. (2013) 'Enhancing preschool children's vocabulary: Effects of teacher talk before, during and after shared reading', *Early Childhood Research Quarterly*. (678) pp. 1–13.

Gopnik, A. (2010) How Babies Think. [online] *Scientific American* pp. 76–81. Available from: www.alisongopnik.com/papers_alison/sciam-gopnik.pdf [Accessed 17 March 2014].

Gross, J. (2012) *Better Communication: Shaping speech, language and communication services for children and young people* [online] Available from: www.thecommunicationtrust.org.uk/media/17889/better_communication_report_-_rcslt_and_jean_gross.pdf [Accessed 26 February 2013].

Hart Research Associates (2009) 'Parenting Interacting with Infants: Strengthening Parent–Child Relationships to Support Social and Emotional Development'. *Zero to Three.* 32(2) November pp. 25–29.

Harvard University (2014) Center on the Developing Child at Harvard University [online] Available from: http://developingchild.harvard.edu/ [Accessed 18 January 2015].

Kuhl, P. (2007) 'Is speech learning 'gated'by the social brain?', *Developmental Science* 1 (10) pp.110–120.

Makaton Charity [online] Available from: www.makaton.org [Accessed 18 January 2015].

Malloch, S. and Trevarthen, C. (eds) (2010) *Communicative Musicality: Exploring the Basis of Human Companionship.* Oxford: Open University Press.

Mathers, S., Eisenstadt, N., Sylva, K., Soukakou, E. and Ereky-Stevens, K. (2014) Sound Foundations: A Review of the Research Evidence on Quality of Early Childhood Education and Care for Children under Three: Implications for Policy and Practice [online] Available from: www.ox.ac.uk/document.rm?id=3215. [Accessed 3 January 2015].

Moylett, H. and Stewart, N. (2012) *Development Matters in the Early Years Foundation Stage.* London: Early Education.

National Association for the Education of Young Children (2012) *Technology and Interactive Media as Tools in Early Childhood Programs Serving Children Through Birth to Age 8.* NAEYC. [online] Available from: www.naeyc.org/files/naeyc/file/positions/PS_technology_WEB2.pdf. [Accessed 5 December 2014].

National Literacy Trust (2014) *Early Words Together* [online]. Available from: www.literacytrust.org.uk/early_words_together [Accessed 10 March 2014].

National Strategies (2009) The crucial role of the Early Years practitioner in supporting young writers with a literacy-rich environment. *Foundation Years.*[online] Available from: www.foundationyears.org.uk/files/2011/11/Gateway-to-Writing-crucial-role-of-the-early-years-practitioner.pdf [Accessed 5 December 2014].

Neaum, S. (2012) *Language and Literacy for the Early Years.* London: Sage.

Piaget, J. (1959) *The Language and Thought of the Child.* London: Routledge.

Rosen, M. (2013) Phonics: a summary of my views. *Michael Rosen blog* [online] 3 January. Available from: michaelrosenblog.blogspot.co.uk/2013/01/phonics-summary-of-my-views.html [Accessed 1 March 2014].

Roulstone S., Law, J., Rush, R., Clegg, J. and Peters, T. (2011) *Investigating the Role of Language in Children's Early Educational Outcomes,* DfE Research Report DFE-RR134, Bristol: University of the West of England.

Skinner, B.F. (1957) *Verbal Behaviour.* Englewood Cliffs, NJ: Prentice Hall.

Smith, R., Purdon, S., Schneider, V, La Valle, I., Wollny, I., Owen, R., Bryson, C., Mathers, S., Sylva, K. and Lloyd, E. (2009) *Early Education Pilot for Two Year Old Children: Evaluation.* National Centre for Social Research: DCSF Publications.

Sylva, K., Melhuish, E., Sammons, P., Siraj-Blatchford, I. and Taggart, B. (2004) *The Effective Provision of Pre-School Education [EPPE] Project.* London: DfES.

Tabors, P. (1997) *One Child, Two Languages: A Guide for Pre-School Educators of Children Learning English as a Second Language.* Baltimore: Paul Brookes Publishing.

Tickell, C. (2011) *The Early Years: Foundations for Life, Health and Learning.* London: The Stationery Office.

Tomasello, M. (2003) *Constructing a Language. A Usage-Based Theory of Language Acquisition.* London: Harvard University Press.

Vygotsky, L. (1962) *Thought and Language.* Cambridge, MA: MIT Press.

Whitehead, M. (2010) *Language and Literacy in the Early Years 0–7* (4th edn). London: Sage.

Whitworth, L. and Carter, C. (2004) The Language Tree. *Bulletin. The official magazine of the Royal College of Speech and Language Therapists.* (628, August) p. 11.

Wyse, D. and Styles, M. (2007) 'Synthetic phonics and the teaching of reading: the debate surrounding England's 'Rose Report'', *Literacy* 41(1) pp. 35–42.

Zucker, T., Justice, L., Piasta, S. and Kaderavek, J. (2010) 'Preschool teacher's literal and inferential questions and children's responses during whole-class shared reading', *Early Childhood Research Quarterly* (25) pp. 65–83.

14 Holistic development: children's health and well-being

Alaina Lally

LEARNING OUTCOMES

After reading this chapter you should be able to:

✔ Explain how our concepts of health influence our health behaviours.
✔ Outline how child health services have evolved in response to changes in health and disease in childhood.
✔ Discuss the determinants of child health and explanations of health inequalities.
✔ Appraise current understandings of mental health and well-being in childhood.
✔ Identify current child health policy and the importance of early intervention.
✔ Have an awareness of health promotion theory and the need for health literacy.
✔ Reflect on your own role and responsibilities working with young children taking into account the provocations in this chapter.

Introduction

Healthier children live longer, experience greater well-being and are more likely to be successful in adulthood (Marmot and Bell, 2010). Renewed effort to 'give every child a healthy start in life' (DoH, 2014) is being made through public policy, such as the 'Healthy Child Programme' (2009) and the 'Healthy Lives, Healthy People' (DoH, 2010) policies. By targeting health in the early years the Early Years practitioner becomes a key health promoter requiring competent understanding of child health and health promotion. However, Ofsted (2013) identified that development and training of Early Years practitioners in 'best practice' in health promotion has been slow to keep pace with the current policy demands. In this chapter we argue that, in order to be successful in promoting young children's health, it is important to explore your own beliefs, values and understanding of health.

PROVOCATION 1

- Do you consider yourself to be healthy, ill, or unhealthy but not ill? Write down your response.
- Make a list of all the facts on which you have based your answer.
- Separate these facts into those relating to physical (your body and its functions), social (your relationships), and **mental health** (your ability to experience and manage positive and negative emotions).
- If you consider yourself to be unhealthy but not ill, write down what you could do to become healthier.
- Is there a pattern in your facts and potential actions to improve your health that suggests how you see and define health?

Concepts of health

The World Health Organization (WHO) defines health as 'complete social, mental, and physical wellness, not just the absence of disease or infirmity' (1946). This is a **holistic view of health** incorporating both positive (wellness) and negative (the absence of disease) constructs of health. In reality, however, not many people can claim to be *completely* well and free from disease at all times.

As you probably saw in your response to Provocation 1 our definitions of health may often focus on physical aspects only. It follows that an Early Years practitioner may only focus on a child's **physical health** ignoring his or her mental and social wellness. This was an early criticism of medical practitioners who used the '**biomedical' model** of care that focused on the '**biological'** or physical functioning of the human body. However, we have become increasingly aware that the physical, social and mental areas of health all influence each other. Understanding the holistic model of health, consisting of the physical (the bio), the mental (the psychic), and the social relationships, provides Early Years practitioners with a framework to use when reflecting on the complexity of child health and health promotion.

PROVOCATION 2

Using the bio-psycho-social model to frame your answer, consider why it is so challenging to change our habits in order to improve our health, such as changing our diet or exercising more.

One of the factors influencing whether we consider changing our health habits is whether we believe health is valuable and important or not. A **'positive concept of health'** views health as an asset that can enhance the quality of our lives, so we may strive to achieve the best health we can, for instance by taking regular exercise we may increase our energy, alertness, and appearance. Conversely, a **'negative concept of health'** views health as the freedom from disease only. With this view we are likely to think that if we are free from disease there is no need to make an effort to be any healthier. We may treat our bodies like cars – as long as we can get them from A to B we don't need to worry about what is happening to the engine as a consequence of our driving or neglect. We only look under the bonnet and see the effects when the car breaks down.

Reflect on which of these views (a **positive concept of health** or a **negative concept of health**) applies to you. If you hold a 'positive' and holistic view of health you are more likely to listen to and act on health promotion messages and adapt your lifestyle to one that is healthy benefiting you socially, emotionally and physically. You are also more likely to see the importance of health promotion. How might a **positive concept of health** or a **negative concept of health** influence the approach of an Early Years practitioner who is trying to promote exercise to young children?

PROVOCATION 3

The holistic definition of health is not only used to understand the health of the individual child. Explore how physical, mental and social definitions of health may be used to evaluate:

- The health of a family.
- The health of a community.
- The health of a nursery, or a school.

A brief history of child health services

How we view health today is a result of a combination of our individual experiences of health and the expectations of health in our society. Although we expect children in the UK to live to adulthood this view is relatively new and specific to western countries. In Victorian times nine out of ten children died before adulthood, mainly due to infectious diseases and poverty but also from complications from the sort of chronic illnesses that children often live with today. A major factor contributing to today's **childhood** survival rates is the existence of the promotion of **Public Health**. Public Health may be defined as: 'The science and art of promoting and protecting health and wellbeing, preventing ill health and prolonging life through the organised efforts of society' (Faculty of Public Health, 2010, p. 1).

Public health services are created in response to the levels of health and types of diseases experienced by the population of a nation. They are influenced by societal and government beliefs about what will improve general health and by how much of the gross national product a nation is willing to spend on the promotion of public health.

Since the nineteenth century there have been three broad phases of focus in public health services in the UK (Green and Thorogood, 1998):

1   *An 'environment focus'*: In the 1800's when it was recognised that poor living conditions influence health, and the spread of infectious diseases that caused so many children's deaths, in the 1800s, Public Health Acts were introduced that focused on providing sanitation, clean water and healthier housing for all. However, poor housing continues to influence the health of many children living in areas of deprivation today (Barnes *et al.*, 2008).

2   *A 'disease prevalence focus'*: As the spread of infectious disease became controlled, it was recognised that the childhood illnesses were exacerbated by malnutrition. In the early1900s the first health visitors and Medical Officers of Health were introduced in 'infant centres' for the purposes of early identification and treatment of disease, and education of the public on disease prevention and management. This was the beginning of 'Childhood Surveillance Programmes' that provide detailed records on a child's health status. Today Early Years practitioners might be employed as health assistants in mother and baby clinics promoting health education and the early detection of disease through surveillance and screening (Blair and Hall, 2006).

3   *A 'social focus'*: As the detection and treatment of disease increased and improved, it became evident that, despite the public health service provisions, the health of children in different groups in society had improved at different rates. The Black Report (1980) highlighted a significant difference between the health of children living in affluence areas and those who were living in poverty. The report used the bio-psycho-social model of health to understand how social and psychological conditions influence people's health behaviours, for instance, identifying socio-cultural differences in the way families access and make use of medical services.

Even today research is still being undertaken to try to understand and address the underlying reasons why children living in affluent families experience better health, and are more likely to have healthy lifestyles than those living in poor families.

The health of UK children

The main indicators used to study the health of children are **life expectancy** at birth (expected number of years of good health) and the **infant mortality rate** (IMR) (the number of infant deaths between 0 and 12 months). Both these indicators have shown an improvement over the past 30 years with progress attributed to a combination of public health policy and advancement in medical services.

Today the main causes of **neonatal** deaths (of newborn infants up to 28 days after birth) are no longer infectious diseases and malnutrition, but are much more likely to be more from 'natural' causes acquired as a result of the infant's health at birth, for example, because of prematurity at birth, injuries sustained during birth or congenital anomalies (conditions with which a baby is born). For children aged 1–18 years the main causes of death tend to be:

*   non-accidental and accidental injuries
*   congenital neurological, respiratory or cardiovascular disorders
*   cancers (Department of Health, 2012)

Despite an overall improvement in health, and a decrease in the numbers of deaths from accidental injury portraying a positive image of the efficiency of health provision in the UK, there are still areas of grave concern. When comparing the Infant Mortality Rate of different groups in the UK it is evident that the public health services are not reaching all groups equally as key health indicators note a: '70% gap in infant mortality between the richest and poorest groups, and rates for some ethnic groups are almost twice the national average' (Department of Health, 2010, p. 18). This is higher than in comparable European countries indicating a failure of the UK to keep pace with the improvements made in other countries (Wolfe *et al.*, 2014). As noted earlier in the chapter the existence of **health inequalities** between different groups in society is not new. However, it is of major concern that the gap between different groups has not narrowed in response to previous health service and public health policies; *on the contrary they have actually widened in some areas.* Understanding why the gap exists and continues to exist and the role they can play in narrowing the gap should be a concern for all Early Years practitioners.

PROVOCATION 4

Visit the Child Health Profiles available from Public Health England government website: www.gov.uk/government/news/phes-2014-child-health-profiles-published.

- Compare the differences in health and disease for children living in areas of affluence and poverty in your region.
- Reflect on how this may be affecting the children in your setting and how you can use your role to engage the services and health promotion required to improve their health.

Risk factors determining children's health

To establish why the gap exists various research studies have attempted to explore the 'determinants' of health. The factors that determine children's health are complex: they may not directly cause ill-health, but may be factors that put children *at risk* of developing ill health. It is essential that Early Years practitioners are aware of these factors as it is much more effective to prevent childhood illness rather than treat problems once they have developed. It is also more socially just. Early years practitioners are aware that the various determinants of children's health (portrayed in the diagram below) interact with each other.

Very young children have no control over their own health, so research focuses controllable factors related to the mother's health and the family context in order to minimise any 'risk factors' that might damage children's future health. As an Early Years practitioner working in settings, schools and communities your role is to play a part in reducing the number of these risk factors through health promotion.

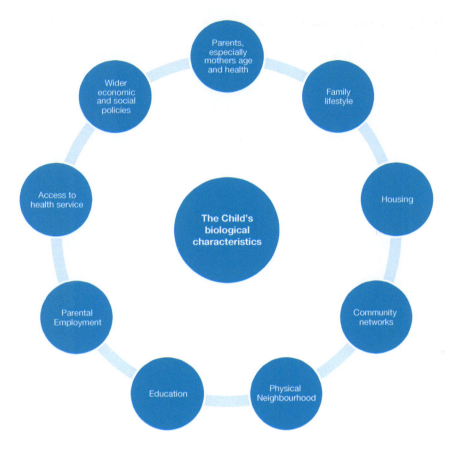

Figure 14.1 The determinants of health. The context of a child's life greatly determines their health at birth, in childhood and in adulthood. Some factors influencing health are amenable to control but others are not controllable

PROVOCATION 5

When reviewing the following factors that may influence children's health, make a note of which determinants explain the differences in the health in individuals and which determinants explain the differences in the health of groups.

As an Early Years practitioner what can you do to promote positive health outcomes for individuals and groups? Consider the list below. How much influence can you have on them? What can you do?

Health risk factors in infancy

The parent's genetic make-up influences the risk of a child being born with a genetically inherited disease, for example, sickle cell anaemia or cystic fibrosis.

The mother's age may influence the biological process of pregnancy. Problems are more likely to occur for teenage mothers and those over 35 years. Mothers aged between 30 and 34 years have the lowest incidence of infant deaths (Office for National Statistics (ONS), 2012). However, an increasing number of pregnancies occur to women over 35; in this age group there are more premature births (born before 35 weeks' gestation) associated with low-birth-weight infants (i.e. below 2.5 kg).

The mother's health and lifestyle influence the risk of health difficulties for babies. Maternal depression and anxiety are linked to a higher risk of low birth-weight babies (ONS, 2012). Lifestyle factors, i.e. a diet lacking folic acid can result in spina bifida; alcohol consumption during pregnancy can cause foetal alcohol syndrome (FAS), while smoking is linked to low birth-weight and has been found to increase the risk of infant death by 40 per cent, and 'sudden infant deaths' (SIDS) by 200 per cent (Salihu and Wilson, 2007; ONS, 2012).

Infant feeding patterns, for example, breastfeeding, may increase a baby's immunity to infection, decrease the likelihood of later development of obesity and type II diabetes and improve resistance to allergies and poor mental health. Breastfeeding is considered to improve health outcomes for children born into low-income families (DoH, 2013 and Unicef, 2012). If it is continued for at least six months there is evidence of some correlation with higher quality parenting interactions with children aged five years (Gutman *et al.*, 2009).

Risk factors are compounded by **socio-economic status** as mothers with lower socio-economic status are more likely to live in poverty, experience depression (Segre *et al.*, 2007; Goyal *et al.*, 2010), smoke, have poor diets, attend antenatal clinics less frequently (Wolfe *et al.*, 2014), and are least likely to breastfeed (UNICEF, 2012). With approximately 30 per cent of families living in poverty today (Barnardo's, 2014) it is important for Early Years practitioners to understand these determinants of health and to facilitate interventions where possible.

Health risks in the Early Years

It has been suggested that children today 'may on average, live less healthy and possibly even shorter lives than their parents' (Olshansky *et al.*, 2005, p. 1143). The major health concerns for young children identified are obesity, increasing mental health issues, accidents and cancers. All these are affected by lifestyle factors of diet, exercise, leisure pursuits and the quality of social relationships (Department of Health, 2010). In studies of exercise the British Heart Foundation found only 21 per cent of boys and 16 per cent of girls met the current recommended levels, and for the first time exercise guidelines for pre-school children have been introduced (BHF, 2012).

Parental exercising habits during pregnancy and the early years are linked to children's physical activity at age 11 years (Mattocks *et al.*, 2008). Similarly, parental diet and use of snacks, and both permissive and coercive discipline strategies were linked to obesity in childhood (Morawska and West, 2013). However, in addition to lifestyle (explicit) influences, obesity is also determined by underlying (implicit) factors, e.g. a family's socio-economic status may affect its access to healthy foods (Currie *et al.*, 2012), and also to safe play areas; while macro aspects e.g. food advertising and labeling, are further powerful forces.

Table 14.1 Determinants of health and Sure Start centres

Children unequally experience two types of health determinants (Figure 1); therefore, to tackle health inequalities both types of determinants require addressing. When Sure Start Local Programmes (SSLP) were introduced in 1995 they had the potential to address both determinants.

EXPLICIT DETERMINANTS AMENABLE TO INDIVIDUAL CONTROL:	Reflection
Individual explicit determinants are the observable health behaviours of individuals and families. For example, smoking, exercising and eating habits. They are a consequence of our choices and are influenced by the cultural habits, customs and context of our social group. Therefore explicit determinants are known as 'behavioural', and 'cultural' explanations (Taylor and Field 2007).	SSLPs were designed to be responsive to local needs and provide services aimed at strengthening the individual parent and child. Each SSLP delivered different campaigns identified by local health needs. For example: classes ranging from infant-led weaning, healthy eating, to baby massage and yoga.	However, if notice is taken only of this 'individual' behavioural explanation health promotion can easily fail as it is in danger of 'blaming' the families for poor child health, and not acknowledging and addressing underlying determinants.

IMPLICIT DETERMINANTS NOT AMENABLE TO INDIVIDUAL CONTROL:		
These are factors that influence a family's lifestyle choices, but which families are not always aware of, and have no direct control over. They include the macro 'social structures' that are influenced by national policies and provision. Examples include: employment, education, health and early-years services, and welfare benefits. These in turn influence a family's material conditions e.g. the type of housing and neighbourhood they live in, and subsequently the children's peer group and social experiences. These underlying determinants are known as the 'structural', and 'material' explanations, as they analyse the **social and environmental circumstances external to individual control** that influence health and health behaviours.

One particular social structure is the 'inverse' health service provision i.e. how health services are more available and accessible for people of higher SES who are the healthiest and have least need of services, whilst families of lower SES with the poorest health find health services functionally and psychologically less accessible. | **The political aspect:** Politicians acknowledged the social and economic aspects of health inequalities by introducing the SSLP policy. It aimed to be a universal service reaching all families and was introduced in three waves that progressed from areas of highest to lowest deprivation.

Structural aspects: SSLP provided education classes for 'return to work' skills for parents in addition to free or low cost childcare e.g. stay and play activities and toy libraries, to allow parents to attend. A high number have provided advice with financial concerns.

Environmental aspects: The SSLPs could not directly change the environment but they could provide safe places for parents to meet and discuss local issues.

Access to health services: In SSLPs health professionals worked in integrated teams to plan and deliver a range of health services, from assessments to advice and education sessions. | Acknowledging the impact of underlying determinants allows more effective health promotion. However, as the benefits of changing health behaviours are not immediately measurable the influence of SSLP's on health inequalities is still being researched.

This allowed the opportunity for social networks to be formed and possibilities for social lobbying action, (thus fostering critical health literacy Figure 3).

Examples of health services are described in 'Delivering health services through Sure Start Children's Centres' (DoH 2007). However, "Healthcare services have been estimated to contribute only a third of the improvements we could make in life expectancy – changing people's lifestyles and removing health inequalities contribute the remaining two thirds" (DoH 2010, p.16). |

Political parties continually debate whether explicit or implicit determinants have the greatest influence on health inequalities, and the evaluation of first phase of SSLP's exposed both strengths and limitations in reaching the most vulnerable in society. The recession prompted changes and a reduction in their provision, although their role as a centre for health service provision may increase (Wolfe *et al.*, 2014). Reviews of the way forward for re-structured Sure Start Children Centre's are found in All Party Parliamentary Sure Start Group (2013) and NCB (2013).

REFLECTIVE PRACTICE
REFLECTIVE PRACTICE

The obese child is often blamed for his or her condition. 'Education' on the benefits of healthy eating and exercise is seen as the solution. To appreciate fully the wide range of forces influencing the health of a child it is useful to use Bronfenbrenner's (1979) ecological theory of the child as nested in a circle of influences. This is a useful framework for illustrating the interrelating influences on a child's health. Use this framework to identify the complexity of behavioural, cultural, material and structural forces influencing childhood obesity. Reflect on how acknowledging all the forces influencing obesity might alter the focus of your health promotion activities in your role as an Early Years practitioner.

Health risks from service provision

In the UK the quality of health service care for children with chronic diseases was found to be less good compared with other northern European countries. Examples of this are seen in relatively poor service provisions for children with epilepsy and preventable emergencies and deaths for children with diabetes (National Children's Bureau (NCB), 2013).

Mental health and well-being

The World Health Organization defines health as 'a state of complete physical, mental and social well-being and not merely the absence of disease or infirmity' and mental health as 'a state of well-being in which every individual realizes his or her own potential, can cope with the **normal** stresses of life, can work productively and fruitfully, and is able to make a contribution to her or his community' (2014).

Use of the term 'well-being' in Early Years practice is a fairly recent phenomenon. It is used to mean a state of being 'comfortable, healthy or happy'. References to being 'prosperous' and 'contented' may be included in some definitions. Some practitioners have found problems with the term asking whether well-being is an absolute state only or whether a person can have some well-being but not complete well-being. Another concern is whether well-being can be judged objectively or whether the state of a person's well-being is only available to another person when it is reported to them i.e. it is subjective. This is problematic for the Early Years practitioner because part of their role is to strive to ensure young children's well-being, which may be difficult if you are not entirely clear what it is and how to measure it.

Earlier on in this chapter the interrelatedness of health factors was discussed. The Department of Health states that 'Mental well-being has a profound role in shaping physical health and contributing to life chances, as well as being important to individuals and as a societal measure' (DoH, 2012 p. 39).

In many Early Years and school documents mental well-being is referred to as 'social and emotional well-being', incorporating psychological development and self-regulation of emotions in conjunction with social relationships. We recognise that in the same way as children grow

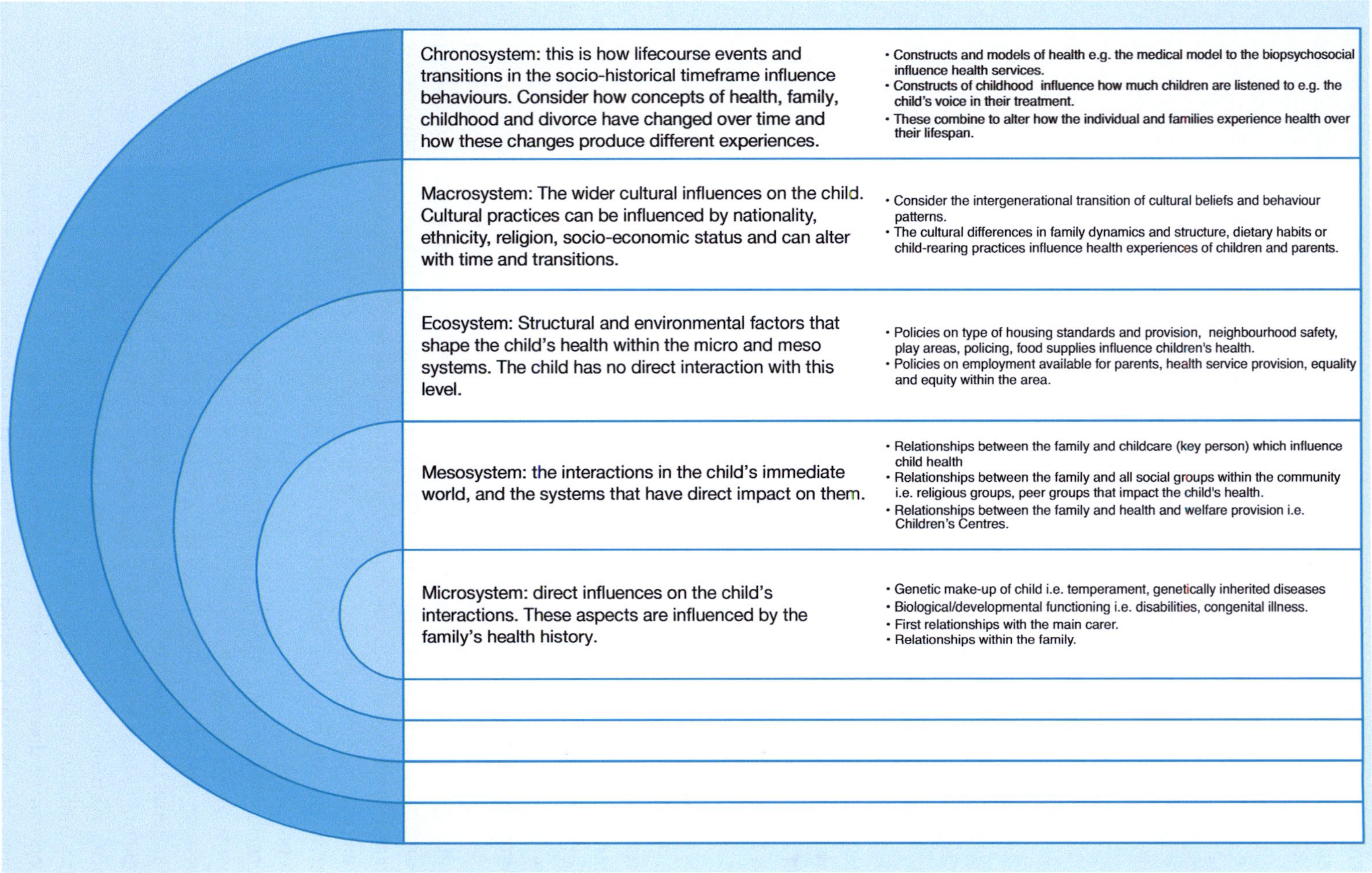

Chronosystem: this is how lifecourse events and transitions in the socio-historical timeframe influence behaviours. Consider how concepts of health, family, childhood and divorce have changed over time and how these changes produce different experiences.

- Constructs and models of health e.g. the medical model to the biopsychosocial influence health services.
- Constructs of childhood influence how much children are listened to e.g. the child's voice in their treatment.
- These combine to alter how the individual and families experience health over their lifespan.

Macrosystem: The wider cultural influences on the child. Cultural practices can be influenced by nationality, ethnicity, religion, socio-economic status and can alter with time and transitions.

- Consider the intergenerational transition of cultural beliefs and behaviour patterns.
- The cultural differences in family dynamics and structure, dietary habits or child-rearing practices influence health experiences of children and parents.

Ecosystem: Structural and environmental factors that shape the child's health within the micro and meso systems. The child has no direct interaction with this level.

- Policies on type of housing standards and provision, neighbourhood safety, play areas, policing, food supplies influence children's health.
- Policies on employment available for parents, health service provision, equality and equity within the area.

Mesosystem: the interactions in the child's immediate world, and the systems that have direct impact on them.

- Relationships between the family and childcare (key person) which influence child health
- Relationships between the family and all social groups within the community i.e. religious groups, peer groups that impact the child's health.
- Relationships between the family and health and welfare provision i.e. Children's Centres.

Microsystem: direct influences on the child's interactions. These aspects are influenced by the family's health history.

- Genetic make-up of child i.e. temperament, genetically inherited diseases
- Biological/developmental functioning i.e. disabilities, congenital illness.
- First relationships with the main carer.
- Relationships within the family.

Figure 14.2 Determinants of child health in an ecological frame

lly, mental health also unfolds slowly over time. It is therefore not always possible to ...preciate the state of a child's social and emotional well-being, although a number of ...eories exist to aid our understanding. Maslow's pyramid of hierarchical needs (1943) is one well-known theory. He considers how well-being needs progress from basic **physiological** needs of food, warmth and safety, through to more psychological needs of security, self-esteem, belongingness, before reaching more intellectual needs of self-actualisation.

A child's mental health is strongly related to parental health, values and beliefs. The development of children's mental health begins with their first relationships. Parents manage their own transition to parenthood in different ways, as their preparedness is related to their own cultural beliefs on parenthood, the existence of social support systems, their economic context and the accessibility of health services (Van Ijzendoorn, 1992). Stress leading to anxiety and post-natal depression in the mother is related to higher levels of behaviour concerns and conduct disorders in children, as the experiences children are exposed to in their early years influence their ability to cope in adverse circumstances (Commons, 2015). Positive mental health develops if children are exposed to increasingly complex experiences in a secure, supportive environment, as they learn to be optimistic and develop the ability to 'bounce back' (Seligman, 2007; Tamminen and Puura, 2014). Children who are able to adapt appropriately to life events are considered to have resilience. Resilience may be defined as: 'the capacity of individuals, schools, families and communities to cope successfully with everyday challenges, including life transitions, times of cumulative stress and significant adversity or risk' (Rutter, 1990, p. 184).

A main protective factor in resilience is the child's first relationship and the formation of a secure attachment bond. The 'goodness of fit' between the child and parent initiates the child's first experiences of self-worth. The formation of a secure attachment is related to both the temperament of the child and the attunement of the parent. The ability to form a secure attachment with a child is in turn related to the parent's own experience of attachment, as intergenerational studies have demonstrated repeated patterns of attachment style (Benoit and Parker, 1994). The child learns to control and self-regulate their emotions in relation to their own temperament by using social referencing and mirroring of the parent (Tamminen and Puura, 2014). If parents have excess stress they may be emotionally unavailable for the infant and have difficulty with attunement. Maternal depression and anxiety has been linked to a higher risk of emotional or conduct disorders in infancy (Office of National Statistics, 2012). Depression is twice as common in mothers living in deprivation, and three times as common in teenage mothers. Thus the quality of parenting influences resilience, for example, in challenging conditions, successful regulation of sleep, emotions, arousal and attention by parents act as protective factors (Timminen and Puura, 2014).

Increasingly, research provides evidence to support early intervention programmes that acknowledge ecological influences on child health (Centre for Social Justice, 2011). The Early Intervention: First Steps (Allen, 2011) and Conception to Age 2: the First 1001 Days (Commons, 2015) propose using specialised multi-agency health and social support services for families. An example of this is where services offering support for sleep and feeding concerns use specialised practices such as 'the Solihull Approach' (Douglas *et al.*, 2009) provided by health visitors working with Early Years practitioners. However, The Centre for Social Justice (2011) warn that for early interventions to work they must be supported by all government parties to avoid 'short termism', and to ensure funding of a well-trained Early Years workforce who can implement evidence based strategies effectively.

REFLECTIVE PRACTICE
REFLECTIVE PRACTICE

The Children's Society report (2012, p. 14) identified six priorities to promote children's well-being:

1 The right conditions to learn and develop;
2 A positive view of themselves and a respect for their identity;
3 Enough of the items and experiences that matter to them;
4 Positive relationships with their family and friends;
5 A safe and suitable home environment and local area;
6 The opportunities to take part in positive activities that help them thrive.

Reflect on your own practice:

1 How well are these promoted in your own practice?
2 What are the implications of these six priorities for you as an Early Years practitioner, parents and the community provision in your area?

Mental ill-health and young children

The mental ill-health of young children is classified as a 'problem' or 'disorder'. 'Problems' are viewed as short-term and may occur in limited contexts, e.g. anxiety, fears, food refusal, temper tantrums, and bedwetting. They are considered to occur in 1 to 5 children. 'Disorders', however, are viewed as more long-term, consistent and occur in multiple contexts e.g. phobias, depression, conduct disorders, and developmental delays (i.e. speech delays), eating disorders and attachment disorders. According to Young Minds (2014) one in every ten children aged 5 to 16 has a diagnosable mental health disorder, one in twelve self-harm (in the past ten years this has risen by 68 per cent), and 7 per cent of three-year-olds have moderate to severe behaviour concerns (Maughan *et al.*, 2004).

The most commonly reported mental health issues in childhood are anxiety, depression, conduct disorders and hyperactivity disorder, such as ADHD (Green *et al.*, 2005). Mental ill health in childhood has serious consequences for a child's future, as it may affect not only their **emotional development** but also his or her social relationships, education, and future prospects. It is thought that half of all adult mental health disorders originate in childhood. This has implications for all Early Years practitioners, as well as mental-health professionals, as a survey of adults in the UK by MindEd identified that 38 per cent of people working directly with very young children did not know how to recognise the signs and symptoms of mental ill-health in children and (worryingly) would not seek help if unsure. They also found that 39 per cent of men considered the signs and symptoms of mental ill-health in children indicative of 'bad behaviour' (The Lancet, 2014). This ignorance of practitioners may mean that children with mental health concerns can miss out on early appropriate support and care during crucial developmental periods.

Provision for mental ill-health in childhood

The Child and Adolescent Mental Health Services (CAMHS), initiated in 1998, has four tiers of support moving from universally available general advice provided by non-specialised professionals e.g. teachers, and social workers, to targeted provision providing individual care by mental-health specialists. CAMHS are often criticised for allowing bureaucracy to limit and slow down the responsiveness of its service. A further area of tension relates to concerns that diagnoses and labelling of mental ill-health in childhood may do more harm than good. Timimi (2004) in his paper 'Rethinking Childhood Depression' argues that childhood has become medicalised. By this he means that understandable behavioural reactions in children are being viewed as disorders and medical problems, as 'childhood depression as a categorical diagnosis cannot be differentiated from normal unhappiness'. Focus on childhood unhappiness in the UK grew following the UNICEF Report (2009) on children's well-being, as the UK was ranked 23rd in the world. Timimi (2004) argues for a multi-perspective approach to children's mental ill-health that uses non-medical treatment to treat 'individual symptoms' of children's unhappiness, as this avoids the stigma that occurs as a consequence of labelling.

Health promotion policy for young children

The twenty-first century has witnessed a collection of government policies aimed at improving the health of children. These reflect the changing focus of child health care from a highly biomedical model concentrating on early recognition and treatment of diseases and development delay, to a preventative model focused on improving the health and well-being of all children.

The Healthy Child Programme in 2009 (HCP) is the most comprehensive overview of guidelines for the delivery of preventative and early intervention services to children from conception to age 19 years. It is formed from the National Service Framework Standard 1 and 2: Children, Young People and Maternity Services 2004, and the Public Health Service Agreement indicators, and incorporates the guidelines from the Health for All Children Report (Hall and Elliman, 2006). The Health for All Children Report highlighted the need for a universal, structured service for children that is evidence-based. This has ensured that a key feature of the Healthy Child Programme is that it is based on the strong evidence obtained from reviews and research conducted by the National Institute for Clinical Excellence (NICE), the Royal College of Pediatrics and academics, for example, research on attachment and parenting by the University of Warwick.

The key focus of the Healthy Child Programme is early intervention by providing universal support to children through services for parents during pregnancy and the early years. This is offered through a multi-agency team led by a health visitor and including Early Years practitioners. **Sure Start** Children's Centres may take an increasing role in the delivery of the Healthy Child Programme in future (Wolfe *et al.*, 2013). The key health aims of the Healthy Child Programme are:

- Improving mental health and well-being by promoting secure attachments and positive parenting from birth.
- Early recognition of risk factors for children's health, e.g. increasing breastfeeding rates, and support to reduce parental smoking and depression.

- Prevention of childhood illness through immunisation programmes and surveillance of risk factors e.g. for obesity.
- Detecting early developmental delay through standardised screening programmes.
- Improving health and safety by health promotion on safety, and a balance between safety and risk.
- Improving the outcomes for children at risk of **exclusion** by a programme of progressive universalism supporting the most vulnerable.

Rather than a universal service the Healthy Child Programme represents a move to one that is more personalised and aimed at increasing provision to individual families with the most need.

PROVOCATION 6

The Early Interventions: The Next Steps document proposed by Allen 2011 is available at: http://media.education.gov.uk/assets/files/pdf/g/graham%20allens%20review%20of%20 early%20intervention.pdf

Review the document to identify the range of evidence-based approved strategies that Early Years practitioners deliver and are recommended for use in the Healthy Child Programme.

Health promotion theory for the Early Years practitioner

Health promotion is defined as 'the process of enabling people to increase control over, and to improve, their health' (World Health Organization, 2014, p. 1).

PROVOCATION 7

In school PSHE you will have experienced health promotion campaigns e.g. healthy eating, sun awareness, sex education, anti-smoking, drug awareness.

- Think of one 'health campaign' that successfully influenced you to change your health behaviours.
- Write down the factors that influenced your decision.
- Now do the same for a 'health campaign' that did not successfully influence you to change.
- Identify the key differences influencing your choices.

Table 14.2 Applying St Leger's (2001) three levels of health literacy (knowing about health) to promote healthy eating

Level of health literacy: ways of knowing	Role of the Professional Practitioner	Application to practice for healthy eating	Approach model	Examples of possible outcomes for healthy eating programmes	Identify the outcomes for a health topic in your field of practice
Level 1: Functional health literacy Functional knowing	**Aim:** 1. To improve practitioners' 'expert' knowledge on the health subject (a determinant of health). 2. To have the ability to nonjudgmentally communicate unbiased information on the health subject to all involved (i.e. children and their families).	**Aim:** 1. Research and identify the knowledge on food to be delivered i.e. to the children and their families. 2. To develop a basic understanding of the factors inhibiting and enhancing health eating for children and families. 3. To explore the most effective transmission method. i.e. – Who is the best person to deliver the message? – What skills and methods are needed to effectively transmit this knowledge to individuals and groups?	'Expert' decides and delivers the 'top-down' knowledge. Although some collaboration over the topic can take place.	**Knowledge of:** 1. Knowledge of food groups and their nutritional value (even sugar has some health benefits). 2. What a balanced meal looks like i.e. identifying a healthy plate. 3. How to cook a healthy meal. 4. How to shop for a healthy meal.	
Level 2: Interactive health literacy Analytical knowing	**Aim:** 1. To develop an understanding of the underlying determinants of health and of the processes involved in using health information to change to a healthier lifestyle. 2. To develop the interpersonal skills for interactive and 'collaborative' approaches to support health behaviours.	**Aim:** 1. To sustain sensitive and meaningful interactions with children and parents that exposes what they see as the barriers preventing change to a healthy diet. 2. To support the children and their families in developing their capacity to become healthy eaters i.e. problem solving and practical skills to overcome the barriers. 3. To listen to the needs of the group/individual and provide opportunities to develop the skills needed to become healthy eaters.	'Client centred': collaborative 'bottom-up'	Respond to the needs identified by the children and families. For example: 1. Skills of adapting current diet to a healthier option i.e. cooking healthier versions of their favourite foods. 2. Skills of cooking healthy food on a budget. 3. Skills of shopping on a budget. 4. Understanding food labels. 5. Working with groups of children and families to promote social capital and support social changes.	
Level 3: Critical health literacy Critical consciousness raising	**Aim:** 1. To develop an understanding of social and political forces underlining determinates of health. 2. Appreciate the role of policy in personal and community empowerment. 3. To develop an attitude towards own health, interagency interactions and social responsibilities.	**Aim:** 1. To be aware of the ethical implications of a health policy and ensure appropriate interpretation and implementation of the policy. 2. To support interagency working that facilitates greater personal and community autonomy and empowerment. 3. To support community action on social issues that aims to change public policy on health determinants. 4. Increase the capacity to promote community and societal action that improves the health of disadvantaged groups.	Democratic: collaborative, but can also take expert approach	1. Acknowledge the cost of healthy foods and take community action on this. 2. EYP working with Health Visitors, Doctors, local food providers to increase availability of cheaper healthy foods. 3. Lobby to reduce fast food outlets near schools. 4. Lobby for appropriate labelling of food.	

One issue in health promotion is to ensure people can access the health promotion offered both physically and psychologically. Your target audience may need a degree of health 'literacy'. **Health literacy** is 'the knowledge and competences of persons to meet the complex demands of health in modern society' (Sørensen *et al.*, 2012, p. 1). An Early Years practitioner with an understanding of health literacy can develop the sensitive and non-judgmental approach to health promotion necessary for empowering children and families to live to their optimal health (UNESCO, Education for All 2009) (see Table 14.2).

Level One Health Literacy takes an Educational Approach (Naidoo and Wills, 2007) in which the practitioner is the 'expert' providing unbiased knowledge on health in a 'top-down' approach. The practitioner identifies the need and content of the health promotion. This approach can be successful when people feel that they are ready and able to make a change. However, it has been criticised, as 'knowledge' alone does not provide the skills and conditions to motivate and support behaviour change effectively. If used too assertively and persuasively it may have the opposite effect to that intended.

Level Two Health Literacy takes an Empowerment Approach that moves beyond information giving to acknowledge the social influences on health behaviours. It uses a 'bottom-up' or collaborative approach where the target audience is supported to identify their own issues and needs in relation to a health behaviour. By listening to the experience of individuals and communities the Early Years practitioner can gain an understanding of the power (perceived 'locus of control') they feel they have to make changes. This is sometimes called **self-efficacy** to indicate our belief in our own capacity to change. The Marmot Report provides an illustration of how social group norms and values may act as a barrier to self-efficacy: 'Through social networks, obesity can actually be 'spread' by person-to-person interaction. **Social norms** affect other health areas too: if more than half of a student's social network smoke, then that student's risk of smoking doubles' (DoH, 2010, p. 19). It is considered an ethical form of health promotion as it is non-judgmental in respecting individual free choice and does not induce guilt or victim-blaming stigma.

Conclusion

This chapter has:

- Explored how concepts of health influence our health behaviours and how changes in understanding from the bio-medical to the bio-psychosocial model can influence your practice.
- Outlined changes in child health services in response to health and disease in childhood.
- Discussed the 'observed' and 'underlying' determinants of children's health, and how the unequal exposure to risk factors influences the existence of health inequalities.
- Highlighted the importance of your promotion of positive mental health and support of children with mental ill-health.
- Identified current child health policy and the renewed focus on early intervention programmes.
- Introduced health promotion theory, the concept of health literacy and the need for you to develop a skill set appropriate for empowering and collaborative approaches to health promotion.

I hope I have made a convincing case to you that as an Early Years practitioner you have an important role to play in securing the health and well-being of the children with whom you work.

Further reading

Burton, M., Pavord, E. and Williams, B. (2014) *An Introduction to Child and Adolescent Mental Health,* Sage.
   This book provides an accessible introduction to CAMHS concepts, theory and practice for any EYP interesting in working in this area.

Mooney, A., Boddy, J., Statham, J. and Warwick, I. (2008) Approaches to developing health in early-years settings, *Health Education,* 108(2), 163–177.
   This study provides an example of research highlighting that much work has already been done in promoting health and well-being in Early Years settings. It also indicates the particular challenges of working within the diversity of the sector, and identifies what needs to be done to further develop health-related work for the Early Years.

St Leger, L. (2001) Schools, health literacy and public health: possibilities and challenges. *Health Promotion International,* 16(2), 197–205.
   This article provides a more detailed explanation of health literacy allowing you to effectively contribute and develop health promotion in educational settings.

Useful websites

Change4Life: www.nhs.uk/change4life/pages/nurseries-childrens-centres-supporters.aspx
   This site provides resources and ideas for promoting healthier lifestyles to all ages. However the section for toddlers and pre-school children and their families provides extra links for further research and resources.

Healthy Development and Integrated Working: www.foundationyears.org.uk/health-integration-in-practice/healthy-development/
   This site provides links to a wide range of health policy and promotions and is a good resource for projects on child health as it gives clear examples of health promotion in practice.

Place2Be: www.place2be.org.uk/
   Although government websites on 'children's mental health in the early years' provide comprehensive information, this website not only provides case studies for current coursework but also guidelines for possible career opportunities.

References

Allen, G. (2011) *Early Intervention: The Next Steps.* Norwich: HMSO. Available at: www.dwp. gov.uk/docs/early-intervention-next-steps.pdf (accessed 10 August 2014).

Barnes, M., Butt, S., Tomaszewski, W. (2008) *What Happens to Children in Persistently Poor Housing?* Shelter NatCen, Eaga London.

Barnardos (2014) Child poverty statistics and facts. Available on www.barnardos.org.uk/what_we_do/our_work/child_poverty/child_poverty_what_is_poverty/child_poverty_statistics_facts.htm (accessed 8 March 2015).

Benoit, D., and Parker, K.C.H. (1994) Stability and transmission of attachment across three generations. *Child Development,* 65(5), 1444–1456.

BHF (2012) *Early Movers – Helping under-5s Live Active & Healthy Lives.* BHF.

Blair, M., and Hall, D. (2006) From health surveillance to health promotion: The changing focus in preventive children's services. *Archives of Disease in Childhood*, 91(9), 730-735.

Bronfenbrenner, U. (1979) *The Ecology of Human Development: Experiments by Nature and Design*. Cambridge, MA: Harvard University Press.

Bunker, J. (2001) Medicine matters after all: Measuring the benefits of medical care: A healthy lifestyle, and a just social environment. *International Journal of Epidemiology*, 30(6), 1260-1263.

Centre for Social Justice (2011) *Making Sense of Early Intervention: A Framework for Professionals*. London: Centre for Social Justice.

Commons, House of (2015) *Conception to Age 2: First 1001 Days*, All Party Parliamentary Group. London: HMSO.

Craig, C. (2007) The Potential dangers of a systemic, explicit approach to teaching social and emotional skills (SEAL), Glasgow. Centre for Confidence and Well-Being.

Currie, C., Zanotti, C., Morgan, A., Currie, D., de Looze, M., Roberts, C., Otto, Oddrun, Smith, R. and Barnekow, V. (eds) (2012) *Social determinants of health and well-being among young people. Health Behaviour in School-aged Children* (HBSC) *Study: International report from the 2009/2010 survey*. Copenhagen, WHO Regional Office for Europe, 2012 (*Health Policy for Children and Adolescents*, no. 6).

DoH (2008) *Children and Young People in Mind: The final report of the National CAMHS Review*. London: HMSO.

DoH (2009) *Healthy Child Programme: Pregnancy and the First 5 Years of Life*. London: HMSO. Available at www.gov.uk/government/publications/healthy-child-programme-pregnancy-and-the-first-5-years-of-life.

DoH (2010) *Healthy Lives, Healthy People: Our Strategy for Public Health in England*. London: HMSO.

DoH (2012) *Report of the Children and Young People's Health Outcomes Forum*. www.gov.uk/government/uploads/system/uploads/attachment_data/file/216852/CYP-report.pdf.

DoH (2013) *Infant Feeding Profiles. in the New National Pledge to Improve Children's Health and Reduce Child Deaths*. HMSO online.

DoH (2014) *Giving Every Child A Healthy Start In Life,* London: HMSO. Available at: www.gov.uk/government/policies/giving-all-children-a-healthy-start-in-life.

Douglas, H., Delaney, J., Cabral, J. and Rheeston, R. (2009) Supporting parenting: the Solihull Approach. *Healthcare, Counselling and Psychotherapy Journal*, 9(3), 17-21.

Ecclestone, K. and Hayes, D. (2009). *The dangerous rise of therapeutic education*. London: Routledge.

Faculty of Public Health (2010) The UK Faculty of Public Health: Working to improve the public's health . Available at www.fph.org.uk.

Goyal, D., Gay, C., and Lee, K.A. (2010) How much does low socioeconomic status increase the risk of prenatal and postpartum depressive symptoms in first-time mothers? *Women's Health Issues*, 20(2), 96-104.

Gray, R., Headley, J., Oakley, L., Kurinczuk, J., Brocklehurst, P. and Hollowell, J. (2009) Towards an understanding of variations in infant mortality rates between different ethnic groups in England and Wales. *Inequalities in Infant Mortality Project Briefing paper 3*. Oxford: National Perinatal Epidemiology Unit.

Green H., McGinnity, A., Meltzer, H., Ford, T. and Goodman, R. (2005) *Mental Health of children and Young People in Great Britain, 2004*. London: Palgrave.

Green, J. and Thorogood, N. (1998) *Analysing Health Policy: A Sociological Approach*. Routledge. London.

Gutman L., M, Brown J, Akerman R (2009) *Nurturing Parenting Capability: The Early Years*, Centre for Research on the Wider Benefits of Learning, The Institute of Education, London.

Gutman, M. and Feinstein, L. (2007) *Parenting behaviour and children's development from infancy to early childhood: Changes, continuities and contributions*. London: Department for Education and Skills,

Hall, D.M., and Elliman, D. (2006) *Health for all Children* (revised 4th edition). Oxford University Press.

Marmot, M. (2013) (Chair) *Review of social determinants and the health divide in the WHO European Region*. WHO, Denmark.

Marmot M. and Bell, R. (2010) *Fair Society, Healthy Lives: Strategic Review of Health Inequalities in England post 2010*. The Marmot Review. London: UCL.

Maslow, A.H. (1943) A theory of human motivation. *Psychological Review*, 50(4), 370-396.

Mattocks, C., Ness, A., Deere, K., Tilling, K., Leary, S., Blair, S. and Riddoch, C. (2008) Early life determinants of physical activity in 11 to 12 year olds: Cohort Study, *BMJ*, 336 (7634), 26–29.

Maughan, B., Brock, A. and Ladva, G. (2004) 'Mental health', in Nessa, N. (ed.), *The Health of Children and Young People*, Office for National Statistics, London, available at: www. statistics.gov.uk/children/downloads/mental_health.pdf (accessed 25 March 2007).

Morawska, A. and West, F. (2013). Do parents of obese children use ineffective Parenting Strategies? *Journal of Child Health Care*, 17(4), 375–386.

Naidoo, J., & Wills, J. (2009). *Foundations for health promotion*. Elsevier Health Sciences.

NCB (2013) *Partnership for a Better Start: Perspectives on the Role of Children's Centres*. NCB. London.

Ofsted (2013) *Not Yet Good Enough: Personal, Social, Health and Economic Education in Schools*, (1 May) Ofsted. Ref: 130065.

Olshansky, S., Passaro, D., Hershow, R., Layden, J., Carnes, B. and Brody, J. (2005) A potential decline in life expectancy in the United States in the 21st century. *North England Journal of Medicine*, 352, 1138–1145.

ONS (2012) *Childhood, Infant and Perinatal Mortality in England and Wales: Cause of Infant Deaths*. ONS www.ons.gov.uk.

Rutter, M. (1990) Psychosocial resilience and protective mechanisms. *American Journal of Orthopsychiatry*. Cambridge: Cambridge University Press, 184–226.

Scheetuga and Zeanah (2001) in Tamminen, T. and Puura, K. (2014) 'Infant mental health', in Rutter, M. (ed.) *Child and Adolescent Psychiatry*. London: Wiley (6th edn in press).

Segre, L.S., O'Hara, M.W., Arndt, S., and Stuart, S. (2007) The prevalence of postpartum depression. *Social Psychiatry and Psychiatric Epidemiology*, 42(4), 316–321.

Seligman, M. (2007) *The Optimistic Child: A proven program to safeguard children against depression and build lifelong resilience*. Boston: Houghton Miffin.

Sørensen, K., Van den Broucke, S., Fullam, J., Doyle, G., Pelikan, J., Slonska, Z., & Brand, H. (2012). Health literacy and public health: a systematic review and integration of definitions and models. *BMC public health*, 12(1), 80.

St Leger, L. (2001) Schools, health literacy and public health: possibilities and challenges. *Health Promotion International*, 16(2), 197–205.

Tamminen, T. and Puura, K. (2014) Infant mental health. In Rutter, M. (ed.) *Child and Adolescent Psychiatry*. London: Wiley (6th edition in press).

Taylor, S. and Field, D. (2007) *Sociology of Health and Health Care* (4th edn). Wiley Blackwell. London.

The Children's Society (2012) *Promoting Positive Well-Being for Children. A Report for Decision-Makers in Parliament, Central Government and Local Areas*. The Children's Society. Available at: www. childrenssociety.org.uk/sites/default/files/tcs/good_childhood_report_2012_final_0.pdf.

The Lancet (2014) Mental health and wellbeing in children and adolescents. *The Lancet*, 383 (9924) 1183.

Timimi, S. (2004) Rethinking childhood depression, *BMJ* 2004, 329, 1398–401.

Unicef (2012) *Guide to The Baby Friendly Initiative* Available at: www.unicef.org.uk/BabyFriendly/Resources/Guidance-for-Health-Professionals/Writing-policies-and-guidelines/guide-to-the-baby-friendly-initiative-standards/.

Van Ijzendoorn, M. (1992) Intergenerational transmission of parenting: A review of studies in nonclinical populations *Developmental Review*, 12(1), 76–99.

WHO (2014) World Health Organization International. Available at www.who.int/topics/health_promotion/en/.

Wolfe, I. (2013) Strengthening children's centres through the universalism of healthcare in National Children's Bureau (NCB) *Partnerships for a Better Start: Perspectives on the role of children's centres*. London, NCB.

Wolfe, I., Macfarlane, A., Donkin, A., Marmot, M., and Viner, R. (2014) *Why Children Die: Death in Infants, Children, and Young People in the UK*. Part A. Report on behalf of Royal College of Paediatrics and Child Health and National Children's Bureau. Royal College of Paediatrics and Child Health, 5–11.

Young Minds (2014) *Young Minds: Child and Adolescent Mental Health*. Available at: www.youngminds.org.uk.

15 Holistic development: the social and emotional needs of children

Tricia Johnson

LEARNING OUTCOMES

After reading this chapter you should be able to:

✔ Support and respond to the emotional and social needs of very young children.
✔ Create links between **attachment** theory and brain development.
✔ Relate the research included throughout the chapter to the social and emotional needs of very young children.
✔ Analyse the factors affecting **social** and **emotional development**.
✔ Analyse and evaluate roles and responsibilities of Key Persons.
✔ Fully articulate and critique the importance of detailed observation.
✔ Reflect upon the role of the environment in promoting the emotional and social needs of very young children.

Introduction

This chapter explores the social and emotional needs of children from birth to five years of age. The aim of the chapter is to expand your current knowledge and understanding from level three through to level five by increasing your ability to compare and contrast, to reflect, to relate theory to practice and to analyse your findings in relation to relevant research. Therefore, while social and **emotional development** is included within the text it is not addressed in detail. It includes aspects of attachment theory and the changes within attachment theory following research, historic and recent, and the current cultures of **childhood** since the work of John Bowlby during the 1950s and 1960s. Reference has been made to the research by Arnold (2010), creating links between children's schemas and their emotions, and that of Gooch and Powell (2013) entitled 'The Baby Room', which examined the practices, attitudes and qualifications of those working with the youngest children in formal daycare settings, very much from the point of view of the childcare professionals. Mention of the expanding field of research into brain development, especially in relation to attachment theory and the experiences of children in the first year of life, has also been included.

The chapter continues with the role of Key Persons and the responsibilities of all Early Years workers in home settings such as Childminders and Nannies, in group settings such as Nurseries, Full Day Care, Children's Centres and Pre-Schools are considered in detail. The effects of National culture, family cultures and cultures within Childcare settings are considered along with factors that may affect the social and emotional development of very young children. You are strongly encouraged to reflect on your practice within your work settings and to fully understand the important role that you, as well qualified, well informed practitioners, have when working with parents and other professionals to support the social and emotional needs of every child in your setting. You are presented with short anecdotes and case studies to consider, discuss, critque and analyse in relation to your own settings and practice. Reference is made to the Chapters in Sections 2, 3 and 4 in order to address areas of childcare and education that overlap and to maintain the holistic approach to child development and learning in relation to the social and emotional needs of each individual child.

Supporting and responding to the emotional and social needs of very young children

The importance of responding sensitively to the emotional and social needs of all children has always been recognised by the majority of childcare professionals, social services, educators, **health** professionals and parents. Throughout the last eleven to twelve years this has become more strongly acknowledged through the findings of research into the development of the brain. Blakemore and Frith (2005) identify three major findings: the dramatic increases in neural connections in the very young, critical periods that are linked to experiences that shape the brain, and enriched environments. Katz, in Dowling (2010), identifies the fact that if we respond effectively to children's social and emotional needs providing them with *social and emotional competence by the age of six . . . we can make a difference for their whole lives'* (2010, p. vii). The findings from research in recent years has had an impact on childcare provision with the specific inclusion of social and emotional development within the areas of learning in Government documents such as: Birth to Three Matters (2003), Every Child Matters (2003), the Early Years Foundation Stage (2008, 2012 and 2014), the National Curriculum (2013, 2014) as Personal, **Social, Health** and Economics, the Children Acts (1989 and 2004) and the Childcare Act (2006). While these documents and policies continue to have a direct impact on the provision of formal day care, registered childminders, nursery and pre-school settings today those such as Birth to Three Matters and every Child Matters, have been archived by the Government. The Early Years Foundation Stage (March 2014) has just been published and is to be used by all registered settings from September 2014.

Personal, social and emotional development involves helping children to develop a positive sense of themselves, and others; to form positive relationships and develop respect for others; to develop social skills and learn how to manage their feelings; to understand appropriate behaviour in groups; and to have confidence in their own abilities (EYFS, 2012, p. 5).

As stated above supporting and responding to the emotional and social needs of children from birth to five years of age is one of the most important roles of all parents and professionals involved in the care, learning, development and education of every individual child. Therefore, we will first consider the immediate emotional needs of all very young children. The moment a baby is born it displays basic needs for food, warmth, love, security and to communicate. These needs are communicated through different cries, body language and facial expressions, that their mother/main carer and you, as professional child carers, learn to interpret and respond to (Trevarthen, 2011, Gerhardt, 2004; Miller 1992 in Elfer *et al.*, 2003. Gradually through the adults' responses to the basic and emotional needs of each child they develop holistically. Thus, their physical development (see chapter 20), communication, language and literacy development (see chapter 17), learning and cognitive development (see chapter 15) and social and emotional development progress. Without appropriate responses to the social and emotional needs of each child by parents and carers the all-round development of the child may well be affected.

Many of you will have already been working with very young children within the age group from birth to five years and will appreciate the importance of social and emotional development. The response to the new born baby, mentioned above, provides the initial sense of love and security which should be gradually nurtured and developed as the child grows and progresses. The positive emotions of love, belonging and feeling secure are very strong but so too are the negative emotions of fear, insecurity and not being responded to. You know how important it is to work closely with parents, in partnership with them and as Bowlby stated: 'A society which values its children must cherish their parents' (Bowlby, 1951 in Steele, 2002, p. 522). Valuing and working with parents also helps to manage transitions and settling-in periods effectively as well as managing the day-to-day changes in health, emotions, learning and development, and the ever-changing related needs of every child and their parents/carers. Consider the following provocation:

PROVOCATION 1

During a visit to a nursery a toddler of approximately eighteen months was crying. It appeared that no one was taking any notice of the toddler who, as well as crying, was looking around for a response from the adults. A comment was made by the visitor, 'oh dear you are not very happy'. An immediate response from one of the adults was, 'He's just having a bad day'.

- What are your initial thoughts when reading this and how does it make you feel?
- Consider how you would manage the situation.
- How would you be responding to the toddler's needs?
- What are the reasons that could be causing the toddler to be miserable?
- Do you think that young children do 'just have bad days' or do you consider that there is always an underlying cause for different displays of emotion such as crying?
- Evaluate the systems that you have in place in your setting to ensure the emotional needs of each child are met.
- What changes would you make to improve the experiences of the children and to help other members of staff manage similar scenarios/situations within your setting?

All children are reliant upon adults throughout their formative years. They will all be influenced by their immediate environments within their family, micro and meso and their external environments, macro and exo as described by Bronfenbrenner (1979) in his **ecobiological** theory. The influence is not only to the immediate material environments but also to the responses and warmth received from the adults with whom they are in contact. They will be influenced by the different cultures within each environment, the culture of the home, the setting and the multicultural influences of our society today. The beginning of the 1990s saw an enormous demographic change to society in Great Britain with the return of many women to the workforce. This has continued to influence the experiences of children and their families and will probably continue to have an influence on society for the foreseeable future. Given this change/evolution within our society and the requirement for different forms of childcare and education we must ensure that we, as Early Years professionals, continue to vary our responses to meet the needs of very young children and their parents/carers whilst providing consistency for each child.

It has been found that attending childcare settings provides better experiences for some children, especially for many of those living in deprived areas, as reported in the Effective Provision of Pre-School Education (EPPE) report (Sylva, 1997–2004), where those children attending settings with highly qualified staff providing high qualitiy learning experiences attained higher levels of learning and development than those attending poor quality provision where there is a risk of poorer outcomes (Mooney and Munton, 1997). Conversely one could say that children experiencing multiple care givers at a very young age may result in inconsistencies of care and education for the children, especially when linked to Bowlby's research in attachment.

REFLECTIVE PRACTICE

Read and reflect on the following statements:

- The fact that many people still consider it essential for very young children to be at home with their Mothers, certainly until the age of two years.
- Whether opinions and attitudes have moved on from this point or whether this attitude still influences many parents and society as a whole?
- It has often been said and observed that parents feel guilty when returning to work and leaving very young children. However, a recent poll involving a group of working mothers has provided opposing evidence. The mothers are saying that they enjoy going to work, do not feel guilty and think that the children benefit from being with parents who want to be with them in the evenings and at weekends. (This was reported in the *Sunday Times* (2014) and related to a poll by Saatchi and Saatchi for MumsNet April 2014.)

Having reflected on the above statements how will you work with a parent/carer who wishes to discuss/has concerns about opinions such as these?

The importance of a child's attachment to parents and carers

The processes of attachment to main carers will now be considered in more detail. John Bowlby's research into attachment between a mother and baby has already been referred to in the introduction and the paragraph above. Initially, and as had already been identified by Freud in the early twentieth century, Bowlby (1979/2005) saw the mother as the most important person for a child to bond with and form a strong attachment to. He identified the need for a strong bond of attachment and saw a difference between the behaviours of children who had secure attachment and those who had insecure attachment to the mother. However, he also recognised that there may be occasions when a mother may be unable to care for the child. On these occasions he advocated sensitive transitions with the new carer spending time with the mother and the child prior to the mother's absence (Bowlby, 1965). Winnicott (1971) suggested that the use of transitional objects, taking a favourite toy or other special item from home to the new setting, provides a very special connection between the two environments and a connection to the mother/carer.

Bowlby's research and attachment theory was supported by the work of Mary Ainsworth who developed the Strange Situation Assessment to determine whether the child was securely or insecurely attached to the mother. Holmes (2001) speaks about Ainsworth's strange situation and also identifies the characteristics of parents who provide their child/children with secure attachment as demonstrating attunement, sensitivity and responsiveness, also recognised by Mooney and Munton (1997). When a baby cries it is seeking positive responses to its needs, which, when received, help the child to feel safe and secure. Humans are born with an innate desire to communicate and to be communicated with (Trevarthen, 2011). If there is no response or a lack of positive response from the mother this begins to affect the baby. Nature provides for the development of attachment bonds in that a baby's vision has a focal length of approximately 200 to 300 millimetres, allowing a feeding baby to focus on his/her mother's face. Most mothers respond to this by gazing at their baby whilst breast or bottle feeding thus making eye contact and helping to ensure that the baby feels secure and loved. However, Holmes (2001) suggests that Bowlby sometimes implied that all that was needed for a secure attachment to develop was a secure base; this was in relation to a psychotherapeutic situation. Can you relate the need for a secure base to childcare settings? Do you as child-carers/educators provide a secure base and do you also, as identified by Holmes (2001), provide the 'empathy and responsiveness' that is required to ensure that children's emotional needs are observed, recognised and met? Holmes identified six domains of attachment theory:

- Secure base – without which survival is impossible
- Exploration and enjoyment
- Protest and anger
- Loss
- Internal working models – are the way in which the child/adult builds up representations of relationships and bases its expectations of current interpersonal interactions on past experiences (Bowlby, 1988 in Holmes, 2001)
- Reflexive function and narrative competence – the ability to be able to talk about oneself and difficult situations.

While these domains do not relate exactly to childcare settings, using the headings of each domain and relating them to your settings, in the broadest sense of their meanings, do you witness them in your settings and can you use them to support the emotional and social needs of the children? Do you see children exploring the environment, enjoying being with their peer groups, making friends, learning and developing within a welcoming environment? How do the children manage **separation**, do they display protest and anger? Again think about this in its broadest sense, from the separation and loss experienced when a parent/carer leaves the setting through to the protest and anger displayed at having a toy snatched or children not sharing toys and books with one another. The thoughts that may have perhaps been evoked here are, 'well these emotions of protest, anger and loss are linked to bereavement'. Yes, they are but they are also linked to separation and the feelings when a toy is snatched away.

The emotions linked to attachment and separation begin to emerge as a baby develops the concept of object permanence, as identified by Piaget (Piaget and Inhelder, 1969) during his research into the sensori-motor stages of development. He found that by the age of approximately nine to ten months a baby will search for a hidden object, thus beginning to understand that although the object cannot be seen it still exists. Through experience, it has been observed that the age of eight to ten months can prove to be a very difficult time for many infants to begin attendance at a setting. However, once the concept of object permanence has fully developed children generally settle and adapt to new environments more easily, provided that the transitions are managed sensitively and responsibly by both the parents/carers and the setting.

REFLECTIVE PRACTICE
REFLECTIVE PRACTICE

Reflect for a few minutes on the environment in your workplace.

- Consider the atmosphere, whether it is generally peaceful, whether the children are involved in the activities or whether it is noisy with little involvement in the activities.
- How would you feel as a visitor or a child and their parent attending the setting for the first time?
- Would they or you yourself like to participate in the activities provided or would you want to hide away?
- Do you think that settings should be calm and quiet at all times?
- Is there evidence of 'respectful care' and the staff responding appropriately to the emotional and social needs of the children?

Having reflected upon these questions would your answers to the situation in Provocation 1 remain the same or have your responses changed?

This was highlighted recently by Marlen (2014) during the 'What about the Children' National Conference (2014) in a presentation entitled 'A Gentle Beginning', when she spoke about children needing time, slowing down time for care routines so that *good attachment and respectful care* can be developed and that a *calm and peaceful carer* results in calm and peaceful children. All children need time and space to play and to experience quality care keeping in mind that *every interaction counts* (Lumsden, 2014) and that the best qualified staff reflect first before reacting (Perkins, 2014). The presentation given by Marlen was very closely linked to work with children at the Pickler Institute in Hungary, founded by Emmi Pikler, a paediatrician who believed all children should be healthy, active, competent and peaceful as infants and who are able to live in peace with themselves and their environment (Tardos, 2010). The research of Emmi Pikler includes working with Day Care Settings and provides insight into the ways that the above can be achieved in these busy settings. We recommend this for further reading, research and analysis in relation to your own setting and your practice.

Research has identified the fact that children are able to form attachments to more than one adult/mother figure. Stern (1998) speaks about the fact that the forming of attachments extends beyond mother/infant attachments; they develop throughout life. Rutter (1993) termed these attachments 'selective attachments' that occur between the ages of one and three years. Whilst Stern (1998) acknowledged the importance of secure attachment he suggested that levels of resitant and avoident attachment differed when subgroupings of attachment are researched across different cultures, e.g.

- resistant or avoident attachment in 12 and 20 per cent of US middle-class samples
- South German samples reflected US norms
- North German showed avoidant attachment
- Japanese children showed resistant attachment

(Stern, 1998, pp. 187–188)

Stern also recognised that differences in these results may well be related to the different approaches used for the research. This is included here to provide you with thoughts about the different cultures and parenting styles that you are meeting with in your settings and wider multicultural communities at the present time. Also the possible effects that the different parenting styles may well have on the level of attachment. In order to put attachment theory into context and create links between the theory and practice, the Overarching Principles of the Statutory Framework for the Early Years Foundation Stage are included here. Four guiding principles should shape practice in early years settings. These are:

- Every child is a **unique** child, who is constantly learning and can be resilient, capable, confident and self-assured.
- Children learn to be strong and independent through positive relationships.
- Children learn and develop well in enabling environments, in which their experiences respond to their individual needs and there is a strong partnership between practitioners and parents and/or carers.
- Children develop and learn in different ways and at different rates. The framework covers the education and care of all children in early years provision, including children with special educational needs and disabilities.

(EYFS, 2012 p. 3 and EYFS, 2014, pp. 5–6)

REFLECTIVE PRACTICE
REFLECTIVE PRACTICE

How are these four principles achieved in your setting?

- Consider your own role and the ethos of your setting.
- Is your Key Person System effectively managed?
- Are the social and emotional needs of the children being responded to and met?
- Use the following information regarding Key Persons and the Role of Key Persons in early years settings to analyse the effectiveness of the Key Person system in your setting.

Key Persons – their role and responsibilities

The recognition that children were able to form attachments to more than one significant adult and the need for an identified 'special person' to aid the separation process by being there for that child when a child was left by a parent/carer in a childcare setting resulted in the practice of ensuring that each child was provided with a Key Person. The need for a **key person** was first identified during the 1980s when research highlighted the fact that many of the children were exposed to care from many different members of staff (Goldschmied and Jackson, 2004; Gooch and Powell, 2013). Initially Key Persons were known as Key Workers and the terms still appear to be used interchangeably. However, Elfer *et al.* (2003) make the point that Key Workers are the persons who liaise with and co-ordinate services provided by other professionals. The Key Person, however, first creates a special relationship with the child and second, but equally important, creates a strong partnership between the parents, staff and other professionals in order to provide for the individual needs of each key child (2003, p. 18). Within the same text there is discussion about childcare settings providing home-from-home experiences. There is also the opinion (Dahlberg *et al.*, 1999) that this is definitely not so, that the nursery experience is definitely different from the home experience. This does not mean that the responses of the adults in nursery settings are not sensitive to the needs of the children. Goldschmied and Jackson (2004) speak about everyone wishing to have 'a special relationship' with someone we trust, who is significant and precious to us', so that we know that we have someone to turn to in times of anxiety, high emotion . . . when we desire to feel close to someone who knows us well. This further emphasises the importance of the Key Person in Early Years Settings. It is also emphasised that the Key Person is not a 'substitute' for the parent. As identified by nursery workers (cited in Elfer *et al.*, 2003) the role is similar to that of a being a parent but 'similarity does not mean the same'.

The important role of the Key Person cannot be stressed enough given recent research involving the cortisol levels of young adults. (Cortisol is a glucocorticoid (hormone) secreted by the adrenal gland in response to stress.) It has been found that cortisol levels are, or tend to be, raised when there has not been a strong mother/mother substitute attachment in the first years of life. There is also fragile evidence of raised cortisol levels throughout the day in children attending day care (Sigman, 2011). However, Sigman acknowledges that this research is still not fully understood in relation to day care and the findings have been questioned by many academics as being tenuous. The reason for including this information here is not to cause concern but again to highlight your importance as Key Persons. Other researchers such as Schore (2013) are beginning to relate back to Bowlby's Attachment Theory, that if a strong attachment bond has developed during the first three years of life children are more able to form other attachment relationships throughout their lives, as being accurate - the internal working model as referred to above (Holmes, 2001). This is because the theory can now be supported by physical and scientific evidence relating particularly to right-sided brain development and development of the orbitofrontal regions which regulate emotions and behaviour.

The EYFS (2014) to be used from September 2014 states as follows in Section 1:

FROM RESEARCH TO PRACTICE

Research into brain development and the findings of projects such as 'Effective Early Learning' (Pascal and Bertram, 1997), where the introduction of the Key Worker system to two day nurseries improved the outcomes for key children and key persons in the nursery (Elfer *et al.*, 2003) where the importance of the role is emphasised throughout, has resulted in the need for Key Persons being embedded within the Statutory Framework for the Early Years Foundation Stage (EYFS, 2014). This is despite the concerns raised by childcare workers and different approaches to childcare and education. The importance of that 'special person' has been fully recognised and supported by the findings in 'The Baby Room Project' (Gooch and Powell, 2013).

1.10. Each child must be assigned a key person (also a **safeguarding** and welfare requirement - see paragraph 3.27). Providers must inform parents and/or carers of the name of the key person, and explain their role, when a child starts attending a setting. The key person must help ensure that every child's learning and care is tailored to meet their individual needs. The key person must seek to engage and support parents and/or carers in guiding their child's development at home. They should also help families engage with more specialist support if appropriate.

(EYFS, 2014, p. 10)

Personal, social and emotional development involves helping children to develop a positive sense of themselves, and others; to form positive relationships and develop respect for others; to develop social skills and learn how to manage their feelings; to understand appropriate behaviour in groups; and to have confidence in their own abilities.

(EYFS, 2014, p. 8)

The learning goals for PSE:

In order to ensure children's personal, social and emotional development children must develop a sence of self-confidence and self-awareness, be able to manage feelings and behaviour and be able to make relationships – to be able to share, take turns and be aware of others' needs.

(EYFS, 2014, p. 11)

Section 3 lists the Safeguarding and Welfare Requirements relating specifically to personal, social and emotional development:

3.6 Providers must train all staff to understand their **safeguarding** policy and procedures, and ensure that all staff have up to date knowledge of safeguarding issues. Training made available by the provider must enable staff to identify signs of possible **abuse** and neglect at the earliest opportunity, and to respond in a timely and appropriate way. These may include:

- significant changes in children's behaviour;
- deterioration in children's general well-being;
- unexplained bruising, marks or signs of possible abuse or neglect;
- children's comments which give cause for concern;
- any reasons to suspect neglect or abuse outside the setting, for example in the child's home; and/or
- inappropriate behaviour displayed by other members of staff, or any other person working with the children. For example, inappropriate sexual comments; excessive one-to-one attention beyond the requirements of their usual role and responsibilities; or inappropriate sharing of images.

(EYFS, 2014, p. 17)

3.27. Each child must be assigned a key person. Their role is to help ensure that every child's care is tailored to meet their individual needs (in accordance with paragraph 1.10), to help the child become familiar with the setting, offer a settled relationship for the child and build a relationship with their parents.

(EYFS, 2014, p. 21)

For further information about working with parents please refer to Chapter 20. The main focus for the Key Person has been very much linked to attachment theory, the development of the brain and the future **mental health** of children who experience or do not experience strong attachment bonds during early childhood. In order to respond to the needs of each individual child and their parents/carers it is now imperative that you ensure that the requirements of the EYFS are met in relation to the role of the key person. Does your setting have a policy or guidelines for all Key Persons and do these documents include support for you as Key Persons? How are you going to meet the needs of each child, recognise changes in behaviour such as exhibiting unwanted behaviours and the signs of possible changes or experiences within a child's life as listed above. How are you going to encourage a child who is showing signs of aggressive behaviours or the child who has withdrawn? How will you help a child to share their toys and not to snatch toys from another child. How will you encourage a child to join in group activities? Are you providing a good 'role model' for the children - remember many behaviours are learned, both wanted and unwanted?

CASE STUDY 1

Charlie, aged two years, attends a Day Care setting three days each week. He appeared to settle quickly after initially showing some expected and age appropriate aspects of separation anxiety such as crying and asking for his Mummy or Daddy. Initially he related well to his Key Person (A) and once settled appeared to enjoy his time playing with the toys and alongside his peers, especially enjoying outdoor play. However, after Charlie had been at the setting for about six months he was away from the setting on a family holiday, followed by a bout of illness which resulted in an absence of four weeks.

On return to the Day Care setting, Charlie did not settle. He no longer related well to (A), he cried and clung very tightly to his Mother or Father. He was observed to relax when another member of the staff (B) came across to talk with him and his parent, and he would settle and play. This reaction was observed by the Day Care Manager and the room leader. Charlie's parents tried to talk to him about the reasons he would not relate to (A) but were unable to discover the reason/s.

In discussion with the parents, manager, key person and staff member (B) it was agreed to give the key person responsibilities to staff member (B). Charlie responded well to this outcome and was gradually better able to respond to (A). This was a sensitive situation for staff that can occur in childcare settings. The manager provided supervision and support for both (A) and (B). See 'From research to practice' section above and compare and contrast the case study with your own experiences.

The importance of **observation**, detailed recording of changes in behaviour while maintaining an open mind and not being judgemental or jumping to conclusions cannot be overstated (see Chapter 26, Observation). It is imperative that you remain objective and do not become subjective in order to analyse your observations, interpret your findings and respond appropriately and sensitively to the needs of all children. There are many factors that affect the social and emotional development of children such as their:

- health and **well-being**
- parental health including maternal depression/post natal depression
- new baby
- moving house
- parents working away from home
- new nanny
- new childcare setting
- abuse - neglect, physical, sexual, emotional and domestic violence

- socio-economic status
- family structure
- the expectations of differing cultures

The effects of a mother's experiences before and during pregnancy may also require consideration when assessing a baby's/child's social and emotional state and their subsequent abilities to socialise, communicate, learn and achieve their full potential.

Can you now think about the resources in your setting? Are these just material resources or do they include human resources, you yourself as the professional early years carer and educator? See Chapters 4 and 9. How is your role changing as you progress through your journey as an undergraduate? Are you relating your new indepth knowledge to the practice within your setting when assessing the social and emotional needs of the children? The importance of rich, appropriate adult responses and interactions cannot be over-emphasised, as identified by Blakemore and Frith (2005) that 'enriched environments' create more opportunities for neural connections to be formed than 'impoverished' ones. We can assume, at this stage that we have high quality provision, you have completed observations of your Key Children during their play and have identified their development and learning needs, in this instance their social and emotional needs. Strong schemas that may have been observed that Arnold (2010) has linked to emotions and emotional need are: connecting by tying or joining objects together, enveloping by covering and wrapping and containing by putting objects into containers such as boxes or bags. How would you interpret this behaviour and support their schemas? Connecting, containing and enveloping may be linked to a sense of safety and security at times when children are, perhaps, feeling insecure. Another schema that is linked to a sense of security is 'transporting' which can include the 'transitional objects' Arnold (2010) referred to earlier in the chapter in relation to Winnicott (1971). When interpreting findings such as these it is also important to consider your knowledge of the children's home situations. Are they experiencing any of the above events that may be affecting their play? How will you respond to the needs of the children and provide the resources that will facilitate their schemas of play and also address their social and emotional needs? Consider the ways that your own experiences, culture and emotions may affect your responses to very young children (refer to Chapter 18).

PROVOCATION 2

On observing a child aged two years playing at home one day, both the Mother and another relative were very concerned when the child lined the dolls up for 'nappy changing' saying, 'Right, you lie there, you lie there and you lie there'.

- What was happening in this short scenario?
- Was the child simply 'playing'?
- Was the child 'playing it out'? (Elfer *et al.*, 2003) or as Rutter (1993) terms it 'actively making sense of the experience'.
- Compare and contrast the child's play with the ideal situation during 'nappy changing'.

Compare this provocation with the schematic play introduced in the above paragraph and ask yourself: is the child actively making sense of the experience?

Conclusion

Margaret Donaldson (1978) recognised that if children are defined as failures, they will ultimately fail and that people have 'a fundamental human urge to be effective, competent and independent, to understand the world and act with skill' (p. 113). The social and emotional needs of all children must be responded to sensitively and appropriately by parents and carers to enable them to learn and develop through the different stages of childhood from birth to adulthood.

This chapter has provided you with varied resources and information to enable you to consider, critique and evaluate your responses and sensitivity to the social and emotional needs of very young children. Linking theory to practice, it has also asked many questions throughout, not only about your own role but that of colleagues to help you to consider ways to develop the practice within your own setting and raise standards. The questions in this chapter aim to extend your knowledge and understanding to enable you to question, critique and interpret behaviours that you observe in the children with whom you work. It has considered levels of attachment, brain development, partnerships with parents and the roles and responsibilities of Key Persons and all Early Years professionals or teachers and has identified related areas of research for you to explore further.

The very important role and responsibilities of all Early Years workers in home settings such as childminders and nannies, practitioners working in group settings such as nurseries, full day care, children's centres and pre-schools cannot be over-emphasised. For example, a secure attachment in the first years of a child's life stimulates the process of brain development which provides a sound base for future learning and development throughout childhood and adolescence through to adulthood. Early Years professionals or teachers need to be fully conversant with current research and practice related to social and emotional development so they are able to respond appropriately to children's needs, for instance in relation to their behaviour choices.

Given that children now experience contact with and care from more than one main carer from a very early age, becoming and being self-aware and having the capacity for effective, positive relationships are key qualities in people working with children that predispose children to sound social and emotional development. It is important that people working with children act professionally, remaining calm and respectful and valuing each child and their parent or carer in their setting. We know that when strong collaborative partnerships are built and evolve between Key Persons, parents/carers and other professionals, children are more likely to progress, not just in their social and emotional development but in all areas of learning and development.

Further reading

Employment law, maternity leave, and paternity leave.

www.education.gov.uk/publications

www.webarchives.gov.uk

www.legislation.gov.uk/

www.uni.edu/universitas/archive/fall06/pdf/art_praglin.pdf

www.sciencemediacentre.org/expert-reaction-to-the-biological-effects-of-day-care-as-published-in-the-biologist-a-journal-of-the-society-of-biology-2-2/

www.who.int/about.definition/en/print.html

While it is not expected that you will know the content of government documents in detail, once in the position of, perhaps a nursery manager, you may be asked about maternity and paternity leave by staff and parents. The length of maternity leave can prove to be an emotive issue that impacts on the whole family and the parent returning to work.

Tardos, A. (2010) Introducing the Piklerian developmental approach: History and principles, pp. 1–4: *The Signal*, World Association for Infant Mental Health, July–Dec. 2010 USA. Available on www.waimh.org/files [Accessed 14/8/15].

This is an interesting article that will help you to reflect on your own practice, link practice to theory and possibly help you to work with staff to achieve an environment where all children, parents and staff feel accepted, valued, have fun and enjoy their experiences.

Paley, V.G. (1999) *The Kindness of Children*, Cambridge, MA: Harvard University Press.

This is one of a series of books written by Vivian Gussin Paley in which she visits a London Nursery School when she uses observation and interaction, including recording in order to bring out the children's stories with the children. She sees amazing, almost humbling acts of kindness and acceptance that an adult may find difficult.

Useful websites

www.whataboutthechildren.org.uk

Includes a variety of research papers related to the social and emotional needs of very young children, also advice, book lists and information which may provide a deepening understanding of the links between theory, current research and practice within this area of children's learning and development.

www.sciencemediacentre.org

Provides up-to-date connections to a very broad range of scientific topics including the brain and neurological development, diet and nutrition, mental health, paediatrics which could enable you to discuss issues relating to social and emotional development in depth resulting in critique and analysis.

www.waimh.org

Provides access to publications and resources that support the aim to promote the mental health, social and emotional development of infants.

References

Abbott, L. and Langston, A. (2005) *Birth to Three Matters,* Berkshire: Open University Press.

Arnold, C. (2010) *Understanding Schemas and Emotion in Early Childhood*, London: Sage.

Blakemore, S.J and Frith, U. (2005) *The Learning Brain - lessons for education,* Oxford: Blackwell.

Bligh, C. et al. (2013) *Well-being in the Early Years*, Norwich: Critical Publishing.

Bowlby, J. (1965) *Child Care and the Growth of Love* (2nd edn), London: Penguin.

Bowlby, J. (1988/2005) *A Secure Base*, London: Routledge Classics.

Bowlby, J. (2005) *The Making and Breaking of Affectional Bonds,* Oxon: Routledge Classics.

Bronfenbrenner, U. (1979) *The Ecology of Human Development: Experiments by Nature and Design* Cambridge, MA: Harvard University Press.

Dahlberg, G., Moss, P. and Pence, A. (1999) *Beyond Quality in Early Childhood Education and Care*. London: Routledge

DfE (2012) *The Statutory Framework for the Early Years Foundation Stage*, Runcorn: DfE [Accessed on line March 2014].

DfE (2012) *The Nutbrown Review – Foundations for Quality*, Runcorn: DfE Publications.

DfE (2013) *The National Curriculum*, UK: DfE [Accessed on line March 2014].

DfE (2014) *The National Curriculum*, UK: DfE [Accessed on line March 2014].

DfE (2014) *The Statutory Framework for the Early Years Foundation Stage*, Runcorn: DfE [Accessed on line March 2014].

DfES (2002) *Birth to Three Matters*, London: DfES Publications.

Donaldson, M. (1978) *Children's Minds*, London: Fontana Press.

Dowling, M. (2010) *Young Children's Personal, Social and Emotional Development* (3rd edn), London: Paul Chapman.

Elfer, P., Goldschmied, E. and Selleck, D. (2003) *Key Persons in the Nursery*, London: David Fulton.

Gerhardt, S. (2004) *Why Love Matters*, East Sussex: Brunner-Routledge.

Goldschmied, E. and Jackson, S. (2004) *People Under Three* (2nd edn), London: Routledge.

Gooch, K. and Powell, S. (2013) *The Baby Room*, Berkshire: Oxford University Press.

Holmes, J. (2001) *The Search for the Secure Base*, East Sussex: Brunner-Routledge.

House, R. (Ed.) (2011) *Too Much, Too Soon?*, Gloucestershire: Hawthorn Press.

Lumsden, E. (2014) Lecture entitled, 'Every interaction Counts', during the 'What About the Children?' National Conference, 13 March 2014 'Building the Brain – What's Love got to do with it?'.

Marlen, D. (2014, March) *A Gentle Beginning*. Presented at The Royal Overseas League.

Mooney, A. and Munton, A.G. (1997) *Research and Policy in Early Childhood Services: Time for a New Agenda*. London: Institute of Education, University of London.

Paley, V.G. (1999) *The Kindness of Children*, Cambridge, MA: Harvard University Press.

Pascal, C. and Bertram, T. (1997) *Effective Early Learning*, London: Hodder and Stoughton.

Perkins, S. (2014) *Separation and Settling – a Personal View*. Presented at What About the Children.

Piaget, J. and Inhelder, B. (1969) *The Psychology of the Child*, New York: Basic Books.

Praglin, L. (2006) The Nature of the 'In-Between', in D.W. Winnicott's *Concept of Transitional Space* and in Martin Buber's Das Zwischenmenschliche in *Universitas*, Vol. 2, Issue 2.

Rutter, M. (1993) *Developing Minds*, London: Penguin, The New Early Years. Available at: www.sciencemedia centre.org/expert-reaction-to-the-biological-effects-of-day-care-as-published-in-the-biologist-a-journal-of-the-society-of-biology-2-2/ [Accessed 27 April 2014].

Schore, A.N. (2013) Bowlby's 'Environment of Evolutionary Adaptedness' Recent studies of the interpersonal neurobiology of attachment and emotional development. In: *Evolution, early experience and human development. From research to practice and policy*. Pages 31–67. Eds: Narvaez, D., Panksepp, J., Schore, A.N. and Gleason, T>R. Oxford: Oxford University Press

Sigman, A. (2011) Mother Superior? The Biological Effects of Day Care in *Research Summary* from *What About The Children*.

Steele, H. (2002) State of the Art Attachment: The Changing Family, pp. 518–522; *The Psychologist* Vol. 15, No. 10, UK BPS/Wiley [Accessed 15 April 2014].

Stern, D.N. (1998) *The Interpersonal World of the Infant*, London: Karnac Books.

Sunday Times (2014) 'What Guilt? Mothers Happy to Got to Work'. *Sunday Times*, 13 April 2014.

Tardos, A. (2010) Introducing the Piklerian developmental approach: History and principles pp. 1–4: *The Signal* International Association for Infant Mental Health July–Dec. 2010, USA. www.waimh.org/files [Accessed 15 April 2014].

Trevarthen, C. (2011) Born for Art, and the Joyful Companionship of Fiction http://network.youthmusic.org.uk/sites/default/files/research/Born%20For%20Art,%20and%20the%20Joyful%20Companionship%20of%20Fiction%20-%20Colwyn%20Trevarthen.pdf [Accessed 25 May 2014].

Winnicott, D.W. (1971/2005) *Playing and Reality* (Routledge Classics), Oxon: Routledge.

16 Holistic development: the physical development of children

Katherine Goodsir

LEARNING OUTCOMES

After reading this chapter, you should be able to:

✔ Understand some of the key theories around physical development; making links to children's holistic development and well-being.
✔ Recognise the significance of movement and physical activity in providing a foundation for later learning and good health.
✔ Reflect on and develop your own attitudes and practice around physical development.

Introduction

The importance of physical development as a foundation for later learning and good health has received renewed attention over the past few years, particularly with the inclusion of Physical Development as one of the prime areas in the Early Years Foundation Stage (Tickell 2011). However, students often comment that it is an area they feel less confident in delivering, often due to a lack of knowledge, concerns over health and safety or their own experiences of physical education.

This chapter aims to provide students with a clear outline of the expected milestones and the **physiological** process underpinning them. Differing theoretical perspectives of physical development will be considered and links made to other key areas such as sensory **perception** and cognition and language acquisition, recognising that each child is **unique** and that these patterns of development can vary from child to child whilst still being 'normal'. Key documents including government reports around health and physical activity will be examined to highlight the importance of movement and a healthy diet. Practitioners' own experiences will be documented and practice based case studies will be used to exemplify good practice in building children's confidence to take manageable risks in their play, develop movement skills and understand what makes them healthy. This chapter will also encourage students to consider their own attitudes to physical activity and reflect on their practice. Encouraging students to analyse their own beliefs, develop a clear understanding of how children acquire key skills and recognise the importance of these to later learning will enable them to better support the holistic development of children in their settings.

The physical development of babies and young children

The newborn and the importance of sensori-motor development

As we know, much of a baby's development occurs in the womb and the majority of babies are born able to survive, with assistance from their mothers. An infant's head accommodates a near adult-sized brain (Doherty and Hughes 2014). New-born babies have a well-developed sense of touch, smell, taste and hearing which enables them to explore their surroundings. Although their sense of vision is poor and limited to seeing objects nearby this is adequate for their early requirements and slowly improves by two years old (Doherty and Hughes 2014). At birth, billions of cells or **neurons** are in place, but are not yet connected. These connections occur, at the base of the brain, in the **sensorimotor** area. Therefore feeling and moving are key to ensuring these connections take place (Pickard and Maude 2014). The importance of physical development for brain function is therefore clear. As practitioners we need to recognise the key messages here and ensure that the environment we create for babies provides opportunities for sensory exploration and movement. The importance of movement in particular is supported by the current guidelines for practice with non-walking babies which state that 'Physical activity should be encouraged from birth through floor-based play and water-based activities in safe environments' (British Heart Foundation 2011).

Proprioception and balance

Neonates have an additional sixth sense which is known as **proprioception**, an internal sense, which relates to position, balance (vestibular sense) movement and posture. This stays with them as they grow and enables children to have an awareness of the position of limbs and what their body is doing, without having to consciously check. Babies rely on proprioception in the womb to explore their environment and will continue to use proprioception throughout their lives to make sense of the world around them (Doherty and Hughes 2014). Balance is one of the first sensory systems to mature and helps the brain to interpret information from the other senses. Good balance supports co-ordination and eye movement and visual perception, all crucial aspects of learning; these skills are needed later when carrying out activities such as catching a ball or following a line of print in a book. Balance, in particular, is important for emotional stability, allowing the child to feel secure and in control as they perceive the outside world (Goddard Blythe 2009).

Reflexes

While sensory experiences aid exploration and support their development, babies have additional physical responses to ensure survival, known as reflexes. The most familiar of these are the 'startle', 'grasp', 'sucking' and 'rooting' as well as' stepping'. These not only support attachment between mother and baby but assist with motor development. These reflexes begin to disappear within the first few months of life as babies become stronger and more independent. Robinson (2008) suggests that these are 'templates' which enable the baby to further develop their movements based on previous experiences, for example the grasp reflex becomes the pincer grip, where children are able to pick up objects using their thumb and finger. She also draws on the work of Spelke and Newport (1998) who suggest that the 'stepping' reflex may persist in a different form when kicking or walking. Changes in the body are supported by alterations within the brain which lead to an increased capacity for more complex skills (Robinson 2008).

Growth and motor development

Different parts of the body grow at different rates. There are two patterns of growth **Cephalo-caudal** which refers to the growth from head to feet, allowing the upper body to increase in strength and control first and **proximo-distal** which proceeds from the centre of the body outwards. Both of these are essential to sensori-motor development and complete physical competence (Pickard and Maude 2014). There are rapid gains in weight and length during the first year, with birth weight doubling by five months and length increasing. Growth continues at a rapid pace but decelerates slowly after the second year so that by four years old birth length has been doubled. By the age of three, the brain is about 75 per cent of its adult weight and almost 90 per cent by age six (Gallahue and Ozmun 2006).

The spontaneous reflexes of the newborn are gradually replaced by co-ordinated movements. These consist of gross motor skills; the use of large muscle groups to perform activities such as running, walking and jumping and **fine motor skills** which use small muscles to perform more dextrous movements such as doing up buttons, writing and using gestures (Gallahue and Ozmun 2006). The importance of developing these vital skills is highlighted by Reunamo *et al.* (2013) whose research shows that children who experience gross motor difficulties also find it difficult to adapt socially, appearing withdrawn and needing support with new and challenging situations. In addition, these children also need more support with cognitive and language skills.

Theories around physical development

Maturation theory

Maturation theory was prevalent between the 1930s and 1950s. Arnold Gesell (1954), amongst others, suggested that new physical skills develop as a result of an internal process and that, as motor development is a result of genetic factors, no amount of stimulation will alter this pattern. Those that adhere to this theory today suggest that motor skills will develop as a result of maturation and do not need to be explicitly taught (cited in Doherty and Hughes 2014).

Contrary to maturation theory, some writers would argue that direct teaching of these fundamental movement skills is imperative to ensure a firm foundation for later participation in sport and recreational activities (Hands 2012; Gallahue and Ozmun 2006). Considering the various theories around physical development shows us that motor development is not merely refining movements which are present before, or at birth and that we need to bear in mind the role of the environment in ensuring that new skills are learnt (Doherty and Hughes 2014).

Gallahue and Ozmun's hourglass model of motor development

Gallahue and Ozmun (2006) suggest that both hereditary and environmental factors impact on our development of motor skills and, while our genetic makeup cannot be changed, the influence of the environment is unknown and changing throughout our life. Gallahue and Ozmun (2006) argue that during the **reflexive** and **rudimentary movement phases** (in utero–2 years old) it is the hereditary factors that have the most impact. However during the **Fundamental Movement phase** it is the environment that is most important and children need to be given instruction and encouragement, together with opportunities for practice to fully master skills such as running, hopping, throwing, catching and jumping.

PROVOCATION

Consider the ideas put forward around Fundamental Movement Skills.

- *Do you agree these needs to be formally taught?*
- *How does this fit in with your beliefs about active learning?*

Reunamo *et al.* (2013)

Sometimes ideas will be presented that will challenge our beliefs about what is important for young children. Some of you when reflecting on the above will remember structured PE lessons in school and the need to practise skills for sports day. This more instructional **discourse** may seem to go against the ideas we are more familiar with as Early Years practitioners. Progressive ideas put forward by Dewey, Piaget and Isaacs encourage us to look at children as active participants who exercise choice and autonomy and learn through exploration and discovery (Wood 2013). However, recent research found 76.3 per cent of 1–3 year olds in day care centres and pre-schools in Finland needed some support in developing gross motor skills (Reunamo *et al.*, 2013) and it could be argued therefore that this approach does not support development of specific skills and a more structured approach is needed. In addition, it is estimated that between 5 per cent and 16 per cent of school age children suffer from a commonly undiagnosed condition known as **Developmental Coordination Disorder** and in order to master movement skills children require lots of practice receiving support through instruction and feedback (Hands 2012).

Developmental task theory

Robert Havinghurst's theory (Havinghurst and Lavine 1979) considers the importance of mastering developmental skills, however not specifically movement skills. He suggests that successful development occurs when children are able to master a series of tasks, arising from physical maturation, cultural pressures of society and the individual's own values and aspirations. This will in turn lead to happiness and success with later tasks, whereas unhappiness, disapproval and difficulty with later tasks result from failure (Gallahue and Ozmun 2006). There is a suggestion here that the value placed on movement skills within society and by the individual will impact on their ability to perform certain tasks. Practitioners' own values and beliefs could also impact on children's abilities and the opportunities afforded to them to learn new skills. Support is also needed to ensure that children can overcome difficulties and that a sense of failure does not impact on their ability to perform certain tasks (McIntyre and McVitty 2004).

Information processing theory

This theory is concerned with the links between the senses and physical development and considers in particular how touch, proprioception and the vestibular sense (balance) work together to ensure information is received and processed. This is known as sensory integration, a theory developed by Ayres (1972) who suggested that children participating in sensorimotor activities have an inner drive which is manifested through obvious effort, confidence and excitement shown by children during movement play (Greenland 2013). Children are bombarded with sensory information from birth and perceive and analyse this in order to make sense of their world. Interestingly, if all the senses are functioning well, this is hardly noticed; however if even just one is affected children's perception will be impaired (McIntyre and McVitty 2004).

Ecological systems theory

Bronfenbrenner's (1979) theory considers that a child's development takes place in the context of influences on their lives, the closest of these being the family, early years setting, peers and the neighbourhood (microsystems). The wider interactions between these (Mesosystems) and additional influences from the political and economic systems (exosystems) as well as the overarching cultural beliefs and values of society (macrosystems) all impact on the child. In terms of physical development the cultural beliefs and values, government policy, the local environments and the attitudes and beliefs of practitioners and family will all affect the provision available to children.

REFLECTIVE PRACTICE

Consider your own attitudes and beliefs around the importance of physical activity.

- How have these been formed?

Consider your experiences of physical activity and your attitude to this as a young child, a teenager and now as an adult. How have your beliefs altered and what has impacted on this?

What are the wider influences on the physical activity undertaken by young children? (Use Bronfenbrenner's model as a framework for discussion.)

- How might these be impacting on the type of provision you provide for children in your setting?

Our own experiences of school sports and the encouragement we received as a child, together with our own beliefs and values around the importance of physical activity, will impact on how we encourage children in our settings to become more active and develop Fundamental Movement Skills. It is considered that physical activity declines with age, particularly with girls as they move into adolescence. Influences you may have considered are peers, opportunities afforded in nurseries and schools, community facilities, cultural practices and government campaigns such as 'Change 4 Life'. Research has shown that physical activity levels are lower in certain ethnic groups and low-income households (Cabinet Office 2014). Levels of physical activity and sedentary behaviour are also linked to parental behaviour (Davies 2013). Making links back to Bronfenbrenner, the Chief Media Officer's report notes the wider influences on children's healthy development such as the neighbourhood environment where there is a lack of safe areas to play, concerns over traffic as well as patchy provision of appropriate sports and leisure facilities; all examples of the exosystem influences on physical development. At the macrosystem level, marketing of unhealthy foods to young children needs to be appropriately regulated (Davies 2013).

It is our responsibilities as practitioners to ensure that any perceived barriers, including our own values and beliefs, do not impact on our provision and that the experiences children receive are positive and encouraging.

Cognitive developmental theory

Jean Piaget (1952) believed that all children's development passes through four periods linked to their age as all possess a similar potential to learn through actively seeking out ways to understand their environment. In the *Sensorimotor period* (birth to 2 years) children explore their world through movement and the use of their senses. In the *Pre-operational period* (ages 2 to 7) children obtain motor skills and verbal language emerges as sensorimotor activity declines. He considered that motor skills and cognitive development were inseparable, a theory supported by Bushnell and Boudreau (1993) who suggested that certain perceptual and cognitive capabilities such as hand-eye co-ordination were dependent on motor development (Doherty and Hughes 2014).

Developmental milestones

Table 16.1 is a summary of a child's developmental milestones as set out in *Development Matters in the Early Years Foundation Stage* (Early Education 2012). These are closely linked to Piaget's stages of development, however it should be noted as stated in the document that children develop in different ways and at their own rates and these variations need to be taken into account when considering individual children. For, example some babies will miss out crawling altogether or may shuffle backwards or forwards instead and some children may not walk until at least 18 months. Humans are equipped with a range of motor skills that assist in survival; however these develop at different times in each individual. There is also no connection between the time a child sits up and the time they walk (Doherty and Hughes 2014). In addition, the brain plays a part as myelination occurs and the pathways in the brain become covered in a protective sheath. This occurs at different rates and may not be in place until the child is much older, possibly resulting in poor co-ordination and movement skills (McIntyre and McVitty 2004).

Table 16.1 A summary of a child's developmental milestones as set out in *Development Matters in the Early Years Foundation Stage.* Adapted from Early Education (2012)

Age range	Gross and fine motor skills
Birth–11 months	• Gradually holds head up unaided. • When lying on tummy, lifts head and then chest, supporting self with forearms. • Rolls over from front to back and then from back to front. • Reaches out and grasps objects, exploring them with the mouth.
8–20 months	• Sits unsupported. • Crawls. • Pulls to standing. • Takes first few steps. • Picks up small objects between thumb and finger. • Holds pencil or crayon with palmar grasp (whole hand).
16–26 months	• Begins to negotiate stairs. • Begins to balance blocks in a small tower.
22–36 months	• Runs with whole foot. • Squats and rises to feet without using hands. • Climbs confidently. • Can kick a large ball. • Begins to use 'tripod' grip to hold writing tools. • Helps with clothing, e.g. unzips zipper.
30–50 months	• Can move in a range of ways including jumping, skipping and hopping. • Can catch a ball. • Can balance on one foot. • Draws lines and circles. • Uses one-handed tools, e.g. scissors.
40–60 months	• Jumps off an object and lands appropriately. • Negotiates space and can change direction to avoid obstacles.

CASE STUDY 1

Emily was working with a group of babies and toddlers aged 6–14 months with varying degrees of mobility; some were able to sit with support, others could roll, crawl or take a few steps. She recognised the importance of sensory play, however wanted to engage all the children. Rather than presenting items in a treasure basket she decided to place them on a large piece of fabric and included items such as feathers, bells, coloured cellophane, ribbons, a jar of marbles and a CD to stimulate, sound, touch and sight. The youngest baby was lying on her back and Emily handed her the cellophane which she scrunched in her hands and mouthed. She giggled as Emily tickled her with a feather. Later when she rolled onto her tummy, Emily placed the jar of marbles just out of her reach encouraging the baby to reach and move towards this, developing the muscles in her neck and arms. Emily was aware that one of the older toddlers (14 months) had shown an interest in placing objects inside containers and therefore provided a shiny, jewelled make-up bag for him to place objects inside. She observed the toddler placing objects such as a toy rabbit and brightly coloured golf ball into the bag. Further, unexpected learning took place when the toddler tried to do up the zip on the bag and Emily commented on his obvious pleasure at completing the task with encouragement from her.

Emily was aware that babies and toddlers learn through using their senses and planned developmentally appropriate activities for a range of abilities and mobility. By providing open ended resources Emily was able to allow the children to take the learning in different directions, with her support there were no fixed outcomes. In this way she was able to use language to support problem solving and prediction as the child tried to fit objects into the bag. Through **observation** Emily also recognised that the child was showing abilities beyond those expected for his age; doing up a zip falls within the 22–36 month category in *Development Matters*. This confirmed her understanding that children learn at different rates and in different ways and that the *Development Matters* should be seen as a guide in this respect.

The importance of physical activity

'Physical activity is often the best remedy for cognitive, social and emotional well-being' (Reunamo *et al.* 2013: 14). The idea that activity is key to both physical and **emotional development** is not a new one. In the early 1900s Margaret and Rachel McMillan, concerned at the poor health of the youngest children and recognising the important link between a healthy body and a healthy mind, set up the first nursery in London, where all activities including meals and rest took place outside (Bilton 2010). However, the importance of physical development declined in the 1970s when school playing fields were sold off (Barclay 2011). In addition, physical education is often considered an 'add-on' in education settings, thereby separating out the development of the body from that of the mind (Bilton 2010).

In 2008 Michael Marmot was commissioned by the then Secretary of State to carry out a review of health inequalities in England. His report 'Fair Society, Healthy Lives' showed that health inequalities were a matter of social justice and that those dying prematurely would have enjoyed between them 1.3 and 2.5 million extra years. In addition, the report recognised the importance of investing in the early years to ensure 'the best start in life' and prevent ill-health in later life (Marmot 2010).

Marmot's Review was followed in 2011 by 'Start Active, stay Active', a report published by the four home countries Chief Medical Officers. The document recognised the importance of regular physical activity in the first five years of life for developing motor skills, promoting healthy weight, enhancing bone and muscular development and for the learning of social skills. Additional benefits were considered, such as growing self-confidence and communication skills as well as establishing good health habits and activity levels throughout life. It also highlighted the risks of **sedentary behaviour**, particularly in the under-fives, a barrier to participation in physical activity (Burns *et al.* 2011). Up until this time, under-fives were not included in government health guidelines and it was considered that those devised for older children were inappropriate for this age group. Therefore, guidelines for the early years were set out as follows:

- Physical activity should be encouraged from birth through floor-based play and water-based activities in safe environments.
- Children of pre-school age who are capable of walking unaided should be physically active daily for at least 180 minutes, spread throughout the day.
- All under-fives should minimise the amount of time being sedentary for extended periods (except for time spent sleeping) (British Heart Foundation 2011).

Tickell (2011) echoed the findings of other reports, recognising the importance of manipulation and movement, noting how many child rearing practices and equipment can restrict this and interfere with optimal physical development. She highlighted the need to understand the importance of healthy choices around activity and food and to manage risk through engaging in lively physical play. She made important links between this and the other prime areas, recognising that physical development supports personal, social and emotional development as children become active agents in their environment. In addition, communication and language develop as children use gesture and the fine motor skills associated with speech (Tickell 2011). Development of the muscles in the neck and good head control are important for the development of speech and language skills (British Heart Foundation 2011). Making physical development a prime area Tickell (2011) considered the importance of developing motor skills as a foundation for later learning such as becoming mathematical or literate; however, these ideas are not new and a decade previously Ouvry (2003) was making important links between the development of arm muscles and being able to manipulate a pencil.

Despite these reviews and a commitment from the government to promote physical activity in the early years, statistics from the recent report from the Chief Medical Officer show that much still needs to be done. Although obesity rates have fallen, around 12.5 per cent of toddlers and 9-10 per cent of children entering school are obese (Davies 2013).

The importance of physical activity has received renewed publicity since the Olympic Games 2012 with a commitment from the government to improve facilities and increase access to physical activity for all ages through a number of different initiatives including safer play areas

FROM RESEARCH TO PRACTICE

A recent longitudinal study of 334,000 European men and women showed a lack of exercise was responsible for twice as many deaths as obesity and highlighted how activity equivalent to a 20 minute brisk walk a day would reduce the risk of premature death (Ekelund *et al.* 2014). As practitioners we are working with children and encouraging them to engage in healthy practices that will support their future health and well-being. We need to ensure that periods of physical activity are built in to our day to day routines and an ethos developed around the importance of physical activity for future health.

and revised guidance on risk in play provision (Cabinet Office 2014). The report draws on research from Public Health England (2014) which states that physical inactivity is the fourth greatest risk factor for poor health in England, contributing to almost 1 in 10 premature deaths, equal to smoking.

Developmentally appropriate practice

How then as practitioners can you ensure that the provision you give our youngest children supports their developmental needs and overcome some of the barriers to physical activity that exist in many settings? Authors already considered document the importance of children being able to move freely and frequently in order to develop muscles and co-ordination and refine motor skills (Goddard-Blythe 2009; McIntyre and McVitty 2004; Gallahue and Ozmun 2006; Hands 2012). 'At home, at school and during all of the activities in between, movement underlies most, if not every, aspect of learning' (McIntyre and McVitty 2004: xiii).

Research by Hulm (2012) identified poor understanding of the government guidelines with only 8 out of 20 practitioners being able to correctly identify these. In addition, barriers within the environment were highlighted such as daily routines, lack of indoors space, too much furniture and lack of specific resources. It is interesting to note also, according to recent studies, that pre-school children are often not as active as their parents and practitioners believe (Tucker *et al.* 2011). The Health Survey for England (2012) also identified that only 9 per cent of boys and 10 per cent of girls aged 2–4 years were meeting these guidelines (Cabinet Office 2014).

Revisiting the current guidelines for under-fives, drawing on ideas from the British Heart Foundation (2011) will provide you with a framework to build on when considering developmentally appropriate practice and in turn enable you to work with parents to support physical activity in the home.

Physical activity should be encouraged from birth through floor-based play and water-based activities in safe environments

Providing non-walking babies with floor-based activities will encourage movement and develop posture, strength and balance. A phrase often used is **'tummy time'** when babies are carried or positioned on their stomachs. This has been shown to help strengthen muscles in the arms, legs and neck and assist with head control. Later movement skills, such as crawling, kicking, rolling and eventually walking, are supported in this way.

How can you support this in your setting?

- Provide colourful, tactile objects that will engage babies' senses
- Clear areas and use mats or blankets inside or outside to allow for 'tummy time'
- Place objects just out of reach to encourage babies to move towards them
- Provide tunnels and create areas with different levels to support crawling and encourage babies to pull themselves up
- Get down on the floor with babies
- Encourage parents to engage in these type of activities at home; perhaps send home bags with suitable equipment to support this

(British Heart Foundation 2011)

Children of pre-school age who are capable of walking unaided should be physically active daily for at least 180 minutes (3 hours) spread throughout the day

Children are naturally active; however this is often in sporadic bouts and allowing for periods of activity throughout the day will support movement development and protect against long periods of inactivity. All types of activity, whether standing up or walking, or more vigorous movement such as dancing, running or climbing can contribute to reaching this target. How can you support this in your setting?

- Ensure there is sufficient space for children to move around freely indoors and outdoors
- Encourage development of motor skills through providing open-ended and every day resources such as balls and boxes
- Consider more structured adult led time such as action songs, music and movement and games to develop fundamental movement skills
- Be good role models through participation as appropriate
- Build in times for activity that encourages raised heart rates and burns calories to support strong cardiorespiratory systems and maintain a healthy weight
- Provide parents with examples of activities in the setting that they could also do at home

(British Heart Foundation 2011)

Woods and Hall (2013) stress the importance of careful planning to adjust environments for children with additional needs, ensuring these are sensitive and do not isolate the child more. She suggests replacing steps with gentle slopes and providing low-level areas with different sensory plants.

All under-fives should minimise the amount of time being sedentary for extended periods (except time spent sleeping)

Sedentary behaviour is associated with activities that take place when seated or lying down and those which require low levels of energy such as watching TV, travelling by bus or car or being strapped into a buggy or high chair. There is emerging evidence of an association with adverse health outcomes such as obesity as well as lower cognitive development (Burns *et al.* 2011).

REFLECTIVE PRACTICE

- Carry out an audit to show how often children are able to engage in periods of sustained activity. Consider daily routines, resources and the layout of your space.
- How can you reduce the amount of time children are sedentary?
- Draw up a list of possible changes.

You may have considered that you allow children plenty of opportunities to move, but carrying out an audit may have helped you to recognise where you could do more. Whole group activities such as registration, snack and meal times and circle time mean that children are sitting for extended periods of time. Even when providing physical activities, consider the time children may spend waiting for their turn and are therefore inactive. Consider removing baby rocking chairs for a day and allowing more floor and tummy time. With your older children take chairs and tables away for a day and allow more movement between activities. Maybe also encourage families to walk or cycle to your setting. A report from the Forestry Commission (2014) outlines how the country's forest could be used to support this through cycling and walking trails. Consider making more use of local forests and green spaces.

CASE STUDY 2

Residents in Bristol hold 'Playing Out' sessions where they apply to close their streets and encourage children to play outside. So far 17 streets across the city have taken part with 80 separate sessions allowing around 500 children and 200 adults to play, chat and enjoy spending time in their street free of traffic. (Playing Out) This initiative is now being supported by the government which has pledged £1.1 million to Play England to encourage take up in other communities, removing and limiting barriers to play and physical activity (Cabinet Office 2014).

Take time to look at the 'Playing Out' website http://playingout.net/inspiration-ideas-and-links/inspiring-news/bristol-trial-a-success/ which contains other case studies. Consider whether you could lobby your local council to do something similar in your area.

A systematic review of research carried out by Caird *et al.* (2011) suggests there may be a link between obesity and poor educational attainment, although this is likely to be part of a broader picture which links poor health and low attainment with socio-economic disadvantage; this supports findings from Marmot (2010). In the recent report by the Chief Medical Officer, concerns were raised about the consumption levels of foods and drinks high in sugar by toddlers. She noted that children's food preferences are often affected by patterns in the home where over-eating is not always controlled and food may be used as a reward (Davies 2013).

The second section of Physical Development in the EYFS is concerned with 'Health and self-care', recognising the link between physical activity and healthy eating patterns (Early Education 2012). Practitioners have a duty not just to ensure children have access to healthy snacks and drinks when in the setting and develop active lifestyles but that they support parents to provide nutritional meals and reduce sedentary behaviour at home. One way to do this is to display daily menus and a collection of leaflets around the importance of healthy eating or hold a parents' evening or cookery workshop.

Risk and resilience

It has been well documented that children need challenges in order to self-regulate their safety (Bilton 2010; Knight 2011). Furthermore, Gill (2007) suggests that children need to experience reasonable risk to prevent them seeking out unmanaged risk. Risk-taking also has many health and developmental benefits including building resilience and self-reliance. Hawkins (2013) notes that risky play encourages and stimulates senses, particularly vision and touch as well as strengthening neural pathways. She draws on the work of Bob Hughes (2012) who comments that children are aware of their own limitations and will not deliberately go beyond these. As adults we need to be aware that although we may judge something as dangerous, children may not. This is echoed in the EYFS, Characteristics of Effective Learning with the following guidance for practitioners: 'encourage children to try new activities and to judge risks for themselves. Be sure to support children's confidence with words and body language' (Early Education 2012: 6). This is further supported by revised government guidelines on risk-taking in play environments (Cabinet Office 2014). Knight (2011) provides the following guidance for practitioners:

- Avoid seeing health and safety and risk assessment as irritating; focus on the beneficial outcomes for children and include children in the process.
- Start with where your children are now and progress together to create manageable challenges.
- Reflect on and evaluate your practice; you will notice that children don't need constant intervention only sensitive and occasional assistance.

CASE STUDY 3

'Free Spirits' – How a beach school supports physical development and risk taking

Harriet and her colleagues take children to the local beach for a weekly two-hour session which takes place all year round, regardless of the weather. The children walk to the station and then travel by train. A link has been made with the local café and train station to use as a 'safe haven' if needed. A risk assessment was completed before the first session and adults always scan the area for hazards before each session. A 'base camp' is established depending on the tides and children are reminded of the health and safety rules.

Activities during the session support children's holistic development; however many of these help develop fine and gross motor skills such as making mud pies and sandcastles, throwing stones, mark making in the sand, collecting natural materials, den building, digging a fire-pit and simply 'running free'. Practitioners and parents comment on how the experience has enabled children to grow in confidence, extended their knowledge and fired their imaginative and creative play.

Conclusion

Physical development concerns not only growth and attainment of developmental milestones but the development of senses, motor skills, muscles, co-ordination and balance. There are several theories around physical development; however it is generally believed that hereditary and environmental factors play an important role in ensuring healthy growth. It is also considered that developing positive attitudes in the early years will provide firm foundations for later health. Several government reports highlight concerns over children's sedentary behaviour and poor diet. It is therefore imperative that practitioners develop environments and activities that encourage a more active and healthy lifestyle with opportunities to promote movement, healthy eating and risk-taking both in the setting and at home.

Acknowledgements

The author would like to thank Harriet Young and Emily Smee from City of Bristol College for providing material for the case studies.

Further reading

Bilton, H. (2010) *Outdoor Learning in the Early Years: Management and Intervention* (3rd edition). Abingdon: David Fulton
Supports practitioners in developing their outdoor area and encouraging staff to engage activity and risk taking.

Gallahue, D.L. and Ozmun, J.C. (2006) *Understanding Motor Development: Infants, Children, Adolescents and Adults* (6th edition). New York: McGraw-Hill
Provides theory around children's growth and physical development including the importance of developing Fundamental Movement Skills.

Woods, A. (2013) (ed.) *Child-Initiated Play and Learning: Planning for Possibilities in the Early Years.* Abingdon: Routledge
Includes chapters on risky play and supporting children with additional needs.

Useful websites

www.gov.uk/government/uploads/system/uploads/attachment_data/file/216370/dh_128210.pdf
Burns, H., Davies, S., Jewell, T. and McBride, M. (2011) *Start Active, Stay Active: A Report on Physical activity for Health from the Four Home Counties.*
Key report on the health of the four home countries with guidelines for physical activity for various age groups.

www.forestry.gov.uk/pdf/Wehavestoppedmoving_FINAL1.pdf/$FILE/Wehavestoppedmoving_FINAL1.pdf
Forestry Commission England (2014) *We have Stopped Moving: Tackling Physical Inactivity – A Role for Public Forest Estate in England?*
Recent report on role of forests in promoting physical activity.

www.playengland.org.uk
Features the importance of outdoor play with ideas on how to support risky play.

References

Ayres, A.J. (1972) *Sensory Integration & Learning Disorders*. Los Angeles: Western Psychological Services.

Barclay, J. (2011) *Playing Fields and Public Open Spaces*. London: House of Commons Library: Science and Environment Section

Bilton, H. (2010) *Outdoor Learning in the Early Years: Management and Intervention* (3rd edition). Abingdon: David Fulton

British Heart Foundation (2011) *UK Physical Activity Guidelines for Early Years (Non-Walkers)*. British Heart Foundation/Loughborough University

Bronfenbrenner, U. (1979) *The Ecology of Human Development: Experiments by Nature and Design*. Cambridge, MA: Harvard University Press

Burns, H., Davies, S., Jewell, T. and McBride, M. (2011) *Start Active, Stay Active: A Report on Physical activity for Health from the Four Home Countries*. Available from www.gov.uk/government/uploads/system/uploads/attachment_data/file/216370/dh_128210.pdf [Accessed 17 March 2014]

Bushnell, E. & Boudreau, J.P. (1993) *Motor development and the Mind: The Potential Role of Motor Abilities as a Determinant of Aspects of Perceptual Development* Child Development 64, 1005-1021.

Cabinet Office (2014) *Moving More, Living More: The Physical Activity Olympic and Paralympic Legacy for the Nation*. Available from www.gov.uk/government/uploads/system/uploads/attachment_data/file/279657/moving_living_more_inspired_2012.pdf [Accessed 1 March 2014]

Caird, J., Kavanagh, J., Oliver, K., Oliver, S., O'Mara, A., Stansfield, C. and Thomas, J. (2011) *Childhood Obesity and Educational Attainment: A Systematic Review*. London: EPPI-Centre, Social Science Research Unit, Institute of Education, University of London

Davies, S. (2013) *Annual Report of the Chief Medical Officer 2012: Our Children Deserve Better: Prevention Pays*. Available from www.gov.uk/government/uploads/system/uploads/attachment_data/file/252656/33571_2901304_CMO_Chapter_6.pdf [Accessed 10 March 2014]

Doherty, J. and Hughes, M. (2014) *Child Development Theory and Practice 0-11* (2nd edition) Harlow: Pearson Education Limited

Early Education (2012) *Development Matters in the Early Years Foundation Stage (EYFS)*. Available at www.foundationyears.org.uk/files/2012/03/Development-Matters-final-print-amended.pdf [Accessed 20 February 2014]

Ekelund, U. et al. (2015) Activity and All-cause Mortality Across Levels of Overall and Abdominal Adiposity in European Men and Women: the European Prospective Investigation into Cancer and Nutrition Study, *American Journal of Clinical Nutrition*. Available from http://ajcn.nutrition.org/content/early/2015/01/14/ajcn.114.100065.full.pdf [Accessed 15 January 2015]

Forestry Commission England (2014) *We have Stopped Moving: Tackling Physical Inactivity – A Role for Public Forest Estate in England ?* Available from www.forestry.gov.uk/pdf/Wehavestoppedmoving_FINAL1.pdf/$FILE/Wehavestoppedmoving_FINAL1.pdf [Accessed 10 January 2015]

Gallahue, D. L. and Ozmun, J.C. (2006) *Understanding Motor Development: Infants, Children, Adolescents and Adults* (6th edition) New York: McGraw-Hill

Gesell, A. (1954) The Ontogenesis of infant behaviour in Carmichael, L. (Ed) *Manual of Child Psychology*. New York: Wiley.

Gill, T. (2007) *No Fear: Growing Up in a Risk Averse Society*. London: Caloustie Gulbenkian Foundation

Goddard-Blythe (2009) In interview with Tracey Stevens. Available at http://abettereducation.blogspot.co.uk/2009/05/interview-with-sally-goddard-blythe-on.html [Accessed 18 February 2014]

Greenland, P. (2013) Physical Development, in Veale, F. (ed.) *Early Years for Levels 4 & 5 and the Foundation Degree*. Abingdon: Hodder Education

Hands, B. (2012) How Fundamental are Fundamental Movement Skills? *Active and Healthy Magazine* 19(1) pp. 11-13

Havinghurst, R.J & Lavine, D.U. (1979) *Society & Education*. Boston: Allyn & Bacon.

Hawkins, C. (2013) Planning for Risky Possibilities in Play in Woods, A. (Ed) *Child-initiated Play and Learning: Planning for Possibilities in the Early Years*. Abingdon: Routledge

Hulm, K. (2012) *Get Up and Go*. Bristol: NHS Bristol and Bristol City Council

Knight, S. (2011) *Risk and Adventure in Early Years Outdoor Play: Learning from Forest Schools*. London: Sage

McIntyre, C. and McVitty, K. (2004) *Movement and Learning in The Early Years: Supporting Dyspraxia (DCD) and Other Difficulties*. London: Sage

Marmot, M. (2010) 'Fair Society Healthy Lives'. Available at www.instituteofhealthequity.org/Content/File Manager/pdf/fairsocietyhealthylives.pdf [Accessed 2 March 2014]

Ouvry, M. (2003) *Exercising Muscles and Minds: Outdoor Play and the Early Years Curriculum* London: National Children's Bureau

Pickard, A. and Maude, P. (2014) *Teaching Physical Education Creatively*. Abingdon: Routledge

Playing Out (2013) *Bristol Trial A Success*. Available from http://playingout.net/inspiration-ideas-and-links/inspiring-news/bristol-trial-a-success/ [Accessed 15 March 2014]

Public Health England (2014). *Everybody Active, Every Day: An Evidence Based Approach to Physical Activity*. London: Public Health England.

Reunamo, J., Hakala, L., Saros, L., Lehto, S., Kyhala A.-S. and Valtonen, J. (2013) Children's Physical Activity in Day Care and Pre-School, *Early Years* (34)1, pp. 32–48

Robinson, M. (2008) *Child Development from Birth to Eight: A Journey Through The Early Years*. Maidenhead: Open University Press

Spelke, E.S & Newport, E.L. (1998) Nativism, Empiricism and the Development of Knowledge in Damon, W (Series ed) & Lerner, R (Vo l ed) *Handbook of Child Psychology: Vol 1 Theoretical Models of Human Development (5th ed)* New York: Wiley pp275-340.

Tickell, C. (2011) *The Early Years: Foundations for Life, Health and Learning: An Independent Report on the Early Years Foundation Stage to her Majesty's Government*, London: Department for Education.

Tucker, P., Van Zandvoort, M., Burke, S. and Irwin, J. (2011) Physical Activity in Daycare: Childcare Providers' Perspectives for Improvement, *Journal of Early Childhood Research* 9(3) pp. 207–219

Wood, E. (2013) *Play, Learning and the Early Childhood Curriculum* (3rd edition) London: Sage

Woods, A. and Hall, V. (2013) Exploiting Outdoor Possibilities for all Children, in Woods, A. (ed.) *Child-Initiated Play and Learning: Planning for Possibilities in the Early Years*. Abingdon: Routledge, pp. 50-67

17 The freedom of the great outdoors

Pam Jarvis and Wendy Holland

LEARNING OUTCOMES

When you have finished the chapter you will:

✔ Understand why outdoor play is so central to holistic Early Years practice.
✔ Be prepared to contribute to and lead innovative activities within the setting.
✔ Be prepared for assignments in which the outdoors is explored as an 'enabling environment', with ideas for resourcing and planning the rich child-led activities which sit at the heart of Early Years 'best practice'.
✔ Recognise the potential of the outdoors to offer a rich experiential environment in which all children, from birth to seven years, can develop holistically, emotionally, socially, linguistically, cognitively and physically.
✔ Understand the potential of the outdoors in offering the ideal situation in which to create free narrative, particularly settings provided by natural environments.
✔ Recognise some gender differences in outdoor play.
✔ Appreciate the special role of the adult in providing high quality experiential learning in the outdoors.

Introduction

This chapter will consider the role of outdoor play within a holistic programme of education and care for children under five. It will assist readers to address the requirements of the Early Years Foundation Stage, while taking a critical and reflective approach to the 'place' that outdoor play is allocated within its framework. At the dawn of modern nursery education in Britain, when opening her pioneering nursery in South London in 1914, Margaret McMillan proposed that her key focus was to 'plan the right kind of environment for [children] and give them sunshine, fresh air and good food' (Stevinson 1954, p. 8), putting the role of the outdoors at the very top of her agenda. In this respect, as in many others, she was ahead of her time, anticipating perhaps Article 31 of the United Nations Convention (1989) on the **rights** of the child to play.

This chapter will consider how outdoor play has slipped down this agenda over the past century, and why its central place in Early Years education needs to be reclaimed. For example, Maynard *et al.* (2011, p. 296) proposed:

> Teachers appeared reluctant to take the children outdoors [because] . . . 'real work' was seen to take place inside the classroom . . . their practice seemed to be influenced by a felt need to remain in control of children's learning in order to protect their own professional identities and to meet prescribed outcomes.

Waite *et al.* (2013) reflected on the culture of English and American education, which they described as 'initiation, student response and teacher feedback' (p. 258), commenting that Nordic countries in which, despite harsh winters, more extensive outdoor free play opportunities are typically provided for children by settings due to their more holistic focus upon 'a general conception of a good childhood', evoking the earlier British ethos pioneered by Margaret McMillan.

Clearly, a 'good **childhood**' will necessarily contain many opportunities for learning directly from adults, particularly with regard to the basic skills that will be required for productive adult life within modern post-industrial societies, for example literacy, numeracy and technological competence. However, this chapter will argue that the skills learned on the playground are of equal importance:

> Social free play and independent discovery activities . . . underpin the inculcation of crucial knowledge and skills which will later enable the individual to cope with the intricate webs of co-operation, collaboration and competition that are characteristic of all adult social arenas, from neighbourhood committees to international negotiations.
>
> (Jarvis *et al.*, 2014, online)

Soderstrom *et al.* (2012) additionally offered compelling evidence that Swedish pre-school children who have more frequent outdoor play in high quality environments gain in physical and psychological fitness, being significantly more likely to have leaner bodies, longer night sleeping times and better overall 'well being' levels than those who do not have such opportunities. This exposure to outdoor environments begins for even the youngest children. It is common practice for infants who are not yet mobile, to be placed on verandas in minus degrees temperatures to experience the myriad sensory richness of fresh air, the sound of birds, the rustle of leaves and the changes of light that naturally occur. How different this good practice seems compared with much UK practice with babies being kept indoors unless the weather is warm and calm. Perhaps this is a little-considered element within the complex set of reasons for the UK's low rating for children's well-being by UNICEF (2007, 2013). In summary, outdoor play is vitally important for the following key reasons:

- Experiential and playful learning within the outdoor environment contains a huge potential for young children's holistic development.
- The ability to play freely and to independently engage with the construction of collective narratives is most productively realised within the outdoor arena.

- The freedom of play in the outdoors is particularly important to the development and learning of boys between the ages of three and seven, due to subtle gendered variations in the typical schedule of development.
- Natural environments hold myriad rich opportunities for holistic, creative development; lack of such experience has led to claims that children may be at risk of suffering 'nature deficit' (Moss 2012).

The potential of the outdoors for developing physical fitness and **gross motor skills** is perhaps the most obvious. It could be proposed that this aspect of outdoor play may at times, in the recent past, have been the only reason that the playground was retained within education and care settings, given the amount of threat that it came under in British and American schools during the last two decades of the twentieth century: 'What children do on playgrounds is typically not considered important by most teachers and parents' (Pellegrini 1995, p. 1). There was a reduction of general break (or play) time during the English school day in the 1990s (Pellegrini and Blatchford, 2002), while Blatchford and Baines (2008) reported shortening of the lunchtime break over the early 2000s and 'a strong anti-recess [playtime] view in US schools' (p. 1). In 1998, the Atlanta public school districts in the USA decided to eliminate recess (playtime) in elementary schools because, in their opinion it was 'a waste of time that would be better spent on schoolwork' (Bishop and Curtis 2001, p. 34).

The value of outdoor play has been recognised to some extent in the English Early Years Foundation Stage Framework (2006, 2012). The statutory framework of 2006 precipitated the building and enhancement of many outdoor facilities and provision throughout UK settings. However, contemporary advice from the revised 2012 framework in fulfilling the requirements of the Early Years Foundation Stage focuses exclusively on the impact of outdoor play on **physical health**, and upon the future rather than the present: 'Encourage children to be active and energetic by organising lively games, since physical activity is important in maintaining good health and in guarding against children becoming overweight or obese in later life' Meggitt (2013). It also presumes that the adult role revolves around 'organising' children's outdoor activities rather than supporting and facilitating them.

The body of academic literature relating to children's development and learning through free play in outdoor arenas supports Harre's (1999) more reflective proposal: 'There must be some other way that words get a meaning than being something that is pointed out by a teacher and noticed by a learner' (p. 50). Such a '**didactic**' approach, which supports the current rush to ensure '**school readiness**' is challenged, by Whitebread and Bingham (2011) as being 'misguided' and, as research demonstrates, 'will not make a difference in the long term' (p. 3).

This chapter will argue that outdoor play creates a forum for children to engage in situations where they can develop and practise the skills of competition, co-operation, and collaboration in moment to moment interaction, which are vital components of human adolescent and adult existence:

> What the playground offers is an enormous scope to initiate, discuss, influence and change the rules in a way that we cannot imagine between children and adults. Indeed, when teachers supervise play it is exactly these types of opportunities that are missing.
>
> (Sluckin 1981, p. 119)

In terms of physical outdoor environment, it has been suggested that children prefer arenas where they can imagine their own play roles and activities, rather than working around environments that have been closely designed and copiously resourced by adults:

> Even though traditional playgrounds are anticipated to promote children's play, their design does not meet children's needs for exploring their environment ... Such playgrounds have not been found to be very challenging and even very young children or those with motor behaviour deficits do not explore their potential on these playgrounds ... Natural environments represent different play opportunities for children. The rough surface provides movement challenges, and topography and vegetation provide a diversity of different designs for playing and moving.
>
> (Fjørtoft 2004, p. 22)

The gender issue

Superficial accounts of outdoor play might suggest that the arena lacks challenge and importance for girls. Nothing could be further from the truth. The point that should instead be centrally considered is that, given the extra freedom that outdoor play affords, this is the arena in which the differences between the genders become most obvious to adult observers, and that boys tend to inhabit a larger area, make more noise and engage in more energetic pursuits (for example consider whether you would expect to find a boy or a girl at the top of the tallest climbable tree!).

The outdoors better facilitates the use of skills that typically develop earlier in boys than in girls, due to slight **biological** differences in brain structure, and different balances of hormones and neurotransmitters (principally serotonin, oxytocin and testosterone), although, as always, human variability must be considered, and individual differences taken into account. In terms of the average gendered development schedule, girls typically develop language and **fine motor skills** earlier than boys, giving them a head start in literacy in particular, and boys typically develop spatial orientation and large motor skills earlier than girls, making the outdoor arena an ideal environment in which to explore these capabilities. Girls, however, equally enjoy the freedom of the outdoors, and may sometimes use their more sophisticated language skills to marshal boys in quite a **Machiavellian** style. Consider the following, drawn from focal child **observations** focusing upon outdoor play activities:

> I observed Elliot hit Francisca on the head with his cap. I thought that the energy with which he did this was rather over-eager, and this was confirmed when she yelled and held her head. Kayleigh immediately snapped, 'I'm telling,' and stalked off; the boys running behind her saying, 'No, no'. This was a game where Kayleigh had been the principal organiser, and had called the boys back into play several times before this incident occurred.
>
> (Jarvis 2014, p. 206)

The role of the practitioner

It is typical that inexperienced practitioners consider outdoor play to be a relatively 'easy' area of practice, albeit sometimes physically uncomfortable with respect to being cold or wet, because they think that outdoor play is unsophisticated compared with the types of activities that are ongoing within a classroom. Again, nothing could be further from the truth. Experienced practitioners realise that the activity taking place in the outdoor environment can be the most complex and subtle play-based learning that they will ever observe. Maynard *et al.* (2013), reporting on their observations of outdoor play, proposed that child-led, open and physically challenging activities were significantly more likely to occur within the outdoor arena, and that effective practice in the outdoors frequently required more skilful responses from practitioners than practice in indoor environments. They subsequently reflected that this higher level of required skill might 'explain why, in our study SST [Sustained Shared Thinking] was observed on only two occasions' (p. 296).

Outdoor play in the setting environment

CASE STUDY 1

A Nursery Class for 3- to 5-year-olds is attached to a primary school, but has its own play space: a small area of hard tarmac, which houses a static metal climbing frame, painted in bright primary colours, situated on and surrounded by a soft tarmac area. There is a larger grassed area, part of which is sloped, that reaches to the stone wall boundary. Against this stand two mature trees, with lower branches that are strong enough to be climbed. The outdoor area has weekly planning, with an individual practitioner responsible for the whole week's timetable. The practice is for one practitioner to 'police' the area while the other is engaged in a focused 'adult-led' activity.

Following the nursery's current theme of 'people who help us' and a recent visit to the nursery from the local 'lollipop' lady, the practitioner has created a 'road safety' scenario, complete with zebra crossing (painted wooden board), traffic lights and the yellow coat and stop sign for the lollipop lady. The nursery has a store of tricycles (some two-seater), scooters and kiddy cars which are always in demand, often leading to arguments about 'fairness', turn taking and the amount of time they are used by individual children. There are also issues about rules and boundaries that those using the wheeled vehicles must adhere to (e.g. not riding on the soft surface near the climbing frame; not riding on the grass or on the path leading up to the school gates).

Once the road safety 'role play' has begun, with agreements about who has first turn at being the lollipop lady and which children have first turn on the wheeled toys, the adult leading the activity stands back and begins to write her observations. Occasionally she will interact with a child if they ask her a question directly.

It is a windy day, as evidenced by the large brick placed at the base of each of the traffic lights to stop them tumbling over. The practitioner who is monitoring the rest of the play is watching some children run up and down the grassy slope with home-made kites made from card and tissue paper streamers. These children are involved in spinning, twirling and running up and down the grass slope. One child begins to cry when his kite becomes tangled up in the branches of a tree. The practitioner 'on watch' immediately goes to free it for him and vestibular play is resumed.

The 'road safety' adult led activity has moments of fluidity, when all the participants agree what their roles should be and the children play within the 'rules'. Wheeled toys stop at the crossing when the lollipop lady holds up her stop sign (and her hand), to help other children cross the road. This play breaks down when children on the wheeled toys become tired of having to stop so frequently, and attempt to circumvent the traffic lights and on occasion 'ram' the lollipop lady. The practitioner focusing on the activity is involved fairly frequently in negotiating apologies, and restating rules.

Because of the limited space 'allowed' to wheeled toys, a few children begin to ride on the grass, which results in collisions with some of the kite flyers. A number of minor accidents have to be written up in the accident book when the play period is over.

On the basis of your current practice:

1 If you were the practitioner leading the adult-focused experience, how would you evaluate the activity?
2 What could the adult monitoring the play have done differently?
3 What kinds of play were the children engaged in?
4 What improvements/changes would you make to the planning of this session?
5 To what extent was the outdoor environment utilised?
6 What aspects of health and safety do you recognise?
7 To what degree could the play be seen as 'risky' or challenging?

An environment of 'loose parts'

Unlike the classroom, an outdoor space has the potential for the child to exist within a 'free' space in which actions can be random and exploratory with unexpected and often exciting results. This applies to the very youngest children in a setting as well as older children. Babies who are not yet mobile will still benefit from daily outdoor experiences (see reference to Soderstrom *et al.* 2012, above). The inclusion of sensory experiences such as shiny, hanging mobiles, sweet-smelling herbs and plants like lavender and thyme, tactile floor spaces on which they can roll, crawl and reach, such as wooden decking or a camomile lawn, natural objects to grasp with different textures, a pine cone, safe glossy leaves, will all stimulate an infant's sensory motor skills. For toddlers, who naturally have a higher centre of gravity, soft places to fall are needed, as well as the experience of vertical and well as horizontal challenges, in order to develop muscle growth.

Outdoor spaces can challenge a child's physicality and problem solving skills, stretching both body and imagination. It is an environment where negotiations can be fiercely entered into, practical problems solved, compromises reached and friendships formed. For the practitioner, however, who might be driven by 'outcome-ised' inspection quality assurance criteria there may be a need to justify how his/her presence outdoors. Such activities raise problems in that they are much harder to assess than adult directed play in the smaller arena of a classroom. This can lead to play that is over-managed and result in far more limiting experiences for children. So what is best practice in the outdoor arena?

A whole body of research (e.g. Soderstrom *et al.* 2012; Fjørtoft 2004; Maynard *et al.* 2011; Bilton 2005) would suggest that children in fact need the freedom and challenge that 'natural outdoors' environments can provide, to collaborate, structure and maintain their activities with the minimum of adult intervention. Clear differences have been observed in the areas of physical, social and intellectual growth when children are given the natural environment to explore as they interact with and are challenged by its varied terrains and vegetation. Few settings in the UK have the advantage of a beach or woodland at or within its boundaries, but imaginative architecture, even in small spaces, can stimulate the enjoyment, risk and challenge these provide, once an understanding of the true benefits of outdoor play have been realised.

The initial planning of early years outdoor areas needs to be focused around the fixed and fluid aspects of any setting's outdoor provision. An ideal here would be the concept of the environment as the 'third teacher' that Malaguzzi speaks of (Edwards *et al.* 1998) and is practised in the Reggio Emilia preschools in Northern Italy. Here, the environment is truly seen from the child's perspective, resourced with provocations and challenges which the child grapples with, as the competent and 'rich' individual he/she is perceived to be (Rinaldi 2006).

Research suggests that 'natural' colours and natural materials support children's sense of well-being, and therefore their ability to absorb the environment (Montessori 1949) more effectively. For babies, in particular, a more monochrome palate is advisable at first. The preference for natural materials therefore should take precedence over brightly coloured plastic installations, which look so inviting to the adult eye. Malaguzzi talks of children being 'a significant chromatic presence' (Ceppi *et al.* 1998) in themselves, so a calm, natural colour palate provides a more soothing environment. The flexibility of the environment, too, is favoured by research findings (Brown 2014), as this allows children to change and own their environment, leading to more creative, open ended play. The kind of 'blue sky' thinking it encourages is a skill that will be vitally needed in the future world of today's young children, given the speed of technological change and their consequent need to become independent lifelong learners to make their way in such societies.

Some fixed resources, like small steps for infants and toddlers, encourage bone density and muscle strength, as well as increasing lung capacity. A wooden climbing frame with a slide attachment provides for the development and practice of gross motor skills and can, depending on its design, provide elements of risk and challenge for preschool children. A large embedded sandpit provides opportunities for early science and mathematics, engineering and design, as well as cooperative and imaginative small world play for all ages. This outdoor area with a purpose built, child-sized ship to house imaginative play is an example of how scale in some areas is important.

Mud kitchens (White 2012), with their essential ingredient of water, support the development of schema and provide essential sensory experience, with the opportunity for messy play which young children find deeply satisfying, exploring ways in which they can independently influence the physical environment. The establishment of raised beds, at child height, provides support for **emergent** walkers, as well as experiences in digging, sowing seeds and growing things. These activities also encourage opportunities for shared experiences with adults.

It must also be remembered that not all play needs to be 'purposeful' in the adult sense of the word. Resources that encourage open-ended play can be the stimulus for highly creative play activities. In terms of non-fixed resources the 'theory of loose parts' (Brown 2014) is an ideal

Figure 17.1 A scaled resource for imaginative play
Source: iStock

concept to apply, as opposed to static, synthetic items that have been designed by adults to be used in very specific ways, and therefore provide short term interest and/or little challenge. Simple materials which have no limits in terms of open ended play are far preferable to over-elaborate resources that are 'one dimensional' or have limited use. Large block play outdoors can take on a new dimension of scale, becoming a castle, a train, a spaceship all in the space of a morning's play. A bucket turned upside down can be a drum, a swathe of material can make a roof for a den and, in the next moment, a gown for a queen in a child's open-ended play. Pebbles, wood, piping, stones, shells or recycled materials are not expensive, yet provide the child with endless possible combinations.

Dens, places to hide, tunnels, quiet, calm spaces are also important for **mental health** and the child's sense of wellbeing at any age. These do not need to be elaborate constructions; a large sturdy cardboard box will provide a crawling infant with instant play opportunities. Space, of course, is important; children move differently in outdoor spaces. They need to be given the space to build on their vestibular sense of balance, to slide, rock, jiggle, spin, teeter, swing until they are dizzy, or balance upside down.

Children ideally need to experience, experiment with and negotiate many different surfaces that test and push their physical skills; for example moving against gravity up a slope, or pushing a pram or tricycle over rough or muddy terrain helps to develop a **proprioceptive sense** of their body's capabilities (Goddard Blythe 2005). In natural surroundings these are easier to come by or import. Piaget describes movement as essential for brain development (Piaget 1962), and this is substantiated by recent findings in neuroscience. A well designed outdoor area, therefore,

Figure 17.2 A large play resource for active play such as balancing, sliding, climbing and hanging upside
down

Source: iStock

develops 'brainpower' as well as 'muscle power'. However, such findings have still to find support in practice. Maynard and Waters (2007) found some head teachers unwilling to defend the positive benefits of child-initiated outdoor play:

> 'I don't like to call it outdoor play; we need to ensure there is real purpose to it.'
>
> (p. 259)

> 'You need a member of staff . . . to bring them back to the focus . . . or it would be a free for all.'
>
> (p. 260)

And when faced with parents' reactions:

> 'Our parents have high expectations . . . they think in levels . . . you have to read by . . . [the age of] five.'
>
> (p. 260)

Risk and challenge

Risk and challenge are issues that all contemporary children's workforce practitioners need to understand, in order to manage them sensitively. An increasingly sophisticated mass media warning parents of myriad perceived dangers in the outdoors, from minor physical injury fears to the carcinogenic effects of sunburn has been a factor in the reduction of opportunities for outdoor free play for children of all ages. For example, a student who worked on a play project explained to us that she dealt with children who had never properly experienced the feeling of rain on their skin, due to panic about a 'need' to go indoors immediately rain began to fall, and a little boy who told her he was 'dying' because his breathing had become laboured and he could feel his heart beating in his chest. It turned out that this was his first experience of running for long enough to become out of breath!

The National Trust has recently claimed that the current generation of children is experiencing 'nature deficit disorder', due to losing touch with the outdoors (Moss 2012, p. 2). In this report, *Natural Childhood,* sponsored by the National Trust, Stephen Moss claims that 'children have less freedom to roam than free-range chickens' (Moss 2012, p. 3). What such children are missing is the vital experience that they need to engage in 'increasing physical control' providing 'experiences of the self as an active agent in the environment, promoting growth in confidence and awareness of control' (Tickell 2011). It is this development of the proprioceptive sense, the child's confidence in his ability to stretch, challenge and yet control his own body, that the practitioner needs to support and encourage. This is particularly true for children with additional needs. The need to develop upper body strength for a child in a wheelchair, for example, would be naturally available in a rich outdoor environment. Too often children with additional needs are over protected, and the 'risks' seen as too daunting, when outdoor play is considered. With some basic adaptations, for example, wider doorways and access slopes and ramps for wheelchairs, children with additional needs can and should be exposed to the same experiential learning as other children outdoors. The benefits are equally as enriching, both for the child with the additional need and their peers in a holistic sense. All areas of development, the social, emotional, cognitive, linguistic and physical skills are extended as well as a growing sense of autonomy.

The 'Forest Schools' of Scandinavia have long promoted a holistic approach to a child's development and learning which involve risk and challenge. In recent years, some areas of the UK have attempted to emulate the Forest School approach. As this movement has gathered pace, from its origins in the 1990s, there are now over 100 Forest Schools in the UK. Research carried out by O'Brian and Murray (2007) together with the Forestry Commission found that Forest School experience had beneficial effects on both children and teachers, in their approach and attitudes towards risk and challenge. Schools that have adopted a 'forest school' approach, with children accessing forest schooling on a weekly basis with trained staff, have reported positive outcomes in terms of children's overall physical development, levels of well-being and independence, social as well as communication and language skills.

The Forest School experience is built around experiences of risk and challenge, involving independent exploration of the woodland environment, tree climbing, fire building and the use of tools for den building. These have been praised by children, parents and practitioners, and positive outcomes have been demonstrated such as children becoming better able to assess risk for themselves, and gaining confidence in their abilities to meet physical and problem solving challenges, following a Forest School experience. Practitioners developed a less negative and more encouraging approach to the concepts of risk and challenge in the everyday outdoor environment (Knight 2011). These positive outcomes are also experienced by children with additional needs, when given the opportunity to engage in the forest school experience (Hill 2013). An increased sense of well-being, confidence and the ability to persevere against difficulty were all evidenced as positive outcomes as a result. Hill also found that this impacted on the professionals who had supported children with additional needs during the forest school experience, in terms of their own understanding of what the children could actually achieve through such experiential learning.

How settings accommodate the idea of providing risk and challenge in outdoor activities will reflect on the individual setting's ideas around safety and risk assessment. In recent times the use of risk assessment both for indoor and outdoor environments has grown substantially, often preventing the exposure of children to more challenging activities and a reduction of out of setting visits. Maynard and Waters (2007) highlighted such concerns from head teachers around parents' complaints if children arrived home dirty or with damp clothing from playing out in the rain. Contemporary parents have a heightened sense of environmental danger compared to previous generations, and are increasingly likely to cite the negligence of other adults when their children suffer accidental injury. Research indicates that modern children are significantly less likely to experience outdoor activities than any previous generation, and that this culture of fear and blame, largely rooted in the mass media, has not only impacted upon children's development of independence and **self-efficacy**, but has also led to an increase in child obesity levels (Gleave 2010).

Responding to increasing concerns, relating principally to children's diminishing physical fitness, the Coalition government (2010–2015) have now developed a focus on increasing physical activity in both the EYFS and the revised National Curriculum. In the EYFS (2012), physical development has become one of the three Prime Areas, and in the revised National Curriculum (2014), more time has been allocated for P.E. in an attempt to address lack of physical fitness. Individual settings do need to take this into account when designing and resourcing their outdoor provision, and planning time for children to access it.

The benefits of a balanced approach to risk and challenge in outdoor play, as opposed to a negative or over cautious approach have been well documented (Gill 2007). Children who are not allowed to engage in such activity tend to have underdeveloped vestibular and proprioceptive senses, making them more prone to accidents, as they have not been able to develop a full conception of their own bodies' capabilities. There are additionally social, physical and intellectual impacts upon children who lack experience in child-led outdoor play activities; such a deficit will inevitably lead to poorly developed confidence in physical and problem solving abilities, poor social skills and poor development of the ability to self-regulate one's own activities.

CASE STUDY 2

An established private day nursery, admitting children from birth to 5 years had recently financed the 'updating' of its outdoor provision, after an Ofsted inspection. As well as using natural wooden materials for a climbing frame and boat swing, there was a 'rest area' with wooden tables for having meals outdoors, a 'hide' made of bamboo, a willow arch, and railway sleepers provided raised beds for the children to dig in and plant seeds. Steps and wooden decking provided access to the 3-5-year-olds' classroom. The work had been carried out during the Spring and children at the nursery enjoyed the new facilities outdoors during a long, warm Summer. A member of staff was also sent on training in 'den and tepee construction', returning with resources to construct a tepee (tarpaulin, long bamboo poles and rope).

Once assembled the tepee was a great success with the children, becoming a semi-permanent feature of the outdoor space, even though it dramatically decreased the area for wheeled toys (not particularly liked by some members of staff due to the shortage of tricycles which led to constant arguments between the children). Eventually, with the advent of a very wet Autumn, the tepee was taken down and stored away in the cellar. Health and Safety issues soon arose around the wet and slippery decking and wooden steps, and the wooden climbing frame, with the manager looking for advice on how to 'weather proof' it, as several children had slipped and fallen when accessing the outdoor area. During a period when heavy snow covered the outdoor area, the practitioner who had been on the tepee training decided to ask the older children for help in erecting the tepee again. It had not been stored with any protective covering and areas of the tarpaulin showed patches of mould, which the practitioner decided she would brush away, once the tepee had been erected.

With one other member of staff, and four of the 4-year-olds, she began to erect the tepee, while other children played in the snow around them, some attempting to push wheeled toys through the snow. The snow provided temporary purchase for the bamboo poles, but once the weight of the tarpaulin was draped around them, they began to collapse with one of the children inside the unfinished structure. As the poles began to slide and the tepee upended in the snow, one of the poles narrowly missed a child pushing a tricycle, head down, looking at the tracks he was making in the snow. Fortunately no child was hurt during the incident.

1. Discuss your views on all-weather access to outdoor provision with others.
2. What action should the setting Manager have taken on discovering the slippery nature of the natural wood finishes?
3. How should this incident be recorded?
4. Who was responsible for maintaining the safety of the outdoor area?
5. What educational benefit was there in erecting the tepee?
6. How might the snow-covered outdoor provision have been more effectively used?

Now return to the first case study, and consider whether your answers to those questions have changed.

The role of the adult in the outdoors: reflective practice

Once a creative, open-ended outdoor play environment is established, the role of the adult in supporting the child's needs has to be considered. An important consideration for the adult is the amount of time the child needs to thoroughly explore the outdoors, and how this might be planned for. Again, the Reggio Emilia approach supports this concept of the importance of time in a child's exploration of the world (Edwards *et al.* 1998).

Creative, imaginative, open-ended play requires prolonged periods of time in which to evolve, and child initiated 'projects' may need to be revisited, and not automatically disbanded at the end of the day. A day broken up by numerous routines will work against this. Research suggests (Bilton 2005) that the practitioner's role is to closely observe such play and provide subtle assistance when invited, for example when a den collapses, and some structural advice is sought, or the child's need to share his/her delight is expressed. Some situations lend themselves to clearer opportunities for deep **sustained shared thinking** (see Maynard 2011), suggested earlier, in gardening activities for example, where adult and child can 'work' together.

By providing such a special and stimulating environment, the adult is working along the same lines as Margaret McMillan planting lavender, roses and herbs in her nursery garden (Bradburn 1989) in order to create an environment where the environment becomes the educator. So providing the environment, planning for sufficient time and space for the child's learning to develop, as well as an interested presence are more effective roles for the adult to inhabit, rather than that of a director, relentlessly imposing [adult] purpose upon children's play. Continued and constant questioning, often in ways that completely disrupt the child's thoughts, is prone to disrupt the independent, exploratory nature of this kind of play and the consequent deep level learning that quality outdoor provision can support.

Within minutes of joining [children's play activities, a temporary member of staff] . . . began firing questions: 'What colour is that?', 'What shape are those?' . . . One after another, with virtually no gap in between. She asked closed questions that she (and most of the children) already knew the answer to . . . Within minutes, some of the group began to drift off . . . One of the children who'd left the activity came up to me and said 'My head hurts, Miss'. So does mine, I thought.

(Olusoga 2014, p. 47)

REFLECTIVE PRACTICE

How would you frame the place for 'sustained shared thinking' in child-led outdoor play in your setting, with an emphasis on the child's immersion in independent, collaborative, open-ended and creative activity?

FROM RESEARCH TO PRACTICE

In 2005, on the basis of a longitudinal study of outdoor-based rough and tumble play which used focal child observations to study a group of children between the ages of four and six years, Pam Jarvis proposed that :

- Much social and gender role development appears to be mediated through social free play, with underpinning narrative becoming an increasingly important underpinning 'driver' for the ongoing physical play.

- Social free play is an important mechanism for the development of complex, **autonomous** social behaviour, allowing children to develop an independent, gendered sense of personal and social competence.
- Young children learn through intricately blended physical and linguistic experiences, crucially including self-directed socio-physical activity, allowing them to develop and practise core skills that underpin social interaction on a lifelong basis, in essence, complex and fluid patterns of competition and collaboration that are often gendered in style.

(see Jarvis 2005, 2006, 2007a and 2007b)

The quite surprisingly sophisticated society that the children created, and the roles in which they placed adults (most frequently as unwitting actors in status competitions between individual children, frequently boys) create some problems for the EYFS concept of 'planned and purposeful play', which presumes that adults would be 'in charge' and 'organising' children in the outdoor arena in the same way that they customarily marshall them within a classroom environment! Indeed, the fact that adults were seldom 'in charge' greatly enhanced the learning experience for the children. Jarvis (2005, p. 262) commented: 'very little of the active playground-based free play behaviour I observed was "conducted with ease, little mental effort and not much care"' (Sylva *et al.* 1980, p. 60). The overall indication was that children had to work very hard to effectively think themselves through the social networks through which they engaged in their outdoor activities and that, indeed, the playground was the only place where children got to engage in such independent and fluid interaction that required them to continually 'think on their feet'.

You will find information about the focal child observation technique in Jarvis *et al.* (2013). Carry out a set of observations of this type, focusing on the outdoor play of both boys and girls. Analyse your observation by considering how much independent thought and action the child had to undertake during the time that you were observing him/her. Compare this observation with others undertaken in a classroom with the same child, and reflect on the different types of learning that unfold within each environment.

Principles, practice and professionalism: reflective practice

There are a number of issues around the use of observation in an early years environment; the main issue being one of **accountability**. Even with the revision of the Early Years Foundation Stage (2012), there is still the expectation that children's play and activities need to be planned, monitored and assessed with sufficient rigor to provide individual detailed profiles at the end of the Reception Year. The effective transition of a child from the Early Learning Goals to Year One assessments in the revised National Curriculum (2014) relies on many formative observations to provide this important summative account of a child's capabilities. Given these expectations, practitioners may tend to engage in and favour planned, 'adult-led' activities. In order to provide balance and validity when using such assessment descriptors as 'emergent', 'achieved' and 'exceeding', children also need to be closely observed in the type of self-initiated play that is routinely seen within high quality outdoor environments.

As suggested earlier in this chapter, there is a growing body of research that highlights the myriad benefits that a child's exploration of his outdoor environment can provide: 'the changing garden with infinite varieties' (Froebel 1974) that can support children in their first fully independent 'excursions' into the world that they will need to inhabit as adults, using the full range of human physical, social and intellectual skills. The role of the practitioner should be on these occasions, one of an 'interested presence', engaging in subtle sustained shared thinking, rather than that of a director of activities designed to meet a relentless adult-imposed agenda.

Nearly a century ago, Emma Stevinson, Principal of the Rachel McMillan Nursery School, reflected: 'When one sees these active little creatures trotting up and down the garden paths in the sunshine, learning in nature's own way, one realises the cruelty of keeping them penned up in the classroom' (Stevinson 1923 online). We leave you with the thought that it is well past time to listen to these voices across the years, and reclaim our heritage of high quality outdoor play for British children in the twenty-first century.

Conclusion

The provision of high quality outdoor play experiences for children is as important as high quality teaching and learning experiences in the classroom. While there clearly needs to be some adult direction in the classroom, for example to frame the types of activities that may develop literacy and numeracy, the development that occurs through outdoor play is only fully realised through child-led activity, preferably in a natural area where the children can use the resources in a highly flexible manner.

The ability to operate independently from moment to moment in collaboration, co-operation and competition is key to successful **engagement** in human adult existence. The place in which these skills are learned is within a playground/outdoor setting where children collaborate and negotiate to construct original play narratives, and to problem-solve within these.

Although the value of outdoor play is generally recognised to some extent as essential for physical fitness, its potential for holistic development, especially social and problem-solving skills is not fully recognised within the Early Years Foundation Stage or, frequently, by individual settings and practitioners (Maynard and Waters 2007). Recent arguments have been raised (for example, Jarvis *et al.* 2014) that this is having an impact upon mental health and sense of well-being in the later stages of childhood and adolescence.

In order to work effectively with children engaged in outdoor play, practitioners need to understand the potential that the outdoors holds for healthy development of a whole variety of skills and competencies, not simply physical fitness. It is hoped that this chapter will help you to develop your practice, reflection and understanding, particularly towards successful engagement in deep sustained shared thinking with children constructing their own play activities in outdoor environments.

Further reading

Durrant, S. (2013) *Outdoor Play: (Play in the EYFS)* London: Pre-School Books.
   Offers a focused look at outdoor play through the EYFS Framework.

Featherstone, S. (2012) *The Little Book of Outside in all Weathers.* London: A&C Black.
Contains some useful ideas for outdoor play, particularly in inclement weather, with a very practical emphasis.

Gould, T. (2014) *Learning and Playing Outdoors.* London: Featherstone Education.
Gives a comprehensive focus on outdoor play and contains many inspiring ideas with a range of visual illustrations, with reference throughout to the EYFS.

Knight, S. (2011) *Risk and Adventure in Early Years Outdoor Play.* London: Sage.
Focuses on the more adventurous and risky elements of outdoor play.

Siren Films (2011) *Two Year Olds Outdoors: play, learning and development.* Newcastle: Siren Films. [Also available at www.sirenfilms.co.uk]
A practical resource from which practitioners can reflect upon outdoor play from a visual perspective.

Tovey, H. (2007) *Playing Outdoors: Space and Places, Risk and Challenge,* Maidenhead: Open University Press.
A critical perspective in the 'Debating Play' series, which examines the history of and rationale for outdoor play, with particular attention to risk and challenge.

White, J. (2014) *Playing and Learning Outdoors.* London: Routledge.
A brand new second edition of a best-selling book, with a comprehensive focus on the outdoors.

Useful websites

www.ltl.org.uk/

Learning through Landscapes, a charity focused on enhancing outdoor play for children.

www.playengland.org.uk/our-work/campaigns/love-outdoor-play.aspx

Love outdoor play, a charity supported by 'Play England', provides ideas and support for outdoor play initiatives.

www.playwales.org.uk/eng/playingout

A portal to the 'Free Range Kids' initiative, focused on reclaiming outdoor areas for children's play.

www.educationscotland.gov.uk/earlyyearsmatters/n/genericcontent_tcm4732299.asp

A web journal called Nurturing Outdoor Play, sponsored by Education Scotland.

References

Bilton, H. (ed.) (2005) *Learning Outdoors: Improving the Quality of Young Children's Play Outdoors.* Oxon: David Fulton.

Bishop, J. and Curtis, M. (2001) *Play Today in the Primary School Playground.* Buckingham: Open University Press.

Blatchford, P. and Baines, E. (2008) *A Follow-up National Survey of Breaktimes in Primary and Secondary Schools.* Final Report to the Nuffield Foundation. Retrieved 22 February 2014 from: www.nuffield foundation.org/sites/default/files/Breaktimes_Final%20report_Blatchford.pdf

Bradburn, E. (1989) *Margaret McMillan, Portrait of a Pioneer,* London & New York: Routledge.

Brown, F. (2014) Playwork. In A. Brock, A., P. Jarvis, P. and Y. Olusoga, *Perspectives on Play: Learning for Life* (2nd edn), pp. 233-243. Abingdon: Routledge.

Ceppi, G. and Zini, M. (eds) (1998) *Children, Spaces, Relations,* Reggio: Domus Research.

Department for Education [DfE] (2012) *Statutory Framework for the Early Years Foundation Stage.* Runcorn: Department for Education. Retrieved 22 February 2014 from www.gov.uk/government/uploads/system/uploads/attachment_data/file/271631/eyfs_statutory_framework_march_2012.pdf

Department for Education (DfE) (2014) *Primary National Curriculum* (from September 2014) www.gov.uk

Early Education (2014) *Development Matters in the Early Years Foundation Stage*. Available at: www.foundationyears.org.uk/files/2012/03/Development-Matters-FINAL-PRINT-AMENDED.pdf

Edwards, C., Gandini, L. and Forman, G. (eds) (1998) *The Hundred Languages of Children – the Reggio-Emilia Approach to Early Childhood Education*. London: Ablex.

Fjørtoft, Ingunn (2004) Landscape as Playscape: The Effects of Natural Environments on Children's Play and Motor Development, *Children, Youth and Environments* 14(2): 21–44. Retrieved 14 February 2014 from www.colorado.edu/journals/cye/

Froebel, F. (1974) *The Education of Man*. Clifton, New Jersey: A.M. Kelly reprint.

Gill, T. (2007) *No Fear: Growing up in a Risk Averse Society*. London: Calouste Gulbenkian Foundation.

Gleave, J. (2010) *Community Play: A Literature Review*. London: Play England.

Goddard Blythe, S. (2005) *The Well Balanced child, Movement and Early Learning*. Stroud: Hawthorn Press.

Harre, R. (1999) The Rediscovery of the Human Mind: The Discursive Approach, *Asian Journal of Social Psychology*, 2, pp. 43–62.

Hill, J. (2013) How can a Nursery School maximise the potential for young children to express Adventure and Challenge access risk for themselves and enjoy a sense of freedom? EECERA 23rd Conference *Values, Culture and Context*.

Jarvis, P. (2005) *The role of rough and tumble play in children's social and gender role development in the early years of primary school*, Unpublished PhD thesis, Leeds Metropolitan University.

Jarvis, P. (2006) Rough and Tumble Play, Lessons in Life. *Evolutionary Psychology* 4, pp. 268–286.

Jarvis P. (2007a) Monsters, Magic and Mr. Psycho: Rough and Tumble Play in the Early Years of Primary School, a Biocultural Approach. *Early Years, An International Journal of Research and Development*, Vol. 27 (2) pp. 171–188.

Jarvis, P. (2007b) Dangerous activities within an invisible playground: a study of emergent male football play and teachers' perspectives of outdoor free play in the early years of primary school. *International Journal of Early Years Education*, 15(3) pp. 245–259.

Jarvis, P. (2014) Building Social Hardiness for Life: Rough and Tumble Play in the Early Years of Primary School. In A. Brock, P. Jarvis and Y. Olusoga, *Perspectives on Play: Learning for Life* (2nd edn), pp. 190, 206–243, Abingdon: Routledge.

Jarvis, P., Newman, S. and Swiniarski, L. (2014) On 'becoming social': the importance of collaborative free play in childhood. *International Journal of Play*. Vol. 3, No. 1, pp. 53–68. DOI:10.1080/21594937.2013.863440. Available at: www.tandfonline.com/doi/pdf/10.1080/21594937.2013.863440"

Jarvis, P., George, J. and Holland, W. (2013) *The Early Years Professional's Complete* Companion (2nd edn). Harlow: Pearson.

Knight, S. (2011) *Risk and Adventure in Early Years Outdoor Play*. London: Sage.

Knight, S. (2013) *Forest School and Outdoor Learning in the Early Years*. London: Sage.

Maynard, T. and Waters, J. (2007) Learning in the outdoor environment: a missed opportunity. *Early Years: An International Research Journal*, 27(3), pp. 255–265.

Maynard, T., Waters, J. and Clement, J. (2011) Moving Outdoors: further explanations of 'child initiated' learning in the outdoor environment. *Education 2-13: International Journal of Primary, Elementary and Early Years Education* 41(3), pp. 282–299.

Maynard, T., Waters, J. and Clement, J. (2013) Moving outdoors: further explorations of 'child-initiated' learning in the outdoor environment. *Education 3-13: International Journal of Primary, Elementary and Early Years Education* Volume 41, Issue 3, pp.282-299.

Meggitt, C. (2013) *Child Care and Education*, London, Hodder Education.

Montessori, M. (1949) *Absorbent Mind*. The Theosophical Publishing House: Madras.

Moss, S. (2012) *Natural Childhood*. Retrieved 16 August 2012 from: www.nationaltrust.org.uk/servlet/file/store5/item823323/version1/Natural%20Childhood%20Brochure.pdf

O'Brian, L. and Murray, R. (2007) Forest School and its Impact on Young Children: Case Studies in Britain. *Urban Forestry and Urban Greening*, 6, pp. 249-265.

Olusoga, Y. (2014) We don't Play Like That Here. In A. Brock, A., P. Jarvis, P. and Y. Olusoga, *Perspectives on Play: Learning for Life (2nd Edn)*, pp.190-206-243, pp.39-59. Abingdon: Routledge.

Pellegrini, A. (1995) *School Recess and Playground Behaviour*. New York State: University of New York.

Pellegrini, A., and Blatchford, P. (2002) Time for a Break. *The Psychologist*, 15(2), pp. 60-62. Retrieved 22 February 2014 from www.thepsychologist.org.uk/

Piaget, J. (1962) *Play, Dreams and Imitation in Childhood*, New York: Norton.

Rinaldi, C. (2006) *In Dialogue with Reggio Emilia*. London: Routledge

Sluckin, A. (1981) *Growing up in The School Playground*. London: Routledge and Kegan Paul.

Soderstrom, M. Boldermann, C., Sahlin, F. Raustorp, A. and Blennow, M. (2012) The quality of the outdoor environment influences children's health – a cross-sectional study of pre-schools. *Acta Paediatrica*, 102, pp. 83-91.

Stevinson, E. (1923) The Open Air Nursery School. London: J.M. Dent. Retrieved 23 February 2014 from www.archive.org/stream/openairnurserysc028518mbp/openairnurserysc028518mbp_djvu.txt

Stevinson, E. (1954) *Margaret McMillan: Prophet and Pioneer*. London: University of London Press.

Sylva, K., Roy, C. and Painter, M. (1980) *Childwatching at Playgroup and Nursery School*. London, Grant McIntyre.

Tickell, C. (2011) *The Early Years Foundation Stage Review: A report on the evidence*. London: Department of Education.

UNICEF (2007) *An overview of child well-being in rich countries*. Florence: UNICEF. Retrieved from www.unicef-icdc.org/presscentre/presskit/reportcard7/rc7_eng.pdf

UNICEF (2013) *Child well-being in rich countries: a comparative overview*. Florence: UNICEF. Retrieved 10 January 2015 from: www.unicef-irc.org/publications/pdf/rc11_eng.pdf

Waite, S. Rogers, S. and Evans, J. (2013) Freedom, flow and fairness: exploring how children develop socially at school through outdoor play. *Journal of Adventure Education and Outdoor Learning*, 13(3), pp. 255-276.

White, J. (2012) *Making a Mud Kitchen*, Sheffield: Muddy Faces. Available at: www.mddyfaces.co.uk.

White, J. (2014) *Learning and Playing Outdoors*. London: Routledge.

Whitebread, D. and Bingham, S. (2011). School readiness: a critical review of perspectives and evidence: Occasional Paper 2. TACTYC Conference, Birmingham: Ready for School? Research, Reflection and Debate, 11-12 November 2011. Retrieved from www.tactyc.org.uk/occasional-papers/occasional-paper2.pdf

Part III

The Child, Family and Society

18 Society's expectations of children

Dawn Evans and Katherine Goodsir

LEARNING OUTCOMES

Within this chapter, we will explore society's expectations of children and aim to inspire you to reflect on these. This will enable you to:

✔ Consider what constitutes and shapes childhood.
✔ Understand different models of society's expectations and perspectives of children, i.e. as workers and an economic necessity, an investment in the future, as innocents, a threat, as consumers, citizens and active participants.
✔ Reflect on the implications on the above for Early Years practice.

Introduction

'Over the last decade children have become increasingly prominent on the national stage and early childhood has become the focus of greater attention than at any time in the past.'
(McDowall-Clark 2013: 81)

In recent years, the topic of **childhood** has reached an unprecedented level of global interest and concern by a range of stakeholders such as parents, practitioners and policy makers. In addition, greater focus on children's **rights** has resulted in recognition of the importance of **listening to children**. This forms the rationale underpinning our chapter. We will invite you to explore and critique some of the issues surrounding the notion of childhoods and in this process challenge your own thinking and understanding of key historical, sociological and global debates. In addition, we will enable you to reflect on your own early years practice and the **engagement** you have with children, their families and the wider community. Reflection should be a key feature of early years practice and will be a prominent feature of your **Sector-Endorsed Foundation Degree in Early Years** programme. Furthermore, 'The reflective practitioner needs also to be curious and willing, indeed eager, to border-cross – into different disciplines, different theories and different paradigms' (Paige Smith and Craft 2011: xv).

What is childhood and what shapes childhood?

'I realise how much childhood has changed and how far society has come with regards their view of children.'

(Laura – City of Bristol College)

It seems sensible to us to first define the concept of 'childhood' before we proceed with our discussion about various perspectives on childhoods. Frone, cited in Waller (2009: 2), provides a helpful initial definition, 'Childhood may be defined as the life period during which a human being is regarded a child and the cultural, social and economic characteristics of that period'. This explanation will be used as a term of reference for this chapter as we explore various historical, cultural and social influences and theories on children and their childhoods. The period of time that a child is viewed as a child varies from country to country and is surrounded by law and legislation and moral values about this. Waller (2009) proceeds further to state that the view of the child is not fixed or universal, it is **unique** in nature and is ever evolving. He considers that childhood is open to multiple perspectives from those that scrutinise it and invest an interest. Additionally, there are diverse childhoods for those that experience it. Childhood is shaped by the past, the present and the future and may be influenced by factors such as time, events and place, social and cultural attitudes and political ideology. The notion of childhood is grounded deeply in a given society by those that live and participate within it, and by those that experience it; so the roles of adults and children are overlapping and blend together. The Libby Brooks text, *The Story of Childhood*, provides a good introduction to this theme as she biographically recounts the experiences of and influences on the children featured. In so doing, she affirms, 'I believe that the arena of childhood will situate some of the most exciting ideological battles of this century, and that progressive thinkers must begin their interrogation of that territory now' (Brooks 2006: 4). With this in mind, we invite you to engage with some of the understandings and debates about childhood that currently exist.

PROVOCATION

What does the concept of 'childhood' mean to you? What do you think shapes and influences children's childhoods? Reflect on your own childhood experiences here.

Read some stories of childhood from the Libby Brooks text; we suggest Rosie, Lois, Allana, Nicholas, Adam, Majid. What do these children's stories inform you about the uniqueness of their childhoods? What has influenced their childhood experiences?

Brooks (2006) *The Story of Childhood: Growing Up in a Modern Britain* Bloomsbury

The child as a worker and economic necessity

'Children have faced struggles throughout history; however they are more resilient than we give them credit for.'

(Jade, City of Bristol College)

'I was shocked to learn that children were capable of long hours, hard labour and work and had such a responsibility.'

(Justine, City of Bristol College)

The idea of a child as a worker often raises strong opinions. In this section the concept of working children will be explored together with some of the issues raised by the idea.

As far back as the 1500s children from around seven years old were expected to work on the land owned by their family, not only to support the family income but with a view to later inheriting the land. This work, particularly agricultural labour, was often seasonal and children would attend school for part of the year or work in other areas. It was also commonplace for parents to send their children away to work as servants or apprentices from as young as seven, regardless of their class (Kremer 2014). Rural industry increased with the household being the centre of economic production during the seventeenth and eighteenth centuries. Not only were children an economic necessity for families but society had become accustomed to seeing young children in regular work; therefore, when the Industrial Revolution in the late eighteenth century moved labour from the home to the factory, it was natural to expect children to be part of that workforce (Cunningham 2005). Children were particularly useful as they were small and nimble and could carry out dextrous tasks, crawling into small spaces in mines, factories and chimneys. In addition child labour was cheap. Although there was opposition to this, the argument was often put forward that their labour was needed to ensure competitiveness in an international market (McDowall-Clark 2013).

Concern over child labour grew with eminent authors such as Charles Dickens and Charles Kingsley raising awareness of the harsh and dangerous conditions in which children worked. Throughout the nineteenth century various Acts were passed to regulate the hours children worked. The Factory Act of 1833, brought in by Lord Shaftesbury, made it illegal for children under nine to work in textile factories and limited working hours to 48 a week for those aged 9–13, as well as stipulating that children should have some form of part-time education. The gradual shift from the workplace to the school room had begun (BBC 2011).

Nowadays, a minority of the world's children work and this is steadily declining, although the figures may still seem horrifying high to those of us living in the western world. The International Labour Organisation (ILO) estimated in 2013 that there were 168 million working children, 11 per cent of all children. It is recognised that many children work around the house or in the family business or take up part-time employment to earn pocket money and that this provides them with skills and valuable experience. However there are also activities that are harmful to children's physical and **mental health**. Organisations such as the ILO and UNICEF campaign tirelessly for the rights of children in work. Although no one would argue that children should work in hazardous conditions, we need to recognise the realities of children's lives and that intervention could actually make things worse. Research by Rahman *et al.* (1999) found that a boycott in the USA of clothes from a Bangladesh factory, following concerns raised about safety there, led to the employer sacking all his child workers. While this might be considered a success, rather than returning home or to school these children were driven into even more hazardous occupations – even prostitution, (cited in O'Dell *et al.* 2013).

The subject of children working is an emotive one and links to our own values and beliefs about whether we consider children need protecting from the adult world of work or see childhood as a time of preparation for adulthood. Linked to this argument is the western view that considers education as the 'norm' for young children and that allowing children to work is therefore wrong. According to McDowall-Clark (2013) this **ethnocentric** assumption is not only condescending but shows an ignorance of what other cultures consider valuable. Wells points out that 'School attendance is so clearly demarcated from work to the extent that, while school is increasingly the only public space that children are recognized as belonging in, work is entirely erased as a legitimate place for children' (Wells 2009: 109).

REFLECTIVE PRACTICE

What images does the term 'child labour' conjure up for you? Examine your own beliefs and values around the importance of work and education. What has led to your own understanding? It is important to recognise that our own beliefs and values impact on our own work with children and that these are often ingrained as a result of our own experiences and background. It is good practice to allow ourselves to challenge this from time to time.

The Child as an Investment in the Future

'Investing in children's earliest years, keeping children alive through vaccination programmes, or ensuring access to clean water, health care and education have been seen as some of the most effective forms of intervention, as well as an investment for the future.'

(Montgomery 2013: 4)

As we can see from the section above, from the end of the nineteenth century increasing value was placed on education. The Forster Education Act of 1870 established a school in every neighbourhood. Although schooling was not made compulsory in England until 1880 for children aged five to ten, many children were receiving some form of education before this time through the church or private schools. Wealthy children had private tutors and governesses. Schools not only provided an education in reading, writing and arithmetic but had a role in ensuring a moral and patriotic upbringing which would instil good habits in children (Cunningham 2005). However, for many, especially the poor, attendance at school was minimal as this was balanced with the demands of work which ensured an income, especially as families were expected to pay a fee for school attendance. In 1891, schooling became free. By the end of the Victorian era it could be seen that state intervention in families' lives was beginning to impose a standardised childhood based on middle-class experiences (McDowall-Clark 2013).

As schooling became more and more important, twentieth-century advances in science and medicine led to improvements in children's health; however as noted by Hendrick (1997) this also led to the scrutinisation of children by professionals such as psychologists, doctors and educationalists as developmental 'norms' emerged. Concerns for the health and welfare of children and consideration of them as an investment for the future could be seen through the evacuation of children during the war and school health programmes (McDowall-Clark 2013). It could be argued that this continues today through the 'Healthy Child Programme' (Department of Health 2009) with its aims to prevent poor health through the education of parents and a robust programme of screening and immunisation, thereby creating a healthier society. In the field of education, testing is also evident. Children in schools are subject to **assessment** throughout their school life from the Early Years Foundation Stage Profile through to 'A' levels and beyond.

Revisiting ideas around the importance of work and education, O'Dell *et al.* (2013) draw on ideas from the sociologist Jens Qvortrup (2001) who argues that through education children are producing economic benefits and, while these cannot be realised immediately, children's achievement at school is being recognised as of future value to themselves, their family and wider society. In the Early Years from the late 1990s policies have been based on a complex set of strategies including a reduction in child poverty, raising standards in young children to improve outcomes on leaving school and relieving pressure on the welfare state (Baldock *et al.* 2013). These policies have been drawn up in response to key reviews such as those of Field (2010), Marmot (2010), Allen (2011) and Tickell (2011) which highlight the importance of investment in the Early Years to prevent problems later in life. As summed up by a UNICEF publication, 'The State of the World's Children, 'A country's position in the global economy depends on the competencies of its people and these competencies are set early in life' (UNICEF 2001: 13).

However, for many countries in the world, support and investment is needed to avoid children dying from preventable diseases and growing up illiterate. The latest review of the Millennium Development Goals (United Nations 2014) shows that globally, 6.6 million children under the age of five died in 2012 – mostly from preventable diseases and that 126 million youth (aged 15 to 24) lack basic reading and writing skills; over 60 per cent of these are young women. Non-governmental organisations such as UNICEF and Save the Children play a large role in education and fundraising to improve the life chances of many young children. In addition, the United Nations Convention of the Rights of the Child (UNICEF 1989) promotes children's rights in terms of participation, protection, prevention and provision.

The child as an innocent

'Childhood should be free from, and protected against the worries and stress of adults and the wider world. It should be a time for exploration, investigation and experimentation; a period of intense emotions – excitement, wonder, joy, dreams, magic and fantasy.'

(Julie, New College)

One perspective on childhood is that children are pure and innocent. This belief is founded on a romantic and nostalgic image of a child that views childhood as a time of happiness, to be nurtured, protected and cherished. The beginnings of this idea can be historically traced back to the 'romantic' philosophers and poets of the eighteenth and nineteenth centuries such as Rousseau, Locke and Blake. More recently, concerns about lost childhoods have been emphasised by

Postman (1994) in his lament on the 'disappearance of childhood' and Kehily (2009) who identifies current concerns being 'stranger danger', bullying and lack of freedom.

The concept of childhood as a time of vulnerability and a need for rescue can be further related to the work of the early missionaries, philanthropists and charities, 'Child rescue or child saving has a long history and is based on the view that children are dependent, weak and powerless victims in need of adult help and protection' (Montgomery 2013: 9). The pioneering work of Lord Shaftesbury in improving children's working lives has previously been considered. Robert Owen was another socialist reformer who during the 1800s wanted to improve the living and employment conditions and education for the families that worked in his mill (Pound 2011). Further examples include the work of Dr Thomas Barnado who founded the first Barnado's children's home in 1870 and Eglantyne Jebb who in 1919 established the Save the Children Fund overseas relief agency for children, providing food, clothing and money to those deemed in need. Both were initially established on the basis that children need saving and rescuing through adult help and intervention. However Montgomery (2013: 9) states that it is important to identify the shift in direction of these long-established charities: 'it is important to note that both have changed radically since their inception and much of their work today is focused on policy change rather than child rescue'. Nevertheless, their charity emphasis remains, as recent campaigns 'Support the Unsupported' (Barnado's 2014) and Syria Appeal (Save the Children 2014) demonstrate this paradigm of support and intervention. In fact, Jebb was instrumental in the development of the United Nations Convention on the Rights of the Child (1989) in the preceding Declaration of the Rights of the Child in 1923. (The concept of children's rights will be further discussed later in this chapter.)

A further past example of social reform can be evidenced through the work of the McMillan sisters in the early part of the 1900s. Margaret and Rachel McMillan established the Deptford Nursery School. Credited as the first nursery school in England, it has recently celebrated its centenary year. The nursery was founded on the philanthropic aims of supporting hungry and poor children by giving opportunities for fresh air, sunshine, play and nourishment in their establishment. Their legacy deserves great praise, including the setting up of free school meals for children (1906). The nursery continues today with the ethos and values of the McMillan sisters at the heart of its practice. A good example therefore, of past and present ideals of children as vulnerable supported through '**educare**'-based practice.

Further examples exist that promote the concept of children as vulnerable and in need of adult protection, including the aforementiond Early Years reviews such as those of Field (2010), Marmot (2010), Allen (2011) and Tickell (2011). These reports all illustrate the current emphasis on intervention in the Early Years, viewing this period as a critical stage. Indeed Tickell reminds us that evidence from the Head Start Programme in the USA, and from France and Sweden, as well as closer to home through the Effective Provision of Pre-School Education (EPPE) research, proves that 'high quality early years interventions provide lasting and significant long-term effects on young children's development' (Tickell 2011: 4). Moreover, the 2011 English coalition government accepted the concept of intervention to improve the life chances of children through their **social policy** document 'Supporting Families in the Foundation Years' (DFE, 2011). This intervention-based policy involves increasing the health visitor workforce, retaining children's centres, and extending provision for 'disadvantaged' two-year-olds. It remains to be seen if the impact of this social policy and political reform work will be as durable and impacting as the work of the McMillan sisters.

PROVOCATION

Consider images of children portrayed in the media:

- What do you think about the romantic image of the child as pure, innocent and vulnerable?
- Do you think the current emphasis on protection and intervention is valuable? Is it achievable?
- Can you link these ideas to your own practice when working with children?

The child as a threat

'Young children are considered rowdy and trouble makers when they play, or run, or laugh loudly in public.'

(Niki, New College)

'Adults have power over children – the justice system shouldn't allow them to be tried at such a young age.'

(Julie, City of Bristol College)

The image of the child as a threat can be seen from the fifteenth century onwards when employing children on the land and in factories was considered a way of keeping children usefully occupied to prevent idleness and mischief. As this became more restricted and children were seen increasingly on the streets, concern was raised amongst the respectable classes about the threat posed by the children of the poor. Many believed that school was the best place to keep children under ten occupied, providing control and discipline (Cunningham 2005; McDowall-Clark 2013).

There are two main discourses which shape our view of children in the western world. The first of these, the romantic **discourse**, which sees children as innocent, has been discussed above. In contrast, the puritan discourse considers the child to be wicked and sinful. This derives from the Christian doctrine of 'Original Sin', which considers all children are inherently evil and need to be punished and controlled in order to become civilised adults. Thomas Hobbes (1588–1679) was one of the main philosophers in this respect, although his views applied to society in general, with his central idea being the need for **authoritarian** rule (Montgomery 2003). Although it is generally considered that the puritan philosophy was superseded by the romantic discourse during the Age of Enlightenment, it could be argued that puritan views still exist today.

In 1993, a child murder case captured the public attention and so began a shift in the way children were viewed. Two-year-old Jamie Bulger was led away from a shopping centre by two ten-year-old boys, having wandered away from his mother, and was assaulted and killed. The media and the public reacted in an emotive way, calling for justice and even the death penalty. Passing sentence at Preston Crown Court the judge described the case as 'an act of unparalleled evil and barbarity' (Goldson 1998: 2 in Goldson 2001). Despite the rarity of the crime the tragedy was considered to be rooted in evil and 'a particularized demonic childhood was constructed' as children were conceptualised as both the cause and product of wider moral and social unease (Goldson 2001: 38). Davis and Bourhill (2004) suggest that while news stories report adult crime as the wrong-doings of an individual, where children are involved in crime there is a suggestion that a whole generation is morally degenerate (cited in McDowall-Clark 2013).

In its recent review of children's well-being, the Children's Society (2012) noted the negative societal attitudes towards children, perpetrated by the media, which considered young people as thugs, vandals and criminals, and called for a change in policy and practice to combat the stereotyping that perpetuates injustice. Payne (2009) documents concerns from the UNICEF committee following the UK Children's Commissioner's Report on the UNCRC. In particular they note a lack of national strategies to tackle the 'general climate of intolerance and negative public attitude towards children'. A survey of 2,021 adults commissioned by Barnardo's (2008) found that 49 per cent agreed that children are increasingly a danger to each other and adults, 43 per cent felt they needed protection from children and 55 per cent considered children were feral.

The child as a consumer

> 'I feel children are being exploited by consumerism, but others could argue it empowers them.'
>
> (Louise, City of Bristol College)

The child as a consumer is not a new concept. 'From early in the twentieth century toy manufacturers realised that they would sell more if they focused on the child as a purchaser rather than some well-meaning adult' Cunningham (2006: 230). Formanek-Brunell (1993) notes how in the 1960s in the USA, a new era began as Barbie and Action Men were produced and a direct relationship was established between children and toy manufacturers (cited in Cunningham 2005). The goods industry aimed at children continues to be influential in the present day; in 2013 the toy market was worth £2.9 billion. Although it saw a fall due to the recession as parents spent less, purchases made by children remained level. The 'pocket money sector', which represents sales of toys under £5, constitutes up to 45 per cent of purchases made either by children or their parents through 'pester power' (Copping 2014). The children's goods market is based around the concept of children and parents as consumers and one view is that this has meant the **adultification** of children as they become the main focus of marketing and media campaigns, almost secondary to their parents. As Buckingham states 'from the moment they are born children today are already consumers' (cited in Gallacher and Kehily 2013: 231). Branding is a powerful influence on children. Webly, cited in Layard and Dunn (2009: 57), considers ' brand loyalties get established early in life: by the age of two, children handle a new toy differently according to whether or not they have seen it on the television screen the previous day. By the age of three, they prefer an advertised brand to another which tastes just the same. It is not until they are 10 to 11 that they can identify the persuasive intent in an advertisement'. Branding and advertising is an interesting concept and prevalent throughout the world. However, in contrast, Layard and Dunn (2006) cite the example of Sweden where television advertising directed at children under twelve is banned.

The concept of dual consumerism between adults and children is evident within some modern-day books and films, such as J. K. Rowling's Harry Potter series whereby, although children are the primary audience, adults are drawn into this world. It could be argued that this allows toy manufacturers to capitalise on the series' popularity by producing and advertising spin-off goods such as action figures, trading cards and dressing-up costumes.

The growth of technology has created further opportunities for children to become consumers in the current 'digital' age. Many children have unprecedented access to television, film, websites, social networking sites and online games. According to recent research by Ofcom (2013) 43 per cent of children aged five to fifteen own a mobile phone. However it is the use of a tablet computer at home that is increasing. Since 2012 this has tripled among 5 to 15-year-olds (42 per cent as opposed to 14 per cent) while one-quarter (28 per cent, of 3 to 4-year-olds use a tablet computer at home. TV continues to be a popular medium; however children are increasingly accessing content on tablets and computers. In addition, 14 per cent of parents of 3 and 4-year-olds felt their children knew more about the Internet than they did. Despite the fact this technology undoubtedly opens up their world of opportunity, there is much discussion around the implications of this trend.

FROM RESEARCH TO PRACTICE

The Ofcom (2013) research above shows not only the increased access children have to various forms of media but provides startling statistics about ownership of mobile phones and tablets, in even very young children. Whether we agree with this on not, children are growing up in an age that is increasingly reliant on digital technology. As practitioners perhaps we need to recognise this more when considering resources available to children for information finding and mark-making. It is interesting to note also, that nearly 1 in 6 parents felt their 3 and 4-year-olds had a greater understanding of the Internet than they did. There is a role in all early years settings, not just children's centres for us to support parents in this respect through reviewing the way we communicate with them and by providing information and support to enable them feel more confident in this respect.

The Byron review acknowledges that there are 'concerns over potentially inappropriate material which ranges from content through to contact and conduct of children in the digital world' (DCSF 2008: 1). Further to this, Cunningham (2006) reflects that with visual media, children can think of themselves as adults. A view is that their childhood may indeed be lost as they become adultified. This endorses the view of Postman (1994) who claimed the advent of technology would signal the 'disappearance of childhood'. However, advocates for technology identify a range of technical and operational skills and knowledge acquired through the use of technology (Marsh *et al.*, 2005; Plowman *et al.*, 2008 cited in Marsh 2010). The digital era is grounded in the context of modern-day childhood and needs to be both supported and embraced by adults; it is within children's worlds even if it collides with our own view about children.

There is a need to explore the complexities embedded within the relationship between childhood and the commercial world in order to identify the ways in which children are positioned within markets and to develop strategies for facilitating their critical **engagement** with this positioning. In this way a reductive and narrow rejectionist agenda is avoided and children's own agency in navigating these waters will be enhanced.

(Marsh 2010: 25)

To conclude, Brooks (2006: 154) argues that 'consumer culture has offered children access to areas of adult life from which they have traditionally been excluded'. Yet consumerism can additionally be seen as a means for children to become active citizens within their society, a topic which will be further discussed below.

The child as a citizen and active participant

'We should allow the child to lead, respecting their independence.'

(Julie, City of Bristol College)

A popular and currently emerging perspective is that children are citizens and participants in their own right. Bronfenbrenner's (1979) ecological theory is formed on the concept that children are part of their socio-cultural, geographical context. He advocates children as part of the structural fabric of their community and neighbourhoods. Clark and Moss (2011), MacLeod (2008) and Alderson (2008) are among some of the contemporary researchers who advocate children's rights using the United Nations Convention on the Rights of the Child (UNCRC) (Unicef, 1989) as an underpinning principle for their beliefs. Their perspectives are founded on the importance of listening to children, hearing their metaphorical voice and enabling children's participation in their own childhoods. The United Nations convention could be criticised as being aspirational; however unless the ethical and legal principles and values are upheld and implemented by the citizens within society, children will be unable to exercise their rights as active participants.

A useful international example of the child viewed as an active participant derives from the Reggio Emilia approach in Northern Italy. Reggio Emilia's founding pioneers Malaguzzi and Rinaldi and today's practitioners from this region have at the heart of their philosophy the concept of children as citizens within their cultural context. In the Reggio Emilia pre-schools and infant toddler centres, children are seen as strong, capable, confident and worthy of rights. Including and involving children as citizens within their settings and local community lies at the core of their practice. The role of the community in the life of the Reggio settings is seen as complementary. According to Katz, cited in Edwards (2012: 44), 'Much has been accomplished by early childhood educators in Reggio Emilia over the period of a generation . . . They show us what can be achieved when a community makes a real commitment to its young children.' Within Reggio Emilia settings, the curriculum evolves, using the children's interests and what fascinates them as a provocation and using creative community members actively engaging with and enhancing children's experiences (Jackson and Fawcett 2009). Malaguzzi's 'hundred languages' (Edwards 2012) is a cultural metaphor for the many ways children play, learn and explore and thus is a celebration of the unique nature of children within their childhoods.

The High Scope philosophy further promotes this idea; the approach derives from the USA and the work of Weikart in the 1960s. In the High Scope approach, children are actively included in the planning, implementation and evaluation of their own learning experiences using a model of plan-do-review (Hohman and Weikart 2002). This puts children at the centre of their learning experience adopting a child-centred approach. You may have examples from your own practice where you have enabled children to have a voice in their care, learning and play.

CASE STUDY 1

Consider the following account from a SEFDEY student:

Louise was looking to buy a house. When she rang the agent about one particular house she was told it was an odd property and wouldn't be suitable for a family. As the agent met Louise his first words were, 'I hope you are not planning to have any children?' When Louise questioned him he told her that the house was dangerous for children as the garden had steps and that there was an open stairway that a baby could fall down. As they moved out into the garden the agent continued to point out tiered areas and 'dangerous' steps, despite Louise's comments that the garden was 'a big adventure for children'. The agent also commented that the house had been empty for years as everyone they showed round felt that it was not suitable for children.

Louise recounted this story to me explaining that her view of the garden was a large area with a tiered slope, a wooded area with fruit trees, a vegetable patch and a large grassy area.

Louise also told me about her practice and how practitioners were often reluctant to allow risk-taking outdoors and would stop children climbing and jumping, saying 'Don't do that or you will fall and hurt yourselves.' This extends to indoors where children are not allowed to use scissors or small tools. When Louise questioned her colleagues they commented on the fact that they had to fill in accident forms and tell the parents. They also worried their practice would be questioned, particularly when reviewing the accident log.

Reflection
- What does this tell us about society's attitudes to risk with young children?
- What is preventing the practitioners from allowing risk-taking?

REFLECTIVE PRACTICE
REFLECTIVE PRACTICE

As a team member consider your response to the concept of risky play.

- What do you think about risky play? What are the barriers in your setting? How can these be overcome and balanced with good health and safety practices?

Contemporary writers view the child through a participant lens by advocating children's experiences of playful adventure and risk-taking. Gill (2007) criticises the risk-adverse nature of modern society and its 'cotton wool' culture. Guldberg (2009) discusses the importance of risk and freedom in an 'age of fear' and opens up a dialogue about the importance of risky play in childhood. Knight (2011) is a supporter of the forest schools approach from Scandinavia which endorses activities such as fire lighting and den building in natural woodland spaces and places. Yet there is a tension here; Brooks (2006) argues that the twenty-first-century child is the 'indoor child' and Palmer (2007: 51) less politely calls the current generation of children 'battery children ... reared in captivity'. The debates from this viewpoint are based on the balance between ensuring children are safe, and allowing opportunities for them to take risks in their play. You may find that you and your team have different views on risky play based on experiences which are commonplace. You will need to work together to ensure practice that is consistent and in the best interests of the children, parents and staff.

Playwork is an example of practice where play has a particularly freedom and agency-based meaning. Else (2009: 150) cites the much praised play worker Hughes who endorses free play as being 'essential for the psychological well-being of the child'. The view of the child as an active change agent, participant and citizen is a **democratic** one and this supports principles related to children's rights.

Conclusion

Throughout this chapter we have shared with you some of the many and varied views and expectations of childhood that exist today. Consideration has been given to perspectives of children. We have also aimed to demonstrate that these have been constructed over time and are subject to political, sociological and global interpretation. We recognise that this is an extensive subject and there is scope for further reflection and debate particularly around the role of the media and the influence of parents. In addition, the changing political landscape impacts on children's experiences not only in the early years but further on as children enter compulsory schooling. We hope this chapter has enabled you to reflect on your own thinking and practice. James and Prout state that 'childhood is an emerging paradigm' (2005: 33) and furthermore, Waller (2009) states that we are still learning about childhood. Perhaps there are views and perspectives on childhood yet to be considered as we move further into the twenty-first century.

Acknowledgements

The authors would like to thank the following students who have kindly contributed to this chapter with their own thoughts: Laura Beese, Jade Mustoe, Justine Walsh, Julie Padfield, Louise Wherlock, Louise Viera, Niki Willows and Julie Kent.

Further reading

Brooks, L. (2006) *The Story of Childhood: Growing Up in Modern Britain* London: Bloomsbury.
  This book provides useful biographical recollections about various childhood experiences in the twenty-first century. The individual chapters recount the case studies of children's social and educational experiences. This book is useful pre-reading for your Foundation Degree.

McDowall-Clark, R. (2013) *Childhood in Society for the Early Years* (2nd edition) London: Sage.
  This book is good as an introduction to the social and global perspectives on children and childhoods. This is an excellent, up-to-date publication to support your thinking and learning about the subject.

Wells, K. (2015) *Childhood in a Global Perspective* (2nd edition) St Ives: Polity Press.
  This is a recently published second edition of this text covering themes such as social policy, politics and rights. A key text for your foundation degree studies.

Useful websites

http://stakeholders.ofcom.org.uk/binaries/research/media-literacy/october-2013/research07 Oct2013.pdf
  This provides a link to the Ofcom (2013) report mentioned above, Children and Parents: Media Use and Attitude, giving you up to date information and statistics on children and media use.

www.open.edu/openlearn/whats-on/radio/ou-on-the-bbc-the-invention-childhood
  This provides information to support Hugh Cunningham's book The Invention of Childhood and is collaboration between Open University and the BBC. It provides links to the episodes and will be an invaluable resource to support your understanding of childhood.

www.unicef.org.uk
  This website provides useful information around global childhoods including several downloadable versions of the UNCRC. Reports on the Millennium Development Goals and The State of the World's children provide statistics on child poverty, global literacy and infant mortality rates and show how progress is being made to ensure greater equity for the world's children.

References

Alderson, P. (2008) *Young Children's Rights: Exploring Beliefs, Principles and Practice* (2nd edition) London: Jessica Kingsley.

Allen, G. (2011) *Early Intervention: The Next Steps* Crown Copyright.

Baldock, P., Fitzgerald, D. and Kay, J. (2013) *Understanding Early Years Policy* (3rd edition) London: Sage.

Barnardo's (2008) *The Shame of Britain's Intolerance of Children* Ilford: Barnardo's.

BBC (2011) *Lord Shaftesbury: The Reformer* (Part 1 of 4 part series) Available from www.youtube.com/watch?v=GV3Z60X6AlO&noredirect=1 [Accessed 24 March 2014]

Bronfenbrenner, U. (1979) *The Ecology of Human Development: Experiments by Nature and Design* Cambridge, MA: Harvard University Press.

Brooks, L. (2006) *The Story of Childhood: Growing Up in a Modern Britain* London: Bloomsbury.

Children's Society (2012) *The Good Childhood Enquiry* Available at www.childrenssociety.org.uk/sites/default/files/tcs/good_childhood_report_2013_final.pdf [Accessed 25 March 2014].

Clark, A. and Moss, P. (2011) *Listening to Children: The Mosaic Approach* National Children's Bureau.

Copping, J. (2014) Toy Industry Suffers as Parents become Resistant to Pester Power *The Telegraph* 27 March.

Cunningham, H. (2005) *Children and Childhood in Western Society since 1500* (2nd edition) Harlow: Pearson Education.

Cunningham, H. (2006) *The Invention of Childhood* London: BBC Books.

DCSF (2008) *Safer Children in a Digital World: The Report of the Byron Review* Crown Copyright.

DFE (2011) *Supporting Families in the Foundation Years* Crown Copyright.

Department for Health (2009) *Healthy Child Programme: Pregnancy and the First Five Years of Life* Crown Copyright.

Edwards, C., Gandini, L. and Forman, G. (2011) *The Hundred Languages of Children: The Reggio Emilia Experience in Transformation* (3rd edition) New York: Praeger.

Else, P. (2009) *The Value of Play* London: Continuum.

Field, F. (2010) *The Foundation Years: Preventing Poor Children Becoming Poor Adults: The Report of the Independent Review on Poverty and Life Chances* Crown Copyright.

Gallacher, L. and Kehily, M.J. (2013) Childhood: A Sociocultural Approach, in Kehily, M.J. (ed.) *Understanding Childhood: A Cross-Disciplinary Approach* (2nd edition) Bristol: Policy Press, pp. 70–92.

Gill, T. (2007) *No Fear: Growing Up in a Risk Adverse Society* England: Calouste.

Goldson, B. (2001) The Demonisation of Children: From the Symbolic to the Institutional, in Foley, P., Roche, J. and Tucker, S. (eds) *Children in Society: Contemporary Theory, Policy and Practice* Basingstoke: Palgrave pp. 34–41.

Guldberg, H. (2009) *Reclaiming Childhood: Freedom and Play in an Age of Fear* Abingdon: Routledge.

Hendrick, H. (1997) Construction and Reconstruction of British Childhood: an interpretive survey, 1800 to the present, in James, A. and Prout, A. (eds) *Constructing and Reconstructing Childhood: Contemporary Issues in the Sociological Study of Childhood* (2nd edition) London: Falmer Press, pp. 33–60.

Hohman, M. and Weikart, D. (2002) *Educating Young Children* High Scope Educational Research Foundation.

International Labour Organisation (2013) *Making Progress Against Child Labour: Global Estimates and Trends 2000-2012* Geneva: International Labour Office.

Jackson, S. and Fawcett, M. (2009) Early Childhood Policy and Services in Maynard, and Thomas (eds) *An Introduction to Early Childhood Studies* (2nd edition) London: Sage, pp. 117–133.

James, A. and Prout, A. (1997) Introduction in James, A. and Prout, A. (eds) *Constructing and Reconstructing Childhood: Contemporary Issues in the Sociological Study of Childhood* (2nd edition) London: Falmer Press, pp. 1–6.

Kehily, M.J. (2009) Understanding Childhood: An Introduction to Some Key Themes and Issues in Kehily, M.J. (ed) *An Introduction to Early Childhood Studies* Maidenhead: Open University Press, pp. 1–16.

Knight, S. (2011) *Risk and Adventure in Early Years Outside Play: Learning from Forest Schools* London: Sage.

Kremer, W. (2014) *What Medieval Europe Did with its Teenagers*. Available from www.bbc.co.uk/news/magazine-26289459 [Accessed 28 March 2014].

Layard, R. and Dunn, J. (2009) *A Good Childhood: Searching for Values in a Competitive Age,* The Children's Society.

McDowall-Clark, R. (2013) *Childhood in Society for the Early Years* (2nd edition) London: Sage.

MacLeod, A. (2008) *Listening to Children : A Practitioner's Guide* London: Jessica Kingsley.

Marmot, M. (2010) *Fair Society: Healthy Lives* The Marmot Review.

Marsh, J. (2010) Young Children's Play in Online Virtual Worlds, *Journal of Early Childhood Research*, 8(1) pp. 23–39.

Montgomery, H. (2003) Childhood in Time and Place in Woodhead, M. and Montgomery, H. (eds) *Understanding Childhood: An Interdisciplinary Approach* Milton Keynes: Open University pp. 45–84.

Montgomery, H. (2013) Interventions and Ideologies in Montgomery, H. (ed.) *Local Childhoods, Global Issues* (2nd edition) Bristol: The Policy Press, pp. 1–52.

O'Dell, L., Crafter, S. and Montgomery, H. (2013) Children and Work in Clark, A. (ed.) *Childhoods in Context* (2nd edition) Bristol: Policy Press, pp. 213–262.

Ofcom (2013) *Children and Parents: Media Use and Attitude Report* Available from http://stakeholders.ofcom.org.uk/binaries/research/media-literacy/october-2013/research07Oct2013.pdf [Accessed 28 March 2014].

Paige Smith, A. and Craft, A. (2011) *Developing Reflective Practice in the Early Years* (2nd edition) Maidenhead: Open University Press.

Palmer, S. (2007) *Toxic Childhood* London: Orion.

Payne, L. (2009) Twenty Years On: The Implementation of the UN Convention on the Rights of the Child in the United Kingdom *Children & Society* Vol. 23, pp. 149–155.

Postman, N. (1994) *The Disappearance of Childhood* New York: Vintage.

Pound, L. (2011) *Influencing Early Childhood Education: Key figures, philosophies and ideas* Berkshire Open University Press.

Qvortup, J. (2001) School-Work, Paid-Work and the Changing Obligations of Childhood in Mizen, P., Pole, C. and Bolton, A. (eds) *Hidden Hands: International Perspectives on Children's Work & Labour*. London: Routledge Farmer.

Rahman, M.M., Khanam, R. and Absar, N.U. (1999) *Child Labor in Bangladesh: A critical Appraisal of Harkn's Bill and the MOU-type Schooling Programme.* Journal of Economic Issues, Voll 33:4 pp 385-1003.

Tickell, C. (2011) *The Early Years: Foundations for Life, Health and Learning: An Independent Report on the Early Years Foundation Stage to Her Majesty's Government* Crown Copyright.

UNICEF (1989) *The United Nations Convention on the Rights of the Child.* Available from www.unicef.org.uk/Documents/Publication-pdfs/UNCRC_PRESS200910web.pdf [Accessed 22 January 2015].

UNICEF (2001) *The State of the World's Children* New York: UNICEF

United Nations (2014) *The Millennium Development Goals Report.* Available from www.un.org/millenniumgoals/2014%20MDG%20report/MDG%202014%20English%20web.pdf [Accessed 22 January 2015].

Waller, T. (2009) Modern Childhood: Contemporary Theory and Children's Lives in Waller, T. (ed.) (2009) *An Introduction to Early Childhood: A Multi-Disciplinary Approach* (2nd edition) London: Sage, pp. 2–15.

Wells, K. (2009) *Childhood in a Global Perspective* Cambridge: Polity Press.

19 The Early Years Foundation Stage (EYFS)

Yasmin Mukadam and Kawal Kaur

LEARNING OUTCOMES

After reading this chapter you will be able to:

✔ Define the term Early Years Foundation Stage and understand what it means in practice.
✔ Identify the features of a curriculum and a framework.
✔ Develop your knowledge about the history of early care and education in the UK leading up to the EYFS.
✔ Compare and analyse key influential approaches and theorists on developing the EYFS.

Introduction

This chapter invites you to explore the EYFS and to comprehend the statutory context for all settings. As an early years practitioner it is essential that you reflect upon your practice, as you consider the nature and implementation of the EYFS as a tool to support young children's learning and development. You will explore the EYFS as both an overarching statutory framework for settings and guidance for early years practice and how to put this into practice. The historical development of early care and education in the UK is briefly explored with a focus on the key influences from international approaches, including Reggio Emilia, Head-start, Steiner and Forest Schools along with an understanding of the impact of major theorists such as Piaget, McMillan and Montessori.

There are case studies within the chapter that will provide differing perspectives for debate and enquiry along with a practical guidance to plan, observe and evaluate activities across the birth to five age range within your setting, using the EYFS documentation.

Understanding what is meant by the Early Years Foundation Stage

The EYFS is the statutory framework that sets the standards for the development, learning and care of children from birth to five (Standards and Testing Agency, 2014). It was first introduced in March 2007 and became a requirement for early years settings and schools from September 2008, replacing the Birth to Three Matters guidance (Department for Education and Skills (DfES), 2003), the Curriculum guidance for the foundation stage (Qualifications and Curriculum Authority) (QCA, 2000) and the National Standards for Day Care (**Sure Start**, DfE, 2003). The emergence of the EYFS, as a statutory policy initiative, aimed to help the sector meet the outcomes of the UK's 2003 Every Child Matters (ECM) agenda. Continued government interest and public debate led to the statutory framework changes in 2012 and 2014 with the aim of continually reviewing and improving the quality in early years provision to help all children achieve their potential (Tickell, 2011: 7). It can be asserted that in practice the EYFS is: 'A holistic and **inclusive** framework that provides a secure foundation and represents a principled approach to children's interests, experiences and being' (Kaur and Mukadam, 2015).

You may agree that the role of **observation** and **assessment** within the EYFS provides a means to continually improve practice and learning opportunities. However, as Palaiologou (2013) suggests, there is a concern that the EYFS assessment scales will overtake practice, and that the early years workforce may feel the need to tick boxes rather than create the innovative practice so important in the early years. Therefore, it needs to be a clear objective to all settings that the EYFS enables a spontaneous play-based curriculum.

PROVOCATION

- Discuss your thoughts and write your own definition of the EYFS.
- What impact has the EYFS had on you in your role and on your practice since implementation?

The EYFS is essentially made up of a macro-level policy guidance and a toolkit to achieve measurable curriculum objectives within a statutory framework to support each individual child's care, learning and development from their **unique** starting points. It also provides a plan and course of action within an educational context supported by a body of theory about effective teaching and learning to meet the needs of individual children, from birth to five. The components within the EYFS framework below are interlinked and must be used cohesively for effective practice:

- The Statutory Framework for the Early Years Foundation Stage
- The Development Matters in the Early Years Foundation Stage (Non-Statutory Guidance)
- The Early Years Outcomes
- The Early Years Foundation Stage Profile Handbook

The Early Years Foundation Stage (EYFS): curriculum or framework?

Originally curriculum models were designed for schools to provide strategies for teaching and learning with a clear structure of what to deliver and how to deliver ensuring that children's learning needs are met. The term 'curriculum' was unfamiliar within the early years sector until the introduction of Qualifications and Curriculum Authority (QCA) curriculum guidance (2000). Even today it remains unclear due to varying interpretations from the media, other professionals and the practitioners in the early years sector. This has led to a range of opinions that can confuse or may give rise to negative comments. As a practitioner studying for a foundation degree how do you define the EYFS to other staff, professionals and parents in your setting?

Today there are many interpretations of a curriculum such as those defined by Tyler (1949), Johnson (1967) and Stenhouse (1965). The following definition is discussed for the purposes of this chapter. 'A curriculum is an attempt to communicate the essential principles and features of an educational proposal in such a form that it is open to critical scrutiny and capable of effective translation into practice' (Stenhouse, cited in Sheehan, 1986). The nature of a curriculum can be explored further by considering two historical approaches below. These models are known as the 'product-based' and the 'process-based' approaches.

Definition of the product-based curriculum model

The product model leads to some kind of desirable end-product. There are a number of features to this model which distinguish it from the process model. It looks at the curriculum as an approach

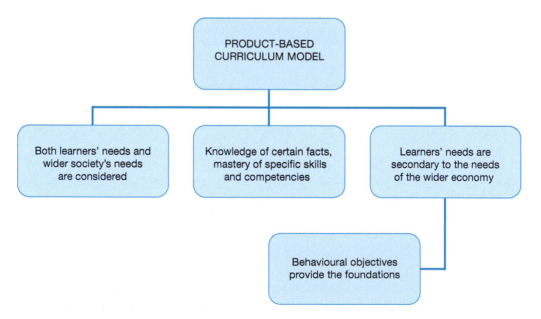

Figure 19.1 The product-based curriculum model

(Adapted from the Further Education Curriculum Review and Development Unit (FEU 1980) as cited in Sheehan (1986: 671)

that must be followed in order to achieve planned desired outcomes. The intended outcomes and learning experiences are prescribed beforehand. Consideration of wider economy needs are fundamental within this model, with learners' needs as a secondary aspect.

Definition of the process curriculum model

The process model can be depicted as being a more open-ended approach to the curriculum than the product approach. Defining features are that it looks beyond the outcomes and focuses on the stages of development and experiences. Ongoing, continuous development is celebrated. This model highlights that the focus of learning is not only to achieve the intended outcomes, but also to celebrate unique abilities of individuals.

Interestingly, both the above curriculum models have strengths and weaknesses which when compared with the EYFS (2012) can enable practitioners to analyse this relatively new model of working. The view of practitioners as identified within recent research suggests 'one of the

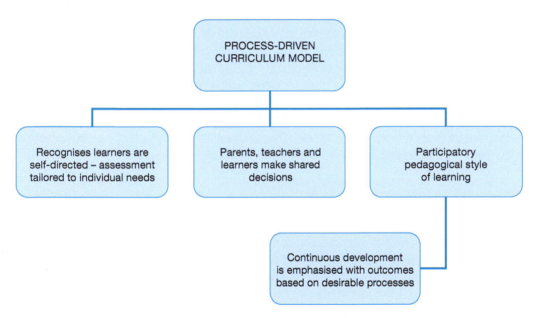

Figure 19.2 The process-driven curriculum model

Adapted from the Further Education Curriculum Review and Development Unit (FEU, 1980) as cited in Sheehan (1986: 671)

PROVOCATION

Critique the above representations of two distinct traditional curriculum models depicting product versus process approaches. Identify their strengths and weaknesses and consider to which version the EYFS is most similar.

intentions of the EYFS was to provide children with smoother transitions on the journey from home, through the pre-school years and into formal schooling' (Brooker *et al.*, 2010). On the other hand, there may be concepts that you will perhaps challenge if they are not congruent with your own values, beliefs and experiences.

Early Years care and education – 1800 to 2014

Interestingly the landscape of early years provision in England is perceived as having seen 'rapid and significant changes in policy and practice, experienced by practitioners, children and their families' (Brooker *et al.*, 2010). The historical links to the EYFS (2012) offer a perspective of underlying values and philosophies of early education and how it has impacted on the system and policies which within a wider landscape frame society and its social issues. In order to speculate about the evolving society and for early identification of interventions and strategies, it is important to associate history with current early years care and education to predict future trends which are highly dependent upon the policies of the government in power.

The importance of good early years' provision was identified as far back as the eighteenth century when Robert Owen opened the first infant school in New Lanark in 1816. Owen based the operation of the school on the principles of what we today call a 'play based curriculum' where children were given opportunities for self-exploration and active learning. Robert Owen's lengthy description of the infants' actual instruction is worth quoting in part:

> The children were not to be annoyed with books; but were to be taught the uses and nature or qualities of the common things around them, by familiar conversation when the children's curiosity was excited so as to induce them to ask questions.
>
> (Donnachie, 2000)

The role of the adult was equally important so that when children became bored or distracted 'a young active teacher would easily find and provide something they were interested in seeing and hearing'. However, even though these were great initiatives by these pioneers of quality early years provision, by and large until the Second World War, home was considered to be the best place for young children. Despite the efforts of practitioners such as Margaret McMillan and Susan Isaacs, the state did not acknowledge the value of education for young children until the Education Act of 1944 which clearly specified the role of local authorities to provide quality nursery education.

> In fulfilling their duties under this section, a local education authority shall, in particular, have regard . . . to the need for securing that provision is made for pupils who have not attained the age of five years by the provision of nursery schools or, where the authority consider the provision of such schools to be inexpedient, by the provision of nursery classes in other schools.
>
> (Education Act, 1944)

Despite this, the local authorities devoted their resources to carrying out the requirements for school-aged children (5-15 years). Subsequent reports highlighted the value of nursery education throughout the 1960 and 1970s. The Plowden Report of 1967 again highlighted the importance of effective nursery education for improving the life chances of children. The Education Act of 1989 impacted upon the Sure Start centres in the form of the National Standards for Under 8s day care and child-minding, which were introduced sector-wide to represent a baseline of quality. The Children Act 2004, Green Paper ECM (2003), Birth to Three Framework (2003) and QCA Curriculum guidance for the foundation stage (2000) provided guidelines for the early years' settings and child-minding networks.

It was identified that the guidance and frameworks were fragmented. This contributed to a lack of parity in practice and the child was placed from one framework (Birth to Three) into another (QCA Foundation Stage). This product-driven model did not consider the child's needs and there were elements that promoted a judgemental view for child development. To ensure that children from all backgrounds have the same opportunities and life chances, the government made The EYFS statutory as laid out within the Children's Plan (2007) and ECM framework. The new EYFS framework was a process-driven approach curriculum as a continuum of development which placed children in a better position where each child is considered 'unique'.

The EYFS (Department for Children Schools and Families (DCSF, 2008) was introduced as a comprehensive framework which sets the standards for care, learning and development for children between ages 0 and 5 years. The EYFS took into account the historical perspectives of education and care in UK and amalgamated the philosophies of the Plowden report (1967) 'value of quality early years education'; the Children's Act 1989 'the welfare of the child is of paramount importance' and The Children's Act 2004 'co-operation between key **agencies** to improve children's well-being and appropriate systems in place to safeguard them'.

The EYFS (DfE 2012) was reformed with particular emphasis on the role of adults in facilitating children's learning and development and to support parents and carers in the home environment.

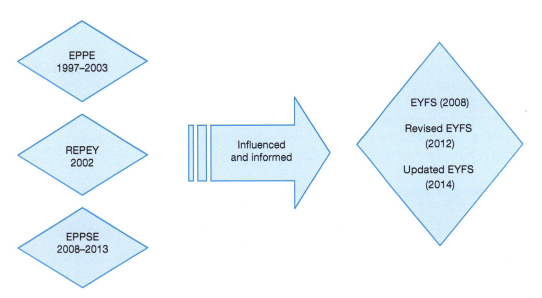

Figure 19.3 The key research influencing and informing the EYFS framework
(Kaur and Mukadam, 2015)

It has taken into account the major findings from the Effective Pre-School and Primary Education (EPPE) and Researching Effective Pedagogy in Early Years (REPEY) project.

The EPPE project was funded by the Department for Education, UK (formerly known as the Department for Education and Skills DFES until 2007 and then DCSF Department for Children, Schools and Families until 2011). It was a longitudinal project which ran in three phases, the first phase from 1997 to 2003 and the second phase from 2003 to 2008. Then it became the Effective Pre-School, Primary and Secondary Education (EPPSE) project and ended in December 2013. The aim of the longitudinal project was to analyse the impact of quality pre-school provision on social-behavioural outcomes for children in their school and later life. Key highlights of the study demonstrated that the quality of pre-school education made a positive impact on the children's long-term academic achievements and favourable social-behavioural outcomes. Additionally the combination of early start (age 2) at pre-school and attending a high quality pre-school had the greatest benefit for Year 1 and 2 outcomes in reading and maths (Sammons *et al.*, 2004a; 2004b).

The REPEY was the DFE funded report which was published in 2002. The REPEY study was done in conjunction with the EPPE project where the settings which were providing good or excellent learning and development opportunities were focused to identify their pedagogy. The study revealed that the practitioners who prioritised on the development of positive dispositions to learning, self-confidence and independence were actually able to achieve positive outcomes for children in cognitive and **social development**. Furthermore, the quality of adult–child interactions played a significant role in learning and development through the process of sustained shared thinking where the adult could identify the child's interests and extend opportunities of thinking through open ended questions, providing further opportunities for discovery learning. In 'excellent' settings more 'sustained shared thinking' interactions were offered compared with the 'good' settings.

The EYFS: curriculum in practice

This section explores the important role of practitioners and their understanding of implementing the EYFS curriculum requirements. Reforms by the DfE in 2012 placed particular emphasis on the role of adults in facilitating children's learning and development and to support parents and carers in the home environment.

Applying the holistic model below ensures that practitioners consider that children are able to achieve four key attributes (Four Cs: Capable, Confident, Caring and Creative) to succeed in

REFLECTIVE PRACTICE
REFLECTIVE PRACTICE

- What is the value of a curriculum/framework for early years provision in the UK?
- Why is it needed now?
- Make a list of the impact it has had on your practice.
- What is the future of the EYFS and the long-term strategy in your setting?

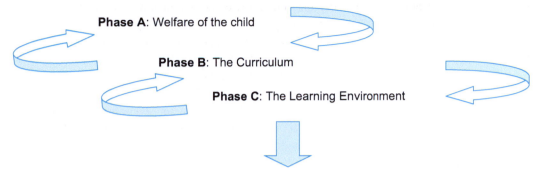

Phase A: Welfare of the child

Phase B: The Curriculum

Phase C: The Learning Environment

Four Cs: **Capable, Confident, Caring and Creative** children who contribute positively to society, achieving economic wellbeing and good health

Figure 19.4 Holistic curriculum model for Early Years
(Kaur and Mukadam, 2014)

life. It is important to remember that the EYFS identifies pedagogical approaches for practitioners to embed that support children in their learning and development.

To implement the EYFS successfully, the holistic curriculum model below provides a phased approach that practitioners can apply in achieving the best outcomes for babies and children.

Phase A: The welfare of the child relates to these aspects: the unique needs of the child; their emotional well-being and health; awareness of **safeguarding** and child protection and consideration of the child's voice

Phase B: The implementation of the EYFS Curriculum relates to these aspects: consideration of the child's interests and needs; understanding of developmental milestones in all areas of learning; observations and assessments to support planning; developing **reflective practice** skills and identifying next steps

Phase C: The Learning Environment relates to these aspects: parents as partners; influential and knowledgeable adults, stimulating environment; multi-professional working; consideration of the child's voice.

It is important that as a setting there are opportunities for each practitioner to identify their key strengths that will enhance the quality of practice and outcomes for children. The EYFS curriculum supports flexibility in devising a pedagogical approach which aims to meet the needs of the children within the setting at a given time.

> We have found overwhelming evidence that children's life chances are most heavily predicted on their development in the first five years of life. It is family background, parental education, good parenting and the opportunities for learning and development in those crucial years that together matter more to children than money, in determining whether their potential is realised in adult life.
>
> (*Report of the Independent Review on Poverty and Life Chances*, Frank Field, 2010)

Read the following case study then evaluate and compare with your practice.

CASE STUDY 1

Annie is a practitioner who has been working in childcare for 27 years. She works predominantly with children aged 2–3 years. There is a free-flow approach to the play-based curriculum within the setting. Annie and her team set up activities in the ICT area, construction area, mark making, painting, sand and water play, role play, small world and musical areas. Children are allowed to transport toys in different areas. However, Annie and the team neither challenge nor support this behaviour of children. This is resulting in resources being scattered in all areas of the nursery. Annie gets very upset with this ongoing situation as she believes that all resources must be used only within the intended area. In addition to this challenge, she also finds writing observations and linking them to planning a complete waste of time. She feels that early years is becoming meaningless paperwork activity. The manager of the setting is striving to support Annie and implement EYFS in a purposeful way.

Consider this situation and reflect on the following questions:

- How suitable is this learning environment for children?
- What should be the role of the adult?
- How can interactions be made effective?
- What aspects of effective learning need to be kept in mind?

Some international approaches to Early Years Foundation Stage

PROVOCATION

- What is your understanding of a curriculum model in the Early Years?
- Read and compare the following curriculum-based models to enhance your understanding of each one.
- Which of these approaches is followed within your setting? How do these approaches compare with the EYFS and its implementation within your setting?
- In your view, which particular approaches either individually or collectively do you think can enhance and improve the quality of provision in the early years sector and why?

The Swedish Curriculum idealises on play and natural explorations. Children develop independence from the outset which prepares them with essential skills required for later life such as self-help and self-awareness. The learning environment created by the 'Pedagogue' is home-like and based upon creating a natural environment where the outdoors is the primary environment for learning. Children spend half the day outdoors regardless of adverse weather conditions, for example babies sleep outdoors as fresh air benefits healthy development. The curriculum is based on three prime aspects: challenge, discovery and adventure. Each experience is based on a quest for fun rather than learning. This philosophy is shared equally by both the parents and the 'Pedagogues'. Currently the adult's role is to deliver the curriculum in a way that interests them rather than one led by statutory drivers and outcomes.

The High-Scope Curriculum approach is based on a landmark Perry School Study in America in the 1960s. The main elements of this approach are similar to EYFS. It is considered by some as the teaching practice while others think that it is a comprehensive curriculum. Five dimensions of 'school readiness' are the key principles, which include: approaches to learning; language, literacy and communication; social and **emotional development**, physical development, health and wellbeing; arts and sciences. It focuses on active participative learning where teachers are as active and engaged as children. Teachers provide a learning environment which promotes independence, curiosity, decision making, co-operation, persistence, creativity and problem solving. The key of High Scope is the Plan-Do-Review cycle where children are involved in planning their own play followed by its implementation and reflection on it. This helps to develop children as thinkers, problem solvers and decision makers. They learn how to act with intentions and reflect on the consequencies of their actions. There is a shared control in adult child interactions. This provides balance of freedom that children need to explore with the limits, for them to feel secure.

The Te Whariki Curriculum was established in New Zealand in 1996 as a bicultural, holistic curriculum. It was regulated in 2008 with a positivist approach taken by the workforce with its implementation. The curriculum promotes active participation of adults which includes both teachers and parents in children's learning and development. The ideology of the curriculum is the weaving of four principles: empowerment, holistic development, family and community and, relationships in children's early life experiences to prepare them for secure development. When compared with EYFS, this curriculum reflects a similar philosophy.

The Montessori Method of education is a widely followed approach which helps children to achieve their maximum potential within a structured learning environment. Maria Montessori pioneered 'discovery learning' which meant that her philosophy was that children are born with an innate capacity to absorb ideas and language within their environment. Montessori developed a structured education programme based upon the developmental stages of a child. She devised special equipment called 'didactic' materials which meant 'intended to instruct'. The aim of this type of learning was to engage children to foster a life-long motivation for learning. This approach suggests that play should have a learning focus.

The Reggio Emilia Approach originated in Italy after the Second World War. Loris Malaguzzi was the founder of this parent-initiated led and driven approach to provide effective learning experiences for pre-school children. This is a classic example of a process-driven approach whereby the curriculum remains fluid, emergent and stems from the child's own unique interests and curiosity. The role of the 'Teacher' is primarily as 'observer' then documenter and finally a partner in the learning process for each child. The 'Teacher' facilitates children to become active learners irrespective of their age or stage of development. Documentation is integral to children's learning. This supports the teacher to understand and to gauge the child's thought process and plan suitable experiences. The environment is considered as the 'third teacher' besides parents and teachers. A well-lit, well-ventilated and orderly environment promotes sense of well-being which helps children to delve in new learning and discover new experiences. All the toys and equipment are accessible to children and are age and stage appropriate.

Implementing the EYFS: a step-by-step process

Now that you have considered the history of the EYFS, studied various curriculum models and understood the range of pedagogical approaches influencing the EYFS you are in a position to work creatively using the approach below.

Step 1

Using the EYFS framework documentation	
Development Matters in the Early Years Foundation Stage (EYFS)	Use this non-statutory guidance material to support you in implementing the statutory requirements of the EYFS.
Statutory Framework	Refer to this across all aspects of your daily practice as this document is a legal requirement.
Early Years Foundation Stage Profile Handbook	This is important because it is the baseline assessment at the end of the Foundation Stage.

Step 2

Concentrate on underpinning the principles into your pedagogical approach in working with children to ensure your daily practice supports the emotional literacy first and the learning as secondary, following a child-centred process-driven approach.

Principles	Practice	Pedagogy
Reflecting daily on the principles provides a secure starting point.	You get to know the child through observation.	Identify learning experiences by interaction with children.
Principles come from the themes and commitments.	Gain knowledge of the child through evaluation of your observations.	Make links to theorists and child development knowledge – translate this knowledge into practice.

Enables you to support their learning and development. ⇨	Planning activities or experiences and identifying next steps. ⇨	Plan a learning-through-play pedagogy - then next steps.
Reflect on practice - does it align with your own values and beliefs? ⇨	Through reflection - what did you do today and why did you do this? ⇨	Consider the needs and interests of the child not the EYFS outcome.

The EYFS themes and principles are one of the best starting points in supporting curriculum delivery.

Step 3

Blend the 'Characteristics of Effective Learning' applying a three-stage process. Start by observing the child, assessing their needs and interests, then plan suitable next steps. Here is a simple Plan, Do and Review style model that is integral to your daily practice.

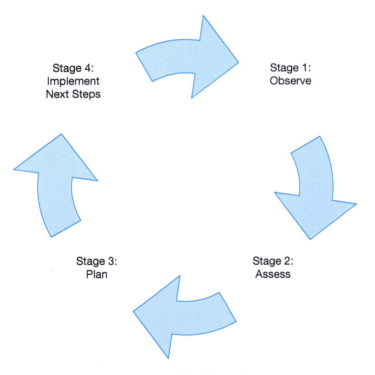

Figure 19.5 Adapted planning cycle for the EYFS

EYFS in practice – the toolkit for reflection

The starting point for successfully implementing the themes and principles requires your ability to critically analyse the vital aspects within the framework. Table 19.1 below gives an overview of some of the critical questions that will support you as you reflect upon your practice. It also provides links of EYFS into practice:

Table 19.1 An overview of critical questions as an aid to reflection

Themes and principles	Critical questions to ask
A unique child Child development Inclusive practice Keeping safe, health and well-being	• Have you considered each child's developmental stage and milestones, individual interests, learning style and communication stage? How do you do this effectively and why is it important? • How can you overcome the challenges of ensuring the needs of every child are fully met? • How can you focus on the child's needs when a parent also has significant needs? • How are you accessing wider community links in order to promote safety, health and well-being?
Positive relationships Respecting each other Parents as partners Supporting learning Key person	• What are your strategies for establishing positive relationships with parents and families? • How do you address concerns sensitively? • Identify key information about child's learning and development that should be shared with parents? • How do you motivate children to experience new learning? • What makes a successful key person? • Do the relationships between key person, parents and team in the room impact children?
Enabling environments Observations, assessments and planning Supporting every child The learning environment The wider context	• Why do you need to plan for both the individual and the group needs? • Why are observations a key responsibility of the early years practitioner? • Do you know what to observe in a child? • What observational skills are required to support every child? • How often do you record observations? • How often should summative reports be done? • What should be included in a summative report?
Learning and development Play and exploration Active learning Creativity and critical thinking Areas of learning and development	• How do you support children's play and learning? • What is your understanding of active learning in practice? • How do you promote sustained shared thinking among different age groups? • What aspects of critical thinking should be promoted?

The following model of practice provides a sound method for all levels of practitioners to aid them in understanding the needs and interests of each child. Practitioners or students with additional learning needs will benefit from this pictorial representation of implementing the EYFS.

My developmental journey through the Early Years Foundation Stage (EYFS)

I am three-months old. Do you know my developmental milestones?

- What preparations will you do for me when I join your setting?
- How will you support my care? How will you promote active learning for me?
- What are the stresses in my life and how will you help me?

I am eighteen-months old now. What are my developmental milestones?

- How will you help me in my transition from baby to this stage?
- What things can I learn at this age and how will you provide me with those opportunities?

I am twenty-six months old now. What are the challenges in my life?

- How will you support me in my toilet training?
- What other things can I learn?
- What kind of learning environment you need to prepare for me?
- Can I think critically and creatively?

I am forty-months old now. What kind of care and learning environment do I need?

- How will you promote early reading and writing skills for me?
- How will you prepare me for school?
- What are the challenges within my age group? How do you help me in resolving them? How do you promote sustained shared thinking for me?

FROM RESEARCH TO PRACTICE

As a manager of the setting, I wanted to evaluate the setting's practice and provision, especially in 2–3s room, to identify how effectively the well-being and involvement of children is supported. Using the Leuven's scale, I devised a data-collection tool which was a table to measure two aspects – well-being and involvement. Leuven's 5-point scale was used with 1 being extremely low and 5 being extremely high. This table was initially used for all new children who were settling into the nursery. The children were observed for their participation in activities and interactions with the key person and graded on the scale. The data collected provided an oversight of the level of needs of each individual child and staff's competence to manage transitions. Furthermore it was identified that staff who were enthusiastic to settle new children were better able than other staff to settle even very emotional children.

> This research was further extended to confirm how the children were interacting at different times of the day. The information collected through the research helped to identify weaknesses in practice such as delegation of responsibilities during key transition times between activities, staff's knowledge about the developmental milestones and challenges for particular age groups. Based on the information collected, an action plan was devised which included rearrangement of the room layout, communication within the team regarding responsibility for activities, training for the team to understand milestones and challenges for each age group. Throughout the whole process an **action research** cycle was applied.
>
> (Research excerpt from a Day Nursery Manager, 2015)

The above action research benefited the setting's practice in many ways. Each and every child's transition was managed sensitively and effectively. Additionally, transitions between activities were much calmer which helped the children's well-being and involvement, which is an important aspect of characteristics of effective learning in EYFS. Furthermore staff's knowledge about developmental milestones improved and the team started working with increased cohesiveness with each staff member understanding the sensitivity of their role.

Conclusion

This chapter has addressed the emergence of an early years curriculum in the UK that has been refined over the last two decades. This distinct phase of care and education, introduced as the EYFS in 2008, is the first integrated statutory curriculum in early years. For the successful implementation of this curriculum within an early years setting an 'enabling adult approach' is fundamental to ensuring the best possible experiences for each child. Therefore it can be concluded that the formula for enabling each child is dependent upon enabling the adult approach which can be summed up as:

Enabling adult = enthusiastic + curious + creative + enquiring + thinker

Within this chapter the EYFS has been likened to a process-driven curriculum that demonstrates a conscious attempt to place the child at the centre of early years practice. The adult role is discussed as critical to the care, learning and development of each child, and the similarities between different curriculum models provide a comparative framework that embeds a child-centred approach. The principles are central to the EYFS curriculum and are emphasised as the starting point for practitioners to critically analyse their practice and understand what to observe and how to provide experiential learning through play with the child at the centre of the curriculum. The political focus of the EYFS has been to provide a smooth transition to school known as 'school readiness'. This has been discussed with theorists such as Steiner, Piaget, Montessori, Vygotsky and Bruner supporting the EYFS as a framework that embraces the areas of learning, characteristics of play and the statutory framework that provides opportunities for children to learn through play.

As history shows, the EPPE findings viewed cognitive and social development as complementary to enabling children to achieve the best outcomes. This merged concept of education and care is at the core of the EYFS as recognised by Robert-Holmes (2012). The revised Early Years Foundation Stage (DfE, 2012) follows on from the success of the first version published in March 2007 and implemented from September 2008 until August 2012. The idea of a model building on and replacing three established frameworks, i.e. the Foundation Stage curriculum for three and four-year-olds (QCA, 2000), the non-statutory Birth to Three Matters guidance (DfES, 2003) and the National Standards for Under 8s Day Care (Sure Start, 2003) was initially met with resistance and mixed reviews from the sector and professionals.

The future direction for early years is a curriculum that focuses on improved quality with opportunities for innovation which need to be fully embraced by the workforce. The role of the adult is paramount. Therefore investment in this key resource should be a priority for the current or future government. A fit-for-purpose workforce will enable a fit-for-purpose curriculum wherever it is delivered. For true impact on children's attainment and future success recognition and understanding of the workforce is vital and must be continually respected and valued by key stakeholders such as policy-makers, parents and other professionals.

Further reading

Early Years outcomes: A non-statutory guide for practitioners and inspectors to help inform understanding of child development through the early years. September 2013, Department for Education. Available at www.gov.uk/government/publications/early-years-outcomes [Accessed 16 August 2015].
  This guidance can be used by practitioners to review children's progress and share a summary with parents for children between the ages of 24 and 36 months. This document supports practitioners and guides them to make best-fit judgements about children's development for their age.

The Early Years Inspection Handbook from 1 April 2015. Available at http://dera.ioe.ac.uk/id/eprint/23060 [Accessed 16 August 2015].
  This guidance from Ofsted is provided for inspectors and sets out what they must do. It explains what early years providers can expect from inspections in early years settings. Reading this document, practitioners will understand the requirements of settings and the judgements made by inspectors.

Palaiologou, I. (2013) *The Early Years Foundation Stage* (2nd edition) London: Sage.
This book contains detailed and reliable information relating to the range of subject matter taught within a foundation degree programme. It provides an insight into the history and philosophy of early childhood education to child development and specific areas of EYFS practice.

Robert-Holmes, R. (2012) 'It's the bread and butter of our practice': Experiencing the Early Years Foundation Stage, *International Journal of Early Years Education* 20(1), pp. 300–342.
This succinct article outlines the complexities of implementing the EYFS. It presents the experiences of both nursery and primary schools following implementation of the EYFS after its first year.

Useful websites

www.gov.uk/government/uploads/system/uploads/attachment_data/file/335504/EYFS_framework_from_1_September_2014__with_clarification_note.pdf
[Accessed 2 February 2015]
Statutory framework for the early years foundation stage: Setting the standards for learning, development and care for children from birth to five. Effective from September 2014.

www.gov.uk/government/uploads/system/uploads/attachment_data/file/237249/Early_Years_Outcomes.pdf
[Accessed 2 February 2015]
This link supports practitioners and guides them to make best-fit judgements about children's development for their age.

www.gov.uk/government/publications/evaluation-schedule-for-inspections-of-registered-early-years-provision
[Accessed 1 January 2015]

http://tactyc.org.uk/
[Accessed 15 September 2014] TACTYC: Association for Professional Development in Early Years.
This website was founded by a group of early years teacher trainers and is a suitable resource for a wide range of early years professionals, early years researchers and education consultants working with children and families in day-care, education, health, play work and social service contexts.

References

Brooker, L. Rogers, S. Ellis, D. Hallet, E. Roberts-Holmes, G. (2010) *Practitioners' Experiences of the Early Years Foundation Stage:* Research Report-DFE-RR029; Department for Education; United Kingdom.

Davis, H. and Bourhill, M. (2004) 'Crisis': The Demonization of Children and Young People in Scraton, P. (ed) *'Crisis' in Childhood'*? Abingdon: Routledge.

Department for Children Schools and Families (DCSF, 2008) [online] Available at: http://www.foundation years.org.uk/files/2011/10/EYFS_Practice_Guide1.pdf.

Department for Education (DfE) (2012). Statutory Framework for the Early Years Foundation Stage. [online] Available at: https://www.education.gov.uk/publications/eOrderingDownload/EYFS%20Statutory %20Framework.pdf [Accessed 12 February 2014].

Department for Education (DfE) (2011) *The Early Years Foundation Stage* (EYFS) Tickell Review. London: HMSO.

Department for Education (2003) Sure Start children's centres: statutory guidance. [online] Available at www.education.gov.uk/publications/eOrderingDownload/SSCC%20statutory%20guidance-2010.pdf [Accessed: 20 March 2014].

Department for Education and Skills (2003) *Birth to three matters guidance.* [online] Available at https://www.gov.uk/government/publications/early-year [Accessed: 18 February 2014].

Donnachie, I. (2000) *Robert Owen. Owen of New Lanark and New Harmony*, Tuckwell Press, pp. 156–171. Available at http://infed.org/mobi/education-in-robert-owens-new-society-the-new-lanark-institute-and-schools/ [Accessed 7 March 2014].

Education Act 1944. Available at www.legislation.gov.uk/ukpga/1944/31/pdfs/ukpga_19440031_en.pdf [Accessed 9 March 2014].

Formanek-Brunell, M., (1993) *Made to Play House: Dolls and the Commercialization of American Girlhood, 1830–1930* New Haven: Yale University Press.

Johnson, M. (1967) Definitions and models in curriculum theory. *Educational Theory* 17, 127–140

Katz, L.G. (1998) What We Can learn From Reggio Emilia in Edwards, C.P., Gandini, L. & Forman, G. 2nd edition *The Hundred Languages of Children: The Reggio Emilia Approach – Advanced Reflections* London: Ablex.

Palaiologou, I. (2013) *The Early Years Foundation Stage* (2nd edition) London: Sage.

Qualifications and Curriculum Authority (2000). [online] Available at http://webarchive.nationalarchives.gov.uk/20040117082828 http://dfes.gov.uk/foundationstage/download.shtml [Accessed: 25 March 2014].

Qvortup, J. (2001) School-Work, Paid-Work and the Changing Obligations of Childhood in Mizen, P., Pole, C. and Bolton, A. (eds) *Hidden Hands: International Perspectives on Children's Work & Labour*. London: Routledge Farmer.

Robert-Holmes, R. (2012) ' "It's the bread and butter of our practice": Experiencing the Early Years Foundation Stage', *International Journal of Early Years Education* 20(1) pp. 300–342.

Sammons, P., Sylva, K., Melhuish, E.C., Siraj-Blatchford, I., Taggart, B., Elliot, K. and Marsh, A. (2004a) *The Effective Provision of Pre-School Education (EPPE) Project: Technical Paper 11. Report on the continuing effects of pre-school education at age 7*. London: DfES / Institute of Education, University of London.

Sammons, P., Sylva, K., Melhuish, E.C., Siraj-Blatchford, I., Taggart, B., Elliot, K. and Marsh, A. (2004b) *The Effective Provision of Pre-School Education (EPPE) Project: Technical Paper 9. Report on Age 6 Assessments*. London: DfES / Institute of Education, University of London.

Sharma, A. and Cockerill, H. (2014) *Mary Sheridan's From Birth to Five Years: Children's Developmental Progress* (4th edition) Oxon: Routledge.

Sheehan, J. (1986) Curriculum models: product versus process, *Journal of Advanced Nursing* 11, pp. 671–678.

Siraj-Blatchford, I., Sylva, K., Muttock, S. Gilden, R. and Bell, D. (2002) *Researching Effective Pedagogy in the Early Years*. Available at: http://dera.ioe.ac.uk/4650/1/RR356.pdf [Accessed 9 March 2014].

Standards and Testing Agency (2014) Early Years foundation stage profile: handbook. [online] Available at: https://www.gov.uk/government/publications/early-years-foundation-stage-profile-handbook [Accessed: 10 March 2014].

Stenhouse, L. (1975) *An Introduction to Curriculum Research and Development*. London: Heineman.

Sylva, K., Melhuish, E., Sammons, P., Siraj-Blatchford, I. and Taggart, B. (2012) *EPPE Project: Effective Pre-School and Primary Education 3-11 Project (EPPE 3-11)*, Available at: www.ioe.ac.uk/Effect_of_starting_pre-school_at_age_2_report.pdf [Accessed 9 March 2014].

Tassoni, P. Hucker, K. (2005) *Planning Play and the Early Years* (2nd edn) Oxford: Heinemann.

Tickell, C. (2011) The Early Years: Foundations for Life, Health and Learning: An Independent Report on the Early Years Foundation Stage to her Majesty's Government, London: Department for Education.

Tyler, R. (1949) cited in Sheehan, J. (1986) Curriculum models: product versus process, *Journal of Advanced Nursing 11*, pp. 671–678.

20 Working in partnership with parents

Ute Ward

LEARNING OUTCOMES

After reading this chapter you should be able to:

✔ Understand the different elements of parental involvement and partnership working.
✔ Identify a range of factors which hinder or facilitate your relationship-building with parents.
✔ Discuss interpersonal and societal influences on the interactions between practitioners and parents.
✔ Understand how practitioners might position themselves in relationships with parents.
✔ Enhance your understanding of your own values and beliefs after examining how these affect your relationships with parents.

Introduction

Practitioners in early years settings have come a long way in recent years regarding working with parents. They are really trying all sorts of things to get parents involved. It just seems as if parents have been left behind. They don't quite get what parental involvement is all about.

(Early Years Foundation Degree student)

The above quote from one student was echoed by others studying on the same degree course. Practitioners' understanding of the role of parents in their children's lives has increased considerably but that does not necessarily mean that there is greater parental involvement in children's learning or in nursery activities. Is this really a question of parents misunderstanding what is required or even deliberately opting out? Or are the changes in practice and the increasing efforts by practitioners still not addressing the underlying issues? This chapter will explore the relationships and interactions between practitioners and parents to develop your understanding of factors which may support or hinder effective partnership working. After a brief description of terms such as parental involvement and partnership working, you will focus on factors that may influence the dialogue between practitioner and parents including internal or personal as well as external or societal issues. You will read about recent research in the area of parent-practitioner relationships, and reflection points and case studies will encourage you to examine your own values, beliefs and practices. This chapter will also support you to develop your study skills in relation to **reflective practice**.

Background

In the last 40 years there have been great changes in the understanding of the role of the parent in early years settings. From a somewhat distant relationship where the parent did not interfere with the practitioners' decisions in the 1960s, we moved to improved communications in the 1970s and attempts for effective participation by and greater **accountability** to parents in the 1990s. These have progressed to the adoption of the concept of partnership working between practitioners and parents to support all children (Rodd, 2006). The Early Years Foundation Stage as well as other government documents and guidance now firmly build on the expectation that practitioners and parents make joint decisions and cooperate for the benefit of young children (DfE, 2012; DfE, 2014).

This emphasis on partnerships between practitioners and parents is supported by findings from research. Desforges and Abouchaar highlighted in their extensive literature review that, 'the impact caused by different levels of parental involvement is much bigger than differences associated with variations in the quality of schools. The scale of the impact is evident across all social classes and ethnic groups' (Desforges and Abouchaar, 2003, pp. 4-5).

The authors stressed that parents are likely to get more involved when their children do well. At the same time teachers' expectations of children increase when they are achieving well (Einarsdottir and Gardarsdottir, 2009). In addition to the child motivating parents and teachers, research has shown that teachers and parents motivate each other in their **engagement** with the child's learning. This leads to a cycle where parent, teacher and child encourage and motivate each other leading to better outcomes for children (Ward, 2013).

What do we mean by partnership?

Parents have long been described as their children's first educators, and you already know that the Early Years Foundation Stage now expects close cooperation between practitioners and parents including joint decisions in relation to the learning and development of the child (DfE, 2014). However, the involvement of parents is not limited to children's learning. In pre-schools and nurseries in the voluntary sector parents are often expected to help during sessions or to serve as members of the management committee. In children's centres and some nurseries **parent forum** meetings enable parents to contribute to evaluations, development plans and decision-making. This broad spectrum of different ways of working in partnership is reflected in Epstein's categories of parental involvement and partnership working:

- basic nursery or pre-school matters (communication between practitioners and parents to help them understand what happens in the setting, how practitioners work etc.);

- volunteering and helping out in the setting;
- contributions to **leadership** and governance (as members of the parent–teacher organisation, the governing body, the pre-school committee, etc.);
- links between the nursery community and other community organisations;
- basic family matters (including parenting skills and children's health and well-being in the home);
- supporting learning activities in the home (Epstein, 2011).

REFLECTIVE PRACTICE
REFLECTIVE PRACTICE

Epstein offers a wide range of areas in which practitioners and parents could work together.

- Which types of parental involvement are already embedded in your practice?
- Which ones do you feel more or less comfortable with?

The first three types of involvement tend to be established in most settings and are part of **normal** practice in the early years sector. In recent years the home learning environment has been stressed much more, and practitioners are now expected to (and often do) advise parents on activities they could do with their children to support learning and development. Some nurseries and many children's centres also offer parenting skills workshops, healthy eating courses and other activities that benefit the family as a whole. However, not all practitioners feel that this is part of their remit. Comments such as 'I became a nursery nurse to work with children, not because I wanted to work with adults' are not uncommon. At the same time there are parents who may interpret the best efforts of a pre-school leader as an intrusion into their lives. These are the dilemmas and attitudes that need to be overcome so that practitioner and parent can work in partnership for the benefit of the child, and this can only happen if the relationship between them is built on trust.

PROVOCATION

If your relationship with parents was a sculpture, what would it look like?

Select a material you feel comfortable with, like clay, play dough, junk boxes, craft materials or natural resources like stones, twigs, pine cones etc. Use these material to make the sculpture. When you have finished, step back and look at it from all angles; question it and reflect on what this sculpture reveals about your attitudes and assumptions about parents.

(You may want to do this on your own at first. Later this could be an activity for a team meeting when colleagues could work in pairs to explain their sculptures and to pose questions to help each other to deepen their understanding of their open and hidden attitudes to parents and the work with them.)

Trusting relationships

If effective partnership working is built on trust, we need to understand what trust is and how it can be developed. There are numerous definitions, and every person may hold a slightly different view. For the discussions here a very general definition has been adopted: 'reliance on and confidence in the truth, worth, reliability, etc., of a person' (Collins, 1979, p. 1557). Trusting relationships build on people's values, beliefs and attitudes. For early years practitioners the following values and beliefs form the basis for a partnership approach. Parents are:

- **experts** on their own children;
- significant and effective teachers of their own children;
- skilled in ways that complement those of practitioners;
- different but have equal strengths and equivalent expertise;
- able to make informed **observations** and impart vital information to practitioners;
- inherently involved in the lives and wellbeing of their children; able to contribute to and central in decision-making;
- responsible and share accountability with practitioners' (Rodd, 2006, p. 226).

These underlying values allow practitioners to approach parents with openness, to listen actively and to engage with them at a level that goes beyond polite conversation.

Before exploring the practitioner's point of view further, it is important to consider what parents' views and expectations are. An overview of family support work revealed that parents value respectful relationships which acknowledge them as the experts on their family and as part of the team supporting their child; they want to feel in control; they want professionals who are emotionally supportive, available and responsive (Quinton, 2004). In the context of early years care and education research showed that parents did not want to be patronized, and they wanted services that meet their individual needs. A generalised view of parents was not beneficial, and structures and procedures should not replace person-to-person relationships. The overall aim ought to be the creation of relationships of equals which are not based on any claim of superiority or authority of the professional (Brooker, 2010). These findings regarding parents' values and expectations echo those of the practitioners' mentioned above. There seems to be agreement that the practitioner should not be in control and dominate the relationship but accept the responsibility, strengths and expertise of the parent. Equally, the parent should not dominate the relationship as it should be a partnership of equals in which trust flourishes on both sides.

Interactions between practitioners and parents

In their daily interactions with parents, practitioners will build on their beliefs and values; their behaviour will be a consequence of what they feel is important and of how they envisage the relationship with the parent. In your practice you may have heard a discussion like the one between Agnes and Jill in Case Study 1, which we now want to examine in more detail.

CASE STUDY 1

Piotr

Piotr, a four-year old Polish boy, has been coming to Rainbow Nursery for almost a year. He is well-settled, enjoys many of the activities and has formed strong friendship bonds with three boys whose first language is English. It is June now and he will soon be leaving the nursery to go into the reception class at the adjoining primary school. Jill, his key worker, is confident that he has the necessary skills and dispositions to settle quickly into the new environment and to do well at school. However, she is a little frustrated with Piotr's mother Agnes who has so far not chosen a day for herself and Piotr to visit the primary school. The reception class teacher has already reminded Jill twice that Piotr and Agnes should come as soon as possible. When Agnes comes to collect Piotr, this is the conversation taking place:

Jill: Hi, Agnes, have you got a moment? There is something we need to sort out.

Agnes: Yes, great. Can Piotr play a bit longer while we talk?

Jill: Of course, Latifa will look after him. Now, we really need to get this school visit sorted out for you and Piotr. The reception class teacher says Tuesday and Thursday mornings would be best. Could you go this Thursday?

Agnes: Yes – no, . . . I am not sure.

Jill: Are you working in the mornings now?

Agnes: No, it's not that . . .

Jill: You seem to be worried about something. Could you tell me about it?

Agnes: It's about Piotr. He hardly ever speaks Polish now; everything he says is in English. He doesn't want to look at his Polish books any more. I so want him to continue speaking Polish. He really needs that so that he can talk to his grandma and aunties and cousins when we go and see them. And when he goes to school he will start reading in English as well. He will lose all his Polish. What am I going to do?

Jill: Oh, right, I see. Well, I am sure that when you are in Poland with him, he will just very quickly pick it up again. He speaks Polish quite well now, doesn't he? So he will just fall back into it when others talk to him in Polish. Now about the school visit – do you know what you need to do to book a slot for the visit?

Consider this exchange between Jill and Agnes. Who is leading the communication? Whose problem is being addressed?

FROM RESEARCH TO PRACTICE

Work with parents in early **childhood** settings is not just a concern in the UK but receives wide-ranging attention in many other countries. For example, recent research in Germany looked specifically at teacher–parent consultations in day-care centres. Although the main focus of this research group is support for children's learning, their work has highlighted some interesting points regarding the interaction between practitioner and parents. They found that in general practitioners show interest in the parents and are willing to engage in discussions with them. During the discussions there seem to be complementary roles:

- the knowledgeable and the person in need of information
- the **expert** and the non-expert
- the speaker and the listener.

However, on closer examination it appears that these pairs simply mask established hierarchies which leave the practitioner in power and control of the interaction and position the parent in a passive, recipient role. The practitioners clearly perceive themselves to be knowledgeable and the parents as being in need of information (Schulz and Kesselhut, 2013).

This imbalance in the practitioner–parent interaction appears to be reflected in the exchange between Jill and Agnes. Agnes appears to have an underlying reason for her hesitation regarding the visit to the school. For her, Piotr's start at school signals a further decline in his Polish identity and language skills, which she is concerned about. Jill, the practitioner, appears to be aware of some unspoken issues and asks for some detail. Reflecting back on what parents' expectations are regarding the relationship with practitioners, Jill's response does not appear particularly emotionally supportive and Agnes' individual needs are barely acknowledged. At the same time, Jill seems so focused on arranging a visit to the school that she does not listen carefully to hear the underlying fear but presses on with her agenda. Jill is the speaker and the knowledgeable person; while Agnes is positioned in the role of the non-expert and the person in need of information.

REFLECTIVE PRACTICE

Think back to a recent difficult conversation with a parent. Who listened and who spoke? Who was the expert and who was the non-expert? Who was the more powerful person in this interaction? Can you identify one or two things you could do differently in future conversation?

The professional and the customer

You have already read that the interactions between early years practitioners and parents are shaped by values and beliefs as they influence how people act and behave and how practitioners position themselves in relation to parents. To some extent this positioning is dependent on external guidelines and regulations, for example, the *Statutory Framework and Development Matters for the Early Years Foundation Stage* (DfE, 2014; Early Education, 2012). These documents set clear expectations regarding the practitioner-parent relationship:

> 'The EYFS seeks to provide ... partnership working between practitioners and parents and/or carers.'
>
> (DfE, 2014, p. 5)

> 'Children learn and develop well in enabling environments, in which their experiences respond to their individual needs and there is a strong partnership between practitioners and parents and carers.'
>
> (*Early Education*, 2012, p. 2)

However, a closer inspection of these two documents does not lead to a clear picture of the nature of the practitioner-parent relationship.

PROVOCATION

Read through the *Statutory Framework for the Early Years Foundation Stage* and highlight all references to the work with parents. Do the same for one or two sections of *Development Matters*. What types of relationship are described? What are the underlying roles or positions assigned to practitioner and parents?

Although there is frequent mention of working, consulting and discussing with parents, there are also many phrases which suggest a more hierarchical relationship:

> 'Talk to parents about the feeding patterns of young babies.'
>
> (*Early Education*, 2012, p. 25)

> 'Use parents' knowledge to extend children's experiences of the world.'
>
> (*Early Education*, 2012, p. 40)

> 'Practitioners must discuss with parents and/or carers how the summary of development can be used to support learning at home.'
>
> (DfE, 2014, p. 13)

At times the practitioner is cast in the role of the expert and the more knowledgeable person, which does not facilitate a relationship of equals. Recent research from Finland found that approximately one-fifth of practitioners adopt this **Professional standpoint** in their relationships with parents: 'The Professional standpoint … highlights the staff's professional capability and skills to decide what is right for each child' (Venninen and Purola, 2013, p. 56). Parents' opinions about the curriculum or regarding appropriate ways to meet their children's needs are not sought regularly, and practitioners are the principal decision-makers. This seems to support some of the findings from the German research mentioned above.

A counterpoint to the Practitioner standpoint is the **Customer standpoint** which has become more prevalent in many countries with the increasing commercialisation of early years education and care: 'The Customer standpoint emphasizes the parents' opinions and wishes, and the staff's actions striving to fulfil them as well as possible' (Venninen and Purola, 2013, p. 56). The parent in the role of the customer (and hence the practitioner as the service provider) is supported by the government's aim to provide choice for parents which leads to increased competition between different early years settings. Many practitioners now feel the need to comply with all parental wishes to avoid negative publicity and to ensure the child remains in their care and provides the income needed for the setting. This appears to position parents in the more powerful role, while practitioners may feel disempowered. In the Finnish research more than half of all practitioners described their relationship with parents in terms of a customer–service provider relationship.

> ## REFLECTIVE PRACTICE
> REFLECTIVE PRACTICE
>
> Do you see elements of the Professional standpoint and the Customer standpoint in your setting and in your own practice? Consider which one may be more prevalent and what impact this has on practitioners on the one hand and parents on the other.

The partnership standpoint

Neither the Professional standpoint nor the Customer standpoint provide a basis for effective interactions between practitioners and staff. This only seems to be possible in a relationship of equals based on values similar to the ones Rodd (2006) advocates and parents are asking for (see above): 'The Partnership standpoint highlights the staff's and parents' mutual activities and concerns in education. Parents and staff search together for solutions in various educational situations' (Venninen and Purola, 2013, p. 56). This reflects the acceptance of parents as equals who bring different and valuable knowledge to the discussions about their children and about the settings as a whole. Research suggests that only about a quarter of practitioners take this standpoint. This is surprising as for the vast majority of practitioners the best interests of children is their core concern. This discrepancy may result from the difficulties and challenges associated with putting partnership-working into practice. However, it is the commitment to partnership practice, rather than the Professional Standpoint or the Customer Standpoint, which firmly moves the focus of the practitioner–parent interactions onto the child.

The child as the focus of the partnership

CASE STUDY 2

Jake started at the nursery 6 months ago. At first he did not settle very well, and he was reluctant to part from his mother Silvie. However, over time his keyworker Rumi has become his trusted adult in the setting and with her support he has got to know some of the other children and made some friends.

One day after the session Rumi complained to her colleague Sarah that Silvie did not come into the pre-school room any longer but stayed in the foyer. Jake always came in on his own and also left the room to meet his mother in the foyer. Rumi felt that Silvie had lost interest in the pre-school and in Jake's learning and development, and she was now quite difficult to engage with. Sarah offered to observe Silvie and Jake for a few days to see whether she could make some suggestions to help Rumi.

A few days later Sarah told Rumi what she had observed: Jake and Silvie were very warm to each other, saying goodbye to each other with hugs and kisses every morning. Silvie stayed in the foyer as Jake walked into the pre-school room. She watched him from the door for several minutes every morning and only left when he had found somebody to talk to. Sarah also noticed that Rumi was rarely near the door when Jake arrived but was already engaged with other children in the wet area (which she is responsible for). Considering the layout of the room Silvie may not have been able to see Rumi from the door.

Rumi was surprised by these observations and at first reacted quite defensively. On reflection (and after testing what parents could actually see from the door) she began to think that she needed to change her behaviour, partly in relation to drop-off time in the morning in general, and partly in relation to Silvie in particular. After some further discussion with her colleague, she shared her observations and thoughts with Silvie and asked her about the changes she had noticed. This was Silvie's response: 'I am so proud; Jake is a big boy now. He feels strong and confident. He can walk into his nursery without me. He is not afraid of other people anymore.'

Consider the different perspectives of Rumi and Sylvie. What did Rumi see and worry about? What did Sylvie see and think? What impact do the adults' perspectives and positions have on Jake?

FROM RESEARCH TO PRACTICE

Depending on your own experience and practice, different aspects of this case study may strike you as important. Here the focus is on the findings from recent research in Italy where researchers explored the difference in the interactions between practitioners and

Italian and non-Italian parents (Bove, 2013). (The difference in nationalities is not relevant for your reflections, as the focus is on the behaviour of practitioners and parents.) The research found that behind the practitioners' complaints that parents do not stay is first and foremost the fact that practitioners miss the dialogue with the parents. This appears to be an indication that the relationship with parents is very important to them and forms part of their understanding of their professional roles.

The act of not coming into the pre-school room is interpreted by the practitioners as showing a lack of interest while parents describe it as allowing their children to be more **autonomous** and independent. When practitioners learnt about the parents' views this led to deep reflections of their own relationships and perspectives. They realised that they had strongly valued their relationships with the children (me and the child) and had been keen to develop and maintain **trusting relationships** with the parents (me and the parent). However, these two relationships had been almost detached from each other and through reflection and discussion they were able to understand that there needed to be a triangular relationship where each interaction between two always holds the third person firmly in mind (Bove, 2013).

Returning to Jake and Rumi's concerns it has become clear that Jake's best interest needs to move more firmly into the foreground. Understanding why Sylvie values her son's independence helps Rumi to see the events quite differently and enables her to build on Sylvie's work to increase Jake's confidence. Based on this new shared understanding Sylvie and Rumi can now develop some strategies for good joint support for Jake.

The impact of childhood experiences

A strong focus on the child tends to facilitate interactions between practitioners and parents, and helps to clarify expectations and boundaries in this relationship. This chapter started with highlighting the need for you to reflect on your own values and beliefs; and at different points the views and beliefs of parents have been mentioned. Our own values and beliefs are shaped at different stages in our lives and they are not necessarily static. As an early years practitioner you know that early experiences shape children not just throughout childhood but also into their adult years.

REFLECTIVE PRACTICE

Consider what events and influences in your early childhood and during your schooling have left a lasting impression on you. Do you think any of those have an impact on how you feel about the work with parents now?

Early childhood experiences shape all adults and also often resonate in the work of early years practitioners and teachers. At the same time, it appears that negative and difficult experiences have a much greater impact than positive ones (Lawrence-Lightfoot, 2003). An early years practitioner who in childhood saw her parents intimidated by a powerful teacher may focus on helping parents to find their voices. This type of experience and the memories of our own childhood and youth can be a very forceful influence on our work, often overriding professional training. Not all experiences may find a positive expression in the sense that you may be trying to avoid a similar mistake or to overcome a wrong. By reflecting on your own early childhood experiences and on your practice you can become more aware of these influences on your own work and you can develop an understanding of their impact.

While it is paramount to be aware of your own experiences, memories and influences, early years practitioners also have to be mindful that parents are similarly shaped by influences and memories from the past. A parent accusing a practitioner of not doing enough to support their child's physical development may be hearing voices from the past telling them that they are hopeless at ball games. Unspoken cultural and religious expectations can also form part of parents' experiences and be vocalised, for example, in gender stereotypical views (I don't want my daughter to play football). The challenge for practitioners lies in developing an understanding of parents' beliefs and values, while being aware of their own values and not losing sight of the fact that the partnership you are striving for is to support the child:

> It is a perilous equilibrium that must be struck between the ghosts of the past and the realities of the present, between adult retrospectives and child perspectives. And although both are important, the exploration of the former should always be in the service of illuminating and informing the latter.
>
> (Lawrence-Lightfoot, 2003, p. 40)

Conclusions

This chapter started with some general information and insight into what is meant by working in partnership with parents by providing a brief historical perspective and an indication of the different forms this partnership can take. Through individual reflection and (hopefully) the creation of your sculpture expressing your approach to the practitioner–parent partnership you started to gradually explore your own views on partnership working. The discussion of some case studies in the light of recent research has provided some vocabulary to express the concepts we often talk about, for example, the customer standpoint, and offered scope to reflect deeply

REFLECTIVE PRACTICE

Revisit your sculpture. What exactly does it say about where you position yourself in relation to the parent? If you did the sculpture again now that you have finished reading this chapter, would it look different?

on the dynamics in practitioner–parent interactions. The case studies also served to gain a better understanding of how practitioner and parent may see the same event from quite different perspectives. Underlying the whole chapter is the understanding that your own values and beliefs shape the way you work with parents. To deepen your learning and understanding it may be useful to return to your sculpture from the first activity.

The Foundation Degree student quoted at the beginning is right: Parental involvement work in the early years has come a long way. The research considered here bears witness to this, as do the many practitioners in all types of settings who are trying different approaches and strategies to engage with parents. But are parents being left behind? Do they just not get what parental involvement is all about? Or do many practitioners position themselves and parents in a way that makes partnership working for the benefit of the child more difficult?

Further reading

Hughes, A. and Read, V. (2012) *Building Positive Relationships with Parents of Young Children*. Abingdon: Routledge.
Building on psychology concepts Hughes and Read provide a thorough guide to effective communication between practitioners and parents. This is an easy-to-read, thought-provoking book with many practical examples.

Lawrence-Lightfoot, S. (2003) *The Essential Conversation: What Parents and Teachers can Learn from Each Other*. New York: Ballantine Books.
This book takes a narrative approach and is easy to read while also offering deep insights into the impact of personal experience, culture and values on practitioner–parent interactions.

Ward, U. (2013) *Working with Parents in the Early Years*. 2nd edn. London: Learning Matters.
This book covers many of the practical aspects of working with parents, for example, engaging with fathers, involving parents in decision-making processes, supporting parental learning and dealing with conflict in the practitioner–parent relationship.

Useful websites

www.familylives.org.uk
This website provides a range of information on family matters and also has a section specifically for professionals working with parents.

www.natcen.ac.uk/our-research/
The National Centre for Social Research website offers research reports in relation to young children, families, early education and care.

References

Bove, C. (2013) 'Observing Interactions between Parents, Children and Teachers during the daily transactions from Home to an Infant-Toddler Centre. Preliminary findings from a study in an Italian Centre'. *23rd EECERA Conference: Values, Culture and Contexts*. 28-31 August 2013. Tallinn, Estonia.

Brooker, L. (2010) 'Constructing the Triangle of Care: Power and Professionalism in Practitioner/Parent Relationships'. *British Journal of Educational Studies*. 58(2): 181-196.

Collins Dictionary of the English Language (1979). London and Glasgow: Collins.

Department for Education (DfE) (2012) *Supporting Families in the Foundation Years* (www.education.gov.uk/childrenandyoungpeople/earlylearningandchildcare/early/b0077836/introduction) [Accessed 30 May 2014].

Department for Education (DfE) (2014) *Statutory Framework for the Early Years Foundation Stage.* Available at: www.gov.uk/government/publications/early-years-foundation-stage-framework–2 [Accessed 31 May 2014].

Desforges, C. and Abouchaar, A. (2003) *The Impact of parental involvement, Parental Support and Family Education on Pupil Achievements and Adjustment: A Literature Review* (research report 443). Nottingham: DfES Publications.

Early Education (2012) *Development Matters in the Early Years Foundation Stage.* Available at: www.early-education.org.uk/sites/default/files/publications/Development%20Matters%20FINAL%20PRINT%20AMENDED.pdf [Accessed 31 May 2014].

Einarsdottir, J. and Gardarsdottir, B. (2009) 'Parental participation: Icelandic playschool teachers' views' in Papatheodorou, T. and Moyles, J (eds) *Learning Together in the Early Years: Exploring Relational Pedagogy.* London: Routledge.

Epstein, J. (2011) *School, Family and Community Partnership.* 2nd edn. Boulder, CO: Westview Press.

Lawrence-Lightfoot, S. (2003) *The Essential Conversation: What Parents and Teachers can Learn from Each Other.* New York: Ballantine Books.

Quinton, D. (2004) *Supporting Parents: Messages from Research.* London: Jessica Kingsley.

Rodd, J. (2006) *Leadership in Early Childhood.* 3rd edn. Maidenhead: Open University Press.

Schulz, M. and Kesselhut, K. (2013) 'Let's just see how Mario is!' Construction of the "Learning Child" and the Parents' Role in Parent–Teacher Conferences.' *23rd EECERA Conference: Values, Culture and Contexts.* 28–31 August 2013. Tallinn, Estonia.

Venninen, T. and Purola, K. (2013) 'Educators' views on parent participation on three different identified levels' in *Journal of Early Childhood Education Research,* 2(1) 48-62.

Ward, U. (2013) *Working with Parents in the Early Years.* 2nd edn. London: Learning Matters.

21 Safeguarding young children

Allison Boggis

LEARNING OUTCOMES

After reading this chapter, you should be able to:

✔ Recognise the signs and symptoms of possible abuse and neglect in young children.
✔ Have a better understanding of the responsibilities of Early Years practitioners when safeguarding young children.
✔ Decide what action should be taken to safeguard a child's well-being.
✔ Develop an understanding of the complexity and sensitivity within this area of practice.
✔ Have a better understanding of current safeguarding policies and procedures.

Introduction

Safeguarding young children from abuse and neglect is a fundamental aspect of Early Years practice. Practitioners who work with and provide care for children are responsible for their well-being and therefore it is vital that they have a good understanding of the legal and policy framework that underpins safeguarding processes.

The discussions in this chapter focus primarily on the core concerns that Early Years practitioners have when safeguarding young children. This practical approach to child protection offers an accessible overview of important issues that relate directly to practice, and the messages inherent within the chapter are significant in that they provide a chance for the reader to anticipate situations in advance of experiencing them for real. However, this chapter is not meant to be a comprehensive guide to safeguarding and protecting young children. While it covers the most basic and important key issues, further study, training and discussions relating to individual setting/schools policies and procedures are necessary. None-the-less, the discussions and opportunities for reflection embedded in the chapter have been designed to help you to engage in a positive resolution approach to this complex and sensitive area of practice and will encourage you to critically reflect on theoretical ideas and concepts as you apply them to real life situations.

The chapter covers two main themes: Principles for Practice and Practical Considerations. The former provides an overview of issues, dilemmas and challenges presented when safeguarding young children, and the latter explores the subsequent actions and roles of practitioners as they raise concerns, identify abuse and work collaboratively to support the child and their family.

Principles for practice

The historical context of safeguarding indicates that serious concerns for children's welfare are neither new nor are they discriminatory: they cut across socio-economic status, religion and culture. While in-depth investigations of serious child case reviews such as those on Maria Colwell, Jasmine Beckford, Victoria Climbie and Peter Connelly have led to **perpetrators** being imprisoned; findings have consistently highlighted failings in communication between support services, ineffective recording, failure to engage and listen to the child, reporting of concerns and insufficient training of frontline support workers (for further information about serious case reviews and to access the national case review repository, go to the NSPCC website and search in the child protection systems in England). Importantly though, these reviews have acted as catalysts for change in policy and practice. For example, the policy development that followed from Victoria Climbie's death in the form of *Every Child Matters* (DfES 2003) was pivotal in changing services for children and young people. The main focus shifted towards safeguarding children, emphasising the need to support earlier interventions so that children might be healthy, safe, have the opportunity to enjoy and achieve, make a positive contribution and achieve economic well-being. Consequently, the Every Child Matters documentation *Working Together to Safeguard Children: A Guide to Inter-agency Working to Safeguard and Promote the Welfare of Children* (originally published by the DH in 2006; updated by the DCSF, 2010 and 2013) clearly placed children at the centre of practitioner interest and concern. It highlighted the preventative processes needed to ensure aspects of children's lives are safeguarded so that they can participate fully in life:

> The process of protecting children from abuse and neglect, preventing impairment of their health and development, and ensuring they are growing up in circumstances consistent with the provision of safe and effective care enables children to have optimum life chances and enter adulthood successfully.
>
> (DCSF 2010: 27)

However, you may recognise that while this statement emphasises a wide-ranging but important set of concerns, the practical application of the processes is not defined in sufficient detail to support you in every-day practice. Indeed, safeguarding young children can be particularly problematic as it is highly unlikely that infants will be able to explain sufficiently what has happened to them. In accordance with the suggestions made within the executive summary of the report for the Office of the Children's Commissioner for England, children's ability to recognise abuse and neglect is linked with increasing age and their gradual understanding that their circumstances are different from those of others tends to become apparent around the ages of eleven or twelve years. Therefore, the responsibility for recognising abuse or ill treatment lies heavily with the practitioner who has a **duty of care** to refer the concerns to social care services.

In practical terms, the *What to Do If You're Worried a Child is Being Abused* (DfES 2003) document is really useful in that it outlines thresholds of what constitutes abuse and harm significant enough to warrant the need for compulsory intervention in the best interests of the child. It also emphasises important concepts in sufficient detail, and the flow-chart diagrams and textual information give detailed guidance on what to do throughout the process. It is based on the premise in Section 47 of the Children Act 1989 whereby local authorities have a duty to make enquiries if there is a 'reasonable cause to suspect a child is suffering or likely to suffer, significant harm'.

PROVOCATION

Before we begin to discuss issues around identification and the recognition of signs and symptoms of abuse, you should proceed with caution.

While you may agree that definitions and categories of abuse are helpful and that they can be usefully applied in particular situations, you should also recognise that the **assessment** of situations as abusive or not may rely on individual practitioner's insights and preconceptions that relate to their personal and professional values, attitudes and experiences.

With this in mind, to what extent do you agree with Powell's (2005) suggestion that each practitioner will approach a specific concern with differing **perceptions** as to what constitutes abuse or ill-treatment?

REFLECTIVE PRACTICE

Consider your own values and beliefs in relation to safeguarding and child protection.

Reflect on how your approval/disapproval of parenting practices influences your decisions and the way in which you interact with the child and his/her parent/carer.

Defining child abuse

The following range of definitions of child abuse are set out in the guidance *Working Together to Safeguard Children* (DCSF 2010: 4.2) and include the failure to prevent harm or the inflicting harm within the family, institutional or community setting. You may already be familiar with the specific types of abuse that are traditionally categorised as:

* physical abuse
* emotional abuse

- sexual abuse
- neglect

Watchful practitioners should be aware of children presenting with some of the following signs and symptoms of abuse.

Physical abuse

This may involve hitting, shaking, throwing, poisoning, burning or scalding, drowning, suffocating or otherwise causing physical harm to a child. Physical harm may also be caused when a parent or carer fabricates the symptoms of illness or deliberately induces symptoms of illness, or deliberately induces illness of a child.

Emotional abuse

This is the persistent emotional ill-treatment of a child such as to cause severe and persistent adverse effects on the child's **emotional development**. For example, it might be conveyed to the child that they are worthless or unloved, inadequate, or valued only in so far as they meet the needs of another person. Emotional abuse may feature age or developmentally inappropriate expectations being imposed on a child or involve seeing or hearing the ill-treatment of another. Serious bullying which causes a child to feel frightened or in danger, or the exploitation or corruption of a child is also categorised as emotional abuse. Although emotional abuse can occur alone, it is expected that some level of emotional abuse is involved in all types of ill-treatment of a child.

Sexual abuse

Sexual abuse involves forcing or enticing a child or young person to take part in sexual activities, including prostitution, whether or not he child is aware of what is happening. The activities may involve physical contact, including penetrative (e.g. rape or buggery) or non-penetrative acts. It may include non-contact activities, such as involving children in looking at, or in the production of, pornographic materials or watching sexual activities, or encouraging children to behave in sexually inappropriate ways.

Neglect

Neglect is the persistent failure to meet a child's basic physical and/or psychological needs, likely to result in serious impairment of the child's health or development. Neglect can occur during pregnancy as a result of maternal substance abuse. Once a child is born, neglect may manifest itself in the parents/carer failing to provide adequate food, clothing and shelter, failing to protect a child from physical and emotional harm or danger, failure to ensure access to appropriate medical care or treatment. It may also include neglect of, or unresponsiveness to, a child's basic emotional needs (DCSF 2010: 4.2).

Please note, the most recent version of the *Working Together to Safeguard Children: a guide to inter-agency working to safeguard and protect the welfare of children* (HM Government, 2013) replaces the 2010 version and came into force on 15 April 2013. However, the new guidance streamlines previous guidance documents to clarify the responsibilities of professionals and strengthen the focus away from processes and onto the needs of the child. Most of the responsibilities and processes in the more recent version remain the same as in the previous guidance but it is presented in a much more succinct and less detailed way. The *Working Together to Safeguard Children* 2010 version can be found in the National Archives (www.webarchive. nationalarchives.gov.uk) and the 2013 version in the gov.uk website in the Department for Education area (www.gov.uk).

PROVOCATION

Practitioners should note that while the above definitions can provide useful guidelines, they should understand that 'there is no absolute criteria on which to rely when judging what constitutes significant harm' (DCSF 2010: 1.28).

With this in mind, you may wish to reconsider the terms used in the above definitions. For example, what do you think 'persistent failure' means? What equates as being 'persistent'? Think back to the previous reflection point; might the interpretation of what constitutes abuse be based on your own personal experiences, values and beliefs?

The legal framework: A child in 'need' or at risk of 'significant harm'?

Once concerns for a child's welfare have been raised, key principles in safeguarding children are outlined within a legal framework which informs policy and practice. The framework includes guidance on when and what action should be taken to protect a child from being maltreated and while *Working Together to Safeguard Children* (DCFS 2013) highlights that all organisations working with children share a commitment to safeguard and promote children's welfare, it also clearly outlines specific roles and responsibilities of statutory **agencies**.

The Children Act 1989 and subsequent legislation suggests that the role of the local authority and other supporting agencies is to help parents uphold their responsibility in providing adequate duty of care in order to ensure the welfare of the child. Under section 17 of the Children Act 1989, the local authority has to perform a delicate balancing act between upholding their duty of safeguarding and promoting the welfare of the child by providing an appropriate range and level of services whilst, at the same time, promote the upbringing of the child by their parents. Section 17 (10) of the Children Act 1989 suggests a child is 'in need' if:

- he/she is unlikely to achieve or maintain, or have the opportunity of achieving or maintaining a reasonable standard of health or development without the provision for him/her of services by a local authority;
- his/her health or development is likely to be significantly impaired, or further impaired, without the provision for him/her of such services; or
- he/she is disabled.

However, before any orders or decisions can be made about the child (excluding emergency orders), the **Welfare Checklist** must be considered (The Children Act 1989, Section 1(3)). It includes the following:

- the ascertainable wishes and feelings of the child (considered in light of his or her age and understanding)
- the child's physical, emotional and educational needs
- the likely effect on the child of any change in circumstances
- the child's age, sex, background and any characteristics that the Court considers relevant
- any harm the child has suffered or is a risk of suffering
- how capable the parents (and any other person in relation to whom the Court considers the question to be relevant) are of meeting the child's needs
- the range of powers available to the Court in the proceedings in question

Sharing information and working together

While it is difficult to anticipate exactly how you might feel and react in particular safeguarding situations (and knowing how or when to intervene is difficult to gauge), the ability to share a professional concern with a colleague is vital. Practitioners need to work effectively with others to consider what might happen to a child if no referral is made, no interventions in place and also to think about the impact that services might have on the child's standard of health and development. You should be prepared to work with other professionals both from within and outside your own organisation and share your concerns with others. The importance of working together was highlighted within Laming's inquiry (2003). He reported poor communication between agencies and inadequate recording of contact and reminded us that 'effective action designed to safeguard the well-being of children and families depends on sharing relevant information on an **inter-agency** basis' (Laming 2003: 1, 45).

Children's rights

The United Nations Conventions of the Rights of the Child (UNCRC 1989) underpins the Children Acts 1989 and 2004 and the Every Child Matters agenda. This aspirational charter (not one that underpins legal entitlement) formulates a consensus of agreed norms concerning the prevention, participation, protection and provision of and for children. It therefore highlights the import-ance for practitioners to keep children central to any safeguarding concerns to ensure that they are given the opportunity to articulate their experience and concern about a range of issues, which directly or indirectly affect them. The application of children's **rights** in practice, however, is complex and practitioners need to give careful consideration as to what children's rights might mean and how to apply them within safeguarding practices. The four central tenets of the UNCRC are:

- *Prevention* in terms of healthcare, discrimination, harm, abduction
- *Participation* in decisions that affect them
- *Protection* from abuse, **conflict** and exploitation
- *Provision* of basic needs, education and security

PROVOCATION

Children clearly have the right to be happy, contented and live a life that is free from neglect, exploitation and abuse. They also have the right to voice their opinions and their perspective should be considered. As a practitioner, you are aware that children develop at different rates and are likely to experience different cultural child-rearing practices and that this could create tensions between the child's right to a family life and the right to be protected from harm and abuse.

How might practitioners translate and apply very young children's rights of participation and protection into practice?

As a watchful and vigilant practitioner, you may have concerns for a child's well-being. This may be before the situation is identified as one that raises concerns of child protection and safeguarding. While the UNCRC (1989) stresses the importance of nurturing children so that they reach their full potential, it also emphasises that parents/carers should take on the responsibility of providing the best care for their children. Where this is not possible, the UNCRC (1989: Article 18.2) suggests that the state should 'render appropriate assistance to parents and legal guardians in the performance of their child-rearing responsibilities and shall ensure the development of institutions, facilities and services for the care of children'. When the child is very young or lacks enough understanding to make appropriate decisions, or when it is clear that parents/carers are not meeting their responsibilities, as a practitioner, you may find yourself in the position where you need to act on the child's behalf.

Practical considerations

Safeguarding children represents a difficult challenge for any practitioner working with young children and their families. However, if you are concerned for a child's safety and welfare and the circumstances are less well defined than you might expect, you are advised to make a note of your concern, date and sign it, and develop discussions with your line manager or the Safeguarding Officer within the setting about the appropriate context and time to intervene. This will not only ensure that the policies and procedures of the setting are followed appropriately but that any implications of making the referral are fully discussed along with any other support that might be necessary and can be put into place promptly. In addition, discussing your concerns in confidence with respected colleagues will help you to reflect on your own values and beliefs and ultimately act in the best interests of the child. While the unfortunate deaths of Maria Colwell, Jasmine Beckford, Lauren Wright and, more recently, Peter Connelly show similarities in that the failure to intervene early enough were due to poor coordination, a failure to share information, poor management and lack of training, the most striking feature is the absence of someone with a strong sense of **accountability** and an overall lack of pro-active interventions. Indeed, Powell and Uppal (2012: 51) stress that due to media coverage, practitioners have become more 'guarded and careful in terms of leaving a paper trail, to ensure, that if the very worst happens and a child that they are responsible for in some way comes to harm, they will feel that there was nothing more they could do'. Munro (2011) implores front-line workers to take a more common-sense approach, to focus their gaze more firmly on the child and the family, and spend less time on bureaucratic systems of recording and reporting so that timely and suitable interventions are in place at the earliest opportunity. This approach echoes that within the DfES (2004: 5), 'Too often children experience difficulties at home or school, but receive too little help too late, once problems have reached crisis point'.

With this in mind, practitioners are asked to use their developing skills of analysis to consider and then later respond to the scenario below.

CASE STUDY 1

Billy brings his little sister Jade to nursery one wet, chilly November morning. He is agitated and shoves his sister through the door, telling Jade's key worker Feride, that he 'can't stop 'cos I'm late for college . . .'. He rushes off, but as he leaves, he tells her that his mum will pick his sister up after work as usual. Feride is aware that Jade's mother is a single parent who works part time at the local supermarket and when she is on an early shift, Billy brings his little sister to Nursery. The family moved into the area a few months ago when Jade's mum found permanent work. Feride noted that this is the third time this week that this young child has arrived cold, hungry and visibly upset. None-the-less, she welcomes Jade to the nursery, and helps her remove her coat. While she does this, Feride notices that her clothing is wet and she has a soiled nappy. She discreetly summons a colleague to take over welcoming the children to the nursery as she attends to Jade.

Jade does not have a spare set of dry clothes and her mother has not provided any nappies, so Feride takes Jade to the nursery cupboard and sorts through some spare clothing to find something suitable for her to wear and tries to coax her to join in. In the changing area, Jade's wet clothing is removed and her nappy is changed, but Feride notices that her bottom is chapped and the skin is sore. She concludes that her nappy has not been changed for some time. She also observes that the child's skin is dirty, her finger nails are long and jagged, and her hair unkempt. Whilst Feride provides routine care to Jade, she chats and sings to her, but the child is not overly responsive. She passively accepts help but appears to be tired and listless. Once she is clean, dry and dressed, Feride asks her if she is hungry and she nods. They go together into the kitchen for toast and juice. She rapidly eats a hearty breakfast and Feride suggests that she goes through to the big room play with the other children. Jade seems reluctant to venture off alone which is unusual as she is normally a confident child so Feride kneels down next to her, smiles and offers to go with her and hold her hand. They go into the big room together.

The importance of observation

Child poverty is very common currently in the UK. It is not unusual to see children wearing inappropriate clothing for the time of year or ill-fitting shoes. The nursery provision in the case study above is located in a deprived part of the town and many of the children that attend have families facing financial difficulties. Many parents seek support and are regular visitors to the food and clothing bank. The socio-economic status of a child and their family however is not an indicator of neglect or abuse. Whatever the social situation, the child's welfare must be considered to be paramount and the reader will have noted that for the third time this week, Jade has arrived at nursery hungry, dirty and cold. There may also have been changes in her behaviour that gave Feride cause for concern. Talking to the child, asking open-ended questions and listening to their views will play a vital role in **observation**, and children's voices should be noted word for word. The observations should contain written evaluations, giving more detail and the date should be recorded. That way, a clear historical picture can emerge. Observations should be kept in a confidential manner and practitioners should be mindful that they may be shared with other professionals or the child's parents/carers depending on the type and severity of the concerns.

While it is important that concerns are shared with colleagues in a professional manner and noted, practitioners should also feel confident to report any concerns they may have if other professionals are not listening/reporting concerns as necessary, or if there are concerns around their behaviour with children. They should also be vigilant in creating a safe working environment, for example by operating an open door practice and telling another colleague when changing a child's nappy, in order to protect themselves from allegations by parents or staff.

REFLECTIVE PRACTICE

It cannot be assumed that all practitioners will have had similar experiences to Feride's. Therefore, you are not expected to reflect on your own practice here, but based on your experience, you are encouraged to consider what you might do if faced with a scenario such as the one in the above case study.

Refer back to the categories of abuse outlined earlier in the chapter. On reflection, are any of the signs/symptoms/indicators inherent in the above case study? Which category/categories of abuse might be indicated? How do you know this?

Raising concerns: 'What should I do?'

Once Feride had settled Jade, changed her nappy, replaced the wet clothing and offered her breakfast, she discussed her concerns with the settings Safeguarding Officer, informing her that this is the not the first time the child has arrived at nursery cold, hungry and fretful. They discuss the case together and agree on the key reasons to intervene:

- The child's rights are not being observed. Provision for their physical and emotional needs has not been made.
- The neglectful situation may persist if no action is taken.
- The setting has a duty of care to protect children from harm and ensure their well-being.

Feride and the nursery's Safeguarding Officer conclude that once they have checked the setting's policies and procedures, they should raise their concerns with Jade's mother in the first instance. Given this is not the first time they have had conversations about Jade's well-being and that the welfare requirements of the EYFS (2014) are clearly not being met, the Safeguarding Officer will refer the gathering concerns to social care who can assess the situation in more depth. Within one working day of the referral being received, the setting would expect that a local authority social worker should make a decision about the type of response that is required and acknowledge receipt to the referrer (DCFS 2013). The primary assessment will gather wider evidence from other professionals such as the GP and the Health Visitor. The individual needs of Jade, and the nature and level of any risk of harm faced by the child will determine the time taken to carry out the assessment. Once this has taken place, a package of appropriate support can be put in place. Practitioners should note however, that if they have concerns about sexual or physical abuse, they should refer to their local Safeguarding Board in the first instance for advice. Safe practice should be reflected in the setting's own policy and procedures where the statement 'all concerns will be discussed with parents/carers in the first instance unless it is thought that this would put the child at further risk of harm' could be used.

How should Feride respond?

Feride may feel uncertain as to how to respond to Jade's mother when she arrives to pick up her daughter from nursery. Depending on how she communicates her concerns, there may be a number of possible outcomes:

- The parent may react defensively, tell Feride to 'mind your own business', argue with her or threaten her.
- The parent may ignore what Feride has said.
- The parent may respond and confide the difficulties that the family are facing.

Jade's mother's response to the concerns is key to determining the direction of future work. If she co-operates, a Common Assessment Framework (CAF) form can be completed collaboratively but if she is resistant, the case will be taken over by Social Care. Whatever happens, Feride needs to be confident that she has consulted with a colleague in her organisation and followed the policies and procedures of the setting and guidance from the Local Safeguarding Board. Sharing concerns in a professional manner and seeking reassurance from colleagues is a form of support that Feride might need herself.

Once Feride has referred her concerns (and is now expected to make a written referral recording her contact with Jade and her mother), there are several steps that should now be taken by the wider agencies. It is likely that she will be asked to contribute to the discussions and help to complete a Common Assessment Framework (CAF) form. For further information, and to gain an understanding of the safeguarding process, please refer back to the non-statutory guidance *What to Do If You're Worried a Child is Being Abused* (DfES, 2003) highlighted earlier in the chapter. This document is also available electronically as a DFES publication on the gov.uk website (www.gov.uk).

Working in a responsive and safe culture – applying theory to practice

Powell and Uppal (2012) advocate an ecological systems approach to underpin a safer culture of working with children, their parents and other professionals. They believe that Bronfenbrenner's (1979) systems model can be usefully applied to safeguarding in that it illustrates how individuals are affected by interactions between varieties of overlapping external systems. Using the 'ripples in a pond' analogy, Jade would be placed in the centre of the ripple and any factors such as inherited genetic conditions, or illness which might affect the child need to be taken into consideration. Within the next and closest ripple to the child are the immediate carers and those that she relies on to maintain her well-being. It could also include siblings, grandparents, church group and nursery, for example. The next ripple would relate to professionals such as health visitors, GPs and educational provision that support Jade's general well-being. These are some of the universal agencies that Jade and her family might be able to access. Finally, the outer ripple relates to socio-cultural, political and environmental factors that indirectly affect Jade. The area in which she lives, the current political climate, the child's ethnicity and religion, for example, all influence Jade and her family.

In terms of the examples of the practical application noted above, practitioners could usefully draw on the work of Gill and Jack (2007) who argue that current approaches to safeguarding typically focus on immediate family circumstances and fail to adequately address the wider community contexts that impact on a child's development. While they acknowledge that current welfare systems do exist, they suggest that the interplay or interaction between them is generally missing. Indeed, they argue that very few professionals focus on examining connections between the well-being of individuals and the external factors that help to shape it. Therefore, they encourage building wider social networking and simultaneously call on community resources to support the child and their family. They also advocate that the voices of the child and the family should be taken into consideration whilst supporting enabling strategies that will overcome areas of difficulty with a positive outcome. For example, it is likely that the local Children's Centre offers breakfast clubs, provides opportunities to seek financial support and advice, and activities that Jade and her mother might like to join in with. This approach is what Powell and Uppal (2012: 61) describe as a 'pro-active ethos'. They go on to outline a number of principles that helpfully guide practitioners to adopt a 'safer cultures' approach:

- The promotion of a positive community ethos.
- Sharing of information.
- A common position regarding establishing ground rules.
- Partnership and cooperation is vital.
- The processes and procedures are relevant and contextual.
- Recommendations should be negotiated and fluid.

PROVOCATION

In relation to the case study, consider what you think is missing from the current situation. What factors need to be present within the following contexts in order that Jade's welfare and future well-being can be promoted?

a. The child's home context
b. The child's close family
c. The child in their local community
d. The practices of the nursery
e. Wider agency involvement

Drawing on your experience, are there any immediate interventions that you can think of that could be offered to Jade and her family?

The ecological systems theory highlights the complexities inherent in safeguarding. No two scenarios are the same and, given the complex nature of child protection and the wilful intentions of some to hurt children, it is not surprising that occasionally tragedies will occur. However, as Early Years practitioners, you should remember that you are responsible for the duty of care for each child. If you have concerns for a child's safety and well-being, you should always take a proactive stance and share them (Children Act 2004).

Conclusion

The discussions in this chapter have offered you an opportunity to explore some of the sensitive and complex issues surrounding safeguarding children in an interactive but 'safe' environment. The first part of the chapter highlighted some of the issues relating to safeguarding children and the latter part offered a practical consideration of upholding the child's rights of protection and participation. While the themes in the chapter cover a range of key issues, there is clearly more extended reading and research that you could engage with to deepen your knowledge and understanding of this important aspect of practice. No one can ever predict when or indeed what safeguarding concerns may crop up on a day-to-day basis in practice and each situation will present you with a new set of challenges, questions and dilemmas. Therefore, it is vital that you are confident in the knowledge of the settings procedures and policies and that you proactively reflect on the need to develop your own skills, work with others collaboratively and adapt your professional practice accordingly in order to promote the welfare of each child that you work with.

Further reading

Gill, O. and Jack, G. (2007) *The Child and Family in Context. Developing ecological practice in disadvantaged communities*, Lyme Regis: Russell House Publishing.
While this text focuses primarily on developing ecological practice in disadvantaged communities, the practical application of the ecological systems theory into ecological practice is thought-provoking and encourages practitioners to think more holistically when considering the wider social context of safeguarding.

Jones, P. and Walker, G. (eds) (2011) *Children's Rights in Practice*, London: Sage.
This text is recommended as further reading as it offers a practical insight into children's rights and how they might be applied in practice.

Chapter 3 'The baby and the young child as the focus for safeguarding' in Powell, J. and Uppal, E. L. (2012) *Safeguarding Babies and Young Children*, Maidenhead: Open University Press.
Practitioners may find this chapter very useful in terms of applying the 'pro-active ethos' as emphasised within this chapter. The textbook as a whole is a useful addition to the student/practitioner's book shelf. It is accessible and focuses on young children and Early Years practice.

Useful websites

www.nspcc.org.uk

The NSPCC is the leading charity in the UK and Channel Islands that is fighting to end child abuse. The information is constantly being changed to reflect current changes in policies and practices. There are some fantastic resources for practitioners and also some research papers that will help to support students.

www.ncb.org.uk

The National Children's Bureau is a national charity whose aim is to improve the lives of children and young people, especially those considered to be the most vulnerable. Apart from providing a source of invaluable and up to date information, the research area of the website will provide many good quality reports that students will find useful for their studies.

www.foundationyears.org.uk

The EYFS Statutory Framework sets standards for the learning, development and care for young children. Look in the Safeguarding area on this site to find out some useful information.

References

Bronfenbrenner, U. (1979) *The Ecology of Human Development*, Cambridge, MA: Harvard University Press.

Children Act 1989, London: HMSO.

Children Act 2014 (www.legislation.gov.uk/ukpga/2004/31/contents) (accessed 21 January 2014).

Department for Children, Schools and Families (DCSF) (2010) *Working Together to Safeguard Children 2010; A Guide to Inter-Agency Working to Safeguard and Promote the Welfare of Children*, London: HM Government.

Department for Children, Schools and Families (DCSF) (2013) *Working Together to Safeguard Children; A Guide to Inter-Agency Working to Safeguard and Promote the Welfare of Children*, London: HM Government.

Department for Education and Skills (2003) *Every Child Matters*, London: HMSO. Also available on webarchive.nationalarchives.gov.uk/20080915105927/everychildmatters.gov.uk/children/.

Department for Education and Skills (2003) *What to Do If You're Worried a Child is Being Abused,* London: HM Government.

Department for Education and Skills (2004) *Every Child Matters: Change for Children,* London: HMSO.

Department of Health (DH) (2006) *Working Together to Safeguard Children: A Guide to Inter-Agency Working to Safeguard and Promote the Welfare of Children,* London: DH.

Gill, O. and Jack, G. (2007) *The Child and the Family in Context: Developing Ecological Practice in Disadvantaged Communities,* Lyme Regis: Russell House Publishing.

Jones, P. and Walker, G. (eds) (2011) *Children's Rights in Practice,* London: Sage.

Laming, H. (2003) *The Victoria Climbie Inquiry: Report of an Inquiry by Lord Laming,* London: HMSO. Available at www.victoria-climbie-inquiry.org.uk/.

Munro, E (2011) *The Munro Review of Child Protection: Interim Report – The Child's Journey.* Available at www.education.gov.uk/munroreview/downloads/Munrointerimreport.pdf (accessed 2 December 2013)

Powell, J. (2005) 'Child Protection', in L. Jones., R. Holmes and J. Powell (eds) *Early Childhood Studies: A Multi-Professional Perspective,* Maidenhead: Open University Press.

Powell, J. and Uppal, E. (2012) *Safeguarding Babies and Young Children,* Maidenhead: Open University Press.

UNCRC (1989) *United Conventions on the Rights of the Child,* Unicef. Available at www.unicef.org.crc. fulltext.htm (accessed 2 December 2013).

22 Supporting inclusive practice in the Early Years

Allison Boggis

LEARNING OUTCOMES

After reading this chapter, you should be able to:

✔ Develop a more nuanced understanding of the concept of inclusion.
✔ Understand the role of the Early Years practitioner in promoting inclusion and celebrating diversity and difference.
✔ Apply your knowledge and understanding to practice.

Introduction

Collective notions of '**normal**' are at the very heart of what is different. As Early Years practitioners, we tend to apply our own expectations of 'normal' to every-day practice; to appropriate behaviours, to ways of being and of presenting ourselves to the contexts in which we find ourselves. However, in order to fully accommodate and celebrate individual differences, we need to disrupt expectations, interrogate views and understanding, and look above and beyond what we deem to be 'normal'. Indeed, if we start by celebrating difference, embracing diversity and work on the basis that inclusion is operational rather than conceptual, the barriers to **equality** and participation will be broken down.

This chapter focuses on supporting those who work with children in Early Years settings in providing an environment that enables *all* young children to learn effectively and with enjoyment, whatever their individual needs. The discussions within this chapter have been designed in such a way as to challenge **perceptions** of difference and consider the ways that diversity can be celebrated and accommodated in Early Years practice. Whilst acknowledging that interrogating your own personal preconceptions can be uncomfortable, by actively engaging with the discussions, concepts and ideas embedded within this chapter, you will be more able to reflect on the confusion that exists around constructs of normality and difference, and thereby develop your professional knowledge and practice to become a more respectful and **inclusive** practitioner.

The chapter is divided into two parts: the first invites the reader to critically engage with debates relating to the concept of inclusion. Then it asks you to consider definitions of inclusion, **contextualise** them in terms of Early Years practice and reflect upon specific factors that make practice inclusive. The second part of the chapter contemplates the application of inclusion in practice and highlights ways in which difference can be celebrated and inclusion embedded as a matter of course.

The concept of inclusion

Practitioners in Early Years settings work with a diverse range of children and their families who represent a wide variety of values and beliefs. On the whole, Early Years settings are and have been, as Nutbrown *et al.* (2013) suggest, at the forefront of inclusive provision of education and care. However, a common assumption of inclusion relates specifically to location, that being spaces that are shared by all children. We should be mindful, however, to differentiate between the terms *integration* whereby the child is physically included within the setting and *inclusion* as an ongoing process that dynamically changes both the environment and attitudes towards individuals. By starting with challenging the terms we use and the preconceptions we have, we can begin to move away from integrating children into the Early Years setting (merely including them into the environment and adhering rigidly to a set of policies or practicalities), to making attitudinal and wilful changes to accommodate and celebrate **diversity.** Indeed, an inclusive practice is not one that looks to change the individual or make him/her 'fit', but one that purposefully makes an effort to *change* the environment. To some, this might suggest a somewhat radical move; to others it makes perfect sense. Notwithstanding, it is one which unapologetically focuses on eradicating inequality, injustice, prejudice and **exclusion**. That said, while we may strive towards openness and critical reflection which allows us to change our practice and challenge **societal norms**, we should also be mindful that in general, we tend to characterise, classify and group things and people together thereby setting boundaries of cultures and communities in order to identify those that sit beyond the classifications.

Defining and contextualising inclusion

Many Early Years settings are now more aware of the importance of inclusion, diversity and equality than ever before. However, there are still some reported instances where tokenistic gestures and insufficient application of inclusion are made and, as a consequence, access is denied to some children. Clearly, inclusion is a complex concept and therefore difficult to define. So where to start? In its broadest sense inclusion encompasses all children, practitioners and parents/guardians in every Early Years community. Inclusive practice seeks to support all children to reach their potential and individually achieve what is possible for them. For the purposes of this chapter, it will be seen as a unified drive towards minimal exclusion from and maximum participation in Early Years settings, schools and society (Booth *et al.*, 2006), and inclusive practices shall be seen to be those that value each person for who they are and appreciate and celebrate difference.

While the process of inclusion should be ongoing, dynamic, engaging and responsive to the contexts in which they operate (and it is agreed that all Early Years settings should be equitable

PROVOCATION

Defining inclusion

Student activity (in pairs)

- Think about what inclusion means to you.
- Write down your own definition of inclusion.
- Swap your definition with your paired colleague.
- Tease out what your definitions actually mean through discussion and give examples from practice to support your definition.
- Develop a shared and agreed definition of inclusion.

The aim of this activity is to find common ground and to understand differences. You should try and reach a mutual understanding and agreed definition of inclusion.

in the ways in which they treat and accommodate young children) Unfortunately in reality this is not always the case. Indeed, Rix *et al.* (in Rix *et al.* 2010) argue that the ways in which we view and treat children can be seen as highly hypocritical. They suggest that children are often accommodated in unsuitable buildings with varying quantities and quality of facilities and that, as individuals they are often formally and informally identified and labelled. In addition, some are grouped according to age, ability and sex and some are withdrawn if they do not achieve targets or are perceived to be 'inherently different according to relative physical, behavioural, emotional, cultural and cognitive parameters' (ibid, p. 2). That said, there is no 'blue print' for the perfect system of inclusion and while we strive towards a universal ideal, it is inevitable that inequity will remain. In terms of its relevance to practice, Elmore (1995: 370) suggests:

> it is possible, indeed highly unlikely, that there is no single best structural solution for any given set of principles for good practice. There may be instead a range of possible solutions that represent various adaptations of principles of good practice to particular conditions.

If a range of possible solutions are applied and practice is adapted and changed as a result, best practice principles do not, and should not, suggest one model of inclusion. This clearly highlights the need for both Early Years settings and Early Years practitioners to respond to differing circumstances in which they operate, in the most suitable manner for the people within them and served by them.

The *Statutory Framework for the Early Years Foundation Stage: Setting the Standards for Learning, Development and Care for Children from Birth to Five* (DfE, 2014) sets out policies for provision supporting inclusive practice. It highlights that practitioners should:

- Respond to 'each child's emerging needs and interests, and guide their development through warm, positive interaction'.

- Develop targeted plans to support a child's future learning and development if there are 'significant emerging concerns, or an identified special educational need or disability' or areas 'where the child's progress is less than expected'.
- Ensure 'quality and consistency in all Early Years settings, so that every child makes good progress and no child gets left behind'.
- Pay close attention to children and if there is any 'cause for concern', practitioners should discuss this with the child's parents and/or carers and agree how to support the child.
- Consider the individual needs and interests of the child in their care and use this information to 'plan a challenging and enjoyable experience for each child in all areas of learning and development'.

What makes practice inclusive?

Upholding children's **rights** to inclusion and participation should be embedded within the duty of care of those working with young children. Early Years practitioners should be prepared to be guided by the rights of the child, as set out by the United Nations (UNCRC, 1989), as a tool for advocacy and employ them to secure recognition and inclusion of all children. Freeman (in Rix *et al.*, 2010) however, argues that giving children rights without them actually being able to access them or denying their rights of representation is of little use. He goes on to suggest that 'rights without remedies of are symbolic importance, no more' (ibid: 103). Therefore, inclusive practices are those that commit to uphold children's rights, respect all children and genuinely engage with them on their own terms. However, while this may seem simple and straightforward, we cannot pretend that it is easy.

REFLECTIVE PRACTICE

In light of the above, reflect on your own practice and think of real examples from everyday practice that 'match' the key points above.

As the first part of this chapter draws to an end, and having considered the above in some detail and reflected on your own practice, let us conclude with a 'good practice' checklist. An inclusive setting is one that has, as a minimum, the elements listed below:

- *An ethos of respect* which includes policies, **leadership** and all stakeholders (adults and children) following it.
- *Effective teaching and learning* that focuses on meeting the needs of all children. The planning process should be effective and focused.
- *Ongoing staff training* that develops the knowledge and understanding of individuals in order to best support the different groups of children they work with.
- *A culturally affirming environment* in which all children's culture, history, language and values are reflected. Positive views of diverse cultures should be portrayed in a variety of ways to reflect inclusion.

REFLECTIVE PRACTICE
REFLECTIVE PRACTICE

How inclusive is your practice?

Daily practice should realise and protect children's rights as enshrined in the United Nations Convention of the Rights of the Child (UNCRC). Much of the reality of putting those rights into practice lies in the hands of the practitioner working in settings with children and their families.

Take time to answer the questions below as fully as possible.

		Yes/No	How?/How not? Use examples from practice to substantiate your claim.
1	Do you see every child in your setting as equal?		
2	Do you respect each child?		
3	Do you provide for all the children's diverse learning and development needs?		
4	Are the children's nutritional needs being met?		
5	Are all the children living in homes that are safe, secure and promote their well-being?		
6	Do all children have access to play, learning and recreation time and to the space they need?		
7	Are all children protected from cruelty, neglect and exploitation?		
8	Are all children loved, understood and cared for in ways which meet their needs?		

Now think of future action points that consider ways in which you could adapt your practice.

Source: Adapted from Nutbrown *et al.* (2013: 16).

- *Parental and wider community involvement* should be encouraged to play a full part within the setting.
- *Induction procedures* should be in place to help settle new children into the setting, welcoming parents and children by offering sensitive support, providing an ethos of respect by offering a gradual introduction to the setting where necessary.

The above list is not exhaustive. Can you add to it?

Celebrating difference and inclusion for all

As Early Years practitioners, you will have come to recognise the responsibility you have to 'get it right' for each child within a differentiated learning experience, for the Early Years of life lay the foundations for not just learning but also for the way in which the child sees him/herself. The environment that you, the children, the parents and the wider community create must incorporate a wide range of needs, providing both challenges and support for all children while enabling and encouraging them to set their own challenges. The discussions within the second section of this chapter will focus on a number of small-scale case studies and you will be asked to consider the ways in which inclusion can be applied in practice.

Including children

At the very heart of including children lies our own individual **perception** of the construction of **childhood**. Indeed, the quality of support and provision will relate to adults' beliefs of what young children 'need', how they should be treated and how they should be educated. This will be influenced to some extent by the life experiences of adults who interact closely with them. It is therefore important for practitioners to articulate their personal constructions of childhood in order that they can reflect on the ways in which their views can influence their responses to and expectations of the children they work with. The following scenarios will help you to reflect on your own constructions of childhood and, in doing so, tease out some alternative strategies for supporting young children.

CASE STUDY 1

A visit to the hospital

Seniz had a moderate hearing loss from birth and during the first three years of her life suffered many painful, recurring ear infections. As a result of a recent heavy cold, her ear drum had burst and after much consultation, it was decided that reconstructive surgery was necessary. In the week prior to the scheduled operation, the paediatric support staff at the hospital explained the procedure to Seniz and her mother and invited them in to visit the children's hospital ward. The visit went well and Seniz was given an illustrated story book to take home about a child of a similar age who was also preparing for a similar operation. Seniz took her book into the playgroup where she shared it at circle time. Her key person took time to listen to Seniz and with the help of her colleagues she transformed the home corner into a hospital ward.

The operation went well and Seniz was discharged the day after her operation. She was proud of the bandage she wore around her head and her mother took a photograph of her, praising her for her bravery. Whilst she recovered at home, Seniz received a card made by the children from playgroup sending her their best wishes.

A short while after the operation, Seniz returned to the hospital to have the staples and stitches surrounding her ear removed. She did not return to the children's ward that she was so familiar with but visited the general Outpatients Clinic instead. As Seniz and her mother waited for their turn, Seniz became anxious and unnerved by the hustle and bustle of this busy hospital department and when she was finally called into the treatment room, she began to whimper quietly. Without any explanation, the medical practitioner started to remove the bandage. Seniz quickly clamped her hand over the bandage and refused to let go. Her mother explained that she needed to let the nurse do her work and take off the bandage so that her ear would 'get better'. After much persuasion, she finally let go and the bandage was removed. The instruments for removing the staples and stitches were laid out with much precision in front of Seniz who began to cry. As the process for removing the staples got underway, Seniz began to sob and whilst the nurse assured her mother that the procedure did not hurt, she did admit that it could be a 'little uncomfortable'. Seniz became so distressed that the process stopped and it was decided that she should visit the children's ward to complete the removal of the staples and stitches.

Seniz and her mother were shown to the children's ward where they were greeted by one of the paediatric nurses that had attended to Seniz during the initial operation. They were taken to a small play room where Seniz was given some pain relief whilst she played with some toys. The nursery nurse played some soothing music and snuggled up on the sofa with Seniz as she read her a story. The practitioner remembered that Seniz had enjoyed blowing bubbles during her previous visit so when she had calmed down, the nurse explained the process and asked Seniz to blow a stream of bubbles each time a staple was removed. Whilst Seniz still showed signs of anxiety during the process, there was much reassurance given and the procedure was completed.

Seniz strongly protested and strongly resisted follow-up appointments at the hospital for some 18 months after her ordeal at the Outpatients Clinic.

There are times when situations dictate what happens or the adult's agenda is prioritised because it is thought to be within the child's 'best interests'. Often young children are not invited to participate in discussions because they are considered too immature or incompetent to understand. While there was nothing deliberately unkind or malicious that went on within the Outpatients Clinic within the hospital, the situation could have been successfully adapted through the use of the resource developed by the Coram Family, *Listening to Young Children*, to ensure that children have a voice so that adults can respond accordingly (Lancaster, 2003). While Seniz could articulate her desires and dislikes, it was clear that her opinions were not valued as highly as they might have been. Indeed, this scenario illustrates how the medical process took priority and in paying little heed to the child's emotional needs it reinforced the proposition that 'very young children represent one of the least powerful groups in society' (Powell, 2005: 79). However, including children is not simple. It is multidimensional, fluid and requires careful planning and developing skills that ensure that the child stays central to practice. It also demands that practitioners should stay alert to all that happens and be prepared to change accordingly so that children are listened to and not 'done unto' without consultation and consideration.

PROVOCATION

Consider how the staff in the paediatric ward prepared Seniz and her mother for the procedure and then compare it with her later experiences. In what ways do you think that the practitioners in the Outpatients Clinic viewed Seniz? How do you think they could have supported her in a more positive way?

Do you always take time to 'listen to children' in your own practice? If you were to record a ten-minute snatch of a day in your setting, what percentage of the recording would be taken up by the children's voices compared with those of the adults?

Including parents and guardians

Over a decade ago, the Rumbold Report (*Starting with Quality*, DES, 1990) promoted the idea that parents were their children's first and most important educators who should therefore be involved in their children's early years learning experiences. This idea is reflected in today's practice and parents' involvement is an expected part of early education and care in all settings. Nutbrown (2011) argued that the more parents know about how their children's learning is developing, the better position they are in to understand what their children are doing and how best to support them. Indeed, many initiatives that have successfully involved parents in their children's learning have developed international acclaim; for example, Pen Green Centre (Whalley *et al.*, 1997; Arnold, 2001) and the Coram Children's Centre (Draper and Duffey, 2001) are mindful that 'one size does not fit all' and that successful initiatives in one setting may not necessarily transfer exactly to another. Some initiatives have focused specifically on education, such as raising literacy standards. Some wish to include fathers more; some concentrate on including families for whom English is not the language of the home; and others have concentrated on providing information about preparing nutritious meals on low incomes. Just as each setting is **unique**, each strategy to promote inclusion will be unique and practitioners should be prepared to change and adapt as necessary. The key points below offer a brief glance into a unique initiative designed to include parents in raising early achievement in literacy.

FROM RESEARCH TO PRACTICE

The Raising Early Achievement in Literacy (REAL) Project

The REAL family literacy programme, developed and implemented by teachers in 11 schools was based on the **conceptual** framework developed by Hannon and Nutbrown (1997) in which parents are seen as providing Opportunities, Recognition, Interaction and a Model of literacy (ORIM). For further information on the literacy outcomes and details of the project, please see the full reports of Nutbrown and Hannon (1997) and Nutbrown, Hannon and Morgan (2005). The framework comprised five components:

- home visits by programme teachers
- provision of literacy resources
- centre-based group activities
- special events
- postal communication

The programme sought to promote children's experiences with family members of early literacy development; writing, reading and rhyming at home and greater awareness of environmental print. Optional adult education classes were also offered.

The project could not have run without parental input and 100 per cent of parents participated in the programme. The reasons for this were twofold: first the programme was open to all, not just those families perceived to be in the most need and, second, it was flexible to family routines and literacy needs. When interviewed, parents highlighted how much more involved they felt in their children's literacy.

The 'take up' of the above programme demonstrates how important it is to ensure that with initiatives that include parents as rightful participations and where practitioners, parents/carers and children can work flexibly and respectfully together, everyone gains positively from the experience.

(Nutbrown *et al.*, 2013: 126)

The above project was probably more ambitious and wide-ranging than a project that you might embark on in your setting. That said, most early years communities constantly re-evaluate their practice in terms of parental involvement.

In terms of your own practice, how do you support and encourage early literacy development both in the setting and at home?

The above study is one of many that illustrate the benefits of including parents/guardians in Early Years settings in order that they are encouraged to become active participants in their children's learning and achievements. With this in mind, please read the case study below and decide how best you might include this child, her mother and grandmother into your setting.

CASE STUDY 2

Just before Christmas, April (aged 3) and her mother moved into the area from Chengdu, a large city in the Sichuan Province, China. April's father had died a year ago and so they decided to move to the UK to live with a maternal grandmother. While April and her mother both speak a little English, her grandmother speaks only Mandarin which is their chosen language in the home environment.

April started at the Nursery in the New Year. Her Grandmother brings her to Nursery every morning; she speaks to no one but she smiles and nods as she hands April to her key worker. April's mother collects her at lunchtime where some limited communication between her and the key worker takes place. April appears to be settling in to the daily routine well. She is a timid, shy girl who watches her peers but as yet has made no friends.

If April started at your setting, what strategies would you have in place to welcome her and her mother and grandmother? How might you encourage their inclusion?

Including Early Years practitioners

Inclusion has most commonly been associated with the participation of children with special educational needs and disability. While it is acknowledged that some children may be more vulnerable to exclusion than others, it is argued that Early Years settings should be responsive to *all* young people within their community, irrespective of their culture, religion, ethnic background or disability. In addition, if settings are to truly embrace and practise inclusion, children as well as adults should be included in this dynamic interaction. However, inclusion can be proclaimed by many and practised by few. Indeed, we sometimes struggle to understand the nuances and complexities of inclusion and may well wonder if we might recognise it when we see it.

In terms of practical application to practice, you might find the *Index for Inclusion* (Booth *et al.*, 2006) useful. It was first published in 2000 and issued to all schools in the UK. Subsequent editions were published and the 2006 version was especially adapted for the use in Early Years settings. The *Index* talks of inclusive values rather than focusing on particular groups of children and it highlights the need for increasing participation for all children as well as adults.

In essence, the *Index* encourages staff to review their current provision, to build on their existing knowledge and to use the set of materials to guide and foster achievement for all. The settings, cultures, policies and practice are self-reviewed and a co-ordinating group is established at the primary stage of the process. The idea is that staff, committee members, trustees, students, parents/guardians and children examine all aspects of practice, identify barriers to learning and review progress. The indicators and questions that arise from the investigation require settings to engage in deep and often challenging explorations of their current position and to think carefully about how they might move forward towards greater inclusion. The process of the *Index* itself calls for collaboration and while settings are required to examine their practice in terms of culture, policies and practices and address issues of gender, class, religion, sexuality and social class, it does not segment, divide or classify these individual elements. It also provides a supportive mechanism to review, develop and suggest ways to work towards creating inclusive cultures, produce inclusive policies and evolve inclusive practices. While Clough and Corbett (2000) evaluated the effects of the *Index for Inclusion* in terms of being instrumental for change within settings, Clough and Nutbrown (2002) concentrated more on how the staff felt included in the process and how they could be supported in facilitating inclusive practice. The results were positive and while some participants were concerned primarily with the implementation of the initiative, the majority felt they learned a great deal personally and it made them think more deeply about inclusion in their own practice and within the setting in which they worked.

Conclusion

The success of any one child is dependent on their experiencing the education and care that meets their individual requirements. To help those working with young children to meet this challenge, this chapter has explored the principles of inclusion and challenged practitioners to review their own perceptions of what inclusion means to them and reflect on how they adopt and enact inclusive policies and practices within their own Early Years setting.

The purpose of this chapter was not to provide a 'how to' guide to inclusion. It was to challenge practitioners to evaluate their own practice, encourage critical thinking about inclusion and to explore difference and embrace diversity. While the discussions did not focus specifically on particular groups of children, it has been suggested that *all* children should be given the opportunity to participate in a range of experiences, particularly those that are motivating, enjoyable and interesting but, most significantly, experiences that meet their individual needs.

The introduction of the *Index for Inclusion* in the latter stages of this chapter brought the discussions to a full circle, concluding where they started: thinking about how collective notions of what is 'normal' and reflecting on how this concept impacts on everyday practice in terms of appropriate behaviours, to our ways of being and of presenting ourselves to the contexts in which we find ourselves. The discussions, case studies and activities presented within the chapters were designed to challenge practitioners to interrogate their own views and look above and beyond what they deem to be 'normal'. Indeed, while we still need to contest and evaluate what we mean by the terms we use, in inclusive environments labels may no longer be necessary for it is suggested that if we celebrate difference and diversity and work on the basis that inclusion is operational rather than conceptual, the barriers to equality and participation will be broken down.

Further reading

Cole, B. (2004) *Mother-Teachers: Insights into Inclusion,* London: David Fulton.
> *This book will challenge preconceptions of inclusion. The stories of six women who are both mothers and teachers of children with SEND provide an insight into their private and public experiences of educational values and teaching practices.*

Nutbrown, C. and Clough, P. with Atherton, F. (2013) *Inclusion in the Early Years* (2nd edn), London: Sage.
> *An essential read for all Early Years students, practitioners and researchers. The text provides an insightful exploration of inclusive and exclusionary practices.*

Rix, J., Nind, M., Sheehy, K., Simmons, K. and Walsh, C. (eds) (2010) *Equality, Participation and Inclusion,* Abingdon: Routledge.
This text provides a rich resource for practitioners as it draws on the writing of academics, practitioners and people who have experienced exclusion. The material draws on lived experience and life stories so students can usefully apply the concepts raised to real life situations and experiences.

Useful websites

www.unicef.org.

UNICEF – this website outlines the ways in which this organisation aims to build a world in which the rights of every child are realised. It provides a wealth of statistical data that emphasises global inequality and outlines children's rights.

www.en.unesco.org

UNESCO – this organisation pursues the goal of establishing worldwide peace and respecting diversity in order to respect human rights to education.

www.csie.org.uk

CISE – Centre for Studies on Inclusive Education. This organisation promotes the development of inclusive education. There is a wealth of resources for practice and academic study.

References

Arnold, C. (2001) 'Persistence pays off: working with "hard to reach" parents', in M. Whalley (ed.) and the Penn Green Team *Involving Parents in Their Children's Learning,* London: Paul Chapman Publishing.

Booth, T., Ainscow, M. and Kingston, D. (2006) *Index for Inclusion: Developing Play, Learning and Participation in Early Years and Childcare* (2nd edn), Bristol: Centre for Inclusive Education.

Clough, P. and Corbett, J. (2000). *Theories of Inclusive Education: A student's guide,* London: Sage.

Department for Education and Department of Health (2014) *SEND Code of Practice: 0-25* years London: DfE DOH.

DES (Department for Education and Science) (1989) *Starting with Quality – Report of the Rumbold Committee,* London: HMSO.

DfE (Department for Education) (2012) The *Statutory Framework for the Early Years Foundation Stage: Setting the standards for Learning, Development and Care for Children from Birth to Five,* London: DfE.

Draper, L. and Duffey, B. (2001) 'Working with parents', in G. Pugh (ed.) *Contemporary Issues in Early Years. Working Collaboratively for Children,* London: Paul Chapman Publishing.

Elmore, R.F (1995) 'Teaching, Learning, and School Organization: Principles of Practice and the Regularities of Schooling' *Educational Administration Quarterly,* vol. 31 no. 3 pp 355-374.

Freeman, M. (2010) 'Why it remains important to take children's rights seriously', in J. Rix., M. Nind., Sheehy, K., Simmons, K. and C. Walsh *Equality, Participation and Inclusion. Diverse perspectives,* Abingdon: Routledge in association with The Open University.

Hannon, P. and Nutbrown, C. (1997) *Preparing for Early Literacy Work with Parents: A Professional Development Manual,* The REAL Project: University of Sheffield.

Lancaster, Y. (2003) *Listening to Young Children: Promoting Listening to Young Children. The Reader,* Maidenhead: The Open University Press.

Nutbrown, C. (2011) *Threads of Thinking: Schemas and Young Children Learning* (4th edn), London: Sage.

Nutbrown, C. and Hannon, P. (eds) (1997) *Preparing for Early Literacy Work with Families: A Professional Development Manual,* Nottingham/Sheffield: NES Arnold/REAL Project.

Nutbrown, C., Hannon, P. and Morgan, A. (2005) *Early Literacy Work with Parents: Policy, Practice and Research*, London: Sage.

Nutbrown, C., Clough, P. and Atherton, F. (2013) *Inclusion in the Early Years* (2nd edn), London: Sage.

Powell, J. (2005) 'Anti-discriminatory practice matters', in L. Abbott and A. Langston (eds) *Birth to Three Matters Supporting the Framework of Effective Practice*, Maidenhead: Open University Press.

Rix, J., Walsh, C., Parry, J. and Kumrai, R. (2010) 'Introduction: another point of view', in J. Rix., M. Nind., K. Sheehy, K. Simmons, and C. Walsh *Equality, Participation and Inclusion. Diverse Perspectives*, Abingdon: Routledge in association with The Open University.

United Nations (1989) *Convention on the Rights of the Child* (UNCRC), New York: UN.

Whalley, M. and the Pen Green Centre Team (1997) *Involving Parents in their Children's Learning*, London: Paul Chapman Publishing.

23 Equality, diversity and the rights of the child

Pere Ayling

LEARNING OUTCOMES

After reading this chapter, you should be able to:

✔ Develop a deeper understanding of diversity and equality and how they relate to rights.
✔ Understand how factors such as gender and ethnicity may lead to inequality in education.
✔ Develop knowledge and understanding of some of the key concepts such as stereotyping and prejudice relating to diversity and equality.
✔ Understand the impact of a policy-informed approach to diversity on practitioners' ability to challenge stereotyping and promote cultural diversity in practice.
✔ Adopt a critical approach to diversity and equality.

Introduction

Diversity, **equality** and **rights** are complex and interrelated concepts. The fact that children have a right to cultural and gender identity and to an educational environment that respects and values their individualities and uniqueness, as well as a learning environment that provides equal opportunity in order that each child can achieve their full potential, illustrates the interconnectedness of these three concepts. This shows that one could not discuss diversity for example, without involving the discourses of equality and rights at the same time. Hence, the primary aim of this chapter is to move beyond a simplistic understanding of diversity and equality to a broader and deeper understanding of these concepts. The chapter does this by examining other concepts such as **social categorisation**, **stereotyping** and **prejudice** and **inclusive pedagogical approach** relating to diversity and equality as well as different theoretical perspectives of diversity and equality.

The chapter is divided into three main sections. The first section analyses the concept of diversity by discussing two approaches to diversity. The section then goes on to discuss the danger of placing children in broad categories in order to 'manage' and 'contain' diversity. The second part of the chapter examines the idea of equality and rights, focusing specifically on two key approaches to equality. That is, 'treating children equally' and 'treating them as equals'.

The third section distinguishes between policy-informed and pedagogical approaches to diversity. The chapter argues that, unlike a policy-informed approach, **inclusive** pedagogy is a critical approach to diversity and therefore more effective in challenging stereotypes while at the same time enabling children to develop respect for cultural differences.

Conceptualising diversity

The term 'diversity' is commonly used to describe and/or acknowledge the 'coexistence of social, cultural and class differences that exist in society' (Robinson and Diaz, 2006: 71). Although diversity is sometimes used to refer to multiculturalism, in actual fact it is now used instead of, and to replace, the term multiculturalism. The reason for this shift in terms might be due to the fact that, unlike multi-*culturalism* which tended to imply only cultural, religious and linguistic differences, diversity is a broader term which allows one to accept other differences such as gender, social class, age, race, lifestyle and (dis)ability. In education, and Early Years education in particular, the term diversity is used to suggest the acceptance and celebration of all types of 'differences'. It is also generally employed to imply equitable education for all pupils, irrespective of their socio-economic and cultural background.

Different approaches to diversity

There are two main approaches to diversity: the **assimilationist** and the multicultural approaches. The assimilationist approach is based on the idea of conformity, with the view that those from ethnic minority groups should adopt the dominant group's values, beliefs and practices. Here, cultural differences are not seen as something to be celebrated but rather they are, at best, considered as something that needs to be glossed over or ignored. At worse, cultural differences may be completely eliminated through policies and practices that forbid the display and/or expression of different cultural practices, language and lifestyle.

Multicultural approaches on the other hand 'explicitly emphasise and acknowledge the existence and importance of culture differences' (Jones *et al.*, 2014: 286). Unlike the assimilationist approach, the multicultural approaches are premised on the idea that cultural differences should

REFLECTIVE PRACTICE
REFLECTIVE PRACTICE

Take a few minutes to reflect on your own views on diversity.

- What does diversity mean to you?
- Do you see diversity as a 'good' or a 'bad' thing? Make a list of what you perceive are the pros and cons of diversity.
- Who do you think benefits from diversity and why?

not only be respected but they are to be preserved as well. From this perspective, cultural and individual differences are also understood as valuable and beneficial to everyone.

As Early Years practitioners, it is imperative that you have an understanding of how your **perception** of diversity will not only impact on how you interact with the children and their parents, but also how it might influence the extent to which you are able to meet the individual needs and interests of the children in your setting. Most Early Years practitioners would claim to espouse multicultural approaches in practice, and many might indeed do. However, the fact that Early Childhood pedagogy in the West 'has been inherently embedded in **mono-cultural** and **mono-lingual** Anglo Saxon cultural practice' (Robinson and Diaz, 2006: 72) would suggest otherwise. How can we claim to respect and embrace cultural and ethnic differences when, for example, the very principles, values and belief systems that underpin the Early Years profession are informed predominantly by Western ideals and **ideologies**?

Even though the EYFS (2014: 15 my emphasis) acknowledges that 'learning English as an additional language is *not a special educational need*' and that 'linguistic diversity is a strength that [should be] recognised and valued', research has found that bilingual children in the UK are often perceived as 'problems' (see Sood and Mistry's (2011) study for example). Similarly, Early Years practitioners often see being bilingual as hindering the child's development. Consequently, rather than support a child's home language, practitioners are keen for the bilingual child to adopt the dominant language, which, in the case of the UK, is the English language. Paradoxically, research has found that a 'child's home language aids the development of English learning and **conceptual** growth' (Siraj-Blatchford, 1996: 30), thus indicating that children with English as an additional language (EAL) can acquire the English language without necessarily abandoning their own culture and language.

Article 30 of the UNCRC states:

> In those States in which ethnic, religious or linguistic minorities or persons of indigenous origin exist, a child belonging to such a minority or who is indigenous shall not be denied the right, in community with other members of his or her group, to *enjoy his or her own culture, to profess and practise his or her own religion, or to use his or her own language.*

To provide children with an environment where they can 'enjoy' and take pride in their culture as well as practise their language, Early Years practitioners need to avoid **tokenistic approaches** to diversity such as the display of words in different languages that are merely superficial and trivialise cultural and linguistic differences.

Early Years practitioners can emphasise the importance of diversity by designing policies and strategies that demonstrate to children and their family that they are welcomed and valued in their setting regardless of their cultural and socio-economic background. One of the ways by which this can be achieved is to ensure that respect for a child's own cultural identity, values and language are part of his/her education. In other words, practitioners must ensure that valuing and respect for diversity is embedded in their everyday practice. In addition, Early Years practitioners must also create an environment that can develop children's ability to respect the different cultures and religion in their settings and community (EYFS, 2014).

The Qualification and Curriculum Authority (QCA) (2009: 10) states:

> learning about identity and cultural diversity can help young people to live and work together in diverse communities in the UK and the wider world. It can also help them develop their identity and a sense of belonging, which are fundamental to personal wellbeing and the achievements of a flourishing and cohesive society.

What is clear in the QCA statement above is the importance and development of a 'culturally responsive curriculum' (Siraj-Blatchford, 2001: 106). Every child has a right to a curriculum that positively reflects and affirms his/her gender, cultural, religious and racial identities. Since the development of identity and the concept of self starts at an early age, it is imperative that Early Years practitioners, whether the setting is ethnically diverse or not: provide children with a culturally responsive curriculum which would raise children's awareness of similarities and differences between and within different groups in their community; help them to develop positive attitudes towards people from different socio-economic backgrounds; and, more importantly, develop in the child the knowledge and confidence to challenge stereotypical ideas and discrimination.

The notion that children learn from the adults around them has been thoroughly argued by many academic scholars. Children's perception of difference, whether positive or negative, is learned from how the adults around them perceive and relate to those with a different gender, culture, religion, race and class from them. Conversely, a child's perception of self is a reflection of how they feel others perceive them and their culture. According to the Swann Report, 'membership of a particular ethnic group is one of the most important aspects of an individual's identity' (DES, 1985: 3). This highlights the importance of a positive representation of 'difference' as well as the role of positive role models in Early Years settings as these can significantly influence children's perception of themselves and their cultural heritage. Moreover, 'children can only learn to be tolerant, change unfair generalisations and learn inclusiveness and positive regards for difference if they see the adults around them do the same' (Siraj-Blatchford, 1996: 24).

'Managing' diversity in practice

Practitioners' awareness of diversity and their understanding of their obligation, as outlined in the Equality Act 2010, to ensure fairness and equality to all children, has resulted in a more positive attitude towards diversity in most Early Years settings. Education practitioners are devising more ways by which they can make their settings inclusive and welcoming to all children. Consequently, positive representation of gender and disability are now common practice in most Early Years settings.

However, in a modern diverse society like the UK, most Early Years settings, particularly those in inner cities such as London, can have large numbers of children from different ethnic groups with different languages and (dis)ability at any one time. Having such a diverse group can make diversity seem like a daunting and complex task; and it is indeed a complex task. As a result, many Early Years practitioners have resorted to 'managing' diversity as a way of making the task less challenging. While this may be a good thing with regard to simplifying the challenge of catering for a diverse group, such an approach to diversity 'contains' rather than allows differences and

PROVOCATION

Who are you?

'Discover' yourself using these sources as a guide:

- Demographic markers – Race, ethnicity, culture, religion, age, gender, language and class.
- Your abilities – what are you good or not good at?
- Your interests and hobbies.
- Your preferred learning style – Do you prefer to learn in groups or one to one? Do you learn better listening or engaging in a debate (auditory), being active by doing (kinaesthetic), or observing others demonstrate (visual), or all of the above?

Now, imagine that this is a rough profile of a child in your setting and come up with a group that you think they belong to or fit in with.

- Is it easy or difficult to come up with a group that you can fit this child in and why is that so?
- How might you promote and ensure that this child, like every child in your setting (with their own individual and cultural differences), feels valued and respected in your setting?
- Do you think this is feasible? Give reasons for your view.

individualities to flourish. Research evidence has shown that the desire to 'manage' diversity will invariably lead to the social categorisation of children (Lawson *et al.*, 2013, Jones *et al.*, 2014).

Social categorisation occurs when professionals like Early Years practitioners uncritically group children into very broad cultural groupings based on 'assumed shared characteristics' (Papatheodorou, 2007: 44) such as ethnicity, (dis)ability, gender and social class. Providing a psychological analysis of social categorisation, Jones *et al.* (2014: 28) explain that;

> [I]n a complex and dynamic world we can't afford to see everyone as a distinct and **unique** person. This would sorely tax our cognitive abilities. Seeing people as a member of a group lets us make decisions quickly. It also helps us feel we understand the world. It gives us a sense of order and the feeling we know more about the person because they belong to a group.

While social categorisation may bring about ease and manageability of limited resources, it also means that individual differences and uniqueness are sacrificed in the process. Jones *et al.* (2014: 28) echo this point, arguing that social categorisation is flawed because it 'focus[es] on group membership, instead of personal qualities'. Furthermore, broad categorisation may also lead practitioners to seek simplistic solutions to issues of diversity (as illustrated in the case study) which research has shown to have significant consequences for children's perception of self and identity formation (Papatheodorou, 2007).

A widely used form of broad categorisation in education is ability grouping, otherwise known as 'streaming'. This is when children are placed into different groups based on their perceived (dis)ability. The main rationale behind this type of categorisation is that it allows teachers to differentiate learning and learning resources appropriately. Providing children with developmentally appropriate learning is important for their self-esteem and confidence. However, educational practitioners should also be aware that such categorisation can be demeaning to the child, particularly those on the lowest rung of the 'ability' ladder, as it has the potential to rob the child of their dignity.

Categorisation based on (dis)ability also constructs those children in the 'top' ability set as '**normal**' and 'intelligent' and others as 'misfits' and 'problems'. Citing Greene (1991), Cassidy and Jackson (2005: 446) argue that such categorisation also 'distances one group from another, sets up barriers of "them" and "us" and serves to undermine notions of community and togetherness'. Greene (1991 in Cassidy and Jackson, 2005: 446) goes further to argue that such broad categorisation is not an act of 'kindness' as some people might argue, but rather a reflection of 'self-serving righteousness'. In other words, there can be no justification for any kind of broad categorisation in education.

Studies have also shown that broad social categorisation, whether based on assumed shared characteristics, traits or (dis)ability can also lead to stereotyping and prejudice (Jones *et al.*, 2014). Stereotypes are 'qualities perceived to be associated with particular groups or categories of people' (Schneider, 2004: 24) while prejudice is 'negatively biased attitudes towards, and general unfavourable evaluations of, a group that is then ascribed to individual members of the group' (Jones *et al.*, 2014: 32).

Prejudice has significant impact on children's perception of self and self-worth. Children with membership to the group that is viewed more favourably and positively may become arrogant and develop a feeling of superiority over others. They may also be disparaging towards children from other groups in order to bolster their sense of self-worth. This group of children may also display a lack of empathy and become insensitive towards those they consider as different and inferior to them. Conversely, those children belonging to the group that is unfavourably evaluated may develop an inferiority complex and a sense of worthlessness, which may in turn lead to self-pity and self-hate.

The idea that cultural diversity is an issue that only practitioners working in multicultural Early Years settings should be concerned with is a fallacy. Indeed, some might argue that the reverse is the case. That is, practitioners in settings such as Debbie's (see case study below) should be as concerned, if not more, about diversity and equality as their colleagues in culturally diverse settings precisely because of their pupils' limited exposure to and interaction with people from different socio-cultural backgrounds. Debbie's simplistic understanding of diversity and the broader implications associated to it has led her to adopt tokenistic approaches to cultural diversity, which invariably only provides her pupils with superficial and very narrow understanding of people of different race and/or ethnicity. Except they are used to engender discussions about diversity and equality (which in Debbie's case is very unlikely due to her view on the issue), with a view to challenging and developing children's appreciation and respect for other cultures, a display of Black people in African attire or the inclusion of a sari in the role play area is more likely to reinforce and perpetuate existing stereotypes and prejudice about ethnic minority groups. Similarly, while giving alms to the poor is a laudable act, if however, her pupils' experience

CASE STUDY 1

Debbie is a Year 1 teacher in a state-funded school, with an outstanding Ofsted report, in an affluent area in rural Suffolk. The village has a predominantly white population and the school is attended mostly by children from white middle-class families. Like Debbie, all the teachers in the school are also white British. Since all of the pupils in her class are white British, like the rest of the teaching staff, Debbie does not think that cultural diversity is necessarily an 'issue' she should be concerned about. Indeed, in her view, issues of cultural diversity and equality are only prevalent in, and specific to, multi-ethnic settings/schools. However, in order to enable her pupils to 'learn' about other cultures, Debbie does the following:

- Displays pictures of people from other cultures; like a picture of black people in traditional African attire.
- Includes some ethnic-type clothing, such as the sari, in the role play area.
- Has 'multicultural' dolls in the resource area.
- Celebrates Chinese New Year with the rest of the school.
- Encourages her pupils to take part in major charity events, such as Red Nose Day and Comic Relief, to raise money for children in poor countries.

of other race and cultural groups is mostly through their charitable acts and/or the media, this will not only skew their perceptions of such groups, for example, Africans and Africa, it may also imbue them with a superiority complex.

Apple (1999 in Robinson and Diaz, 2006: 72) asserts that 'education is precisely the social field where possibilities of critique and interrogation of social inequality are more likely to be explored'. Therefore, regardless of whether or not they are in a multi-ethnic school, one of the roles of Early Years practitioners is to provide children with a safe environment where they can engage in critical thinking in order to challenge stereotypical ideas relating to gender, class, race, ethnicity and (dis)ability. Such an environment will also enable children to 'understand the importance of human rights and the consequences of intolerance and discrimination and how to challenge these' (QCA, 2009: 11).

Furthermore, a critical understanding of diversity and equality allows the practitioner to understand how differences based on gender, ethnicity, social class and (dis)ability, are used to discriminate against individuals and groups and perpetuate inequality. For example, males and females have historically been constructed as fundamentally different, with boys more favourably constructed as stronger, tougher and more adept at problem-solving (although, these constructions are gradually being deconstructed). This type of gender construction has permeated our psyche to the extent that boys and girls are raised differently. Consequently, boys and girls have also come to have markedly different aspirations, believing that some professions, for example, engineering, are only for 'boys'. Such construction has profound impact on children's experience and attitude in education as well as their inspiration and aspiration.

Equality and rights

Equality and rights cannot be divorced from diversity. It could indeed be argued that 'equality' and 'rights' should be central to debates on, and understanding of, diversity since research has shown that cultural, gender and socio-economic differences can lead to some people being excluded and marginalised. When we value diversity, we invariably seek equality and want to protect individuals' rights.

The EYFS (2014) states that inclusion not only concerns children with special educational needs (SEN) but is also about providing equal opportunity to all children irrespective of their gender, social class, ethnicity, (dis)ability, culture and ethnicity. Extending this point, Papatheodorou (2007: 48 my emphasis) contends that inclusion 'is a *right* based on equitable treatment and social justice for all'. To put it more simply, inclusive settings are those that promote equality by **safeguarding** children's rights in, and through, education.

Equal opportunity is an approach based on the idea that individuals should be treated fairly or equally but not necessarily as equals or the same. As Smith and Lusthaus (1995: 380) aptly point out, there is a fundamental difference between 'treating people *equally* and treating them *as equals*'. Rather, equal education opportunity is about meeting the individual child's needs and celebrating their individual strengths.

Treating children as equals or the same is a very narrow understanding of the equal opportunity model. This is because to treat children the same, particularly in terms of the type of support given in education, is to assume that every child enters education with the same amount of 'valuable' resources and experiences. To put it yet another way: to treat children the same is to ignore the fact that children do not have *equal* access to social, cultural and economic capitals, which can put individuals at an advantage or disadvantage depending on the volume of their capitals (Bourdieu and Passeron, 1990). For example, a recent study by Stahl (2015) found that children from a working-class family are less likely to succeed in education.

More significantly, treating children as equal without taking into account socio-economic factors such as class and ethnicity, for example, will result in some children being blamed for underachieving. Here, the onus is on the individual to overcome whatever adversity they may be facing and take advantage of the opportunities provided in education (Lawson *et al.*, 2013). It is no wonder critics have argued that in societies that espouse such an approach to equality, the less fortunate are 'free to try [but] born to lose' (Bayefsky, 1985: 5 in Smith and Lusthaus, 1995: 380).

In contrast, treating individuals equally rather that as equals is a more generous and broader way of understanding equal education opportunity. This approach to equality of opportunity goes beyond respecting individual differences, to seeing these differences as strengths while

PROVOCATION

How often do you explore factors such as class, gender, culture and race when considering factors that may be contributing to a child's underperformance in your setting?

acknowledging that factors such as ethnicity, gender and class can inhibit children's capacity to fully participate in education at the same time. The chief aim here is to reduce or completely remove, where possible, class, gender, (dis)ability and race related barriers in education so that all children have an equal chance at developing to their full potential.

Article 2(1) of the UN Convention on the Rights of the Child (1989) states:

> The State Parties to the present Convention shall respect and ensure the rights set forth in the Convention to each child within their jurisdiction without discrimination of any kind, irrespective of the child's or his or her parent's or legal guidance's race, colour, sex, language, religion, political or other opinion, national, ethnic or social origin, property, disability, birth or other status.

Yet research has found that there is a link between racism and class prejudice and under-performance in education. Crucially, studies have shown that inequality in education occurs because practitioners fail to acknowledge the interaction between individual differences such as gender, and socio-cultural differences such as ethnicity, race and class (Stahl, 2015). In their research, which explores equality in education, Cassidy and Jackson (2005) explain how factors such as disability, race, gender and class intersect and expose children to multiple layers of discrimination.

It is important to mention at this juncture that promoting equality in education is not something practitioners can *choose* to do or not to do but, rather, as something they are obliged to do under European and UK law. Under the Equality Act 2010, which has replaced previous equality legislation in the UK, schools in the UK are required by law to provide a learning environment that respects children's rights, values their cultural and gender differences, and provides them with equal opportunity.

Promoting diversity and equality through an inclusive pedagogy

It is now commonplace, mainly due to legislative requirements and Ofsted inspections, to see a display of an array of policies in most Early Years settings. Some of these policies are very detailed and comprehensive while others are brief, highlighting key aspects. Having a policy is important as it is one of the ways by which settings can demonstrate their commitments to, and responsibilities towards, important issues such as diversity, equality and rights. A good policy will also outline the plans and procedures in place to enable staff to put policy into practice.

While it is imperative that policy is put into practice, policy should not be rigidly and uncritically adhered to, neither should it be the singular element on which practice is based. In other words, policy should certainly not be adhered to at the expense of good pedagogy. As Papatheodorou (2007: 49) accurately argues, when policy takes precedence over 'pedagogy and [broad] categorisation determines action, there is a danger of practitioners reacting to situations rather than dealing proactively with complex and diverse needs'. Reliance on policy and procedure in meeting and dealing with children's complex and diverse needs would result in practitioners simply looking and 'adopt[ing] tips for teaching rather than engaging with pedagogy' (Epstein, 1993 in Papatheodorou, 2007: 49).

Similarly, practitioners who adopt a policy-driven approach to their practice tend to be more concerned about adjusting the physical environment and less concerned about the 'modification of approaches to teaching and learning and schools policies' (Riddell, 2009: 8). What is clearly apparent here is that policy-informed approaches to issues of diversity, equality and rights stifle critical reflection in practitioners.

In order to meet the diverse needs of each child, Early Years practitioners must not only make structural changes, but also change their pedagogical approach. Although pedagogy is often mistaken for the act of teaching, it is a much broader concept than teaching. While 'teaching is the act and performance of presenting curricular subjects' (Papatheodorou, 2007: 49), pedagogy goes beyond the act of teaching to include the **ideologies**, beliefs and theories that inform and shape the way we teach. Alexander (2004: 11) defines pedagogy as: 'What one needs to know, and the skills one needs to command, in order to make and justify the many different kinds of decisions of which teaching is constituted'.

Early Years settings in the UK are typically organised in the same way. Adhering strictly to the **continuous provision model of teaching**, a typical Early Years setting would organise the learning environment to reflect the seven areas of learning and development as stipulated in the EYFS (2014). This organisation of the learning space in such a manner exemplifies the act of teaching (it is also a good example of policy-informed approach to teaching). A pedagogical approach on the other hand is the critical examination of the rationale behind the continuous provision model of teaching and whether such provisions positively reflect the diverse ethnicities, languages, (dis)ability, gender and cultures in the settings and community. In other words: 'pedagogy offers the lenses and filters through which policy, statutory regulation and guidance, and practice may be critically examined, critiqued, questioned and appropriated to meet the needs of all and every individual child' (Papatheodorou, 2007: 50). Article 29 of the UNCRC states that education should ensure:

> 'the development of respect for the *child's parents*, his or her own *cultural identity, language and values*, for the *national values* of the country in which the child is living, the country from which he or she may *originate*, and for *civilizations different from his or her own.*

Highlighted in the article are very important and complex issues that cannot be met entirely by policy-informed approaches to teaching which are more concerned with ticking the boxes. Ensuring that every child in your setting feels that their '*own cultural identity, language and values*' are respected and valued while simultaneously developing the child's knowledge of, and respect for, '*civilizations different from his or her own*' would require a critical rather than a simplistic approach to teaching. A pedagogical approach to teaching allows education practitioners to 'adopt a reflexive critical stance towards their work with children and their relationship with families and local communities' (Robinson and Diaz, 2006: 79).

The intention here is not to devalue policy or to suggest that it does not have a role in Early Years settings, because it does. Rather, as I hope has become clear, the aim here is to stress the importance of pedagogy in Early Years practice. While statutory and non-statutory guidelines are helpful tools, it is only by adopting a pedagogical approach to teaching that Early Years practitioners can 'interrogate and negotiate subtle cues of difference and, consequently, make judgements about children's need that may require targeted additional and/or special support' (Papatheodorou, 2007:53).

Conclusion

This chapter has critically analysed the concepts of diversity and equality. In doing so, it has provided you with a deeper understanding of these concepts by identifying and examining the issues and concepts such as stereotyping and prejudice as well as theoretical perspectives relating to diversity and equality. An understanding of these concepts and, more specifically, how they are connected to rights, will enable you to understand how inequalities are created and perpetuated by social structures.

In explaining the differences between 'treating children equally' and 'treating them as equals' as well as those between 'teaching' and 'pedagogy', the chapter has shown the complexity of the concepts of diversity and equality. While the challenges of meeting the diverse needs and interests of children were acknowledged in the chapter, the chapter cautioned against employing simplistic solutions such as 'streaming' or ability grouping that merely 'manage' and 'contain' rather than celebrate diversity.

The chapter also cautioned against uncritically adhering to policy. Rather, Early Years practitioners are advised to adopt an inclusive pedagogical approach to diversity and equality. The chapter argued that a pedagogical approach would not only enable educational practitioners to reflect on their own beliefs and values, it would also give them the confidence to challenge, question and interrogate policies, ideologies and theories that inform and shape the way in which they deliver the curriculum, organise the learning environment and relate to children and their families. In other words, by adopting an inclusive pedagogy, Early Years practitioners might be able to develop a critical approach to diversity and equality.

Further reading

Sood, K. and Mistry, M.T. (2011) 'English as an additional language: Is there a need to embed cultural values and beliefs in institutional practice?', *Education 3-13 International Journal of Primary, Elementary and Early Years Education*, 39(2), pp. 203-215, DOI: 10.1080/03004270903389913.
  This article investigates the hidden assumptions that teachers and other professionals, e.g. Ethnic Minority Achievement Coordinators (EMAC) may have about EAL children and the implications of these assumptions on teaching and learning. The authors provide a three-stage model that they believe might help teachers to better support EAL children.

Aguado, T. and Malik, B. (2001) 'Cultural diversity and school equality: Intercultural education in Spain from a European perspective', *Intercultural Education*, 12:2, 149-162, DOI: 10.1080/14675980120064791.
  This article provides a European perspective on diversity and equality, specifically, focusing on the concept of 'intercultural education' and how this approach effectively and comprehensively addresses the issue of cultural diversity in schools.

Lawson, H., Boyask, R. and Waite, S. (2013) 'Construction of difference and diversity within policy and practice in England', *Cambridge Journal of Education*, 43(1): 107-122, DOI: 10.1080/0305764X.2012.749216
  This article provides a critical analysis of how the concepts of diversity and difference are constructed within English educational policy.

Devarakonda, C. (2013) *Diversity and Inclusion in Early Childhood: An Introduction*. London: Sage.
This book offers a comprehensive analysis of diversity and inclusion in early childhood.

Lane, J. (2008) *Young Children and Racial Justice: Taking Action for Racial Equality in the Early Years: Understanding the Past, Thinking about the Present, Planning for the future*. London: National Children's Bureau.
This book examines issues of fairness and equality and their implementation in Early Years services and settings.

Useful websites

www.education.gov.uk/
Department of Education.

www.multilingualfamily.gov.uk/
Multilingual family.

www.ncb.org.uk/media/74042are_equalities_an_issue.pdf
Young children's Voices Network.

www.crae.org.uk/media/26362/Equality-Matters-for-Children-CRAE-Equality-Act-guide.pdf
Equality Matter for children: a guide for children's services on the Equality Act 2010 (2011). London: Children's Rights Alliance for England (accessed 2 May 2014).

www.gov.uk/government/uploads/system/uploads/attachment_data/file/315587/Equality_Act_Advice_Final.pdf
Equality Act 2010: (2014) Departmental advice for school leaders, school staff, governing bodies and local authorities (accessed 2 May 2014).

References

Alexander, R. (2004) 'Still no pedagogy? Principle, pragmatism and compliance in primary education'. *Cambridge Journal of Education*, 34(1) pp.7–33

Bayefsky, A.F. (1985) 'Defining equality rights', in Smith, W.J. and Lusthaus, C. (1995) The Nexus of Equality and Quality in Education: A Framework for Debate, *Canadian Journal of Education*, 20(3) McGill University. Available at www.csse-scee.ca/CJE/Articles/FullText/CJE20-3/CJE20-3-11Smith.pdf (accessed August 2015).

Bourdieu, P. and Passeron, J. (1990) *Reproduction in Education, Society, and Culture*. London: Sage

Cassidy, W. and Jackson, M. (2005) 'The need for equality in education: An intersectionality examination of labelling and zero tolerance practices'. *McGill Journal of Education*, (3) pp. 435–455.

DES (1985) *The Swann Report Education for All*. London: Her Majesty's Stationery Office. Available at www.educationengland.org.uk/documents/swann/swann1985.html (accessed 2 May 2014).

Early Years Foundation Stage Profile Handbook (EYFS) (2014) www.foundationyears.org.uk/files/2014/05/2014_EYFS_handbook.pdf (accessed February 2015).

Jones, J.M., Dovidio, J.F. and Vietze, D.L. (2014) *The Psychology of Diversity: Beyond Prejudice and Racism*. West Sussex: Wiley Blackwell.

Lawson, H., Boyask, R. and Waite, S. (2013) 'Construction of difference and diversity within policy and practice in England', *Cambridge Journal of Education*, 43(1), pp. 107–122, DOI: 10.1080/0305764X.2012.749216.

Norwich, B. (2002). 'Education, inclusion and individual differences: recognising and resolving dilemmas'. *British Journal of Education Studies*, 50(4) pp. 482–502.

Papatheodorou, T. (2007) 'Difference, culture and diversity: challenges, responsibilities and opportunities', in Moyles, J. (2007) *Early Years Foundations: Meeting the challenge.* Maidenhead: Open University Press.

Qualification and Curriculum Authority (QCA) (1994) 'Cross-curriculum dimensions: A planning guide for schools'. Available at http://schoolsonline.britishcouncil.org/sites/default/files/el/98010.pdf (accessed 2 May 2014).

Qualification and Curriculum Authority (QCA) (2009) Cross-curriculum Dimensions – A planning Guide for Schools. London: QCA.

Rhedding-Jones, J. (2005) 'Questioning diversity', in Yelland, N. (ed.) (2005) *Critical Issues in Early Childhood Education.* Berkshire: Open University Press.

Riddell, S. (2009) 'Social justice, equality and inclusion in Scottish education', *Discourse* 30(3) pp. 283–297.

Robinson, K. and Jones Diaz, C. (2006) *Diversity and Difference in Early Childhood Education: Issues for theory and practice.* Berkshire: Open University Press

Schneider, D.J. (2004) *The Psychology of Stereotyping.* London: Guilford Press.

Siraj-Blatchford, I. (1996) 'Language, culture and difference: challenging inequality and promoting respect', in Nutbrown, C. (1996) *Children's Rights and Early Education.* London: Paul Chapman.

Siraj-Blatchford, I. (2001) 'Diversity and Learning in the Early Years', in Pugh, G. (2001) *Contemporary Issues in the Early Years.* London: Paul Chapman.

Smith, W.J. and Lusthaus, C. (1995). 'The Nexus of Equality and Quality in Education: A Framework for Debate'. *Canadian Journal of Education*, 20(3) McGill University. Available at www.csse-scee.ca/CJE/Articles/FullText/CJE20-3/CJE20-3-11Smith.pdf (accessed 17 August 2015).

Sood, K. and Mistry, M.T. (2011) English as an Additional Language: is there a need to embed cultural values and beliefs in institutional practice?, *Education 3-13 International Journal of Primary, Elementary and Early Years Education*, 39:2, 203-215, DOI: 10.1080/03004270903389913.

Stahl, G. (2015) *Identity, Neoliberalism and Aspiration: Educating White Working-Class Boys.* London: Routledge.

UN Convention on the Right of the Child. (1989) Available at www.unicef.org.uk/UNICEFs-Work/Our-mission/UN-Convention/ (accessed 2 May 2014).

24 Special Educational Needs and Disability (SEND) in the Early Years

Allison Boggis

LEARNING OUTCOMES

After reading this chapter, you should be able to:

✔ Consider the impact of value-based approaches to SEND.
✔ Have a clearer understanding of provision and practice in relation to SEND.
✔ Understand the need for early intervention.
✔ Appreciate the importance of collaborative working when supporting a child with SEND.

Introduction

We are living in a time of unprecedented change underpinned by the effects of global economic recession, changes in government and sweeping reforms to our education and welfare systems. It is not surprising then that as Early Years practitioners, we find ourselves in what Hallett and Hallett (2010: 9) describe as a 'changing landscape' in terms of providing support to young children with special educational needs and disability (SEND). While these changes are undoubtedly underpinned by political motivation, there is also a recognised need to overhaul existing systems that support pupils with special educational needs (SEN) and/or disabilities. Arguably, however, current systems are based on an outdated model of society and are now not considered as being 'fit for purpose' (House of Commons, 2006: 12). Indeed, as Rix *et al.* (2010: 4) point out, 'nearly everything about the construction of our current social system is based on **separation** and **segregation**. It is not a system which is well suited to the delivery of **equality**, participation and disability'.

Clearly, if we are to work towards a more **inclusive** society, cultural changes are necessary. However, it is unlikely that the implementation of such changes will be straightforward. It is therefore essential that Early Years practitioners take time to challenge existing practice, critically consider opportunities for change and develop practice in order that the outcomes and life chances for young children with SEN and/or disabilities can be improved.

This practical approach to SEND offers practitioners an accessible overview of important issues that relate directly to Early Years practice. The discussions are significant in that they provide the reader with opportunities for critical **engagement** with and consideration of the ways in which a child with SEND and their family can be supported. The opportunities for reflection are designed to help you engage in a positive, resolution approach to this complex area of practice, and will encourage you to critically reflect on theoretical ideas and concepts as you apply them to real life situations.

This chapter is not directed solely towards Special Educational Needs Co-ordinators (SENCOs) nor those involved in specialist provision. It is meant to be read by all practitioners working with young children in Early Years settings so that they gain a greater understanding of SEND and engage with the contentious and emotive issues relating to it. It reflects the principle that for systems to change sufficiently to enable improvements in provision for young children and their families, *all* practitioners need to be actively involved in regular reviews of practice.

Terminology

It is important to reflect on the terminology used throughout this chapter before we proceed. Special educational needs (SEN) is a complex and ambiguous term. The concept of disability is equally complex, meaning different things to different people. Indeed, according to Etkins (2012), accurately defining and consistently identifying pupils with SEN and/or disability is confusing, problematic and inconsistent. While there is considerable overlap in the use of both terms, it does not always follow that all disabled children have SEN and all children with SEN are defined as disabled (House of Commons, 2006: 16). Large variations in the use of terminology among regions, local authorities and even within local authorities have added to this confusion.

Currently, children are considered to have SEN 'if they have greater difficulty in learning than the majority of children their age which calls for an additional or different educational provision to be made for them' (DfE, 2011: 18). The term SEN originated from the Warnock Report (1978) which introduced the idea of special educational needs, statements of SEN and an integrative approach to education, which later became known as inclusion. The rationale of this process was to move away from categorisation of pupils' needs under medical terms where children were considered 'uneducable' or 'educationally sub-normal' and move towards a system where children with identified SEN could be educated in mainstream schools. However, using SEN as a single category and grouping all children with SEN together as a homogenous group regardless of their actual needs and difficulties soon became problematic. Some years later, Warnock herself identified that:

> One of the major disasters of the original report was that we introduced the concept of special educational needs to try and show that disabled children were not a race apart and many of them could be educated in the mainstream ... But the unforeseen consequence is that SEN has come to be the name of a single category, and the government uses it as if it is the same problem to include a child in a wheelchair and a child with Asperger's, and that is conspicuously untrue.
>
> House of Commons (2006: 16)

In addition, the language of SEN has become contentious and confusing; health services refer to 'disabled' children, education services to children with 'special educational needs', and social care to children 'in need'. While children may find themselves belonging to more than one category, the terms do not mean the same and have different consequences in terms of the support that young children will need and receive.

Special Educational Needs is a term used widely in England and according to Ofsted (2010: 5), there were 'just over one in five pupils – 1.7 million school children identified as having Special Educational Needs'. Etkins (2012) argues that due to its common [over]use (my emphasis), the real meaning of SEN has been lost. She goes on to suggest that a more explicit understanding of the term is required, referring to a continuum of need, not a single category. She believes that any approaches to identification and assessment of need and provision of support should take account of differing needs. Lamb (2009) added that the single use of the term 'SEN' can lead to lowering expectations of children and there is danger, as Florian (2010: 65) notes, that an 'intractable cycle is formed' whereby children are assigned membership of a group because they are 'judged to possess the attributes of the group membership and they are believed to have the attributes of the group because they are members of it'.

You are defined as disabled under the Equality Act 2010 (www.nidirect.gov.uk) if you have a physical or mental impairment that has a substantial and long-term negative effect on your ability to do **normal** daily activities. The term 'substantial' is taken to mean that minor or trivial and 'long-term' means 12 months or more. However, Oliver (1983: 261) observes that 'it has been suggested that the term 'people with disabilities' should be used in preference to 'disabled people' because this prioritises people rather than disability. He goes on to explain that 'disabled people' is the preferred term adopted by those within the disabled movement because it makes a political statement: they are not people with 'disabilities', but people that are disabled or disadvantaged by society's response to their differences (Oliver, 1990).

The intention of this chapter is not to add to the ongoing debate in terms of reference. Therefore, the terms 'disabled children' and 'children with disabilities' are used interchangeably and intentionally with 'disability' placed purposefully either before or after 'children' to emphasise social barriers and/or individual impairment.

REFLECTIVE PRACTICE
REFLECTIVE PRACTICE

Having read the above, take a moment to reflect on your own practice and answer the following questions:

- How are SEN and/or disability conceptualised within your setting?
- What terms/language do you use?
- Do you place the 'disability' before or after the child?
- Does it lead to a lowering of expectations of the child?
- By staff members?
- By the child him/herself?
- By the parents/carers of the child?
- By other children?

While acknowledging the tensions that the terms 'SEN' and 'disability' present, for ease of purpose SEND (which represents special educational needs and/or disability) will be used throughout this chapter.

Identifying SEND in the Early Years

Some children have identified complex needs from birth. Health assessments enable very early identification of a range of medical and physical difficulties and early support is usually provided by health-related services which work with families to help support them understand their child's individual needs and work on their behalf to access the support they need. When the child reaches an age to access Early Years provision, an Early Support Programme should already be in place and this will consider Education, Health and Care needs (EHC) of the individual.

CASE STUDY 1

Edward is 3 years old. He has Down's syndrome. He needs some support to feed himself but is enjoying finger foods and drinks out of a cup unaided. He started walking 6 months ago and while he is quite steady, he falls easily if jostled. The physiotherapist has identified this need and advised that he wears orthopaedic boots to help stabilise his ankles. The family have been working with the Speech and Language therapist and between them they are encouraging Edward to use Makaton and verbalisation to communicate. Recently, he has been getting upset if his nappy is wet or soiled and started to sign when he wants to use the potty.

He is a very sociable child who has many friends. His mother has contacted Little Ted's Playgroup to enquire about a place starting in the Autumn Term.

PROVOCATION

Looking back at the discussion about terms used to define SEN and Disability as outlined earlier in this chapter (terminology), consider the following:

1 Does Edward have SEN? How do you know this?
2 Is Edward disabled? How do you know this?
3 What are his **unique** needs?
4 What provision might you need to put in place to support Edward?

REFLECTIVE PRACTICE

Did the label/categorisation of Down's syndrome help you to answer the above questions?

Practitioners should be aware of the possible **debilitating** *effects of labelling. They may place unrealistic expectations on the child or simply assume that they will demonstrate unacceptable behaviours and wait for it to happen. Labels may also infer that the child has/is a 'problem' and we may view they child in terms of 'deficit'. In Edward's case, his diagnosis is medically determined, but his overall characteristics are not.*

Children that start at Early Years settings with identified special educational needs may already have programmes of support in place. (From September 2014, Education, Health and Care plans replaced and phased out the statements of special educational needs and Learning Difficulty assessment). This has made it clear that all **agencies** should work together to enable children and young people to achieve their goals and be supported in the best way possible. It is up to practitioners to communicate with parents/guardians to establish which professionals have been involved to date and gather information that will help them support the child. However, practitioners should be mindful that parents who have disabled children are often asked to recount their stories on many occasions, and this is one of the criticisms that parents have of service providers. The Early Support programme, supported by the National Children's Bureau and the Council for Disabled Children, aims to alleviate this by bringing service providers together with parents, and place children and young people at the centre of the holistic and integrated planning services. There are resources and further training available (www.ncb.org.uk).

PROVOCATION

All parents/guardians of children that start at 'Little Teds' have a home visit prior to their first 'Taster Session'. During this visit, the key person will explain all about the group and answer any questions the family may have. They usually leave the family with an 'All About Me' booklet to complete and bring to their first 'Taster Session'. The questions are not overly onerous and provide details such as family members' names, the child's likes/dislikes, favourite toy, favourite foods, allergies, preferred routines, etc. The key workers find them invaluable during the 'settling in' period.

Lisa has been allocated as Edward's key worker. She has organised a home visit to see Edward, his mother and his sister. She is aware that parents who have disabled children are often asked to repeat their stories over and over again and so she is unsure whether to ask Edward's family to complete the 'All About Me' booklet. On the other hand, if she doesn't ask them to complete it and she does not have the information she needs, it might compromise him settling into the group or stigmatise him and his family.

- What should Lisa do?
- Why?

Whether the child arrives at the setting with an identified need or not, careful observations and assessment are integral to the role of an Early Years practitioner. The ongoing recording and monitoring systems utilised within Early Years settings should be acknowledged as crucial to effective planning. Wall (2011: 114) suggests that the usefulness and power of observations can:

- inform planning;
- inform understanding of a child's current competence levels;
- support reflection of the appropriateness of provision;
- enable the sharing of information with other parties;
- enable assessment of specific children, groups, interactions, the learning environment and the staff.

However, she warns that while purposeful observations should offer benefits to practitioners, parents and children, for those children who are experiencing difficulties, the focus should rest on the child, not the difficulties. She advocates that when working with a young child with **cerebral palsy** for example, the practitioners need to understand the impairment but focus their attention of the child's current strengths, skills, likes and dislikes which will inform planning. The cerebral palsy is of secondary consideration. In order to use their best endeavours to ensure that the necessary provision is made for each child, practitioners should increase their knowledge of individual children and consider them as **unique**.

Observations should be part of the everyday work of the provision. If concerns are raised, observations can clarify thinking and identify specific areas of difficulty as well as strengths. It is important that where SEND is identified, appropriate evidenced-based interventions are put into place. Indeed, the interventions will rely heavily on the observations and consequently, observations will play a key role in future planning.

Initiatives such as Early Support and **Sure Start** demonstrate that the policy context and legislation has developed consistently in line with the theme of identifying and providing support as early as possible.

Policy and practice

Since 2003, the Early Support programme has been implemented in England and it was developed within the climate established by the Every Child Matters Agenda. By 2007, the Early Support policy document *Aiming High for Disabled Children: Better Support for Families* (DCSF/DoH, 2007) was put in place. Clearly, policy makers have increasingly made the connection between intervening as early as possible to support young children and their families for the all-round long-term benefits for the wider community (HM Government, 2011). Early intervention has been well supported by governments which have been motivated to increase access to pre-school education for all children, and in addition to being the theme of general policy it has also been a focus for disabled children and children with SEN. Indeed, the DfES (2011: 29) goes as far as to suggest that: 'Through effective early identification and intervention – working with parents and families – we can reduce the impact that SEN or disability may have in the long run, and enable more young people to lead successful and independent adult lives.'

Most young children aged 0-5 attend some form of Early Years provision and so equal opportunities and anti-discriminatory practices are central to Early Years practice. It is vital that all children and families have access to a standard of care and education that ensures that they are supported and valued. However, practitioners should note that equal opportunities are not about treating every child and their family in the same way, but that the support they receive is tailored to their individual and specific needs. Similarly, equality of opportunity is based on the belief that *all* children and their families are supported in terms of their gender, race, culture, faith, sexual orientation, family background and ability. Kay (2012: 92) argues that if this is not achieved in the early years of a child's life, it can be detrimental, inhibiting them from achieving full potential as they progress. She continues by suggesting that children need to see difference as a positive, rather than a negative.

Two decades ago, the Disability Discrimination Act (1994) set out requirements that schools and colleges should make provision for children and young people with disabilities. Following on from this, the SEN Code of Practice (2001) and Article 23 of the UN Convention on the Rights of the Child (1989) stated the need for children to have access to education and to be able to live a full life. In addition, the SEN Code of Practice placed a greater emphasis on the need for very young children to receive both support before they start nursery, through early intervention programmes, and then when they move into a mainstream early years setting.

The SEN Code of Practice (2001) (later replaced by the SEND code of Practice for 0-25 years in September 2014) set out the need for each Early Year's setting to have a Special Educational Needs Co-ordinator (SENCO) in place to ensure that the needs of children with disabilities in their settings are met. In addition, it stated that practitioners should work closely with all agencies involved so that the planning and activities on offer meet the needs of all children within the setting. Emphasis is clearly placed on early identification, assessment and provision of SEND in early education settings. (For further information and extended reading, please see Chapter 1 'Legislation and Policy' in Kate Wall's comprehensive text book, *Special Needs and Early Years*, 2011). This chapter gives a detailed outline of the key developments of policies and legislation that have been pivotal for Early Years provision. The detailed timeline from 2000 demonstrates the expanse of documentation published).

At the time of writing, radical changes to the SEN code of practice were taking place and the DfE (2011) paper 'Support and aspiration: A new approach to special educational needs and disability. Progress and Next Steps' set out plans for the radical reformation of the current system for identifying, assessing and supporting children and young people who are disabled or have SEN. The Children and Families Act 2014 was given royal approval in March 2014 and Part Three of the Act is dedicated especially to SEN emphasising the commitment to Special Educational Needs. The extent of the ways in which the Act and the green paper are applied in practice remains to be seen.

As an Early Years practitioner, you will have a good working knowledge of the Early Years Foundation Stage (DfE 2012/14) framework and understand that if a child is not showing typical development for their age, they may be at risk of delay or ahead for their age. You are required to review their progress in the prime areas between the ages of 24 and 36 months also at the end of the EYFS in the EYFS profile and to make a summative assessment to share with parents, colleagues and other settings. These are often the first, but very important, steps in supporting a child with SEND and their family.

REFLECTIVE PRACTICE
REFLECTIVE PRACTICE

Take time to reflect on a scenario in your setting where you felt concerned about a child's individual progress. Think back and answer the points below:

- How did you raise the concerns?
- Who did you share the information with?
- Can you describe the strategies you had/may put into place to support the child?
- Were you aware of your settings policies that underpin good practice?

On reflection:

- Were your concerns justified?
- What were the outcomes?
- What might have happened if further steps had not been taken to support the child and their family?

Support for children with SEND and their families

It has already been established that individualised early interventions are crucial if the child is to be supported appropriately. However, practitioners are reminded not to adopt the 'deficit' model that illustrates what the child cannot do. For example, you might imagine that a practitioner's observation notes might state the following; 'Edward can't use a pencil' or 'Ayesha can't put her coat on by herself yet'. While this may be true, imagine how this categorisation might impact on the parents/carers and how it might impact on the expectations of their child. In addition, the observations do not say anything that informs future actions. Rather than note what the child cannot do, make detailed notes of what they can do. For example, 'Edward can grasp chubby sticks of chalk using a palmer grip and can mark make with them on the playground surface or on secured paper on the sloped writing easel', or 'Ayesha can put her arms in the sleeves of her coat if an adult holds it for her'. This stance not only facilitates more constructive communication with parents/carers and other professionals, it also provides a starting point from which to set realistic targets.

There are no hard and fast rules about approaching parents/carers for the first time if you have concerns about their child's progress. Every situation is different so practitioners are advised to think through the scenario first and consider their communication techniques and choice of words. Parents/carers may or may not have recognised that their child has difficulties in a specific area/s of their development. However, it is not uncommon for parents/carers to actively resist acknowledging that their child is not progressing along the usual path of development and to refuse or avoid further investigation. Practitioners should be mindful of this. While it is beyond the remit of this chapter to outline the reasons for parental denial, suffice it to say practitioners should maintain a dialogue with the family and help to facilitate acceptance of the child's needs over time. Expressing concerns or indicating some difficulty formally might not be the best approach as informal discussions with parents/carers often reveal the most. Initially, positive conversations about the child are really important to demonstrate you are not just concentrating on the deficits and difficulties that their child is experiencing, that you are not attempting to 'label' their child but that you are committed to supporting their child by providing an appropriate and positive environment in which they can achieve.

Whatever the outcome, practitioners should be mindful that supporting the child's needs should come first and while partnership with parents is the cornerstone of special educational needs legislation, and should be promoted whenever possible, it is not necessary to gain a parent's permission to put support programmes in place where they only involve staff who work within the setting. Parents and carers should be notified, of course, about what is happening within the setting, but it is only when external agencies are involved that parent's permission will need to be given.

PROVOCATION

Let us return to Edward. Observations have indicated that Edward has recently begun to get upset if his nappy is wet or soiled and started to sign when he wants to use the potty.

- As he is about to start at Little Ted's and you are his designated key worker, how might you approach Edward's parents about this?
- For the sake of continuity, might you be able to work out a strategy for home and playgroup between you?
- How might you combine the parents' knowledge of Edward and your knowledge of child development to support him?
- Do parents know best?
- Do practitioners know best?
- What are the benefits of working together?
- What might happen if you adopt one strategy at Little Ted's and his parent's adopt a different strategy at home?
- How might this affect Edward?

Practitioners should have the welfare of the child at the centre of their practice. They should be non-judgemental when working in partnership with parents and be able to demonstrate high levels of sensitivity, paying attention to the processes as well as the communication itself. While interpersonal skills are highly important, organisational structures and policies that underpin good practice for SEND are crucial if a healthy, effective relationship between home, school and/or nursery is to be maintained.

PROVOCATION

What do children know? How can we gain Edward's voice? How do we know what is important to him?

Why not consider the Mosaic Approach (Clarke and Statham, 2005) to listen to Edward. This is when a variety of tools are used to elicit opinion and evidence child participation. Verbal and visual tools are needed, so you might wish to utilise the following:

- Observations
- Photographs
- Drawings/paintings
- Voice recording
- Video recording
- Circle time

Can you add to this?

What do parents know? Parents know their children best. What contributions can parents make?

- Their child's history
- What they can do at home and what they are learning to do
- What they like and are good at
- How they communicate
- What strategies have worked well in supporting their child

Can you add to this?

What do Early Years practitioners know? What do you know about the child?
- Their developmental needs
- A range of teaching and learning methods
- What resources you have available
- Expectations of behaviour
- Policies and practices
- Roles and responsibilities

Can you add to this?

Now make a list of any other professionals from external agencies that might be involved with Edward and his family.

- What might they know?

A 'joined up' approach

Early Years practitioners should acquire the skills necessary to co-ordinate, implement and evaluate provision for children with SEND. It is important that they work effectively with colleagues from other disciplines and external agencies to support children and their families (Children and Families Act 2014). Before planning takes place, however, practitioners need to think through the needs of individual children and consider how these can be met in practice. What interventions and activities are appropriate? Initial meetings are vitally important and all contributions should be valued.

There are many voices that are needed to be heard in assessment processes and what better place to begin than starting with the child?

When all opinions and professional judgements have been gathered, clearly there is much to do in terms of building a holistic picture of Edward in order that you can continue to support his current and ongoing needs. The key points of all reports need to be collated and summarised before a range of appropriate interventions can be put in place. Many of the adaptations and interventions may be quite small, some may already be in place and others will soon become part of the daily routine. It is helpful to know who is doing what, by when and how the effectiveness of the strategies will be monitored. Checklists like the one below (from Roffey and Parry, 2014: 80) can help with general planning and setting targets for the child:

- Are there any physical adaptations needed? What are they?
- What curricular adaptations are needed?
- Do any adaptations to the usual routine need to be made? What are they?
- Is any additional equipment needed? What are these?
- What specific support is needed from inside and outside of the setting?
- Are there any training needs that have been identified?
- Who will be responsible for monitoring the child's progress?
- What arrangements for continuing communications are to be put in place? How often?

We must be mindful that the plans should not be stigmatising but be fluid and take into account the progress of the child. A holistic, multi-agency approach that responds to the child's changing needs will make a difference to a child's wellbeing and progress in their early lives.

Conclusion

Every child is unique and as such **bespoke** provision should be put in place in order that they reach their full potential. Each scenario presents a new set of challenges, questions and dilemmas. There is no blue print for working with young children with SEND and there are no tried and trusted ways of working universally with children. Therefore, in order to develop the skills of working collaboratively and adapt their professional practice accordingly to support a child with SEND, it is vital that practitioners are confident in their own knowledge and understanding of child development and in the procedures and policies adopted by their settings.

The purpose of this chapter was not to provide a 'how to' guide to working with children who have special educational needs and/or disability and their families. It was to provoke thought, engage in critical reflection and challenge practitioners to evaluate their own values and practice. While the discussions did not focus specifically on particular aspects of SEND, they have offered an opportunity for readers to explore some of the complexities of the terms and concepts that surround special educational needs and disability per se. As Early Years practitioners, you were asked to consider the value base of the terms used, to reflect on the appropriateness of labelling children and to contemplate the implications of this in practice. Moving on from here, you were encouraged to critically engage with processes of identifying SEN in Early Years settings and consider the changes in policy that underpin and support provision. Finally, the latter part of the chapter offered a series of provocations as a means of practical self-evaluation when supporting a child with SEND. All in all, the themes cover a wide range of key issues and there is clearly more reading and research that you could engage with to deepen your knowledge and understanding of this important subject area.

Further reading

Ekins, A. (2012) *The Changing Face of Special Educational Needs* Abingdon: Routledge.
    This text helps practitioners make sense of the rapid pace of change within SEND in an accessible and logical way. It also emphasises the exciting opportunities that these changes will provide for developing new, innovative and creative working practices.

Roffey, S. and Parry, J. (2014) *Special Needs in the Early Years* (3rd edn) London: Routledge.
    This book contains a wealth of information about how Early Years practitioners can work effectively with professionals and parents to help identify and support a range of special educational needs.

Wall, K. (2011) *Special Needs and Early Years* (3rd edn) London: Sage.
    This accessible text blends theory and practice to provide a detailed analysis of provision for young children with SEND.

Useful websites

www.councilfordisabledchildren.org.uk
    The Council for Disabled Children aims to make a difference to the lives of disabled children and children with special educational needs by influencing government policy, working with local agencies to translate policy into practice and produce guidance on issues affecting the lives of disabled children.

www.nasen.org.uk
    The National Association for Special Educational Needs (NASEN) aims to promote the education, training, advancement and development for those with special and additional needs. The journals and training opportunities are very helpful for students and practitioners.

www.csie.org.uk
    The Centre for Studies on Inclusive Education (CSIE) is a national charity that works to promote equality and eliminate discrimination in education. This site offers a wide range of resources for schools, parents and students.

References

Children and Families Act (2014).

Clarke, A. and Statham, J. (2005) Listening to young children; experts in their own lives *Adoption and Fostering*, Vol 29 (10) pp. 45-56.

Disability Discrimination Act (1994).

DCSF/DoH (2007) *Aiming High for Disabled Children: Better Support for Families* London: Department for Education.

DfE (2010) *The Importance of Teaching* London: Crown Copyright.

DfE (2011) *Support and Aspiration: A new approach to special educational needs* Norwich: TSO.

DfE (2012) *Statutory Framework for the Early Years Foundation Stage: Setting the Standards for Learning, Development and Care for Children from Birth to Five* London: Department for Education.

DfE (2014) *Special Educational Needs and Disability Code of Practice: 0 to 25 years* available at: www.gov.uk/government/uploads/system/uploads/attachment_data/file/398815/SEND_Code_of_Practice_January_2015.pdf (Accessed 25 August 2015).

Etkins, A (2012) *The Changing Face of Special Educational Needs: Impact and implications for SENCOs and their schools* London: Routledge.

Florian, L. (2010) 'The concept of inclusive pedagogy', in Hallet, F. and Hallet G. (eds) *Transforming the Role of the SENCO: Achieving the National Award for SEN Co-ordination* Maidenhead: Open University Press.

Hallett, F. and Hallett, G. (2010) *Transforming the Role of the SENCOs: Achieving the National Award for SEN Co-ordination* Maidenhead: Open University Press.

HM Government (2010) *Equality Act 2010* London: Office of Disability Issues.

HM Government (2011) *Early Intervention: The Next Steps* London: Cabinet Office.

House of Commons Select Committee (2006) 'Special Educational Needs: Third report of session 2005-2006' London: TSO.

Kay, J. (2012) *Good Practice in the Early Years* London: Continuum.

Lamb, B. (2009) *SEN and Parental Confidence* London: Crown Copyright.

Ofsted Review (2010)*The Special Educational Needs and Disability Review: A statement is not enough* Manchester: Crown Copyright.

Oliver, M. (1983) *Social Work and Disabled People* Basingstoke: Macmillan.

Oliver, M. (1990) *The Politics of Disablement* Basingstoke: Macmillan.

Rix, J., Walsh, C., Parry, J. and Kumrai, R. (2010) 'Introduction: Another point of view', in Rix, J., Nind, M., Sheehy, K., Simmons, K., Parry, J. and Kumrai, R. (eds) *Equality, Participation and Inclusion: Diverse Perspectives* Abingdon: Routledge.

Roffey, S. and Parry, J. (2014) *Special Needs in the Early Years: Supporting Collaboration, Communication and Co-ordination* (3rd edn) London: Routledge.

United Nations (1989) *Convention on the Rights of the Child*, UNICEF: London.

Wall, K. (2011) *Special Needs and Early Years. A practitioner's guide* (3rd edn) London: Sage.

Warnock, M. (1978) *Warnock Report: Special Educational Needs, Report of the Committee of Enquiry into the Education of Handicapped Children and Young People*, London: HMSO.

Part IV

The Senior Practitioner-Professional

25 Legal and professional responsibilities

Carol Hayes

LEARNING OUTCOMES

After reading this chapter, you will be able to:

✔ Recognise the difference between legislation, regulation and **professionalism.**
✔ Demonstrate an understanding of the basic principles of policy writing and development within an early years setting.
✔ Review information and legislation concerning respect, confidentiality and security of data, in the light of a need for information sharing and policy development.
✔ Reflect upon policies, procedures, roles and responsibilities existing in a particular childcare/education setting, including the effects of legislation and external regulation.
✔ Demonstrate an understanding of the boundaries of your own role within health and safety policy development, and the potential impact of the issues for children, adults, families and agencies when working with children at an early years setting.

Introduction

This chapter will look briefly at some of the legal and professional responsibilities which bind you as a practitioner in early years along with some discussion of policy development and the relationship between policy and legislation. The chapter explains some of the differences between legislation, policy development and **professionalism** and how national policy development can influence policy writing within an early years setting. Examples of policy development considerations are explored and issues of health and safety and risk **assessment** are used to illustrate some of the concerns. Along the way there are reflective passages and practice examples to support your involvement, and at the end of the chapter is a list of recommended reading and suggested websites to enable you to **contextualise** the material and pursue your particular area of interest.

Childcare providers in England must comply with a set of legal requirements set out in the Childcare Act 2006, and this pivotal piece of English legislation established the Early Years Foundation Stage as the framework for education of our youngest children, in early years settings. The Childcare Act 2006 also laid out the safeguards and welfare requirements for each individual working with children *(further information about this can be found in Chapter 21)*.

Legislation versus regulation and professionalism

Before progressing further with this chapter you need to be sure that as an early years practitioner you are familiar with the terminology of the law. It is not necessary for you to have detailed knowledge of the complexities of English law and the legal system of this country, but a basic understanding will help you to comprehend what responsibilities you do have when caring for and educating young children.

In the British legal structure there are a number of graduated steps that the laws of the land must pass through before they become enshrined in enforceable legislation. Usually legislation comes about through an Act of Parliament, and in this country we have two houses of Parliament, the Commons and the Lords. Any potential legislation will need to be considered and voted upon, by both Houses before receiving Royal Assent and becoming law, such as the Childcare Act 2006. Before reaching this stage there is generally a Green Paper (such as Every Child Matters, 2003) which is a paper for consultation and anyone can make a contribution to this, it is a 'test of public opinion'. Following the Green Paper is often a White Paper laying out the philosophy and rationale behind the proposal and explaining to Parliament, and the public, the need for this new legislation. On its passage through the two Houses it is called a Bill, such as the new Child Care Payments Bill (sponsored by the Treasury) that is now an Act of Parliament and legally enforceable. Only when this has been fully approved by Parliament will it go for Royal Assent and become an Act of Parliament and legally enforceable.

Acts of Parliament are often accompanied by a series of regulations which detail the way in which a specific requirement of that law is enforced by the appointed regulators, such as Ofsted. Such regulations are likely to focus upon areas such as health and safety or child protection, for example the Childcare Act 2006 legislated that we must reduce inequalities between children; Ofsted, as the Government regulator, then developed a series of regulations to ensure that the law is strictly complied with, such as the requirement to develop an equal opportunities policy in every setting.

Legislation is all about Acts of Parliament, but is not necessarily the law. The law is the set of rules or regulations which society has deemed necessary to maintain its existence. The distinction between the law and legislation is that the law applies to us all, such as the speed limits, murder and theft, regardless of our circumstances. Legislation however, in the form of a statute, may favour one element of society, for example equal opportunities legislation, which may give certain sectors of society additional rights or privileges.

Professionalism

How many of you can truthfully say that you have never broken the law? How many of you have never dropped litter, never driven over the speed limit, have not immediately informed a shop

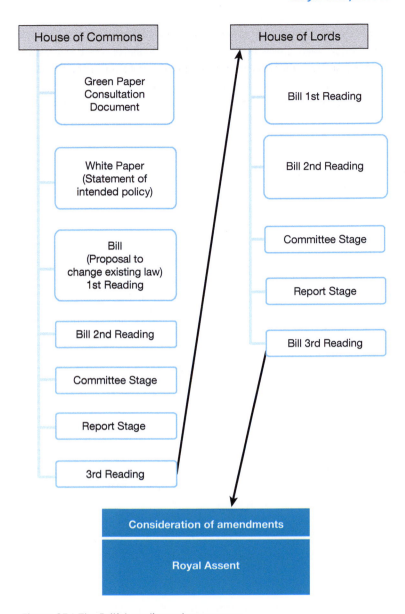

Figure 25.1 The British parliamentary process

assistant when you know that they have undercharged or not charged for an item in your shopping trolley? I suspect that very few of you can be sure that you have never overstepped the mark, and do not lose sleep over the issue. However, what happens when you think that you are being observed? Driving down the motorway with cars rushing past at 80, 90 and even 100 miles an hour, suddenly they all slow down to 70 miles per hour as they see a police car ahead of them. Does this mean that for the law to be effective it needs to be policed by government legislators? What happens when the police car is not there? Although clearly some will break the law, the majority of you are usually law abiding and this is where the law is superseded by your professional responsibilities, this is what takes over when the government legislators are not around to police the process. Ofsted are clearly the government legislators in early years, enacting their role to ensure that Government legislation is being enforced and that childcare settings are following their legal responsibilities. When Ofsted is not there each practitioner has to call upon their professional conscience, or their professionalism, to ensure that their legal, moral and ethical responsibilities are dispatched to the best of their abilities.

There is often confusion amongst early years practitioners regarding their legal requirements and their moral and professional responsibilities. This dichotomy is one which those responsible for developing policy need to be clear about. Jones and Welch (2010) suggest that professional and moral responsibilities are those which we feel are *right*, they are operational, but legal requirements are what we are compelled to do by the law of the land.

> So although we say that someone has a right to food, water and shelter, unless there are legal imperatives that someone has to provide these, the safeguarding of that right will depend on the voluntary action of others.
>
> (Jones and Welch, 2010, p. 36)

It is therefore likely that your views of professional responsibilities will vary and is likely to be heavily influenced by culture, religion, political climate etc. Your understanding of your own professionalism is a key factor in determining how you carry out your role, but the whole concept of professionalism is complex and ambiguous, probably meaning different things to different individuals and different professional **agencies**. Moyles (2001) talked about 'passion' and 'paradox'. Moyles (2010) believed that professionalism meant that practitioners needed passion, or at least a deep belief and commitment to their role. However the legal and political constraints within the early years sector produce a paradox, which means being able to walk the tightrope between the potential dilemma of legal constraint and belief, to produce a rigorous approach to the work with integrity and firm ethical principles.

> Passion for young children is part of the culture of practitioners. Passion must be allowed, both as a **panacea** for coping with challenging **paradoxes** and also for inspiring professionalism in those who work and play with the youngest members of our society.
>
> (Moyles, 2010, p. 93)

Part of that paradox is to conceptualise professionalism in the light of increased legislation, regulation and control, through critical and dynamic reflection, expanding our knowledge and understanding. It also means being what Osgood (2006) calls a 'passive recipient' of the legislation and regulatory frameworks, but also able to interpret them creatively and become active enough within the process to be able to challenge established practice, statutory and regulatory standards and to develop a set of firm ethical values, to act as a baseline for further practice.

Legal responsibilities

Developing policy within early years requires those working in the sector to juggle a complex mix of legal requirements, political agenda and professional and ethical responsibilities. Each setting is required to have its own set of policies. Developing policy can be viewed from two perspectives or categories:

1   Government policy making, both national and local, (including Ofsted).
2   Organisational policy making.

Each of these becomes interdependent, depending upon how we view the policy making process, from a top-down experience to a bottom-up experience, for example, a situation where politicians decide upon a policy which is imposed on practitioners for implementation, or where practice informs the policy development and Government policy is shaped by the views of practitioners, the general public and interested organisations. Policy makers are part of the decision making process and are responsible for developing a clear vision and relevant interpretation of strategies to take up the challenge of the mission they have been given. Educational policy making is a vastly complex and political process, and owes its complexity not only to the fact that childcare and education is a sector where it is difficult to identify and define terms, such as 'what is quality?', but also the diversity of interests that the sector represents for the different stakeholders. Any policy development within a setting involves difficult and multi-dimensional problems. Faced by financial constraints for example, governments are not able to meet all the social demands without adopting restrictive measures within the sector or 'robbing Peter to pay Paul', in order to rationalise the use of allocated resources. So also within the dynamics of management and the effective and efficient allocation of finance, managers of settings have to make difficult decisions to regulate the utilisation of scarce resources, without leading to service disruptions and dysfunctions.

A policy statement should define good practice and be clearly set out for all practitioners, parents, carers and children about how this good practice can be delivered, maintained and evaluated. A clear policy statement should offer unambiguous guidelines to ensure that all staff come into contact with a child and their family in a professional context, and are aware of how to understand the **ethos** and culture of the setting and therefore how to proceed. This will involve detailed planning, **vertical planning** between national government, local government, outside interested agencies, research and settings, and horizontal integration of ideas from parent partnerships, practitioners and the children.

Of course not all policies are written down, but may be adopted customs of practice. This is more likely in the case of organisational policies than in Government policy formation. Baldock *et al.*, (2013) suggest that there are certain features of any policy whether written or not:

*   It will coherently detail the assumptions and values of an issue.
*   It will have clear objectives.
*   The costs of implementation will be acceptable.
*   Available resources will match the objectives.
*   Implementation strategies will be clear.
*   Communication with interested parties will be effective and open.
*   It is compatible with other related policies.
*   It is regularly reviewed and updated.

Practitioners need to understand the varied and interrelated factors influencing policy development in early years, in order to be able to understand their own and others roles in the process. It is also important to recognise that policy is neither exempt from trends nor made in isolation, but that it is a product of the prevailing social context within which it develops.

(Baldock *et al.*, 2003, p. 34)

There is clearly a strong relationship between policy and legislation, and as you have already seen most legislation comes as a result of an Act of Parliament, but this is a long and complex process. Alternatively the Government of the day may ask for a report to be produced, for example the Nutbrown Review (2012), where Cathy Nutbrown was asked to investigate qualifications and standards in early years. This may be followed by a White Paper stating the philosophy behind the proposed legislation and only then will it be considered by Parliament. However, legislation is only one way of developing Government policy; initiatives such as **Sure Start** and Children's Centres were implemented by the Government of the day, making additional money available to departments to lead on particular policies.

REFLECTIVE PRACTICE
REFLECTIVE PRACTICE

Since the 1980s there has been an enormous expansion in the quantity of government legislation and policy related to early years. Legislation should reflect the needs of society, the culture and the community it serves.

With a colleague reflect upon the place of legislation in your professional practice.

(For example, does health and safety legislation affect what you do with the children in the outdoor play area?)

Policy development

A policy is a collectively agreed statement of beliefs and a recommended course of action; it is a document to inform procedures. Procedures are the way to do something, usually written but not necessarily, they are usually context specific. Policy is therefore a way for settings to translate their vision into workable programmes to deliver their objectives. Within any early years setting having a clearly written policy to inform procedures allows a baseline to underpin day-to-day decision making, and ensures consistency between staff and settings. It allows parents and other professionals to understand the culture and ethos of your setting, and the services that you offer. To adhere to the legal requirements of the Childcare Act 2006, some specific polices in early years settings, including childminders, do need to be in written format, for example:

- Safeguarding
- Equal Opportunities

- Administration of Medicines
- Risk assessment
- Health and Safety
- Behaviour Management
- Concerns and Complaints from Parents
- Smoking
- Parent failing to collect at appointed time
- Child going missing
- Emergency Evacuation
- Identification of visitors

These legally required policies are likely to fall into a number of broader categories:

- Anti-discriminatory legislation. [*more information on this area can be found in Chapter 23 of this book*]
- Learning and development requirements, given legal force by the Early Years Foundation Stage (amendment) order 2012 under section 39 (1)a of the Childcare Act 2006.
- Safeguarding and Welfare requirements, Early Years Foundation Stage (welfare requirements) 2012, section 31 (1)b of Childcare Act 2006. [*more information on this area can be found in Chapter 21 of this book*]
- Employment law.
- Health and Safety legislation.
- Data collection legislation.
- Duty of care.

However, despite their legal origins, these policies can be made context specific and relate to your particular setting, thereby allowing a personalised approach for their implementation. Clearly for this to work communication is a key issue, with all staff, parents and children fully aware of their existence, and accessible to all, all of the time. Considerable thought and consideration needs to be given to how the policies, and policy implications, will be communicated effectively to all staff, parents, children and other stakeholders. Attention needs to be given to how this level of communication will continue following the initial roll-out and 'fanfare', to new staff, students, children and parents etc. Faded copies of 'dog-eared' policies on the wall of the nursery cloakroom, does not constitute honest and clear communication procedures. This may require adaptation or even simplification for a wide range of people, abilities and situations.

Baldock *et al.*, (2013) defined policy as: 'An attempt by those working inside an organisation to think in a coherent way about what it is trying to achieve (either in general or in relation to a specific issue) and what it needs to achieve it' (p. 3). They go on to say that for such a considered approach to practice to take place, the writer of a policy needs to think on three levels, First, on the basic and relevant facts and values that need consideration; second, broad objectives; and third, a consideration of the procedures needed to enact these objectives. Arguably the most difficult of these is the first one because it is like shifting sand, constantly moving, changing and developing at a personal level but also at local, governmental and political levels.

PROVOCATION

In 2012, the Government announced a series of possible measures to reduce the cost of childcare. Booth, Kostadintcheva, Knox and Bram (2013) undertook a research project to examine parental views: 87 per cent of the parents surveyed said that the government should set limits for child–adult ratios in settings and 95 per cent suggested that this might be affected by the age of the child and whether the children had special needs. There was also some support for considering regulation of the qualifications and experience of practitioners. The following results were recorded:

Parents who believed current ratios were about right (%)	Age groups	Current agreed ratios
72	Under 2 years old	3
80	2 years old	4
46	3–5-year-olds with no teacher present	8
59	Child-minders with children under 8 years	6

With a colleague consider the following questions:

1   If there were an increase in the numbers that you could care for at one time, how would this affect your practice and that of your setting?
2   What factors should affect how many children a carer is allowed to care for at one time?
3   Should the current Ofsted rating define the numbers admitted to the setting?
4   Do you believe that this increase in ratios would result in a reduction in childcare fees?

For access to the full report please go to: www.gov.uk/government/uploads/system/ uploads/attachment_data/file/212614/DFE-RR285

Policy development is not 'rocket science' but, according to Kingdon and Gourd (2014), it is rarely done well and requires the policy writer to strike a balance between a wide range of complex interests, views and opinions without losing sight of the original desired objectives. With the advent of the Internet and social media, early years settings today are dynamic and ever changing institutions, they are also complex, and at times unpredictable. For example, parents are often better informed than in the past, and Governments have rising expectations of staff and are therefore making growing demands on settings within social need, manipulation of society, educational achievement and health.

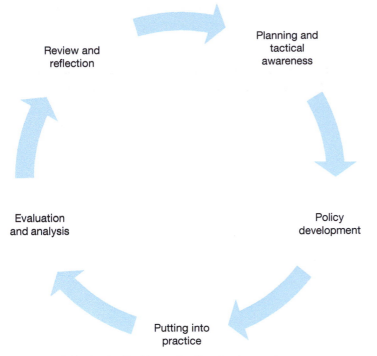

Figure 25.2 Cycle of reflection and policy development

Policies rarely start from a blank sheet and policy writers need to be aware of pre-existing conditions and possible bias from over familiarity. This whole process can be seen as a cyclical and ever changing and reviewing process. Policy development, whether at government or at setting level, is not a one off activity but a continuum or cycle of review and reflection, as we see in Figure 25.2.

The process needs to start with a close review of current practice, and the policy writer needs to be fully aware of the long-term view, taking into account the demographics of the setting and of the government's political, economic and cultural trends. This will demand a holistic view of local, national and international perspectives, drawing on the policy writer's experience of theoretical perspectives and up-to-date research. This is a creative, flexible and reflective process, questioning established ways of doing things and considering new and alternative perspectives on an issue. It may involve bringing in people and expertise from outside the setting, consulting with other professional agencies and with other settings. So the most effective policies are based on taking account of the best available evidence from a wide range of sources. All the stakeholders need to be involved throughout the policy development process; this may involve:

- Reflecting on existing research and practice.
- **Action research** projects to ensure a targeted approach to development.
- Consideration of financial and commercial options.
- Consideration of the lessons learned from prior experience, current experience and good practice sharing.

It is the responsibility of policy makers to provide an **inclusive** approach, taking into account the needs of all the children, families, staff and volunteers who will be affected, either directly or indirectly, by the interpretation of the policy. To ensure this level of inclusivity, policy makers may need to take account of the following:

* All those who will potentially be responsible for administering the policy, allowing them to take ownership of the decisions made. That will include all staff or volunteers working within a setting, for example mid-day supervisors, caretakers, catering staff, volunteer parents, etc.
* All those who will be affected by the policy implementation, for example parents collecting their children, staff taking breaks, children's risk assessment for outdoor play, etc.
* Seeking regular feedback from all stakeholders as to the consequence and outcome of the policy. This may mean setting dates for regular reviews of the practical working of the policy, but also being able to respond quickly and flexibly if it becomes apparent that a policy is in need of revision.
* Evaluation processes will therefore need to be built into the policy to know whether the policy has been successful. Criteria for measuring success or meaningful performance measures will need to have been defined, and the use of pilots to influence and enhance a rigorous approach to the policy document development. This will also ensure that there are mechanisms to jettison old and redundant policies, for scrapping or reconfiguration.

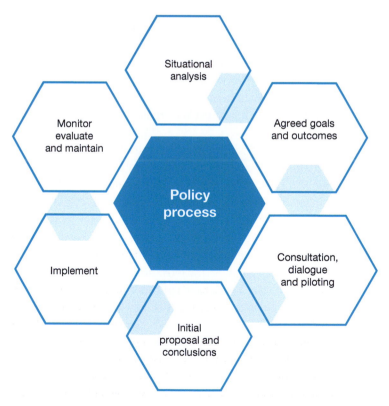

Figure 25.3 Policy process

Such a process allows a holistic or 'joined-up' approach to policy development ensuring an ethical, moral, cultural and legal basis for the process. This requires policy makers to consider beyond the boundaries of the setting to other professionals, cutting across other departments or other neighbouring settings and barriers to allow for integration and co-operation.

Respect and confidentiality

The ultimate public **perception** of a professional is one of trustworthiness and integrity. To ensure this you need to understand your responsibilities regarding confidentiality and the law. This is a major issue when working with children and families and is legally guided by a number of pieces of legislation, for example:

- Data Protection Act (1998)
- Freedom of Information Act (2000)
- Access to School Records
- Children Act 1989
- Children Act 2004

Those working with young children need to be aware that any individual in this country has the right to access any information held about them. So parents can request sight of any records that you hold about their children, indeed children can ask to see their records if it is deemed that they can understand their request, this includes the Early Years Foundation Stage Profiles. If an individual is refused access to their information they can appeal through the courts to gain appropriate access, and can, in exceptional circumstances, have data amended if they feel that it is inaccurate or portrays them in a way that might be detrimental to their health and well-being (DCSF 2008).

Storing personal data relating to other individuals needs careful consideration and should usually be password protected if it is digital information, or in physically locked storage if in hard copy format. This will include all the children's Early Years Foundation Stage Profiles. If such information is to be useful for practitioners to plan for children or share with other appropriate professionals (such as the Reception/Year 1 teacher), it needs to be up to date, relevant and accurate and appropriate in content and quantity. According to the Data Protection Act (1998), it also needs to be used only for a 'specific purpose'. Contained within the policy needs to be reference to how long the data is to be kept and how it will eventually be disposed of. As a practitioner you need to be aware that anything that you write about an individual may be read by that person next week!

It is important that you do not get confused by this and understand that you still have an obligation to reveal any information to another appropriate professional agency if, in your 'professional judgement', a child may suffer 'significant harm' by not revealing a confidence (Children Act 1989 and Children Act 2004). (Further information relating to this is discussed in Chapter 21 of this book). It is essential to remember that the Data Protection Act (1998) is *not* a barrier to information sharing, but before sharing confidential material the practitioner needs to consider whether it is 'Necessary, proportionate, relevant, timely and secure' (DCSF 2008, p. 11).

CASE STUDY 1

Marsha is the owner/manager of an inner-city private day nursery. She has eight members of staff all qualified to Level 2 or 3 and she prides herself on the levels of professionalism within the setting. As she walked into the toddler room two Level 3 members of staff were laughing uproariously, one of them was the room manager. When she questioned what was happening one of the staff members told her in a loud voice and across the heads of a group of two-year-olds, that one of them had just told her that she had a 'new daddy' as her 'old daddy' had gone away. The children were playing and were apparently unconcerned about the revelations.

1   *How do you think that Marsha should react?*
2   *Should the members of staff be disciplined in any way?*
3   *Was this a breach of confidentiality? Is this a legal issue or one of professionalism?*
4   *What sort of policy could Marsha introduce into the setting to ensure that such behaviour is not seen as acceptable in the future?*

Health and safety

An example of one of your major legal responsibilities in a childcare setting is the health and safety of all those who access your setting. Health and safety legislation in England generally falls into four main areas:

1   Promoting and encouraging good health and safe working practices.
2   The control of potential infection.
3   Risk assessment (a careful examination of what could potentially cause harm to staff, volunteers, children, visitors, etc.).
4   Continuous professional development and training in health and safety practices for all staff.

The main pieces of legislation associated with these are:

- Health and Safety at Work Act 1974
- Childcare Act 2006
- Manual Handling Operations Regulations 2004
- Control of Substances Hazardous to Health 2002 Regulations (COSHH)
- Reporting of Injuries, Diseases, Dangerous Occurrences Regulations 2013 (RIDDOR)
- Early Years Foundation Stage 2014
- Food Safety 1990

CASE STUDY 2

Pattercakes Nursery is a Children's Centre on the outskirts of a rather run-down area of a city in the Midlands. The nursery is committed to a Forest School approach and believes that access to a positive outdoor environmental experience is a way to develop self-awareness, communication, independence and empathy in their children, who often have low self-esteem and do not always understand the boundaries of their behaviour.

There is a small outside area attached to the Children's Centre, with a few trees and a stone circle for the children to sit. The staff want to undertake a story-telling session around a camp fire which the children will have helped to build and light.

All staff have attended the Forest School training and training for risk assessment.

Under the following headings what do you think needs to be considered before this activity can be undertaken?

- What are the possible hazards?
- What harm could the children and staff come to if these are not controlled?
- Who will be at risk?
- What measures need to be put in place to prevent harm?
- Who will take ultimate responsibility?

Dilemma

The staff recognise that while every effort needs to be made to minimise the risk to the children, there is always a balance between risk and benefit, and focusing only on risk could create negative attitudes to adventurous play.

Clearly every early years setting is **unique** and will bring with it particular health and safety issues for those who access it, but it is important to realise that although the manager/leader may have ultimate responsibility for what goes on in their setting all employees, paid or unpaid, have a personal responsibility for health and safety. As a consequence everyone in the setting needs regular training in issues related to health and safety and risk assessment, to ensure the safety of all children and adults, and this needs to be clearly written into any policy document related to this area.

The concept of risk assessment and how this can affect the quality of the activities undertaken needs to be closely written into any health and safety policy in a setting. Risk assessment is a careful evaluation of what could cause harm to those who access your setting. However, once again you see how the policy writer needs to walk the tightrope and deal with the dilemma. How far does the limitation of risk also eliminate the possibility of allowing children to grow and expand their world view? Could, for example, your whole philosophy of what it is to be a child be challenged by the implementation of an over rigorous health and safety policy?

REFLECTIVE PRACTICE
REFLECTIVE PRACTICE

Please take some time to read the following passage, which is an excerpt from Johnston and Nahmad Williams (2009) pp. 256–257:

According to today's regulators and bureaucrats, those of us who were kids in the 60s, 70s, and early 80s probably shouldn't have survived because our baby cots were covered with brightly coloured lead-based paint which was promptly chewed and licked.

We had no childproof lids on medicine bottles, or latches on doors or cabinets and it was fine to play with pans.

When we rode our bikes, we wore no helmets, just flip flops and fluorescent 'spoky-dokies' on our wheels.

As children, we would ride in cars with no seat belts or air bags – riding in the passenger seat was a treat.

We drank water from the garden hose and not from a bottle and it tasted the same.

We ate chips, bread and butter pudding and drank fizzy juice with sugar in it, but we were never overweight because we were always outside playing.

We shared one drink with four friends, from one bottle or can and no one actually died from this.

We would spend hours building go-carts out of scraps and then went top speed down the hill, only to find out we forgot the brakes.

After running into stinging nettles a few times we learned to solve the problem.

We would leave home in the morning and could play all day, as long as we were back before it got dark. No one was able to reach us and no one minded.

We did not have PlayStations or X-Boxes, no video games at all. No 99 channels on the TV, no videotape movies, no surround sound, no mobile phones, no personal computers, no DVDs, no internet chat rooms and no TVs for those of us a wee bit older.

We had friends – we went outside and found them.

We played elastics and rounders, and sometimes that ball really hurt!

We fell out of trees, got cut, and broke bones, but there were no law suits.

We had full-on fist fights but no prosecution followed from other parents.

We played knock-the-door-run-away and were actually afraid of the owners catching us.

We walked to friends' homes.

We also, believe it or not, WALKED to school; we didn't rely on mummy and daddy to drive us to school, which was just around the corner.

We made up games with sticks and tennis balls.

We rode bikes in packs of seven and wore our coats by only the hood.

The idea of a parent bailing us out if we broke the law was unheard of . . . they actually sided with the law.

This generation has produced some of the best risk takers and problem solvers and inventors, ever. The past 50 years has been an explosion of innovation and new ideas. We had freedom, failure, success and responsibility, and we learned how to deal with it all.

With a colleague reflect upon this concept of childhood. Is it the changing notion of what childhood really is that has changed the legislation surrounding childhood, or is it the legislative process that has changed our concept of what it is to be a child in the twenty-first century?

Conclusion

This chapter has outlined some of the legal and professional responsibilities faced by early years practitioners when caring for and educating our youngest children. There is currently an explosion of new legislation and initiatives coming from Government, and practitioners often find it difficult to negotiate all the requirements and distinguish between what they are legally required to do, and what could be referred to as just good practice from a professional industry. It is not possible to include even a fraction of this in this book, which is why recommended reading has been included at the end of the chapter to enable you to further guide your knowledge and understanding. Although negotiating the legislation may seem daunting to policy developers, the emphasis in this chapter is on the practice of policy development being a collaborative and co-operative process, using the expertise from within and without the immediate setting. A rigorous approach to development will help you to establish a bank of policy documentation which will guide the practice within your setting, and ensure that all members of staff (paid and unpaid) feel included and involved, and therefore more able to implement the policies to ensure a quality and safe approach to practice. Such involvement will empower all members of staff to feel able to express opinions and concerns about the policies in practice, and to keep such policy documents under constant review, thereby responding to the changing face of theoretical research, government ethos and community conditions. This chapter highlights the challenges that policy makers face to travel together with staff, children, families, local and national governments to reach the goals of a world class quality service for children. Attempting to define the nature of a 'quality service' is material for a whole new book, and such a fluid concept of the 'shifting sands' of party political government and theoretical understanding will mean that we will probably never be able to. What is clear is that your policy development process needs to be set within the cultural, ethical and professional context of your early years setting, and those within the system need to be investing in that policy-making process.

This chapter is clearly a very brief overview of the issues concerning policy development, and given the limits of one chapter, has attempted to look at the main issues and relate these to one area of policy writing. Kingdon and Gourd (2014) believe that in most cases early years practitioners are thrown into the position of co-ordinating policy development with often negligible training or help. There is therefore need for some well-grounded information to guide the process.

One of the biggest challenges is to ensure that the intentions of the written policy are translated into practice as envisioned by the policy writers. This poses challenges for issues of practical organisation, administration, training, development and research. In order to ensure a smooth roll-out of policy, all involved need to be fully engaged and committed to good communication and dissemination of information and materials, and to develop strategies for keeping ahead of initiatives from local and national Government sources. 'Early years workers need to recognise their potential role in the policy process and to build their professional confidence on a set of values explicitly directed to achieving positive outcomes for the children' (Kingdon and Gourd 2014, p. 16).

Further reading

Kingdon, Z. and Gourd, J. (2014) *Early Years Policy: The Impact on Practice*, Oxon: David Fulton Books.
   This text provides an up-to-date look at the global and political aspect of policy making, accountability and policy makers. While the book is firmly embedded within practice development it also examines, in some detail, the theoretical perspectives and looks at early years policy development in context.

Keeping up to date with Government initiatives can be hard but the long-standing magazines for early years practitioners, *Nursery World* and *The Early Years Educator*, usually have articles for policy makers with summaries and reviews of the latest legislation and opportunities, allowing you to engage in critically reflective dialogue with other practitioners across the country through the letters pages and on-screen presence,

Useful websites

www.education.gov.uk/publications/standard/AllPublications/
   This website will give you access to the latest Department for Education publications, including up to the minute research which has been commissioned by the Department for Education.

www.hse.gov.uk/pubns/hsis1.htm
   This website offers advice and guidance to early years workers and the general public on health and safety law, regulation, risk assessment and safety. This also gives access to a range of leaflets and posters which may be useful to those working within early years or managing settings.

www.ofsted.gov.uk/
   This is the official Office for the Standards in Education website for inspection processes. It will provide you with access to early years inspection reports and approved publications, including information regarding requirements for inspection, and a range of resources and framework guidance.

References

Baldock, P., Fitzgerald, D. and Kay, J. (2013) *Understanding Early Years Policy* (3rd edn), London, Sage.

Booth, C., Kostadintcheva, K., Knox, A. and Bram, B. (2013) *Parents' Views and Experiences of Child Care: research project,* Ipsos MORI. www.gov.uk/government/uploads/syatem/uploads/attachment_data/file/212614/DFE-RR285 [accessed 28 November 2014]

DfE (2008) *Information Sharing: Guidance for Practitioners and Managers*, ref. DCSF-00807. Available at www.gov.uk/ . . . / [accessed 18 August 2015].

DfE (2014) *Statutory Framework for the Early Years Foundation Stage: Setting the standards for learning, development and care for children from birth to five,* https://ww.gov.uk/government/uploads/system/uploads/attachmnt_data/file/335504/EYFS_framework_from_1_september_2014_with_clarification_note.pdf (accessed 15 November 2015).

DfES (2003) *Every Child Matters – Summary*, London, DfES.

DfES (2004) Children Act 2004, London HMSO.

DoH (1989) Children Act 1989, London, HMSO.

Great Britain Parliament (1974) Health and Safety at Work Act (Act of Parliament), London: TSO.

Great Britain Parliament (1998) Data Protection Act 1998 (Act of Parliament), London: HMSO.

Great Britain Parliament (2000) Freedom of Information Act 2000 (Act of Parliament), London: HMSO.

Great Britain Parliament (2006) Childcare Act 2006 (Act of Parliament), London, Crown.

Health and Safety Executive (2002) *Control of Substances Hazardous to Health 2002 Regulations*, GB, HSE Books.

Health and Safety Executive (2004) *Manual Handling Operations Regulations*, GB, HSE Books.

Health and Safety Executive (2013) *Reporting Injuries, Diseases and Dangerous Occurrences in Health and Social Care: Guidance for employers,* Health Services Information Sheet HSIS1(rev3), HSE Books. www.hse.gov.uk/pubns/hsis1.htm [accessed 20 March 2014].

Johnston, J. and Nahmad-Williams, L. (2009) *Early Childhood Studies*, Essex, Pearson Longman.

Jones, R. and Welch, S. (2010) *Rethinking Children's Rights,* London, Continuum Books Ltd.

Kingdon, Z. and Gourd, J. (2014) *Early Years Policy: The Impact on Practice*, Oxon, David Fulton Books.

Moyles, J (2001) Passion, Paradox and Professionalism in Early Years Education, Oxford: Routledge. *Early Years: Journal of International Research and Development*, Vol 21, Number 2, 1 June 2001, p 81-95 (15).

Nutbrown C. (2012) *Foundations for Quality: The Independent Review of Early Education and Childcare Qualifications Final Report*, London DfE.

Ofsted (2013) Records, Policies and Notification Requirements of the Early Years Register, www.ofsted.gov.uk/resources/factsheet-childcare-records-policies-and-notification-requirements-of-early-years-register [accessed 20 March 2014].

Osgood, J. (2006) Deconstructing Professionalism in Early Childhood Education: Resisting the regulatory gaze, *Contemporary Issues in Early Childhood Education*, 7(1) 5-14.

26 Observation

Janet Harvell and Samantha McMahon

LEARNING OUTCOMES

After reading this chapter you will have:

✔ Considered the purpose of observation in recognising and supporting children's learning.
✔ Explored some of the ethical considerations to be considered when observing children.
✔ Examined a number of different observation methods, considered the advantages of these and when to use each method.
✔ Considered how to use shared observations to effectively inform Self Evaluation and support the inspection process.

Introduction

In this chapter we outline the purposes of **observation** and provide an overview of some of the different observation methods available to practitioners, encouraging the reader to expand on their existing practice. To ensure authenticity, demonstrate relevance to practice and to support reflection, key learning points and concepts are illustrated through examples provided by practitioners. We move the discussion on to explore some of the ethical dilemmas faced by the observer and reflect on the importance of the language used in observations. The reader is encouraged to consider the child's perspective when reading the different examples. The need to be aware of bias, and the impact this could have when observing children, is explored. Ultimately we consider how peer observation can support continuous improvement in practice and provision by linking it to the Self Evaluation Process for Ofsted inspection. Throughout the use of Case Studies, Reflective Practice and Provocations are used to support the reader in developing a deeper understanding of the topics being examined.

What is observation and why do we observe young children?

Observation has a long tradition in early years and underpins many theoretical perspectives which offer explanations of how children develop e.g. Piaget and Bronfenbrenner (Hedegaard 2009). Frederick Froebel (1782–1852) first saw observation as an opportunity for staff to understand how play supported children's thinking and learning (Nutbrown and Clough 2014). Observation now supports a more holistic role, with evidence from this being used by researchers to inform current policy and develop practice. For example, the longitudinal study into *The Effective Provision of Pre-School Education (EPPE)* by Kathy Sylva *et al.* (2004) was significant in demonstrating the positive impact of having a graduate-led workforce, resulting in the consequent development of a graduate pathway with the emergence of the *Early Years Professional* (CWDC 2009) and *Early Years Teacher* (2013). Papatheodorou and Luff (2012) also point out that students use observation for a variety of reasons as they learn about the child, further their own learning and acquire skills. In routine early years practice observation is used most often to assess, and then plan for the learning, development and care needs of the child. It is an invaluable tool to help the adult match provision to need and enhance cognitive process (Glazzard *et al.* 2010). Similarly, observations to assess the effectiveness of the environment and adult-child interactions, to mention just two opportunities, can be used effectively to inform the setting when conducting its self-evaluation, and also provide confidence when engaging in shared observations during the inspection process. Nutbrown, in her review of early years qualifications, highlighted the criticality of having well qualified practitioners who have a secure knowledge and understanding of how children develop and use this 'to make careful observations of each individual child, applying what they know about how children develop and play in a reflective and considered way' (2012: 19).

CASE STUDY 1

Sarawat aged 37 months has been attending nursery for three sessions per week for a period of 4 weeks. Her Key Person has noticed that Sarawat spends most of her time in the home corner and tends to interact with any adults who are close by. Here are two of her observations.

Observation 1: Sarawat plays in the kitchen area where two other children and a practitioner are playing. She moves freely around the area collecting food and says 'I don't have all the ingredients'. She then picks up the whisk and asks the practitioner what it is; the practitioner tells her and demonstrates how it works. Sarawat then uses the whisk on her food and puts the pan on the stove, 'Now it's hot' she says, and 'I need oven gloves'. She takes the pan of food to the practitioner and says 'Be careful it's hot'. The practitioner asks if she would like to share her food with the other children in the kitchen area. Sarawat looks towards the other children then replies 'No it's for mum'. She puts down the pan and takes out some of the fruits and vegetables, hands them to the practitioner and says 'This is a chilli, what's this?' The adult replies 'It's a kiwi'. 'Kiwi' copies Sarawat and returns the fruit and vegetables to her pan.

Observation 2: Sarawat is in the kitchen area, there are three other children who move in and out of the area. Sarawat is at the sink and hands a piece of fruit to the baby, 'No don't eat that, it's disgusting' and she then washes the fruit. She repeats this three times then gets a pan and says 'I'll make some porridge'. She then spends several minutes trying to see how much of the food she can fit into the pan. She takes different pieces of fruit and vegetable out until the lid firmly closes. She then takes the pan over to the Key Person, 'I've made porridge'. She lifts off the lid and says 'I need oven gloves, it's hot'. Keira, one of the other children, comes over to look; Sarawat puts the lid back on the pan saying 'It's for the baby'.

Consider these observations, and the insight which might be gained by the Key Person into Sarawat's thinking and meaning-making. The practitioner must interpret this data and can identify the areas of learning and development which might focus initially on the prime areas; personal social and **emotional development**, physical development and communication and language, matching to the child's age from Development Matters (Early Education 2012). This enables the practitioner to track Sarawat's progress and makes it easy to spot if the child's level of learning and development is emerging, developing or secure. Try this for yourself and identify the Characteristics of Learning. How might the practitioner use this information to offer support and sustain Sarawat's learning and development? Can you identify any reasons to be cautious when using this information for **assessment** and planning?

In the Early Years Foundation Stage (EYFS) observation is recognised as integral to the ongoing or formative assessment process whereby practitioners observe 'children to understand their level of achievement, interests and learning styles, and to then shape learning experiences for each child reflecting these observations' (DfE 2012: 10). It is a statutory requirement for the Early Years Foundation Stage Profile to be completed in the final term of the year in which the child reaches five years of age (DfE 2012: 11). This must provide a picture of the child's progress against the expected levels of learning and development and the key to this will be ongoing observations. Accurate observational data will also be integral to the progress check at age two whereby practitioners must provide parents with a summary of the child's progress in each of the prime areas and, in the future, this will be used to inform the Healthy Child Programme development review (DfE 2012: 11).This progress check is a vital component of the government's early intervention agenda as proposed in Supporting Families in the Foundation Years (DfE 2011) and central to facilitating links with parents and other professionals thus underpinning practice which safeguards children (Marsden *et al.* 2013). One student on the Foundation degree, an experienced childminder, provided an example of a progress review she had completed for a two year old in her care, commenting that the review was very useful as it helped her to pull all the child's learning and development together, stating that 'It makes any areas they exceed in, and any gaps in their development or my planning evident and I know the parents found it really useful and were keen to add their comments. It was also used as a transition form when the child started a local playgroup – 2 birds in one stone'. However the childminder also acknowledged that it was very time-consuming and that she relied very heavily on up-to-date tracking forms based on systematic observation.

CASE STUDY 2

Jennie is visiting the setting for the first time with her mum, she is 18 months old and, apart from attending a weekly stay and play session, she spends most of her time at home with mum. Mum is due to start work in two weeks' time.

During the first 10 minutes Jennie spends most of the time sat on mum's knee or standing very close to her. She sucks her fingers but looks round at the lights and toys in the room. She does look over at the practitioner on several occasions but does not respond when she asks a question. The practitioner places a few toys, including a bear, on the table. After a minute or two Jennie climbs down and touches the toys, she picks up the bear and kisses it and while still holding the bear loads the toys in and out of the basket. She passes the basket to the practitioner, quickly turns and says to mum 'go up' indicating her desire to get back on her mum's knee. Jennie kisses the bear and offers it to her mum for a kiss; she says 'kiss bear' and also offers her own face for a kiss. Jennie then remains on her mum's knee eventually falling asleep holding the bear. Reflect on the observation. How might the Key Person use this observation and apply relevant theory to support the child and reduce any risk associated with a difficult transition into the setting?

FROM RESEARCH TO PRACTICE

Observation can be a very powerful tool and in this instance a practitioner might draw on theory and research relating to transitions to support the interpretation of the data and suggest practical strategies to support the child. Brooker (2008) reminds us that transitions can have a cumulative impact on the child and can be a source of anxiety for the child and their parents. To minimise this anxiety Brooker (2008) emphasises the importance of relationships between the child, practitioner and parents. In practice the Key Person is the essential link between home and the setting and a significant form of support to the child and parents. In the case of Jennie, mum might be encouraged to stay for several sessions and to talk about Jennie. The Key Person might try to identify if Jennie has a transition object, something which is familiar, comforting and offers continuity.

Observation is an accepted and indeed expected aspect of early years practice. However it is important that practitioners continue to take a reflective approach to observation.

Different observation methods

At this stage it would be useful to consider some of the different observation methods that are available for practitioners to use. The previous examples have illustrated a narrative method of observation, arguably the most commonly used format.

REFLECTIVE PRACTICE
REFLECTIVE PRACTICE

Spend a few minutes listing the different methods of observation used in your setting.

- Which is the preferred method?
- Why do you think this is?

After completing this activity it is likely that most people will have identified the use of just one or two methods that are used on a regular basis. Discussions with practitioners suggest that the Snapshot, Photograph and Narrative methods are the most familiar as they can be used instinctively (if there is pen, paper or a camera to hand). They do not need the observer to follow any specific time scales, or to be familiar with detailed codes such as those used when completing Target Child observations. In a busy setting where time is of an essence, practitioners will naturally revert to those methods that they feel most confident in using.

The chart on the following page provides an outline of some of the most common observation techniques together with a brief description of how they can be used in practice. With all observations, particularly those that are completed spontaneously, it is important to remember to include the date and name of the child being observed to support an accurate picture to demonstrate a child's development and progress over a period of time.

Using observations effectively to understand children

The key to effective observation is the productive use of a range of these techniques when helping us to assess a child's level of development, emotional well-being and interests (to name a few). Too often time constraints mean that observations are used to inform a more generic 'tick list', such as progress against the early learning goals (DfE 2014), in order to inform the identification of the 'next steps' in a child's learning. Spend a few minutes looking at the following photograph of a young child and make a note of what you are seeing and what this can tell us about the child.

The next time you are updating a child's development records and considering areas for progression, allow time to reflect upon the different observation methods that are available. Ask yourself whether one of the alternative methods could provide a different perspective, and richer detail, when considering all facets of a child's development. For example the Tracking Method could identify which resources or activities a child visits the most often, while a Time Sample could indicate the length of time spent on different activities. When considered together, these observations could support more effective planning when reflecting on how best to support children in their next stages of learning and development. The Event Sample could be used to analyse any factors that could be contributing to behaviour that is of concern, while a Sociogram could help when planning how to help a child to become more integrated within the setting.

Table 26.1 **Different observation methods**

Snapshot	A brief, spontaneous record of what the child is doing. These observations are often used to record significant events/achievement of milestones. Post-it notes are commonly used to record the information.
Photograph	These can provide visual evidence of children's engagement (or non-engagement) in activities and also record significant events and milestones.
Time sampling	These are brief observations carried out at regular periods during an identified period of time; for example every 10 or 15 minutes. This can give practitioners a holistic overview of a child's experience, the variety of activities they engage with and range of social interactions.
Event sample (also referred to as ABC)	This method can be helpful when trying to identify the cause of repeated behaviours. A log is completed whenever a particular behaviour is observed: making a note of what was happening immediately before the behaviour (the **A**ntecedent), what occurred (the **B**ehaviour) and what happened afterwards as a result (the **C**onsequence). This can then be analysed to see if there is an underlying cause/pattern to the behaviour being observed.
Target child	This method uses a range of codes to collect data related to children's behaviour, social and emotional development and language.
Narrative	This involves watching child/ren or an activity and recording objectively everything that happens.
Tracking	Practitioners 'track' a child's movement around the setting. This could use a chart that identifies the available resources and activities that a child visits and engages with, together with the time spent. Some settings use a room plan to track the child's activity. These can be used to analyse how effectively children use the range of resources available and the time spent engaged with these activities.
Sociogram	A Sociogram records the different children/groups of children that a child interacts with during a session. This can be used to identify children who may be isolated/not part of a subgroup, or identify social groups that children are a part of, or special friendships.
Longitudinal study	A series of planned observations of one child taken over an extended period of time.
Levels of involvement	This uses a number of key factors that identify children's levels of engagement in their activities. There are five levels with level five being the highest level of involvement represented by sustained intense activity (Laevers 1996). This could be useful when analysing children's Characteristics of Effective Learning (DfE 2012) and Sustained Shared Thinking.
Checklist/Tick list	A chart that has been pre-populated with a series of key information targets such as children's skills, development milestones, progress towards the early learning goals. Staff will observe children completing different activities and 'tick' when a certain skill has been observed (DfE 2012).

Figure 26.1
A photograph of a young child.
Source: iStock

PROVOCATION

Examine a selection of observations of children. Have they been used to accurately assess the children's stage of development? Is it clear how the observation has been used to plan for the children's next steps? What evidence is there to show how the observations have been used to inform planning?

CASE STUDY 3

Staff were concerned at the regression observed in two-year-old Bella's emotional development and used an Event Sample to see if they could identify any contributory factors for this. The Event Sample showed that changes in behaviour were particularly noticeable at the beginning of the week. Discussion with her mother, who had recently separated from Bella's father, identified that Bella spent the weekends with her father before returning home to her mother on Sunday evening. Bella's Key Person was able to use the information to inform a supportive discussion with both of Bella's parents. She also borrowed a range of story books from the local library that included different family groups and used these to support Bella's understanding of her new family make-up. Staff were also more attuned to Bella's emotional development and external factors impacting upon this. How does this example relate to your understanding of current theory? How might the key person use this to support Bella and her parents?

FROM RESEARCH TO PRACTICE

Bowlby (1907-1990) was the first person to make reference to attachment theory and the impact that significant events could have on children and their families. The concept of the Key Person developed as a result of this, recognising the important role the key person can have in providing continuity of care between the setting and the home (Bruce *et al*. 2015; Jackson and Needham 2014). The EYFS (DfE 2014) has made it a statutory requirement for each child to be allocated a key person who will support the development of secure relationships between the child and their parents. These positive relationships will contribute towards the child's successful transition into the setting and ensure that individual needs are being planned for. How does your setting support children's attachment?

Ethical dilemmas

PROVOCATION 2

Imagine that you are sitting with a small group of friends engaged in conversation and someone, uninvited, sits down next to you and without speaking to you begins to observe you and make notes.

- How would you feel?
- How might you react?

You ask them what they are doing; they reply just observing, please ignore me and behave normally.

- How do you feel, what do you think?
- Do you behave normally?

Stephen Brookfield (1995) calls for the reflective practitioner to hunt out and challenge their assumptions, and that is what the provocation above is designed to do. As an adult I might have a number of reactions to this situation ranging from embarrassment, disbelief, resentment at my privacy being invaded, even anger and I doubt I would behave normally. As an adult I would be able to ask searching questions as to why I was being observed and ultimately move away. This is a rather simplistic example, nevertheless it is a reminder that the reflective practitioner should not take for granted their 'right' to observe children, and to be mindful that the act of observation can disturb a child's feelings and change their behaviour. The United Nations Convention on the Rights of the Child (UNCRC 1989) has changed the status of children, acknowledging the child's right to voice their views on matters which affect them. Papatheodorou *et al.* (2011) state unequivocally that ethical practice, which exercises the **rights** of the child, means that the child should give informed consent to be observed. This is not a straightforward process, how do you get informed consent from a one-year-old? With older children you might be able to explain what you want to do and why, but a one-off consent, a rather abstract concept would not be appropriate. Consequently, children of three, four and five years old need to be asked every time; this is known as receiving the child's assent (Papatheodorou *et al.* 2011). In turn seeking the child's assent every time may mean that their awareness of being observed is heightened and thus their behaviour changes. In practice obtaining written informed consent from the parents is often considered adequate but practitioners should still carry out observations in a way which is sensitive to, and respectful of, the rights of the child. Try to be alert to cues, both verbal and non-verbal, that mean the child does not want to be observed or that your presence is intrusive. Be culturally aware, thoughtful and open minded. There is rarely only one way of doing something or one interpretation of the data. It is possible to consider observation, or looking and listening-in, as described by Sumsion and Goodfellow (2012), as a naturalistic process which offers great insight into the world of the infant, and mirrors how children themselves learn. On balance the practitioner strives to ensure that the child being observed will not be harmed, and ultimately that the child and other children will benefit from the observations. While observing children, practitioners and

REFLECTIVE PRACTICE
REFLECTIVE PRACTICE

In addition to gaining informed consent from parents and practitioners while carrying out observations at a number of Chinese kindergartens the researcher was conscious of giving children the opportunity to agree to, or withdraw from, the observations. Laminated cards with universally recognised 'happy' and 'sad' faces, together with Chinese characters and the Pinyin form for 'yes' and 'no', were available for children to signify their consent or dissent to being observed. They had the opportunity to look at photographs that were taken and were also given the camera to take their own photographs and videos.

What ethical considerations do you consider have been addressed within this case study? What other strategies might you use to gain children's consent?

是

Wěi Yes

没有

Bù No

students may face many ethical dilemmas, which are too numerous to include here, but guidance can be sought at the British Educational Research Association (BERA) in their *Revised Ethical Guidelines for Educational Research*.

Bias in observations and why language matters

When we first meet someone, including children, we form a first impression which is often long-lasting; this is explained by 'impression formation' theory (Papatheodorou *et al.* 2011). Furthermore this theoretical framework suggests that some characteristics have a stronger effect than others and that observers can often distort the evidence to fit their first impressions and these dominant characteristics. We also tend to categorise people based on prior knowledge and, while this helps us understand and make sense of the person, problems can occur when an observer records behaviours which only fit preconceived ideas about a child. Such preconceptions might be based on knowledge about the child's family, where they live and assumptions about their upbringing, meaning that the child's **unique** characteristics are overlooked. Furthermore in becoming early years practitioners we may draw on our own **childhood** experiences. The emotional state of the observer can alter their **perceptions** of the child and their learning (Dubiel 2014). First impressions and preconceived ideas and attitudes can lead to bias in observations which the observer can guard against by being self aware and re-examining their values and beliefs. There are practical steps the observer can also take to check for and to counteract bias such as: ensuring that they record accurately the child's actions using objective, neutral language. The observer should record what they see and hear – 'look, listen and note' – while their own feelings can be recorded separately in a reflective journal. Once the observer has described objectively and in detail the child's actions, then they can begin to analyse and offer an explanation of the child's behaviour, learning and development. In the first instance the practitioner will often refer to the non-statutory guidance provided in Development Matters and the elements of effective learning (Early Education 2012) and, more recently, the Early Years Outcomes (DfE 2013) to assess children's progress towards the early learning goals (DfE 2014).

Observations should be accessible to all concerned and understood by all, including the children, parents, colleagues and other professionals. Practitioners may be called upon to share information about a child with a range of other professionals and, while it is essential that the practitioner highlights any concerns, they must provide accurate evidence based on systematic observations (Marsden *et al.* 2014). The type of language you use matters. It can lead to the generation of set responses and prejudice the way children are seen by busy professionals. Furthermore the child and parents have feelings and the words used in an observation can have a powerful and emotive impact. Practice which is attentive to the child's rights and acknowledges that the child is an expert in their own learning will seek to involve the child in their observations and the assessment process. Today this is facilitated by access to a range of digital media which can be used by the child or the practitioner to record their actions, provide evidence and importantly support dialogue. Listening to the child and if possible using their words can serve to check that the language used is understandable, accessible, less biased and sensitive to the emotional dimension. This dialogue is also key to meaningful analysis of the data and should be extended to include parents and other members of the team.It is good practice for members of the team to share observational data and discuss possible interpretations and to have an opportunity to share their feelings about the process. Deeper analysis will be informed by practitioner knowledge and understanding of a range of **contextual** elements that could have an effect upon a child's current stage of learning and development and provide a more accurate picture of the progress a child is making. Rogoff (2003) explores in greater detail the impact of culture on children's lives while Hedegaard (2009) reflects on a diverse range of theories available to help us make sense of children's learning.

Observing practice and the role of shared observations

Observation in the early years is not confined to the observation of children. In the same way that practitioners gain valuable information about children through the observation process, the effectiveness of the early year's environment, activities and practitioner interaction can be similarly informed through peer observation. This is reflected in the revised early years inspection framework which encourages joint observations between the inspector and the setting (Ofsted 2014a; 2015). The opportunity for shared professional **discourse** on observed practice can inform on the effectiveness of the setting in recognising its strengths and areas for development and, through analysis, demonstrate a realistic understanding of how to further develop existing practice (Ofsted 2014a); the role of supervision was also formalised in the revised EYFS (DfE 2012). 'High-quality professional supervision is provided, based on consistent and sharply focused evaluations of the impact of staff's practice' (Ofsted 2013, p. 16).

REFLECTIVE PRACTICE
REFLECTIVE PRACTICE

How prepared are you and/or your setting for making the most effective use of the opportunity that shared observations provides? How often does peer observation take place in your setting? How is feedback given? How is this used to inform the setting's self-assessment? Do you provide allocated time where you can share observations, discuss assessments and plan for individual children's learning? Are resources for observations readily available to staff, e.g. post-it notes, observation sheets, writing tools, cameras? How do you ensure that all areas of learning are being observed over time? How are observations and assessment monitored within the setting?

Effective practice is linked to outstanding **leadership** and management where senior staff have a realistic understanding of the setting and its strengths and areas for development. This should be informed by reflection on traditional observations of staff and children, or more informal 'learning walks' followed by a professional conversation with staff involved in the observed activity/routine. The following questions could be used to prompt/support such discussion:

- How do you think that session/activity went?
- What did you intend for the children to learn from this activity? Do you think the activity was successful? What has/ve the child/ren learned?

- Why did you choose that activity? (Was it developmentally appropriate ... for all levels of children?)
- How was it adapted for different needs and ages of children?
- How did you think the children benefited?
- Was the outcome different from what you expected? Why?
- How is this going to inform planning for the next steps in children's learning?
- What would you identify as the strengths and weaknesses of the session/activity?
- What feedback would you give to staff to support them in developing their practice?

Conclusion

There can be no doubt that observation is fundamental to supporting accurate and informed understanding of children's current stage of learning and development. This cannot be allowed to override ethical considerations and you have been prompted to reflect on some of the ethical implications when observing children within their environment. You have also considered some of the different observation methods that are available and been encouraged to engage with these to support a more holistic understanding of children's development. Finally there has been the opportunity to consider the implications for settings in putting into place effective systems to ensure accurate self-assessment and self-evaluation.

Further reading

Elfer, P. (2005) *Observation Matters* in Abbott, L. and Langston, A. (eds) *Birth to Three Matters: Supporting the Framework of Effective Practice*. Maidenhead: Open University Press.
Peter Elfer explores the emotional dimensions of observing young children and explains the Tavistock method of observation.

Hedegaard, M. (2009) Children's Development from a Cultural–Historical Approach: Children's Activity in Everyday Local Settings as Foundation for Their Development. In *Mind, Culture, and Activity*, 16: 64–81.
This article explores childhood theories linking these to practice; includes examples of observations and discussions.

Useful websites

http://ecrp.uiuc.edu/v7n2/forman.html
Forman, G. and Hall, E. (2009) Wondering with Children: The Importance of Observation in Early Education, in *Early Childhood Research and Practice* 7(2) [online]. Available from [accessed 12 March 2014].
This article explores the role of observation in understanding children's learning and provides short video clips to support discussion and develop understanding.

www.ioe.ac.uk/EPPSE_epublications_April2013_-_new_links.pdf
Effective Pre-school, Primary and Secondary Education (EPPSE) Project (1997–2013) [accessed 12 March 2014].
This site provides a list of additional sources of information and a useful publication list linked to EPPE and EPSE projects.

www.sirenfilms.co.uk
Siren Films offer some free content, videos and articles plus DVDs to purchase showing children's learning and development which offer opportunities to practise observation.

References

Andrews, M. (2013) *Exploring Play for Early Childhood Studies*. London: Sage.

Brooker, L. (2008) *Supporting Transitions in the Early Years*. Maidenhead: Open University Press.

Brookfield, S. (1995) Becoming a critically reflective teacher. San Francisco: Jossey-Bass.

Bruce, T., Louis, S. and McCall, G. (2015) *Observing Young Children*. London: Sage.

CWDC (2009) [online] Available from: http://webarchive.nationalarchives.gov.uk/20091118212822/cwd council.org.uk/eyps [accessed 22 March 2014].

DfE (2014) Statutory Framework for the Early Years Foundation Stage. Cheshire: DfE.

DfE (2013) *Early Years Outcomes. A non-statutory guide for practitioners and inspectors to help inform understanding of child development through the early years* [online] available from: www.foundation years.org.uk/files/2012/03/Early_Years_Outcomes.pdf [accessed 12 March 2014].

DfE (2012) *Statutory Framework for the Early Years Foundation Stage*. Cheshire: DfE.

DfE and DoH (2011) *Supporting Families in the Foundation Years*. London: DfE and DoH.

Dubiel, J. (2014) Effective assessment in the early years foundation stage. London: Sage.

Early Education (2012) *Development Matters in the Early Years Foundation Stage* (EYFS). London: Early Education.

Early Years Teacher (2013) [online] Available from: www.education.gov.uk/childrenandyoungpeople/early learningandchildcare/h00201345/eyitt/graduate-leaders/eyps/eligibility [accessed 21 March 2014].

Glazzard, J., Chadwick, D., Webster, A. and Percival, J. (2010) *Assessment for Learning in the Early Years Foundation Stage*. London: Sage.

Hedegaard, M. (2009) Children's Development from a Cultural–Historical Approach: Children's Activity in Everyday Local Settings as Foundation for Their Development. In *Mind, Culture, and Activity*, 16: 64-81.

Jackson, D. and Needham, M. (2014) *Engaging with Parents in Early Years Settings*. London: Sage.

Laevers, F. (1996) The concept of involvement and the Leuven Involvement Scale: an analysis of critical reflections. In: Laevers F. (ed.) *An exploration of the concept of involvement as an indicator for quality in early childhood care and education*. (Cidree vol. 10.) Dundee: CIDREE (Consortium of Institutions for Development and Research in Education in Europe) pp. 59-72.

Leuven Scale of Well-being and Involvement [online] available from: www.tes.co.uk/teaching-resource/Well-being-and-Involvement-Leuven-Scale-6340990/.

Marsden, F., McMahon, S. and Youde, A. (2014) Interagency Working, Observation and Assessment, in Reid, J., and Burton, S. (eds) *Safeguarding and Protecting Children in the Early Years*. London: Routledge.

Nutbrown, C. (2012) *Foundations For Quality*. Cheshire: Crown Publications.

Nutbrown, C. and Clough, P. (2014) *Early Childhood Education: History, Philosophy and Experience*. London: Sage.

Ofsted (2015) Early Years Inspection Handbook [online] Available from: https://www.gov.uk/government/publications/early-years-inspection-handbook-from-september-2015 [accessed 7 November 2015].

Ofsted (2014a) *Conducting Early Years Inspections* [online] Available from: www.gov.uk/government/uploads/system/uploads/attachment_data/file/379137/Conducting_20early_20years_20inspections_20from_20 September_202014.pdf [accessed 31 December 2014].

Ofsted (2014b) *Evaluation Schedule for Inspections of Registered Early Years Provision* [online] Available from: www.gov.uk/government/uploads/system/uploads/attachment_data/file/379123/Evaluation_20schedule_20for_20inspections_20of_20registered_20early_20years_20provision_20from_20September_202014.pdf [accessed 31 December 2014].

Ofsted (2013) *Evaluation Schedule for Inspection of Registered Early Years Provision* [online]. Available from: www.ofsted.gov.uk/resources/120086 [accessed 12 March 2014].

Papatheodorou, T., Luff, P. with Gill, J. (2011) *Child Observation for Learning and Research*. Essex: Pearson Education.

Rogoff, B. (2003) *The Cultural Nature of Human Development* (Reprint) USA: OUP.

Sumsion, J. and Goodfellow, J. (2012) 'Looking and Listening in': a methodological approach to generating insights into experiences of early childhood education and care settings, in *European Early Childhood Education Research Journal* 20(3) pp. 313–327.

Sylva, K., Melhuish E., Sammons P., Siraj-Blatchford I. and Taggart B. (2004) *The Effective Provision of Pre-School Education (EPPE) Project: Findings from the Early Primary Years* [online] Available from: www.ioe.ac.uk/RB_Findings_from_early_primary(1).pdf [accessed 12 March 2014].

Tickell, C. (2011) *The Early Years: Foundations for Life, Health and Learning.* London: DfE.

UNCRC (1989) United Nations Convention on the Rights of the Child [online] Available from: www.unicef.org.uk/Documents/Publication-pdfs/UNCRC_PRESS200910web.pdf [accessed 21 March 2014].

27 Leadership

Shan Lockwood

LEARNING OUTCOMES

After reading this chapter you will:

✔ Understand why leadership is important.
✔ What the characteristics of an effective leader are.
✔ The differences between a leader and manager.
✔ How a team can be developed and motivated.
✔ How to deal with conflict and change.

Introduction

This chapter aims to encourage you to look at different models of **leadership**. By the end of the chapter you should have a clear understanding of leadership in early years and the skills, qualities and attributes needed to be a successful leader. Additionally you will be encouraged to consider how to develop effective leadership to motivate and inspire others to develop quality practice. Current leadership roles in early years have distinct characteristics and need a wide variety of skills, including collaboration, the development of pedagogy and a shared vision (Kagan, 1994). We shall reflect on particular problems within our sector, including the reluctance of some to take on the role of leader and the lack of **professional status**. Nevertheless, due to the disparate nature of the role and the diverse but challenging responsibilities, the early years sector requires well trained and visionary leadership.

Why is leadership so important?

Leadership is an important area of study because of its link to effective provision. Research projects such as *The Effective Provisions on Pre-School Education* (EPPE) (Sylva et al., 2004), *Researching Effective Pedagogy in Early Years* (REPEY) (Siraj-Blatchford et al., 2002) and *Effective Leadership in the Early Years Sector* (ELEYS) (Siraj-Blatchford and Manni, 2006) have identified that efficient and successful leadership is essential to the delivery of quality provision because 'children made better all-round progress in settings where: there was strong leadership and relatively little staff turnover' (Blatchford and Manni, 2006: 6). Therefore to improve practice as a current or potential leader it is essential that you consider the skills necessary to be successful in that role.

The difference between leadership and management

Bennis (1989) suggested that there are some significant differences which characterise these roles. He proposed that a **manager** administers, maintains the current systems, has a short-term view and relies on control of staff whereas a leader innovates, inspires trust through focusing on people and considers the long-term development of the setting, thus challenging the **status quo**. Smith and Langstone (1999) draw similar conclusions, describing the manager as someone who controls but accepts current practice and the leader as an individual who **motivates** and initiates change. Additionally Law and Glover (2000) compare the two roles by suggesting that managers plan, organise and control, whereas leaders give direction, offer inspiration and build a team through collaboration. Rodd suggests that the roles are 'inherently linked and interwoven' (2006: 21) but those taking on leadership roles do need to be able to inspire others and take the setting forward.

> ## REFLECTIVE PRACTICE
> REFLECTIVE PRACTICE
>
> Reflect on the individual roles in your setting.
>
> - Can you identify individuals who manage and those who lead?
> - Do they reflect the above characteristics?

Distinctive features of Early Years leadership

Differences

Some of the attributes necessary for successful work in early years are similar to those needed by any leader, for example the ability to care for and develop other people. However, Solly (2003) suggested that the female character of the sector leads to warm and kind leadership focusing on advocacy, passion, inspiration and team **ethos**, quite different from one based on **hierarchy** and power. Leadership in early years involves inspiring others with a **vision**, a capacity for **reflection** and dedication to provide the best quality care and education. Morgan (1997) described leadership as being **multi-faceted,** involving **reciprocal** relationships highlighting the ability to promote collaboration and teamwork. Additionally early years leaders need to have the ability to interpret **legislation** and guidance into effective practice requiring high level skills and understanding. This is why Nutbrown (2012) and Sylva *et al.* (2004) strongly argue that well qualified practitioners who have high levels of pedagogical awareness and who can guide others are essential in developing quality early years education and care.

Challenges

The challenges of leadership in early years are also diverse. The range of teams for which a leader may be responsible could be wide-ranging. Pilcher (2009) identified that teams in early years may include the childcare providers themselves, partners such as other **agencies** (such as social services), parents and children. The skills required to work in such an extensive range of teams are significant, particularly when working in a multi-agency manner and with individuals who may have completely different professional values and priorities. The female nature of the sector may actually be beneficial. Scrivens cites Shakeshaft's work (1987/89), 'women's leadership style tends to be more **democratic** and participatory' (Scrivens, 2002 cited in Siraj-Blatchford and Manni, 2006: 13).

However, other issues have been identified as being problematic, such as lack of consistency in leadership effectiveness (Siraj-Blatchford and Manni, 2006: 4) as well as there being a general reluctance to take on such roles. Rodd (1997) argued this reluctance may stem from the fact that early years staff are ill-prepared to take on such complex leadership roles. Waniganayake *et al.* (2000) suggested that early years practitioners found managing other adults more difficult as their training is directed at skills in managing children. A supplementary problem for early years settings is that many who do complete further training do not stay in early years but move into education, as Taggart *et al.* (2000) identified, exacerbating the problem of access to experienced and encouraging role models.

REFLECTIVE PRACTICE

- Have you identified any distinct characteristics of leaders in early years?
- Do you feel the members of staff in your setting are willing and prepared to take on leadership roles?
- What would enable staff to take on extra responsibilities?
- What might the barriers be to taking on leadership roles?

Models of leadership

Leadership models

There is a range of leadership models that consider leadership from different perspectives.

Table 27.1

Theory	Description
Shared /participatory leadership	Holistic style of management requiring respect and trust among the team to enable shared responsibility. Generally collaborative in style because the group is more important than the individual, but some individuals may need to lead in particular situations.

Theory	Description
Transformational leadership	Individuals are motivated by emotional or affective rather than intellectual factors. However this is a highly empowering model because it encourages individuals to take responsibility for making their own decisions.
Distributive leadership	Several people can simultaneously fulfil a leadership role in the same early childhood pre-school setting.
Contextual leadership	The most effective leadership style depends on the context of the situation. Therefore different styles are necessary: • Community leadership • Pedagogical leadership • Administrative leadership • Advocacy leadership • Conceptual leadership

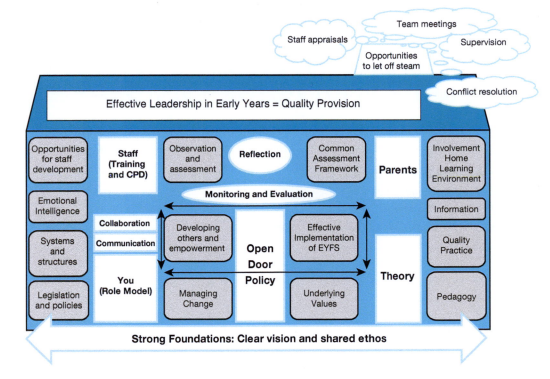

Figure 27.1 House

This model of leadership was devised by the BA (top-up) students as a model of leadership and the skills required. They felt that having a clear ethos was the foundation to effective leadership. Can you draw your own image of leadership in early years reflecting on the complexity of the role?

Distributed leadership

Many individuals see the role of a leader similar to Mullin's (1993) authoritarian leader who holds the power and makes all the decisions. However, there is now a move towards a more collective vision of leadership because, as Siraj-Blatchford and Manni (2006) identified, the most effective settings are those with a shared ethos challenging the view that authority is always linked to power. Distributed leadership defines leadership in terms of 'influence' (Rodd, 2006: 17) which may then help make leadership seem more accessible and help overcome an individual's reluctance to take on such roles. Osgood (2004, 2006) supports this type of leadership because it leads to more collaborative strategies which are more likely to develop high levels of **professionalism** and promote inclusion. However, distributed leadership may not be a simple remedy to improving quality unless a commitment is made to increasing expertise as 'it may be irresponsible for the manager to delegate too much responsibility' (Siraj-Blatchford and Manni, 2006: 21) where staff may be young, inexperienced and under-qualified. However, although the new Early Years Educator qualification does not make any specific reference to leadership it does emphasise the importance of 'continued professional development to improve own skills and early years practice' (NCTL, 2013a: 7) and additionally the Early Years Teacher qualification highlights the need to 'Take responsibility for leading practice through appropriate professional development for self and colleagues' (NCTL, 2013b: 5), so this may change.

REFLECTIVE PRACTICE
REFLECTIVE PRACTICE

Early years settings already have distributed leadership by having designated practitioners responsible for special educational needs, behaviour management and **safeguarding**.

- Do you think this system works?
- What are the benefits?
- What are the problems?
- How does your setting address these issues?

Desirable skills, qualities and attributes of a leader in Early Years

Personal qualities

Many feel leaders need to be powerful, dynamic and 'larger than life' characters but this **perception**, which Meindl (1995) calls the 'romance of leadership', may add to practitioners' hesitancy in taking on such roles. However, the main quality needed by any leader is to lead and motivate others, 'to get others to do what the leader wants because they want to do it' (Rodd, 2006: 11). Therefore the emphasis should be on the development and **empowerment** of others rather than on the leaders themselves. One of the most important attributes of a leader is having a clear vision for the team and the ability to develop a shared ethos with both staff and parents (Daly *et al.*, 2004).

REFLECTIVE PRACTICE
REFLECTIVE PRACTICE

- Do you feel all leaders need to be dynamic?
- Would this perception prevent you from applying for a promotion?
- How do you think your setting could encourage more staff to take on leadership roles?

Vision

The role of any leader is to lead a team forward and motivate them to achieve their full potential and support children and families effectively. In early years this would undoubtedly mean leading a team to offer quality childcare provision. Thus any leader in the early years sector must have a clear vision of what is meant by quality care and education (Siraj-Blatchford and Manni, 2006). Additionally, Sylva *et al.* (2004) identified that the most effective settings were those who had a shared ethos that was clearly communicated with both staff and parents. It is this set of principles or beliefs that brings staff together and informs every aspect of practice with everyone working to the same aim. This philosophy will usually be developed as the team is formed and storming and norming take place (Tuckman and Jensen, 1977).

Team development

An effective leader needs to be aware of the type of team they are managing but also the stage their team is at in order to help them work cohesively and successfully. Tuckman and Jensen (1977) identified that teams are evolutionary and go through different stages in their development. These stages are:

- *Forming*: This describes how the team comes together, gets to know each other and plans how to work together. This means team leaders need to develop a listening culture where individuals can speak freely and honestly. At this stage the team needs to learn how to deal with differences and therefore may rely heavily on guidance.
- *Storming*: This is where the team engages in discussion, reflect on their work, perhaps even challenging each other in order to develop the shared ethos which should bring them together. This stage may have to deal with **conflict** so the leader needs skills such as conflict resolution.
- *Norming:* At this stage the team should settle down and pull together under the shared vision.
- *Performing:* This is where the team fulfils its roles and responsibilities and starts functioning.

The team may have to revert to earlier stages at times of change, for example if a new member of staff joins the team or a new form of practice is introduced. Daly *et al.* (2004) suggest that there are characteristics of an effective team, including: a sense of purpose, a balance of roles within the team, commitment from team members and effective leadership and good communication. Thus a leader needs to develop all these skills to support and develop efficient team work in their setting. Edgington (2004) highlights the need for a leader to be aware of the type of team they are managing because it will affect the behaviour of the individuals involved.

- *The rigorous and challenging team* can be analytical and respond to changes well. However they may never be satisfied and therefore the leader may have to manage dissatisfaction within the team and individuals not feeling valued.
- *The turbulent team* may appear to be meeting its aims but the leader may have to manage unresolved conflict because the turbulence in the team may make cohesiveness difficult.
- *The cosy team* appear to get on well together and may have been together a long time and know each other very well. However, this is a team that may make it difficult for a new manager or leader in particular to establish any new ways of working because they are unable to reflect critically.

Additionally Belbin (1981) argues that for a team to work successfully together they need to be well balanced fulfilling a range of roles, including:

- *Action-orientated roles*, like the shaper who keeps on task, the implementer, and completer/finisher to meet deadlines
- *People-orientated roles* like the co-ordinator who pulls it together, the team-worker who is supportive to others, and resource investigator who brings people together
- *Cerebral roles* like the planter who is creative but not good at detail, the monitor evaluator for detail and analysis, and the specialist for particular knowledge and skills

Therefore when recruiting or developing their team a leader can use Belbin's team role reports to develop a well-balanced team. However, they must also be careful not to stereotype individuals into certain roles which may limit their development, highlighting the importance of professional judgement in an effective leader.

For more information on Belbin: www.belbin.com/

Collaboration

Leaders need to be able to develop collaborative ways of working with others and build a culture where change is seen as exciting and motivating. Rodd outlines the complexity of the role highlighting that they need the ability to 'balance concern for work, task, quality and productivity with concern for people, relationships, satisfaction and morale' (2006: 12) reflecting Adair's theory (1987) that effective leaders balance the needs of the task, the individuals involved and the team to avoid frustration and be successful.

Bloom (2000), cited in Dunlop (2008), suggested that leaders need to have knowledge of a range of subjects including organisational theory, child development and pedagogy. Additionally they require technical, human and **conceptual** skills and a clear moral purpose. Furthermore they need to be responsive to everyone they deal with, including parents, staff and other professionals, requiring high-level communication skills. Bloom and Bella (2003) describe this diversity as a cluster of required skills such as interpersonal, communication, group facilitation, for example facilitating meetings, staff development and the ability to make decisions.

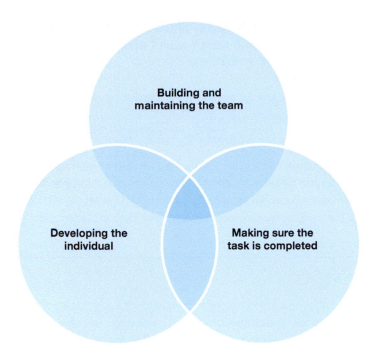

Figure 27.2 Adair's model for teamwork. This diagram illustrates that a leader needs to be aware of the needs of the team and the individual in order to complete the task and therefore needs a clear vision and strategy.

Context

Southworth (1998) highlights the need for situational leadership, which means that any leader must have a good understanding of the context in which they are working. This **contextual** literacy helps leaders to understand the dynamic nature of the sector and the diverse and fluctuating nature of the circumstances they are required to work in. Thus leaders in early years are faced with many challenges from implementing new legislation, curricula and ever-changing **social policy** while maintaining staff morale and motivation. Siraj-Blatchford and Manni argue that leaders also need to support staff in overcoming their resistance to change (2006: 17) as the ability to accept and be motivated by change is one of the characteristics of an effective setting. Thus early years leaders need to engage with social policy so they can clearly articulate any need for change so staff have a clear idea of the way forward.

Emotional intelligence

Emotional intelligence (Goleman, 1996) is an essential characteristic of an effective leader because they need to be self-aware but also have empathy with their team as this leads to more effective and productive relationships. This may be important in the day-to-day management of a setting but is absolutely essential when leading in a period of change. Behaviour is a function of personality and social context, and when people are in a challenging situation they revert to deep-seated behaviour patterns, often making them more difficult to manage. Emotional intelligence is also related to **reflective practice** which helps a leader develop a more realistic perception of situations and therefore manage more effectively.

FROM RESEARCH TO PRACTICE

Emotional Intelligence may be used during supervision with staff because 'supervision should foster a culture of mutual support, teamwork and continuous improvement, which encourages the confidential discussion of sensitive issues' (DfE, 2014: 20). In order for staff to 'open up' during supervision the leader needs to have empathy with their situation and be approachable.

Motivation

Motivating staff is an important skill but there are many theories to consider. In order to help employees reach their full potential, Maslow's *Hierarchy of Needs* (1943) suggested that leaders and managers need to meet their team's **physiological** and basic needs first through having a comfortable and safe working environment where they feel they belong and are valued. Additionally Herzberg (1959) agreed that members of staff are motivated by recognition and opportunities for self-development. This may support the case for distributed or shared leadership which allows individuals to take on more responsibility and gain satisfaction from increased achievement. This is also supported by McGregor's 'Y theory' (1960), which states that individuals naturally seek responsibility because they are motivated by self-fulfilment.

ACTIVITY

Self-assessment questionnaire: Are you a good leader?

- www.mindtools.com/pages/article/newLDR_50.htm
- You can take part in this on-line quiz by clicking on those statements that describe you to identify what you already do well.

Dealing with conflict

Conflict can arise from a range of different aspects of practice but is particularly prevalent at times of change, and as early years is constantly changing as a sector this then becomes an important issue. Conflict is not necessarily a negative factor as it can be creative and a dynamic force in the process of change, however it also needs to be addressed so it does not undermine practice.

Strategies such as team meetings, staff **appraisals**, coaching and supervision (see Chapter 28) can be used to address conflict. Leaders need to be aware of their central role in developing the culture of the setting. Dickins describes a listening culture as somewhere that 'practitioners and managers value the importance of listening' (2010: 1). To develop such a culture a leader needs to use an open style of management, develop a no blame culture where individuals feel safe to experiment, be a good role model in their own listening skills and develop collaborative and reflective ways of working.

Conflict resolution is essential to effective management (Boardman, 2003). Thomas and Kilmann's (1974) conflict mode instrument helps you identify how you usually respond to conflict.

Table 27.2 **Thomas and Kilmann's (1974) conflict mode instrument**

		Yes	No
1	Know what you want and take a firm stand?		
2	Try to meet everyone's needs, co-operate effectively but also try to be assertive?		
3	Try to encourage individuals to partially give in so everyone has some form of satisfaction?		
4	Be willing to meet the needs of others at the expense of your own?		
5	Avoid conflict where possible?		

1 If you answered yes to Question 1 you may tend towards a competitive style which may leave people feeling bruised or resentful. However it may be necessary in urgent situations.
2 If you answered yes to Question 2 you tend to have a collaborative style which collates a variety of viewpoints in order to identify the most effective solution.
3 If you answered yes to Question 3 you tend to use a compromising style which may partially satisfy everyone and may be the only solution when a situation is at a standstill or there is an urgent time frame.
4 If you answered yes to Question 4 you tend to have an accommodating style where you know when it is necessary to be co-operative for the good of the team and sometimes surrender your own position. However, this may not lead to the best outcomes as individuals may not respect your concession.
5 If you answered yes to Question 5 you tend to have an avoiding style where you might delegate controversial decisions because you do not want to offend or upset anyone. Although this may not matter if the situation is trivial or someone else can solve the issue, it is usually seen as weak when other individuals try to take advantage which could lead to more conflict in the long term.

Conflict resolution involves a range of strategies and the most effective will depend on the situation concerned. However, it is usually best to address the situation, gather information and include others in identifying solutions and then negotiate the most effective procedure.

Leadership of practice and its challenges

Developing leadership within the sector

One of the most significant dilemmas we are faced with in early years is how we can encourage more individuals to embrace the challenges of additional responsibility in a profession which has low status, poor pay and limited expectations of staff in terms of qualifications and training. Nutbrown recommended that by September 2022, all staff (counting in adult-child ratios) should be qualified to Level 3 and there should be an increase in graduate pedagogical leadership. Additionally, Sylva et al. (2004) identified a clear link between good practice and high levels of training so the debate about leadership needs to take into account social policy and legislation. Current policy with a lack of commitment to increasing qualification requirements is a clear barrier to professional development. Additionally, greater **accountability** by government may cause a reluctance to 'let go', placing more emphasis on the managerial role (Webb, 2005) and limiting creativity within early years. Furthermore, such a focus may lead to dissatisfaction because early years workers are mainly motivated by their contact with the children, parents and staff (Siraj-Blatchford and Manni, 2006; Jeffery and Troman, 2004). However, investing in training and leadership may allow the sharing of administrative duties and increase achievement to enthuse leaders further (Rodd, 1997). There does seem to be a move towards this as the Early Years Teacher Standards state that one of the roles is to 'take a lead in establishing a culture of cooperative working . . . and support and lead other practitioners including Early Years Educators' (NCTL, 2013a: 5).

It is possible for other members of the team to take on leadership roles, perhaps leading a change in provision. Certainly, as a tutor on the degree programme, I have witnessed first-hand how students have led various research projects which have resulted in changes to practice. Hard (2004) has identified the importance of both formal leaders, who are recognised because of their position, and informal leaders, who may just show leadership qualities motivating their team to develop.

CASE STUDY 1

This is a discussion about leadership in early years that took place in an Fda (Foundation Degree in Young Children's Learning and Development) meeting.

S1   A good leader is someone who can support staff, is able to accommodate their needs and listen to them. However, sometimes this is hard when you are only the manager and the owners, who have no childcare experience, undermine your decisions.

S2   I agree, good leaders value their staff.

S3   Yes, an effective leader is someone who is able to build a team and they can do this by delegating more because this gives you more confidence.

S4   Yes, I agree, but you have to make sure that everyone is clear on their roles and responsibilities because one of the things that leads to conflict is people not fulfilling their roles, for example, not completing their learning journeys. In that case leaders do need to take action as if they don't deal with problems they just get worse.

S1 In my setting when I became manager I set up a green/amber and red monitoring and evaluation tool for that situation. Observations and assessments are reviewed every month and if staff are not up to date they go on amber and are given help and support where necessary. They are set a target to get up to date and then if they don't meet it they go on red and disciplinary action is started.

S2 Yes, I agree, but also managers need to listen to staff as sometimes they may have problems at home.

S3 One of the problems in my nursery is when staff back-bite about each other. Many of them are young and haven't done a lot of training since they finished college. Some have got no qualifications and so they don't have the same understanding about what effect this can have on staff and children.

S5 At our pre-school because we have a lot of older staff who don't want to do any more training because they just see it as a job that fits in with the family. Some staff form cliques which exclude the others and stop us from moving forward.

S2 Sometimes it can be frustrating though when you come back from college with all these ideas and no-one is willing to support you in changing things because 'it is too much hassle and other people won't like it'.

- What issues does this focus group meeting highlight?
- Can you think of any ways the students could change the situation using theory already discussed?
- Is there any evidence within current government policy that the situation is about to change?

Developing a strong team

The main challenge of leadership in early years is how to lead a team forward effectively and inclusively. Many of my Fda and BA top-up students are very concerned that when Ofsted come to inspect they are often judged on their weakest member of the team, confirming to them the old saying that 'a team is only as strong as its weakest link'. Nutbrown (2012) highlights the need for early years workers to develop confidence in their own practice, their ability to engage with other professionals and their skills of pedagogical leadership develop. Therefore leaders need to have a good understanding of both motivation and reflective practice in order to develop a strong and cohesive team, particularly at a time when only fifty per cent of the team need to be qualified (DfE, 2014: 20).

Leading change

Early years practice is constantly developing, so 'change management' (Andrews, 2009) is an essential skill of any leader in the sector. The type of change being experienced may dictate the type of leadership required. Rodd (2006) describes six key types of change: incremental, induced, routine, crisis, innovative and **transformational**. Sometimes at a time of crisis a leader may have no other option but to use an authoritarian style of management, but they still need to use their emotional intelligence to be aware of the potential impact on staff. Some members of staff may react to change with fear, disbelief and concern whereas others may see it as an opportunity to develop. Fullan (2005) highlights the need for positivity as negativity can be '**debilitating**' (2005: 16) and advocates using change as an opportunity for personal development. However, in order to achieve this it is essential to develop a 'no blame' culture where there are 'leaders at all levels'. In fact many (Aubrey, 2011 and Siraj-Blatchford and Manni, 2006) argue that the most effective leaders are those who encourage a culture of change, while Rodd (2006) and Aubrey (2011) highlight the need for staff consultation, regular reviews of working practices and decision-sharing to reduce any potential resistance.

CASE STUDY 2

You have just been appointed a manager of a setting which has a 'Cosy Team' which has been together a long time. You wish to introduce some changes to their working practices. How would you approach this situation and motivate them to help you implement this change?

Commitment to Continuing Professional Development (CPD)

One of the tools open to an effective leader is that of **Continuing Professional Development**. The Statutory Framework for the Early Years Foundation Stage (EYFS) (2014) supports the idea of a highly skilled workforce:

> Providers must support staff to undertake appropriate training and professional develop-ment opportunities to ensure they offer quality learning and development experiences for children.

> (DfE, 2014: 20)

Siraj-Blatchford and Manni (2006: 19) highlighted the importance of monitoring and appraisal because it allowed the identification of 'the strengths and limitations of the staff' which also allowed 'on-going support' to staff 'who had been given extra responsibility' (2006: 21). Supervision is also an effective support strategy to enable staff to manage the emotional stress involved in such a complex and demanding role (see Chapter 28).

Gaining appropriate qualifications is an important element in developing leadership skills because the ELEYS project identified that the most effective settings were those where 'a good proportion of the staff were (graduate- or teacher-) qualified' (Siraj-Blatchford and Manni, 2006: 6). This is also linked to other necessary characteristics such as reflection and high levels of **articulation**. The government has just announced its new Level 3 Early Years Educator

PROVOCATION

'A number of survey respondents were in favour of these tougher early years entry requirements as they felt they would help raise the overall standard of early years practitioners and boost the profile of the early years as a professional sector.'

(Hawthorne, 2014: 37)

- Do you agree? Will higher qualifications lead to better leadership?
- After reading *More Great Childcare* (Truss, 2013) do you feel the government is committed to raising the quality of the workforce?
- What are their dilemmas?

qualification which requires students to have a C in English and Maths at GCSE and an Early Years Teacher qualification as recommended by Nutbrown (2012). This may help improve the **professional status** of Early Years practitioners if the requirement is then reflected in the Statutory Framework of the Early Years Foundation Stage.

Engagement in social policy

Another challenge for Early Years leaders is to engage in the development of the profession. Professionalism relates to more than just having certain skills, competence and expertise, it also refers to how the role is perceived in society. However, promoting a professional image for Early Years workers has been problematic. As Angela Nurse identifies, practitioners come from 'a much wider educational and social background' (2007: 3) and do not fit the traditional image of a professional. Thus the debate about professionalism in early years has to be placed in the context of social policy within the UK and the continued reluctance of governments to support a clear career structure.

Conclusion

There is no denying that leadership in early years is challenging but at the same time it can be stimulating and rewarding. Leaders need to be able to manage people effectively but also have a thorough knowledge of pedagogy in order to articulate it coherently to others to engage and motivate their staff team. However, as a sector we cannot develop a professional status on our own. We need a commitment from Government to increase expectations, and thus **engagement** in social policy can be seen to be an essential requirement for those committed to good practice. As Hawthorne argues 'consulting with the early years sector should be the first step of policy development, not the last' (2014: 53).

Further reading

Nutbrown, C. (2012) *Foundations for Quality: An Independent Review of Early Education and Childcare Qualifications Final Report.* Runcorn: Department of Education.
Based on extensive consultation a structured argument is provided about why there is a need to improve the level of qualifications within early years.

Rodd, G. (2006) *Leadership in Early Childhood* (3rd edn) Maidenhead: Open University Press.
A classic text with a clear outline of leadership theory and advice and support to those taking on leadership roles.

Siraj-Blatchford, I. and Manni, L. (2006) *Effective Leadership in the Early Years Sector (The ELEYS Study)* London: Institute of Education, University of London.
A summary of information from settings which have been judged to be effective and which explore the concept of leadership from 'the bottom up'.

Useful websites

www.gov.uk/government/organisations/national-college-for-teaching-and-leadership
The National College for Teaching and Leadership offers advice and support for those leading both schools and early years settings. They aim to improve the quality of the education workforce. The change facilitator's handbook also offers useful advice about how to implement change successfully.

www.ncb.org.uk/areas-of-activity/early-childhood/resources/publications/leadership-and-quality-improvement
The National Children's Board provides some clear, well written resources on effective leadership.

www.foundationyears.org.uk/eyfs-statutory-framework/
Contains excellent links to many area of early years practice.

References

Adair, J. (1987) *Not Bosses but Leaders*, London: Kogan Page.

Andrews, M. (2009) 'Managing change and pedagogical leadership', in Robins, A. and Callan, S. *Managing Early Years Settings*, London: Sage.

Aubrey, C. (2011) *Leading and Managing in the Early Years*, London: Sage.

Belbin, R. M. (1981) *Management Teams: Why They Succeed Or Fail*, London: Butterworth, Heinemann.

Bennis, W. (1989*) On Becoming a Leader*, Cambridge: Perseus Books.

Benson, L. (2010) 'Leading and managing others', in Bruce, T. *Early Childhood: A Guide for Students,* London: Sage.

Bloom, P.J. and Bella, J. (2003) 'Investment in leadership training: The payoff for early childhood education', in *Young Children*, 60(1), pp. 32–40.

Boardman, M. (2003) 'Changing times: Changing challenges for early childhood leaders', *Australian Journal of Early Childhood*, (28)2, pp. 20–25.

Daly, M., Byers, E. and Taylor, W. (2004) *Early Years Management in Practice*, Oxford: Heinemann.

Department for Education (DfE) (2014) *The Statutory Framework for the Early Years Foundation Stage: Setting the standards for learning, development and care for children from birth to five,* Runcorn: Department for Education.

Dickins, M. (2010) *Leadership for Listening*, London: National Children's Board.

Dunlop, A.W. (2008) *A Literature Review on Leadership in the Early Years* [online] Available at: www.educationscotland.gov.uk/resources/a/leadershipreview [accessed 2 September 2015].

Ebbeck, M. and Waniganayake (2003) *Early Childhood Professionals: Leading Today and Tomorrow,* Sydney: MacLennan & Petty.

Edgington, M. (2004) *The Foundation Stage Teacher in Action* (3rd edn), London: Paul Chapman Publishing.

Fullan, M. (2008) *The Six Secrets of Change: What the Best Leaders Do to Help their Organisations Survive and Thrive,* San Francisco: Jossey-Bass.

Goleman, D. (1996) *Emotional Intelligence: Why it Can Matter More Than IQ,* London: Bloomsbury.

Hard, L. (2004) 'How is leadership understood in early childhood education and care?', *Journal of Australian Research in Early Childhood Education,* 11(1), pp. 123-131.

Hawthorne, S. (2014) *Early Years Agenda: Interim Report,* London: Pre-School Learning Alliance.

Herzberg, F. (1959) *The Motivation to Work,* New York: Wiley.

Jeffery, B. and Troman, G. (2004) 'Time for ethnography', *British Educational Research Journal,* 30(4) pp. 535-548.

Kagan, S.L. (1994) 'Leadership: rethinking it – making it happen', *Young Children,* 49(5), pp. 50-54.

Kagan, S.L. and Bowman, B.T. (1997). 'Leadership in early care and education: Issues and challenges', in Kagan, S.L. and Bowman, B.T. (eds) *Leadership in Early Care and Education* (pp. 3-8), Washington, DC: National Association for the Education of Young Children.

Law, S. and Glover, D. (2000) *Educational leadership and learning: practice, policy and research,* London: Open University Press.

McGregor, D. (1960) *The Human Side of Enterprise,* New York: McGraw-Hill.

Maslow, A.H. (1943) 'A theory of human motivation', *Psychological Review,* 50(4), pp. 370-396.

Meindl J. (1995) 'The romance of leadership as a follower-centric theory: a social constructionist approach', *Leadership Quarterly,* 6, pp. 329-341.

Morgan, G. (1997). 'Historical views of leadership', in *Leadership in Early Care and Education,*Washington, DC: National Association for the Education of Young Children, pp. 9-13.

Mullins, L. (1993) *Management and Organisational Behaviour,* London: Pitman Publishing.

NCTL (National College for Teaching and Leadership) (2013a) *Teachers' Standards (Early Years),* Crown copyright.

NCTL (National College for Teaching and Leadership) (2013b) *Early Years Educator Level: Three Qualifications Criteria,* Crown copyright.

Nurse, A. (2007) *The New Early Years Professional: Dilemmas and Debates,* London: Routledge.

Nutbrown, C. (2012) *Foundations for Quality: An Independent Review of Early Education and Childcare Qualifications Final Report,* Runcorn: Department of Education.

Osgood, J. (2004) 'Time to get down to business? The responses of early years practitioners to entrepreneurial approaches to professionalism', *Journal of Early Childhood Research,* 2(1), pp. 5-24.

Osgood, J. (2006) 'Deconstructing professionalism in early childhood education: resisting the regulatory gaze', *Contemporary Issues in Early Childhood Journal,* 7(1), pp. 5-14.

Pilcher, M. (2009) 'Making a positive contribution', in Robins, A. and Callan, S. *Managing Early Years Settings,* London: Sage, pp. 83-99.

Rodd, G. (1998) *Leadership in Early Childhood: The Pathway to Professionalism* (2nd edn), Buckingham: Open University Press.

Rodd, J. (2006) *Leadership in Early Childhood* (3rd edn), Maidenhead: Open University Press.

Rodd, J. (1997) 'Learning to be leaders: Perceptions of early childhood professionals about leadership roles and responsibilities', *Early Years* 18(1) pp. 40-46.

Scrivens, C. (2002) 'Constructions of leadership: Does gender make a difference? – Perspectives from an English speaking country', in Nivala, V. and Hujala, E. (eds) *Leadership in Early Childhood Education: Cross-cultural Perspectives.* Department of Educational Sciences and Teacher Education: University of Oulu.

Siraj-Blatchford, I. and Manni, L. (2006) *Effective Leadership in the Early Years Sector* (The ELEYS Study) London: Institute of Education, University of London.

Siraj-Blatchford, I., Sylva, K., Muttock, S., Gilden, R. and Bell, D. (2002) *Researching Effective Pedagogy in the Early Years (REPEY)* Norwich: Department for Education and Skills.

Smith, A. and Langstone, A. (1999) *Managing Staff in Early Years Settings,* London: Routledge.

Solly, K. (2003) *What do Early Childhood Leaders do to Maintain and Enhance the Significance of Early Years?* London: Institute of Education, University of London.

Southworth, G. (1998) *Leading Improving Primary Schools*, London: Falmer Press.

Sylva, K., Melhuish, E. Sammons, P., Siraj-Blachford, I. and Taggart, B. (2004) *The Effective Provision of Pre-School Education (EPPE) Project: Final Report*, London: DfES and Institute of Education, University of London.

Taggart, B., Sylva, K., Siraj-Blatchford, I., Melhuish, E., Sammons, P. and Walker-Hall, J. (2000) *Characteristics of the Centres in the EPPE Sample: Interviews. Technical Paper 5.* London: DfEE.

Thomas, K.W. and Kilmann, R.H. (1974) *Thomas-Kilmann Conflict Mode Instrument*, Mountain View, CA: Xicom, a subsidiary of CPP, Inc.

Truss, E. (2013) *More Great Childcare: Raising quality and giving parents more choice*, London: Department for Education.

Tuckman, Bruce W. and Jensen, Mary Ann C. (1977) 'Stages of small group development revisited', *Group and Organizational Studies*, 2, pp. 419–427.

Waniganayake, M., Morda, R. and Kapsalakis, A. (2000) 'Leadership in child care centres: Is it just another job?' Special Issue: *Management and Leadership. Australian Journal of Early Childhood*, 28(1), pp. J13-19.

Webb, R. (2005) 'Leading teaching and learning in the primary school: from "educative leadership" to "pedagogical leadership" ', *Educational Management Administration & Leadership* January, 33, pp. 69–91.

Whalley, M. (2001) 'Working as a team', in Pugh, G. *Contemporary Issues in the Early Years. Working Collaboratively for Children,* London: Paul Chapman.

28 Mentoring, coaching and supervision

Samantha McMahon, Mary Dyer and Catherine Barker

LEARNING OUTCOMES

By the end of the chapter you will have:

✔ Considered the purpose of coaching, mentoring and supervision.
✔ Examined a number of different approaches to coaching, mentoring and supervision.
✔ Considered the key skills and ethical practices required for effective coaching, mentoring and supervision.
✔ Considered how coaching, mentoring and supervision can contribute to overall quality improvement in the setting.

Introduction

All early years settings are concerned with improving practice, and continuous improvement is underpinned by the **continuing professional development** of all staff, as this helps to support staff to ensure they are competent and up to date with the constantly changing requirements within the Early Years sector. Continuous professional development is a requirement of all early years professionals to ensure consistency within their job role. Coaching, mentoring and supervision can be understood as techniques which support professional development. As a student reading this chapter you are likely to be concerned with your own professional journey, making changes and improvements to enhance your own professional practice. This will be a major part in achieving goals within your working environments and also as a student learning and developing from the input of staff and peers.

This chapter will raise your awareness and understanding of techniques which should be available to you and other practitioners to support your professional journey. Coaching, mentoring and supervision are often used interchangeably and it can be difficult to draw a clear distinction between the concepts as they are usually based on one-to-one discussions and the focus is normally on improving performance. Nevertheless in this chapter we will discuss the differences between these concepts, highlight some areas of overlap and provide an overview of coaching, supervision and coaching as they might be understood and experienced from an early years perspective. We will also consider the role of coaching, supervision and mentoring in supporting overall quality improvement in the setting. With careful evaluation of all the roles we can achieve a cohesive overview of the professional development achievable.

Coaching

Brockbank and McGill (2012) argue that the purpose of coaching is to change behaviour. They suggest that its place lies within managing the performance of staff and ensuring that tasks are completed in the 'right' way. Earlier definitions also point to coaching being a very directive process focusing on performance rather than on understanding or knowledge, where staff are encouraged and supported to complete work tasks in prescribed ways and adopt management solutions to problems (Parsloe and Leedham, 2009).

Approaches to coaching

In general, coaching considers specific areas of performance of an individual and the overall job outcomes, all the while focusing on the improvement of practice and development of the individual to ensure that they are working to the best of their ability and enhancing the team as a whole. When coaching is undertaken it is normally with an agreed time span with a specific goal which will normally be set by the team leader or management of the setting. This does not always treat the practitioner as an equal partner in the process, and it can be quite a formal process in comparison with mentoring. There will usually be regular, formal meetings with a record-keeping process completed from the start of the coaching. Coaching is often linked to performance reviews, target setting and **appraisals** within the workplace, hence the role of the team leader or management in the involvement of the target setting within the coaching role.

As the case study illustrates, coaching in the early years setting may take the form of induction programmes for new staff, the following of set processes and procedures for specific tasks, and the training of apprentices following NVQs requiring competence-based **assessment**. It is often evidenced in the creation of tick lists and set pro-formas to support routine tasks such as the setting up of areas of continuous provision within the setting, planning learning activities and carrying out **observations** of children, and performing regular, routine tasks such as preparing simple snacks.

PROVOCATION

Create a tick list/process sheet for nappy changing for new staff to follow.

CASE STUDY 1

Linda is the deputy manager of a private day nursery and she has responsibility for all students who are on placement at the setting. She has set up an induction programme to ensure that all the students are familiar, from the outset, with essential policies and procedures including health and safety and **safeguarding**. Linda also observes students, checks their activity plans, liaises with other members of staff and checks with the student each week on their progress. The weekly sessions are an opportunity for the students to reflect and Linda, who describes herself as coach, mentor and supervisor for the students said 'the sessions are an opportunity for them (the students) to gain constructive feedback from me, this gives them an insight into their abilities, how we expect things to be done, and the areas they need to work on'.

- *What do you think are the benefits of Linda's approach? Are there any challenges? As a student how would you prepare for the weekly meeting with Linda?*

In the plan below, the management team have provided instructions on how to set out the role play area, including where to hang posters and the price list. This is an example of top-down prescriptive management.

Example: plan for layout of role play area for all staff to follow:

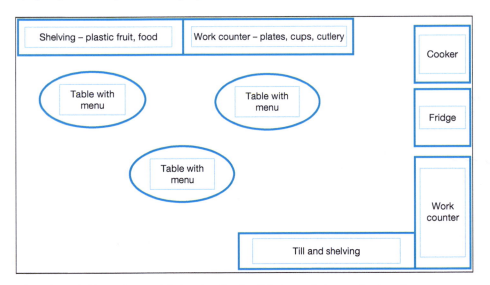

Fruit and vegetable posters on left-hand wall; price list above shelves on back wall.

While this can be useful to novice practitioners and could ensure a measure of continuity in the basic quality of provision, such a performative approach to coaching does not support staff in dealing with the less predictable aspects of early years practice. Nor does it support practitioners in developing their own understanding of their practice. Furthermore, if practitioners are only ever coached in meeting management-set objectives, they will remain on the edge of any possible community of practice, only able to copy rather than make their own contribution to notions of what good practice is, reducing their sense of belonging to the team and their responsibility for maintaining good practice, and limiting their potential to develop their own personal effectiveness.

A more modern approach to the purpose of coaching is to see the coach as someone who supports the practitioner to identify and realise their own potential, to believe in their own ability to do their job and do it well, and to increase their self-awareness and responsibility for their own practice (Parsloe and Leedham, 2009). The following illustrates how this might be achieved in practice, and brings the process closer to the concepts of mentoring and supervision.

REFLECTIVE PRACTICE

Rather than asking all staff to comply with a single plan for the layout of the role play area, which is only ever changed by a manager, consider how you can encourage them to develop and share their ideas for its layout and use. What guidance and support might you need to provide?

Mentoring

Mentoring is often regarded as a process where a more experienced individual leads the less experienced – a Vygotskyian model, where the experienced teach and the inexperienced learn. Brockbank and McGill (2012) define it as a process that leads to change in thinking, and Pask (2004, cited in Pask and Barrie, 2007) defines a mentor as someone who supports a mentee in the process of thinking things through, someone who is respectful and empowering. Mentoring, then, can be seen as a process that requires individuals to examine their values, attitudes and professional ambitions, and set appropriate goals around these to further their professional development. These goals may be individually focused, on personal career development within and outside a particular organisation, or may be set within the context of a management vision of the effectiveness and purpose of the organisation. Within the early years setting, this may be about the professional development that takes a practitioner from their entry level qualification at NVQ Level 2 or 3 to acquiring experience and qualification that may advance them within their organisation or outside it.

Parsloe and Leedham (2009) regard mentoring as a less directive process than coaching, less performance driven and more of an equal relationship between colleagues where the professional development of the 'mentee' is the focus for both parties. The mentee is encouraged to feel more ownership of the process, contributing or even leading the setting of goals and achievement criteria. However, while it may be a more respectful and enabling relationship, for many early years practitioners, mentoring, especially where it is linked to the identification and fulfilling of training needs, is a process run by line managers, so that while it may be a less overtly directive process, it remains one where they are required to meet specific goals within specified time-frames, and are held accountable if this does not happen. Mentoring, for many practitioners, remains a performance management tool.

CASE STUDY 2

Setting X has introduced a mentoring system where senior colleagues mentor less experienced staff and apprentices undertaking Early Years qualifications. Jo is Room Leader for the Baby Room and has two permanent staff and a trainee to mentor. Consider what records it would be useful for her to keep. How can she make the process less 'managerial' for her mentees and encourage their involvement and ownership of the process?

Approaches to mentoring

Usually mentoring is undertaken by an experienced member of staff from the setting, who is able to guide and offer support. However, since mentoring may involve deeper personal concerns or aims, boundaries need to be established from the outset to ensure an appropriate professional relationship is maintained. Mentoring is something that can be developed and nurtured over a long period depending on the nature of the mentoring process, and may seem a less formal process than coaching or supervision.

As a process, it is often supported by systems of appraisal (including 360° appraisal), Performance Development Reviews, or Performance Management Reviews. However, the key principle remains the same in all these processes: the setting of goals, targets, achievement criteria and timescales. For this, accurate records and a commitment to action from both the mentor and mentee is essential. Although records of meetings can be recorded for the purpose of both the mentor and mentee it is vital that an agreement is drawn up at the start between the mentor and mentee to ensure that the boundaries of the role are clear and agreed by both parties. The mentee should always have access to the records of the meetings recorded. It is usually found that mentoring is undertaken on a 'needs-based' requirement and meetings between the mentee and mentor are set on the needs of the mentee. To be effective, goal setting should be used from the start of the process. This should be with the mutual consent of the mentor and mentee. The mentee should be involved in their own goal setting and the goals set should be SMART (Specific, Measurable, Achievable, Realistic and Timely), and recorded and reviewed regularly to ensure the process is effective. This in turn can lead to the identification of continuous professional development (CPD) requirements to enhance the mentee's skills, if required.

One final consideration that must be addressed in the mentoring process lies in whose goals are being met. Where goals are management-led and organisational in nature, individuals should be encouraged to see a personal value in achieving them for mentoring to be effective. Where goals are individually led, then the setting will need to see some benefit from supporting these in terms of its own operation. This is the eternal paradox of professional development in any field – persuading an individual to do what their employer wants/needs them to do and persuading an employer to support (financially or in terms of time and other practical measures) the achievement of goals that may seem to have more benefit for the employee than the organisation (Megginson, 2003).

Both mentoring and coaching are used to identify areas of strength and also areas of development where support and guidance can be given to ensure practice is improved. The idea is that through continuous professional development (CPD) opportunities, which can be identified through coaching, mentoring and supervision, the individual member of staff will show improvement and feel supported by the setting as a whole. If this is identified through the mentoring role then this can lead to coaching from either the same member of staff or a more suitable staff member usually from the setting but in certain situations outside **agencies** may be involved and brought in to support individuals or groups.

However it can easily be seen from the Table below (adapted from Connor and Pakora, 2007, p. 16) that there are a number of differences between the two areas of coaching and mentoring.

Coaching	Mentoring
The relationship usually has a time-span.	The relationship can be on-going and be over an extended period of time.
Structured, scheduled and regular meetings.	Informal meetings on a 'need' basis.
Short term and tailored for specialist needs.	Longer term and more personal with a broader outlook.
It is not essential to have formal experience of the Early Years role to coach unless it is a specialist area.	Mentor is usually an experienced member of staff based within the setting – this can be a member of staff with a senior role.
Work-based issues are a focus	Personal issues can be discussed as these often impact on the role and career of the Early Years worker.
There are specific goals and targets to be achieved – can be set by management or the coach.	Guidance-based and usually set by the individual mentee rather than management. Helps support and develop the mentee professionally.

Supervision

Both mentoring and coaching as described above can appear to be processes within which the focus is on performance and development but where there is limited space for the discussion of personal feelings towards one's role. In the Tickell Review (2011) successful supervision is also described as a tool which should allow staff to raise professional queries, discuss career progression, clarify roles, support performance management and build confidence in supporting children's development. However in other caring professions such as nursing and health visiting, supervision is an established strategy to support practitioners in dealing with the emotional impact of their work. Working in early years can have an enormous emotional impact on practitioners; often it is very rewarding but as Elfer (2012) highlights it sometimes brings a significant emotional cost. Therefore Ward *et al.* (2012) suggest that supervision must address emotions and that it should relieve stress, prevent burnout and provide an opportunity to solve problems. Ultimately this is to ensure that practitioners can continue to safeguard children. Consider the following case study:

CASE STUDY 3

Kate has recently been promoted in her setting and has taken on board additional responsibilities including SENCO, and partnership-working with parents and a range of external professionals. Kate is keen to embrace the challenge presented by the new role but recognises that the best interests of the children and their families rest on her judgements and decisions. Kate is anxious that she will make a mistake and she begins to doubt her ability to cope. There is no existing system of supervision in place in the setting so Kate arranges a meeting with her manager to discuss her feelings. Her manager simply did not realise that Kate felt anxious and needs support; they now meet every six weeks for a supervision meeting.

Spend a few minutes thinking about Kate in her new role, have you ever experienced similar feelings of anxiety at work or placement and worried about how your decisions might be affecting a child or their family? How might supervision help?

Supervision should be intrinsic to effective **leadership** and is a key part of staff support systems (Tickell, 2011). However, as the case study illustrates, supervision is not yet embedded as part of Early Years practice and its purpose is not fully understood by leaders and managers. The Safeguarding and Welfare Requirements in the EYFS offer only limited guidance on supervision, stating that supervision should provide opportunities for staff to:

- discuss any issues – particularly concerning children's development or well-being;
- identify solutions to address issues as they arise; and
- receive coaching to improve personal effectiveness.

(DfE, 2012)

However this does not provide hard-pressed leaders and managers with much information on the benefits of supervision or what supervision might look like in their setting.

Benefits of supervision

There are many routine policies which are integrated into practice to ensure that settings are compliant with the legal requirements and these practices, such as adult:child ratios are accepted and seen as necessary to keep children safe. Supervision should be viewed as another aspect of routine practice to keep children safe. Sometimes in a busy setting it can appear to be an unnecessary luxury to allocate time for supervision and it is not until there is an incident in the setting that time is given to reflect and talk. The Plymouth Serious Case Review (Plymouth Safeguarding Children's Board, 2010) highlighted how practitioners had felt unable to express their uncertainties and discomfort in a safe way.

Supervision should be an opportunity for practitioners to raise concerns about the children in their care and to receive support to help them deal with difficult situations at work (Tickell, 2011). Talking things through can help organise thoughts, feelings and actions. Good supervision can add value to the organisation, ultimately it should ensure that children and their families receive a quality service. Effective supervision ensures the implementation of policies and procedures and that the practitioner meets the settings objectives and standards. It should assist in staff retention by valuing the practitioner's work and building self-confidence. It is an opportunity to identify learning needs and to promote the health and well-being of the practitioner.

CASE STUDY 4

Examples of supervision in practice

Mel is a Higher Level Teaching Assistant with some teaching responsibility mostly in Reception and Key Stage 1. Supervision takes place formally, on an annual basis, and is linked to performance management and results in a documented development plan.

Mel said '*I'm not sure of the purpose other than it's a statutory requirement, I certainly did not feel motivated as the development areas were not my choice*'.

Angela who is employed in a Children's Centre as a family support worker has a supervision meeting every six weeks. Recently new paperwork has been introduced which prompts the supervisor to ask about the individual's welfare and their relationships with colleagues and their manager. Actions are written down and agreed and these are revisited briefly at the start of the next supervision meeting.

Angela said '*I find supervision valid and useful; these are times when I can be honest about how things are going. However I have a good relationship with my manager, I'm not sure how things would work if the relationship was a bit . . . tense*'.

These examples illustrate how supervision is carried out in two settings, each of the practitioners has a very different experience and for Mel it is not entirely successful. What works in one setting may not work in another, there is no one-size-fits-all model or approach, it must grow and develop in the setting (McMahon and Percival, 2014). A reflective approach to supervision might be modelled on the approach suggested by Bernstein and Edwards (2012) which was adapted from work in Head Start in the United States.

FROM RESEARCH TO PRACTICE

A reflective approach to supervision

From the outset supervision time is protected and is not related to appraisal, meeting deadlines or organisational matters and there is a mutually constructed agenda which can be worked through flexibly. Each party has a responsibility to prepare for the session and can draw upon notes, a journal or diary. The supervisee is allowed to share their account focusing on their experiences with children and families. However findings from research conducted by Peter Elfer (2012) and The Plymouth Serious Case Review (2010) suggest that relationships between staff can be a cause for concern and materially impact on practice; therefore the supervision meeting, with boundaries, may provide a forum to discuss staffing matters. The supervisor listens, asks open questions and may share some past experiences, it is important to look for positives as well as concerns. Supervision does provide the leader or manager with an oversight of practice and they must identify instances where immediate action is needed. However resolution is normally sought by working together on a plan of suggested actions these are recorded and the supervisee is asked for feedback on the session. This feedback should consider the following:

- What understandings of practice have been developed?
- What response, emotionally and practically is being planned?
- How does this affect the family? (McMahon and Percival, 2014)

It is important that both parties keep accurate and timely records and that the next session starts with an update. This type of approach takes time to develop and relies on **trusting relationships** between the parties and is perhaps what Tickell (2011) had in mind when she asks for supervision to encourage reflective practice, so that it is more than an opportunity to check what practitioners are or are not doing.

(Bernstein and Edwards, 2012)

Other approaches to supervision include more formal links to the appraisal process and will be based on a joint review of progress against an agreed set of objectives and goals. In the meeting learning resources, training and coaching can be identified for the achievement of the agreed goals. Whichever model is adopted it must always be seen as a two-way process allowing the free discussion of any aspect of work or development that the individual member of staff or manager wishes to raise.

Key conditions for coaching, mentoring and supervision

PROVOCATION

Consider the following common barriers to effective coaching, mentoring and supervision:

1   Lack of organisational policies or standards to provide guidance for each process
2   Lack of time and space
3   Interruptions
4   Poor recording of meetings, inadequate training for coaches, mentors and supervisors
5   Lack of supervision for coaches, mentors and supervisors
6   Unplanned and infrequent meetings

Now draw up a list of key conditions for delivering effective coaching, mentoring and supervision.

Adapted from Care Council Wales (2011)

The activity above is designed to encourage consideration of the organisational and structural conditions needed to support effective coaching, mentoring and supervision. However the coach, mentor and supervisor also need the following qualities to provide effective supervision: integrity, empathy, good listener, honesty, anti-discriminatory, reflective and respect.

It is essential that through each process the individual has their thoughts and feelings recognised and is able to learn from their mistakes. In turn they must also be willing to contribute to the process, to come to the meeting prepared, and to be honest, listen and seek advice. Disagreements may occur and may not be easily resolved within the meeting; this should be recorded and followed up in the next meeting.

In any system of coaching, mentoring and supervision, the development of an effective relationship is essential to ensure that the individual benefits from the process and this supports continuous improvement within the setting. To ensure that the processes of coaching, mentoring and supervision are mutually beneficial then both sides need to be aware of their responsibilities at the start of the process with those involved. Practitioners need to understand that coaching, mentoring and supervision is there to support them within their role and help to improve and develop their practice.

Whether it is mentoring, coaching or supervision that is being implemented within the setting, some basic ground rules will help to ensure effectiveness. These assume a more transformative approach to these processes that is concerned with the development of the individual practitioner and the quality of the setting as a whole, rather than the superficial improvement of performance on routine, everyday tasks (Brockbank and McGill, 2012).

1	Make sure you meet	Time management is key. Share responsibility and commitment to this. Make appointments to meet and keep to them.
2	Agree what to talk about	Set ground rules and keep the meeting focused.
3	Keep it brief	Meetings should take from 30-75 minutes to maintain focus and purpose and allow sufficient time for meaningful dialogue.
4	Stick to the basic process	Agree ground rules and an agenda, then keep to them. Come away with agreed action points.
5	'Ask not tell'	Adopt a non-directive style. Move away from being a manager.
6	It's all about learning	The emphasis is on personal development and reflection based on experience/performance, i.e. the importance of the learning relationship; it does always have to be finding the right training course to send someone on.
7	Be aware of boundaries	Coaching/mentoring/supervising is not counselling or therapy. Share and agree boundaries, and respect them.

Adapted from Parsloe and Leedham (2009)

Ethical considerations

Coaching, mentoring and supervision should be conducted within an ethical framework of mutual respect for the parties concerned and also the fundamental beliefs and values which shape early years practice. The values, principles and objectives of the setting should be clearly articulated within their policies and mission statement and these are grounded in an ethic of care for children, their families and staff. Ultimately for coaching, mentoring or supervision to be effective requires trusting and supportive relationships which requires a mutual understanding of the following ethical issues.

Confidentiality

It is important for staff to feel comfortable in discussing all aspects of their work (Care Council Wales, 2011) and confidentiality plays a huge part in the trust between the parties concerned. While the documentation from the meetings is confidential they are also organisational documents and may be open to scrutiny in particular circumstances such as audit, grievance or internal/external enquiry. It is essential that all parties are aware of and understand what will happen to the information discussed; it is private but not necessarily secret.

Power

Another consideration is the potential power imbalance between the parties, if the coach, mentor or supervisor has a more senior role in the organisation they need to recognise that they are in a powerful position. They need to remember that the other party may say things to try to please them and be unwilling to be honest about their practice in order to avoid recrimination or **conflict**. Any agenda, goals or targets discussed should be by mutual agreement and any notes should be written up and actions agreed. Both parties should have a signed copy and the next session should begin with revisiting the agreed actions.

Coaching, mentoring and supervision – their contribution to quality improvement

The impact of having these in place within the setting contributes to:

- The development of sharing knowledge and skills – this has an impact on the whole team as a community of practice. Working together and sharing good practice helps to refine skills and has the advantage of working to individuals' strengths.
- Recruitment, retention and career development of staff – knowing that support is available to staff from the onset of employments will not only make them feel reassured but will help retain them in their employment and in turn help support career development within the setting.
- Developing **reflective practice** – practitioners often need support to develop reflective practice and coaching, mentoring and supervision can help to support this as areas of development can be discussed and reflected on between individuals to ensure the appropriate steps are taken to ensure improvement.

Professional development of all staff within the early years setting can make a significant contribution to its overall continuous quality improvement, especially if the focus is on a transformative approach (Brockbank and McGill, 2012) rather than simply the management of performance in routine tasks. Transformative development, as the name implies, is a process which changes the nature and quality of the organisation – an approach which can support practitioners in developing their practice based on personal and individual professional goals, and putting children and their development, families and their needs at the heart of their practice.

By moving from the initial performance management coaching of induction and basic training for new staff and apprentice early years assistants, to encouraging their participation in developing processes and procedures and requiring them to identify their own learning goals, even the least experienced of practitioners can contribute to the quality improvement of a setting. By taking a developmental approach (Brockbank and McGill, 2012) to mentoring and supervising individual practitioners, where goals and targets are identified by practitioners in discussion with their managers, and issues of values, confidence and personal responses to practice are discussed through reflective dialogue, deeper learning is possible that supports the practitioner in understanding their role and its place within the setting. By extending this to an examination of the values of the organisation and inviting discussion and evaluation of the overall mission statement for the setting, a more systemic change becomes possible for the organisation (Brockbank and McGill, 2012), where the whole team takes ownership of the values of the organisation, and responsibility for embedding these in their practice, thus driving up the overall quality of the setting.

If the overall quality of the setting is improved, children and their families will benefit, which can be a great source of satisfaction for the practitioner. Furthermore, staff and even students on placement are more likely to feel pride in their workplace and highly motivated in their practice, if they feel valued; effective coaching, mentoring and supervision sends a clear message to staff that they matter. The individual practitioner is supported in their learning and professional development and, importantly, those who have experienced effective coaching, mentoring and supervision are likely to emulate this as future leaders of early years practice.

REFLECTIVE PRACTICE

What would be the benefits to you, your role and your setting of having coaching, mentoring or supervision?

Conclusion

In this chapter we have considered the purposes of coaching, mentoring and supervision. Parsloe and Leedham (2009) summarise it all succinctly stating that it's all about the learning, with the emphasis on reflection and personal development, which in turn can improve quality in the setting. We examined a number of different approaches to each technique and it is clear that one size does not fit all. However to be most effective each should be undertaken from a standpoint of mutual respect and reciprocity. Trusting relationships built on a strong ethic of care for children, families and each other are the essential foundations to each approach. While the chapter has drawn attention to the need for both parties to be organised and to keep accurate records, other key skills required include the ability to listen, reflect and a belief that coaching, mentoring and supervision can be transformative. Finally the chapter considered how taking a developmental approach can lead to systematic changes in a setting and drive up quality, thus leading to better outcomes for children and their families and a greater sense of satisfaction for students and practitioners.

Further reading

Brockbank, A. and McGill, I. (2012) *Facilitating Reflective Learning: coaching, mentoring and supervision* (2nd edition). London: Kogan Page.

This book considers different approaches to mentoring and coaching, also the different levels of support that can be achieved for both the individual and their organisation. The authors consider these from the perspective of the individual engaging in CPD and the outcomes they seek as well as from the perspective of the organisation and how it pursues its own continuous improvement. This is a generic text book, aimed at a range of different organisations, but sheds light on universal issues faced by leaders and managers in mentoring and coaching their staff, stressing the importance of personal as well as organisational ownership of the purposes and learning outcomes attached to the process.

Lawlor, D. (2013) 'A transformation programme for children's social care managers using an interactional and reflective supervision model to develop supervision skills', in *Journal of Social Work Practice* 27(2), 177–189.

This paper stresses the importance of the tone and relationship underpinning the supervision meeting, following an interactional model to create a positive, and trust-based relationship between the supervisor and supervisee. Lawlor acknowledges the importance of promoting reflective practice in a profession where this is essential if positive outcomes are to be achieved for service users and where practitioners need support that goes beyond target-driven performance management and audit cultures, making his work of relevance to those working in the early years sector. He offers an overview of how an interactional model offers an opportunity for leaders and managers to understand and apply reflective supervision as a discursive and interactional process. The paper ends with an explanation and analysis of training that will support supervisors in developing the necessary trust-based relationship with their supervisees. While this may seem rather large for smaller early years organisations to consider for themselves, he does identify key learning points about the development of a supervisory relationship that would apply to all settings, no matter what the size of their organisation.

Wenger, E. (1998) *Communities of Practice: Learning, Meaning and Identity.* Cambridge: Cambridge University Press.

Wenger explores and explains the importance of the situated nature of professional learning in developing expertise and sharing good practice. He places great emphasis on the individual as a creator of knowledge and stresses the importance of opportunities for all workers, including new members in professional teams, to contribute to this creation of knowledge within the workplace. This book encourages the reader to consider how knowledge can be shared within the workplace, offering a context within which leaders and managers can set their supervision and mentoring and promote individual and collective reflection.

Useful websites

www.cipd.co.uk/hr-resources/factsheets/coaching-mentoring.aspx
You have to register for this but it is free to do so and has some excellent resources.

http://new.coachingnetwork.org.uk/information-portal/what-are-coaching-and-mentoring//
This website is easy to read and has great resources.

www.kelsi.org.uk/__data/assets/pdf_file/0006/28860/Supervision-booklet-early-years.pdf
This is a very useful starting point to think about supervision.

References

Bernstein, V. J. and Edwards, R.C. (2012) 'Supporting Early Childhood Practitioners through Relationship-based Reflective Supervision', in *NHSA Dialogue: A Research-to-Practice Journal for the Early Childhood Field,* 15(3): 286–301.

Brockbank, A. and McGill, I. (2012) *Facilitating Reflective Learning: coaching, mentoring and supervision* (2nd edn). London: Kogan Page.

Care Council Wales (2011) *Supervising and Appraising Well: A Guide to Effective Supervision and Appraisal.* Care Council Wales [online]. Available from: www.daycaretrust.org.uk/data/files/Projects/Volunteering/Supervising_and_Appraising_Well.pdf [Accessed 15 April 2014].

Connor, M. and Pakora, J. (2007) *Coaching and Mentoring at Work – Developing Effective Practice* (2nd edn). Berkshire: Open University Press.

Department for Education (DfE) (2012) *Statutory Framework for the Early Years Foundation Stage.* Crown Publications [online]. Available from: www.education.gov.uk/publications/eOrderingDownload/EYFS%20Statutory%20Framework.pdf [Accessed 15 April 2014].

Elfer, P. (2012) 'Emotion in nursery work: work discussion as a model of critical professional reflection', *Early Years: An International Journal of Early Childhood Research and Development*, 32(2): 129-141 [Accessed 15 April 2014].

McMahon, S. and Percival, J. (2014) 'Supervision and Reflective Practice', in Reid, J. and Burton, S. (eds) *Safeguarding and Protecting Children in the Early Years*. Oxon: Routledge.

Megginson, D. (2003) *Continuing Professional Development*. UK: Chartered Institute of Personnel and Development.

Megginson, D. and Whitaker, V. (2007) *Continuing Professional Development*. UK: Chartered Institute of Personnel and Development.

Parsloe, E. and Leedham, M. (2009) *Coaching and Mentoring: Practical Conversations to Improve Learning* (2nd edn). London: Kogan Page.

Pask, R. and Barrie, J. (2007) *Mentoring and Coaching: A Handbook for Education Professionals*. Berkshire: Open University Press.

Plymouth Safeguarding Children Board (2010) *Serious Case Review in Respect of Nursery Z*. Plymouth: Plymouth SCB.

Tickell, C. (2011) *The Early Years: Foundations for Life, Health and Learning: An Independent Report on the Early Years Foundation Stage to her Majesty's Government*. London: Department for Education.

Ward, H., Brown R. and Westlake, D. (2012) *Safeguarding Babies and Very Young Children from Abuse and Neglect*. London: Jessica Kingsley.

29 Quality

Danielle Carey

LEARNING OUTCOMES

After reading this chapter, you should:

✔ Recognise that quality in the early years sector is a contested concept.
✔ Have raised awareness of the differing perspectives of the key stakeholders regarding quality within the early years.
✔ Have raised awareness of the recent Government changes to qualifications within the early years sector.
✔ Recognise the impact of practitioners' personal values in relation to providing high quality early years provision.

Introduction

This chapter poses the question: What does high quality early years provision really mean in England in the twenty-first century? I feel it is important to set this chapter in context as I am aware that my lived experiences both personally and professionally impact upon my views and opinions. I am very proud to have worked as a nursery nurse in the early years sector for the majority of my career, a career spanning twenty years. For the past seventeen years I have worked in further and higher education with early years practitioners studying for qualifications ranging from Level 2 to Level 7. I am passionate about high quality early years provision and believe high quality care and education for young children is crucial.

In recent years the early years sector in England has undergone unprecedented change. These changes have been underpinned by statute and regulatory frameworks such as: *The National Childcare Strategy* (DfEE, 1998), *Every Child Matters* (DfES, 2003) and the previous Government's *Ten Year Strategy for Childcare* (HM Treasury, 2004). In addition, in 2012 the coalition government commissioned the influential Nutbrown Review (Nutbrown, 2012) which emphasised the need for further improvement in enhancing the quality of early years provision and providing a high standard of care and education for all. Cottle and Alexander (2012, p. 637) interestingly, 'note the number of times "quality" is cited [in Government documentation] but [highlight that quality] is rarely if ever, defined, suggesting an assumption that there is an explicit and agreed model of what constitutes quality childcare and quality practitioners'.

It is accepted that providing high quality early years provision is important to young children's development and their future life chances and therefore it is somewhat disappointing that the latest figures available indicate that only 13.3 per cent of the early years provision based in schools and 22.2 per cent of provision in the Private, Voluntary and Independent (PVI) sector were judged by the Office for Standards in Education (OfSTED) to be outstanding after inspection by OfSTED between September 2010 and August 2011 (OfSTED, 2011).

The **discourse** relating to the nature of high quality early years provision is not new and has been ongoing since the work of Froebel in the nineteenth century. One of the most influential pieces of research regarding the impact of high quality early years provision in England on children's long-term outcomes is the **Effective Pre-School Provision Education** (EPPE) Project (Sylva *et al.*, 2004, 2008 and Sylva, 2010). This project followed a cohort of children aged three and four from pre-school through to the end of Key Stage 3, aged fourteen. The findings highlighted that the impact of early years provision on children's long-term outcomes is greatest for those children who attended early years settings where a qualified teacher was present.

It is clear that the goal of both the coalition government and of the previous Labour government was to provide high quality, affordable early years provision for young children and their families leading to long-term improvements in outcomes for children. Gambaro *et al.* (2013, p. 1) acknowledge that the language relating to policy in England repeatedly refers to high quality but suggests that 'questions remain about how far provision is indeed high quality, and the extent to which quality is consistent across the sector'.

Issues of quality are further complicated by the complex and fragmented diversity of the early years sector in England. The Daycare Trust (2011, p. 1) identify that the sector operates 'a mixed market approach . . . with private, voluntary and independent (PVI) providers operating alongside the maintained sector provision. Two-thirds of full day care provision is privately run'.

What constitutes 'high quality' within the early years sector in England is a contested concept and the subject of contemporary debate among stakeholders. This debate is underpinned by **perceptions** of high quality provision and how this can be provided and measured. Gambaro *et al.* (2013, p. 3) identify 'quality care as care which best advances children's cognitive, social and behavioural development', highlighting that there are two measures of this type of quality, these being structural and process measures. Structural measures relate to the resources available in the setting, for example: child to staff ratios, group size, staff qualifications and training, and the space available. Process measures relate to the type of activities available in the setting including the relationships between children and staff, the environment and other children; this is supported by Blau and Currie (2006) and Sylva (2010). The key stakeholders considered in this chapter are:

- children and their parents
- practitioners
- the Government
- OfSTED

It is important to acknowledge that regardless of stakeholders' views and opinions OfSTED (2013, p. 5) are legally responsible for the inspection and regulation of early years provision and subsequently for making judgements on 'the overall quality and standards of the early years' provision inspected, taking into account three key judgements:

1   How well the early years provision meets the needs of the range of children who attend.
2   The contribution of the early years provision to the children's well-being.
3   The **leadership** and management of the early years' provision.

(OfSTED, 2013, p.5)

Following inspection, grades are assigned based on the findings, these being: outstanding, good, requires improvement or unsatisfactory. OfSTED judgements are useful to benchmark quality but it is important to remember that stakeholders' definitions of quality are also based on their personal values and beliefs which may differ significantly from those judged within the OfSTED inspection framework.

There are multiple theories regarding the acquisition of values (Freud, 1965, Erikson, 1968, and Gilligan, 1982), which is understandable as values are underpinned by different philosophical positions based on ideological beliefs. Anderson and Arsenault (1999, p. 32) provide a useful definition of values stating they are 'the intrinsic beliefs we hold as people ... values are held close to our hearts and impact on the decisions we make, the way we approach situations, the way we look at the world'.

It should be acknowledged that when discussing quality in early years provision the ideological beliefs and values of the stakeholders may support or differ from those of OfSTED, 'problematising' perceptions of quality and highlighting the difficulties of defining high quality early years provision.

It is considered important to question definitions of quality and in doing so to consider the views of children, their parents and practitioners and to explore how these relate to OfSTED's contemporary auditing practices, which it is suggested is a 'top-down perspective' in order for settings to achieve compliance, which is driven by the Government.

REFLECTIVE PRACTICE
REFLECTIVE PRACTICE

•   **What do you think constitutes high quality in the early years?**
•   **How is this achieved in your setting? Could it be improved?**
•   **If so, how?**

This chapter will now explore quality from the perspectives of the aforementioned stakeholders.

Children and their parents

Legislation and guidance such as the Children Act (DfES, 2004) and Every Child Matters (DfES, 2003) highlight that children's agency is acknowledged by their interests being considered paramount and by giving children a voice. Therefore it is considered imperative that children's views and opinions are taken into consideration. Coleyshaw *et al.* (2010, p. 11) support this view, highlighting the importance of **listening to children**, adults and families arguing that 'recognising the perspective of young children is part of a culture of respect'.

It is clearly important to take children's views of quality into account but also recognised that practitioners may consider this to be quite difficult to achieve, questioning how might children's views be gathered and how can these results be interpreted? One way of doing so is to adopt a Mosaic research approach (Clark and Moss, 2001) as used by Harcourt (2012, p. 20). The Mosaic research Approach made use of traditional methods such as **observations** which were complemented with 'participatory tools such as photography, drawings, conversations, mapping, art and storytelling'.

It is acknowledged that there is limited literature regarding children's views of the quality of their early years provision. However Harcourt's research (2012, p. 20) demonstrates that children understand the word quality as being what is 'important or good'. She notes that 'young children are capable of making powerful and persuasive contributions to our knowledge about the quality of their prior to school settings and suggesting appropriate strategies for improving their experiences'. This perception is supported by Gambaro *et al.* (2013, p. 3) who acknowledge that children have the ability to assess quality based on 'how much they enjoy their day.' Children have the capacity to make judgements regarding the quality of their setting, and listening to children provides powerful messages for practitioners. This is supported by Coleyshaw *et al.* (2010 p. 19), who maintain that consultation with children 'is vital to improving provision and keeping provision at its best level because unless you are listening to children, you are missing out on a whole part of the picture'.

PROVOCATION 1

Provide the children in your setting with resources to take photographs (cameras, Ipads, tablets) and ask them to capture pictures of things that they enjoy at the setting and things that they don't enjoy.

Talk to them about their photographs. Consider whether simple changes could be made to improve the children's enjoyment of their time at your setting.

It is also important to consider parents' views. It is acknowledged that there is limited research regarding what parents understand high quality provision to be and recent research into parents' perceptions of quality is somewhat contradictory. Waldegrave (2013, p. 29) identifies that while 'quality of care is important to parents ... it is not always the kind of quality parents can judge from OfSTED reports', concluding that when considering quality the most important things for parents are 'How caring or competent the staff seem (98%), number of children to staff (94%)

CASE STUDY 1

Charlotte's story

When Charlotte decided to return to work her two children were aged three and one. As an early years practitioner herself she decided she wanted her children to attend day nursery. I asked Charlotte how she chose the setting her children attend. She explained that she visited a number of settings and that a range of factors influenced her choice: whether she had to make an appointment or was invited to 'just pop in', staff interaction with the children, if the children seemed happy, if she was made to feel welcome, her first impression, the location and the cost. Charlotte told me that the biggest influence when deciding the setting her children would attend was:

> *'the feel of the place, I just knew it was the right place for my children. My son immediately wanted to play whereas at other settings he wouldn't leave my side. It wasn't the smartest, cheapest or nearest but it had a lovely atmosphere I just knew my children would be happy there and they are.'*

I asked Charlotte if she had read the OfSTED Reports for the settings she had visited, she replied that she had not, adding: *'I'm not really bothered about OfSTED; it's just a snap shot and focuses mainly on the three- to four-year-olds.'*

CASE STUDY 2

David's story

When deciding which nursery to send his daughter to David told me he knew that he

> *'had to find the right one for her. I visited five different nurseries before deciding which one she would attend'.*

When asked why he chose the nursery he explained,

> *'the children were confident, they came up to me and said hello. The most important things though were the interaction between the staff and the children which was excellent and all the children seemed really happy'.*

David explained that his partner had reviewed OfSTED reports but he had not. Clearly for Charlotte and David their experience at the settings was more important than OfSTED's judgements; this view is echoed in the previously mentioned research (Waldegrave, 2013 and Gambaro *et al.*, 2013).

[and the] qualifications of staff (84%)'. Interestingly these three quality components were all deemed by the parents to be more important than the settings OfSTED report (82%) (ibid., p. 31).

The complexity of defining parents' perceptions of quality is highlighted by drawing comparisons between Waldegrave's research (2013) and that of Gambaro *et al.* (2013, p. 3). The latter research highlights the following components as being the most important: 'staff quality (54%), warm and caring atmosphere (43%) [and] good quality buildings and facilities (32%)'. While there is some agreement between Waldegrave (2013) and Gambaro *et al.*'s (2013) findings, such as staff quality, it is important to note that a high percentage of parents did not rank the aforementioned components in their top three, supporting the perception that parents have diverse views regarding what quality is, highlighting the complexity of defining high quality early years provision.

PROVOCATION 2

- Ask the parents at your setting why they chose it.
- Do their responses relate to OfSTED definitions of quality? Do they focus on structural or process measures or something else? Is quality the same regardless of the child's age?

Practitioners

Practitioners have the complicated task of trying to ensure their setting provides high quality care and education, while keeping all the stakeholders happy. This is a complex task. Cottle and Alexander (2012, p. 638) recognise this dilemma, suggesting practitioners have been left 'to struggle with the tensions between the principled practice of working with children within a framework of policies that aim to provide flexibility and an inflexible system of prioritising targets, inspections and **accountability**'. This tension is evident in the transcript of an interview with a reception teacher, 'We believe that some of the targets for young children are totally inappropriate. So there's a constant juggling of needing to fulfil certain requirements but stay true to what we believe as well' (Reception teacher, Edgehill School. ibid., p. 644). Cooke and Lawton (2008) identify that practitioners and managers have mixed views regarding quality, identifying a range of skills and personal qualities that they deem to be important for practitioners, including patience, confidence in building strong relationships with parents, and emotional resilience. These attributes cannot be measured by OfSTED.

The core values underpinning early years practice relate to **equality** and diversity, inclusion, and children learning through play and enabling environments, all of which support children's development of positive self-image and high self-esteem. During my career I have lost count of the different curricula that have been imposed, but I would argue that by staying true to these core values and having a good knowledge of child development, practitioners can ensure all children achieve their potential regardless of the curricula or inspection regime. I believe this is achieved by providing enabling environments, knowledgeable and caring staff and ensuring the starting point when planning for children is what they can do and not what they cannot. If this is accepted I would suggest that all children would achieve positive outcomes and the former coalition government's aim for early years provision to support children's 'School Readiness' can be achieved (Truss, 2013).

Cottle and Alexander's research (2012, p. 644) also highlights the importance of the '**ethos** [of a setting], a feel, something that is hard to see because you are involved in it'. It is interesting that Charlotte (in the above case study) also identified the importance of this but acknowledged that this important component of quality is intangible and cannot be measured by OfSTED.

It is important to question whether there is a dilemma in balancing what parents want and what practitioners think high quality early years should be. Waldegrave (2013, p. 29) thinks not, acknowledging that while parents want caring providers, practitioners talk more explicitly about child development: 'when it comes down to what that means in terms of child-carer interactions [it] is actually quite similar, namely good levels of interaction between child and practitioner'.

Practitioners have to balance their personal values and beliefs with the requirements of the stakeholders, it is recognised this may be challenging but important to acknowledge that this can be achieved.

PROVOCATION 3

- As a staff team do you all have a shared view of what high quality provision is?
- Plan a staff meeting to discuss this.

Government policy

As the introduction to this chapter highlighted, since 1998 there has been a plethora of policy developments in the early years sector which it is contended have continually shifted the goal posts. Alongside these developments the sector has also experienced unprecedented growth and Government funding has increased significantly. This growth and investment relates to the previously identified notion that high quality early years provision will improve long-term outcomes for children. Therefore there is an expectation that this investment should pay dividends in the future.

The aforementioned strategies alongside societal changes, for example in maternal employment, have led to the expansion of the sector. This, coupled with the 95 per cent take-up of the entitlement to 15 hours of free childcare for children aged three and four and more recently two-year-old funding, for those from disadvantaged backgrounds (DfE, 2011) has created pressure on the sector in terms of recruitment and retention of staff, increasing qualifications and skills and promoting diversity in the workforce, all of which are recurring themes regarding workforce composition (Kendall *et al.*, 2012)

As stated earlier, Professor Cathy Nutbrown, (Nutbrown, 2012) was commissioned by the coalition government to lead an independent review of early education and childcare qualifications, in order to improve the quality of qualifications and to develop career pathways for early years practitioners. This was supported by Tickell (2011) who argued a well qualified early years practitioner has the ability in the long term to improve children's educational attainment, social behaviour and employment prospects. It is evident from the political discourse that providing quality early years provision is deemed to be reliant on improving the academic qualifications of the workforce.

As previously mentioned, the EPPE Project (Sylva et al., 2004) identified that the greatest positive impact is evident in those children who attended maintained nursery school settings in which Level 3 practitioners were managed by a qualified teacher. This differs considerably from the staff composition in the majority of PVI settings where there is no requirement for a qualified teacher and only half the practitioners are required to be qualified to Level 3 with the remaining holding Level 2 qualifications or no qualifications at all.

Cottle and Alexander (2012, p. 648) state that practitioners recognise the importance of having 'quality' staff and relate this (to some extent) to staff having achieved qualifications. Interestingly though, practitioners have raised concerns regarding the achievement of qualifications, maintaining that having qualifications is not 'an absolute guarantee of quality'. This is supported by Chaplin (2013) who is critical of the discourse regarding the necessity for qualifications, arguing that government has become obsessed with qualifications and that this does not take into account the importance of experience. While this is accepted, it is suggested that experienced staff that are also well qualified would provide the optimum quality.

Following the Nutbrown Review (Nutbrown, 2012), the Department for Education (DfE, 2013a) have taken the decision that from September 2014 only qualifications accredited by the National College for Teaching and Leadership (NCTL) will be deemed to be 'full and relevant', these being the Early Years Educator, at Level 3 and Early Years Teacher at Level 6. Truss (2013) suggests that by building a vigorous qualification system the status of the early years sector will be raised, and will therefore attract more high quality graduates. It is contended that this view is somewhat naive as for this aim to be achieved issues relating to pay and conditions also need to be addressed (Kendall *et al.*, 2012).

Early Years Educator

Between 2007 and 2011 there was significant growth in the number of staff working in early years settings who hold 'full and relevant' Level 3 qualifications: from 72 per cent to 84 per cent (Truss, 2013). Unfortunately Nutbrown (2012) raised concerns regarding the lack of depth, intensity and content of some Level 3 qualifications, maintaining that some did not equip practitioners with the skills and knowledge to enable them to provide high quality care and education.

From September 2014, the only qualifications that will be deemed 'full and relevant' at Level 3 will be the Early Years Educator (EYE). This qualification aims to build on the richer underpinning knowledge recommended by Nutbrown (2012) to ensure that work-based practice becomes a central part of all training. As a result, all students' training must encompass the acquisition of knowledge alongside the application of theory to practice. This should result in those achieving EYE status being highly skilled professionals. Staff who have previously achieved Level 3 qualifications will not be required to undertake additional training, but will not be able to refer to themselves as Early Years Educators.

It has been confirmed that EYEs will also be required to hold GSCE grade A*-C in Maths and English. The impact of this requirement on recruitment and longer term on the workforce is concerning as nationally only 61 per cent of school leavers achieve these grades (DfE, 2013b). While no one would argue that practitioners should have a minimum standard of Maths and English to support children effectively, as the Dean of a School of Education which offers Level 3 Early Years courses, research of the current cohort's qualifications indicates that almost 50 per cent do not currently hold a GCSE grade A*-C in Maths. It is suggested that this rigid requirement could affect recruitment and lead to staffing shortages within the sector.

Early Years Teacher Status

In accepting some of the recommendations of Nutbrown (2012), the Coalition Government continued the work started by the previous Labour Government who were working towards their stated aim of having 'a graduate leader in every full day care setting by 2015' (CWDC, 2010, para. 9). The rationale underpinning this aim was recognition that graduates with expertise in early **childhood** have the greatest impact on pedagogical leadership (Sylva *et al.*, 2004 and Nutbrown, 2012). To achieve their aim, in 2005 the previous Labour Government introduced Early Years Professional (EYP) Status (EYPs specialise in leading and shaping practice). Evaluation of the impact of EYPs indicates that the quality of provision for pre-school children aged three and four improved significantly in those settings where an EYP was employed (Mathers *et al.*, 2011). It is interesting that this aim became only an 'aspiration' of the Coalition Government. In addition, withdrawal of government funding for part-time Foundation Degrees and BA (Hons) top-up programmes has impacted significantly on recruitment. Therefore it is contended this aspiration may be unachievable.

Building on the success of the EPPE Project (Sylva *et al.*, 2004), Nutbrown (2012) recommended that all early years settings should be managed by an early years teacher with **Qualified Teacher Status** (QTS) rather than EYPs. It is unfortunate that this recommendation was rejected and instead EYP was replaced with **Early Years Teacher Status**. While at first glance Early Years Teacher status and Qualified Teacher Status (QTS) appear equitable as they have similar entry criteria (GCSE Maths, English and Science above grade C and successful achievement of the Maths and English Skills Tests), the degree classification required differs. In order to access a PGCE in Early Years with QTS an applicant must hold an honours degree (360 credits) with a minimum of a 2:2 classification. In contrast to access Early Years Teacher Status, an ordinary degree (300 credits) is sufficient. In addition Early Years Teacher Status does not confer QTS so those who achieve it are not entitled to the terms and conditions attached to QTS, specifically pay and pension **rights**. This disparity is highlighted by a survey into EYP pay that found individuals earned at most £9.00 per hour while a Newly Qualified Teacher with QTS earned a minimum of £16.80 per hour (Murray, 2009).

Nutbrown (2013, p. 7) was highly critical of the Coalition Government's decision not to create parity between all early years teachers, maintaining that 'those who work with young children are offered a lesser status and, we should realistically anticipate, poorer pay and conditions than those who work with older children'. It is contended that this should be reconsidered and that Early Years Teacher Status should confer QTS, valuing the work that EYTs currently undertake and creating equality between teachers of all children. It is contended that this would ensure

FROM RESEARCH TO PRACTICE

Professor Cathy Nutbrown, in response to the government's lack of acceptance of the recommendations of her government-commissioned report, *Foundations for Quality* (2012), produced a paper 'Shaking the foundations of quality?' (Nutbrown, 2013). In this paper she clearly highlights why 'childcare policy must not lead to poor quality early education and care'.

This paper is important because high quality early years provision is crucial and should be led by well qualified staff who understand, respect and value the importance of childhood.

that one is not perceived as being superior to the other. It is acknowledged that this would significantly increase the cost of early years provision due to the increase in pay and suggested that this is the real reason for not conferring QTS on those gaining Early Years Teacher Status.

Ofsted

Early years provision in England is inspected by Ofsted; this involves **assessment** of performance based on the assessment of academic and other measured outcomes held by Ofsted, followed by a visit to the setting. Inspectors speak to staff, children and parents and carry out observations of practice (Ofsted, 2011). While all inspections follow this broad format, the way inspections are carried out varies. School inspections are announced, last two days and cover the whole school. Since 2012, when early years provision is inspected as part of a school inspection there is no longer a requirement to make a separate judgement on the early years provision. In contrast, inspections of early years provision not based in schools are unannounced, usually last half a day and judgements are made relating to the Early Years Foundation Stage and aspects of health and safety. Layzer and Goodson (2006, p. 565) are critical of this 'one-time snapshot' approach maintaining that 'it only measures what happens on a particular day. The activities and interactions in any setting may vary greatly over a week or a month, [highlighting that] our research procedures for the most part ignore this basic fact'.

Wilkinson (2009, p. 73) highlighted that local authorities previously shared responsibility for monitoring the quality of early years settings but they did not rely on 'Ofsted data in isolation', maintaining staffing, qualifications and foundation stage assessments were also important components when drawing conclusions. In 2014 the shared responsibility between Ofsted and Local Authorities was withdrawn (DfE, 2013a) resulting in Ofsted now being the sole arbitrator of quality judgements. It is considered that this is detrimental to ensuring high quality provision.

The findings of inspections are important. On the one hand they can identify outstanding provision, but conversely they also have the power to find a setting unsatisfactory, requiring it to improve which could result in registration being suspended or withdrawn.

The relationship between Ofsted and providers is underpinned by a power dimension. Quality is judged in terms of Ofsted definitions which may be at odds with practitioners', parents' and

Quality continues to improve ...

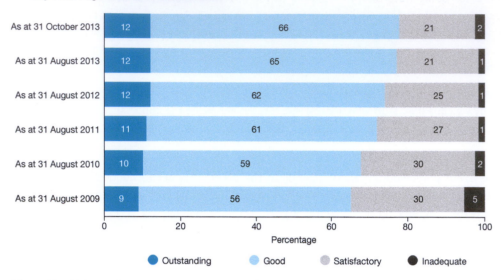

State of nation: most recent inspection judgements for overall effectiveness of all providers on the Early Years Register as at 31 October 2013

Figure 29.1 Ofsted early years annual report, 2012/2013

Source: Ofsted early years annual report: 2012/13, page 11: https://www.gov.uk/government/uploads/system/uploads/attachment_data/file/386504/Ofsted_Early_Years_Annual_Report_201213.pdf

children's definitions. Recent guidance from Wilshaw (2014), the chief inspector of Ofsted, urges early years inspectors to 'be clear about the extent to which a provider prepares children for school'. This is concerning as practitioners have raised concerns that some inspectors may not have the relevant skills and competencies to make such judgements.

It is contended that this focus on educational attainment and school readiness marginalises the important care element of provision and fails to acknowledge that preparation for school and young children's learning are complex issues which involve much more than just developing early reading, writing and maths skills.

Conclusion

It is hoped that this chapter has helped you to recognise that there are multiple definitions of quality which are underpinned by the diverse stake holders' perceptions, values and experiences and that all of these are important when making judgements about quality.

Quality measures indicate that there is a relationship between structural and process aspects of quality with research indicating that early years provision with highly qualified staff (teachers with QTS), has the greatest impact on children's long-term outcomes.

Debate continues regarding the essential elements of high quality early years provision. These relate to issues such as diversity of provision, qualification requirements, government policy and the form and function of Ofsted. In addition it is evident that parents', practitioners' and Ofsted definitions of quality can differ significantly. While these debates continue, it is suggested that when considering quality the most important issue is the experience of the child and the impact this has on the child's long-term outcomes.

As practitioners you are responsible for promoting the early years core values which I contend aim to ensure the individual needs of all children are met ensuring they achieve their full potential. I believe the most important thing for children is to have fun and enjoy their day, and in doing so I know from experience that children develop high levels of confidence, self-image and self-esteem. I remain confident that as practitioners you will ensure that for the children in your care this is the case and in doing so I believe they will be well prepared for their transition to school.

Further reading

Barber, J. and Paul-Smith, S. (2012) *The EYFS in Practice: The step-by-step guide to help you prepare for and manage your early years inspection with confidence.* Practical Pre-School Books. London.

This book reflects the revised EYFS 2014 and includes changes to the requirements of the Self-Evaluation Form (SEF). The book will be useful to you as it will help you to prepare effectively for your Ofsted inspection to ensure your inspection is a positive and stress-free experience.

Cottle, M. and Alexander, E. (2012) Quality in early years settings: government, research and practitioners perspectives. *British Educational Research Journal.* Vol. 38 No. 4 (pp. 635–654).

This article examines the reality of parent partnership in relation to providing quality early years services and highlights that partnerships are understood and enacted in very different ways. This article will help you to understand the tensions parents feel relating to Government policy and will cause you to question the purpose and priorities of your setting.

Harcourt, D. (2012) Standpoints on quality: Listening to children in Verona, Italy. *Australasian Journal of Early Childhood* Vol. 37, Part 2 (pp. 19–26).

This article provides insight into how you as a practitioner might capture young children's views and opinions regarding the quality of your setting with the intention of improving practice based on the children's views and opinions.

Useful websites

http://eyfs.info/home

The Early Years Foundation Stage Forum website is a vibrant online community for passionate EYFS professionals from a range of early years settings, including nursery practitioners, early years professionals, childminders, teachers, advisers and consultants, educators and writers and provides a platform to discuss and debate contemporary early years practice.

http://reports.ofsted.gov.uk/

This website provides a database of Ofsted reports carried out in early years settings. Reviewing Ofsted reports is a useful tool to support your knowledge and understanding of how to become an outstanding provider.

References

Anderson, G. and Arsenault, N. (1999) *Fundamentals of Educational Research,* (2nd edn). Falmer Press. London.

Blau, D. and Currie, J. (2006) Pre-School, Day Care and After-School Care: Who's Minding the Kids? In Hanushek, E. and Welch, F. (eds) *Handbook of the Economics of Education,* Elsevier. Amsterdam.

Chaplin, G. (2013) *Qualification Vs Experience*. Uncategorized. Available from: http://garychaplain.com/2013/06/27/qualifications-vs-experience (accessed 18 March 2014).

Clark, A. and Moss, P. (2001) *Listening to Young Children: The Mosaic Approach*. National Children's Bureau and Joseph Rowntree Foundation. London.

Coleyshaw, L., Whitmarsh, J., Jopling, M. and Hadfield, M. (2010) *Listening to Children's Perspectives: Improving the quality of provision in early years settings*. Department for Education Research Report DFE-RR239b. London.

Cooke, G., and Lawton, K. (2008) *For Love or Money: Pay, progression and professionalization in the 'early years workforce'*. Institute of Public Policy Research. London.

Cottle, M. and Alexander, E. (2012) Quality in early years settings: government, research and practitioners' perspectives. *British Educational Research Journal*, Vol. 38, No.4 (pp. 635–654).

CWDC (2010) *Memorandum submitted by the Children's Workforce Development Council*. www.publications.parliament.uk/pa/cm200910/cmselect/cmchilsch/275/275we46.htm (accessed 25 March 2014).

Daycare Trust (2011) *Choosing Quality – Supporting parents to access high quality childcare*. Policy insight paper 4. Daycare Trust. London.

Department for Education and Employment (1998) *The National Childcare Strategy*.

Department for Education and Skills (2003) *Every Child Matters: Change for Children*. HMSO. Nottingham.

Department for Education and Skills (2004)*The Children Act*. HMSO. London.

Department for Education (2011) *Provision for Children under Five Years of Age in England: January 2011* Statistical First Release. Department of Education. London.

Department for Education (2012) *Early Years Foundation Stage Framework*. Department for Education. London.

Department for Education (2013a) *More Great Childcare: Raising Quality and Giving Parents More Choice*. Department for Education. London.

Department for Education (2013b) *Raise on Line. Key Stage 4 Results. Available from:* www.education.gov.uk/schools/performance/group (accessed 25 March 2014).

Erikson, E.H. (1968). *Identity: Youth and Crisis*. Norton. New York.

Freud, S. (1965) *New Introductory lectures on Psychoanalysis*. Norton. New York.

Gambaro, L. Stewart, K. and Waldfogel, J. (2013) *A Question of Quality: Do children from disadvantaged backgrounds receive lower quality early years education and care in England?* Centre of Analysis of Social Exclusion. School of Economics. London.

Gilligan, C. (1982) *In a Different Voice: Psychological theory and women's development*. Harvard University Press. Cambridge.

Harcourt, D. (2012) Standpoints on quality: Listening to children in Verona, Italy. *Australasian Journal of Early Childhood*, Vol. 37, Part 2 (pp. 19–26).

HM Treasury (2004) *Choice for Parents, the Best Start for Children: A Ten Year Strategy for Childcare*. Department for Education and Skills, Department for Work and Pensions and the Department for Trade and Industry. HMSO. Nottingham.

Kendall, A., Carey, D., Cramp, A. and Perkins, H. (2012) Barriers and Solutions to HE Progression for Early Years' practitioners. *Journal of Vocational Education, and Training* Vol. 64, No.4. (pp. 543–560).

Layzer, J.I., and Goodson, B.D. (2006) The 'Quality' of Early Care and Education Settings: Definitional and Measurement Issues. *Evaluation Review*, Vol. 30, No.5 (pp. 556–576).

Mathers, S., Singler, R. and Karemaker, A. (2011) *Improving Quality in the Early Years: A Comparison of Perspectives and Measures*. Daycare Trust. London.

Murray, J. (2009) Value-based Leadership and Management, in Callan, S. and Robins, A. (eds) *Managing Early Years Settings*. Sage. London.

Nutbrown, C. (2012) *Foundations for Quality. The independent review of early education and childcare qualifications. Final Report*. Department for Education. London.

Nutbrown, C. (2013) *Shaking the Foundations of Quality? Why 'childcare' policy must not lead to poor-quality early education and care.* The University of Sheffield. Sheffield.

Ofsted (2011) *The Annual Report of Her Majesty's Chief Inspector of Education.* Children's Services and Skills 2010/2011. Ofsted. Manchester.

Ofsted (2013) *Conducting Early Years Inspections. Guidance for inspecting early years provision required to deliver the Early Years Foundation Stage.* Ofsted. Manchester.

Sylva K., Melhuish, E.C., Sammons, P., (2004) *The Effective Provision of Pre-School Education (EPPE) Project: Final Report: A Longitudinal Study Funded by the DfES 1997–2004.* London: DfES/Institute of Education, University of London.

Sylva, K., Melhuish, E., Sammons, P., Siraj-Blatchford, I., and Taggart, B. (2008). *Effective Pre-school and Primary Education 3-11 Project (EPPE 3-11) Final report from the primary phase: pre-school, school and family Influences on children's development during Key Stage 2 (age 7-11).* DCSF Publications. Nottingham.

Sylva, K. (2010*)* Quality in Childhood Settings, in *Evidence from the effective pre-school and primary project,* edited by Sylva, K. Melhuish, E. Siraj-Blatchford, I. and Taggart, B. Routledge. Oxon.

Tickell, C. (2011) The Early Years: Foundations for life, health and learning. *An Independent Report on the Early Years Foundation Stage to Her Majesty's Government.* www.education.gov.uk/tickellreview (accessed 2 March 2014).

Truss, E. (2013) Elizabeth Truss sets out the reforms to childcare published in the paper 'More great childcare'. Elizabeth Truss speaks at the Policy Exchange on childcare. 30.01.13 Available from: www.gov.uk/government/speeches/elizabeth-truss-speaks-at-the-policy-exchange-on-childcare (accessed 2 March 2014).

Waldegrave, H. (2013) *Quality Childcare Improving Early Years Childcare,* Lee, L. (ed.). London Policy Exchange. London.

Wilkinson, D. (2009) Quality Assessment of Early Years Education: Introduction *National Institute Economic Review,* Vol. 207 (pp. 73–74).

Wilshaw, M. (2014) *Letter from HMCI to early years inspectors – March 2014.* Available from: www.ofsted.gov.uk/resources/letter-hmci-early-years-inspectors-march-2014 (accessed 27 March 2014).

30 The effects of poverty on Early Years attainment

Jonathan Doherty and Caroline Tobbell

LEARNING OUTCOMES

After reading this chapter you should be able to:

✔ Understand what is meant by poverty and its effects on children, families and society.
✔ Understand the link between the achievement gap and social disadvantage.
✔ Be aware where underachievement is evident in the EYFS outcomes for vulnerable groups.
✔ Understand that well trained and knowledgeable Early Years practitioners can make a difference to vulnerable children's achievement.
✔ Be introduced to some strategies Early Years practitioners could employ to address the issues of attainment and disadvantage.

Introduction

Educational achievement is high on the political agenda. Children from poor backgrounds achieve less well than those from more advantaged families and this is the case in children as young as two. In a speech in 1999, Prime Minister Tony Blair said, 'the child born in the run-down estate, should have the same chance to be healthy and well educated as the child born in the leafy suburbs'. Fifteen years later in the Early Years Annual Report (2014) Ofsted argued that the pre-Reception age settings best equipped to help break 'the cycle of disadvantage' are those which are focused on helping children to learn at the earliest age. In a keynote speech to mark the launch of the report, HM Chief Inspector, Sir Michael Wilshaw, announced recently that too many of this country's poorest children are getting an inadequate start because the early years system is failing them. His solution for those children facing serious disadvantage to break the cycle of disadvantage? Putting two-year-olds in schools. If only the solution were that simple! The factors that affect children's achievement, and in particular the achievement of those children in disadvantage, are much more complex and require solutions involving families and communities, the early years and school sectors, and society as a whole. In this chapter we explore the following themes:

- Poverty and social inequality
- The achievement gap and social disadvantage
- Underachievement in the EYFS
- Strategies to improve educational disadvantage

Poverty and social inequality

What comes into your head when you hear the term 'child poverty'? Your first thoughts might conjure up images of starving children in underdeveloped countries sustained for days on meagre portions of rice and drinking contaminated water, or families riddled by disease living in squalid shanties with survival a constant struggle. You would be right of course. But **poverty** also exists much closer to home. In the UK today, 3.5 million children are living in poverty. That is 27 per cent of children, or one in four (DWP, 2013). The Government has a statutory requirement, enshrined in the Child Poverty Act 2010, to end child poverty by 2020. Predictions are, however, that this target will not be reached and another 1 million children will be pushed into poverty.

Definitions of poverty include 'absolute poverty', that is where basic needs such as food, drinking water, sanitation and access to services like health and education are lacking. It also is defined as 'relative income' which is 60 per cent of average income. Families and individuals who fall below this are deemed to be in poverty. In reality, this means homes which lack heating, where clothes are handed down from older siblings, food is scare and often mothers do without so that their children are fed. Eligibility for free school meals (FSM) is commonly used as a measure of disadvantage. Other approaches emphasise deficits in 'capabilities' or 'well-being'. Early research by Townsend (1979) argued that for those in poverty, resources are so below those of the average that individuals are excluded from **normal** activities and patterns of living and are therefore socially at a disadvantage. Oppenheim's definition really strips this down, 'Poverty means going short materially, socially, and emotionally . . . Poverty means staying at home, often being bored, not seeing friends . . . not being able to take the children out for a treat or on holiday' (1993, p. 4).

The causes of poverty are complex but its effects are far-reaching. It imposes costs on broader society, estimated to be at least £29 billion a year (Hirsh, 2013). Families with children are more likely to be poor than those without children. Families from ethnic minorities are more likely to live in poverty. In 2010, families with at least one disabled member were 30 per cent more likely to live in poverty than families without disabilities. Poverty is a blight to a healthy, thriving **childhood**. Three-year-olds in households with incomes below about £10,000 are 2.5 times more likely to suffer chronic illness than children in households with incomes above £52,000. Infant mortality is 10 per cent higher for infants in the lower social group than the average. There is a higher risk of unemployment and a higher probability of being involved in crime (Holtermann, 1997). Children in those communities are much more likely to be victims of accidents in the home and are nine times less likely than those living in affluent areas to have access to green space, places to play and to live in environments with better air quality. Far from being a time of happy exploration, childhood for many disadvantaged children means spending less time discovering the world around them and more time struggling to survive it (Jensen, 2009). Poverty and its associated risk factors damage children's cognitive, physical and socio-emotional well-being (Klebanov and Brooks-Gunn, 2006). The linked effect of disadvantage on children's educational achievement presents a grim picture and it is to this that we now turn.

PROVOCATION

Do you agree with the definitions of poverty given above? What would your personal definition be?

It is important to addresses the issue of poverty as its consequences for children, families and society are hugely detrimental. Who do you see as the main stakeholders?

How can we realistically reduce the levels of poverty in this country? What steps are needed to make this happen?

The achievement gap and social disadvantage

Raising the educational achievement of children from low-income families has been a key priority of past and present governments and is very much 'everyone's business' (DCSF, 2010). Poverty corrodes educational achievement. It is during the early years when poverty has the greatest influence on outcomes. The **achievement gap** begins early and widens steadily. Schools do not close this gap. Poorer children arrive at school less prepared for formal education (less 'school-ready') and frequently less equipped to build upon the rich environments for early learning experienced in the EYFS. Children from disadvantaged backgrounds are less likely to achieve **a good level of development** at age 5, to achieve well at school age 11 and do well in their GCSEs at 16 compared with children from affluent backgrounds. Important work by Feinstein (2003) showed the strong influence of social class on achievement. He found that social class attainment gaps are in evidence by age 5. More alarming was that achievement by children from higher socioeconomic status (SES) groups had overtaken children from lower socioeconomic status groups at 22 months. At age 5, children who are eligible for free school meals (FSM) have lower literacy and numeracy achievement. At age 7, the achievement of children eligible for FSM is lower (Sammons *et al.*, 2002). At Key Stage 1, 94 per cent of children who reach a good level of development at age 5 go on to achieve the expected levels of reading in Key Stage 1 and are five times more likely to achieve the highest levels – strong evidence that disadvantage and underachievement are linked through the pre-school years and beyond.

Underachievement in the EYFS

The new Early Years Foundation Stage Profile (EYFSP) introduced in September 2012 brought changes as to how children are assessed at the end of the EYFS. The 'good level of development' (GLD) measure has changed. Now, children reach a GLD at the end of the EYFS if they achieve at least the expected level in the early learning goals in the **Prime Areas of learning** and in the Specific Areas. In 2013, 52 per cent of children overall achieved a 'good level of development' (DfE, 2013). Articles in the press have painted a picture of decline in standards and the wide disparities in achievement of certain groups of children. The 2012–13 EYFSP results show 36 per cent of pupils eligible for **FSM** achieved a GLD compared with 55 per cent of other pupils. They show a lower proportion of pupils from Asian, Chinese and black backgrounds achieving a 'good level of development' and Gypsy/Roma and travellers of Irish heritage significantly lower than the rest. The gap between girls and boys is 16 percentage points and between summer-borns and those born at other times of the year is 23 percentage points. The **SEN** attainment gap is 42 percentage points. Free School Meal attainment gaps are widest in the literacy areas of learning. This means there are clear differences in achievement in terms of gender, ethnicity and social class.

There are large attainment gaps among **disadvantaged groups** nationally. Have we made progress over the years for the most disadvantaged groups of children and narrowed the achievement gap? There is some evidence that the gap has closed slightly but there are still disparities between children at different levels of deprivation (Bradbury, 2013) In the UK levels of poverty continue to rise, and the achievement for the most disadvantaged children is still below that of more affluent peers. Both of these are unacceptable. In the section that follows we suggest five strategies to tackle these important issues.

Strategies to move forward and improve educational disadvantage

1 Have high aspirations

> '*The greater failure is not the child who doesn't reach the stars, but the child who has no stars that they feel they are reaching for.*'
>
> (Gordon Brown, 2007)

To improve educational achievement for all children we need to look beyond EYFSP data to how we as professionals and parents inspire our children. Findings suggest (e.g. Goodman and Gregg, 2010) that aspirations and attitudes have an important part to play in explaining why poor children typically achieve poor educational outcomes. Gypsy, Roma, Traveller families often have lower aspirations for their children than other groups. Conversely some other minority groups have very high aspirations (Strand, 2007).

High aspirations are linked to good educational outcomes. 'Poverty of expectations' is as limiting as material poverty. Children in disadvantage have the odds stacked against them. Some poor children have low aspirations of themselves. They view themselves as less able academically and are more inclined to believe that academic results are unimportant to them and consequently have less focus in their learning. But disadvantage does not determine life courses: many children from impoverished backgrounds do achieve very well at school and in the world of work. When parents have high aspirations for their children and provide encouragement from an early age, children achieve good outcomes.

2 Develop communication and language skills

Communication underpins educational development and oral language is a key ingredient for academic achievement. Many children from the poorest families do not have a basic grasp of language, literacy and numeracy and as a consequence struggle to access the EYFS curriculum and flourish in it. In this country, children from low income backgrounds are 19 months behind their better-off peers. This compares with only 10.6 months in Canada (Waldfogel and Washbrook, 2012). Early deficits in language are indicators of poor later outcomes. Hart and Risley's groundbreaking research in 2003 found that by age 3, children from disadvantaged homes hear three million fewer words than those from affluent homes. Children from the most advantaged backgrounds were a year ahead in their vocabulary than those less advantaged. Projects such as Talk to your Baby, and Raising Early Achievement in Literacy (REAL) have already made a difference. After one year of language interventions, children from disadvantaged families with delayed linguistic development showed improvement in their language skills (Opie *et al.*, 2004). Interventions targeted at emergent literacy (coming before reading and writing make real differences to 'at risk' pre-school children.

What role is there for practitioners? We need informed and sustained attempts to improve language and communication development by creating language-rich preschool environments with frequent opportunities for communication (Potter, 2007). Early years staff need a good understanding of how language is developed and the means to promote it. These include talking to children about topics that interest them, using open-ended questions in conversation, asking children to elaborate and extending their vocabulary. Collaboration between practitioners and parents is vital. It means **inter-agency** working across children's services. In many settings there are increasing numbers of children for whom English is not their first language. Children who enter these settings are at a disadvantage without good levels of support for them and their families. Here are some ways in which one Nursery tackled the issues.

CASE STUDY 1

English as an additional language

A busy Nursery in a disadvantaged area had children from a variety of backgrounds including refugees and asylum seekers and a large number of recently arrived immigrants into the local community. Children who speak little or no English at home are at a disadvantage when they enter an Early Years setting without support in the language with which they are most familiar. They feel isolated and often scared. The EYFS emphasises the role of the first language in laying firm foundations for language development. Supporting children and their families where English was not the first language was a priority for the setting. This was seen as an excellent opportunity for practitioners to explore strategies in their practice to meet individual needs and ensure progress and achievement was high.

An Audit of Need document for the settings was created. Strategies were discussed that valued and used the first language, extended vocabulary in English and provided a platform of trust for children, their parents and carers. Staff greeted children and parents at the beginning and end of each day. The setting policy is that where parents are not able to bring their child to school they set up systems to contact parents at least weekly using phone, email and text. They arranged for a bilingual support worker to come into the setting regularly to meet and greet parents. The Bilingual Community Officer from the Ethnic Minority Achievement Team undertook visits to jointly observe the children in their routines and arranged for whole staff training to take place.

They arranged for information to be translated and for parents who don't read they have sensitively found ways of explaining important information to them. They had times each month for parents to come into the setting and meet their child's key person and discuss progress in a relaxed setting. Story-telling in the home language was stressed. Musical activities provided opportunities to learn new words; language learning through games increased and every opportunity was taken to promote language in the everyday routines of the setting.

Consider the following questions:

- *What strategies would you use to encourage a child to learn English but not lose their first language?*
- *What different strategies do the nursery practitioners use to communicate with parents?*
- *Why is it so important to build relationships and trust and how might this be done?*

3 Employ well-qualified professionals to deliver high quality early learning

Children achieve best at the hands of well qualified and experienced professionals qualified at least to Level 3 with access to ongoing professional development. This is a vital key to closing the achievement gap between children from poorer homes and their peers. The Nutbrown Review (2012) recommended that all early years staff should be qualified to Level 3 at a minimum by September 2022 and that students should have Level 2 qualifications in English and Mathematics before they begin a Level 3 early education or childcare course.

Since 1997 over £20 billion has been spent on early years and childcare services. As part of the strategy to tackle disadvantage the Labour government introduced SureStart in 1998 in disadvantaged areas, an initiative aimed at providing support and information for parents and giving access to quality childcare based on the Head Start initiative in the USA. The Coalition government maintained an expectation that Children's Centres' core purpose is to reduce inequalities between families in greatest need by helping to improve parenting skills, raise aspirations and improve life chances. Where they are most effective is as hubs for the local community sharing expertise and resources with local families. High-quality affordable childcare provision makes a significant contribution to children's outcomes and sets them on the path to success in later life. High quality early education and care has an enormous impact on outcomes for disadvantaged children, through improved language, cognitive and social gains. In the UK, children from low income families are less likely to attend high quality early education and care programmes than their peers and so are already at a disadvantage (Pascal and Bertram, 2012).

REFLECTIVE PRACTICE
REFLECTIVE PRACTICE

Practitioners need to be skilled and knowledgeable to deliver high quality pedagogy.

We suggest five 'key conditions' that directly impact on educational outcomes:

1   Strong **leadership**, steering curriculum and planning with a clear educational focus.
2   Knowledgeable and capable practitioners with good understanding of the children they care for and knowledge of what a developmentally appropriate curriculum looks like in practice.
3   Pedagogic approaches which promote play, high levels of adult–child verbal interactions and 'sustained shared thinking'.
4   Safe and stimulating physical environments that promote learning indoors and outdoors and that allow children to play and have choice about their activities alongside adult-supported activities.
5   Significant levels of parental **engagement** where parents are involved in decisions about their child's learning, which build partnerships and support them to continue children's learning experiences at home.

Take each of these in turn. Reflect on the three questions below.

- *What does each of the above conditions mean for you currently?*
- *What will each of the above conditions mean for you in the future?*
- *Are there actions you can take now to help you become as knowledgeable as you can so that you deliver effective and appropriate pedagogy?*

FROM RESEARCH TO PRACTICE

Sound Foundations

Mathers *et al.* (2014) *Sound Foundations. A review of the research evidence on quality of early childhood education and care for children under three: Implications for policy and practice.*

What is this? A review of research (mainly from the USA, New Zealand, Australia and UK) to collate what is known about quality education and care for children from birth to three. The research focuses its findings on supporting young children from the most disadvantaged backgrounds.

Why is it important? It demonstrates the importance of knowledgeable, well trained practitioners with good understanding of pedagogical practices for under-threes.

What does it tell us? Good quality settings will make a difference to young children and narrow gaps in attainment if the quality is good. Pedagogy for under-threes is specialised and different from what may be provided for over threes.

Key findings:

Four key dimensions of good quality pedagogy for all children under three:

1 Stable relationships and interactions with sensitive and responsive adults.
2 A focus on play-based activities and routines which allow children to take the lead in their own learning.
3 Support for communication and language.
4 Opportunities to move and be physically active.

Reflection

1. *How would you interpret the statements in the key findings?*
2. *In what ways could you apply them in your setting?*
3. *How does this fit with the recommendations from OFSTED to encourage more schools to provide places for 2-year-olds?*

4 Invest early to counter disadvantage

Investing in the early years leads to improved educational outcomes, better health outcomes and a reduction in poverty. Investing early results in a stronger economy with less crime, higher earnings and a more stable and productive workforce. Society as a whole benefits from investing in young children. Recent initiatives such as the **Pupil Premium** introduced in 2011 provides extra funding for disadvantaged children and increases social mobility to enable more pupils from disadvantaged backgrounds to attend university and reduce the attainment gap nationally.

Currently, all 3 and 4-year-olds in England are entitled to 15 hours of free early education and childcare each week for 38 weeks a year. Free early education for disadvantaged 2-year-olds began in 2006 in response to growing evidence that high quality early education can counter the potential negative effects of disadvantage and positively influence children's cognitive and **social development**. The 'two-year-old programme' is already playing a pivotal role in improving disadvantaged children's outcomes through increasing confidence and independence, verbal skills and reasoning ability, and in ensuring that by the age of 5 children are as ready as their more advantaged peers to start and fully benefit from school (Gibb *et al.*, 2011).

5 Work in partnership with parents

Parents and carers play a vital role in their children's early development and learning. Evidence (e.g. Desforges and Abouchaar, 2003; Gutman and Feinstein, 2007) suggests that when parents engage in learning activities with their children from an early age, it has more of a positive impact on outcomes than any other factor. This is why it is so important for all settings to engage with parents and to support them in creating good home learning environments (HLEs). Such research advocates the following type of activities at home:

- reading with the child
- teaching songs and nursery rhymes
- painting and drawing
- playing with letters and numbers
- visiting the library
- teaching the alphabet and numbers
- taking children on visits
- creating regular opportunities for them to play with their friends at home.

PROVOCATION

- How would you go about helping parents develop an environment for learning at home?
- How would you advise them incorporate some of the above ideas into everyday activities?
- There will be barriers to this work. Can you identify them and suggest solutions to overcome these?

There is much work to be done. It is also vital that parents and early years practitioners work in partnership together. The All Party Parliamentary **Sure Start** Group (2013) emphasised this in the recent review of Sure Start centres. Settings that do this effectively build a fuller picture of children's achievements as well as their interests. They share what children are doing in settings and guide parents on how to build upon this at home. Where practitioners build relationships with parents and help them to understand how children learn best and help them see how they can support their own child more effectively this in turn can help them parent their children more effectively at home. However, this is not always easy. The following case study describes how one setting tries to build relationships and trust in challenging circumstances.

CASE STUDY 2

A private day nursery has set up a toy library for children to choose toys and story books to take home. At first they had a regular slot towards the end of a session where the library was open and parents were invited to join their child to choose something to take home. Initially when they opened the library children and parents were enthusiastic but they found interest from parents soon dropped off. When they asked the parents about it they found they did not really see the point of the library and they indicated it was a worry that they had to remember the toy or book or were concerned it may get damaged or lost.

The practitioners then decided to re-launch the library and instead of putting it on at the end of the session they made it at a particular time each week to coincide with a drop-in slot where they welcomed parents anyway. During these sessions they used the toys and books with children and modelled how parents could use the toys and books with the children. They created some 'suggestions for using' cards to go with the toys and books to give the parents some ideas for what to do at home. They also encouraged parents to take photos of themselves and the children playing with the toys and to share their experiences the following week. They also bought some bags to take the toys home in safely. They reassured parents that loss and damage was not a reason not to use the library. They found interest from both children and parents picked up and they added the photos and parents' and children's comments about their play at home to the children's profiles.

Consider the following questions:

- *Why didn't the toy library go so well at first?*
- *What do you think made a difference after the re-launch?*
- *In what ways do you think the toy library will encourage a good home learning environment?*
- *In what ways do you think the toy library may support the children's learning?*

Conclusion

Tackling poverty and improving outcomes for children have been priorities for previous UK governments. Without tackling this issue we cannot have a world-class education system. Despite a variety of initiatives, educational achievement for the most disadvantaged children remains below that of more advantaged peers. Children from poor backgrounds are disadvantaged from the start. Gaps already evident at 22 months continue to widen through school and into adulthood. There are many complex factors relating to children's underachievement. In this chapter, however, we presented five strategies offering the potential to close the achievement gap for children in most disadvantage. Poverty impacts negatively on educational outcomes. More needs to be done to remove inequalities in our system so that all of our children have a fair and equal chance to flourish, regardless of their gender, ethnicity or social class.

It is essential that Government really commits to tackling the issue. It requires a clear and sustained approach to implement policies and procedures which provide good quality support in childcare provision, schools, housing, health and social and welfare support. We believe this is urgently required. In this chapter we argued for Government commitment through policy and financial backing, and for strategies based on research evidence that will ensure that poorer children are no longer inherently disadvantaged in their lives. Initiatives such as those discussed in the chapter are effective and have made a difference to the lives of children. What is now needed is to take stock of what really does work (programmes, initiatives and interventions) and to cause these to happen immediately.

We feel the fuse is lit for early years. Initiatives such as free early years places for 2, 3 and 4-year-olds are essential. We must also maintain the thrust for high quality settings where pedagogy and practice with our youngest children is no less than excellent. Practitioners make a difference to children's lives but they must be highly qualified, knowledgeable about child development and strive to fulfil every child's aspiration and potential. In these ways, we can break the link between poverty and underachievement and improve outcomes for all children.

Further reading

Bradbury, A. (2013) *Understanding Early Years Inequality. Policy, assessment and young children's identities.* London: Routledge.

One of the very few books to tackle this issue. Detailed and well informed, drawing upon current policy, EYFS data and offering a sharp sociological critique of the issue of educational underachievement. Not an easy introduction to the topic though.

Roberts, K. (2009) *Early Home Learning Matters – a good practice guide.* London: Family and Parenting Institute.

A short book but full of excellent information. Chapters include working with parents, a good home learning environment and working inclusively. Easy to read and well worth doing so.

Field, F. (2010) *The Foundation Years: Preventing Poor Children Becoming Poor Adults.* The report of the independent review on poverty and life chances. London: Cabinet Office.

Commissioned by the Prime Minister in 2010 to review poverty in the UK, this report is thorough and makes a number of urgent recommendations. Long but well worth reading in sections.

Useful websites

www.literacytrust.org.uk/

The National Literacy Trust: This site supports the development of children's communication, language and literacy and has many excellent resources for the Early Years sector.

www.suttontrust.com/

The Sutton Trust: An organisation which aims to influence policy and practice in relation to breaking the link between family background and educational inequality and as such conducts research and supports a range of programmes to this effect.

www.educationscotland.gov.uk/supportinglearners/additionalsupportneeds/eal/

Education Scotland: Guidance and advice on supporting learning for children with English as an additional language including case studies in early years settings.

References

All Party Parliamentary Sure Start Group (2013) *Best Practice for a Sure Start: The Way Forward for Children's Centres.* London: 4Children.

Blair, T. (1999) 'Beveridge revisited: a welfare state for the 21st century'. In R. Walker (ed), *Ending Child Poverty: Popular Welfare for the 21st Century,* Bristol: The Policy Press.

Bradbury, A. (2013) *Understanding Early Years Inequality. Policy, assessment and young children's identities.* London: Routledge.

Brown, G. (2007) Education Speech. University of Greenwich. 31 October 2007.

Department for Children, Schools and Families (DCSF) (2010). *Breaking the Link Between Disadvantage and Low Achievement in the Early Years. Everyone's business.* London: DCSF.

Department for Education (DfE) (2012) *Statutory Framework for the Early Years Foundation Stage. Setting the standards for learning, development and care for children from birth to five.* London: DfE.

Department for Education (DfE) (2013) *Early Years Foundation Stage Profile Attainment by Pupil Characteristics, England. Statistical First Release 47*. London: DFE.

Department of Work and Pensions (DWP) (2013) *Households below Average Income. An analysis of the income distribution 1994/95-21/11/12*. Available at *www.gov.uk/ . . . /* Accessed 20 August 2015.

Desforges, C. and Abouchaar, A. (2003) *The Impact of Parental Involvement, Parental Support and Family Education on Pupil Achievement and Adjustment: A Literature Review*. London: DfES.

Feinstein, L. (2003) Inequality in the early cognitive development of children in the early 1970 cohort. *Economica,* Vol. 70, (277), pp. 73-97.

Gibb, J., Jelicic, H. and La Valle, I. (2011) *Rolling out free early education for disadvantaged two year olds: an implementation study for local authority and providers*. Research Report DFE-RR131. National Children's Bureau with National Centre for Social Research.

Goodman, A. and Gregg, P. (2010) *Poorer Children's Educational Attainment: How important are attitudes and behaviour?* York: Joseph Rowntree Foundation (www.jrf.org.uk/publications/educational-attainment poor-children).

Gutman, L. and Feinstein, L. (2007) *Parenting Behaviours and Children's Development from Infancy to Early Childhood: Changes, Continuities, and Contributions*. London: Centre for Research on the Wider Benefits of Learning.

Hart, B., and Risley, T. (2003) The early catastrophe: The 30 million word gap. *American Educator,* 27, pp. 4-9.

Hirsh, D. (2013) *Estimating the Costs of Child Poverty, 2013*. Child Poverty Action Group website. Available at www.cpag.org.uk. Accessed 14 April, 2014.

Holtermann, S. (1997) All our futures: the impact of public expenditure and fiscal policies on children and young people. In A. Walker and C; Walker (eds), *Britain Divided: The growth of social exclusion in the 1980s and 1990s*. London: CPAG.

Jensen, E. (2009) *Teaching with poverty in mind. What being poor does to kids' brains and what schools can do about it*. Alexandria, Virginia USA: ASCD.

Klebanov, P. and Brooks-Gunn, J. (2006) Cumulative, human capital, and psychological risk in the context of early intervention: Links with IQ at ages 3, 5, and 8. *Annals of the New York Academy of Sciences,* 1094, pp. 63-82.

Mathers , S., Eisenstadt, N., Sylva, K., Soukakou, E. and Ereky-Stevens, K. (2014) *Sound Foundations . A Review of the Research Evidence on Quality of Early Childhood Education and Care for Children Under Three. Implications for Policy and Practice*. University of Oxford and Sutton Trust. Available at: www.suttontrust.com/ourwork/research/item/sound-foundations. Accessed April 2014.

Nutbrown, C. (2012). *Review of Early Education and Childcare Qualifications: Interim Report*. London: Department for Education DfE.

Ofsted (2013) *Early years. The report of Her Majesty's Chief Inspector of Education, Children's Services and Skills 2012-13*, Manchester: Ofsted.

Opie, M., Steele, H. and Ward, S. (2004). 'Cognitive outcomes of Sally Ward's early language-based intervention with mothers and babies in longitudinal perspective: lessons of Head Start revisited', *Educational and Child Psychology*. Vol. 21, (2), pp. 51-66.

Oppenheim, C. (1993) *Poverty: the facts*. London: CPAG.

Pascal, C. and Bertram, A. (2012) 'The impact of early education as a strategy for counteracting socio economic disadvantage'. Background paper prepared for Ofsted's Access and Achievement 2013 review, Birmingham: CREC. Available at: www.ofsted.gov.uk/accessandachievement. Accessed February 2014.

Potter, C.A. (2007) Developments in UK early years policy and practice: can they improve outcomes for disadvantaged children? *International Journal of Early Years Education*. Vol. 15, (2), pp. 171-180.

Sammons, P., Sylva, K., Melhuish, E., Siraj-Blatchford, I., Taggart, B. and Elliot, K. (2002) *Technical paper 8a: measuring the impact of pre-school children's cognitive progress over the pre-school period* (The Effective Provision of Pre-School Education (EPPE) project), London: DfES/Institute of Education, University of London.

Strand, S. (2007) *Minority Ethnic Pupils in the Longitudinal Study of Young People in England* (LSYPE): University of Warwick.

Townsend, P. (1979) *Poverty in the United Kingdom*. London: Allen Lane & Penguin Books.

Waldfogel, J. and Washbrook, E. (2012) *Achievement gaps in childhood: A cross-national perspective'*. Paper prepared for the Sutton Trust/Carnegie Corporation Summit on Social Mobility, London. May 2012.

Wilshaw, M. (2014) *Unsure Start. HMCI's Early Years Annual Report 2012/13 Speech,* 3 April. Westminster.

31 Working collaboratively

Anne Rawlings and Jo Dallal

LEARNING OUTCOMES

After reading this chapter, you should:

✔ Have a raised awareness of the context for collaborative working.
✔ Recognise the policy context for multi-professional through 'interprofessional' practice.
✔ Recognise the various terms that are used to denote collaborative working.
✔ Have a raised awareness of how and why working collaboratively is a hope for the future for Early Years practitioners.

Introduction

It is widely accepted that all employees of the children's workforce (birth to 19 years) should work collaboratively, but before moving further forward there needs to be a consideration of related terminology. This chapter attempts to explore the nuances surrounding this enigma and hopes to find a way forward for all those professionals working in the field by means of case studies and reflection.

The *Working Together to Safeguard Children* (March 2013); *The Framework for the Assessment of Children in Need and their Families* (2000); and statutory guidance on making arrangements to safeguard and promote the welfare of children under Section 11 of the Children Act 2004 (2007) have all been published to enable a framework for more effective collaboration but there is still a long learning curve to negotiate. A good start would be for different disciplines to work together on an agreed definition for 'inter-professional practice'.

A number of terms are used to describe the practice of working with a range of professionals; these include multi-agency, multi or inter-disciplinary, integrated working, multi-professional and inter-professional. These terms have different meanings for different professional groups and all have relevance in varying contexts. However, in order to safeguard and protect children and young people effectively the drivers for each discipline will need to reflect on the impact of those drivers and the language used by each different professional group, for example those working in health, education, social care and the voluntary and third sectors.

CASE STUDY 1

Children with additional needs in particular are especially vulnerable to the vagaries of partnership working.

John is nine years old and has such severe mental and physical disabilities that he needs full-time care. The following identifies all those involved in his care:

Family members: Mother, father, two siblings and grandparents.
Health professionals: General Practitioner, Medical Centre Nurse, Incontinence Officer, Home Nursing Support.
Social services: Social Worker, Respite Care Worker, Family Support Worker, Occupational Therapist
Voluntary services: Hospice, outreach support, charities.
School: Local Education Authority link person, Educational Psychologist, Speech Therapist, School Nurse, Doctor, Teachers and Teaching Assistants.

The challenge is for all these people to work together in partnership for the benefit of the child and they do, to a point. The reality is that although each tries their best to provide services for John and his family the professions do not seem to share information. This leads to the family feeling the pressure of repeating issues time and time again. Fusion becomes elusive. Information becomes lost amongst all the attempts to achieve well-being for the child. The family forgets, as anyone might, which information has been shared with which professional and becomes anxious when those involved do not seem to be aware of all their difficulties. However, it is said that 'multi-agency working enables different services to join forces in order to prevent problems occurring in the first place. It is an effective way of supporting children, young people and families with additional needs and helping to secure improved outcomes' (CWDC 2007: 5).

How would you describe the care given to John bearing in mind the following definitions?

Multi-disciplinary: This involves more than one agency working with a family but not really transcending professional boundaries. The child moves from one professional to another and the professionals within each discipline work in separate ways with a limited amount of sharing information. *Is this the type of care John is receiving?*
Multi-professional: This involves many professionals, hopefully working together. *Is this the type of care John is receiving?*
Multi-agency working: This involves many agencies, hopefully working together. *Is this the type of care John is receiving?*
Inter-disciplinary: This involves professionals working in parallel with others but with some co-operation. There is recognition here that there is a need for more than one profession to be involved. Ideally parents take the initiative and pass on information from one professional to another. This is a skills-based response rather than a child-centred one. However 'a child is a whole person whose life cannot be divided into different segments' (Foley and Rixon 2014: 53). *Is this the type of care John is receiving?*

Trans-disciplinary: This highlights that child development is linked. Therefore it involves all professionals working together across disciplines. The needs of the family as well as those of the child must be considered and information sharing and coming to an agreed decision is essential. Here a Key Person system must be implemented (Peter Elfer) and might be considered to be akin to the concept of a lead professional. *Is this the type of care John is receiving?*

Context for collaborative working

This should be where all agree to work towards a common goal, to share relevant information, to respect and understand job roles and professional boundaries and to focus on a mutually agreed programme of health and well-being. 'Integrated working is at the centre of making a real difference to the lives of children, young people and their families' and is still a central tenet of the *Every Child Matters* (DfE 2003) agenda not yet rescinded in law. However, for collaboration to occur there must be trust and mutual respect between disciplines and all must work towards

PROVOCATION

(a) *Name all the professionals who might be involved in a serious case review covering safeguarding and child protection.*

Before doing so it is appropriate to emphasise that serious case reviews (SCRs) should shed light on whether lessons can be learned about the way local professionals and agencies work together. They are not inquiries into how a child dies or who is to blame, they focus on improving practices that safeguard and promote the welfare of children (Radford 2010) 'SCRs shed light on whether lessons can be learned about the way local professionals and agencies work together in the light of a serious injury or child death where abuse or neglect is suspected' (Wonnacott 2008/2011: 1). This process is sometimes seized upon by the press who are determined to name those they feel have failed the child, always bearing in mind that the press needs to ascertain what sells copy.

(b) *If these professionals can be named, what might be stopping them from producing trans-disciplinary teamwork?*

The problem might possibly be **epistemological**. If so there is a need to discover whether this is an important barrier to working collaboratively or whether there are fundamental principles that create too much of a challenge for the work force involved. We know we should all work together in the best interests of the child which should be paramount (Children Act 1989). However there must be an 'acceptance that there are multiple ways of understanding' (Cartmel, Macfarlane and Nolan 2013: 399) and that the knowledge base of each discipline is equally valuable.

openness, honesty and transparency. 'Interprofessional working involves working in an integrated way rather than in parallel or in sequence' (Payler and Georgeson 2013: 380–397). This should all be possible, but in reality there is a hierarchy among professions. It is debateable as to whether equal value is placed on the opinion of a childcare worker or a paediatrician, a health visitor or the Head of a Social Services' department. Recommendations of a consultant in an accident and emergency unit might be considered to be more important than those of a childminder in cases of potential child abuse. This is exemplified in the Climbié case of 2000 when the child-minder raised the alarm and highlighted a cause for concern.

Prevention and early intervention must be a priority to safeguard and protect children because by the time a Serious Case Review (SCR) is needed it is too late for that child. A SCR is when a child dies or sustains significant harm, and abuse or neglect are known or suspected to have been a factor. However, SCRs are retrospective and primarily used to identify lessons about how agencies work individually and together to safeguard and promote the welfare of children, and to ensure that interagency working is improved as a result.

A recent DfE-commissioned report entitled 'A Study to Investigate the Barriers to Learning from Serious Case Reviews and Identify Ways of overcoming these Barriers' (DfE July 2014) was conducted by an inter-professional research team from Kingston University's Institute for Child Centred Inter-professional Practice (ICCIP). The team agreed with some aspects of the Munro Report (2011) in that the current system is too focused on what happened and not why it happened. A central principle for a professional working in any area is that they are able to refer to their own skills, knowledge and understanding and have the ability to make decisions sometimes under pressure in the middle of very complex and emotional situations. The sharing of the build-up to significant incremental events in order to support each other when making crucial decisions is key to protecting and **safeguarding** children.

It is the on-going *incremental events* that should be shared across disciplines that will highlight the on-going cause for concern which is key to the early identifying of cases for further investigation. For example in the Daniel Pelka case every primary school teacher knows that children will take food from another child's lunch box for a variety of reasons and it may not be unusual. However, in Daniel's case his 'search for food was excessive' and he was 'becoming a secretive eater'. This, linked to other indications such as speech and language delay, aggressive

PROVOCATION

An overwhelming finding from previous Serious Case Reviews indicates, for those practitioners that work in early years (birth to five years), that 'two thirds of SCRs concern children under the age of five (and half are for infants under twelve months)' (Brandon *et al.*, 2012; NSPCC, 2012; Ofsted, 2011). This means that services for a large number of 'these children fall under the Private, Voluntary, Independent (PVI) and third sectors, or are looked after by families/carers, which adds to the complexity and transparency of information sharing' (DfE July 2014).

Consider why this might be.

behaviour towards his mother, Daniel's poor attendance at school (below 64%) and missed appointments, all indicated a grave cause for concern (Coventry LSCB - Final Overview Report of Serious Case Review re Daniel Pelka - September 2013: pp. 23-24).

Those disciplines that work in the children and young people's services have their own multiplicity of complex rules and relationships with each other within their own organisations and outward facing activities. The complexity of revealing learning in order to acquire and synthesise information from each other is acknowledged and depends on building a picture of how combinations of the varying contexts, use of a common shared language, sustainable relationships and infrastructures amalgamate in order to create new and smarter ways of working through their differing lived experiences.

Challenges highlighted in several research publications indicate a 'power imbalance' recognised to exist within and between professions. Issues such as equal status, demarked hierarchy in job titles or perspectives of individuals' levels of management responsibility appear to determine the extent of an individuals' propensity to engage with embedding learning in practice (Martin *et al.*, 2010). This can result in potential implications of one profession determining policy which could lead to inconsistencies and/or misunderstandings within and across other professions that could bring about risk adverse practices or raised awareness of risk identified by Anning *et al.* (2006). However, Ecklers *et al.* (2006: 250) cautions that '*learning together has not always resulted in working together.*'

CASE STUDY 2

'Colin, aged seven, arrives at school on Monday morning with two black eyes and a bruised nose. He has always been rather aggressive with other children, bullying the smaller ones and often getting into fights. He is new to the school and so far neither of his parents has had contact with the staff. He boasts about his new father being a black belt in karate. On the morning in question, he is obviously in pain from the bruising and sits quietly by himself suffering, not roused by the taunts and questions of the other children nor responding to the teacher when she asks how he got hurt' (OU 1989).

What should be the starting point? Which professionals might need to be involved when investigating this case? Should there be a lead professional? Which professional do you feel might play the most important role in supporting Colin?

Cartmel *et al.* (2013: 398) argue that 'the workforce' should be 'challenged to reconsider ways of working'. In each sector there needs to be support, recognition and encouragement for those working at operational level. Managers should be considered as accountable as those whom they line manage. This being one of the issues in the Victoria Climbié case. 'The landmark public inquiry that followed this case provided a salutary example of how the network of agencies charged with safeguarding vulnerable children were not able to successfully protect a child' (Foley and Rixon 2014: 60).

CASE STUDY 3

P. was well known to the local social services department. For a number of months she would appear at the local social services office on a Monday or Tuesday morning. She would be injured either with bruises or broken bones. She had a child of three who came with her to the offices.

By examining the situation it was decided to offer her a place at a Refuge so as to distance her from her abusive boyfriend. She often accepted this offer and would stay away from her home for a few days only to return later. She was in danger and her child was a witness to violent behaviour.

Being mindful of links between domestic violence and child abuse what might you suggest as the way forward for this family?

- *Was there a dilemma for the social services department?*
- *Which other professionals might be involved in this case?*

A vital practice for all practitioners is to listen to children and their families and this is enshrined in the Children Act (2006) in that they are to 'listen to children, young people and their families and to draw on their insights when engaged in their other functions'. Local Safeguarding Children Boards (LSCBs) must act on the duties outlined in the Act. It is an imperative that owing to the vulnerability issues relating to babies and young children, particularly those that may have additional needs, that all disciplines should be rigorous, not only about ethical aspects, but also the appropriateness of how evidence of their health and well-being is collected, monitored and acted upon (The Children Act 2006: 3.2, p. 9). Additionally, there may be those older children who might have parenting responsibilities but who could have competency and capability needs.

Policy context for multi-professional working

The *Munro Review of Child Protection* (2011) put forward the proposal to use a 'systems approach' for all Serious Case Reviews (SCRs). Munro suggests that a **systems approach**, used in aviation engineering, will counteract a 'blame culture' and develop a way of working that encourages people and processes to collaborate more closely. The new *Working Together* Document (2013) revised in the light of the Munro Review clearly states that when: 'Safeguarding children – the action we take to promote the welfare of children and protect them from harm – is everyone's responsibility. Everyone who comes into contact with children and families has a role to play' (*Working Together to Safeguard Children: a guide to interagency working to safeguard and promote the welfare of children*, April 2013: p. 7).

The Children Act 1989 introduced the concept of partnership with parents recommending that local authorities should attempt to work in partnership with parents wherever possible. This can be problematic when the main carers of a child are determined to avoid contact and home visits from the appropriate professionals. This appears to be an area of commonality in most of the recent serious case reviews. The Children Act 2004 considered that all professions 'are now required to establish co-operative partnership working, Section 10 in particular talking about the 'duty to co-operate'. This 'is a common thread running through all government documents ... services and agencies need to work together to make the delivery of services more effective' (Crown Copyright 2007: 01). 'Mono-disciplinary approaches ... restrict the opportunities for knowledge exchange, create duplication of services and contribute to increased costs' (Cartmel *et al.* 2013: 398).

We have discussed some of the barriers that need to be addressed but what about the enablers to effective interprofessional practice? It is essential that all current practitioners give a commitment to interprofessional practice and that the government consider for future practitioners a 'foundation entry year' where all practitioners, no matter what discipline, train together in order to begin to understand the complexities of safeguarding and protecting children and young people from the different disciplinary standards and perspectives. The Kingston University SCR research team's 10 recommendations point the way forward for the government and practitioners, whether at operational or strategic level, to consider building on the emerging themes and recommendations from the study. Four of these are mentioned below :

1   How the safeguarding, child protection and SCR process might be made less onerous, less blaming and more practical;
2   How the findings and learning from SCRs nationally might be made more easily available and useable locally;
3   How the findings and learning might be better shaped and used to have a positive impact on learning for practice;
4   How the embedding of practice changes might be checked and consolidated.

More importantly, consideration should be given to developing a set of mandatory 'National Safeguarding and Child Protection Standards', applicable to all professions, agencies and disciplines working with children and young people (DfE, July 2014: p. 11). Collaboration and interprofessional practice can only happen when practitioners discuss and reflect upon the different disciplinary perspectives that impact on their working practices.

The aim of this chapter is to emphasise that integrated working acts as a powerful safeguarding component protecting young children and young people at risk. We know that most safeguarding cases involve babies under the age of one (Brandon *et al.* 2008) therefore integrated working means being able to identify additional needs of children and young people with accuracy and speed.

PROVOCATION

Discuss the similarities between the terms mentioned in provocation 1 and choose which would be in the best interests of the child.

Throughout child care cases there needs to be a strong emphasis on reflection which, in this instance, will be done through an examination of selected case reviews in order to tease out why we are continually getting things wrong and children continue to remain at risk. Reflection highlights the fact that 'all aspects of children's lives are inextricably linked' (Foley and Rixon 2014: 53) 'Emancipatory reflection involves looking at structures and power issues. In this type of reflection it is encouraged to look at the constraints on practice and how they can be challenged (Thomas 2004 cited in Foley and Rixon 2014).

Frost (2005: 13) spoke about cooperation, collaboration, coordination and integration. None of these ideas seem impossible to achieve. More recently, multi-agency and multi-professional terms are utilised and can be used to identify the requirements of working together. One of the glaring challenges is the idea of bringing teams together, one team can provide a focus for helping the child and the family but the challenge is several teams working on the same case. This links back to the social model of looking at disabilities when we must attempt to change society rather than dealing with medical issues. Here we must change the way professionals work rather than change the professions. All practitioners need to develop 'the opportunities to develop confidence when working with other people' (Payler and Georgeson 2014: 394); this can only be achieved through a trans-disciplinary approach.

Meredith Belbin, the great proponent on teams and how they work, stresses 'that a team is not a bunch of people with job titles, but a congregation of individuals each of whom has a role which is understood by other members'. This being true of one team should be true of those coming from other teams and reconstituting as a new one. Belbin's philosophy is about creating and making the most of individual differences. Trans-disciplinary teams could fit this aspiration.

When bringing professionals together they must each understand the other's job role. If this can be done then it avoids duplication of work and/or the avoidance of not so palatable sections of responsibility. It facilitates **accountability**; it also means that all are privy to relevant information. In a 2014 study looking at 'Multi-agency working in the Early Years' undertaken by Payler and Georgeson, 52 Early Years Practitioners were interviewed and 'expressed uncertainties over roles'.

Respect for boundaries is essential, as is patience and tolerance. The work load of professionals varies, the social worker with many different cases or the health visitor having the responsibility to visit so many clients springs to mind. It might be argued that all case loads need to be reduced and specialisms need to be reintroduced.

In the 1970s there were dedicated teams dealing with child protection issues. Their expertise was second to none. They held an overriding picture of the circumstances. This enabled them to move quickly and appropriately if it was felt to be necessary. 'Collaborative relationships were characterised by a high degree of cooperation and problem solving' (Farmakopoulou 2002: 49). This must be the essence of trans-disciplinary working.

Rita Cheminais (2009) cites Atkinson *et al.* (2007), identifying the features of good practice in multi-agency partnership working as:

- Good **leadership** – a good leader is someone who is inspirational, is knowledgeable and willing to take risks. It is someone who displays all the attributes of emotional intelligence (Goleman). The leader needs to provide a clear focus and direction.

- Commitment from those involved – there needs to be the ability to devote the time to attend meetings and to work in partnership with those from other professions.
- A good working relationship based on trust and mutual respect – no one profession should consider itself to be superior to another. There is a need for all to be proud of their work and to realise that they all have something to contribute with regards to the interests of the child. There should be no hierarchy. An Early Years' Educator (EYE) is equally as important as a professor of paediatrics. That EYE has direct daily contact with the child and is able to be sensitive to any changes in behaviour or demeanour. The professor might only see the child on one occasion.
- Regular meetings need to be organised and dates agreed in advance.
- Continuity of attendance at meetings by relevant professionals – this is hard to achieve due to staff turnover and workload but if this is the case there needs to be an effective handover of information.
- Joint ownership of the case – that is to say joint aims and objectives should be agreed.
- Joint funding, which ideally leads to equal resource distribution. This is a real problem as funding is squeezed and reduced annually.

PROVOCATION

Consider the above points.

- Are they all equally important?
- Are there any that you might omit or add?
- Would you place them in this order? Are they achievable?

In order to work in the best interests of the child there needs to be effective Information-sharing. Six key points on information-sharing need to be considered:

1 All involved need to know that information will be shared. Gaining permission for this to happen is desirable.
2 The safety and welfare of the child must be the overriding consideration.
3 If possible the wishes of the protagonists must be respected.
4 Advice on what to share should be sought wherever doubt is a factor.
5 All information should be checked for accuracy and must be as current as possible.
6 All reasons for the sharing of information or otherwise should be recorded (DFES 2006).

The Common Assessment Framework (CAF) is a key part to delivering frontline services that are integrated and focused around the needs of children and young people (CWDC 2008: 4) This has been introduced as a result of many SCRs and links to many of the above points.

In response to safeguarding and when children have sadly and tragically died, the government responds by commissioning serious case reviews. The key principles underlying serious case reviews are: urgency, impartiality, thoroughness, openness, confidentiality, co-operation, resolution (Sheffield Safeguarding Children Board 2008). Chapter 8 of *Working Together to Safeguard Children* (Department of Health 2006) requires the Local Safeguarding Children Board and individual agencies to review their involvement with the child and their family in cases that meet the criterion for a Serious Case Review. These are required following a child's death in which abuse of any kind is thought to be the cause.

CASE STUDY 4

The following cases give some opportunity to discuss and reflect on the issues raised so far:

1   Sheffield, Child D – 2008
2   Haringey, Baby P – 2009
3   Birmingham, Child K, case number 14 – 2010
4   Bristol, Child M – 2011

1 Child D, Sheffield, 2008

Child D died two weeks after her third birthday. Cause of death was given as broncho-pneumonia due to malnutrition. The mother and her partner pleaded guilty to child cruelty and neglect. Child D had been attending a nursery for a short period of time. A health visitor and a midwife had attempted to visit. No concerns were logged from any of the professionals. The family was 'deliberately untruthful, evasive and manipulative of visiting professionals' (Sheffield Safeguarding Children Board). Throughout the case there are examples of good practice from the health professionals, but the child's life ended in tragedy.

Lessons learnt: All health professionals should keep detailed records which highlight attempts to visit a family. Attention needs to be paid to evasive behaviour but large case loads make it difficult to focus on one or two missed visits. Primary Care trusts should provide support and guidance to health visitors about visits to families. Child D was withdrawn from the nursery and fees had not been paid. The panel suggested that management of the setting needed to explore the reasons for non-payment and try to offer a payment package. However, the nursery was a private concern dependent on fees being paid and no further investigation from this avenue was forthcoming.

In an ideal world alarm bells would have rung shortly after the birth of Child D. A protection package should have been developed identifying the appropriate professionals and their input and a senior member of staff should have led the intervention.

2 Baby P, Haringey, 2009

This was a high profile case which ended in the death of baby P in 2007. The cause of death was documented as a 'fracture/dislocation of the thoraco-lumbar spine' (Haringey 2009). All three protagonists in this case (the mother, her boyfriend and another friend) were all found guilty of 'causing or allowing the death of a child' (Haringey 2009). Baby P was already the subject of a child protection plan. Ten agencies were involved with Baby P and/or his family.

Lessons learnt: There should have been a willingness to challenge the credibility of information given by the mother and her partner. All professionals involved need to attend child protection conferences. Those at this conference were not specialists in child protection issues. The severity of the child being on a child protection plan was not emphasised sufficiently. Missed appointments should have been challenged and a need to consider care proceedings rather than trying to avoid them should have been considered. There should be an absolute requirement to improve inter-agency communication and an improvement of knowledge about safeguarding and more staff support from senior management.

3 Child K, case number 14, Birmingham, 2010

Death of a school-aged Child K in 2008. Cause of death bronchial pneumonia and septicaemia. Mother and male partner convicted of manslaughter. There were six children in the family. The partner was not the **biological** father. The child attended school where there were incidents of him stealing food from other children. Over time the school tried to report concerns to Children's Social Care. A suggestion was made to complete an **assessment** using the Common Assessment Framework. Attempts were made to visit the family but these were rebuffed. The child was removed from school and the mother seemingly undertook home education thus removing the child from the school environment. Several agencies however were aware of concerns over the family.

Lessons learnt: Agencies did not have all the facts concerning the family circumstances. Assessments which were made were not adequate or sufficiently frequent. Some professionals seemed unaware of their responsibility to share concerns.

4 Child M - Bristol, 2011

Various causes of death logged. This case involved a teenage mother known to a variety of agencies. She attended college for a short time while her child in was in nursery. Places at both the nursery and the college were lost through non-attendance of the mother. There was poor hygiene in the family home and an issue over alcohol abuse. A variety of agencies were involved in helping the mother. Three adults were charged with manslaughter and child cruelty.

Lessons learnt: All agencies needed to understand their respective roles. The attendance of all professionals involved in meetings would have facilitated information sharing.

There seems to be a common thread running through all the above cases.

- *What is it?*
- *Can you see any others?*

Conclusion

Short-term solutions have not proved effective. Legislation is in place but is not truly followed. In the long term it might be prudent to look at the training of all those professionals involved with children.

Training might be the solution. All training should include a generic either first or final year at university. The relevant professions should receive the same teaching and learning. This would facilitate familiarisation with the various disciplines and foster understanding and respect. Each would understand alternative job roles and each would be able to network, forge alliances and support networks.

PROVOCATION

Try this – It's a mini adventure

Form groups of five. You are locked in an underground cave. Each person has an object. The water is rising fast (remember that you are all in the same place and in the same rising water so you need to be constantly thinking about where the level of the water is – up to your knees, shoulders. It will look silly if one of you is wading up to your ankles while the other is drowning, etc.). You have to get out. To do this you have to work as a team and each use the following objects together: a whistle, a length of rope, two paper clips, a newspaper, and a bucket.

You have 15 minutes to work out a mini adventure to present to the group!

The aim of this activity is to see how you would work together as a team in a situation where you only have limited resources.

Relate this to working together as required via instructions given in *Every Child Matters* (2003).

This chapter focuses a great deal on safeguarding issues as suggested in the brief submitted. There is further suggested reading below that might widen this remit. However, suffice it to say that challenges are similar throughout all services whether it be health, social care or education. For the client dependent on these services it is essential to understand the roles of each professional so that they are aware of what each may be able to provide. The client must be aware that although information is shared not everything is documented so some issues might be missed. An unavoidable problem arises should there be a need, especially for those with health issues at night, weekends and bank holidays. Invariably, conflicting advice is given.

Trans-disciplinary working might be the only answer; technology should be focused on enabling all information to be shared in a timely and accurate manner. It should be clear and concise with the receiver being able to paraphrase what has been said by the professional in order for the latter to ensure that it has been completely understood.

Further reading

Gasper, M. (2010) *Multi-agency Working in the Early Years*: London, Sage.
  This focuses on what working in partnership looks like.

Davis, J.M. and Smith, M. (2012) *Working in Multi-professional Contexts:* London, Sage.
  This covers roles, policies and practices in integrated working.

Useful websites

www.foundationyears.org.uk/health-integration-in-practice/partnership-working-integration/
  There are some good resources on this site.

www.nfer.ac.uk/publications/CSS02/CSS02.pdf
  This is a detailed study of mul*ti-agency working in the Early Years*

References

Anning, A., Cottrell, D., Frost, N., Green, J. and Robinson, M. (2006) *Developing Multi-professional Teamwork for Integrated Children's Services: Research, Policy and Practice*. Maidenhead: Open University Press.

Brandon, M., Belderson, P., Warren, C.,Howe, D., Gardner, R., Dodsworth, J. and Black, J. (2008) *Analysing child deaths and serious injury through abuse and neglect: What can we learn? A biennial analysis of serious case reviews 2003–2005* (DCSF-RR023). Available at: webarchive.nationalarchives.gov.uk/20130401151715/ and www.education.gov.uk/publications/eOrdering Download/DCSF-RR023.pdf (Accessed 2 May 2014).

Brandon, M. Sidebotham, P., Bailey, S. Belderson, P., Hawley, C., Ellis, C. and Megson, M. (2012) *New learning from serious case reviews: a two year report for 2009–2011*. Department for Education.

Cartmel, J., Macfarlane, K. and Nolan, A. (2013) 'Looking to the future', *Early Years*, 33(4), pp. 398–412.

Cheminais, R. (2009) *Effective Multi-agency partnerships*. London: Sage.

Children's Workforce Development Council (CWDC) (2008) *Integrated Working Explained*. Leeds: Children's Workforce Development Council.

Coventry LSCB (September 2013) *Final Overview Report of Serious Case Review re Daniel Pelka*. Available at: www.lgiu.org.uk/wp-content/uploads/2013/10/Daniel-Pelka-Serious-Case-Review-Coventry-LSCB.pdf (Accessed 25 August 2015).

Department for Education and Skills (2014) *A Study to Investigate the Barriers to Learning from Serious Case Reviews and Identify Ways of overcoming these Barriers*. London: Department for Education and Skills.

Department for Education (2006) *Safeguarding Children and Safer Recruitment in Education*. U.K. Department for Education.

Department for Education (2003) *Every Child Matters*. Available at: webarchive.nationalarchives.gov.uk/20101220152656/ and www.dcsf.gov.uk/everychildmatters/ (Accessed 25 August 2015).

Department for Children, Schools and Families (2015) *Information Sharing: Guidance for practitioners and managers*. Available at: www.gov.uk/government/publications/safeguarding-practitioners-information-sharing-advice (Accessed 20 August 2015).

Department for Education and Skills (2006*) Information Sharing: Practitioners' Guidance*. London: Department for Education and Skills.

Department of Health, (2006) *Departmental report- The Health and Personal Social Services Programmes,* U.K.: The Stationary Office.

Ecklers, L., Gibbs, T., Mayers, P., Alperstein, M. and Duncan, M. (2006) Early involvement in a multi-professional course: An Integrated Approach to the Development of Personal and Interpersonal Skills. *Education for Primary Care*, 17, pp. 249–257.

Farmakopoulou, N. (2002) Using an integrated theoretical framework for understanding inter-agency collaboration in the SEN field, *European Journal of SEN*, 1(17) pp. 49–59.

Foley, P., Rixon, A. (2014) *Changing Children's Services: Working and Learning Together (Working together for Children's Services)*. Bristol: Open University.

Local Safeguarding Board, Haringey (2009) *Serious Case Review: Baby Peter. Executive Summary*. London: Department for Children, Schools and Families.

Martin, K., Jeffes, J. and Macleod, S. (2010) *Safeguarding Children-Literature review*. Slough: NFER.

Munro, E. (2011) *The Munro Review of Child Protection: Interim Report: The Child's Journey*. Available at: www.gov.uk/government/uploads/system/uploads/attachmentdata/file/206993/DFE-0010-2011.pdf (Accessed 2 May 2014).

NSPCC (2011) *New learning from serious case reviews: a two year report for 2009–2011*, Department for Education.

OfSTED (2011) *The voice of the child: learning lessons from serious case reviews: A thematic report from Ofsted's evaluation of Serious Case Reviews from April 1st to September 30th 2010*.

Payler, J. and Georgeson, J. (2013) Multiagency Working in the Early Years: Confidence, Competence and Context. *Early Years: An International Research Journal*, 33(4) pp. 380–397. Abingdon: Routledge.

Radford, J. (2010) *Serious Case Review in Respect of the Death of a Child Case Number 14* Available at: http://northumberlandscb.proceduresonline.com/pdf/kyhra ishaq scr.pdf (Accessed 20 October 2014).

Ward, P. (2008) *Sheffield Safeguarding Children Board, Serious Case Review. Child D. Executive Summary*. London: Department for Children, Schools and Families.

Wonnacott, J. (2008/2011) *Serious Case under Chapter VIII 'Working Together to Safeguard Children' in respect of the serious injury of case no. 2010-11/3*. Available at: www.nsch.norfolk.gov.uk/documents/Birmingham%20Nursery%20SCR.pdf (Accessed 2 May 2014).

GLOSSARY OF TERMS

Abuse (and neglect) Abuse and neglect are forms of maltreatment of a child. Somebody may abuse or neglect a child by inflicting harm or by failing to act to prevent harm. Children may be abused in a family or in an institutional or community setting, by those known to them or more rarely, by a stranger. They may be abused by an adult or adults or another child or children.

Accommodation To modify existing ideas to include new information.

Accountability Being answerable or responsible for a situation or procedure.

Achievement gap The difference between the highest attainders and the lowest attainders in assessments of learning and development.

Action research Type of research where the researcher instigates a change in practice in an attempt to improve provision within a specific organisation.

Adultification The process by which children prematurely take on adult roles.

Agencies Other organisations or groups the setting may work with which may include health, social care or education.

Agent of change Someone who develops and uses their skills, knowledge and understanding to initiate change with the purpose of making a positive difference for themselves and others.

Appraisal Evaluation, judgement and assessment. It is often a one-to-one meeting with a manager where a member of staff can discuss their progress and development.

Articulation Being able to express and verbalise one's thoughts and opinions.

Assent The term used to indicate a willingness to participate in research by children who are too young to give full informed consent. In the UK this is currently all children under the age of 18.

Assessment The gathering of information in order to make informed decisions. Assessment is an integral part of most early childhood programmes.

Assimilate The process of incorporating new knowledge into the existing knowledge base.

Assimilationist Refers to a view that requires ethnic minority groups to adopt the dominant group's values, beliefs and practices.

Attachment An affectionate bond linked to dependency of one person upon another, as is usually the bond of attachment between and Mother/Father and their child.

Authoritarian Controlling, rigid, strict and often demanding.

Autonomous Independent, self-directed and self-governing.

Behaviourists A school of thought that advocated studying human development by evidence that could be observed, e.g. behaviour, rather than internal thought.

Bespoke Specially made for a particular purpose.

Bilingualism   Speaking and/or understanding two languages.

Biological   The science of the body, its formation, chemical processes within the body and the nature of the person. The effect of nature combined with nurture is a long standing discussion point within childcare and education.

Biomedical model   A conceptual model of illness that excludes psychological and social factors and includes only biological factors in an attempt to understand a person's medical illness or disorder.

Bio-psycho-social model   A conceptual model that assumes that psychological and social factors must also be included along with the biological in understanding a person's medical illness or disorder.

Blended learning   Formal education programme in which a student learns, at least in part, through delivery of content and instruction via digital and online media with some element of student control over time, place, path, or pace.

Case study   A process or record of research into the development of particular persons, groups, or situations over a period of time.

Catalyst   A person, occasion or thing that precipitates an event or change.

Catalyst   An event or person causing a change.

Cephalo-caudal   Sequential growth from head to toe.

Cerebral palsy   A general term for a number of neurological conditions that affect movement and co-ordination, typically caused by damage to the brain before or at birth.

Characteristics of effective learning   Describes factors identified in the EYFS which play a central role in a child's learning and in becoming an effective learner. The characteristics of effective learning are processes that run through and underpin all seven areas of learning and development. They are: playing and exploring; active learning; creating and thinking critically.

Childhood   The period of life during which a human being is regarded as a child, taking into consideration the social, political and cultural influences at that time.

Cognitive   A school of thought that advocated studying human development by examining the development of thought, particularly reasoning, thinking or remembering.

Cognitive qualities   Acts and processes of knowing.

Collaborative   Working together with others to inform developments, decisions and solutions to issues in practice.

Conceptual   Widely accepted norms of theories and related events within a particular discipline.

Conflict   Disagreement.

Contextual   Background or circumstances to a situation.

Contextualise   To put into context. In this case to apply the specifics of theory to practice.

Contingent strategies   Recognition that the amount of support provided by the adult depends on assessment of the child's capability.

Continuing professional development (CPD)   Includes staff training, self-reflection and up skilling.

Continuous provision model of teaching   Enables children to explore recent learning, practice new skills, and follow their own interests. Practitioners are able to enhance the continuously offered activities to make more overt links to adult-initiated and adult-directed, focused sessions.

Co-participation   Joint decision-making by adult and child.

Criticality   A disciplined thinking process of actively examining thoughts and evidence, questioning their reasoning, purpose, concepts, philosophical roots, grounds for acceptance and belief, conclusions, implications and consequences.

Culture   A social group, in a broad sense, assumed to have shared models of the world in terms of perceptions, attitudes and values.

Customer standpoint   A position in which the parent is seen as highly influential and in control due to his/her commercial power.

Data collection methods   The techniques which are used to gather data in order to answer the research question(s), for example, observations and questionnaires.

Debilitating   Weakening, draining or hampering.

Democratic   This is a view that leadership can be shared and individuals can be self-governing in their work.

Developmental Coordination Disorder   A chronic neurological disorder characterised by poor movement and co-ordination skills; also known as dyspraxia.

Diagogy   Learning by child and companion together.

Didactic   Means intending to teach or instruct.

Disadvantaged groups   Identified groups who have circumstances which lead to a less favourable position economically and socially to the majority of the population.

Discourse   An accepted view based on a set on ideas, beliefs and values.

Diversity   Suggests the acceptance and celebration of all types of 'differences' and implies equitable education for all pupils, irrespective of their socio-economic and cultural background.

Dualism   The division of something conceptually into two opposed or contrasted aspects.

Duty of care   Everyone who works with children has duties under the law to ensure the safety and welfare of all children in their care.

Early Education Entitlement   A free Education Entitlement is provided for all 3 and 4-year-olds in England who are entitled to 570 hours of free early education or childcare a year. This is often taken as 15 hours each week for 38 weeks of the year. Some 2-year-olds are also eligible.

Early Support   This programme is for parents and carers of disabled children and young people from birth to adulthood. It coordinates support for health, education and social care.

Early Years Educator (EYE)   Early Years Educator qualifications were introduced in September 2014. They are the only Level 3 qualifications from that date that that will be deemed 'full and relevant' for working in the early years.

Early Years Foundation Stage (EYFS)   The statutory framework and guidance that sets standards for the learning, development and care of children from birth to 5 years old. All schools and Ofsted registered early years providers must follow the EYFS, including childminders, preschools, nurseries and school reception classes.

Early Years Teacher Status (EYTS)   Early Years Teachers will be specialists in early childhood development and will have Early Years Teacher Status (EYTS) reflecting the specialist role that they have in working with babies and children from birth to five years old. Early Years Teachers make the education and care of babies and children their first concern. They are accountable for achieving the highest possible standards in their professional practice and conduct.

e-brary   An online digital **library** of full texts of over 700,000 scholarly e-books.

Ecological Systems Theory   Used to explain how a child's environment affects how he or she develops. This approach often focuses on interrelated processes and structures within four environmental systems. These include the micro-, meso-, exo-, and macrosystems.

Educare   To train or lead, often considered a mix of education and care.

Educational research   Research undertaken within the field of education, usually to inform change and improvements in education policy or practice.

Effective Pre-School Provision Education (EPPE)   This project was the first major European longitudinal study of young children's development and the impact of the various child care provisions experienced. It was conducted by researchers at the Institute of Education, London, UK. www.ioe.ac.uk/research/66736.html.

e-learning   Learning conducted via electronic media, typically on the Internet.

Emergent   Means coming into being or notice.

Emotional development   Is the development of and ability to manage and express one's feelings such as happiness and sadness, being calm or angry, anxious or relaxed. Therefore, it is closely linked to children's behaviours, attachment and separation.

Emotional intelligence   The ability to recognise one's own and other people's **emotions**, to discriminate between different feelings and label them appropriately, and to use **emotional** information to guide thinking and behaviour.

Empathy in advance   The ability to see the world as another person might, to share and understand another person's feelings, needs, concerns and/or emotional state in advance of meeting them.

Empowerment   Enablement and confidence building to allow individuals to become autonomous practitioners.

Engagement   A term used to describe parents' interest in and contribution to their children's learning and/or early years setting.

Epistemological   Concerning the nature of knowledge, its presuppositions and foundations, and its extent and validity.

Epistemology   Of a branch of philosophy that examines the nature of knowledge.

Equality   Refers to a state of being equal, especially in status, rights or opportunities.

Ethics   The framework which researchers need to consider to ensure research does no harm to any participant and is grounded in respect and sensitivity for the needs and feelings of all those involved.

Ethnocentric   Judging other cultures against the beliefs and values of your own.

Ethnography   Type of research which focuses on the detailed experiences and perspectives of a particular community or society. In educational research this is usually centred on a single institution.

Ethos   The underlying characteristic that informs practice.

Evaluation research   Type of research which aims to assess the effectiveness of an aspect of practice, policy or process.

Exclusion   In simple terms, the deliberate act of leaving someone out.

Experts, parents as   A term used to recognise parents' comprehensive knowledge and understanding of their own children.

Experts, practitioners as   A term used to acknowledge the knowledge and understanding of practitioners often masking that practitioners are positioned as more knowledgeable than parents.

Extrinsic motivation   When you do something for external reward or to avoid negative consequences.

Feminist   The belief that women are and should be treated as potential intellectual equals and social equals to men. Feminists can be either male or female human beings, although the ideology is commonly (and perhaps falsely) associated mainly with women.

Fine Motor Skills   Motor skills that require use of small muscle groups and are more dextrous; movements such as doing up buttons or writing.

Free school meals (FSM)   Are available to children whose families are on very low incomes.

Fundamental Movement Phase   Movement development from 2–7 years which includes acquisition of skills such as running, jumping and kicking.

Gatekeepers   Individuals in positions of authority who give permission for research studies to take place in their institutions, for example, headteachers and centre managers.

Good level of development   A measure of children's attainment in the Early Learning Goals at the end of Foundation Stage in England.

Gross Motor Skills   Motor skills that require use of large muscle groups e.g. running, walking and jumping.

Health   A state of complete physical, mental and social well-being and not merely the absence of disease or infirmity (WHO 1946).

Health inequalities   Preventable and unjust differences in health status or in the distribution of health determinants between different population groups.

Health literacy   'The knowledge and competences of persons to meet the complex demands of health in modern society'.

Heuristic play   Discovery learning through play.

Hierarchy   An organisational structure based on grading with a clear chain of command.

Holistic   characterised by the belief that the parts of something are intimately interconnected and explicable only by reference to the whole.

Holistic health   A 'whole' person model of health that encompasses the physical, mental, social and spiritual aspects of health.

Homogenous   Consisting of parts of all the same kind.

Ideologies   Systems of ideas and ideals, especially those which form the bases of social, educational, economic or political theory and policy.

Inclusive   All-encompassing and ensuring no one is excluded.

Inclusive pedagogical approach   One that promotes access to and provision of education to all regardless of background, and a curriculum responsive to the needs of all learners.

Infant Mortality Rate (IMR)   Death rates between 0-1 years

Informed consent   The ethical principle which involves participants voluntarily agreeing to take part in a research study. Researchers need to ensure that all information relevant to the study is shared with everyone involved, this includes parents and carers.

Institutional based learning   Student learning experiences, including work related learning and academic learning, within the Higher Education (HE) classroom context, for example, at a Further Education (FE) College or at a University.

Intellectual adaptation   Ability to change ideas to fit with situational demands.

Interagency   The bringing together of different agencies and expertise in a co-ordinated and integrated effort to support the child.

Interpretivism   A way of viewing the world where knowledge is contextual and created by social interactions. Interpretivists believe that knowledge is fluid and cannot be objectively determined.

Interprofessional   Describes interactions and relationships of groups of individuals from different disciplines working and communicating with each other individuals in order to ensure the best outcomes for children and their families.

Intersubjectivity   The ability to share meaning in an interaction between individuals.

Intrinsic motivation   The desire to do something for internal satisfaction.

Involvement   A term used to describe parents' interest in and contribution to their children's learning in the early years setting and/or at home.

Joint involvement   Purposeful engagement in conversations or activities.

Key Person   A significant adult/special person for a child to relate to within a childcare setting, or, as explained by Elfer (2003) the Key Person first creates a special relationship with the child and second, but equally important, creates a strong partnership between the parents, staff and other professionals in order to provide for the individual needs of each key child (2003 p. 18).

Key Person Approach   A reciprocal relationship between a member of staff, individual child and their family. It provides the child with a sense of security so that they feel confident to explore their world and form further relationships.

Leadership   Guidance, giving direction, governance.

Legislation   A law which affects practice.

Leuven Involvement Scale for Young Children (LIS-YC)   This scale, devised by Professor Ferre Laevers, measures the quality of individual children's involvement in activities, which is strongly related to learning outcomes. There are five levels of involvement: 1 No activity, 2 Interrupted activity, 3 Activity without intensity, 4 Activity with intense moments, and 5 Continuous intense activity.

Life expectancy   The average years a person is expected to live at birth.

Listening to children   Listening comes in many forms. In this context it means providing children with opportunities for communication and responding to what they are saying.

Machiavellian   Cunning, scheming, and unscrupulous.

Management   Organising, running, controlling, administration, supervision.

Marginal gains   Small improvements that make an incrementally big difference.

Maturation theory   A theory that considers humans develop through a genetically determined sequence.

Mental health   A state of emotional and psychological well-being in which an individual is able to use his or her cognitive and emotional capabilities to function appropriately in society.

Metacognition   Thinking about thinking.

Methodology   The philosophy or set of principles which underpin the research design. It will inform all aspect of the research including the research question, data collection methods and analysis of findings.

Mono-cultural   Relates to a single culture that is the same across a group, organisation or society.

Monolingual   Refers to a person, group or society using only one language.

Motherese   The specific tone, intonation, sounds and words between a mother and a baby or young child that encourages communication in many forms. Also referred to as 'parentese' or 'infant directed speech'.

Motivation   Impetus, spur, drive, inspiration, incentive or stimulus.

Multi-faceted   Having many aspects to a situation.

Multilingualism   Speaking and/or understanding more than one language.

National Service Frameworks   Policies set by the National Health Service in the United Kingdom to define standards of care.

Nativist   A theory that learning, and in this case language, is innate rather than acquired by learning.

Negative health   A 'negative concept' of health only considers health as freedom from disease, so if we are free from disease we need not strive to be any healthier.

Negative mind set   A fixed attitude of low expectations.

Neonatal   The time around birth or the newborn infant.

Neonate   A new-born child.

Neurological   Relating to the nerves and nervous system.

Neuron   A brain cell that processes and transmits information through electrical and chemical signals.

Neuroscience   The study of the brain and the nervous system.

Non-governmental Organisation   A non-profit organisation set up independently of government to support a civil society, including voluntary and charity organisations.

Non-traditional entrants   Those entrants to higher education who have population characteristics not normally associated with entrants to higher education, that is, they come from social classes, genders, ethnic groups or age groups that are under-represented.

Non-verbal communication   Communication that takes place without words using visual clues, it could include sounds, gestures, looks, body movements, pictures and diagrams.

'Normal'   The usual, typical, or expected state or condition. Staying within the standard measure, the 'normal' distribution.

Observation   The action or process of closely observing or monitoring something or someone.

Operant conditioning   A form of learning in which a person or animal individual changes his or her behaviour because of the consequences (results) of the behaviour. The person or animal learns that certain behaviours have specific consequences which might be positive or negative.

Panacea   A solution or remedy for all difficulties or diseases.

Paradigm   A set of ideas or points of view.

Paradoxes   Statements that seem to contradict themselves but may, however, be true or statements that are self-contradictory or logically untenable even though they are based on a valid deductions from acceptable premises.

Parent forum   A committee made up of parents with children in school or nursery. The parent forum fosters discussion and participation in the life of the school or nursery community on a variety of different levels.

Participatory   Taking part and being involved.

Participatory early years research   Research which actively involves children's voices, opinions and actions within the data collection and design of the study. This type of research upholds the view that children's views are as important as those of adults.

Partnership standpoint   A position which acknowledges the equal power of parent and practitioner.

Pedagogical qualities   Effective teaching and learning processes.

Pedagogical values   Views and attitudes relating to professional practice with children in education.

Perception   Insight, awareness and sensitivity.

Perpetrator   A person who perpetrates, or commits, an illegal, criminal, or evil act. In the case of safeguarding, the act is committed against a child or young person.

Physical health   Relating to the physical body.

Physiological   The normal, healthy functioning of the human body and its organs.

Positive health: A 'positive concept of health' views health as an asset that can enhance our lives, so we strive to achieve health as best we can.

Positivism   Positivists view knowledge as fixed and objective and believe that the social world can be measured in the same way as natural phenomenon. Statistical and mathematical approaches are often used in positivist research.

Possibility thinking   Considering creative and different ways to do things.

Post-structuralist   Rejecting definitions that claim to have discovered absolute 'truths' or facts about the world.

Poverty   When families have inadequate money to fund adequate daily living.

Practitioner-researcher   A role where the researcher has a dual function where research is undertaken alongside their professional role, for example as an early years practitioner.

Prediction (also inference, deduction and interpretation)   The skills of finding meaning in a text, understanding the intention of the writer beyond the literal reading or sounding out of the words, thinking about the story and what might happen.

Prejudice   Occurs when unfounded negative attitudes towards groups are ascribed to individuals.

Prime areas of learning   The three prime areas of focus for 0–3-year-olds are Personal, Social and Emotional Development, Physical Development and Communication and Language.

'professional artistry'   A comprehensive knowledge and understanding of your profession and being creative in using this for your own practice development.

Professional standpoint   A position which ascribes the practitioner the more powerful role in relation to parents because of professional training and experience.

Professional Status   How a profession is regarded when compared with others.

Professional value base   The specific moral, ethical and philisophical stance that informs your theory for and in practice.

Professionalism   The combination of all the qualities that are connected with highly trained and skilled people.

Proprioception (or Proprioceptive sense)   An internal sense of balance, position, posture and movement which enables bodily awareness.

Proximo-distal   Sequential growth from the centre of the body outwards.

Psychological perspectives   Different ways of evaluating the abilities, behaviours, and personal qualities of children.

Public Health   The regulation and promotion of societal health by the state. The health of the population as a whole, especially as monitored, regulated, and promoted by the state.

Pupil Premium   Extra money provided to schools and early years settings to support learning for children from impoverished and disadvantaged households.

Qualified Teacher Status (QTS)   Required in England and Wales to work as a teacher of children in state schools under local authority control, and in special education schools. A similar status exists under a different name in Scotland and Northern Ireland.

Qualitative research   A research approach which uses non-numerical methods such as observations and interviews. Qualitative research often produces data which captures the voices and feelings of participants.

Quantitative research   A research approach which uses numerical data such as scales and statistics. Quantitative research typically produces data which can be analysed for patterns and comparisons.

Reciprocal   Mutual relationship that is equal.

Reflection   Looking back on a situation or incident and analysing what went well but what could have been improved.

Reflective 'way of being'   An instinctive way of thinking, learning and 'being' in practice that involves continual consideration of varied perspectives and influences on how you think and act, including your own values and principles.

Reflective activist/activism   'An active engagement in continual review and repositioning of assumptions, values and practice in light of evaluation of multiple perspectives, including the wider socio cultural perspectives influencing the context; transforming and transcending self and practice in order to effect change and improvement' (Hanson 2012: 144).

reflective disposition   Involves being naturally curious, asking questions and seeking alternative views on situations and self to inform your learning and actions.

Reflective identity   Your role as a reflective practitioner is integral to your 'way of being' in practice. You are a reflective thinker, learner and activist.

Reflective learner   Being a reflective learner implies a disposition and capacity to learn from critical reflection. This includes being able to articulate change in understanding or perspective and the significance of this for your own professional development; your identity, role and practice.

Reflective practice   Practice which has been informed by a process of reflective thinking and learning, either individually or collaboratively with others.

Reflective thinker   Being a reflective thinker implies a disposition and capacity to engage in 'open exploration' (Moon, 2008: 26) of assumptions, ideas, knowledge and experiences. Being a critically reflective thinker involves the exploration of a particular themes or issues from different perspectives or 'lenses' (Brookfield 1995, Hanson 2012). This process is also described as **critical reflection**.

Reflexes   Automatic physical responses to stimuli which ensure survival.

Reflexive Movement Phase   Initial movements which include reflexes.

'reflexive' practitioner   Someone who has the disposition and capacity to continuously re-examine their own assumptions and actions from the perspective of others.

Rights   The basic rights and freedoms that belong to every person in the world.

Rudimentary Movement Phase   Movement development that occurs between birth and two years.

Safeguarding   Protecting children from harm using appropriate measures.

Scaffold   The skill of being able to break down the learning of a concept into small, consecutive steps that build on each other; can be demonstrated by anyone who has prior knowledge of the skill or concept. A practitioner may support a child to enable them to achieve without taking over the task.

School readiness   When a child possesses the skills, knowledge and attitudes necessary for success in school and for later learning and life.

Sector-Endorsed Foundation Degree in Early Years (SEFDEY)   A Foundation Degree in early Years that has been designed and is delivered in order to meet the requirements of employers and national guidelines.

Sedentary Behaviour   Activities that take place when sitting or lying down and require low levels of energy to perform such as watching TV or travelling by bus.

Segregation   Setting someone or something apart from others because they are different.

Self-concept   Ideas about self, constructed from own beliefs and the responses of others.

Self-efficacy   Refers to people's beliefs about their capabilities to produce designated levels of performance in order to exercise influence over events that affect their lives.

Sensori-motor   The relationship between motor activity and the stimulation from the senses.

Separation   The act or process of moving apart or forcing something apart.

Social categorisation   Occurs when people uncritically group others into very broad cultural groupings based on 'assumed shared characteristics'.

Social constructivist   Theory of cognitive development developed by Vygotsky and others. Social constructivists believe that children learn and develop through social interactions with others.

Social development   The development of the desire and ability to communicate with, to relate to others and to become part of a group or community.

Social health   Concerns the quality of relationships. This can be considered on an individual, community or societal level.

Social learning theory   The view that people learn by observing others.

Social matrix   Complex mix of personal and cultural values and beliefs.

Social norms   Define accepted behaviours in social groups. These are the rules that a group uses to display appropriate and inappropriate values, beliefs, attitudes and behaviours. These rules may be explicit or implicit.

Social policy   This can refer to legislation, guidelines or regulations that affect individual lives in society.

Social research   The systematic study of social phenomena which typically examines the attitudes, assumptions or beliefs of a particular society or group.

Socio-cultural context   Social and cultural influences on the context in which you live and work.

Special Educational Needs (SEN)   Children whose learning and development is delayed or impaired in some way.

Status quo   The current state of affairs.

Stereotyping and **stereotypes** are in evidence when there is a perception that certain qualities are associated with particular groups or categories of people.

Stimulus and response   A learning process by which an external event can provoke a change in the subject; in behaviourism a positive reinforcement of praise or reward is likely to have more effect in provoking a repeat response.

Sure Start   A UK government-based initiative aimed at improving outcomes for children through early education, health and family support, with an emphasis on outreach and community development.

Sustained shared thinking   Occurs when two or more individuals work together in an intellectual way to solve a problem, clarify a concept, evaluate an activity or extend a narrative.

Systems approach   Emphasises the interdependence and interactive nature of elements within and external to an organisation. It is based on the concept that an organisation is a system. A system is defined as a number of interdependent parts functioning as a whole for some purpose.

Teacher-parent consultations   Meetings between teachers and parents to discuss children's progress, learning and achievements.

Temperament   A person's nature and effect on behaviour.

The Communication Chain   This chain describes the complex process of communication from the initial hearing and attending to understanding and finally providing a response.

The National Institute for Health and Care Excellence (NICE)   Provides national guidance and advice to improve **health** and social care.

The unique child   This is both a concept and a value in the EYFS. It holds that each child is different and through observation and listening to the child, each child's needs must be recognised and met differently when required.

Therapeutic ethos   A culture which prioritises curing illness or difficulties and maintaining health and well-being.

Tokenistic approaches   Occur when only a perfunctory effort or symbolic gesture towards the accomplishment of a goal, such as racial integration, is made.

Transformational   This refers to a leader identifying the need for change and creating a vision for the whole setting which transforms practice and individuals within the setting.

Transformative learning   Learning from experiences that challenge and develop existing understanding and assumptions and stimulate a different and more informed perspective or insight.

Transformative   Changing the way people interpret their experiences and their interactions with the world.

Transition   A change from one situation or state of being to another. Transitions entail adjustments that can sometimes be challenging for children.

Triangulation   The comparison of different forms of data in order to reach more rounded conclusions. For example, a researcher may combine data from observations, interviews and questionnaires to deepen analysis.

Trusting relationships   Relationships between equal or unequal partners where each party believes and relies on the other to act in the best interest of the child.

Tummy Time   Providing opportunities for babies to be placed on their stomachs in order to strengthen muscles and assist with head control.

Unique   One of a kind. Unlike anyone else.

Valid   Validity in research refers to how accurate or logical conclusions are based on the data provided. What makes research valid depends on the attitude of the researcher. For example, positivists feel research is valid if it can be replicated by another researcher and the same results found.

Verbal communication   Communication that involves words and speech.

Vertical planning   The planning of education and services between teachers and professionals responsible for different groups and classes in a hierarchical structure.

Vision   Idea or concept about what is good practice.

Welfare checklist   When decisions on any matters that will have an effect on the child, the welfare of the child is of paramount concern. The seven criteria included in the checklist can be found under s1(3) Children Act 1989.

Well-being   The state of feeling mentally and physically healthy and content.

Work-based learning (WBL)   Learning taking place in your work context, where the workplace as opposed to the classroom is the learning environment but where there is a strong link between the two.

Zone of Proximal Development (ZPD)   Devised by Lev Vygotsky this has been defined as 'the distance between the actual developmental level as determined by independent problem solving and the level of potential development as determined through problem solving under adult guidance, or in collaboration with more capable peers' (Vygotsky, 1978, p. 86).

INDEX